KT-178-717

A PRIMER OF DRUG ACTION
TENTH EDITION

A comprehensive guide to the actions, uses,
and side effects of psychoactive drugs

ROBERT M. JULIEN M.D., PH.D.

St. Vincent Hospital and Medical Center
Portland, Oregon

WORTH PUBLISHERS

Senior Sponsoring Editor: Laura Pople
Marketing Manager: Renee Altier
Project Editor: Penelope Hull
Art Director and Cover Designer: Barbara Reingold
Photo Editor: Ted Szczepanski
Production Manager: Barbara Anne Seixas
Composition and Illustrations: Macmillan India Ltd
Manufacturer: R.R. Donnelley & Sons Company

ISBN 0-7167-0615-6   (EAN 9780716706151)

Printed in the United States of America

Second printing

Library of Congress Cataloging-in-Publication Data

Julien, Robert M.
  A primer of drug action: a concise, nontechnical guide to the actions, uses, and
side effects of psychoactive drugs / Robert M. Julien.—10th ed.
        p. cm.
      ISBN 0-7167-0615-6 (pbk.)
      1. Psychotropic drugs. 2. Psychopharmacology. I. Title.

  RM315.J75 2005
  615'.788—dc22   2004055358

Worth Publishers
41 Madison Avenue
New York, NY 10010
www.worthpublishers.com

Contents

v

Preface

In the thirty years since the publication of the first edition of *A Primer of Drug Action,* there has been an explosion of knowledge about drugs, the underlying disorders for which drugs are used, and the receptor substrates on which drugs act. The accumulation of drug knowledge continues to accelerate, and remarkable advances are occurring. In the three years since the publication of the ninth edition, I have witnessed the introduction of new drugs for treating schizophrenia, depression, bipolar illness, Alzheimer's disease, parkinsonism, and other neurological and psychological disorders. I have been more and more impressed with the chronic and disabling nature of untreated and persistent anxiety, dysthymia, depression, and pain. I have witnessed the explosion in the prescription of medications for the treatment of psychological disorders of children and adolescents, and I have gained new understanding of the biochemical abnormalities in behavioral and psychological disorders.

The pharmacology of 2005 is vastly different from the pharmacology of 2002. New anxiolytics, antidepressants, mood stabilizers, and antipsychotics have continued to appear, and more are on the horizon. The use of currently available drugs for "off-label" use continues to expand, offering new hope for the treatment of psychological disorders and the prevention of substance abuse relapse.

In 1975, when the first edition of *A Primer of Drug Action* was published, we had few drugs to treat many of the psychological disorders discussed in the tenth edition. We had little idea of the structure or roles of drug receptors. Child and adolescent psychopharmacology was embryonic, and most of the drugs presented in the tenth edition had not even been conceived of. As the twenty-first century progresses, we will describe the human genetic code and explore the mechanisms by which gene expression can be modified by drugs. We will develop new and better drug delivery systems. We will develop remarkable new treatments for mental disorders, and we will see vast improvements in drug design and delivery and in the therapeutic uses of drugs as phenotype-specific agents. Drug abuse and dependence will undoubtedly continue to be problems; however, we will develop new medications to help people escape the ravages of drug dependency. We will develop new analgesic agents that are clinically efficacious yet devoid of reinforcing potential. I hope we will develop new treatments to prevent, delay, or ameliorate neurodegenerative disorders and to protect neurons after injury or insult.

Each of the ten editions of *A Primer of Drug Action* has managed to mirror and document scientific and clinical advances. A *Primer of Drug Action* discusses the general principles of each class of psychoactive drugs and provides specific information about each drug in the class. The book also addresses the mechanisms of action of each drug and drug class, current theories about the etiology of major psychological disorders and rationales for drug treatment, and the uses and limitations of psychopharmacology in patient care. Drugs of compulsive abuse are given equal time with drugs for therapeutic purposes. Often a drug of abuse has many and valid therapeutic uses. Theories of drug-induced behavioral reinforcement, comorbidity of substance abuse with other psychological disorders, and the treatment of substance abuse and relapse prevention are presented. In essence, the major changes that have occurred since the publication of the ninth edition in 2001 necessitated a complete revision of the book. More than 50 percent of the research literature cited in the tenth edition was published between 2001 and 2004.

The goal of the first edition in 1975 was to provide pharmacological information that was concise, accurate, and timely. Information in the first edition (as well as in subsequent editions) was presented in clear language as free as possible of technical jargon so that even readers with only modest backgrounds in the biological sciences could easily understand it. In general, this philosophy continues, although recent advances in molecular biology and psychopharmacology necessitate discussion at a somewhat deeper level.

Current research into the mechanism of action and pharmacology of psychoactive drugs is fully discussed and referenced. The pharmacological and psychotherapeutic treatments of psychological disorders are integrated, and the interface between psychopharmacotherapy and the various professions of counseling, psychology, and psychotherapy is addressed. Prescribing and nonprescribing rofessionals working with either people who are taking psychotropic medications or people who suffer from drug dependency disorders now must be knowledgeable about and conversant in the pharmacology of the drugs their clients are taking. This has become even more important since the publication of clinical practice guidelines for the treatment of major psychological disorders, so each chapter contains a brief discussion of the clinical interface between pharmacological and psychological treatments.

FEATURES OF THE TENTH EDITION

In its first thirty years of publication, *A Primer of Drug Action* helped shape knowledge about psychopharmacology, drug abuse, and psychopharmacotherapy. In the tenth edition, *A Primer of Drug Action* is completely revised and updated with the aim of keeping its place as the most current, objective, and understandable introduction to the pharmacology of drugs that affect the mind and behavior. Each of the 21 chapters has been completely rewritten and updated. Included in each presentation are not only the traditional and newly available drugs but also discussions of both current and future directions in drug research (including new drugs that are on the horizon but not yet available for clinical use).

Two new chapters have been added. Chapter 12 addresses child and adolescent psychopharmacology, with critical review of the literature on the use of prescribed drugs in this population. Chapter 13 addresses geriatric psychopharmacology, with emphasis on drugs used in the treatment of Parkinson's and Alzheimer's diseases. These disorders are both considered neurodegenerative diseases, so discussion of drug-induced slowing or prevention of them is emphasized.

It is my hope that the tenth edition of *A Primer of Drug Action* will serve the needs of readers who want a concise, clearly presented, and comprehensive introduction to psychopharmacology, drug education, and psychopharmacotherapy. Each chapter includes study questions and extensive references suitable for use by everyone interested in learning about the actions of psychopharmacological agents.

Robert M. Julien, M.D., Ph.D.
Portland, Oregon
drjulien.com

Available from the publisher is the *Test Bank* (ISBN 0-7167-8913-2) by Peter E. Simson of Miami University, Oxford, Ohio. The new edition of the *Test Bank* contains almost 800 items in multiple-choice, true-false, and short-answer formats. Each question is keyed to the page in the book where the answer is located.

Introduction to Psychopharmacology: How Drugs Interact with the Body and the Brain

Pharmacology is the science of how drugs affect the body. *Psycho-pharmacology* is a subdivision of pharmacology and is the study of how drugs affect specifically the brain and behavior. To understand the actions, behavioral uses, therapeutic uses, and abuse potentials of psychoactive drugs, one must necessarily understand how the body responds to the taking of a drug. This involves the basic principles of drug absorption, distribution, metabolism, and excretion (collectively termed *pharmacokinetics*) as well as the interactions of a drug with its "receptor," or the structure with which the drug interacts to produce its effects (the area of study termed *pharmacodynamics*).

This book is specifically oriented to drugs that affect the brain and behavior. It begins with three chapters devoted to the fundamentals of drug action. Chapter 1 explores the area of pharmacokinetics, the movement of drug molecules into, through, and out of the body. It addresses such questions as the following: Once a drug arrives in the stomach (if taken orally), how and why does it gain access to the bloodstream? Once in the bloodstream, how is it distributed throughout the body? Is it distributed evenly? How is distribution reflected in the actions of the drug? Finally, how does the body eventually get rid of the drug?

Chapter 2 explores the area of pharmacodynamics. It examines the interaction between drugs and the receptors to which the drugs attach, as well as how the attachment results in alterations in cell function and behavior. Receptors are described both structurally and functionally, and how drugs alter receptor structure and function is discussed. Finally, the ways such actions underlie the therapeutic effects and the side effects of drugs are illustrated.

1

Chapter 3 applies knowledge about basic pharmacology to the specifics of drug action on the brain and behavior. For readers without background in neuroscience, the structure and function of the neuron is introduced because it is on various parts of neurons that psychoactive drugs act to produce their effects. We focus on the point of connection between two different neurons, an area called the *synapse*. By studying the process of synaptic transmission and specific neurotransmitters, we begin to understand the mode of action of psychoactive drugs as well as the complexity of brain functioning in both health and disease.

Chapter 1

Pharmacokinetics: How Drugs Are Handled by the Body

When we have a headache, we take for granted that after taking some aspirin our headache will probably disappear within 15 to 30 minutes. We also take for granted that, unless we take more aspirin later, the headache may recur within 3 or 4 hours. This familiar scenario illustrates four basic processes in the branch of pharmacology called *pharmacokinetics*. Using the aspirin example, the four processes are as follows:

1. *Absorption* of the aspirin into the body from the swallowed tablet

2. *Distribution* of the aspirin throughout the body, including into a fetus, should a female patient be pregnant at the time the drug is taken

3. *Metabolism* (detoxification or breakdown) of the drug as the aspirin that has exerted its analgesic effect is broken down into metabolites (by-products or waste products) that no longer exert any effect

4. *Elimination* of the metabolic waste products, usually in the urine

The goal of this chapter is to explore these processes of pharmacokinetics, concluding with discussion about how pharmacokinetics can be used to determine the time course of action for drugs. The chapter also explores the steady-state maintenance of therapeutic blood levels of drugs in the body and the usefulness of therapeutic

3

drug monitoring. Finally, the chapter introduces the concepts of drug *tolerance* and drug *dependence*.

The understanding of pharmacokinetics, along with knowledge about the *dosage* taken, allows determination of the concentration of a drug at its *receptors* (sites of action) and the *intensity* of drug effect on the receptors as a function of time (Wilkinson, 2001). Thus, pharmacokinetics in its simplest form describes the time course of a particular drug's actions—the time to onset and the duration of effect. Usually, the time course simply reflects the amount of *time* required for the rise and fall of the drug's concentration at the target site. Figure 1.1 illustrates the complexity of drug movement through the body and its equilibrium at its site of action.

The root *kinetics* in the word *pharmacokinetics* implies movement and time. As each of the drugs in this book is discussed, the focus is first on the time course of the drug's movement through the body, particularly

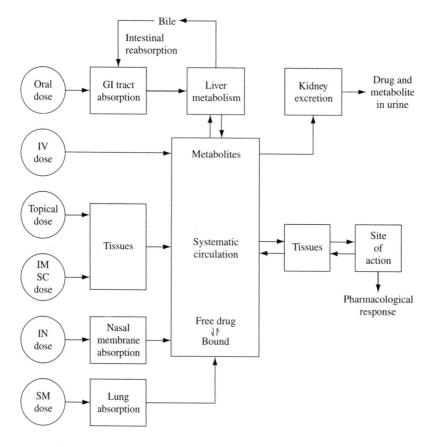

FIGURE 1.1 Schematic representation of the fate of a drug in the body. IM = intramuscular; IV = intravenous; IN = intranasal; SC = subcutaneous; SM = smoked.

its *half-life* and any complications that arise from alterations in its rate of metabolism. Knowledge of movement and time offers significant insight into the action of a drug. At the very least, it helps distinguish a particular drug from other related drugs. For example, the main difference between two benzodiazepines (Chapter 6), lorazepam (Ativan)[1] and triazolam (Halcion), is in their pharmacokinetics. Both these drugs depress the functioning of the brain, causing sedative and antianxiety effects. However, lorazepam persists for at least 24 hours in the body, while triazolam persists for only about 6 to 8 hours. If lorazepam is administered at bedtime for treatment of insomnia, daytime sedation the next day can be a problem, since lorazepam persists in the body through the next day. However, for longer, steady action (as might be useful in treating anxiety), lorazepam would be the superior agent to use.

The kinetic differences between lorazepam and triazolam are illustrated in Figure 1.2, which shows three ranges: an ineffective range (where not enough drug is present to produce either sedative or antianxiety effects), a therapeutic range, and a toxic range (where sedation becomes excessive). Triazolam reaches peak blood level rapidly and is of short duration. Lorazepam, on the other hand, reaches peak blood level later and persists longer in the therapeutic range. In essence, pharmacokinetic differences account for these results and allow two similar drugs to be used for quite different therapeutic goals.

Drug Absorption

The term *drug absorption* refers to processes and mechanisms by which drugs pass from the external world into the bloodstream. For any drug, a route of administration, a dose of the drug, and a dosage form (liquid, tablet, capsule, injection, patch, spray, or gum) must be selected that will both place the drug at its site of action in a pharmacologically effective concentration and maintain the concentration for an adequate period of

---

[1]Most drugs used in medicine are known by two or even three names. The most complicated name for a drug is its *structural* name, which accurately describes its chemical structure in words. In this book, the chemical names for drugs are not used. The second name for a drug is its *generic* name, which is a somewhat easier-to-remember name given to the drug by its discoverer or manufacturer. After a drug's patent protection runs out (usually 17 years after the date of its patent registration by the manufacturer), any other generic drug manufacturer may legitimately sell the drug under this name. The third name is the drug's *trade* name, a unique name placed on the drug by its original patent holder. Only that manufacturer can ever sell the drug under that name, even after the patent runs out and others sell the drug under its generic name. For example, many companies sell aspirin, a generic name for acetylsalicylic acid, the structural name. However, only Bayer Pharmaceuticals (the original company that patented acetylsalicylic acid) can call it Bayer Aspirin. In this book, when a drug is introduced, the generic name is given first, and the generic name is not capitalized. The trade name follows in parentheses, is capitalized, and usually is not given again,

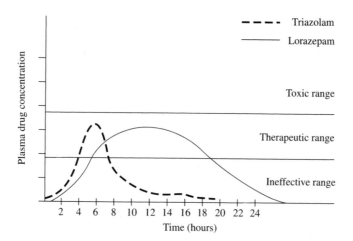

FIGURE 1.2 Theoretical blood levels of triazolam (a short-acting benzodiazepine) and lorazepam (a longer-acting benzodiazepine) over time following oral administration. Approximations for ineffective, therapeutic, and toxic blood levels are shown.

time. Drugs are most commonly administered in one of six ways:

- Orally (swallowed when taken by mouth)
- Rectally (drug embedded in a suppository, which is placed in the rectum)
- Parenterally (given in liquid form by injection with a needle and syringe)
- Inhaled through the lungs as gases, as vapors, or as particles carried in smoke or in an aerosol
- Absorbed through the skin (usually as a drug-containing skin patch)
- Absorbed through mucous membranes (from "snorting" or sniffing the drug, with the drug depositing on the oral or nasal mucosa)

Oral Administration

To be effective when administered orally, a drug must be soluble and stable in stomach fluid (not destroyed by gastric acids), enter the intestine, penetrate the lining of the intestine, and pass into the bloodstream. Because they are already in solution, drugs that are administered in liquid form tend to be absorbed more rapidly than those given in tablet or capsule form. When a drug is taken in solid form, both the rate at which it dissolves and its chemistry limit the rate of absorption.

After a tablet dissolves, the drug molecules contained within it are carried into the upper intestine, where they are absorbed across the intestinal mucosa by a process of *passive diffusion*. This process necessitates that the drug molecules, at least to some degree, be soluble in fat (be *lipid soluble*). In reality, even a small amount of lipid solubility allows for absorption after oral administration; the most lipid soluble drugs are merely absorbed faster than less lipid drugs. However, as we will see later, to penetrate into the brain, a drug must be quite lipid soluble; less soluble drugs (penicillin, for example) simply do not have sufficient lipid solubility to enter the brain. Since psychoactive drugs have good solubility in the lipid linings of the stomach and intestine, about 75 percent of the amount of an orally administered psychoactive drug is absorbed into the bloodstream within about 1 to 3 hours after its administration.

Although oral administration of drugs is common, it does have disadvantages. First, it may lead to occasional vomiting and stomach distress. Second, although the amount of a drug that is put into a tablet or capsule can be calculated, how much of it will be absorbed into the bloodstream cannot always be accurately predicted because of genetic differences between individuals and because of differences in the manufacture of the drugs. Finally, the acid in the stomach destroys some orally administered drugs, such as the local anesthetics and insulin, before they can be absorbed. To be effective, those drugs must be administered by injection.

Rectal Administration

Although the primary route of drug administration is oral, some drugs are administered rectally (usually in suppository form) if the patient is vomiting, unconscious, or unable to swallow. However, absorption is often irregular, unpredictable, and incomplete, and many drugs irritate the membranes that line the rectum. In psychopharmacology, some phenothiazines (Chapter 11) are administered rectally to treat nausea and vomiting and some "narcotics," such as morphine, are administered by suppository when oral and injectable routes are not possible.

Administration by Inhalation

In recreational drug misuse and abuse, inhalation of drugs is a popular method of administration. Examples of drugs taken by this route include nicotine in tobacco cigarettes and tetrahydrocannabinol in marijuana, as well as smoked heroin, crack cocaine, crank methamphetamine, and the various inhalants of abuse, all of which are discussed at length later in the book. The popularity of inhalation as a route of administration follows from two observations:

1. Lung tissues have a large surface area through which large amounts of blood flow, allowing for easy and rapid exchange of drugs between lung and blood (often within seconds).

2. Drugs absorbed into pulmonary (lung) capillaries are carried in the pulmonary veins directly to the left side (arterial side) of the heart (Figure 1.3) and from there directly into the aorta and the arteries carrying blood to the brain.

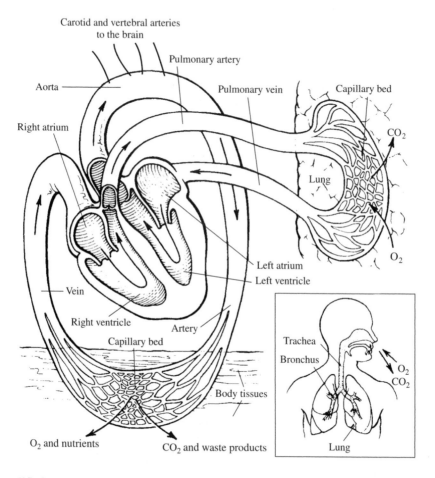

FIGURE 1.3 Heart and circulatory system. Blood returning from the systemic venous circulation to the heart enters the right atrium and flows into the right ventricle. With contraction of the heart, this blood is pumped into the pulmonary arteries leading to the lungs. Once in the pulmonary capillaries, carbon dioxide (CO_2) is lost and replaced by oxygen. This oxygenated blood returns to the heart in the pulmonary veins, which empty into the left atrium. With heart contraction, the oxygenated blood is pumped from the left ventricle into the aorta and is carried to the body tissues and brain, where oxygen and nutrients are exchanged in the systemic capillary beds. Oxygen and nutrients are supplied to the body tissues through the walls of the capillaries; CO_2 and other waste products are returned to the blood. The CO_2 is eliminated through the lungs, and the other waste products are metabolized in the liver and excreted in the urine.

As a result, drugs administered by inhalation may have an even faster onset of effect than drugs administered intravenously. If drugs administered in this fashion are behaviorally reinforcing, intoxicating, and subject to compulsive abuse, the rapid onset of effect can be intense, to say the least.

The various anesthetic gases (such as nitrous oxide) and vaporized liquids (such as halothane) are absorbed across lung membranes into the arterial circulation nearly as fast as they are inhaled, allowing for the rapid onset of anesthesia.

Administration Through Mucous Membranes

Occasionally, drugs are administered through the mucous membranes of the mouth or nose. A few examples:

- A heart patient taking nitroglycerine places the tablet under the tongue, where the drug is absorbed into the bloodstream rapidly and directly.

- Cocaine powder, when sniffed, adheres to the membranes on the inside of the nose and is absorbed directly into the bloodstream. (Cocaine is discussed in Chapter 7.)

- Nasal decongestants are sprayed directly onto mucous membranes from which they both are absorbed and also act locally to constrict mucous membranes, relieving nasal congestion.

- Nicotine (Chapter 8) in snuff, nasal spray, or chewing-gum formulations (Chapter 6) is absorbed through the mucosal membranes directly into the bloodstream.

- Caffeine (Chapter 8) became available in 1999 in chewing-gum form; the caffeine is rapidly absorbed as the gum is chewed.

- For use before and after surgery in children, the opioid narcotic fentanyl (Sublimase; Chapter 15) became available in 1998 in lollipop form, so this pain-relieving drug can be provided without subjecting a child to a painful injection. As the lollipop is sucked, the drug is released and absorbed through the mucous membranes of the mouth. This form of administering fentanyl has also become popular for patients with disabling pain conditions when orally administered pain relievers are insufficient.

- Recently introduced is a sublingual (placed under the tongue) combination of buprenorphine (an opioid narcotic) and naloxone (an opioid antagonist) for the office treatment of opioid dependency. The combination product is called Suboxone, and it is discussed in Chapter 15. The buprenorphine is absorbed through the mucous membranes, but the antagonist, naloxone, is not. Used in this fashion, the desired narcotic effect is achieved. However, should the pill be crushed, dissolved, and injected, the antagonist, naloxone, precipitates drug withdrawal. This effect should discourage abuse of the buprenorphine and reduce illicit use. It is yet another example of how knowledge of pharmacokinetics can be used to therapeutic benefit.

Administration Through the Skin

In the 1990s, several prescribed medications were incorporated into *transdermal patches* that adhere to the skin. This is a unique bandage-like therapeutic system that provides continuous, controlled release of a drug from a reservoir through a semipermeable membrane (Figure 1.4). The drug is slowly absorbed into the bloodstream at the area of contact. Some examples of drug-containing patches:

- Nicotine (used to deter smoking)
- Fentanyl (used to treat chronic, unrelenting pain)
- Nitroglycerine (used to prevent the symptoms of angina pectoris in patients with coronary artery disease)
- Clonidine (used to treat hypertension)

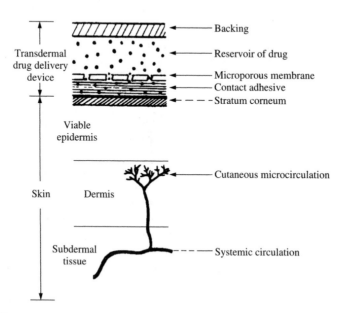

FIGURE 1.4 Diagrammatic representation of a transdermal "patch" delivery system placed on the skin.

- Estrogen (used to replace reduced hormones in postmenopausal women)
- Scopolamine (used to prevent motion sickness)

In 2003, a new form of an older antidepressant drug, selegiline (Chapter 9), was marketed as a transdermal skin patch that allows for slow, continuous absorption and minimization of side effects. In all cases, the drug is slowly, predictably, and continuously released from the liquid in the patch and absorbed into the systemic circulation over a period of days, allowing the levels of drug in the plasma to remain relatively constant.

Administration by Injection

Administration of drugs by injection can be *intravenous* (directly into a vein), *intramuscular* (directly into a muscle), or *subcutaneous* (just under the skin). Each of these routes of administration has its advantages and disadvantages (Table 1.1), but all share some features. In general, administration by injection produces a more prompt response than does oral administration because absorption is faster. Also, injection permits a more accurate dose because the unpredictable processes of absorption through the stomach and intestine are bypassed.

Administration of drugs by injection, however, has several drawbacks. First, the rapid rate of absorption leaves little time to respond to an unexpected drug reaction or accidental overdose. Second, administration by injection requires the use of sterile techniques. Hepatitis and AIDS are examples of diseases that can be transmitted as a drastic consequence of unsterile injection techniques. Third, once a drug is administered by injection, it cannot be recalled.

Intravenous Administration. In an intravenous injection, a drug is introduced directly into the bloodstream. This technique avoids all the variables related to oral absorption. The injection can be made slowly, and it can be stopped instantaneously if untoward effects develop. In addition, the dosage amount can be extremely precise, and the practitioner can dilute and administer in large volumes drugs that at higher concentrations would be irritants to the muscles or blood vessels.

The intravenous route is the most dangerous of all routes of administration because it has the fastest speed of onset of pharmacological action. Too-rapid injection can be catastrophic, producing life-threatening reactions (such as collapse of respiration or of heart function). Also, allergic reactions, should they occur, may be extremely severe. Finally, drugs that are not completely solubilized before injection cannot usually be given intravenously because of the danger of

TABLE 1.1 Some characteristics of drug administration by injection

Route	Absorption pattern	Special utility	Limitations and precautions
Intravenous	Absorption circumvented Potentially immediate effects	Valuable for emergency use Permits titration of dosage Can administer large volumes and irritating substances when diluted	Increased risk of adverse effects Must inject solutions slowly as a rule Not suitable for oily solutions or insoluble substances
Intramuscular	Prompt action from aqueous solution Slow and sustained action from repository preparations	Suitable for moderate volumes, oily vehicles, and some irritating substances	Precluded during anticoagulant medication May interfere with interpretation of certain diagnostic tests (e.g., creatine phosphokinase)
Subcutaneous	Prompt action from aqueous solution Slow and sustained action from repository preparations	Suitable for some insoluble suspensions and for implantation of solid pallets	Not suitable for large volumes Possible pain or necrosis from irritating substance

blood clots or emboli forming. Infection and transmission of infectious diseases are an ever-present danger when sterile techniques are not employed.

Intramuscular Administration.   Drugs that are injected into skeletal muscle (usually in the arm, thigh, or buttock) are generally absorbed fairly rapidly. Absorption of a drug from muscle is more rapid than absorption of the same drug from the stomach but slower than absorption of the drug administered intravenously. The absolute rate of absorption of a drug from muscle varies, depending on the rate of blood flow to the muscle, the solubility of the drug, the volume of the injection, and the solution in which the drug is dissolved and injected.

In general, most of the precautions that apply to intravenous administration also apply to intramuscular injection, but as a rule, drugs that are intended for intramuscular administration are prepared in amounts much larger than those intended to be given intravenously. Accidental intravenous injection of doses intended for intramuscular use can be catastrophic.

Subcutaneous Administration. Absorption of drugs that have been injected under the skin (subcutaneously) is rapid. The exact rate depends mainly on the ease of blood vessel penetration and the rate of blood flow through the skin. Irritating drugs should not be injected subcutaneously because they may cause severe pain and damage to local tissue. The usual precautions to maintain sterility should be applied.

Self-administration of any drug by injection is to be discouraged except when oral administration is not effective or when the drug is being taken therapeutically under the direction of a physician (injection of insulin by a diabetic is a prominent example). The risks associated with injection of a drug (infection, overdose, allergic responses, and transmission of the AIDS virus) are far greater than those associated with oral administration of the same drug.

Drug Distribution

Once absorbed into the bloodstream, a drug is distributed throughout the body by the circulating blood, passing across various barriers to reach its site of action (its receptors). At any given time, only a very small portion of the total amount of a drug that is in the body is actually in contact with its receptors (see Figure 1.1). Most of the administered drug is found in areas of the body that are remote from the drug's site of action. For example, in the case of a psychoactive drug, most of the drug circulates outside the brain and therefore does not contribute directly to its pharmacological effect. This wide distribution often accounts for many of the side effects of a drug. *Side effects* are results that are different from the primary, or therapeutic, effect for which a drug is taken.

Action of the Bloodstream

Every minute in the average-size adult, the heart pumps a volume of blood that is roughly equal to the total amount of blood within the circulatory system. Thus, the entire blood volume circulates in the body about once every minute, and once absorbed into the bloodstream, a drug is rapidly (usually within this 1-minute circulation time) distributed throughout the circulatory system.

A schematic diagram of the circulatory system is presented in Figure 1.3. Blood returning to the heart through the veins is first pumped into the pulmonary (lung) circulation system, where carbon dioxide is removed and replaced by oxygen. The oxygenated blood then returns to the heart and is pumped into the great artery (the aorta). From there blood flows into the smaller arteries and finally into the capillaries, where nutrients (and drugs) are exchanged between the blood and the cells of the body. After blood passes through the capillaries, it is collected by the veins and returned to the heart to circulate again. Psychoactive drugs quite quickly become evenly distributed throughout the bloodstream, diluted not only by blood but also by the total amount of water contained in the body.

Following are a few examples of how the blood circulation handles drugs differently.

- If a drug is taken orally, it passes through the cells lining the gastrointestinal (GI) tract into what is called the "portal system" and through the liver; from there the drug enters the central circulation and enters the heart. Occasionally, drug-metabolizing enzymes in either the cells of the GI tract or the liver can markedly reduce the amount of drug that reaches the bloodstream. This process is called *first-pass metabolism*. Two examples regarding enzymes in the GI tract are unusual and interesting. First, the enzyme *alcohol dehydrogenase* is found both in the cells lining the GI tract and in cells of the liver. As we will see in Chapter 4, women have less of this enzyme in the GI tract cells and therefore exhibit higher blood alcohol levels for a given amount of alcohol ingested (corrected for body weight) than do men.

- The second example involves the antianxiety drug buspirone (BuSpar; Chapter 6). As we will discuss later, there are different drug-metabolizing enzymes; one of these is called CYP3A. This enzyme metabolizes so much buspirone that only about 5 percent of the drug is able to cross the GI tract and enter the portal circulation. Blocking this enzyme by drinking grapefruit juice (Lilja et al., 1998) allows more absorption of buspirone, markedly increasing the amount of drug in the bloodstream and thus improving its therapeutic action (Figure 1.5). Greenblatt and coworkers (2001) review this unusual situation with grapefruit juice and discuss the enzyme mechanism responsible for the interaction. While many drugs are affected by this interaction, buspirone is the most affected of all the psychoactive drugs. In a recent report, this same group of researchers (Greenblatt et al., 2003) illustrate the increases in absorption of the antianxiety drug diazepam (Valium) when taken with grapefruit juice (Figure 1.6). Note that the increase in diazepam absorption is not as great when it is taken with grapefruit juice as is the increase of absorption when buspirone is taken with grapefruit juice. The substance in grapefruit juice that inhibits the enzyme that normally would metabolize the buspirone and diazepam as they are being absorbed has not been identified, although Greenblatt and coworkers (2003) discuss possibilities.

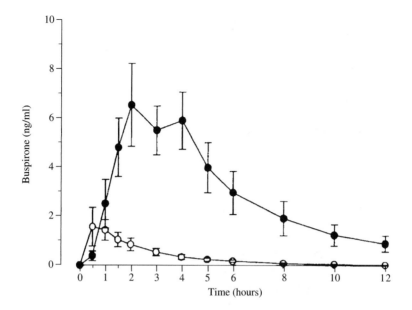

FIGURE 1.5 Plasma concentrations (mean and SEM) of buspirone (in nanograms per milliliter of plasma) in ten healthy volunteers after a single oral dose of 10 mg buspirone, after ingestion of 200 mL (about 7 oz) grapefruit juice (*solid circles*) or water (*open circles*) three times a day for 2 days, and on day 3 with buspirone administration 30 and 90 minutes later. [Data from Lilja et al. (1998).]

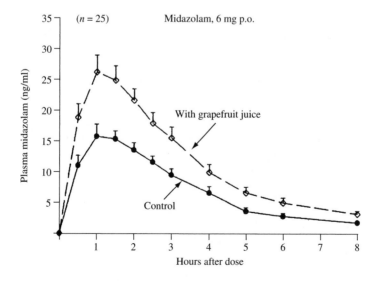

FIGURE 1.6 Plasma concentrations of diazepam (Valium) after a 6-mg oral dose on day 1 (control trial prior to grapefruit juice) and on day 3 (when midazolam was taken 2 hours after grapefruit juice. [From Greenblatt et al. (2003).]

- Injected (by whatever route), absorbed transdermally, or absorbed from mucous membranes, a drug enters systemic veins and returns to the right side of the heart (usually with minimal amounts passing initially through the liver). The drug is then circulated through the pulmonary vessels, returns to the left side of the heart, and finally distributes through the aorta to the brain and the body. Sodium pentothal is an example of an injected general anesthetic. Injected intravenously, it circulates to the heart, then the lungs, and then the brain (see Figure 1.3). After injection, consciousness is lost within about 30 seconds.

- Inhaled drugs absorbed from the lungs are carried in pulmonary veins directly to the left side of the heart and, from there, rapidly to the brain. The effects of smoked tobacco or smoked marijuana are felt within a breath or two.

Body Membranes That Affect Drug Distribution

Four types of membranes in the body affect drug distribution: (1) the cell membranes, (2) the walls of the capillary vessels in the circulatory system, (3) the blood-brain barrier, and (4) the placental barrier.

Cell Membranes. To be absorbed from the intestine or to gain access to the interior of a cell, a drug must penetrate the cell membranes. What is known of the structure and properties of cell membranes that determines their permeability to drugs? In Figure 1.7, the two layers of circles represent the water-soluble head groups of complex lipid molecules called *phospholipids*. The phospholipid heads form a rather continuous layer on both the inside and the outside of the cell membrane. The wavy lines that extend from the heads into the membrane are the lipid chains of the phospholipid molecules. Therefore, for our present purposes, the interior of the cell membrane can be considered to consist of a sea of lipid in which large proteins are suspended.

Cell membranes, consisting of protein and fat, thus provide a physical barrier that is permeable to small, lipid-soluble drug molecules but is impermeable to large, lipid-insoluble drug molecules. Cell membranes (as barriers to the absorption and distribution of drugs) are important for the passage of drugs (1) from the stomach and intestine into the bloodstream, (2) from the fluid that closely surrounds tissue cells into the interior of cells, (3) from the interior of cells back into the body water, and (4) from the kidneys back into the bloodstream.

Capillaries. Within a minute or so of entering the bloodstream, a drug is distributed fairly evenly throughout the entire blood volume. From there, drugs leave the bloodstream and are exchanged (in equilibrium)

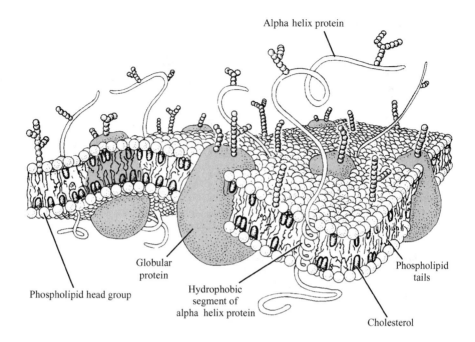

Alpha helix protein

Globular
protein

Phospholipid head group

Hydrophobic
segment of
alpha helix protein

Phospholipid
tails

Cholesterol

FIGURE 1.7 Diagrammatic representation of the cell membrane, a phospholipid bilayer in which cholesterol and protein molecules are embedded. Both globular and helical kinds of protein traverse the bilayer. Cholesterol molecules tend to keep the tails of the phospholipids relatively fixed and orderly in the regions closest to the hydrophilic phospholipid heads; the parts of the tails closer to the core of the membrane move about freely. [From M. S. Bretscher, "The Molecules of the Cell Membrane," *Scientific American* 253 (1985): 104.]

between blood capillaries and body tissues. In Figure 1.8 is a cross-sectional diagram of a capillary. Capillaries are tiny, cylindrical blood vessels with walls that are formed by a thin, single layer of cells packed tightly together. Between the cells are small pores that allow passage of small molecules between blood and the body tissues. The diameter of these pores is between 90 and 150 angstroms, which is larger than most drug molecules. Thus, most drugs freely leave the blood through these pores in the capillary membranes, passing along their concentration gradient until equilibrium is established between the concentrations of drug in the blood and in body tissues and water.

The transport of drug molecules between plasma and body tissues is independent of lipid solubility because the membrane pores are large enough for even fat-insoluble drug molecules to penetrate. However, the pores in the capillary membrane are not large enough to permit the red blood cells and the plasma proteins to leave the bloodstream. Thus, the only drugs that do not readily penetrate capillary pores are drugs

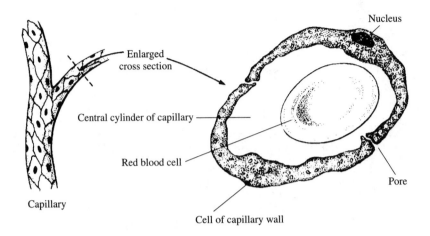

FIGURE 1.8 Cross section of a blood capillary. Within the capillary are the fluids, proteins, and cells of the blood, including the red blood cells. The capillary itself is made up of cells that completely surround and define the central cylinder (or lumen) of the capillary. Water-filled pores form channels, allowing free flow of blood plasma and extracellular fluid.

that bind to plasma proteins. The rate at which drug molecules enter specific body tissues depends on two factors: the rate of blood flow through the tissue and the ease with which drug molecules pass through the capillary membranes. Because blood flow is greatest to the brain and much less to the bones, joints, and fat deposits, drug distribution generally follows a similar pattern (Figure 1.9). An example might

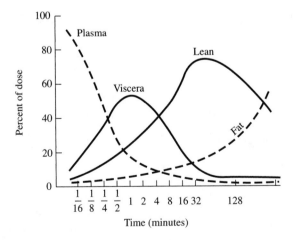

FIGURE 1.9 Diagrammatic representation of the distribution of a lipid-soluble drug (thiopental, a barbiturate discussed in Chapter 5) in blood plasma, body fat, lean body mass (muscle), and visceral tissues at various times after intravenous injection of the drug. Time scales (in minutes) progress geometrically.

be appropriate. When marijuana is smoked, the active drug, tetrahydro-cannabinol (THC, Chapter 18) achieves plasma concentrations of about 10 to 20 nanograms of drug per milliliter of plasma (ng/ml) soon after initiation of smoking. Within about 30 minutes, it achieves levels of about 50 to 100 ng/ml, which falls off within 1 hour to less than 5 to 10 ng/ml because the drug is rapidly taken up into body fat. From there, it slowly returns to plasma and is metabolized to an inactive metabolite (carboxy-THC) that is excreted in the urine.

Blood-Brain Barrier. The brain requires a protected environment in which to function normally, and a specialized structural barrier, called the *blood-brain barrier* (BBB), plays a key role in maintaining this environment. The BBB involves specialized cells in the brain that affect nearly all its blood capillaries (Figure 1.10). In most of the rest of the body, the capillary membranes have pores; in the brain, however, the capillaries are tightly joined together and covered on the outside by a fatty barrier called the *glial sheath*, which arises from nearby astrocyte cells.

Thus, to reach the cells in the brain, a drug leaving the capillaries in the brain has to traverse both the wall of the capillary itself (because there are no pores to pass through) and the membranes of the astrocyte cells. Therefore, as a general rule, the rate of passage of a drug into the brain is determined by two factors: (1) the size of the drug molecule and (2) its lipid (fat) solubility. Large, highly ionized drugs penetrate poorly, while small, fat-soluble drugs penetrate rapidly. The molecules of almost all psychoactive drugs are small enough and sufficiently lipid soluble to cross the blood-brain barrier, exerting their actions on neurons in the brain. Drugs that cannot cross the BBB are restricted in action to structures located outside the central nervous system (CNS). CNS actions are usually not of major significance. Penicillin is an example of such a drug. It does not cross the BBB and is not of use in treating infections located in the CNS: its effectiveness as an antibiotic is restricted to infections located outside the brain.

Pardridge (2003) discusses the difficulties that the blood-brain barrier presents when one attempts to develop new drugs for CNS diseases:

> Only a small class of drugs—small molecules with high lipid solubility and a low molecular mass—actually cross the BBB. There are only a few diseases that consistently respond to this category of small molecules and these include depression, affective disorders, schizophrenia, chronic pain, and epilepsy. In contrast, many serious disorders of the brain do not respond to the conventional lipid-soluble small-molecule model and these include Alzheimer disease, stroke/neuroprotection, brain and spinal cord injury, brain cancer, HIV infections of the brain, various ataxia-producing disorders, amyotropic lateral sclerosis, multiple sclerosis, Huntington disease, and childhood inborn genetic errors of the brain. (p. 91)

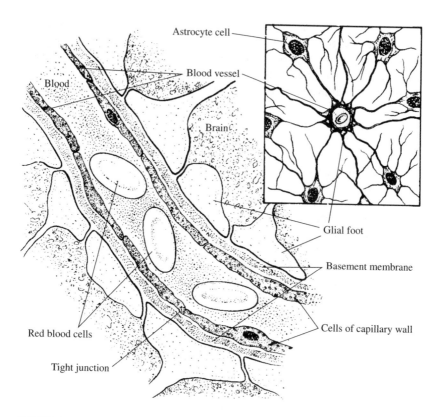

Astrocyte cell

Blood vessel

Blood

Brain

Glial foot

Basement membrane

Cells of capillary wall

Red blood cells

Tight junction

FIGURE 1.10 Blood-brain barrier. Blood and brain are separated by capillary cells packed tightly together and by a fatty barrier called the glial sheath, which is made up of extensions (glial feet) from nearby astrocyte cells (*inset*). A drug diffusing from blood to brain must move through the cells of the capillary wall because there are tight junctions rather than pores between the cells; the drug must then move through the fatty glial sheath.

Pardridge concludes that the development of new therapeutic modalities for brain diseases is hampered by our inability to solve the problems of drug transport across the BBB and that the absence of an academic research infrastructure is the single most important limiting factor on the future of brain drug development.

Placental Barrier. Among all the membrane systems of the body, the placental membranes are unique, separating two distinct human beings with differing genetic compositions and differing sensitivities to drugs. The fetus obtains essential nutrients and eliminates metabolic waste products through the placenta without depending on its own organs, many of which are not yet functioning. The dependence of the fetus on the mother places the fetus at the mercy of the placenta when foreign substances (such as drugs or toxins) appear in the mother's blood (Gilstrap and Little, 1998). The placental barrier is discussed further in the discussions of individual drugs.

A schematic representation of the placental network, which transfers substances between the mother and the fetus, is shown in Figure 1.11. In general, the mature placenta consists of a network of vessels and pools of maternal blood into which protrude treelike or fingerlike villi (projections) that contain the blood capillaries of the fetus. Oxygen and nutrients travel from the mother's blood to that of the fetus, while carbon dioxide and other waste products travel from the blood of the fetus to the mother's blood.

The membranes that separate fetal blood from maternal blood in the intervillous space resemble, in their general permeability, the cell membranes that are found elsewhere in the body. In other words, drugs cross the placenta primarily by passive diffusion. Fat-soluble

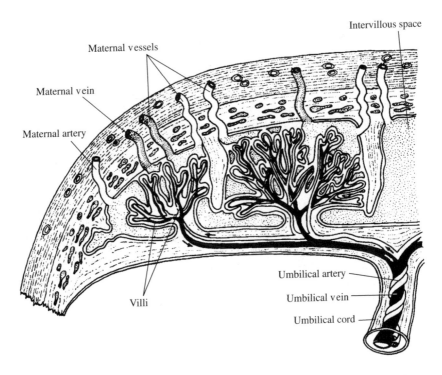

FIGURE 1.11 Placental network separating the blood of mother and fetus. Note the close relationship between fetal and maternal blood in the villus.

substances (including all psychoactive drugs) diffuse readily, rapidly, and without limitation:

> The view that the placenta is a barrier to drugs is inaccurate. A more appropriate approximation is that the fetus is to at least some extent exposed to essentially all drugs taken by the mother. (Wilkinson, 2001, p. 11)

As a general rule, any psychoactive drug will be present in the fetus at a concentration quite similar to that in the mother's bloodstream. This is not meant to imply that the presence of the drug in the fetus is necessarily detrimental to the fetus. Certainly some psychoactive drugs adversely affect the developing fetus, but most do not appear to be detrimental. Examples of drugs that can adversely affect a fetus include ethyl alcohol (Chapter 4), lithium, and several anticonvulsant drugs used in the treatment of both epilepsy and bipolar disorder (Chapter 10). Garland (1998) discusses in detail the transfer of drugs across the placenta.

Termination of Drug Action

Routes through which drugs can leave the body include (1) the kidneys, (2) the lungs, (3) the bile, and (4) the skin. Excretion through the lungs occurs only with highly volatile or gaseous agents, such as the general anesthetics and, in small amounts, alcohol ("alcohol breath"). Drugs that are passed through the bile and into the intestine are usually reabsorbed into the bloodstream from the intestine. Also, small amounts of a few drugs can pass through the skin and be excreted in sweat (perhaps 10 to 15 percent of the total amount of the drugs). However, most drugs leave the body in urine, either as the unchanged molecule or as a broken-down *metabolite* of the original drug. More correctly, *the major route of drug elimination from the body is renal excretion of drug metabolites produced by the hepatic (liver) biodegradation of the drug.*[2]

Psychoactive drugs are usually too lipid soluble to be excreted passively with the excretion of urine. They have to be transformed into metabolites that are more water soluble, bulkier, less lipid soluble, and (usually) less biologically active (even inactive) when compared with the parent molecule (the molecule that was originally ingested and

---

[2]When evaluating urine for the presence of drugs of abuse, inactive drug metabolites rather than active drug are found in the urine. It is often unclear whether there is correlation between the presence of the metabolite in urine and active drug in plasma *at the time the urine sample was taken.*

absorbed).[3] Thus, for a lipid-soluble drug to be eliminated, it must be metabolically transformed (by enzymes located in the liver) into a form that can be excreted rapidly and reliably. Such biotransformation relieves the body of the burden of foreign chemicals and is essential to our survival. Such mechanisms are not new. Biotransformation of foreign substances probably originated millions of years ago when humans invented fire and began to eat the char of barbecued meat, ingesting and absorbing substances that were foreign and potentially toxic to the body.

Role of the Kidneys in Drug Elimination

Physiologically, our kidneys perform two major functions. First, they excrete most of the products of body metabolism; second, they closely regulate the levels of most of the substances found in body fluids. The kidneys are a pair of bean-shaped organs that lie at the rear of the abdominal cavity at the level of the lower ribs. The outer portion of the kidney is made up of more than a million functional units, called *nephrons* (Figure 1.12). Each nephron consists of a knot of capillaries (the *glomerulus*) through which blood flows from the renal artery to the renal vein. The glomerulus is surrounded by the opening of the nephron (*Bowman's capsule*), into which fluid flows as it filters out of the capillaries. Pressure of the blood in the glomerulus causes fluid to leave the capillaries and flow into the Bowman's capsule, from which it flows through the tubules of the nephrons into a duct that collects fluid from several nephrons. The fluid from the collecting ducts is eventually passed through the ureters and into the urinary bladder, which is emptied periodically.

In an adult, about 1 liter (1000 cubic centimeters) of plasma is filtered into the nephrons of the kidneys each minute. Left behind in the bloodstream are blood cells, plasma proteins, and the remaining plasma. As the filtered fluid (water) flows through the nephrons, most of it is reabsorbed into the plasma. By the time fluid reaches the collecting ducts and bladder, only 0.1 percent remains to be excreted. Because about 1 cubic centimeter per minute of urine is formed, 99.9 percent of filtered fluid is therefore reabsorbed.

Lipid-soluble drugs can easily cross the membranes of renal tubular cells, and they are reabsorbed along with the 99.9 percent of

---

[3]Some drugs are exceptions: an administered drug may be metabolized into an "active" metabolite, which is at least as active and possibly more active and may have a longer duration of action than the parent drug. Examples in psychopharmacology include diazepam (Valium; Chapter 6), which is metabolized to nordiazepam, and fluoxetine (Prozac; Chapter 9), which is metabolized to norfluoxetine. In both cases, the parent drug has an effect that lasts for two or three days, while the metabolite is active for over a week, until it is eventually biotransformed to an inactive compound that can be excreted.

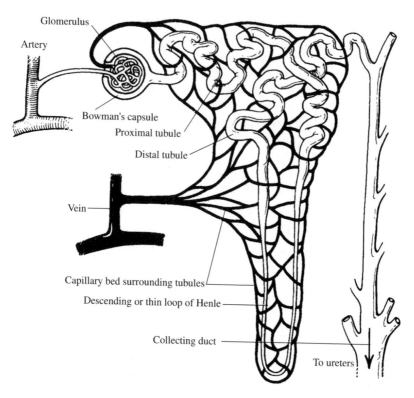

FIGURE 1.12 Nephron within a kidney. Note the complexity of the structure and the intimate relation between the blood supply and the nephron. Each kidney is composed of more than a million nephrons.

reabsorbed water. Drug reabsorption occurs passively, along a developing concentration gradient—the drug becomes concentrated inside the nephrons (as a result of water reabsorption), and the drugs are themselves reabsorbed with water back into plasma. Thus, the kidneys alone are not capable of eliminating psychoactive drugs from the body, and some other mechanism must overcome this process of passive renal reabsorption of the drug.

Role of the Liver in Drug Metabolism

Since the kidneys are not capable of ridding the body of drugs, the reabsorbed drug is eventually picked up by liver cells (*hepatocytes*) and is enzymatically biotransformed (by enzymes located in these hepatocytes) into metabolites that are usually less fat soluble, less capable of being reabsorbed, and therefore capable of being excreted in urine. As the drug is carried to the liver (by blood flowing in the hepatic artery and portal vein), a portion is cleared from blood by the hepatocytes and metabolized to by-products that are then returned to the bloodstream (Figure 1.13). The metabolites are then carried in the bloodstream to the kidneys, filtered into the renal tubules, and are poorly reabsorbed, remaining in the urine for excretion. Mechanisms involved in drug metabolism by hepatocytes are complex, but they have gained increased importance in psychopharmacology because of recently described drug interactions involving certain antidepressant drugs (Chapter 9) (Greenblatt et al., 1999).

The *cytochrome P450 enzyme family*, physically located in hepatocytes (with, as discussed above, a few located in the cells lining the GI tract), is the major system involved in drug metabolism. This gene family originated more than 3.5 billion years ago and has diversified to accomplish the metabolism (detoxification) of environmental chemicals, food toxins, and drugs—all foreign to our needs. Thus, the cytochrome P450 enzyme system (of which hundreds exist and about 50 of which are functionally active in humans) can detoxify a chemically diverse group of foreign substances. Several P450 enzyme families can be found within any given hepatocyte.

A few of these enzyme families, particularly cytochrome families 1, 2, and 3 (designated *CYP1*, *CYP2*, and *CYP3*), encode enzymes involved in most drug biotransformations. By definition, since these three families promote the breakdown of numerous drugs and toxins, enzyme specificity is low (the enzymes are nonspecific in action).

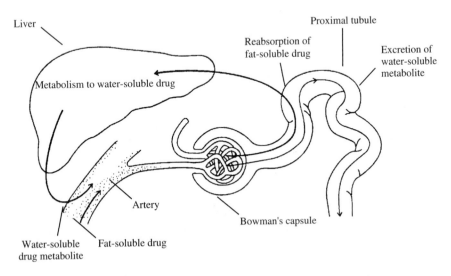

FIGURE 1.13 How the liver and kidneys interact to eliminate drugs from the body. Drugs may be filtered into the kidney, reabsorbed into the bloodstream, and carried to the liver for metabolic transformation to a more water-soluble compound that, having been filtered into the kidney, cannot be reabsorbed and is therefore excreted in urine.

Thus, the body is enzymatically capable of metabolizing multiple different drugs.

CYP-3A4 (a subfamily of CYP3) catalyzes about 50 percent of drug biotransformations (Figure 1.14); this variant is found not only in liver but also in the GI tract, as we saw with the metabolism of buspirone by CYP3. CYP-2D6 catalyzes about 20 percent of drugs, and CYP-2C variants catalyze an additional 20 percent. CYP-1A2, CYP-2E1, and CYP-3A3/4 each catalyze about 5 percent of drug biotransformations. While certainly of academic importance, the fact that the same family of enzymes metabolizes multiple drugs results in drug interactions that are of practical and therapeutic importance. Drug interactions are discussed further in Chapter 2.

Factors Affecting Drug Biotransformation

Several different factors can alter the rate at which drugs are metabolized, either increasing or decreasing the rate of drug elimination from the body. In general, multiple *genetic, environmental,* and various *physiological factors* can be involved. This is a huge area of study. Here is an example, that of drug interactions at the metabolic level.

Intuitively, if the body increases the amount or activity of CYP drug-metabolizing enzymes, then the rate at which all drugs metabolized by these enzymes are broken down should increase. Therefore, drug *tolerance* develops as the blood level of drug for a given amount taken falls more rapidly than would be expected if tolerance had not developed.

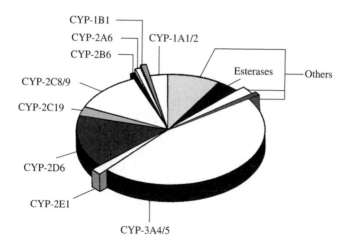

FIGURE 1.14 The approximate proportion of drugs metabolized by the major hepatic CYP enzymes. The relative size of each pie section indicates the estimated percentage of metabolism that each enzyme contributes to the metabolism of drugs. [From Wilkinson (2001), p. 15.]

Thus, increasing doses of a drug must be administered to both maintain the same level of drug in the plasma and produce the same effect as previously administered smaller doses. *Carbamazepine* (Tegretol; Chapter 10) is particularly effective in stimulating the production of the drug-metabolizing enzyme CYP-3A3/4 within hepatocytes, inducing tolerance to both itself and other drugs metabolized by CYP-3A3/4. Carbamazepine markedly reduces the blood levels and subsequent therapeutic efficacy of many of the selective serotonin reuptake inhibitor (SSRI) antidepressants (Chapter 9). The phenomenon of the association of tolerance to one drug with apparent tolerance to another is termed *cross-tolerance*.

Conversely, some psychoactive drugs depress the activity of the CYP enzyme that metabolizes other drugs metabolized by the same enzyme. This process serves to *increase* the blood level of these other drugs and unexpectedly increase their toxicity (Kashuba et al., 1998; Ozdemir et al., 1998; Wetzel et al., 1998). For example, SSRI-type antidepressants, such as fluoxetine (Prozac, Chapter 9), inhibit the enzymes CYP-1A2 and CYP-2C, increasing the toxicity of several other types of antidepressants, certain antiasthma drugs, certain antipsychotic drugs (Figure 1.15), and many heart medications. Such drug interactions are often severe and have been fatal. Conversely, the analgesic drug codeine needs to be metabolized by CYP-2D6 into morphine, which is codeine's active metabolite responsible for its analgesic effect. Patients taking an SSRI antidepressant do not experience the metabolism of codeine to morphine, and therefore codeine in these persons is ineffective as a pain-relieving agent.

Other Routes of Drug Elimination

Other routes for excreting drugs include the air we exhale, bile, sweat, saliva, and breast milk. Many drugs and drug metabolites may be found in these secretions, but their concentrations are usually low, and these routes are not usually considered primary paths of drug elimination. Perhaps clinically significant, however, is the transfer of psychoactive drugs (such as nicotine) from mothers to their breast-fed babies.

Time Course of Drug Distribution and Elimination: Concept of Drug Half-Life

Knowledge about the relationship between the time course of drug action in the body is essential for (1) predicting the optimal dosages and dose intervals needed to reach a therapeutic effect, (2) maintaining a therapeutic drug level for the desired period of time, and (3) determining the time needed to eliminate the drug. The relationship between the pharmacological response to a drug and its concentration in blood is fundamental to pharmacology. With psychoactive drugs, the level of

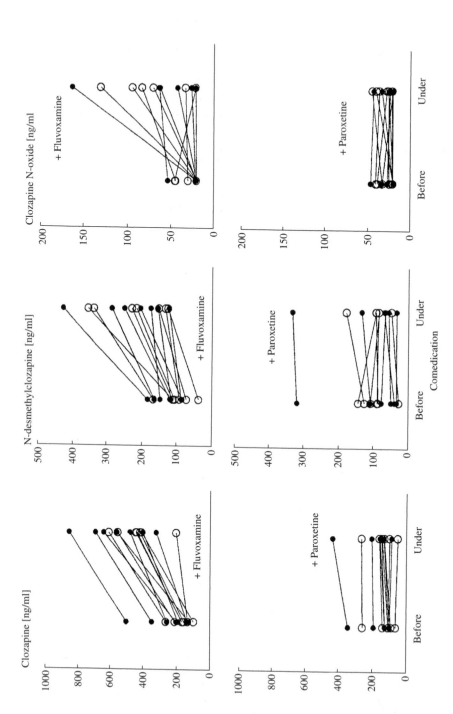

FIGURE 1.15 Blood level (in nanograms per milliliter plasma) of clozapine (Clozaril, an antipsychotic drug discussed in Chapter 11) and two of its metabolites (N-desmethylclozapine and N-oxide) before and one week after the start of coadministration of either fluvoxamine (Luvox) or paroxetine (Paxil) in patients with schizophrenia. Both fluvoxamine and paroxetine are SSRI-type antidepressants (Chapter 9). Note that fluvoxamine but not paroxetine increased clozapine blood levels since paroxetine does not inhibit CYP enzymes to any significant degree. [From Wetzel et al. (1998).]

drug in the blood closely approximates the level of drug at the drug's site of action in the brain.

Figure 1.16 illustrates the time-concentration relationship for a drug that is injected intravenously and therefore reaches peak plasma concentration immediately. For our purposes here, intravenous injection removes the variability involved with oral absorption and slow attainment of peak blood levels. Note that after the immediate peak in the plasma concentration, it appears to fall very rapidly, followed by a slower decline in concentration. The rapid fall reflects the rapid redistribution of the drug out of the bloodstream into body tissues. This process of *redistribution* takes only minutes to spread a drug nearly equally throughout the major tissues of the body. The early portion of the line illustrated in Figure 1.16 represents this rapid-distribution phase, which lasts only a few minutes. The slower, prolonged decrease in the level of drug in the blood represents the time required for the body to detoxify the drug by hepatic metabolism. (The plasma concentration of the drug metabolites is not illustrated.) The calculated

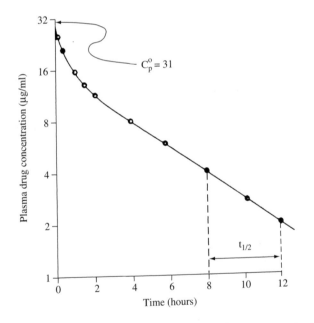

FIGURE 1.16 Plasma concentration time curve following intravenous injection of a drug. In this example, drug concentrations are measured in plasma every 30 minutes for the first 2 hours following drug injection, then every 2 hours until 12 hours after injection. Over the first 2 hours, redistribution exists as the drug leaves plasma and enters body tissues and equilibrates with those tissues. After redistribution, the fall in plasma level is linear, exhibiting a metabolic half-life of 4 hours, regardless of the plasma concentration of the drug. [From Wilkinson (2001), p. 21.]

elimination half-life is a measure of this process, and it allows the time course of drug action to be calculated.

Figure 1.16 shows that the elimination half-life of the drug is about 4 hours (the time for the blood level to fall from 4 µg/ml to 2 µg/ml. This 4-hour half-life then remains constant over time. In other words, it takes the same amount of time for the blood level to fall from 8 µg/ml to 4 µg/ml as it does to fall from 4 µg/ml to 2 µg/ml or from 2 µg/ml to 1 µg/ml. Thus, a different absolute amount of drug is metabolized within each half-life; the time interval remains constant.

The knowledge of a drug's half-life is important because it tells us how long a drug remains in the body. As shown in Table 1.2, it takes four half-lives for 94 percent of a drug to be eliminated by the body and six half-lives for 98 percent of the drug to be eliminated. At that point, a person is, for most practical purposes, drug free. It is important to remember that even though the blood level of the drug is reduced by 75 percent after two half-lives, the drug persists in the body at low levels for at least six half-lives. The so-called drug hangover is a result.

Throughout this book, drug half-lives are cited to describe the duration of action of psychoactive drugs in the body and allow comparisons between drugs with similar actions but differing half-lives. Most drug half-lives are measured in hours; others are measured in days, and recovery from the drug may take a week or more. For example, the elimination half-life of diazepam (Valium; Chapter 6) is about 30 hours in a healthy young adult (Figure 1.17), much longer in the elderly. The half-life of its active metabolite (nordiazepam, not illustrated in Figure 1.17) is even longer, on the order of several days to a week. The elderly exhibit even more prolongation of the half-lives of both diazepam and nordiazepam; the duration of action can be 4 weeks or even longer.

Note that drug half-life is the *time* for the plasma level of drug to fall by 50 percent. Thus, half-life is independent of the absolute level of

TABLE 1.2 Half-life calculations

Number of half-lives	Amount of drug in the body	
	Percent eliminated	Percent remaining
0	0	100
1	50	50
2	75	25
3	87.5	12.5
4	93.8	6.2
5	96.9	3.1
6	98.4	1.6

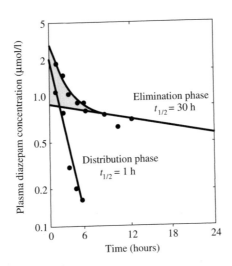

FIGURE 1.17 Plasma levels of diazepam (Valium, a benzodiazepine) following a single intravenous dose. The fast (distribution) phase has a half-life of about 1 hour. The slower, metabolic elimination phase shows a half-life of 30 hours. The long half-life of the active diazepam metabolite, nordiazepam, is not shown.

drug in blood: the level falls by 50 percent every half-life, regardless of how many molecules of drug were actually metabolized during that time. Therefore, a varying amount of drug is metabolized with each half-life (fewer actual molecules are metabolized per half-life as the plasma level of drug falls).

One of the rare exceptions to this concept is the metabolism of ethyl alcohol by the enzyme alcohol dehydrogenase. Here, a constant amount of alcohol is metabolized per hour, regardless of the absolute amount of alcohol present in blood, and the blood level falls in a straight-line manner.[4] (The metabolism of alcohol is discussed in Chapter 4.)

Drug Half-Life, Accumulation, and Steady State

The biological half-life of a drug is not only the time required for the drug concentration in blood to fall by one-half, but it is also the determinant of the length of time necessary to reach a steady-state concentration (Figure 1.18). If a second full dose of drug is administered before the body has eliminated the first dose, the total amount of drug in the body and the peak level of the drug in the blood will be greater than the total amount and peak level produced by the first dose. For

---

[4]Usually, about 10 cc of absolute alcohol are metabolized per hour, regardless of blood level. The significance of this rate is discussed in Chapter 4.

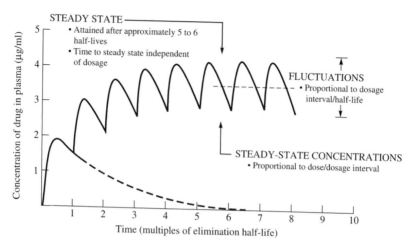

FIGURE 1.18 Plasma drug concentrations during repeated oral administration of a drug at intervals equal to its elimination half-life. The heavy dashed line illustrates the elimination curve if only a single dose is given. Because only 50 percent of each dose is eliminated before the next dose is given, the drug accumulates, reaching steady-state concentration in five to six half-lives. The sinusoidal curve shows the maximal and minimal drug concentrations at the beginning and end of each dosage interval, respectively. The light dashed line illustrates the average concentration achieved at steady state.

example, if 100 milligrams (mg) of a drug with a 4-hour half-life were administered at 12 noon, 50 mg of drug would remain in the body at 4 P.M. If an additional 100 mg of the drug were then taken at 4 P.M., 75 mg of drug would remain in the body at 8 P.M. (25 mg of the first dose and 50 mg of the second). If this administration schedule were continued, the amount of drug in the body would continue to increase until a plateau (steady-state) concentration was reached.

In general, the time to reach *steady-state concentration* (the level of drug achieved in blood with repeated, regular-interval dosing) is about six times the drug's elimination half-life and is independent of the actual dosage of the drug. In one half-life, a drug reaches 50 percent of the concentration that will eventually be achieved. After two half-lives, the drug achieves 75 percent concentration; at three half-lives, the drug achieves the initial 50 percent of the third dose, the next 25 percent from the second dose, plus half of the remaining 25 percent from the first dose. At 98.4 percent (the concentration achieved after six half-lives), the drug concentration is essentially at steady state. This is the rationale behind our general rule. The steady-state concentration is achieved when the amount administered per unit time equals the amount eliminated per unit time. The interdependent variables that determine the ultimate concentration (or steady-state blood level of drug) are the dose (which determines the blood level but not the time to steady state), the dose interval, the half-life of the drug, and other, more complex factors that can affect drug elimination.

In summary, steady, regular-interval dosing leads to a predictable accumulation, with a steady-state concentration reached after about six half-lives; the magnitude of the concentration is proportional to dose and dosage interval. Clinically, these factors guide drug therapy when blood levels of the drug are monitored and correlated with therapeutic results.

Therapeutic Drug Monitoring

Therapeutic drug monitoring (TDM) can aid a clinician in making critical decisions in therapeutic applications. In psychopharmacology, TDM can dramatically improve the prognosis of psychological disorders, making previously difficult-to-treat disorders much more treatable (Preskorn et al., 1993).

The basic principle underlying TDM is that a threshold plasma concentration of a drug is needed at the receptor site to initiate and maintain a pharmacological response. Critically important is that plasma concentrations of psychoactive drugs correlate well with tissue or receptor concentrations. Therefore, TDM is an indirect although usually quite accurate measurement of drug concentration at the receptor site. To make the correlation between TDM, dosage, and therapeutic response, large-scale clinical trials are performed, and blood samples are drawn at multiple time periods during both acute (short-term) and chronic (long-term) therapy. Statistical correlation is made between the level of drug in plasma and the degree of therapeutic response. A dosage regimen can then be designed to achieve the appropriate blood level of a drug.

The goals of TDM are many. One goal is to assess whether a patient is taking medication as prescribed; if plasma levels of the drug are below the therapeutic level because the patient has not been taking the required medication, therapeutic results will be poor. Another goal is to avoid toxicity; if plasma levels of the drug are above the therapeutic level, the dosage can be lowered, effectiveness maintained, and toxicity minimized. A third goal is to enhance therapeutic response by focusing not on the amount of drug taken but on the measured amount of drug in the plasma. Other goals include possible reductions in the cost of therapy (since a patient's illness is better controlled) and the substantiation of the need for unusually high doses in patients who require higher-than-normal intake of prescribed medication to maintain a therapeutic blood level of a drug.

Drug Tolerance and Dependence

Drug tolerance is defined as a state of progressively decreasing responsiveness to a drug. A person who develops tolerance requires a larger dose of the drug to achieve the effect originally obtained by a smaller dose. At least three mechanisms are involved in the development of drug tolerance—two are pharmacological mechanisms, one is a behavioral mechanism.

Metabolic tolerance is the first of the two classically described types of pharmacological tolerance. As discussed earlier, the presence of a drug in blood perfusing the liver can induce the synthesis of hepatic cytochrome P450 drug-metabolizing enzymes. Thus, the drug is metabolized at a faster rate, and more drug must be administered to maintain the same level of drug in the body.

Cellular-adaptive or *pharmacodynamic tolerance* is the second type of pharmacological tolerance. Receptors in the brain adapt to the continued presence of the drug, with neurons adapting to excess drug either by reducing the number of receptors available to the drug or by reducing their sensitivity to the drug. Such reduction in numbers or sensitivity is termed *down regulation*, and higher levels of drug are necessary to maintain the same biological effect.

Behavioral conditioning processes are the third type of drug tolerance. The exposure of drugs to receptors does not account for the substantial degree of tolerance that many people acquire to opioids, barbiturates, ethyl alcohol, and other drugs. Instead, tolerance can be demonstrated when a drug is administered in the context of usual predrug cues but not in the context of alternative cues. Poulos and Cappell (1991) proposed a *homeostatic theory* of drug tolerance. They found that, with morphine analgesia, testing in an environment in which tolerance had developed affected the manifestation of tolerance, and an environmental cue could maintain the tolerance. This *contingent tolerance* is pervasive and represents a general process underlying the development of all forms of systemic tolerance.

The environmental cues routinely paired with drug administration will become conditioned stimuli that elicit a conditioned response that is opposite in direction to or compensation for the direct effects of the drug. Over conditioning trials, the compensatory conditioned response grows in magnitude and counteracts the direct drug effects; that is, tolerance develops.

Physical dependence is an entirely different phenomenon from tolerance, even though the two are often associated temporally. A person who is physically dependent needs the drug to avoid withdrawal symptoms if the drug is not taken. The state is revealed by withdrawing the drug and noting the occurrence of physical and/or psychological changes (withdrawal symptoms). These changes are referred to as an *abstinence syndrome*. Readministering the drug can relieve the symptoms of withdrawal.

Because physical dependence is often manifested following cessation of use of drugs of abuse such as alcohol and heroin, the term has been linked with "addiction," implying that withdrawal signs are "bad" and observed only with drugs of abuse. This is certainly far from the truth: rather severe withdrawal signs can follow cessation of such therapeutic drugs as the SSRI type of clinical antidepressants[5] (Chapter 9). Therefore, the occurrence of withdrawal signs after drug removal is not necessarily a sign of drug "addiction" that is usually associated with "bad" drugs such as heroin. Rather, physical dependence is an indication that brain and body functions were altered by the presence of a drug and that a different homeostatic state must be initiated at drug withdrawal. It takes time (from a few days to about two weeks) for the brain and the body to adapt to this new state of equilibrium where drug is absent.

STUDY QUESTIONS

1. What is meant by the term *pharmacokinetics*? What does the term imply?

2. Why must a psychoactive drug be altered metabolically in the body before it can be excreted?

3. Discuss the advantages and disadvantages of the various methods of administering drugs.

4. List the various membrane barriers that may affect drug distribution.

5. Discuss the blood-brain barrier as a limitation to drug transport.

6. Discuss the placental barrier as it affects the distribution of psychoactive drugs. What are the cautions for the use of psychotropic medication during pregnancy?

7. If a drug has an elimination half-life of 6 hours, how long does it take for the drug to be effectively eliminated from the body after administration of a single dose?

8. What is drug tolerance and why does it occur? Discuss three mechanisms underlying the development of tolerance.

9. What are the various routes through the body whereby a drug can be eliminated?

10. Define *half-life*. How does *half-life* apply to steady state?

11. What is meant by the term *therapeutic drug monitoring*? In what instances might it be of value?

---

[5]Removal of SSRI-type antidepressants is followed in many individuals by withdrawal signs that can be organized into five core somatic symptoms: (1) disequilibrium (dizziness, vertigo, ataxia), (2) GI symptoms (nausea, vomiting), (3) flulike symptoms (fatigue, lethargy, myalgias, chills), (4) sensory disturbances (paresthesias, sensation of electric shocks), and (5) sleep disturbances (insomnia, vivid dreams).

REFERENCES

Garland, M. (1998). "Pharmacology of Drug Transfer Across the Placenta." *Obstetrics and Gynecology Clinics of North America* 25: 21–42.

Gilstrap, L. C., and B. B. Little (1998). *Drugs and Pregnancy*, 2nd ed. New York: Chapman & Hall.

Greenblatt, D. J., et al. (1999). "Human Cytochromes and Some Newer Antidepressants: Kinetics, Metabolism, and Drug Interactions." *Journal of Clinical Psychopharmacology* 19, Supplement 1: 23S–35S.

Greenblatt, D. J., et al. (2001). "Drug Interactions with Grapefruit Juice: An Update." *Journal of Clinical Psychopharmacology* 21: 357–359.

Greenblatt, D. J., et al. (2003). "Time Course of Recovery of Cytochrome P450 3A Function After Single Doses of Grapefruit Juice." *Clinical Pharmacology and Therapeutics* 74: 121–129.

Kashuba, A., et al. (1998). "Effect of Fluvoxamine Therapy on the Activities of CYP-1A2, CYP-2D6, and CYP-3A as Determined by Phenotyping." *Clinical Pharmacology and Therapeutics* 64: 257–268.

Lilja, J. J., et al. (1998). "Grapefruit Juice Substantially Increases Plasma Concentrations of Buspirone." *Clinical Pharmacology and Therapeutics* 64: 655–660.

Ozdemir, V., et al. (1998). "The Extent and Determinants of Changes in CYP-2D6 and CYP-1A2 Activities with Therapeutic Doses of Sertraline." *Journal of Clinical Psychopharmacology* 18: 55–61.

Pardridge, W. M. (2003). "Blood-Brain Barrier Drug Targeting: The Future of Brain Drug Development." *Molecular Interventions* 3: 90–105.

Poulos, C. X., and H. Cappell (1991). "Homeostatic Theory of Drug Tolerance: A General Model of Physiological Adaptation." *Psychological Reviews* 98: 390–408.

Preskorn, S. H., et al. (1993). "Therapeutic Drug Monitoring: Principles and Practice." *Psychiatric Clinics of North America* 16: 611–641.

Wetzel, H., et al. (1998). "Pharmacokinetic Interactions of Clozapine with Selective Serotonin Reuptake Inhibitors: Differential Effects of Fluvoxamine and Paroxetine in a Prospective Study." *Journal of Clinical Psychopharmacology* 18: 2–9.

Wilkinson, G. R. (2001). "Pharmacokinetics: The Dynamics of Drug Absorption, Distribution, and Elimination." In J. G. Hardman, L. E. Limbird, and A. G. Gilman, eds., *Goodman and Gilman's The Pharmacological Basis of Therapeutics*, 10th ed. (pp. 3–29). New York: McGraw-Hill.

Pharmacodynamics: How Drugs Act

While the body is trying to rid itself of an ingested psychoactive drug, the drug is exerting effects by attaching to receptors in cells in both the brain and the body. As a result of the interactions, the body experiences effects that are characteristic for the drug. *It is a basic principle of pharmacology that the pharmacological, physiological, or behavioral effects induced by a drug follow from their interaction with receptors.* The study of the interactions is termed *pharmacodynamics* and involves exploring the mechanisms of drug action that occur at the molecular level. It provides the basis for both the rational therapeutic use of a drug and the design of new and superior therapeutic agents (Ross and Kenakin, 2001).

To produce an effect, a drug must bind to and interact with specialized receptors, usually located on cell membranes. In the case of psychoactive drugs, these receptors are usually located on the surface of neurons within the brain. The occupation of a receptor by a drug (*drug-receptor binding*) leads to a change in the functional properties of the neuron, resulting in the drug's characteristic pharmacological response. In most instances, drug-receptor binding is both *ionic* and *reversible* in nature,[1] with positive and negative charges on various portions of the drug molecule and the receptor protein attracting one to

[1]Reversible ionic binding is contrasted with the formation of a permanent, irreversible, covalent bond between a drug and a receptor. One of the rare instances in psychopharmacology where an irreversible covalent bond forms is between certain antidepressant drugs and the enzyme monoamine oxidase (Chapter 9).

the other. The strength of ionic attachment is determined by the fit of the three-dimensional structure of the drug to the three-dimensional site on the receptor.

Receptors for Drug Action

Since drugs exert their effects by forming reversible ionic bonds with specific receptors, exactly what are receptors? A *receptor* is a fairly large molecule (usually a protein[2]) that is present on the surface of or within a cell that furnishes the site or sites where biologically active, naturally occurring, endogenous compounds (called *ligands,* or *neurotransmitters*) induce their normal biological effects. While literally hundreds of different types of ligand receptors are known (each a unique protein molecule), the ability to recognize one specific neurotransmitter characterizes each one (Feldman et al., 1997, p. 13). Thus, only one neurotransmitter might be specific enough to fit or bind to a specific receptor protein. For example, if only serotonin binds to a specific protein receptor, the protein is called a serotonin receptor. But although the receptor is specific for serotonin, serotonin (as a neurotransmitter) also binds to other, structurally different receptors. To date, more than 15 different serotonin receptor proteins have been identified.[3] In pharmacology, such diversity makes it possible to develop closely related drugs, each with slightly different degrees of affinity for the different serotonin receptors. For example, a specific drug might have affinity for a serotonin-1 receptor but not for any of the other serotonin receptors. Until recently it was not possible to develop such a drug. However, with the understanding that drug receptors are proteins, it became possible to isolate a specific receptor protein from the rest of the brain, purify it, determine its amino acid sequence, isolate the portion of DNA responsible for making the protein, and clone the protein receptor to produce sufficient quantities of receptor against which drugs could be screened for affinity and activity. This is the pharmacology of the new millennium!

It is now known that a given drug may be more specific for a given set of receptors than is the endogenous neurotransmitter. Serotonin,

[2]A protein is a complex chain of various amino acids. Proteins are essential to life, functioning, among other things, as metabolic enzymes and receptors.

[3]Each receptor protein that binds serotonin, for example, has a slightly different amino acid composition; despite this, their three-dimensional structures are similar enough that serotonin, for example, still fits a "slot" (like a lock-and-key arrangement) and ionically binds to the protein. Pharmacologists have named these different protein receptors serotonin-1, serotonin-2, serotonin-3, and so on; in earlier years, multiple receptors for a single neurotransmitter were given more exotic names (for example, muscarinic and nicotinic for acetylcholine receptors, alpha and beta for adrenergic receptors, and mu, delta, and kappa for opioid receptors).

for example, must necessarily attach to all its more than 15 different serotonin receptors (it has to because it is the endogenous neurotransmitter at each receptor). However, a given drug might attach to only one receptor. For example, fluoxetine (Prozac) binds to and blocks the presynaptic serotonin reuptake receptor. It does not bind to any of the many postsynaptic serotonin receptors. Fluoxetine is therefore called a *selective serotonin reuptake inhibitor* (SSRI) and is used clinically as an antidepressant.

Another drug, buspirone (BuSpar) has no affinity for the presynaptic serotonin transporter; it attaches with great specificity to postsynaptic serotonin 1_A receptors, which results in an antianxiety action. This specificity implies that buspirone might not have the side effects of fluoxetine that follow from increased activity of serotonin at all postsynaptic receptors (Chapter 9).

Figures 2.1 through 2.4 demonstrate six important points about drug-receptor interactions:

1. A receptor is usually a membrane-spanning protein (Figure 2.1) that has binding sites for an endogenous neurotransmitter and appropriate drug molecules.

2. This membrane-spanning protein is not a simple globule (as suggested by Figure 2.1) but a continuous series of either 7 or 12 alpha helical coils (loops of amino acids) embedded in the membrane (Figure 2.2).

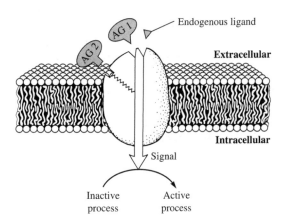

FIGURE 2.1 Diagrammatic representation of the classical concept of a receptor. One type of agonist (AG 1) fits the receptor site for an endogenous ligand and mimics the action of the ligand. Another type of agonist (AG 2) binds to an adjacent receptor site, thereby influencing (amplifying) signal transmission. Signal transmission activates intracellular processes that are inactive without receptor activation.

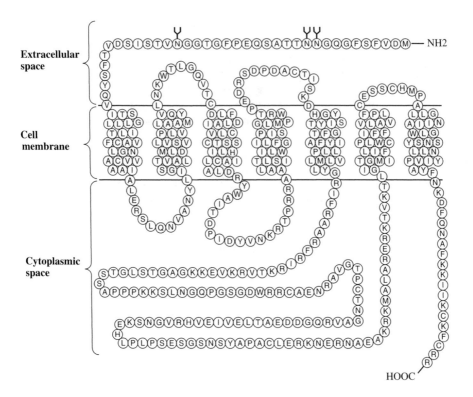

FIGURE 2.2 Schematic representation of the primary structure of the serotonin 1$_A$ postsynaptic receptor. Each circle represents an individual amino acid; the letter is the initial of the name of the amino acid. This receptor is one member of a large "family" of postsynaptic neurotransmitter receptors containing 7-transmembrane alpha helical coils.

3. The endogenous neurotransmitter (and presumably drugs also) attaches inside the space between these coils (Figure 2.3) and is held in place by ionic attractions.

4. This reversible ionic binding of the neurotransmitter specific for that receptor may activate the receptor, usually by changing the structure of the protein (Figure 2.4). This change allows a "signal," or "information," to be transmitted through the receptor to the inside of the cell.

5. The intensity of the resulting transmembrane signal is thought to be determined by the percentage of receptors that are occupied by molecules of neurotransmitter.

6. A drug can affect the transmembrane signal by binding either to the receptor for the endogenous neurotransmitter or to a nearby site. ·

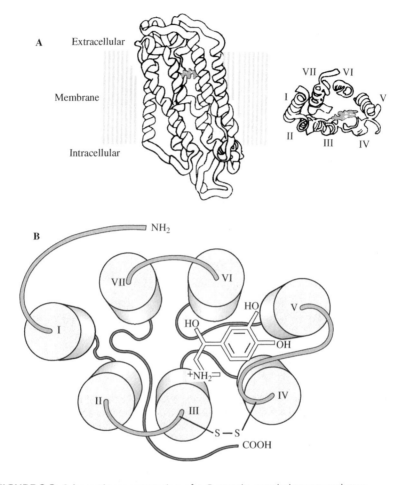

FIGURE 2.3 Schematic representation of a G protein-coupled transmembrane receptor, with a molecule of neurotransmitter (norepinephrine) lying in its binding site. Note the arrangement of the 7-transmembrane helical coils and the site of the transmitter attachment deep within the structure. The ionic interactions between the transmitter and particular amino acid side chains are not illustrated. In **A**, the membrane and continuous coils are shown. In **B**, the helical coils are represented as cylinders with the molecule of norepinephrine interacting with four of the coils.

Binding of a drug to a receptor results in one of three actions:

1. Binding to a receptor site normally occupied by the endogenous neurotransmitter can initiate a cellular response similar or identical to that exerted by the transmitter. The drug thus mimics the action of the transmitter. This is termed an *agonistic action* and the drug is termed an *agonist* for that transmitter.

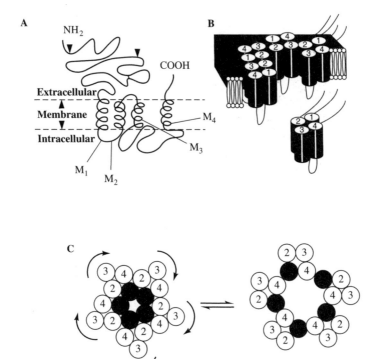

FIGURE 2.4 Presumed topology of the GABA$_A$ receptor. **A.** Single subunit with its large extracellular terminal part, and four transmembrane helical coils. **B.** Arrangement of the transmembrane domains of five subunits to form a central channel. **C.** Transmembrane domain in a transverse section through the membrane when the channel is closed (*left*) and open (*right*). [From W. E. Haefley et al., "The Multiplicity of Actions of Benzodiazepine Receptor Ligands," *Canadian Journal of Psychiatry* 38, Suppl. 4 (1993): 5102–5107.]

2. Binding to a site near the binding site for the endogenous transmitter can facilitate transmitter binding. This is also an agonistic action.

3. Binding to a receptor site normally occupied by a neurotransmitter but not initiating a transmitterlike action blocks access of the transmitter to its binding site, which inhibits the normal physiological action of the transmitter. This is called an *antagonistic action* and the drug is termed an *antagonist* for that neurotransmitter or receptor site.

Thus, directly binding to the receptor either blocks the access of the transmitter to its receptor (an antagonistic action) or else mimics or facilitates transmitter action (agonistic actions).

It is also a general rule of psychopharmacology that drugs do not create any unique effects; they merely modulate normal neuronal functioning, mimicking or antagonizing the actions of a specific neurotransmitter. Binding accompanied by drug-induced mimicry or facilitation of neurotransmitter action is an agonistic action.[4] Drug occupation of a receptor that is not accompanied by neurotransmitter-like activation blocks the access of the neurotransmitter to the receptor and is an antagonistic action.[5]

Receptor Structure

What does a receptor look like? As stated earlier, most receptors are membrane-spanning proteins, each having 7 or 12 alpha helical coils. Following are three different types of membrane-spanning proteins, as well as a fourth type of drug-receptor protein: enzymes.

Ion Channel Receptors.   The first type of membrane-spanning receptors are those that form an *ion channel;* the central portion of the receptor forms a pore, or channel, that enlarges in size when either an endogenous neurotransmitter or a specialized intracellular G protein attaches to the receptor. The attachment allows flow of a specific *ion* (such as chloride ion) through the enlarged pore. A drug may also bind to this receptor, acting to either facilitate or block the action of the neurotransmitter.

Figures 2.4 and 2.5 illustrate the neurotransmitter gamma aminobutyric acid (GABA) and a drug (a benzodiazepine) opening a channel and allowing inward flow of chloride ions through an enlarged pore within a GABA-activated receptor. Benzodiazepines (Chapter 6) serve as agonists at this site by binding to a site near the GABA-binding site and by facilitating the action of GABA. This action allows flow of chloride ions into the neuron, hyperpolarizing the neuron and inhibiting neuronal function. This action underlies the use of benzodiazepines as sedative, antianxiety, amnestic, and antiepileptic agents.

In contrast, the drug flumazenil (Romazecon) attaches to the benzodiazepine-binding site but does not facilitate the action of GABA. It does, however, compete with any benzodiazepine that is present, displacing the benzodiazepine from the receptor and reversing the actions of the benzodiazepine. Flumazenil is classified pharmacologically as a

---

[4]Example: Buspirone attaches to the serotonin 1_A receptor and activates it, mimicking serotonin action on the receptor, which results in an antianxiety action of clinical significance.

[5]Example: Fluoxetine competes with serotonin for the reuptake protein, blocking access of serotonin to the receptor and prolonging serotonin's presence in the synaptic cleft (Chapter 3). This allows more serotonin stimulation of postsynaptic receptors, eventually leading to down regulation in the number of serotonin receptors and relief of clinical depression (Chapter 9).

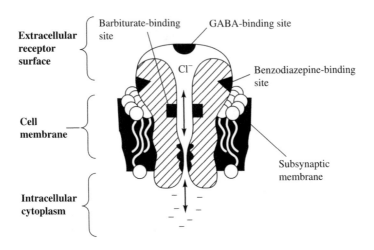

FIGURE 2.5 GABA$_A$ receptor in a perpendicular section through the membrane. The localization of the various binding sites is purely hypothetical. [From W. E. Haefley et al., "The Multiplicity of Actions of Benzodiazepine Receptor Ligands," *Canadian Journal of Psychiatry* 38, Suppl. 4 (1993): 5102–5107.]

benzodiazepine antagonist and is used clinically to treat benzodiazepine overdoses.[6]

Figure 2.6 illustrates the opening of a channel as a result of neurotransmitter attachment to an adjacent membrane-spanning receptor protein (a G protein-coupled receptor). Receptor activation releases an intracellular G protein that in turn activates other proteins that ultimately open an adjacent ion channel. Obviously, this can be quite confusing.

Carrier Proteins. The second type of membrane-spanning receptor protein is a *carrier* (or *transport*) *protein*. This type of receptor transports small organic molecules (such as neurotransmitters) across cell membranes against concentration gradients. Important in psychopharmacology are the presynaptic carrier proteins that function to bind dopamine, norepinephrine, or serotonin in the synaptic cleft and transport them back into the presynaptic nerve terminal, terminating the synaptic transmitter action of these three neurotransmitters (Chapter 9). Cocaine and methylphenidate (Ritalin) (both covered in

[6]Also shown in Figure 2.5 is a barbiturate-binding site on the GABA receptor complex. Barbiturates (Chapter 5) act like benzodiazepines in increasing the effect of GABA on the chloride channel within the GABA receptor. Thus, with a site and mechanism of action similar to that exerted by benzodiazepines, the two classes of drugs might be expected to demonstrate similar clinical and behavioral effects. In general, that is true.

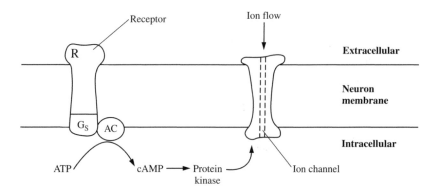

FIGURE 2.6 Hypothetical model of a G protein-coupled receptor functioning to open an adjacent ion channel. A neurotransmitter binds to its receptor site (R). A conformational change results, and a second-messenger enzyme, adenylate cyclase (AC), is activated through the action of a released G protein (G_s). G_s forms cyclic adenosine monophosphate (cAMP), which activates a protein kinase (functioning as a second messenger), which ultimately acts on the ion channel to cause it to open, allowing a flow of ions into (or out of) the cell. This is but one model of an intracellular function being modulated by a G protein-coupled transmembrane receptor activated by a neurotransmitter.

Chapter 7) block the carrier protein that is specific for transporting dopamine. Fluoxetine (Chapter 9) blocks the carrier protein that is specific for transporting serotonin. Imipramine (Tofranil) blocks the carrier protein that is specific for transporting norepinephrine. These molecular actions result in similar but still distinctly different effects.

Figure 2.7 illustrates the structure of the presynaptic transport receptor for dopamine. The presynaptic transport protein receptor is arranged as 12 helical arrays of amino acids, contrasted with the 7 helices present in postsynaptic serotonin (and other neurotransmitter) receptors, as shown in Figure 2.2.

G Protein-Coupled Receptors. A third type of membrane-spanning receptor protein is called a *G protein-coupled receptor.* It is a postsynaptic receptor, activation of which induces the release of an attached intracellular protein (a *G protein*) that, in turn, controls enzymatic function within the postsynaptic neuron. Figure 2.2 illustrates the structure of one of the more than 15 such receptors for serotonin (here, the serotonin 1_A receptor). Figure 2.8 illustrates some of the intracellular alterations that can be induced as a result of activation of this receptor.

G protein-coupled receptors are discussed throughout this book because they are involved in the actions of many neurotransmitters, such as acetylcholine, norepinephrine, dopamine, serotonin, and opioid endorphins, all of which are sites of action of psychoactive drugs. The

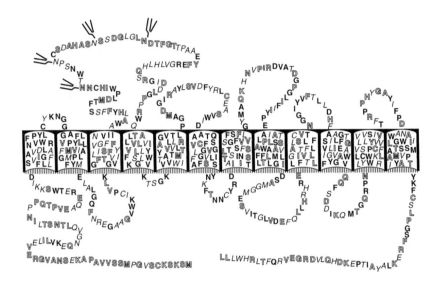

FIGURE 2.7 Schematic representation of the dopamine transporter showing proposed orientation in the presynaptic membranes. [From S. Shimada et al., "Cloning and Expression of a Cocaine-Sensitive Dopamine Transporter Complimentary DNA," *Science* 254 (1991): 576–578.]

molecular structure of G protein-coupled receptors (more than 50 have been identified, and more keep coming!) consists of a single protein chain of 400 to 500 amino acids possessing seven transmembrane alpha helices (see Figure 2.2). Both the extracellular and the intracellular terminal portions of the protein chain vary in length and in amino acid composition. G protein-coupled receptors are the middlemen (the *second messenger*[7]), able to communicate between the neurotransmitter-receptor complex and intracellular enzymes or adjacent ion channels (Figures 2.8 and 2.9). The protein consists of three functional subunits, which taken together have historically been called G protein because they interact with guanine nucleotides within the cell. G proteins control many cellular functions, among them control of ion channels, energy metabolism, cell division and differentiation, and neuronal excitability. Simmonds (1999) reviewed the interaction between G proteins and *adenylate cyclase*, a key intracellular regulatory enzyme.

Enzymes. A fourth type of receptor protein for psychoactive drugs is *enzymes*, in particular enzymes that regulate the synaptic availability of certain neurotransmitters. These enzymes function to break down neurotransmitters, and their inhibition by drugs increases transmitter

---

[7]The endogenous neurotransmitter is the first messenger, carrying information between presynaptic and postsynaptic neurons across the synaptic cleft (Chapter 3).

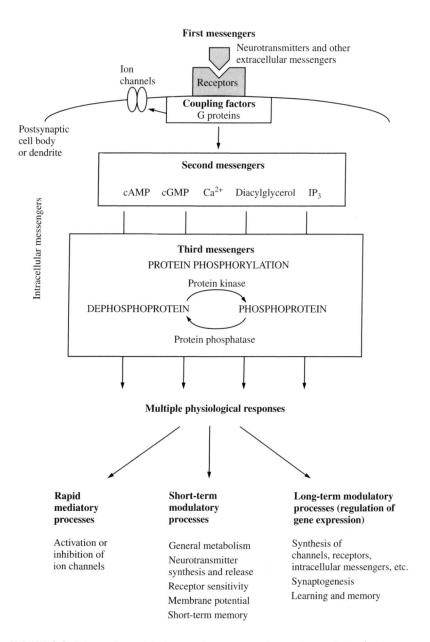

FIGURE 2.8 Schematic model of transmitter-receptor interaction and the resulting second-messenger action. Second messengers are intracellular proteins, molecules, or ions that are regulated by transmitter-receptor activation. The neurotransmitter is the first messenger, and binding is a recognition action. Receptor alteration with G protein release represents transduction of first-messenger binding. As shown here, second messengers amplify the signal and serve to turn on or turn off numerous rapid and long-term physiological responses.

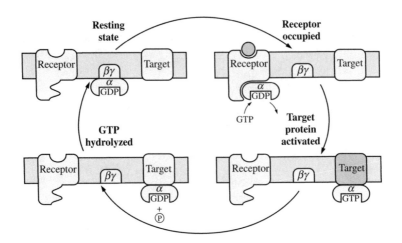

FIGURE 2.9 Function of the G protein. The G protein consists of three subunits, alpha, beta, and gamma, which function to anchor the G protein to the transmembrane helical protein-receptor molecule. Coupling of the alpha subunit to an agonist-occupied receptor causes the bound GDP (guanine diphosphate) to exchange with intracellular GTP (guanine triphosphate); the alpha-GTP complex dissociates and interacts with adenylate cyclase. The original complex then regenerates through hydrolysis of the GTP. [From H. P. Rang et al., *Pharmacology* (New York: Churchill Livingstone, 1995), Figure 2.9.]

availability. Following are two examples: *acetylcholine esterase,* the enzyme that breaks down acetylcholine within the synaptic cleft (Chapter 3). The second example is *monoamine oxidase,* the enzyme that breaks down norepinephrine and dopamine within presynaptic nerve terminals, controlling the amount available for release (Chapters 3 and 9).

Drugs known as *irreversible acetylcholine esterase inhibitors* form covalent bonds with the enzyme and are used as insecticides and as lethal "nerve gases." Drugs that *reversibly* inhibit the enzyme *acetylcholine esterase* are used clinically as cognitive enhancers, delaying the onset of Alzheimer's disease (Chapter 13). Drugs that irreversibly inhibit the enzyme *monoamine oxidase* are called monoamine oxidase inhibitors (MAOIs) and are used primarily as antidepressants.

Drug-Receptor Specificity

As discussed, receptors exhibit high specificity both for one particular neurotransmitter and for certain drug molecules. Making only modest variations in the chemical structure of a drug may greatly alter the intensity of a receptor's response to it. For example, amphetamine and methamphetamine (Chapter 7) are both powerful psychostimulants.

Although their chemical structures are very close, they differ by the simple addition of a methyl ($-CH_3$) group to amphetamine, forming methamphetamine. Methamphetamine produces much greater behavioral stimulation at the same milligram dosage. Both drugs attach to the same receptors in the brain, but methamphetamine exerts a much more powerful action on them, at least on a milligram basis. The drug molecule with the "best fit" to the receptor (methamphetamine, in this example) elicits the greatest response from the cell. In pharmacologic terms, methamphetamine is more *potent* than amphetamine, because a lower absolute dose achieves the same level of response as a higher dose of amphetamine. Importantly, as we will see next, a more *potent* drug is not necessarily a more *effective* drug. It merely produces its effects at a somewhat lower dose.

As a consequence of drug binding to a receptor, cellular function is altered, resulting in observable effects on physiological or psychological functioning. The total action of the drug in the body results from drug actions either (1) on one specific type of receptor or (2) at multiple different types of receptors. The use of a drug for a given therapeutic (or recreational) effect also results in other effects, called *side effects*.

As an example of the side effects produced by the first mechanism, fluoxetine-induced blockade of presynaptic serotonin reuptake increases serotonin availability at all postsynaptic serotonin receptors. This single action results not only in relief of depression but also in such side effects as anxiety, insomnia, and sexual dysfunction (Chapter 9).

As an example of the side effects produced by the second mechanism, certain other antidepressants (the tricyclic antidepressants; Chapter 9) increase both serotonin and norepinephrine availability (reducing depression). They also produce sedation as a result of their blocking histamine receptors; dry mouth and blurred vision can result. A balance between wanted effects and inevitable but unwanted side effects is always desirable.

Dose-Response Relationships

One way of quantifying drug-receptor interactions is to use *dose-response curves*. In Figure 2.10, two different types of dose-response curves are illustrated. In graph A, the dose is plotted against the percentage of people (from a given population) who exhibit a characteristic effect at a given dosage. In graph B, the dose is plotted against the intensity, or magnitude, of the response in a single person. These curves indicate that a dose exists that is low enough to produce little or no effect; at the opposite extreme, a dose exists beyond which no

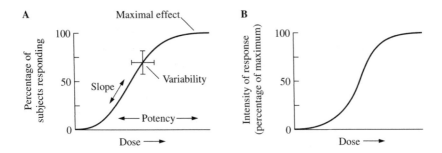

FIGURE 2.10 Two types of dose-response curves. **A.** Curve obtained by plotting the dose of drug against the percentage of subjects showing a given response at any given dose. **B.** Curve obtained by plotting the dose of drug against the intensity of response observed in any single individual at a given dose. The intensity of response is plotted as a percentage of the maximum obtainable response.

greater response can be elicited. Dose-response curves demonstrate important characteristics:

1. *Potency* refers to the absolute number of molecules of drug required to elicit a response, a measurement of the dose required.

2. *Efficacy* refers to the maximum effect obtainable, with additional doses producing no more effect.

3. *Variability* and *slope* refer to individual differences in drug response, with some persons responding at very low doses and some requiring much more drug.

The location of the dose-response curve along the horizontal axis reflects the potency of the drug. If two drugs produce an equal degree of sedation, but one exerts this action at half the dose level of the other, the first drug is considered to be twice as *potent* as the second drug (Figure 2.11). As stated, however, potency is a relatively unimportant characteristic of a drug, because it makes little difference whether the effective dose of a drug is 1.0 milligram or 100 milligrams as long as the drug is administered in an appropriate dose with no undue toxicity.

Slope refers to the more or less linear central portion of the dose-response curve. A steep slope on a dose-response curve implies that there is only a small difference between the dose that produces a barely discernible effect and the dose that causes a maximal effect. The steeper the slope, the smaller the increase in dose that is required to go from a minimum response to a maximum effect. This can be good, as it may indicate that there is little biological variation in the response to the drug. Conversely, it may be a disadvantage if it indicates that untoward toxicity occurs with only minimal increases in dose.

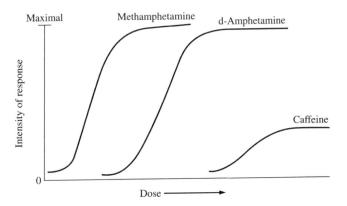

FIGURE 2.11 Theoretical dose-response curves for three psychostimulants to illustrate equal efficacy of methamphetamine and dextro-amphetamine; increased potency of methamphetamine; and reduced potency and efficacy of caffeine.

The *peak* of the dose-response curve indicates the maximum effect, or efficacy, that can be produced by a drug, regardless of further increases in dose. Not all psychoactive drugs can exert the same level of effect. For example, caffeine, even in massive doses, cannot exert the same intensity of central nervous system (CNS) stimulation as amphetamine (see Figure 2.11). Similarly, aspirin can never achieve the maximum analgesic effect of morphine. Thus, the maximum effect is an inherent property of a drug and is one measure of a drug's efficacy.

Most psychoactive drugs are not used to the point of their maximum effect because side effects and toxicities limit the upper range of dosage, regardless of whether the drug is administered for a therapeutic purpose or taken for recreational use. Therefore, the usefulness of a compound is correspondingly limited, even though the drug may be inherently capable of producing a greater or more intense effect.

Drug Safety and Effectiveness

For a drug to be approved by the federal Food and Drug Administration (FDA), its manufacturer must demonstrate both that the drug is *effective* for the claimed therapeutic use and that it is *safe* to use in a wide population. Effectiveness is determined in animal experiments and in human trials. Effectiveness is further assessed as the drug undergoes wider use in the general population. Safety refers to the potential for the drug to cause adverse effects, effects that vary from predictable and tolerable side effects to serious and unpredictable toxicities such as serious, unpredictable, and unrecognized allergic reactions to the drug. Also, when a drug is introduced into a general population, there is variability in response because of genetic or other population variances. Drug-drug interactions are also a common and important type of adverse effect, often predictable and often underappreciated during clinical trials (Jurrlink et al., 2003; Khatib et al., 2003).

Variability in Drug Responsiveness

The dose of a drug that produces a specific response varies considerably between individuals. Interpatient variability can result from differences in rates of drug absorption and metabolism, previous experience with drug use, various physical, psychological, and emotional states, and so on. Despite the etiology of the variability, any population of individuals will have a few subjects who are remarkably sensitive to the effects (and side effects) of a drug, while a few will exhibit remarkable drug tolerance, requiring quite large doses to produce therapeutic results. The variability, however, usually follows a predictable pattern, resembling a Gaussian distribution (Figure 2.12). In a few instances, however, a specific population of individuals (following a genetically predetermined pattern) will skew this distribution by exhibiting a unique pattern of responsiveness, usually due to genetic alterations in drug metabolism.

From Figure 2.12, it is obvious that, although the average dose required to elicit a given response can be calculated easily, some individuals respond at doses that are very much lower than the average and others respond only at doses that are very much higher. Thus, it is extremely important that the dose of any drug be individualized. Generalizations about "average doses" are risky at best.

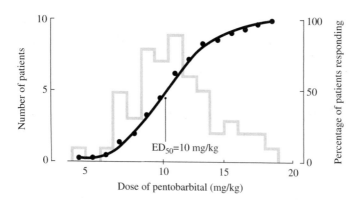

FIGURE 2.12 Example of biological variation. Histogram (*left ordinate*) and cumulative frequency histogram (*right ordinate*) following intravenous administration of pentobarbital, used to cause drowsiness in hospitalized patients. An ED_{50} of about 11 mg/kg body weight is shown. Note, however, that some patients exhibited sedation at about 4 mg/kg, while others required a dose of about 18 mg/kg The stairstep bars illustrate the data behind the dose-response curve.

The dose of a drug that produces the desired effect in 50 percent of the subjects is called the ED_{50}, and the lethal dose for 50 percent of the subjects is called the LD_{50}. The LD_{50} is calculated in exactly the same way as the ED_{50}, except that the dose of the drug is plotted against the number of experimental animals that die after being administered various doses of the compound. Both the ED_{50} and the LD_{50} are determined in several species of animals to prevent accidental drug-induced toxicity in humans. The ratio of the LD_{50} to the ED_{50} is used as an index of the relative safety of the drug and is called the *therapeutic index*.

To illustrate, two dose-response curves are shown in Figure 2.13. The curve at the left illustrates the dose of drug necessary to induce sleep in a population of mice, and the one at the right illustrates the dose of drug necessary to kill a similar population. In this example, the $LD_{50}:ED_{50}$ ratio is seen to be 100:10, or 10. This may seem like a rather large margin, but note that at a dose of 50 milligrams, 95 percent of the mice sleep while 5 percent of the mice die. This overlap demonstrates both the difficulty in assessing the relative safety of drugs for use in large populations and the biological variation in individual responses to drugs. With this particular compound, a dose cannot be administered that will guarantee that 100 percent of the mice will sleep and none will die. Thus, a more useful indication of the margin of safety is a ratio of the lethal dose for 1 percent of the population to the effective dose for 99 percent of the population ($LD_1:ED_{99}$). A sedative drug with an $LD_1:ED_{99}$ of 1 would be a safer compound than the drug shown in Figure 2.13. Note that the clinical usefulness of indices obtained from laboratory animals is limited because these indices do not reflect the occasional unexpected response (from the causes listed earlier) that can seriously harm a patient.

Drug variability is also intimately associated with drug toxicity. Therefore, the side effects that are invariably associated with a drug, as well as its more serious toxicities (including those that can be fatal), must always be considered.

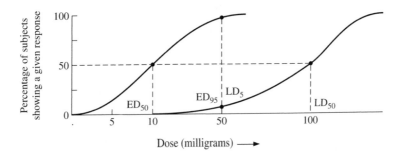

FIGURE 2.13 Two dose-response curves. *Left:* Dose of drug required to induce a given response. *Right:* Lethal dose of the compound. See text for discussion.

Drug Interactions

The effects of one drug can be modified by the concurrent administration of another drug. These relationships are particularly important in psychopharmacology. For example, Chapter 1 explained how certain drugs might either increase or decrease the rate of hepatic metabolism of other drugs, and this interaction affected the plasma levels of other drugs metabolized by the same enzymes. Another common mechanism of drug interaction involves drugs that can interact through an *additive mechanism,* where the effects of one drug potentiate the effects of another. For example, alcohol taken after a benzodiazepine tranquilizer has been ingested or after smoking marijuana increases sedation and loss of coordination. This action may have little consequence if the doses of each drug are low, but higher doses of either or both drugs can be dangerous both to the user and to others. Even though a person may normally be able to ingest a limited amount of alcohol and still drive a car without significant loss of control or coordination, the concurrent use of tranquilizers or marijuana may profoundly impair driving performance, endangering the driver, passengers, and other motorists. Logan (1996) reports the interaction between alcohol, marijuana, and methamphetamine on driving performance, noting additive impairments during both methamphetamine intoxication and withdrawal. Drug use was inconsistent with safe driving. Numerous other examples of additive drug interactions are reported in the medical literature and almost daily in the newspapers.

Drug Toxicity

All drugs can produce harmful effects as well as beneficial ones. The nature of these unwanted effects falls into two categories:

1. Effects that are related to the principal and predictable pharmacological actions of a drug (for example, the sedation caused by drinking alcohol or the dry mouth experienced while taking certain antidepressants)

2. Effects that are unrelated to the expected actions of a drug (for example, a severe allergic reaction to a drug)

It is important to categorize harmful effects of drugs in terms of their severity and to distinguish between effects that cause a temporary inconvenience or discomfort and effects that can lead to organ damage, permanent disability, or even death.

Most drugs exert effects on several different body functions. To achieve the desired therapeutic effect or effects, some side effects often must be tolerated. This is possible if the side effects are minor, but if they are more serious, they may be a limiting factor in the use of the drug. The distinction between therapeutic effects and side effects is relative and depends on the purpose for which the drug is administered: one person's side effect may be another person's therapeutic effect. For example, in one patient receiving morphine for its pain-relieving properties, the intestinal constipation that morphine induces may be an undesirable side effect that must be tolerated. For a second patient, however, morphine may be used to treat severe diarrhea, in which case the constipation induced is the desired therapeutic effect and relief of pain is a side effect.

In addition to side effects that are merely irritating, some drugs may cause reactions that are very serious, including serious allergies, blood disorders, liver or kidney toxicity, or abnormalities in fetal development. Fortunately, the incidence of serious toxic effects is quite low.

Allergies to drugs may take many forms, from mild skin rashes to fatal shock. Allergies differ from normal side effects, which can often be eliminated or at least made tolerable by a simple reduction in dosage. However, a reduction in the dose of a drug may have no effect on a drug allergy because exposure to any amount of the drug can be hazardous and possibly catastrophic for the patient.

Damage to the liver and kidneys results from their role in concentrating, metabolizing, and excreting toxic drugs. Examples of drug-induced liver damage include that caused either by alcohol or certain of the inhalants of abuse (Chapter 4). Certain of the major tranquilizers (for example, the phenothiazines) may induce jaundice by increasing the viscosity of bile in the liver (Chapter 11).

The toxicity to a fetus of both socially abused and some therapeutic drugs should be mentioned. Data quite clearly show the adverse effects of nicotine and ethyl alcohol on the fetus. Similarly, the effects of cocaine abuse on the fetus have received much attention (Konkol and Olsen, 1996). These three drugs are responsible for a majority of preventable fetal toxicities and are three of the major health hazards in the country today.

Placebo Effects

As stated by Nies (2001):

> The net effect of drug therapy is the sum of the pharmacological effects of the drug and the nonspecific placebo effects associated with the therapeutic effort. Although identified specifically with administration of an inert substance in the guise of medication, placebo effects are associated with the taking of any drug, active or inert. (p. 57)

About 1950, so-called *double-blind, randomized, controlled clinical trials* of medications became the gold standard for studying drug effects in humans. Controlled trials were intended to remove the bias, expectations,

and even fraud associated with clinical trials where uncontrolled variables led to much subjective and presumably biased inputs (Lakoff,
2002). Throughout this book, reference will be made to the results obtained from recent drugs trials that continue to use the double-blind,
randomized, controlled, trial model.

Recently, however, the placebo effect of drugs has come under
scrutiny, especially in trials of antidepressant medication. Indeed, recent papers confirm that placebo effects, even in double-blind, randomized, controlled trials, are significant and are increasing at a rate of
about 7 percent per decade (Figure 2.14). As summarized by Walsh and
coworkers (2002), in the analysis of double-blind, randomized, controlled clinical trials of drugs used to treat depression, about 28 percent
of patients treated with placebo respond positively and significantly.
This compares with 50 percent of patients who respond similarly when
treated with active medication. At a minimum, this illustrates that
placebo contributes significantly (perhaps half) to clinical response.

What then is a placebo? Commonly it is a sugar pill (a dummy
pill), although this is only one type of placebo responsible for beneficial effects. Hrobjartsson and Gotzsche (2001) state, "A placebo could

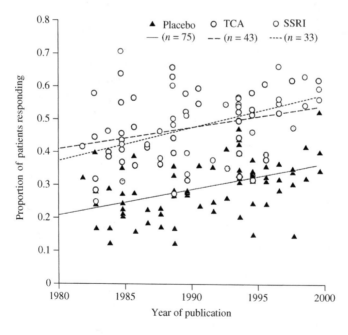

FIGURE 2.14 Proportion of patients assigned to placebo, tricyclic antidepressants
(TCAs), and selective serotonin reuptake inhibitor antidepressants (SSRIs) who showed
a 50 percent or greater improvement in their depression as measured by the Hamilton
Rating Scale for Depression Score by the year of publication of results of clinical trials.
[From Walsh et al., (2002), p.1843.]

be pharmacological (e.g., a tablet), physical (e.g., a manipulation), or psychological (e.g., a conversation)" (p. 1594). It may also be as simple as altering the therapeutic environment (Mayberg et al., 2002). Obviously then, placebo is active treatment, whether it is administering a sugar pill, manipulating or touching a patient, or talking to or otherwise counseling a patient. In clinical trials of medication, placebo treatment should be controlled, and often it is not. For example, in a recent study of placebo effects on brain function in depressed persons, those who received placebo pills still received "brief sessions of supportive psychotherapy with a research nurse," presumably to avoid relapse to depression when active medication was withheld (Leuchter et al., 2002, p.123).

Placebos seem to work best on symptoms or diseases that vary (wax and wane) over time. Perhaps the most prominent examples are major depression and chronic pain. The placebo action is independent of any chemical property of the drug; it arises largely because of what the patient or the prescriber expects or desires or from the complex interactions associated with the therapeutic alliance. A placebo response may result from either the patient's or the physician's mental set or from the entire environmental setting in which the drug is taken. Placebos can therapeutically empower patients to stimulate their psychophysiological self-regulation abilities.

Swartzman and Burkell (1998) discuss the influence of expectations on the response to placebo medication. Expectations guide the search for information and organize information obtained from the search. Both the patient and the prescriber may have expectations regarding anticipated benefits possibly resulting from drug administration. In therapeutics, expectations of improvement at the start of drug therapy can predict subsequent therapeutic effectiveness and response. Perhaps even the "feeling" of side effects serves to verify the expectation that the drug is "working." Lakoff (2002) and Faries and coworkers (2001) describe a double-blind placebo run-in period as perhaps the best way to reduce the placebo effect in drug trials. Placebo pills are administered, unbeknownst to either the doctor or the patient, for a week and then patients who responded positively are eliminated from the trial. In studies using a single-blind run-in period (the doctor knew a placebo was being given), only 5 percent of subjects exhibited a placebo response and were eliminated from the study, compared to 28 percent of patients responding positively to placebo when neither the doctor nor the patient knew that only placebo was being given. Thus, the double-blind run-in before drug treatment may be a better model for reducing placebo response rates. Unfortunately, this technique has not been used in reported drug trials to date (it is a new model). It may become a model for the future. At least, however, these results demonstrate that the health care practitioner is an important contributor to the placebo response. It is not just inherent in the patient.

STUDY QUESTIONS

1. What is meant by the term *pharmacodynamics*? What does the term imply?

2. What is a receptor? What is a drug receptor?

3. Discuss the structure of a drug receptor.

4. Distinguish between *agonist* and *antagonist* as they relate to drug-receptor interactions.

5. Compare and contrast a presynaptic receptor and a postsynaptic receptor.

6. List the four types of receptors discussed in this chapter.

7. Discuss drug-receptor specificity. Can a drug ever be more specific for a receptor than is the endogenous neurotransmitter? Explain.

8. What is meant by a dose-response relationship? Draw a hypothetical example of such a relationship.

9. Discuss the factors that influence the time course of drug action in the body.

10. Discuss how two drugs might interact with each other in the body.

11. Which factors contribute to the intensity of drug effects?

12. What are two important functions of neuronal receptors? How do drugs affect receptors?

13. Discuss the placebo response as it relates to drug trials and to therapeutic response and the therapeutic alliance between patient and health care worker.

REFERENCES

Faries, D. E., et al. (2001). "The Double Blind Variable Placebo Lead-In Period: Results from Two Antidepressant Clinical Trials." *Journal of Clinical Psychopharmacology* 21: 561–568.

Feldman, R. S., J. S. Meyer, and L. F. Quenzer (1997). *Principles of Neuropsychopharmacology*. Sunderland, MA: Sinauer.

Hrobjartsson, A., and P. C. Gotzsche (2001). "Is the Placebo Powerless? An Analysis of Clinical Trials Comparing Placebo with No Treatment." *New England Journal of Medicine* 344: 1594–1602.

Jurrlink, D. N., et al. (2003). "Drug-Drug Interactions Among Elderly Patients Hospitalized for Drug Toxicity." *Journal of the American Medical Association* 289: 1652–1658.

Khatib, S. M. al-, et al. (2003). "What Clinicians Should Know About the QT Interval." *Journal of the American Medical Association* 289: 2120–2127.

Konkol, R. J., and G. D. Olsen, eds. (1996). *Prenatal Cocaine Exposure*. Boca Raton, FL: CRC Press.

Lakoff, A. (2002). "The Mousetrap: Managing the Placebo Effect in Antidepressant Trials." *Molecular Interventions* 2: 72–76.

Leuchter, A. F., et al. (2002). "Changes in Brain Function of Depressed Subjects During Treatment with Placebo." *American Journal of Psychiatry* 159: 122–129.

Logan, B. K. (1996). "Methamphetamine and Driving Impairment." *Journal of Forensic Sciences* 41: 457–464.

Mayberg, H. S., et al. (2002). "The Functional Neuroanatomy of the Placebo Effect." *American Journal of Psychiatry* 159: 728–737.

Nies, A. S. (2001). "Principles of Therapeutics." In J. G. Hardman, L. E. Limbird, and A. G. Gilman, eds., *Goodman and Gilman's The Pharmacological Basis of Therapeutics*, 10th ed. (pp. 45–66). New York: McGraw-Hill.

Ross, E. M., and T. P. Kenakin (2001). "Pharmacodynamics: Mechanisms of Drug Action and the Relationship Between Drug Concentration and Effect." In J. G. Hardman, L. E. Limbird, and A. G. Gilman, eds., *Goodman and Gilman's The Pharmacological Basis of Therapeutics*, 10th ed. (pp. 31–43). New York: McGraw-Hill.

Simmonds, W. F. (1999). "G-Protein Regulation of Adenylate Cyclase." *Trends in Pharmacological Sciences*, 20: 66–73.

Swartzman, L. C., and J. Burkell (1998). "Expectations and the Placebo Effect in Clinical Drug Trials: Why We Should Not Turn a Blind Eye to Unblinding, and Other Cautionary Notes." *Clinical Pharmacology and Therapeutics* 64: 1–7.

Walsh, B. T., et al. (2002). "Placebo Response in Studies of Major Depression: Variable, Substantial, and Growing." *Journal of the American Medical Association* 287: 1840–1847.

Chapter 3

The Neuron, Synaptic Transmission, and Neurotransmitters

All our thoughts, actions, memories, and behaviors result from biochemical interactions that take place in and between *neurons*. Drugs that affect these processes are, in general, called *psychoactive drugs*. In essence, psychoactive drugs are chemicals that alter (mimic, potentiate, disrupt, or inhibit) the normal neuronal processes associated with neuronal function or communication between neurons. To understand the actions of psychoactive drugs, therefore, it is necessary to have some idea of what a neuron is and how neurons interact with each other.

Overall Organization of the CNS

The human brain consists of perhaps 90 billion individual neurons located in the skull and the spinal canal. The *spinal cord* extends from the lower end of the medulla to the sacrum. The spinal cord consists of neurons and fiber tracts involved in the following:

- Carrying sensory information from the skin, muscles, joints, and internal body organs to the brain

- Organizing and modulating the motor outflow to the muscles (to produce coordinated muscle responses)

- Modulating sensory input (including pain impulses)
- Providing autonomic (involuntary) control of vital body functions

The lower part of the brain, attached to the upper part of the spinal cord, is the *brain stem* (Figure 3.1). It is divided into three parts: the *medulla*, the *pons*, and the *midbrain*. All impulses that are conducted in either direction between the spinal cord and the brain pass through the brain stem, which is also important in the regulation of vital body functions, such as respiration, blood pressure, heart rate, gastrointestinal functioning, and the states of sleep and wakefulness. The brain stem is also involved in behavioral alerting, attention, and arousal responses. Depressant drugs, such as the barbiturates (Chapter 5), depress the brain-stem activating system; this action probably underlies much of their hypnotic action.

Behind the brain stem is a large, bulbous structure—the *cerebellum*. A highly convoluted structure, the cerebellum is connected to the brain stem by large fiber tracts. The cerebellum is necessary for the proper integration of movement and posture. Drunkenness, which is

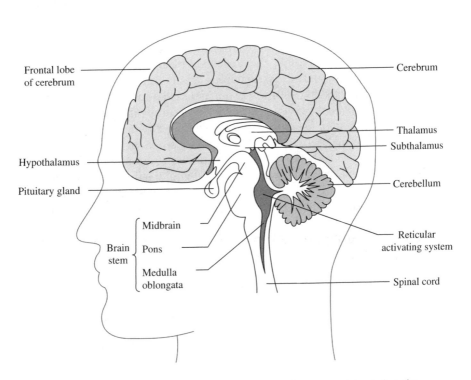

FIGURE 3.1 Midline section of the brain illustrating several structures lying below the cerebral cortex.

characterized by ataxia (loss of coordination and balance, staggering, and other deficits), appears to be caused largely by an alcohol-induced depression of cerebellar function.

The area immediately above the brain stem and covered by the cerebral hemispheres is the *diencephalon*. This area includes the hypothalamus, pituitary gland, various fiber tracts (bundles of axons that travel as a group from one area to another), subthalamus, and thalamus. Three of these areas are discussed here: the subthalamus, the hypothalamus, and the limbic system.

The *subthalamus* is a small area underneath the thalamus and above the midbrain. It contains a variety of small structures that, together with the basal ganglia, constitute one of our motor systems, the *extrapyramidal system*. Patients who have Parkinson's disease (Chapter 13) have a deficiency of the neurotransmitter dopamine in the terminals of their nerve axons, which originate in cell bodies in the substantia nigra (one of the subthalamic structures).

The *hypothalamus* is a collection of neurons in the lower portion of the brain near the junction of the midbrain and the thalamus. It is located near the base of the skull, just above the pituitary gland (the function of which it largely modulates). The hypothalamus is the principal center in the brain responsible for the integration of our entire autonomic (involuntary or vegetative) nervous system. Thus, it helps control such vegetative functions as eating, drinking, sleeping, regulation of body temperature, sexual behavior, blood pressure, emotion, and water balance. In addition, the hypothalamus closely controls hormonal output of the pituitary gland. Neurons in the hypothalamus produce substances called *releasing factors,* which travel to the nearby pituitary gland, inducing the secretion of hormones that regulate fertility in females and sperm formation in males. The hypothalamus is a site of action for many psychoactive drugs, either as a site for the primary action of the drug or as a site responsible for side effects associated with the use of a drug.

Closely associated with the hypothalamus is the *limbic system,* the major components of which are the *amygdala* and the *hippocampus*. These structures exert primitive types of behavioral control; they integrate emotion, reward, and behavior with motor and autonomic functions. Because the limbic system and the hypothalamus interact to regulate emotion and emotional expression, these structures are logical sites for the study of psychoactive drugs that alter mood, affect, emotion, or responses to emotional experiences.

The hypothalamic and limbic areas contain structures important in psychopharmacology and the abuse potential of drugs. Included here are the dopamine-rich reward centers that involve the *ventral tegmental area,* the *median forebrain bundle,* and the *nucleus accumbens*. Throughout this text, this system is discussed as a site of the behavior-reinforcing action of psychoactive drugs that are subject to compulsive abuse.

Almost completely covering the brain stem and the diencephalon is the *cerebrum*. In humans the cerebrum is the largest part of the brain. It is separated into two distinct hemispheres, left and right, with numerous fiber tracts connecting the two. Because skull size is limited and the cerebrum is so large, the outer layer of the cerebrum, the *cerebral cortex,* is deeply convoluted and fissured. Like other parts of the brain, the cerebral cortex is divided by function; it contains centers for vision, hearing, speech, sensory perception, and emotion. The various regions of the cerebral cortex can be classified in several ways, among them, the type of function or sensation that is processed. Figure 3.2 illustrates some of this categorization.

The Neuron

The neuron is the basic component of the CNS, and each neuron shares common structural and functional characteristics (Figure 3.3). A typical neuron has a *soma* (cell body), which contains the nucleus (within which is the genetic material of the cell). Extending from the soma in one direction are many short fibers, called *dendrites* (hundreds of

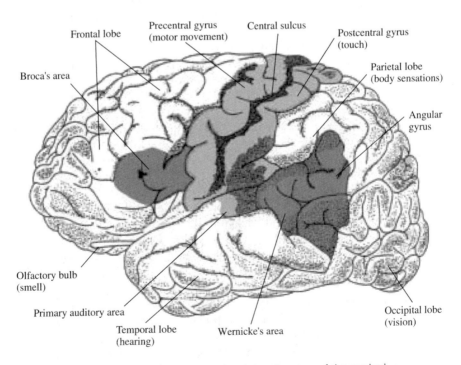

FIGURE 3.2 Surface structure of the brain showing major areas of the cerebral cortex.

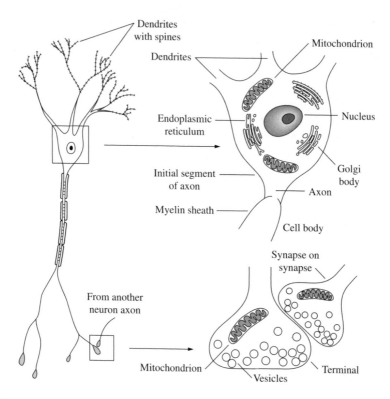

FIGURE 3.3 Major parts of a neuron. The genetic material (DNA) is contained in the nucleus, and several specialized organelles are present in the cytoplasm, the material of the cell outside the nucleus. The cell is covered by a thin wall, or membrane. Mitochondria are present in the cell body, the fibers, and the terminals. The terminals also contain small, round vesicles that contain neurotransmitter chemicals. Synaptic connections from the fibers of other neurons cover the cell body and dendrites. In many neurons the synapses on dendrites can be seen as little spines. The axon itself has no synapses on it except sometimes at its synaptic terminals, where other neuron axon terminals may form synapses on synapses. [From Thompson (1993), p. 31.]

widely branched extensions), that receive input from other neurons through *receptors* located on the dendritic membrane. On receipt of a signal from another cell, an electrical current is generated and travels down the dendrite to the soma. Extending in another direction from the soma is a single elongated process called an *axon*, which varies in length from as short as a few millimeters to as long as a meter (meter-length examples are the axons that run from the motor neurons of the spinal cord out to the muscles that they innervate). The axon, in essence, transmits electrical activity (in the form of *action potentials*) from the soma to other neurons or to muscles, organs, or glands of the body. Normally, the axon conducts impulses in only one direction—from the soma down the axon to a specialized structure that, together with one or more dendrites from another neuron, forms a complex microspace called a *synapse* (Figure 3.4).

> A given neuron in the brain may receive several thousand synaptic connections from other neurons. Hence if the human brain has 10^{11} neurons, then it has at least 10^{14} synapses, or many trillions. The number of possible different combinations of synaptic connections among the neurons in a single human brain is larger than the total number of atomic particles that make up the known universe. Hence the diversity of the interconnections in a human brain seems almost without limit. (Thompson, 1993, pp. 2–3)

It was once thought that the brain has the maximal number of neurons at birth; once a neuron dies, it is not replaced. This concept has been debunked as we now realize that new neurons form every day (a process called *neurogenesis*) and existing neurons need to be maintained in a state of health (Johansson et al., 1999). Certainly what continues to develop during our lifetime are the number and pattern of synaptic connections,

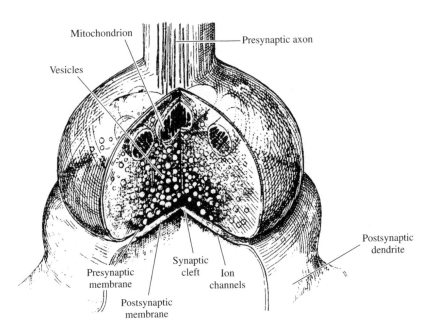

FIGURE 3.4 Three-dimensional drawing of a synapse. The axon terminal is the top knoblike structure, and the spine of the receiving neuron is the bottom one. Note that there is a space (synaptic cleft) between the presynaptic terminal membrane and the postsynaptic cell membrane.

which are continually being reshaped, resynthesized, and "sculpted" by experience and appear to form the anatomical basis of memory and the maintenance of a normal state of mood (Sossin, 1996). The relationship between neuronal "health" and mood is discussed in Chapter 9.

A synapse is the point of functional contact between an axon terminal and another cell (see Figure 3.4). A synapse consists of a minute space (the *synaptic cleft*) between the presynaptic membrane (which is the axon terminal) of one neuron and the postsynaptic membrane of the receiving neuron. The presynaptic terminal contains numerous structural elements, the most important of which (for our purposes) are the small synaptic vesicles, each of which contains several thousand molecules of neurotransmitter chemical (a "ligand," or *first messenger)* that transmits information from one neuron to another). These vesicles store the transmitter, which is available for release (Figure 3.5). Through a process called *exocytosis*, and under the influence of calcium ions, vesicles fuse with the presynaptic membrane and molecules of transmitter are released into the synaptic cleft. The transmitter substance diffuses across the synaptic cleft and attaches to various types of receptors on the postsynaptic membrane (located on dendrites of the next neuron), thereby transmitting information chemically from one neuron to another. The neurons do not physically touch each other; synaptic transmission is a chemical rather than an electrical process.

The process of synaptic transmission takes a remarkably short time (Clements, 1996). In the case of the ligand-gated *ion channel receptors,* the entire process may occur over a time span as short as a millisecond for transmitter release (from presynaptic vesicles), diffusion (across the cleft), receptor attachment, channel opening, and ion influx. *G protein-coupled receptors* are slow-response receptors— they produce activation responses that may last from hundreds of milliseconds to perhaps many seconds. These responses are generally thought to be modulatory; the neurotransmitter either dampens or enhances intracellular enzymatic functions. Through release of the intracellular *second messenger* (Chapter 2), slow-response receptors trigger the cell's internal machinery, leading to effects as diverse as modulation of ion channel activity to protein transcription from genetic material (a process described later as being involved in mechanisms of long-term memory formation in glutamate-releasing neurons). Thus, activation of these receptors can produce long-lasting, even permanent changes in the postsynaptic neuron.

Termination of Synaptic Transmission

As discussed, the arrival of an action potential at the synapse induces release of a neurotransmitter into the synaptic cleft, and the transmitter then reversibly binds to postsynaptic receptors. Certain mechanisms must be present to get rid of neurotransmitter; otherwise

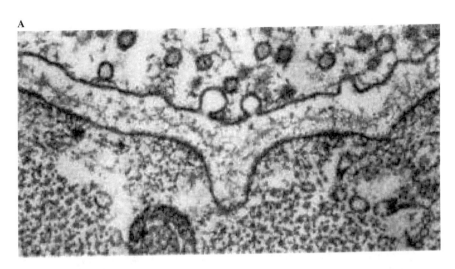

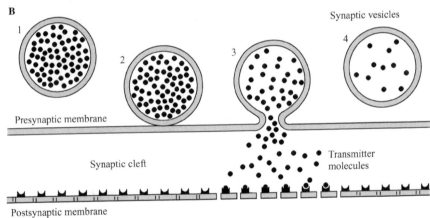

Synaptic vesicles

Presynaptic membrane

Synaptic cleft

Transmitter
molecules

Postsynaptic membrane

FIGURE 3.5 A. Photomicrograph of a synapse in action taken with the electron microscope. Vesicles are releasing their transmitter chemical into the synaptic cleft. **B.** Schematic of the process.

transmitter would remain in the synaptic cleft and continually bind to the postsynaptic receptors. Every synapse is able to accomplish the removal of transmitter from the synaptic cleft. In most cases, transmitter removal occurs through either of three mechanisms:

1. An enzyme present in the synaptic cleft breaks down any neurotransmitter lingering within the synapse.

2. The transmitter is taken back into the presynaptic cell through the 12-helix reuptake transporter receptor present on the presynaptic membrane (see Figure 2.7).

3. In the case of glutamate neurotransmission, after release the gluta-mate is taken up into an adjacent glial cell, reprocessed, and re-turned to the presynaptic nerve terminal.

Examples of neurotransmitters removed by the second mechanism (presynaptic reuptake) include the following:

- Norepinephrine, uptake of which is blocked by the *tricyclic antidepressants* and *atomoxetine* (Strattera)
- Serotonin, uptake of which is blocked by the *selective serotonin reuptake inhibitor* (SSRI) *antidepressants*
- Dopamine, uptake of which is blocked by *bupropion* (Welbutrin, Zyban) and *cocaine*.

These neurotransmitters will be described in this book. In the case of the neurotransmitter acetylcholine, the enzyme *acetylcholine esterase* breaks down the transmitter into acetate and choline, which are then taken up into the nerve terminal and the acetylcholine resynthesized.

Receptor Specificity

It would be nice to think that for each specific neurotransmitter there is a single receptor type. In actuality, virtually every transmitter has multiple distinct receptor subtypes to which it binds. For example, norepinephrine, serotonin, and dopamine bind to (have affinity for) multiple postsynaptic receptors as well as a presynaptic transporter. On the postsynaptic membrane, a neurotransmitter may bind to both fast-response (ion channel) receptors and slow-response (G protein-coupled) receptors. A transmitter may bind to different types of G pro-tein-coupled receptors, each initiating different intracellular processes. For example, for serotonin receptors, at least 18 different subtypes of receptors have been described. All this leads to immense opportunity for the development of drugs with incredible specificity—for example, for blocking one specific subtype of postsynaptic serotonin receptor, reducing or eliminating the side effects that limit the clinical useful-ness of existing psychotherapeutic agents. Table 3.1 lists a few of the commonly recognized neurotransmitters, some of the receptor sub-types that have been identified, and some of the brain functions thought to be under the control of each transmitter.

The Soma

Present in all cells of the body (except red blood cells), the soma has a *nucleus* that contains the basic genetic material (the DNA) for the cell (see Figure 3.3). Because the neuron is a specialized type of cell, its DNA

TABLE 3.1 Selected neurotransmitters in the CNS

Neurotransmitter	Receptors	Function[a]
Acetylcholine (ACh)	Muscarinic (M_1 through M_5) Nicotinic (N_N and N_M)	Memory function, sensory processing, motor coordination, neuromuscular junction neurotransmission, and ANS and PANS function
Norepinephrine (NE)	Alpha$_1$ and alpha$_2$; beta$_1$, beta$_2$, and beta$_3$.	CNS sensory processing, cerebellar function, sleep, mood, learning, memory, anxiety, and SANS
Dopamine (DA)	D_1 through D_5 in two families designated D_1 and D_2	Motor regulation, reinforcement, olfaction, mood, concentration, hormone control, and hypoxic drive
Serotonin (5-HT)	Currently 18 receptors have been identified and broken into 8 families designated 5-HT$_1$ through 5-HT$_8$	Emotional processing, mood, appetite, sleep, pain processing, hallucinations, and reflex regulation
Glutamate (Glu)	NMDA, quisqualate, and kainate	Long-term potentiation, memory, major excitatory function within the CNS and PNS
Gamma amino-butyric acid (GABA)	GABA$_A$ and GABA$_B$	Major inhibitory neurotransmitter in the CNS
Histamine (H)	H$_1$ and H$_2$	Sleep, sedation, and temperature regulation
Glycine (Gly)		Major inhibitory function within the spinal cord

[a]ANS = autonomic nervous system, PANS = parasympathetic autonomic nervous system, SANS = sympathetic autonomic nervous system.
From P. M. Carvey, *Drug Action in the Central Nervous System* (Oxford: Oxford University Press. 1988), p. 7.

expresses a subset of genes that encode the special structural and enzymatic proteins that endow the neuron with its size, shape, location, and other functional characteristics (Cooper et al., 2003). Also located in the soma are the *mitochondria*, which provide the biological energy for the neuron. This energy, in the form of *adenosine triphosphate* (ATP), is made available for all the various chemical reactions carried out in the cell (such as neurotransmitter synthesis, storage, release, and reuptake).

In response to stimuli (perhaps initiated by a second-messenger action), the DNA in the nucleus is transcribed into a second similar molecular form as strands of ribonucleic acid (RNA), which is then "edited" by several rapid steps and exported from the nucleus to the cytoplasm of the soma. The edited RNA is called *messenger RNA*, and this nuclear material is then translated from the nucleic acid code of the RNA into the amino acid sequence of the protein that is to be expressed (Figure 3.6). Expression, or translation, occurs on the *endoplasmic reticulum*, where the neurotransmitters are synthesized and then "packaged" into vesicles that are then transported in specialized *microtubules* down the axon to the synaptic terminals, where they await release (Figure 3.7). Even the

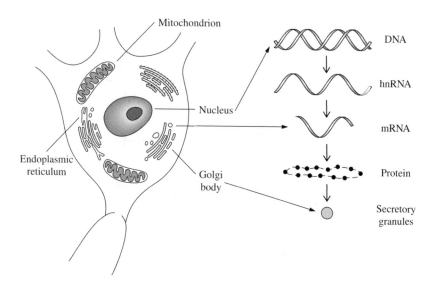

FIGURE 3.6 Formation of transmitter substances and "packaging" in vesicles from genetic material in the nucleus. DNA-encoded information is transcribed in the nucleus to a primary transcript form (hnRNA), which is edited and exported from the nucleus to the cytoplasm as messenger RNA (mRNA). The information is then translated from the genetic nucleic acid code of RNA into the amino acid sequence of the protein that is to be expressed. Within the Golgi body portion of the endoplasmic reticulum, the transmitter is packaged into secretory organelles for transport down the axon to the neuron terminals.

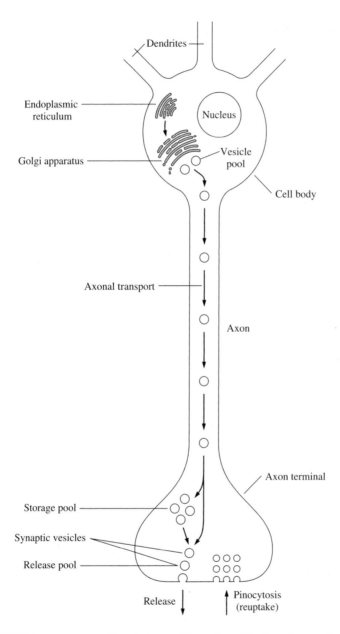

FIGURE 3.7 Axon transport. Chemicals travel from the cell body to the terminals. It is believed that they move along the axon in microtubules that fill the axon.

presynaptic receptors (such as the dopamine transporter) are made in the soma and carried down the axon, embedding in the cell membrane where they exert their synaptic functions.

Specific Neurotransmitters

Neurons release specific chemical substances from their presynaptic nerve terminals, and it is the interaction between psychoactive drugs and these chemicals (and the receptors on which they act) that underlies the actions of the drugs. Therefore, it is important to introduce these chemicals as neurotransmitters. The earliest chemicals identified as CNS neurotransmitters were acetylcholine and norepinephrine, largely because of their established roles in the peripheral nervous system. In the 1960s, serotonin, epinephrine, and dopamine were added. In the 1970s, gamma aminobutyric acid (GABA), glycine, glutamate, and certain neuropeptides (such as the endorphins) were identified. In the late 1980s, the lipid amide anandamide was identified as the endogenous transmitter for the tetrahydrocannabinol receptor. Today, dozens (and perhaps hundreds) of neurotransmitters are recognized (Snyder, 2002).

Acetylcholine

Acetylcholine (ACh) was identified as a transmitter chemical first in the peripheral nervous system and later in brain tissue. Deficiencies in acetylcholine-secreting neurons have classically been associated with the dysfunctions seen in Alzheimer's disease. Certainly drugs that either potentiate or inhibit the central action of acetylcholine exert profound effects on memory. For example, scopolamine is a psychedelic drug (Chapter 19) that blocks central cholinergic receptors and as a result produces amnesia. Conversely, drugs that increase the amount of acetylcholine in the brain appear to improve memory function and are used to delay the onset of Alzheimer's disease (Chapter 13).

ACh is synthesized in a one-step reaction from two precursors (choline and acetate) and then is stored within synaptic vesicles for later release. This reaction and the dynamics of ACh release, metabolism, and resynthesis are shown in Figure 3.8. Like other neurotransmitters, ACh is released into the synaptic cleft, rapidly diffuses across the cleft, and reversibly binds to postsynaptic receptors. Once ACh has exerted its effect on postsynaptic receptors, its action is terminated by *acetylcholine esterase* (AChE).

The enzymatic reaction that degrades ACh is important not only in the treatment of Alzheimer's disease but in agriculture and in the military. Drugs that inhibit the action of AChE are referred to as *AChE inhibitors* and include both "reversible" AChE inhibitors and "irreversible" AChE inhibitors. *Irreversible AChE inhibitors* form a permanent covalent

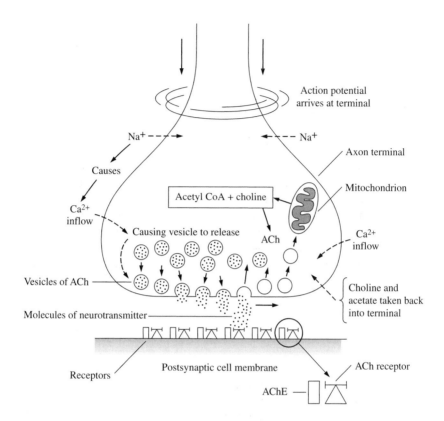

FIGURE 3.8 Chemical synapse. Acetylcholine (ACh) is used as the example. It is made in the axon terminal from acetyl coenzyme A (acetyl CoA) and choline, stored in vesicles, and released. When the action potential arrives at the terminal, closed calcium channels in the terminal are opened and Ca^{2+} rushes into the terminal, triggering vesicles to fuse with the membrane and release ACh molecules into the synaptic cleft. They attach to ACh receptors on the postsynaptic membrane and trigger the opening of Na^+ channels. ACh is immediately broken down at the receptors by acetylcholine esterase (AChE) into choline and acetate, which are taken back up by the terminal and reused.

bond with the enzyme and totally inhibit enzyme function. Usually administered in "toxic" doses, the result is usually fatal. Some of these toxic drugs (such as *malathion* and *parathion*) are exploited in gardening and agriculture as insecticides because they kill insects on contact. Other irreversible AChE inhibitors (such as *Sarin* and *Soman*) are used in the military as lethal nerve gases.

Less toxic and shorter acting are the *reversible AChE inhibitors,* used to more modestly increase ACh levels in the brain. They increase ACh levels and clinically are used as cognitive enhancers, delaying the decline in cognitive function in patients with Alzheimer's disease. Individual agents are discussed in Chapter 13.

ACh is distributed widely in the brain (Figure 3.9). The cell bodies of cholinergic neurons in the brain lie in two closely related regions. One involves the *septal nuclei* and the *nucleus basalis*. The axons of these neurons project to forebrain regions, particularly the hippocampus and cerebral cortex. The second originates in the midbrain region and projects anteriorly to the thalamus, basal ganglia, and diencephalon and posteriorly to the reticular formation, pons, cerebellum, and cranial nerve nuclei. In addition to its generally agreed-on role in learning and memory, the diffuse distribution of ACh is consistent with suggestions that ACh is involved in circuits that modulate sensory reception; in mechanisms related to behavioral arousal, attention, energy conservation, and mood; and in REM activity during sleep (Cummings, 2000).

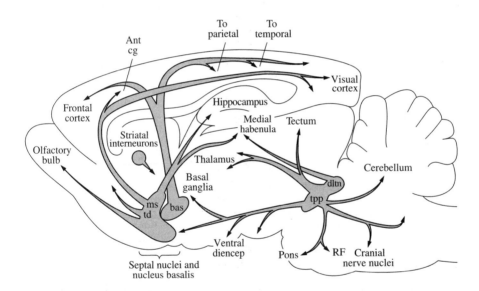

FIGURE 3.9 Representation of the cholinergic systems in the rat brain. As illustrated, central cholinergic neurons exhibit two basic organizational schemata: (1) local circuit cells (those that morphologically are arrayed wholly within the neural structure in which they are found) exemplified by the interneurons of the caudate-putamen nucleus; (2) projection neurons (those that connect two or more different regions). Of the cholinergic projection neurons that interconnect central structures, two major subconstellations have been identified: (1) the forebrain cholinergic complex composed of neurons in the medial septal nucleus (ms) and nucleus basalis (bas) and projecting to the entire nonstriatal telencephalon; (2) the pontomesencephalotegmental cholinergic complex, composed of cells in the pendunculopontine (tpp) and laterodorsal (dltn) tegmental nuclei and projecting ascendingly to the thalamus and other diencephalic loci and descendingly to the pontine and medullary reticular formation (RF), cerebellum, and cranial nerve nuclei.

Catecholamine Neurotransmitters: Dopamine and Norepinephrine

The term *catecholamine* refers to compounds that contain a catechol nucleus (a benzene ring with two attached hydroxyl groups) to which is attached an amine group (Figure 3.10). In the CNS, the term usually refers to the transmitters *dopamine* (DA) and *norepinephrine* (NE). In the peripheral nervous system, *epinephrine* ("adrenaline") is a third catecholamine transmitter. In the brain, a large number of psychoactive drugs (both licit and illicit, therapeutic and abused) exert their effects by altering the synaptic action of NE and DA.

The chemical synthesis of DA is illustrated in Figure 3.10. NE is produced by an additional step that involves oxidation of the proximal carbon of the ethyl side chain. Biosynthesis of the catecholamines begins with the amino acid tyrosine and is a complicated process involving genetic and enzymatic regulation. Following synthesis, the transmitter is stored in vesicles for release into the synaptic space. Interestingly, such release is tightly controlled (modulated) by *presynaptic receptors* (autoreceptors) that are activated not only by NE or DA but by such substances as ACh, prostaglandins, other amines, and possibly glutamate and/or endorphins. Such autoreceptors are an important target for the action of the antidepressant drug *mirtazapine* (Remeron; Chapter 9). In addition, drugs such as the amphetamines (Chapter 7) can cause the release of stored catecholamines.

Following release, NE and DA attach to postsynaptic receptors. As discussed earlier, inactivation in the synaptic cleft occurs primarily by reuptake of the transmitter from the synaptic cleft into the presynaptic nerve terminal. Within the nerve terminal, catecholamines can be inactivated by enzymes, such as monoamine oxidase (MAO). The products of inactivation are further metabolized and eliminated from the body through the urine. The class of antidepressants referred to as MAO inhibitors (Chapter 9) act by inhibiting MAO and thereby increasing the amounts of DA and NE available for synaptic release.

Postsynaptic Catecholamine Receptors. Unlike transmitters such as ACh and GABA, which affect ion channels, postsynaptic binding of DA or NE triggers a sequence of chemical events in the postsynaptic cell membrane, eventually affecting either ion channels or intracellular metabolic activity. It is likely that the slow onset of action of antidepressant drugs (several weeks to achieve a therapeutic effect) follows the down regulation of postsynaptic catecholamine receptors as an adaptation to the presence of increased amounts of transmitter present in the synaptic cleft (because the reuptake elimination of the transmitter was blocked by the drug).

Each catecholamine transmitter exerts effects on a number of different postsynaptic receptors. Norepinephrine and epinephrine exert effects at two primary types of receptors (alpha and beta), each of which has at

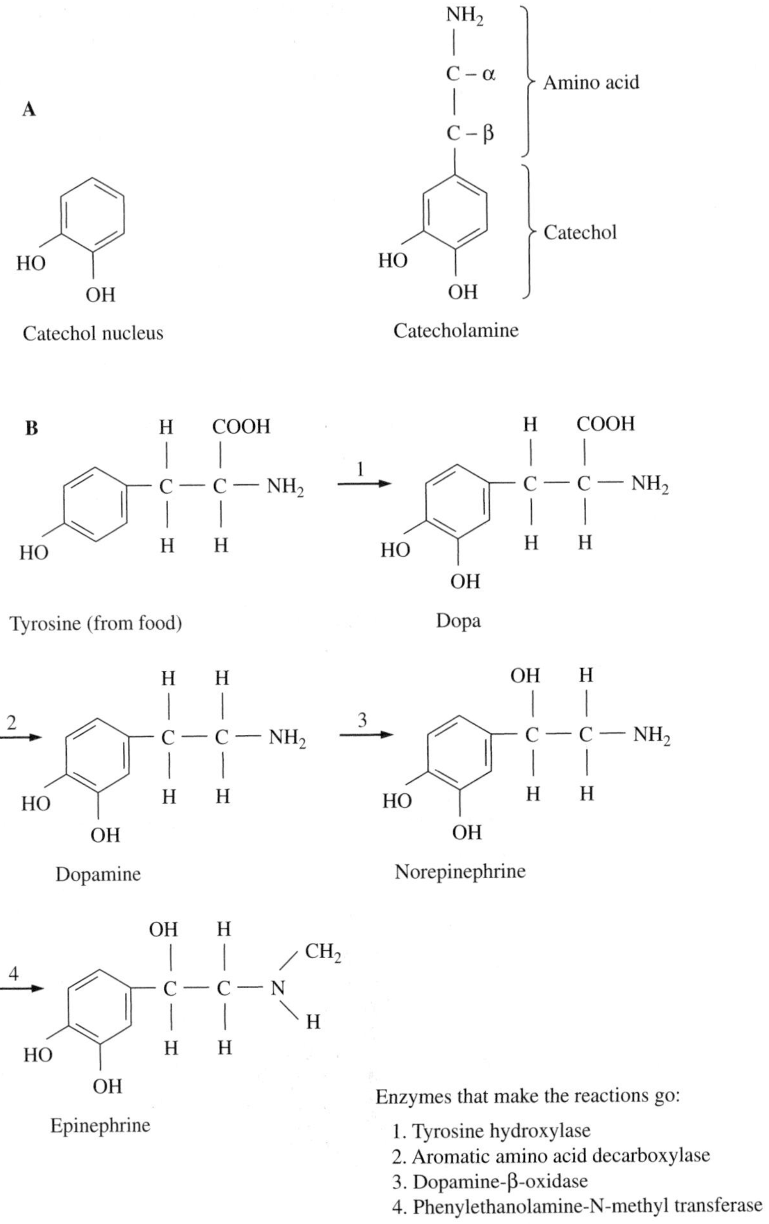

FIGURE 3.10 A. Catechol and catecholamine structure. All catecholamines share the catechol nucleus, a benzene ring with two adjacent hydroxyl (OH) groups. **B.** Structures and synthesis of the catecholamines. Tyrosine, an amino acid found in foods, is converted into dopa, then into dopamine, next into norepinephrine, and, finally (in the peripheral nervous system) into epinephrine, depending on which enzymes (1–4) are present in the cell.

least two subtypes. Dopamine exerts postsynaptic effects on at least six receptors, divided into two families (D_1 and D_2). Confusingly, D_1 receptors are subdivided into two subtypes—D_1 and D_5—and D_2 receptors into four subtypes—D_{2A}, D_{2B}, D_3, and D_4. Postsynaptic dopamine receptors of the D_2 family are responsible for at least part of the antipsychotic activity of the drugs discussed in Chapter 11. Alterations in dopamine receptor function have been implicated in numerous diseases and behavioral states including schizophrenia, Parkinsonism, Huntington's chorea, affective disorders, sexual activity, reward, attention deficit hyperactivity disorder, and others.

Norepinephrine Pathways.   The cell bodies of NE neurons are located in the brain stem, mainly in the locus coeruleus (Figure 3.11). From there, axons project widely throughout the brain to nerve terminals in the cerebral cortex, the limbic system, the hypothalamus, and the cerebellum. Axonal projections also travel to the dorsal horns of the spinal cord, where they exert an analgesic action (Chapter 15). The release of

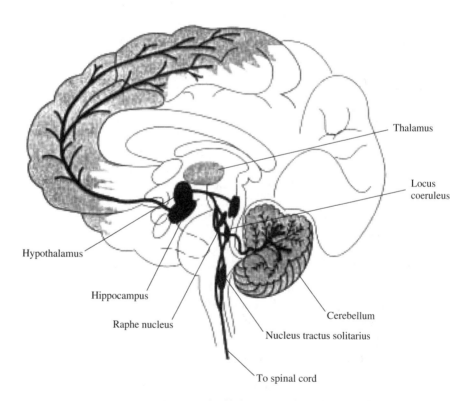

FIGURE 3.11 NE projection system in the human brain. The cell bodies are in the locus coeruleus and adjacent regions of the brain stem and project widely to the forebrain and cerebellum and to the brain stem and spinal cord.

NE produces an alerting, focusing, orienting response, positive feelings of reward, and analgesia. NE release may also be involved in basic instinctual behaviors, such as hunger, thirst, emotion, and sex.

Dopamine Pathways. Dopamine pathways in the brain originate in the brain stem, sending axons both rostral to the brain and caudal to the spinal cord. Three dopamine circuits are classically described (Figure 3.12):

1. Cell bodies in the hypothalamus send short axons to the pituitary gland. These neurons are believed to function in the regulation of certain body hormones. Alterations in hormone function are commonly seen in people with schizophrenia taking phenothiazine antipsychotics, which block these dopamine receptors (Chapter 11).

2. Cell bodies in the brain-stem structure called the substantia nigra project to the basal ganglia, playing a major role in the regulation of movement. Parkinsonism, its treatment with l-DOPA (Chapter 13), and antipsychotic-induced extrapyramidal side effects (Chapter 11) all involve this pathway.

3. Cell bodies in the midbrain (ventral tegmentum), near the substantia nigra, project to higher brain regions including the cerebral cortex (especially the frontal cortex) and the limbic system, including the limbic cortex, nucleus accumbens, amygdaloid complex, and the entorhinal cortex; the entorhinal cortex is the major source of neurons projecting to the hippocampus. Alterations in the development of this pathway may be involved in the pathogenesis of schizophrenia and its amelioration by neuroleptic drugs. In addition, this dopaminergic pathway involving the ventral tegmentum, nucleus accumbens, and frontal cortex appears to underlie our "central reward pathway" (Figure 3.13), augmentation of which appears necessary to induce compulsive abuse and sustain continued use of most drugs of abuse (Chapter 21).

Serotonin (5-Hydroxytryptamine, 5-HT)

Serotonin was first investigated as a CNS neurotransmitter in the 1950s when lysergic acid diethylamide (LSD) was found to structurally resemble serotonin and block the contractile effect of serotonin on the gastrointestinal tract. At that time, it was hypothesized that LSD-induced hallucinations might be caused by alterations in the functioning of serotonin neurons and that serotonin might be involved in abnormal behavioral functioning. Today, drugs that potentiate the synaptic actions of serotonin are widely used as antidepressants and as antianxiety agents useful in treating such disorders as obsessive compulsive disorder, panic disorder, and phobias. Some of these *serotonergic drugs* fall under the category of *selective serotonin reuptake inhibitors* (SSRIs;

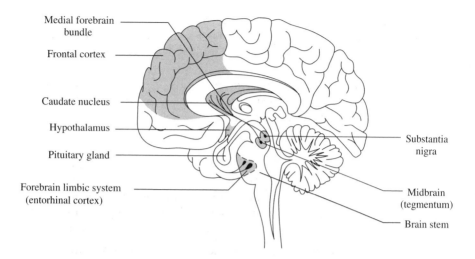

Medial forebrain bundle
Frontal cortex
Caudate nucleus
Hypothalamus
Pituitary gland
Forebrain limbic system (entorhinal cortex)
Substantia nigra
Midbrain (tegmentum)
Brain stem

FIGURE 3.12 The three dopamine systems in the brain. One is a local circuit in the hypothalamus; another is the pathway from the substantia nigra to the caudate nucleus of the basal ganglia, which is involved in motor functions and Parkinson's disease; the third consists of cell bodies in the brain stem and midbrain (tegmentum) that project widely to the cerebral cortex and forebrain limbic system (entorhinal cortex).

Chapter 15). Serotonin plays a role in depression and other affective states, sleep, sex, and the regulation of body temperature; use of an SSRI to treat depression can be associated with such side effects as insomnia, anxiety, and loss of libido (Jacobs, 1999).

Significant amounts of serotonin are found in the upper brain stem, particularly in the pons and the medulla (areas that are collectively called the *raphe nuclei*). Rostral projections from the brain stem terminate diffusely throughout the cerebral cortex, hippocampus, hypothalamus, and limbic system (Figure 3.14). Serotonin projections largely parallel those of DA, although they are not as widespread. Serotonin seems to have an effect that is opposite that of DA, and altered serotonin function has been postulated to augment the behavioral stimulant actions of cocaine (Rocha et al., 1998a); serotonin receptors have been postulated to modulate the activity of dopaminergic reward pathways and thus the effects of various drugs of abuse (Rocha et al., 1998b). Axons of serotonin neurons projecting to the spinal cord from cell bodies located in the raphe nuclei may be involved in the modulation of both pain (Chapter 15) and spinal reflexes.

In addition to the presynaptic serotonin transporter (blocked by SSRIs), more than 18 subtypes of postsynaptic serotonin (5-HT) receptors have been identified. They have been classified in families (designated by a number) and subtypes within a family (designated by a

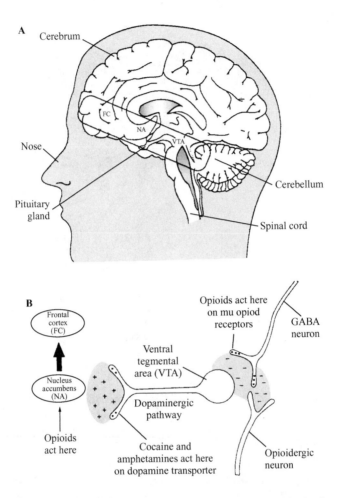

FIGURE 3.13 The limbic dopaminergic reward pathway. **A.** Human brain sliced open lengthwise, showing the relevant midbrain and forebrain area, outlined by an oval, with ventral tegmental area (VTA), nucleus accumbens (NA), and frontal cortex (FC) labeled. **B**. Diagram of the area outlined in **A.** Heavy dots = stored neurotransmitter at nerve endings; + = excitatory neurotransmitter; − = inhibitory neurotransmitter.

letter). Note that this is a different type of designation than the one for dopamine. The four main families of 5-HT receptors are designated 5-HT$_1$, 5-HT$_2$, 5-HT$_3$, and 5-HT$_4$. The 5-HT$_3$ receptor is a ligand-gated ion channel; the others use a G protein-coupled second-messenger system. Beyond this, receptor function becomes exceedingly complicated (Feldman et al., 1997).

Throughout this book, reference will be made to drugs that affect serotonin neurotransmission by acting at one or more receptors for serotonin. These drugs range from anxiolytics and antidepressants to psychedelics.

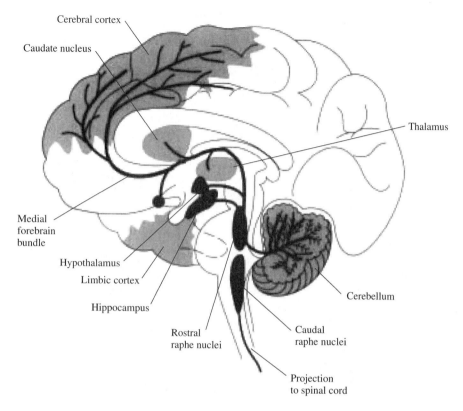

FIGURE 3.14 Serotonin pathways in the human brain. Cell bodies and fiber tracts (axonal projections) are shown in black. Serotonergic terminals are represented by the shaded areas.

Amino Acid Neurotransmitters

The "classical" neurotransmitters (ACh, NE, DA, and serotonin), although important in behavioral regulation and in the actions of psychotropic drugs, are nevertheless used by only a small proportion of the neurons in the brain (Snyder, 2002). Dozens, if not hundreds, of other neurotransmitters exist in the brain, and many of them have been implicated in the actions of psychoactive drugs. Many of these transmitters will be discussed as appropriate throughout this book. Examples include *endorphins* and their receptors, involved in the action of opioid narcotics (Chapter 15), and *anandamide* and its receptors, involved in the action of tetrahydrocannabinol (Chapter 18). Snyder (2002) reviews the history of the development of our concepts of synaptic transmission.

Here we introduce two amino acid neurotransmitters that are widely distributed in the brain. The first, *glutamic acid* (or *glutamate*), is the major universally excitatory neurotransmitter, present on virtually all neurons within the brain. The second is *gamma aminobutyric acid* (GABA), which is the major inhibitory neurotransmitter in the brain. Most other amino acids in the brain do not serve as neurotransmitters (with the exception of aspartate and glycine) but function as precursor molecules for the biosynthesis of other transmitters (for example, tyrosine for catecholamines and tryptophan for serotonin).

Both glutamate and GABA function to modulate a number of ion channels and G protein-coupled receptors, maintaining a balance between excitation and inhibition in the brain. This balance is vital to behavioral control mechanisms. The following sections focus on glutamate and GABA as they are involved in the actions of several psychoactive drugs ranging from the benzodiazepine antianxiety agents (Chapter 6) to the mood stabilizers (Chapter 10).

Glutamate. Glutamate is a major excitatory neurotransmitter in the brain. Glutamate receptors are found on the surface of virtually all neurons. Interestingly, glutamate is also the precursor for the major inhibitory neurotransmitter GABA. GABA is formed from glutamate under control of the enzyme *glutamic acid decarboxylase.*

Glutamate neurotransmission plays a critical role in cortical and hippocampal cognitive function, pyramidal and extrapyramidal motor function, cerebellar function, and sensory function. Research is focusing on the importance of glutamate dysfunction in the pathogenesis of schizophrenia, especially the negative symptoms, and the cognitive dysfunction associated with the disorder (Chapter 11). Glutamate also plays a role in "synaptic plasticity," or learning and memory. However, glutamate excesses can be a potent neuronal "excitotoxin," triggering either rapid or delayed death of neurons. This excitotoxicity may play a role in the neuronal injury that accompanies alcoholism (Chapter 4), Alzheimer's disease (Chapter 13), head injury, and a variety of other disorders as reviewed by Weeber and coworkers (2002).

Glutamate is a nonessential amino acid, meaning that it is easily synthesized in the body and is not required in the diet. It does not readily penetrate the blood-brain barrier, and it is produced locally by specialized neuronal mechanisms (Figure 3.15). It can be synthesized by a number of different chemical reactions, among which is the normal breakdown of glucose. A second reaction is synthesis from glutamine. In this mechanism (which might be the more important for neuronal glutamate), there is a glutamine cycle in which synaptically inactive glutamine serves as a reservoir of glutamate. In this cycle, after glutamate is released from a neuron and exerts its excitatory effect, it is transported (taken up) into astrocytes (neighboring support cells in the brain) and converted to glutamine, which is stored in the astrocyte. Eventually, the glutamine diffuses out of the astrocytes and

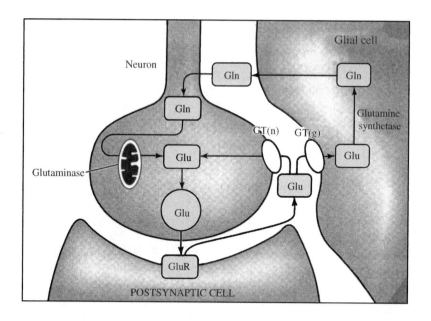

FIGURE 3.15 Pathways for glutamine release, reuptake, and reutilization. Glutamate (Glu) is released into the synapse and recaptured by a glutamate transporter located on adjacent glial cells. Within these glial cells, glutamate is convereted to glutamine (Gln) by the enzyme *glutamine synthetase*. Gln then returns to the CSF, where it is present in high concentrations. It diffuses into neuronal terminals to replenish the Glu after conversion to Glu from Gln by the enzyme *glutaminase*. [From Cooper et al. (2003), p. 133].

enters the presynaptic nerve terminals, where it is converted to glutamate, the active neurotransmitter. The cycle then repeats (Feldman et al., 1997).

Postsynaptic glutamate receptors are many and can be subdivided into two major types: *ionotropic receptors* (directly coupled to membrane ion channels permeable to sodium and/or calcium) and *metabotropic receptors* (coupled to G proteins). The ionotropic receptors subtypes can be further divided into three: NMDA, kainate, and AMPA (the latter two are sometimes referred to as "non-NMDA" receptors; Figure 3.16). In the adult human brain, NMDA and AMPA receptors are colocalized in about 70 percent of their synapses. These receptors mediate rapid excitation of postsynaptic neurons, with especially high concentrations in the cerebral cortex, hippocampus, striatum, septum, and amygdala.

NMDA receptors are activated by glutamate in the presence of another amino acid, either glycine or serine. At resting potential, the NMDA ion channel is blocked by magnesiaum ions (Mg^+). Only when the membrane is depolarized (by the activation of AMPA or kainite receptors on the same postsynaptic neuron) is the Mg^+ blockade of the ion channel relieved. Then the NMDA receptor channel opens and permits the entry of both sodium and calcium ions (see Figure 3.16). Within the NMDA receptor ion channel is a binding site for phencyclidine and ketamine (two "psychedelic" drugs discussed in Chapter 19). These two drugs are noncompetitive antagonists at this NMDA receptor: they inhibit NMDA functioning. Other nonpsychedelic drugs of this type have neuroprotective and antidepressant properties.

NMDA receptors also play a critical role in regulating synaptic plasticity and play vital roles in learning, memory, and cognitive ability. To form memory, high-frequency presynaptic activity in cerebral cortical and limbic neurons leads to the presynaptic release of glutamate, which activates a host of glutamate receptors on the postsynaptic dendritic spines (Figure 3.17). This activity produces a large postsynaptic depolarization, which allows for activation of NMDA ionoptropic receptors, ultimately leading to calcium ion influx into the neuron. The

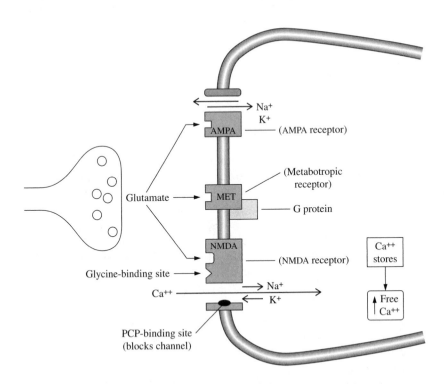

FIGURE 3.16 Glutamate receptor family. The AMPA receptor controls fast sodium and potassium channels; the NMDA receptor controls calcium channels; the metabotropic receptor controls a second-messenger system via a G protein that acts on the intracellular machinery of the cell. (PCP is discussed in Chapter 19.)

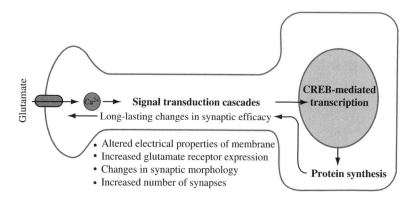

FIGURE 3.17 Processes involved in memory formation. Formation of memory is a complex process that requires several aspects of neuronal function. Memory formation begins with activation of NMDA-type glutamate receptors allowing Ca^{++} to flow into the cell. The Ca^{++} flux activates several intracellular second-messenger signaling cascades. Ultimately, these signaling processes activate the transcription factor CREB, which leads to the modulation of several genes required for consolidation of long-term memory. Translation of newly synthesized mRNAs leads to production of proteins required to affect long-term changes in neuronal physiology. [From Weeber et al. (2002), p. 377.]

high levels of glutamate also activate metatropic receptors, which are coupled via a phospholipase enzyme to a cascade of signal transduction pathways, terminating in activation of a cyclic AMP response-element-binding protein (CREB), which in turn is vital to initiate transcription of new proteins vital for the formation of long-term memory. These new memory proteins are carried out of the nucleus and are translated into functional proteins that effect lasting changes in synaptic strength by altering the electrical properties of the synaptic membrane. These memory proteins do so by "increasing the responsiveness to neurotransmitter, and even changing the number and size of synapses" (Weeber et al., 2002, pp. 377–378). Disruption of this process can be deleterious, being expressed as deficits in memory formation (Chapter 13) or in a state of depression (Chapter 9).

While NMDA activity plays an important role in synaptic plasticity (neuronal "health"), excessive glutaminergic signaling is also involved in neuronal toxicity. For example, ethanol (Chapter 4) reduces glutamate activity, and alcohol withdrawal markedly increases glutamate release from neurons; excesses of glutamate can lead to neuronal destruction through overactivity of NMDA receptors. Attempts to treat alcoholism aim to prevent such neuronal injury by preventing repeated relapses and withdrawals (Chapter 4). Also, traumatic head injury results in massive release of glutamate, and attempts to provide "brain protection" after head injury are aimed at preventing glutaminergic overactivity. Anoxia and hypoglycemia are other glutamate-releasing events that can lead to neuronal damage. Apparently, the entry of large excesses of calcium ions into cells via the NMDA receptors is an important step in the rapid cell death that occurs with excitotoxicity. Finally, new treatments to prevent the progression of Alzheimer's disease and other dementias are aimed at protecting neurons through blockage of NMDA receptor activity (Chapter 13). In 2004, the first anti-Alzheimer's drug that acts through a glutaminergic mechanism became available for clinical use (Chapter 13).

Gamma Aminobutyric Acid (GABA). GABA, a universally inhibitory transmitter, is found in high concentrations in the brain and spinal cord. Two different types of GABA receptors are described, $GABA_A$ and $GABA_B$.

$GABA_A$ receptors are fast receptors and have four transmembrane helical complexes; five receptors join to form an ion channel receptor for chloride ions (see Figure 2.4). Activation of this receptor by GABA opens the channel and leads to an influx of chloride into the cell, hyperpolarizing the cell and reducing its excitability. Barbiturate and benzodiazepine binding to this receptor facilitates the action of GABA (Chapters 5 and 6). Such action is associated with the anxiolytic, amnestic, and anesthetic effects of these sedative drugs (Tomlin et al., 1999). $GABA_A$ receptors are found in high density in the cerebral cortex, hippocampus, and cerebellum.

Important for future pharmacologic research, about ten different subtypes of the $GABA_A$ receptor occur, certainly allowing for the development of agonists and antagonists of specific $GABA_A$ receptor subtypes (Chapter 6). Such drugs might be novel antianxiety agents, anticonvulsants, or cognitive enhancers. Buggy and colleagues (2000) reported that certain anesthetic drugs exert their sedative and amnestic actions by activating $GABA_A$ neurons that in turn reduce the functioning of glutamate neurons on which they synapse.

$GABA_B$ receptors are slow-response receptors of the G protein-coupled type. Activation of $GABA_B$ receptors in the amygdala is associated with the membrane-stabilizing, antiaggressive properties of valproic acid, a drug widely used to treat bipolar disorder (Chapter 10).

Peptide Neurotransmitters

Most of the newly identified neurotransmitters are peptides, which are small proteins (chains of amino acid molecules attached in a specific order). Peptide transmitters can be classified into several groups; one important group is the opioid-type peptides. Other groups include the hypothalamic-releasing hormones, the pituitary hormones, and the so-called gut-brain peptides. Feldman and colleagues (1997) and Cooper and colleagues (2003) discuss these peptides and their possible implications in psychopharmacology.

In this book, one peptide transmitter of interest is the type involved in the actions of the opioids, such as morphine. *Opioid peptides* include the *endorphins* (about 16 to 30 amino acids in length) and the shorter-chain *enkephalins* (5 amino acids in length). These substances are formed from a larger protein produced elsewhere in the body. The endorphins may be involved in a wide variety of emotional states, including pain perception, reward, emotional stability, energy "highs," and acupuncture. Narcotics such as morphine, codeine, and heroin activate (are agonists at) receptors for endorphins and enkephalins (Chapter 15).

Opioid receptors are termed *mu, kappa,* and *sigma*; the mu receptor mediates most of the analgesic and reinforcing properties of morphine and other narcotics. These receptors are the usual 7-transmembrane-spanning proteins, consisting of about 370 to 400 amino acids. They are G protein-coupled receptors; activation of the receptor by a neurotransmitter or an exogenous opioid serves to either activate adjacent ion channels (increasing potassium conductance or decreasing calcium conductance) or inhibit the intracellular function of the enzyme adenylate cyclase. From here, the intracellular consequences become quite complicated (see Cooper et al., 2001).

Another peptide transmitter of interest in this book is *substance P,* a *gut-brain peptide* (11 amino acids in length) that plays an important role as a sensory transmitter, especially for pain impulses that enter the spinal cord and brain from a peripheral site of tissue injury. Opioids, serotonin agonists, and norepinephrine agonists exert much of their analgesic effect by acting on substance P nerve terminals to limit the release of this pain-inducing peptide. Substance P antagonists are also being developed as antidepressant drugs (Chapter 9).

Receptors for substance P appear to be G protein-coupled receptors; activation appears to result in inhibition of adjacent potassium channels and activation of intracellular second messengers (phospholipase C or adenylate cyclase). The role of substance P in pain transmission is discussed in Chapter 15.

STUDY QUESTIONS

1. Define a psychoactive drug.
2. What are some of the functions of the spinal cord?
3. What is a neuron? Describe the following parts of a neuron: dendrites, soma, axon, synaptic terminal.
4. What is a synapse? How does it function?
5. How is the synaptic transmitter action of a released chemical terminated? Give two examples.

6. Name a drug that blocks the action of acetylcholine as a neuro-transmitter. What are the consequences of the blockade? Name a drug that potentiates the action of acetylcholine as a transmitter. What might such a drug be used for?

7. Name three catecholamine neurotransmitters. How is their neuro-transmitter action terminated? What drugs block this process?

8. Describe the various types of serotonin receptors. What drugs might either stimulate or block them? How might these drugs be applied for therapeutic benefit?

9. Name two amino acid neurotransmitters. Describe any drugs that might potentiate or block the actions of each one. How might these drugs be used therapeutically?

10. What is substance P? How does it relate to neuropharmacology?

REFERENCES

Buggy, D. J., et al. (2000). "Effects of Intravenous Anesthetic Agents on Glutamate Release: A Role for $GABA_A$ Receptor-Mediated Inhibition." *Anesthesiology* 92: 1067–1073.

Clements, J. D. (1996). "Transmitter Time-Course in the Synaptic Cleft: Its Role in Central Synaptic Function." *Trends in Neurosciences* 19: 163–171.

Cooper, J. R., et al. (2003). *The Biochemical Basis of Neuropharmacology*, 8th ed. New York: Oxford University Press.

Cummings, J. L. (2000). "Cholinesterase Inhibitors: A New Class of Psychotropic Compounds." *American Journal of Psychiatry* 157: 4–15.

Feldman, R. S., et al. (1997). *Principles of Neuropsychopharmacology*. Sunderland, MA: Sinauer.

Jacobs, B. L. (1999). "Special Supplement Issue: Serotonin 50th Anniversary." *Neuropsychopharmacology* 21(25).

Johansson, C. M., et al. (1999). "Identification of a Neural Stem Cell in the Adult Mammalian Central Nervous System." *Cell* 96: 25–34.

Rocha, B. A., et al. (1998a). "Cocaine Self-Administration in Dopamine-Transporter Knockout Mice." *Nature Neuroscience* 1: 132–137.

Rocha, B. A., et al. (1998b). "Increased Vulnerability to Cocaine in Mice Lacking the Serotonin-1B Receptor." *Nature* 393: 175–178.

Snyder, S. H. (2002). "Forty Years of Neurotransmitters: A Personal Account." *Archives of General Psychiatry* 59: 983–994.

Sossin, W. S. (1996). "Mechanisms for the Generation of Synapse Specificity in Long-Term Memory: The Implications of a Requirement for Transcription." *Trends in Neurosciences* 19: 215–218.

Thompson, R. F. (1993). *The Brain: A Neuroscience Primer*, 2nd ed. New York: Freeman.

Tomlin, S. L., et al. (1999). "Preparation of Barbiturate Optical Isomers and Their Effects on $GABA_A$ Receptors." *Anesthesiology* 90: 1714–1722.

Weeber, E. J., et al. (2002). "Molecular Genetics of Human Cognition." *Molecular Interventions* 2: 376–390

Drugs That Depress Brain Function: Sedative-Hypnotic Drugs

The sedative-hypnotic drugs (or central nervous system—CNS—depressants) are drugs that affect neurons so that the functioning of the brain is depressed, resulting in a behavioral state of calm, relaxation, disinhibition, drowsiness, and sleep as doses of drug increase. These agents are ingested to ease anxiety, tension, and agitation and to induce a soporific state. Behaviorally, what is observed is a dose-related state of anxiolysis (relief from anxiety), release from inhibitions, sedation, sleep, unconsciousness, general anesthesia, coma, and, eventually, death from respiratory and cardiac depression.

Drugs that can produce this state include ethyl alcohol and the inhalants of abuse (Chapter 4), the barbiturates (Chapter 5), general anesthetics and antiepileptic drugs (also covered in Chapter 5), the benzodiazepines, and several of the newer "second-generation" antianxiety and hypnotic drugs (all covered in Chapter 6). Compared with alcohol and the barbiturates, the benzodiazepines have a lesser capacity to produce potentially fatal CNS depression. Because of this improved margin of safety, the benzodiazepines have replaced the barbiturates for the treatment of anxiety and insomnia and have found use in the treatment of a wide variety of psychological disorders. Even the benzodiazepines, however, are not devoid of the potential for causing significant problems, such as dependency and abuse. Therefore, the search continues for hypnotic and anxiolytic drugs with increased efficacy and possibly lower potential for toxicity and abuse.

The terms *sedative, tranquilizer, anxiolytic,* and *hypnotic* can be applied to any CNS depressant. These drugs, including alcohol, diminish environmental awareness, reduce response to sensory stimulation, depress cognitive functioning, decrease spontaneity, and reduce physical activity. Higher doses produce increasing drowsiness, lethargy, clouding of consciousness with amnesia, hypnosis, and unconsciousness. Some of these sedatives have been implicated as "date rape" drugs.

The uniformity of action of all CNS depressants correctly implies that the effects of any CNS depressant potentiate the effects of any other CNS depressant. For example, alcohol exaggerates the depression induced by benzodiazepines, and benzodiazepines intensify the impairment of driving ability in a person who has been drinking alcohol. The depressant effects of sedative drugs are certainly additive; frequently they are supra-additive. Thus, the depression that is observed in a person who has taken more than one drug is greater than would be predicted if the person had taken only one. Such intense depression is often unpredictable and unexpected, and it can lead to dangerous or even fatal consequences. Depressant drugs should not be used in combination, especially if one of the drugs is ethyl alcohol.

All the CNS sedative-hypnotic agents carry the risk of inducing physiological dependence, psychological dependence, and tolerance. *Physiological dependence* is characterized by the occurrence of withdrawal signs and symptoms when the drug is not taken. Signs and symptoms range from sleep disturbances (rebound insomnia, for example) to life-threatening withdrawal convulsions. *Psychological dependence* follows from the positive reinforcement effects of the drugs. *Tolerance* occurs as a result of both the induction of drug-metabolizing enzymes in the liver and the adaptation of cells in the brain to the continuous presence of drug. In addition, a remarkable degree of *cross-tolerance* may occur: tolerance to one drug results in a lessened response to another drug. *Cross-dependence* also may be exhibited, in which one drug can prevent the withdrawal symptoms that are associated with physical dependence on a different drug. This observation underlies the clinical use of benzodiazepines to help moderate the signs and symptoms associated with withdrawal from alcohol.

Chapter 4

Ethyl Alcohol and the Inhalants of Abuse

ETHYL ALCOHOL

The term *alcohol* socially applies to *ethyl alcohol* (ethanol)—a psychoactive drug that is similar in most respects to all the other sedative-hypnotic compounds that are discussed in Chapters 5 and 6. The main difference from the other depressants is that ethanol is used primarily for recreational rather than medical purposes. Because ethanol is the second most widely used psychoactive substance in the world (after caffeine), its use as a sedative and intoxicant has created special problems for both individual users and society in general.

Pharmacology of Alcohol

Ethyl alcohol is not merely a recreational beverage; it is a drug that, like any other psychoactive agent, affects the brain and behavior. Therefore, in discussing alcohol, we need to address its basic pharmacology (pharmacokinetics and pharmacodynamics) as well as its side effects, teratogenic effects, and toxicities. In addition, since alcohol ingestion is widely associated with drug dependence, treatment of alcohol dependence must be addressed.

Pharmacokinetics

Since alcohol is so rapidly and well absorbed orally, its major route of administration is the drinking of beverages containing the drug. Alcoholic beverages include beer, wine, and hard liquors; hard liquors, such as gin and whiskey, are fortified to alcohol levels beyond those achievable with fermentation.

Absorption. Ethyl alcohol is a simple two-carbon molecule (Figure 4.1). It is rarely drunk in its pure form; rather, it is found in 12 to 14 percent concentrations in wines, usually 3.2 to 5 percent in beers (as much as 7 to 10 percent in some "microbrews"[1]), and 40 to 50 percent in "hard" liquors. In the latter, concentration is usually expressed as alcohol "proof," which is twice the percent concentration (for example, 80 proof = 40 percent ethanol). The appendix at the end of this chapter addresses the amount of alcohol that is present in many different forms of alcohol-containing beverages.

Alcohol is soluble in both water and fat, and it diffuses easily across all biological membranes. Thus, after it is drunk, alcohol is rapidly and completely absorbed from the entire gastrointestinal tract, although most is absorbed from the upper intestine because of its large surface area. The time from the last drink to maximal concentration in blood ranges from 30 to 90 minutes. In a person with an empty stomach, approximately 20 percent of a single dose of alcohol is absorbed directly from the stomach, usually quite rapidly. The remaining 80 percent is absorbed rapidly and completely from the upper intestine; the only limiting factor is the time it takes to empty the stomach.

It now appears that women absorb more ethanol than do men. Because of this, women become more impaired than men after drinking equivalent amounts of alcohol and may suffer more alcohol-related organ damage (Agartz et al., 2003; Hommer et al., 2001) and more traumas resulting from traffic crashes and interpersonal violence (Mumenthaler et al., 2003). This phenomenon appears to result mainly from a lower amount of drug-metabolizing enzyme in the wall of the stomach of the female.

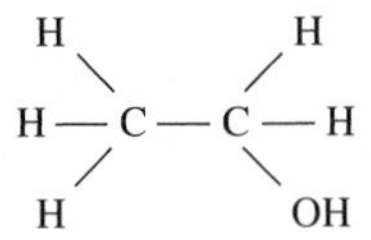

FIGURE 4.1 Structure of ethanol (CH_3CH_2OH).

---

[1]Micobrewed beers contain anywhere from 4.5 to 10 percent alcohol, depending on the product. Lighter brews contain about 4.5 to 6 percent; heavier bocks and porters may contain 7 to 9 percent alcohol; specialty products, triple beers, and barley wines may contain 10 percent or even more alcohol. Thus, some microbrewed beers may easily contain twice (or three times) as much alcohol as ordinary 3.2 percent beers. See the appendix at the end of this chapter for more information.

Distribution. After absorption, alcohol is evenly distributed through-out all body fluids and tissues. The blood-brain barrier is freely perme-able to alcohol. When alcohol appears in the blood and reaches a per-son's brain, it crosses the blood-brain barrier almost immediately. Alcohol is also freely distributed across the placenta and easily enters the brain of a developing fetus. Fetal blood alcohol levels are essen-tially the same as those of the drinking mother.

Metabolism and Excretion. Approximately 95 percent of the alcohol a person ingests is enzymatically metabolized by the enzyme *alcohol dehy-drogenase*. The other 5 percent is excreted unchanged, mainly through the lungs.[2] About 85 percent of the metabolism of alcohol occurs in the liver. Up to 15 percent of alcohol metabolism is carried out by a gastric alcohol dehydrogenase enzyme, located in the lining of the stomach, which can decrease the blood level of alcohol by about 15 percent, obvi-ously attenuating alcohol's systemic toxicity. The metabolism of alcohol by gastric alcohol dehydrogenase is part of what was called *first-pass me-tabolism* in Chapter 1. Rapid gastric emptying (as by drinking on an empty stomach) reduces the time that alcohol is susceptible to first-pass metabolism and results in increased blood levels. Drinking on a full stomach retains alcohol in the stomach, increases its exposure to gastric alcohol dehydrogenase, and reduces the resulting blood level of the drug.

Several years ago, Frezza and coworkers (1990) reported that whenever women and men consume comparable amounts of alcohol (after correction for differences in body weight), women have higher blood ethanol concentrations than men (Figure 4.2). The reasons ap-pear to be threefold:

- Women have about 50 percent less gastric metabolism of alcohol than men because women, whether alcoholic or nonalcoholic, have a lower level of gastric alcohol dehydrogenase enzyme. Since the gastric enzyme metabolizes about 15 percent of ingested alcohol, the blood alcohol concentration (BAC) is increased by about 7 percent over that in a male drinking the same weight-adjusted amount of alcohol.

- Men may have a greater ratio of muscle to fat than do women. Men thus have a larger vascular compartment (fat has little blood supply). Therefore alcohol is somewhat more diluted in men, again increasing blood alcohol levels in women compared to men.

---

[2]Small amounts of alcohol are excreted from the body through the lungs; most of us are familiar with "alcohol breath." This excretion forms the basis for the breath analysis test because alcohol equilibrates rapidly across the membranes of the lung. In the "breathalyzer" test, a ratio of 1:2300 exists between alcohol in exhaled air and alcohol in venous blood. The blood alcohol concentration is easily extrapolated from the alcohol concentration in the expired air.

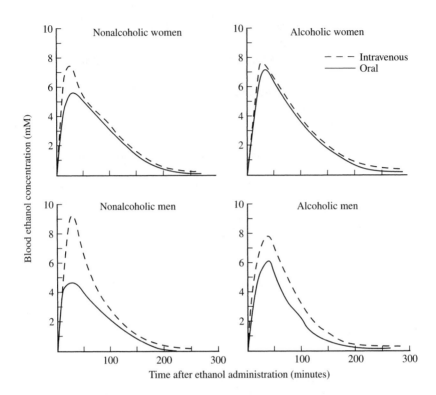

FIGURE 4.2 Effects of route of administration and gender on BAC. Ethanol was administered in a dose of 0.3 milligram per kilogram of body weight either by intravenous injection (dashed lines) or orally (solid lines) to nonalcoholic and alcoholic men and women. The higher BAC after oral alcohol intake by women compared with men shows that first-pass metabolism (in the stomach) is lower in women than in men. This is especially noticeable in alcoholic women compared with all other groups of men and women. [Modified from Frezza et al. (1990), p. 97.]

- Women, with higher body fat than men (fat contains little alcohol), concentrate alcohol in plasma, drink for drink, more than men, raising the apparent blood level.

The metabolism of alcohol by alcohol dehydrogenase is only the first step in a three-step metabolic process involved in the breakdown of alcohol (Figure 4.3):

1. Alcohol dehydrogenase functions to convert alcohol to acetaldehyde. A coenzyme called *nicotinamide adenine dinucleotide* (NAD) is required for the activity of this enzyme. The availability of NAD is the rate-limiting step in this reaction; enough is present so that the maximum amount of alcohol that can be metabolized in 24 hours is about 170 grams (Feldman et al., 1997)

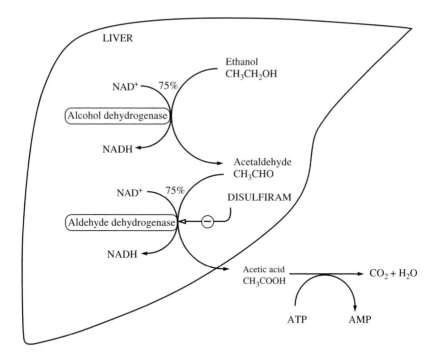

FIGURE 4.3 Metabolism of ethanol. Ethanol is oxidated by the enzyme alcohol dehydrogenase using NAD^+ as a cofactor to form acetaldehyde. A second oxidative step converts acetaldehyde to acetic acid, which, in turn, is broken down to carbon dioxide and water. The first step involving alcohol dehydrogenase is the rate-limiting step. The drug disulfiram (Antabuse) blocks the second step by blocking the activity of aldehyde dehydrogenase.

2. The enzyme *aldehyde dehydrogenase* converts acetaldehyde to acetic acid. The drug *disulfiram* (Antabuse) irreversibly inhibits this enzyme.

3. Acetic acid is broken down into carbon dioxide and water, thus releasing energy (calories).

The average person metabolizes 7 to 8 grams (about 10 milliliters) of 100 percent alcohol per hour, independent of the blood level of alcohol. This rate is fairly constant for a given individual and among individuals.[3] Thus, it would take an adult 1 hour to metabolize the amount of

---

[3]In biochemical terms, this is called zero-order metabolism. Virtually all other drugs are metabolized by first-order metabolism, which means that the amount of drug metabolized per unit time depends on the amount (or concentration) of drug in blood (see Chapter 1). Perhaps zero-order metabolism occurs because the amount of enzyme (or a cofactor required for activity of the enzyme) is limited and becomes saturated with only small amounts of alcohol in the body.

alcohol that is contained in a 1-ounce glass of 80 proof (40 percent) whiskey, a 3.5-ounce glass of 12 percent wine, a 12-ounce bottle of 3.2 percent beer, or a 6-ounce glass of 7 percent microbrew. Consumption of 3.5 ounces of wine, 12 ounces of 3.2 percent beer, 8 ounces of 5 percent beer, or 1 ounce of 80 proof whiskey per hour would keep the blood levels of alcohol in a person fairly constant. If a person ingests more alcohol in any given hour than is metabolized, his or her blood concentrations increase. Consequently, there is a limit to the amount of alcohol a person can consume in an hour without becoming drunk.

One must therefore know or ask, "what is a drink equivalent?" Once, beers contained 3.2 percent alcohol and a 12-ounce beer, containing about 10 cc of absolute alcohol, was considered to be a drink equivalent. Today, only a couple of states are 3.2 percent beer states; most allow 4.5 percent to 5.2 percent beers, more in "ice" beers and certain microbrews. Fortified beers and some microbrewed beers contain about 8 to 9 percent ethanol. A 12-ounce 5 percent beer therefore is 1.5 drink equivalents. A 16-ounce 5 percent beer is almost 2 drink equivalents. A 12-ounce, 5.5 percent "ice" beer is 1.7 drink equivalents. Often, alcoholic beverage products do not list the alcohol percentage on their label, certainly a flaw in our system. It is incumbent on both the server and the imbiber to know the concentration of alcohol in the product being drunk. Why? Because a person metabolizes one drink equivalent per hour. Ingesting more per hour will result in drug accumulation resulting in a rise in blood alcohol concentration. The appendix at the end of this chapter expands on the topic of drink equivalents.

These kinetics permit not only estimation of BAC after drinking a known amount of alcoholic beverage but also estimation of the fall in blood concentration over time after drinking ceases. The following may serve to explain the relationship between the amounts of alcohol consumed, the resulting BAC, and the impairment of motor and intellectual functioning (here, driving ability). Most states define a BAC of 0.08 gram percent (grams%)[4] as intoxication, and a person who drives with a BAC above this amount can be charged with driving while under the influence of alcohol. Thus, one might assume that a level of 0.07 grams% is acceptable but a level of 0.09 grams% is not. However, the behavioral effects of alcohol are not all or none; alcohol (like all sedatives) progressively impairs a person's ability to function. Thus, the 0.08 grams% blood level is only a legally established, arbitrary value. A person whose BAC is under 0.8 grams% yet functions with impairment detrimental to operation of a motor vehicle can still suffer

---

[4]Grams% is the number of grams of ethanol that would be contained in 100 milliliters of blood.

criminal penalties. Driving ability is minimally impaired at a BAC of 0.01 grams%, but at 0.04 to 0.08 grams%, a driver has increasingly impaired judgment and reactions and becomes less inhibited (Ridderinkhof et al., 2002). As a result, the risk of an accident quadruples. The deterioration of a person's driving ability continues at a BAC of 0.10 to 0.14 grams%, leading to a sixfold to sevenfold increase in the risk of having an accident. At 0.15 grams% and higher, a person is 25 times more likely to become involved in a serious accident.

Figure 4.4 illustrates the correlation between the number of drink equivalents imbibed, gender, body weight, and the resulting blood alcohol concentration. First choose the correct chart (male or female). Then find the number that is closest to your body weight in pounds. Look down the left column to find the number of drinks consumed. BAC is found by matching body weight with number of drinks ingested. Then note that BAC falls about 0.015 percent every hour since the first drink was ingested. From the total number of drinks ingested, subtract the amount of alcohol that has been metabolized over the number of hours since drinking began (remember that approximately 1 drink equivalent is metabolized in 1 hour). The final figure is the approximate BAC. By calculating this number, the degree to which driving ability is impaired can be predicted.

Some agencies and organizations have even more stringent BAC standards than the states. For example, the Federal Department of Transportation regulations test and prevent truck drivers from driving at 0.04 grams% and airline pilots from flying at 0.02 grams% after 24 hours of abstinence.

Factors that may alter the predictable rate of metabolism of alcohol are usually not clinically significant. With long-term use, however, alcohol can induce drug-metabolizing enzymes in the liver, thereby increasing the liver's rate of metabolizing alcohol (and so inducing *tolerance*) as well as its rate of metabolizing other compounds that are similar to alcohol (termed *cross-tolerance*).

Pharmacodynamics

Identifying the mechanism of the action of alcohol continues to be difficult. For many years, it was presumed that alcohol acted through a general depressant action on nerve membranes and synapses. Because it is both water soluble and lipid soluble, ethanol dissolves into all body tissues. This property led to a unitary hypothesis of action—that the drug dissolves in nerve membranes, distorting, disorganizing, or "perturbing" the membrane, similar to the action of general anesthetics (Chapter 5). The result is a nonspecific and indirect depression of neuronal function. This mechanism would certainly account for the nonspecific and generalized depressant behavioral effects of the drug.

Blood Alcohol Concentration—A Guide

One drink equals 1 ounce of 80 proof alcohol; 12-ounce bottle of beer; 2 ounces of 20% wine; 3 ounces of 12% wine.

Men

Drinks	Approximate blood alcohol percentage (grams%) Body weight (pounds)								
	100	120	140	160	180	200	220	240	
0	.00	.00	.00	.00	.00	.00	.00	.00	Only safe driving limit
1	.04	.03	.03	.02	.02	.02	.02	.02	Impairment begins
2	.08	.06	.05	.05	.04	.04	.03	.03	Driving skills significantly affected
3	.11	.09	.08	.07	.06	.06	.05	.05	
4	.15	.12	.11	.09	.08	.08	.07	.06	Possible criminal penalties
5	.19	.16	.13	.12	.11	.09	.09	.08	
6	.23	.19	.16	.14	.13	.11	.10	.09	
7	.26	.22	.19	.16	.15	.13	.12	.11	Legally intoxicated
8	.30	.25	.21	.19	.17	.15	.14	.13	
9	.34	.28	.24	.21	.19	.17	.15	.14	Criminal penalties
10	.38	.31	.27	.23	.21	.19	.17	.16	

Alcohol is "burned up" by the body at .015 grams% per hour, as follows:

Number of hours since starting first drink   1   2   3   4   5   6
Percent alcohol burned up   .015 .030 .045 .060 .075 .090

Calculate BAC
Example:
180 lb. man – 6 drinks in 4 hours
BAC = .130 grams% on chart
Subtract .060 grams% burned up in 4 hours.
BAC equals .070 grams% – DRIVING IMPAIRED.

Women

Drinks	Approximate blood alcohol percentage (grams%) Body weight (pounds)									
	90	100	120	140	160	180	200	220	240	
0	.00	.00	.00	.00	.00	.00	.00	.00	.00	Only safe driving limit
1	.05	.05	.04	.03	.03	.03	.02	.02	.02	Impairment begins
2	.10	.09	.08	.07	.06	.05	.05	.04	.04	Driving skills significantly affected
3	.15	.14	.11	.10	.09	.08	.07	.06	.06	
4	.20	.18	.15	.13	.11	.10	.09	.08	.08	Criminal penalties
5	.25	.23	.19	.16	.14	.13	.11	.10	.09	
6	.30	.27	.23	.19	.17	.15	.14	.12	.11	
7	.35	.32	.27	.23	.20	.18	.16	.14	.13	Legally intoxicated
8	.40	.36	.30	.26	.23	.20	.18	.17	.15	
9	.45	.41	.34	.29	.26	.23	.20	.19	.17	Criminal penalties
10	.51	.45	.38	.32	.28	.25	.23	.21	.19	

Alcohol is "burned up" by the body at .015 grams% per hour, as follows:

Number of hours since starting first drink   1   2   3   4   5   6
Percent alcohol burned up   .015 .030 .045 .060 .075 .090

Calculate BAC
Example:
140 lb woman – 6 drinks in 4 hours
BAC = .19 on chart
Subtract .060 grams% metabolized
BAC =.13 – LEGALLY INTOXICATED

FIGURE 4.4 Relation between blood alcohol concentration, body weight, and the number of drinks ingested for men and women. See text for details.

This hypothesis, however, does not explain the evidence that alcohol may disturb both the synaptic activity of various neurotransmitters, especially major excitatory (glutamate) and inhibitory (GABA) systems, and various intracellular transduction processes.

Glutamate Receptors. Ethanol is a potent inhibitor of the function of the NMDA-subtype of glutamate receptors (Tsai et al., 1998). Ethanol disrupts glutaminergic neurotransmission by depressing the responsiveness of NMDA receptors to released glutamate. This attenuation of glutamate responsiveness may be exacerbated by its known enhancement of inhibitory GABA neurotransmission. With chronic alcohol intake and persistent glutaminergic suppression, there is a compensatory up regulation of NMDA receptors. Thus, on removal of ethanol's inhibitory effect (as would occur during alcohol withdrawal), these excess excitatory receptors would result in withdrawal signs, including seizures.

The drug *acamprosate*, a structural analogue of glutamate (Figure 4.5), is an anticraving drug used to maintain abstinence in alcohol-dependent individuals, an action postulated to be produced by interaction with glutaminergic NMDA receptors, attenuating neuronal hyperexcitability induced by chronic alcohol ingestion and withdrawal (Al-Qatari and coworkers, 1998; Dahchour and DeWitte, 2000). The use of acamprosate in the treatment of alcoholism is discussed later in this chapter.

GABA Receptors. Ethanol activates the GABA-mediated increase in chloride ion flows, resulting in neuronal inhibition (Feldman et al., 1997). The behavioral results of this inhibition include sedation, muscle

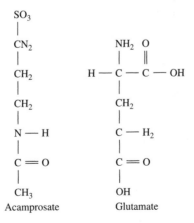

FIGURE 4.5 Structures of acamprosate and glutamate.

relaxation, and inhibition of cognitive and motor skills. A GABAergic antianxiety effect was illustrated by Kushner and coworkers (1996), who demonstrated that low doses of ethanol act acutely to reduce both panic and the anxiety surrounding panic. This finding lends support to the view that drinking by those with panic disorder, stress, and anxiety is reinforced by this GABAergic agonistic effect. Thus, the use of alcohol to self-medicate one's panic or anxiety disorder may contribute to the high rate at which alcohol-use disorders occur with anxiety and panic disorders. Matsuzawa and Suzuki (2002) discuss the interaction between ethanol and stress in the mechanism of psychological dependence on ethanol. They invoke a mechanism in which GABAergic inhibition results in activation of opioid receptors that ultimately activates behaviorally rewarding dopaminergic neurons.

Ethanol binds to a different subunit on the GABA$_A$ receptor than do other GABA agonists (Wan et al., 1996). A chronic adaptive effect seems to involve changes in intracellular mRNA, suggesting that chronic alcohol can affect gene expression. As a result of the GABAergic agonistic action, the activity of other transmitter systems is ultimately affected.

The GABA agonistic action of ethanol has been linked to the positive reinforcing effects of the drug (Matsuzawa and Suzuki, 2002). Indeed, the abuse potential of alcohol follows from an ultimate action to augment dopamine neurotransmitter systems, particularly the dopaminergic projection from the ventral tegmental area (VTA) to the nucleus accumbens and to the frontal cortex (Chapter 3). Such action is probably an indirect effect rather than a direct action exerted on dopamine-secreting neurons.

Opioid Receptors. Wand and coworkers (1998) present data consistent with a dysfunctional brain opioid system as part of a neurocircuitry involved in heavy alcohol drinking and alcohol dependence. Alcohol-dependent individuals and their offspring may have a deficit in brain opioid activity. Ethanol may induce opioid release, which in turn triggers dopamine release in the brain reward system. Administration of *naltrexone* (ReVia, Trexan) blocks opioid release and may reduce alcohol craving. Indeed, naltrexone is approved for the treatment of alcohol dependency.

Serotonin Receptors. There is a growing literature on the role of serotonin in the actions of alcohol. Chronic alcohol consumption results in augmentations in serotoninergic activity, and serotonin dysfunction may play a role in the pathogenesis of some types of alcoholism. Today, emphasis is on the role of serotonin 5-HT$_2$ and 5-HT$_3$ receptors in the central effects of ethanol; these receptors are located on dopaminergic neurons in the nucleus accumbens. Antagonistic drugs that block these receptors reduce ethanol intake in patients with early-age onset of alcoholism, presumably by ameliorating an underlying serotonergic abnormality (Johnson and coworkers, 2000). In addition, presynaptic serotonin transporter dysfunction can be correlated with predisposition to early-onset alcoholism (Heinz and coworkers, 1998). Consistent with this are the observations that serotonin reuptake-inhibiting antidepressants such as *sertraline* (Zoloft) reduce alcohol drinking in alcoholics of lower risk and/or severity (Pettinati et al., 2000).

Cannabinoid Receptors. Within the past four or five years, important information has been gathered on the probable role of cannabinoid receptors (Chapter 18) in the actions of alcohol, especially in postwithdrawal cravings and in the relapse to drinking. Chronic ingestion of ethanol stimulates the formation of the endogenous neurotransmitter for cannabinoid receptors, a substance called *anandamide*. This neurotransmitter activates the cannabinoid receptors and, with continued ethanol ingestion, eventually leads to down regulation of these receptors (Hungund and Basavarajappa, 2000). Down regulation then disinhibits the nucleus accumbens, our endogenous reward system. Removal of ethanol by cessation of drinking leads to a hyperactive endocannabinoid reaction, which appears to result in a craving for alcohol and a return to drinking.

Mice that are genetically inbred to lack cannabinoid receptors do not voluntarily consume alcohol and also lack alcohol-induced dopamine-mediated reward responses in the nucleus accumbens (Hungund et al., 2003). Similarly, administration of drugs that block cannabinoid receptors (cannabinoid antagonists) prevents relapse to alcohol ingestion (Serra et al., 2002). Therefore, it now appears that ethanol and cannabinoid agonists (for example, tetrahydrocannabinol in marijuana) activate the same reward system. Down regulation of cannabinoid receptors may be involved in the development of tolerance and dependence on ethanol, and an active response from cannabinoid receptors after alcohol detoxification may lead to alcohol craving and eventual compulsion to relapse (Hungund et al., 2002; Wang et al., 2003). Perhaps our greatest hope for truly effective anticraving drugs to help prevent relapse to voluntary drinking in withdrawn alcoholics lies in the development of cannabinoid antagonists such as rimonabant (Chapter 18).

Pharmacological Effects

The graded, reversible depression of behavior and cognition is the primary pharmacological effect of alcohol. Respiration, although transiently stimulated at low doses, becomes progressively depressed and, at very high blood concentrations of alcohol, is the cause of death. Alcohol is also anticonvulsant, although it is not clinically used for this purpose. On the other hand, withdrawal from alcohol ingestion is accompanied by a prolonged period of hyperexcitability, and seizures can occur; seizure activity peaks approximately 8 to 12 hours after the last drink.

In the CNS, the effects of alcohol are additive with those of other sedative-hypnotic compounds, resulting in more sedation and greater impairment of motor and cognitive abilities. Other sedatives (especially the benzodiazepines) and marijuana are the sedative drugs most frequently combined with alcohol, and they increase its deleterious effects on motor and intellectual skills (for example, driving ability) as well as alertness. Patients suffering from insomnia find alcohol to be an effective hypnotic agent (Roehrs and coworkers, 1999).

Alcohol also affects the circulation and the heart. Alcohol dilates the blood vessels in the skin, producing a warm flush and a decrease in body temperature. Thus, it is pointless and possibly dangerous to drink alcohol to keep warm when one is exposed to cold weather. Long-term use of high doses of alcohol is associated with diseases of the heart muscle, which can result in heart failure. However, recent observations have demonstrated that *low* doses of alcohol consumed daily (up to 2 drink equivalents per day for men and 0.5 to 1.0 daily drink equivalents for women) *reduce* the risk of coronary artery disease (Mukamal et al., 2003a) and peripheral artery disease (Djousse et al., 2000). This protective effect on coronary and peripheral blood vessels occurs because of an alcohol-induced increase in high-density lipoprotein in blood with a corresponding decrease in low-density lipoprotein. (The higher the concentration of high-density lipoprotein and the lower the concentration of low-density lipoprotein, the lower the incidence of development of arteriosclerosis and occlusive vascular disease.) Unfortunately, the cardioprotective effect of low doses of alcohol is lost on people who also smoke cigarettes.

Light to moderate doses of alcohol have also been shown to reduce the incidence of ischemic strokes (Figure 4.6). Ischemic strokes are strokes due to loss of oxygen delivery to specific areas of the brain. This protective action can reduce the risk of dementia among older adults (Mukamal et al., 2003b). The mechanisms responsible for the protective effect of low doses of alcohol on ischemic stroke appear to involve alcohol-induced increases in (protective) high-density cholesterol and an aspirinlike decrease in platelet aggregation. Higher amounts of alcohol (more than 14 drinks per week) were associated with an increased risk of stroke.

Alcohol (like all depressant drugs) is not an aphrodisiac. The behavioral disinhibition induced by low doses of alcohol may appear to cause some loss of restraint, but alcohol depresses body function and interferes with sexual performance. As Shakespeare says in *Macbeth:* "It provokes the desire, but it takes away the performance."

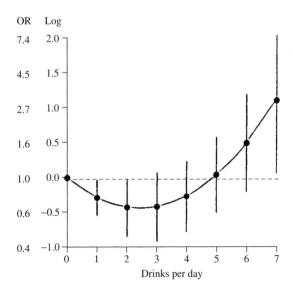

FIGURE 4.6 Relationship between alcohol and stroke. The reference group (indicated by the dashed horizontal line) is those not drinking during the past year. Analysis is matched for age, sex, and race/ethnicity and adjusted for hypertension, diabetes, heart disease, cigarette use, and education. OR = odds ratio for having a stroke. Log = logarithmic scale of stroke incidence. Vertical lines indicate 95 percent confidence intervals. [From R. L. Sacco et al., "The Protective Effect of Moderate Alcohol Consumption on Ischemic Stroke," *Journal of the American Medical Association* 281 (1999), p. 57.]

Psychological Effects

The short-term psychological and behavioral effects of alcohol are primarily restricted to the CNS, where a mixture of stimulant and depressant effects is seen after low doses of the drug. Figure 4.7 correlates the effects of alcohol with levels of the drug measured in the blood. The behavioral reaction to disinhibition, which occurs at low doses, is largely determined by the person (Holdstock and deWit, 1998), his or her mental expectations, and the environment in which drinking occurs. In one setting a person may become relaxed and euphoric; in another he or she may become withdrawn or violent. Mental expectations and the physical setting become progressively less important at increasing doses because the sedative effects increase and behavioral activity decreases.

At low doses, a person may still function (although with less coordination) and attempt to drive or otherwise endanger self and others. Memory, concentration, and insight are progressively dulled and lost. Perceptual speed is an important component of task performance and

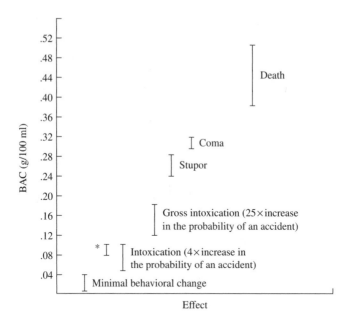

FIGURE 4.7 Correlation of the blood level of ethanol with degrees of intoxication. The legal level of intoxication (*) varies by state; the range of values is shown. BAC = blood alcohol concentration.

is markedly impaired by ethanol (Schweizer et al., 2004). At BAC values of about 0.05 to 0.09 grams%, some common clinical symptoms are sociability, talkativeness, decreased inhibitions, diminution of attention, judgment, and control, slowed information processing, and loss of efficiency in critical performance testing. As the BAC increases, the drinker becomes progressively more incapacitated.

Alcohol intoxication, with its resulting disinhibition, plays a major role in a large percentage of violent crimes, including fighting, rape, sexual assault, and certain kinds of deviant behaviors. Alcohol is implicated in more than half of all homicides and assaults; about 40 percent of violent offenders in jail were drinking at the time of the offense for which they have been incarcerated. Many of these offenses probably would not have occurred if the offender, the victim, or both had not been intoxicated (McClelland and Teplin, 2001). Martin (2001) studied how alcohol use by men affects intimate-partner violence. She states that alcohol intoxication may contribute to aggressive and criminal behavior through its mediating effects on the physiological, cognitive, affective, or behavioral functioning of the drinker. Through effects on the GABA system, alcohol reduces the anxiety about the consequences of aggressive behavior. Through dopaminergic activation, impulse control is reduced, which increases the likelihood of aggression. Through glutamate depression, cognitive functioning is impaired, reducing the drinker's ability to find peaceful (nonviolent) solutions to difficult situations. Many drinkers develop a type of "alcohol myopia," defined as shortsightedness in which superficially understood, immediate aspects of experience have a disproportionate influence on behavior and emotion. Cognitive and attentional deficits cause a focus on the present, reduce fear and anxiety, and impair problem solving. Finally, alcohol use increases concerns with power and dominance, linked to male violence generally and to intimate-partner interactions in particular. The effect can be an inappropriate sense of mastery, control, or power. A recent symposium addresses this issue (Abbey et al., 2002). The issue of violence and crime applies to women as well as to men (Martin and Bryant, 2001).

Hindson and coworkers (2001) surveyed 42,000 adults as part of a U.S. Census Bureau survey about alcohol use/abuse and physical fighting. Relative to those who did not begin drinking until age 21 or older, those who started drinking before age 17 were three to four times more likely ever in their lives and at least three times more likely in the past year to have been in a fight after drinking. Thus, early-age onset of drinking is associated with alcohol-related violence not only among persons under 21 but among adults as well.

More than 50 percent of all motor vehicle highway accidents are alcohol related, a number that has changed little in 20 years. More than 10 million individuals in the United States currently suffer the consequences of their alcohol abuse, which include arrests, traffic accidents, occupational injuries, violence, and health and occupational losses. This number does not include the 10 million individuals considered to be alcohol dependent (and suffering their own negative consequences). About 10 percent of our society is personally afflicted with (or suffers the consequences of) another's alcohol use. Untreated alcohol problems lead to death, disability, and $185 billion each year in avoidable health, business, and criminal justice costs.

Noel and coworkers (2001) studied 30 recently detoxified male alcoholics (with matched controls) to assess "frontal lobe" or "executive" functioning and the vulnerability of the frontal lobes to alcohol abuse. In all tests of executive function, withdrawn alcoholics performed poorly compared with controls. They stated:

> Chronic alcohol consumption is associated with severe executive function deficits, still present after a protracted period of alcohol abstinence. This supports the idea that cognitive deficit in detoxified, sober alcoholics is due, at least partly, to frontal lobe dysfunction. (p. 1152)

Furthermore:

> These findings could have important implications, particularly
> concerning relapse. Since drug use is largely controlled by auto-
> matic processes, executive functions are needed to block this and
> maintain abstinence. Thus, the existence of persistent executive
> function deficits could affect the capacity to maintain abstinence.
> (p. 1152)

Persistent alcohol use can harm even adolescents. Brown and
coworkers (2000) studied alcohol-dependent adolescents (who developed dependency in early adolescence) and found that recent detoxification was associated with poor visuospatial functioning (as might be
expected), whereas alcohol withdrawal early in life was associated
with persistence of poor retrieval of verbal and nonverbal information.
This finding reflect long-term effects on working memory.

Long-term effects of alcohol may also involve many different organs of a person's body. Long-term ingestion of only moderate
amounts of alcohol seems to produce few physiological alterations. As
noted earlier, low to moderate doses can even be protective to the heart
and vascular system. On the down side, long-term ingestion of larger
amounts of alcohol leads to a variety of serious neurological, mental,
and physical disorders. These disorders are described in the section on
alcoholism and its pharmacological treatment.

Alcohol is quite caloric but has little nutritional value; consumption of a high-alcohol diet (and little else!) slowly leads to vitamin deficiencies and nutritional diseases, which may result in physical deterioration. Indeed, alcohol abuse has been suggested as the
most common cause of vitamin and trace element deficiencies in
adults.

Tolerance and Dependence

The patterns and mechanisms for the development of tolerance of,
physical dependence on, and psychological dependence on alcohol are
similar to those for other CNS depressants (Chapter 5). The extent of
tolerance depends on the amount, pattern, and extent of alcohol ingestion. Persons who ingest alcohol only intermittently on sprees or more
regularly but in moderation develop little or no tolerance. Persons who
regularly ingest large amounts of alcohol develop marked tolerance.
The tolerance is of three types:

1. *Metabolic tolerance,* where the liver increases its amount of drug-
   metabolizing enzyme. This type of tolerance accounts for at most
   25 percent of the tolerance to alcohol that develops.

2. *Tissue, or functional, tolerance,* where neurons in the brain adapt to the amount of drug present. Individuals who develop this type of tolerance characteristically display blood alcohol levels about twice those of a nontolerant individual at a similar level of behavioral intoxication. Note, however, that despite behavioral adaptation, impairments in cognitive function are similar at similar blood levels in both tolerant and nontolerant persons. In other words, at a BAC of 0.15 grams%, both tolerant and nontolerant persons display marked deficits in insight, judgment, cognition, and other executive functions. The tolerant person may just *appear* less intoxicated.

3. *Associative, contingent, or homeostatic tolerance.* A variety of environmental manipulations can counter the effects of ethanol, and counterresponses are a possible mechanism of tolerance.

When physical dependence develops, withdrawal of alcohol results, within several hours, in a period of rebound hyperexcitability that may eventually lead to convulsions. Alcohol abuse is one of the most common causes of adult-onset seizures; seizures occur in about 10 percent of adults during alcohol withdrawal. Alcohol withdrawal seizures are a life-threatening consequence of alcohol cessation in alcoholic persons. The period of seizure activity is relatively short, usually 6 hours or less, but seizures can be very severe. Blocking seizure activity during withdrawal is a major goal of detoxification and usually involves two classes of agents: the benzodiazepines and the anticonvulsants. As early as 1978, Ballenger and Post noted that the severity of alcohol withdrawal seizures is correlated with the number of years of alcohol abuse and perhaps with the number of detoxifications. A "kindling" model of alcohol withdrawal seizures suggests that repeated alcohol withdrawals may lead to an increase in the severity of subsequent withdrawals and a greater likelihood of withdrawal seizures with each detoxification. Brown and coworkers (1988) expanded on this theory by offering data supporting the theory that the number of detoxifications is an important variable in the predisposition to withdrawal seizures (Figure 4.8). Malcolm and coworkers (2000) applied this concept to a postulate that holds that repeated detoxifications might also cause neurobehavioral alterations that may affect alcohol craving. Patients who had experienced multiple detoxifications had higher scores on tests that measure obsessive thoughts about alcohol, drink urges, and drinking behaviors. Thus, recurrent detoxifications may lead to increased rates of relapse due to a "kindling" of behaviors and thoughts leading to a compulsion to return to drinking. The researchers concluded by adding that the kindling effect persists despite treatment with benzodiazepines or other traditional sedative-hypnotic drugs.

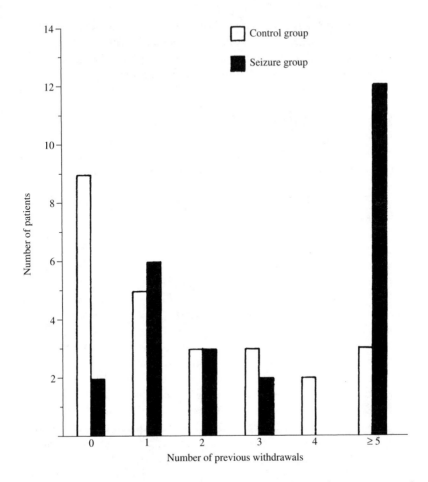

FIGURE 4.8 Number of previous withdrawals (prior detoxifications) in two groups of alcoholics. Fifty male alcoholics were divided into two groups. The control group had not experienced alcohol withdrawal seizures, while the seizure group comprised individuals who had experienced one or more withdrawal seizures in their past history. This figure demonstrates that 12 of 25 of the alcoholics with a history of withdrawal seizures had undergone five or more detoxifications, compared to only 3 of 25 of the control group. [From Brown et al. (1988), p. 511.]

In addition to withdrawal seizures and cravings, the alcohol withdrawal syndrome can consist of a period of tremulousness, with hallucinations, psychomotor agitation, confusion and disorientation, sleep disorders, and a variety of associated discomforts—a syndrome that is sometimes referred to as *delirium tremens* (DTs).

Fadda and Rossetti (1998) reviewed withdrawal as a sign of alcohol-induced neuroadaptation and the neurodegeneration that may play a role in the persistent cognitive deficits that result from alcohol dependence. Markianos and coworkers (2000) assessed dopamine receptor responsiveness in alcoholic patients during their usual alcohol consumption and after detoxification. Detoxification was accompanied by a normalization of low responsiveness of dopamine receptors during alcohol abuse. The Markianos team postulated that the dopamine system is involved in alcohol dependence and withdrawal.

Side Effects and Toxicity

Many side effects and toxicities associated with alcohol have already been mentioned; following is a summary and expansion. In acute use, a *reversible drug-induced dementia* is induced. This syndrome is manifested as a clouded sensorium with disorientation, impaired insight and judgment, anterograde amnesia (blackouts), and diminished intellectual capabilities. The person's affect may be labile, with emotional outbursts precipitated by otherwise innocuous events. With high doses of alcohol, delusions, hallucinations, and confabulations may occur. In social functioning, these alterations result in unpredictable states of disinhibition (drunkenness), alterations in driving performance, and uncoordinated motor behavior.

Liver damage is the most serious physiological long-term consequence of excessive alcohol consumption. Irreversible changes in both the structure and the function of the liver are common. For example, ethanol produces active oxidants during its metabolism by hepatocytes; this then results in oxidative stress on liver cells. The significance of alcohol-induced liver dysfunction is illustrated by the fact that 75 percent of all deaths attributed to alcoholism are caused by cirrhosis of the liver, and cirrhosis is the seventh most common cause of death in the United States.

Long-term alcohol ingestion may irreversibly cause the *destruction of nerve cells,* producing a permanent brain syndrome with dementia (Korsakoff's syndrome). More subtle and persistent cognitive deficits may be present whether or not a diagnosis of Korsakoff's syndrome is made. This situation is termed *alcohol dementia,* which can cause long-term problems with memory, learning, and other cognitive skills

The *digestive system* may also be affected. *Pancreatitis* (inflammation of the pancreas) and *chronic gastritis* (inflammation of the stomach), with the development of peptic ulcers, may occur.

A great deal of epidemiological evidence now shows that chronic excessive alcohol consumption is a major risk factor for *cancer* in humans. Although ethanol alone may not be carcinogenic, it is a cocarcinogen, or a tumor promoter. The metabolism of ethanol leads to the generation of acetaldehyde and free radicals. Acetaldehyde has been shown to promote tumor growth, promoting cancers of the oral pharynx, stomach, and intestine (Harty and coworkers, 1997). Statistically, heavy drinking increases a person's risk of developing cancer of the tongue, mouth, throat, voice box, and liver. The risk of head and neck cancers for heavy drinkers who smoke is 6 to 15 times greater than for those who abstain from both. The risk of throat cancer is 44 times greater for heavy users of both alcohol and tobacco than for nonusers.

Although the finding is controversial, ethanol may increase the risk for breast cancer by still unidentified means; it may produce free radicals that cause oxidative stress to cells in breast tissue (Hamajima and coworkers, 2002). Alcohol-associated breast cancers appear with highest frequency in postmenopausal women who report regular consumption of alcohol before the age of 40 years (Lenz et al., 2002). The increased risk of breast cancer offsets the beneficial effects of moderate alcohol consumption on cardiovascular disease

Teratogenic Effects

For years we have known that alcohol is both a physical and a behavioral teratogen (National Institute on Alcohol and Alcoholism, 1987). Drug-induced alterations occur in brain structure and/or function (Roebuck and coworkers, 1998). *Fetal alcohol syndrome* (FAS) is a devastating developmental disorder that occurs in the offspring of mothers who have high blood levels of alcohol during critical stages of fetal development; it affects as many as 30 to 50 percent of infants born to alcoholic women (Little et al., 1998a). The rate of FAS is about 3 to 5 per 1000 live births. Clearly, a relatively large number of otherwise biologically normal infants may be irreversibly damaged by maternal alcohol abuse during pregnancy, and alcohol abuse during pregnancy appears to be the most frequent known teratogenic cause of mental retardation.

Although the amount of alcohol that must be consumed to cause fetal injury is not known, it is generally accepted that more than 3 ounces of absolute alcohol daily, especially in conjunction with binge drinking, poses a special risk of FAS to the fetus (Finnegan and Kandall, 1997). Even very low daily doses of alcohol taken early in pregnancy can be associated with smaller body size (height and weight) in offspring even as late as their teenage years (Day and coworkers, 2002). Whether neurodevelopmental alterations accompany this long-term effect is unknown at this time. Because subtle intellectual and behavioral effects of low-level alcohol consumption may go unnoticed, no safe level of alcohol intake during pregnancy has been established.

Features of the full fetal alcohol syndrome include the following:

- CNS dysfunction, including low intelligence and microcephaly (reduced cranial circumference), mental retardation, and behavioral abnormalities (often presenting as hyperactivity and difficulty with social integration)

- Retarded body growth rate (fetal growth retardation)
- Facial abnormalities (short palpebral fissures, short nose, wide-set eyes, and small cheekbones)
- Other anatomical abnormalities (for example, congenital heart defects and malformed eyes and ears) (Sampson et al., 1997, p. 317)

In the United States, an estimated 2.6 million infants are born annually following significant in utero alcohol exposure. While many display the full features of FAS, about one newborn out of every hundred live births may display a "lesser degree of damage, termed *fetal alcohol effects*" (Finnegan and Kandall, 1997) or perhaps more correctly termed *alcohol-related neurodevelopmental disorder* (ARND) (Sampson et al., 1997). Taken together, the combined rate of FAS and ARND is estimated to be at least 9 per 1000 live births. This would make alcohol ingestion the third leading cause of birth defects with associated mental retardation; it is the only one that is preventable. Perhaps a new term should be utilized to encompass the full spectrum of fetal damage that can follow ingestion of ethanol by pregnant women. "Fetal alcohol spectrum disorder" would include both fetal alcohol syndrome and fetal alcohol effects, covering that gray line between the infants with facial abnormalities and those with "milder" effects, such as hyperactivity and aggressive behaviors.

While the structural abnormalities and growth retardation of FAS are well described, the behavioral and cognitive effects of alcohol exposure are less appreciated. Affected and subject to deficits are intelligence (IQ), activity, attention, learning, memory, language, and motor and visuospatial activities in children prenatally exposed to varying amounts of alcohol (Mattson and Riley, 1998; Willford et al., 2004). Also present can be sensory problems involving ocular, auditory, vestibular, and speech and language development. Carmichael and coworkers (1997) studied a cohort of 500 children, 250 of whom were infants of "heavier" drinkers who typically drank at "social drinking levels." The other 250 children were infants of infrequent drinkers and abstainers. There were significant alcohol-related differences in behavioral and learning difficulties during adolescence. Exposure to alcohol during pregnancy was associated "with a profile of adolescent antisocial behavior, school problems, and self-perceived learning difficulties." Thus, brain function can be markedly affected in offspring of alcohol-drinking mothers in the absence of the observable structural abnormalities.

In a study in Finland, Autti-Ramo (2000) followed 70 children with fetal alcohol exposure (42 with recognized cognitive and other deficits, 10 with physical growth restrictions only, and 18 classified as normal). They were assessed at age 12 years for psychosocial well-being. The longer the alcohol exposure during pregnancy, the more likely the child was to have significant cognitive and social impairments. Of the 42 children with early recognition of cognitive deficits, 29 (69 percent) were in permanent foster or institutional care. Even among the children in the normal and growth-restricted groups, 10 (36 percent) were temporarily or permanently in alternative care. Behavioral problems were significant. Thus, alcohol exposure in utero can be associated with social disadvantages, including alternative care and behavioral problems.

Baer and coworkers (2003) reported results of a 21-year longitudinal study in which they followed offspring of 500 women who, in 1974–1975, drank during their pregnancy (30 percent binge drank). Offspring of 2 women displayed FAS and 31 offspring were identified as having components of ARND. When offspring attained the age of 21 years, 21 percent of their fathers and 11 percent of their mothers were identified as having had a history of alcohol problems. The offspring of mothers who binge drank during pregnancy exhibited three times the likelihood of at least mild alcohol dependence (14.1 percent versus 4.5 percent).

The mechanisms responsible for the production of FAS and ARND are unclear. Ikonomidou and coworkers (2000) reported that ethanol-treated rats had reduced neuronal densities in their developing forebrain; the effects occurred during the time period of synaptogenesis. The authors postulated that the neurodegeneration followed both from NMDA receptor blockade and from positive $GABA_A$ receptor activation.

The prevention of FAS and ARND obviously involves abstinence from alcohol by women who are, plan to become, or are capable of becoming pregnant. Screening questionnaires may be effective in helping to protect not only the unborn infant but also the long-term health of the mother (Bradley and coworkers, 1998). Because alcohol screening can effectively identify women and infants at risk, it is recommended for women during prenatal visits.

Alcoholism and Its Pharmacological Treatment

The recognition of alcoholism as a multifaceted disease and behavioral process is relatively recent. In 1935, Alcoholics Anonymous was founded based on a *moral model* of alcoholism; it offered a spiritual and behavioral framework for understanding, accepting, and recovering from the compulsion to use alcohol. In the late 1950s, the American Medical Association recognized the syndrome of alcoholism as an illness. In the mid-1970s, alcoholism was redefined as a *chronic, progressive, and potentially fatal disease*. In 1992, the description was expanded as follows:

> Alcoholism is a primary, chronic disease with genetic, psychosocial, and environmental factors influencing its development and manifestations. The disease is often progressive and fatal. It is characterized by impaired control over drinking, preoccupation with the drug alcohol, use of alcohol despite adverse consequences, and distortions in thinking, most notably denial. Each of these symptoms may be continuous or periodic. (Morse and Flavin, 1992, p. 1012)

In this definition, "adverse consequences" involve impairments in physical health, psychological functioning, interpersonal functioning, and occupational functioning, as well as legal, financial, and spiritual problems. "Denial" refers broadly to a range of psychological maneuvers that decrease awareness of the fact that alcohol use is the cause of a person's problems rather than a solution to those problems. Denial becomes an integral part of the disease and is nearly always a major obstacle to recovery. Feldman and colleagues (1997) discussed a *behavioral model* of alcoholism:

- Alcohol consumption ranges from complete abstention to levels that induce chronic intoxication, and individuals can move up and down the continuum of intoxication as a function of varying circumstances.

- The consequences of alcohol ingestion (at least in the short term) are behaviorally reinforcing.

- Alcohol drinking is subject to the same control mechanisms that govern other reinforced behaviors.

- Alcoholism is a learned but maladaptive behavior pattern.

- This behavior pattern can be altered by appropriate reinforcement contingencies, allowing for the possibility of controlled drinking in former alcoholics.

To this behavioral model, one must add inherent genetic factors that confer heightened vulnerability to alcoholism in some people. Prescott and Kendler (1999) provide data and review the evidence for the strong role of genetic factors in the development of alcoholism among males; environmental factors seem to be much less important.

Regardless of a genetic, behavioral, or medical cause of alcoholism, it is now obvious that the *age of onset* of drinking behaviors markedly affects long-term outcomes and societal functioning. Heavy users of alcohol at early ages have, as might be predicted, the poorest outcomes as adults. Heavy drinking as early as age 13 years predicts a high risk for subsequent alcohol dependency, low levels of academic achievement, and poor interactions in family and social activities. Binging at age 15 years and continuing through age 18 results in an even higher rate of alcohol dependency (Hill and coworkers, 2000).

Rohde and coworkers (2001) followed a large cohort of adolescents (14 to 18 years old) through age 24 years. Approximately three-quarters of the adolescents at initial interview had tried alcohol; those who drank often consumed large quantities of alcohol. Problematic alcohol use occurred in 23 percent. Of the latter group, 80 percent had some form of comorbidity with alcohol use: increased rates of depression, disruptive behavior, drug use disorders, and daily tobacco use. By age 24, problem-drinking adolescents exhibited increased rates of substance abuse disorders, depression, and antisocial and borderline personality disorders. The researchers concluded that early adolescent excessive alcohol use is not a benign condition that resolves over time.

In many cases, alcohol may (at least at first) be ingested in an attempt at *self-medication* of psychological distress. A person who, before drinking alcohol, experiences anxiety, depression, bipolar, or other responsive psychological disorders may find the symptomatology alleviated by ethanol. This then leads to unregulated and unmonitored drug ingestion (the drug is not taken under a physician's supervision). Either the positive reinforcing effects of the drug or drinking to avoid the unpleasantness of withdrawal then trap the person. In support of this concept, Goodwin and Gabrielli (1997) stated:

> A good deal of evidence now indicates that many, and perhaps most, alcoholics do *not* have primary alcoholism. Their alcoholism *is* associated with other psychopathology, including addiction to other drugs, depression, manic-depressive illness, anxiety disorder, or antisocial personality. (p. 144)

They further state that 30 to 50 percent of alcoholics meet criteria for major depression; 33 percent have a coexisting anxiety disorder; many have antisocial personalities; some are schizophrenic; and many (36 percent) are addicted to other drugs. Some, if not many, alcoholics may have first used alcohol and become psychologically dependent on the drug as a self-prescribed medication to treat their primary disorder.

Lapham and coworkers (2001) studied psychiatric diagnoses in over 1000 males and females aged 23 to 54 years who were convicted of driving while impaired. Eighty-five percent of female and 91 percent of male offenders reported a lifetime alcohol use disorder; 32 percent of female and 38 percent of male offenders had a drug use disorder. Fifty percent of female and 33 percent of male offenders had at least one additional psychiatric disorder, mainly posttraumatic stress disorder or major depression. Woody (2001) discussed the implications and need to implement treatment interventions for these offenders. Court and diversionary programs focus on alcohol use, not on drug use and other psychological problems. The costs of treatment are high, and most offenders are unwilling to enter treatment (usually denial is present). Psychological assessments are rare, and education is ineffective. Rearrest rates are high. New incentives are needed, including biweekly urine and blood tests as a condition for driving.

Holder and coworkers (2000) discuss community-based interventions to reduce alcohol-related traffic crashes and violence. Kushner and coworkers (1999) demonstrate that in a college-age population,

> cross-sectionally, the odds of having either an anxiety disorder or an alcohol use disorder were two- to fivefold greater when the other condition was present. . . . Alcohol use disorders (especially alcohol dependence) and anxiety disorders demonstrate a reciprocal causal relationship over time, with anxiety disorders leading to alcohol dependence and vice versa. (p. 723)

Lejoyeux and coworkers (1999) noted that 38 percent of alcohol-dependent patients presented had an impulse-control problem. The cooccurrence of pathologic gambling (one type of impulse-control disorder) was associated with a younger age of onset of alcohol dependence, a higher number of detoxifications, and a longer duration of dependence. Both alcohol dependence and pathologic gambling are pleasure-seeking dependencies, and alcohol use may provide much the same reinforcement as gambling. Frye (2003) discusses the cooccurrence of alcoholism and bipolar disorder. An overwhelmingly positive association exists between alcohol use disorder and personality disorders, especially antisocial, histrionic, and dependent disorders (Grant et al., 2004). *Dual diagnosis* (or *comorbid illness*) must always be presumed (until proven otherwise).

Alcoholism is a major public health problem. Of the 160 million Americans who are old enough to drink legally, 112 million do so. As many as 14 million Americans may have serious alcohol problems, and about half that number are considered to be alcoholic. Alcoholism costs about 100,000 Americans lives each year and in excess of $166 billion annually in direct and indirect health and societal costs. Older people who drink are at risk for their own set of problems. In 1996 the American Medical Association published "Alcohol in the Elderly," an update on alcohol use in this population (Council on Scientific Affairs, 1996).

Pharmacotherapies for Alcohol Abuse and Dependence

Because alcoholism involves the ingestion of alcohol, eliminating the ingestion of alcohol is an obvious therapeutic strategy. Achieving success, however, is an extremely difficult task. Vaillant (1996) performed a 50-year follow-up of two cohorts of men who abused alcohol at an early age. One group consisted of university undergraduates and the second consisted of nondelinquent inner-city adolescents. By 60 years of age, 18 percent of the college alcohol abusers had died, 11 percent were abstinent, 11 percent were controlled drinkers, and 60 percent were still abusing alcohol. By 60 years of age, 28 percent of the inner-city alcohol abusers had died, 30 percent were abstinent, 12 percent were controlled drinkers, and 30 percent were still abusing alcohol. As alcohol abuse after age 60 can be devastating, the greater levels of abuse by college-educated males certainly need to be addressed. Barrick and Connors (2002) discuss approaches to the treatment of older adults with alcohol use disorders.

The ideal goals of pharmacotherapy for alcohol dependence and abuse include the following:

1. Reversal of the acute pharmacologic effects of alcohol

2. Treatment and prevention of withdrawal symptoms and complications

3. Maintenance of abstinence and prevention of relapse with agents that decrease craving for alcohol or the loss of control over drinking or make it unpleasant to ingest alcohol

4. Treatment of coexisting psychiatric disorders that complicate recovery

Can these goals be met? First, at this time, no agent that can reverse the acute pharmacologic effects of alcohol is available. Some feel that caffeine can antagonize alcohol intoxication and increase alertness. This is not true, as a behavioral stimulant can only increase activity and cannot reverse the motor, cognitive, or other dysfunctions induced by alcohol (Fillmore et al., 2003). Therefore, acute alcohol intoxication is usually treated with supportive care to protect both the intoxicated person and others placed at risk of injury.

Pharmacotherapies are available to treat and prevent withdrawal symptoms, to reduce relapse to drinking behaviors, and to treat complications in alcohol-dependent people who are decreasing or discontinuing alcohol. Medication can also effectively prevent and treat the symptoms, seizures, and DTs associated with withdrawal. In addition, medications are available to help address and treat the comorbidities observed in alcohol-dependent persons. These include anxiolytics, antidepressants, and mood stabilizers. The use of pharmacologic agents to reduce the rates of relapse to renewed drinking remains the most difficult problem. Myrick and coworkers (2001) reviewed the therapies commonly used in alcohol-dependent persons.

Pharmacotherapies for Management of Alcohol Withdrawal

At its simplest, if taking alcohol reduces glutamate activity and increases GABA activity in the brain, alcohol withdrawal then results in the opposite: reduced GABA activity and increased glutamate activity. These changes result in uncontrolled excitation and can damage cognitive functioning (Duka et al., 2003). The major therapeutic goal of managing acute alcohol withdrawal or detoxification is to prevent uncontrolled excitation by either reducing glutamate activity or increasing GABA activity.

Benzodiazepines. Increasing GABA activity is the mechanism underlying the use of the benzodiazepines as current drugs of choice for the treatment of acute alcohol withdrawal; they ameliorate the symptoms of withdrawal and also prevent seizures and DTs (Daeppen et al., 2002; D'Onofrio et al., 1999). It may not seem logical to substitute one potentially addictive drug (a benzodiazepine) for another (ethanol). An explanation follows. The short duration of the action of alcohol and its narrow range of safety make it an extremely dangerous drug from which to withdraw. When alcohol ingestion is stopped, withdrawal symptoms begin within a few hours. Substituting a long-acting drug prevents or suppresses the withdrawal symptoms. The longer-acting benzodiazepine is then either maintained at a level low enough to allow the person to function or is withdrawn gradually. Preferred drugs are the benzodiazepines with long-acting active metabolites—chlordiazepoxide (Librium) or diazepam (Valium)—while acute seizure activity is well controlled with the faster-onset, shorter-acting benzodiazepine lorazepam. The pharmacology of the benzodiazepines is discussed in Chapter 6.

Currently, treatment strategies for management of alcohol withdrawal recommend benzodiazepines as first-line therapy and other drugs (beta blockers, clonidine, carbamazepine, and antipsychotics) only as adjunctive therapy (Holbrook et al., 1999). Beta blockers and clonidine are drugs that block the functioning of the sympathetic nervous system; they help ameliorate some of the autonomic signs and symptoms of withdrawal. Their use is not without problems.

Antipsychotic Drugs. Antipsychotic drugs (Chapter 11) can alleviate delirium and hallucinosis, but they lower the seizure threshold and can increase the propensity for withdrawal seizures.

Anticonvulsants. Malcolm and coworkers (2001) reviewed several small studies relevant to the use of anticonvulsants in acute alcohol withdrawal and dependence. They note the limitations of benzodiazepines for this use: sedation, psychomotor deficits, additive interactions with alcohol, and abuse and dependence liabilities. While older anticonvulsants have significant limitations that can be deleterious in alcoholics (contributing to liver and pancreatic problems, for example), they are effective. For example, carbamazepine (Tegretol) and valproic acid (Depakote) have been successfully used in place of benzodiazepines, despite potentially significant adverse side effects (Malcolm et al., 2002). Newer anticonvulsants—for example, gabapentin (Neurontin), oxcarbazepine (Trileptal), topiramate (Topomax), and tiapride—have significant potential and are less toxic than carbamazepine and valproic acid, which may make them a better choice than benzodiazepines for the treatment of alcohol withdrawal.

Recently, Komanduri (2003) and Johnson and coworkers (2003) have demonstrated the efficacy and safety of topiramate (Topomax) in the treatment of alcohol dependency (Figure 4.9). With this demonstration of

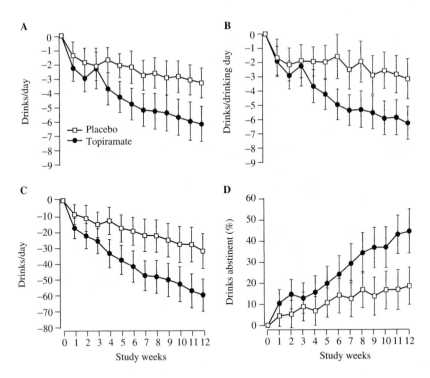

FIGURE 4.9 Change in self-reported drinking outcomes from baseline (week 0) forward for 12 weeks. **A.** Absolute reductions in drinks per day. **B.** Absolute reductions in drinks per drinking day. **C.** Percentage reduction in heavy drinking days. **D.** Percentage of days abstinent. The number of participants for each value varied from 48 to 75. Topiramate positively affected all four measurements. [From Johnson et al. (2003), p. 1681.]

efficacy, topiramate is now one of the very few effective drugs currently available for treating alcohol dependence; others include disulfiram, naltrexone, and acamprosate. Those are discussed next. The pharmacology of the anticonvulsants is presented in Chapter 10, where they are discussed as mood stabilizers for the treatment of bipolar disorder.

Pharmacotherapies to Help Maintain Abstinence and Prevent Relapse

Numerous drugs to decrease daily consumption of ethanol and prevent clinical relapse to continued drinking have been tried; many of these are listed in Table 4.1. Some have been successful and many are of limited use.

Alcohol-Sensitizing Drugs. Among others, *disulfiram* (Antabuse) and *calcium carbimide* (Temposil, available in Canada only) are used to deter a patient from drinking alcohol by producing an aversive reaction if the patient drinks. These drugs alter the metabolism of alcohol, allowing acetaldehyde to accumulate. If the patient ingests alcohol within several days of taking the aversive drug, the accumulation results in an acetaldehyde syndrome, characterized by flushing, throbbing headache, nausea, vomiting, chest pain, and other severe symptoms. It is felt that calcium carbimide may have fewer side effects than does disulfiram. If taken daily, aversive agents can result in total abstinence in many patients. However, controlled trials of disulfiram therapy to reduce alcohol consumption have been disappointing, demonstrating that disulfiram fares little better than placebo treatment (Garbutt et al., 1999; Swift, 1999).

Opioid Antagonists. *Naltrexone* (ReVia, Trexan) was approved by the FDA in 1994 for use in the treatment of alcohol dependence to reduce the craving for alcohol, even though the effect was small. The hypothesis of action is that the reinforcing properties of alcohol involve the opioid system; blockade of the opiod system by naltrexone should reduce craving by reducing the positive reinforcement associated with alcohol use. Initial studies with naltrexone were encouraging; however, more recent studies (Gastpar et al., 2002; Krystal et al., 2001) determined that the efficacy of naltrexone in the prevention of alcohol relapse is no better than placebo. The drug caused no decrease in the time to relapse, the percentage of days on which drinking occurred, or the number of drinks per drinking day. If the drug is to be effective as single-drug therapy, it will probably be in patients who have been drinking heavily for 20 years or less and who have stable social support and living situations (Fuller and Gordis, 2001).

TABLE 4.1 Drugs used to decrease alcohol consumption, reduce craving, maintain abstinence, or prevent relapse in alcohol-dependent individuals

Drug	Mechanism	Comments
Disulfiram	Inhibits aldehyde dehydrogenase to allow acetaldehyde accumulation	Clinical efficacy in question as a result of controlled trials. Effective in special situations.
Calcium carbimide	Same as disulfiram	May have fewer side effects than disulfiram. Available in Canada, not in USA.
Naltrexone	Endogenous opioid antagonist	Approved by FDA for treating alcohol dependence. Reduces consumption in heavy drinkers.
Acamprosate	NMDA and GABA$_A$ receptor modulator	Reduces unpleasant effects of alcohol abstinence, reduces craving. May have adverse fetal effects. Approved in Europe, not in USA.
Fluoxetine and other serotonin antidepressants	SSRI-type serotonin agonist	Reduces depression and anxiety occurring comorbid with alcohol dependency.
Buspirone	Serotonin 5-HT$_{1A}$ agonist	Little demonstrable efficacy may be due to inadequate amounts in blood.
Ondansetron, Ritanserin	Serotonin 5-HT$_3$ antagonists	May reduce craving. Poorly demonstrated efficacy.
Carbamazepine	Mood stabilizer, anticonvulsant	Can reduce unpleasant withdrawal effects.
Gamma-hydroxy-butyrate (GHB)	NMDA antagonist	Sedative-euphoriant. Can alleviate withdrawal symptoms. Subject to abuse.
Bromocriptine	Dopamine agonist	Can reduce craving. Little documented efficacy in reducing relapse.

Compliance with therapy is essential. Injectable long-lasting (depot) forms of naltrexone can be effective in preventing relapse to heroin use (Comer et al., 2002). It will be interesting to see whether or not this preparation of naltrexone will be effective in preventing relapse to alcohol.

Mason and coworkers (1999) studied a related opioid antagonist, *nalmefene* (Revex). In 105 adults with alcohol dependence, nalmefene was effective in preventing relapse to heavy drinking compared with placebo therapy (Figure 4.10); no medically serious side effects were observed. Large-scale, final phase, multicenter, placebo-controlled investigations into the use of nalmefene in the treatment of alcohol dependence are currently in progress. The pharmacology of naltrexone, nalmefene, and other opioid antagonists is discussed further in Chapter 15.

Acamprosate.   Acamprosate (calcium acetylhomotaurinate) has been used for many years as an anticraving drug in many European countries. In late 2004, acamprosate was approved in the United States (under the trade name *Aotal*) for the treatment of alcoholism. Acamprosate is the

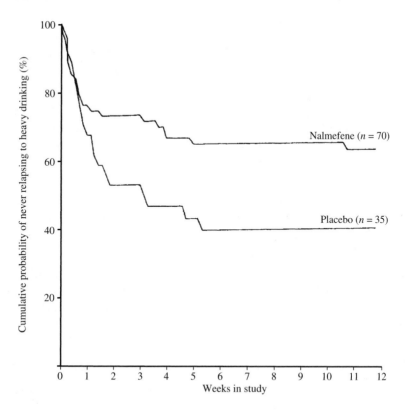

FIGURE 4.10 Rates of never relapsing to heavy drinking from randomization (week 0) through the end of double-blind treatment. [From Mason et al. (1999), p. 722.]

first pharmacologic agent specifically designed to maintain abstinence in ethanol-dependent people after detoxification. With a chemical structure similar to that of GABA, acamprosate is thought to exert both a GABA-agonistic action at GABA receptors and an inhibitory action at glutaminergic NMDA receptors, actions similar to those exerted by ethanol. The drug is poorly absorbed orally and therefore is given in relatively high doses (about 2 grams per day). Acamprosate has a half-life of about 18 hours, and it is excreted unchanged by the kidneys; it is not metabolized before excretion.

In early human studies, acamprosate was thought to be about three times as effective as placebo, with drinking frequency reduced by 30 to 50 percent. Today, it is thought to be comparable to naltrexone, with efficacy increased by adding the drug to established, abstinence-based, cognitive-behavioral rehabilitation programs (Feeney et al., 2002) or by combining the drug with naltrexone (Keifer et al., 2003) (Figure 4.11). In both situations, naltrexone and acamprosate, although less than impressive individually, are quite effective used together and/or added to intensive psychotherapies. Since combination

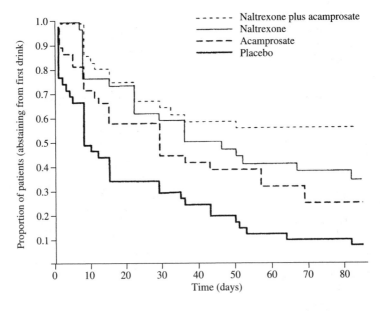

FIGURE 4.11 Relapse rates to relapse to drinking following a 2-week period of detoxification, then started on one of four regimens: placebo therapy, acamprosate (2 grams per day), naltrexone (50 milligrams per day), or combined acamprosate/naltrexone. Each group consisted of 40 patients. The three medication groups were significantly different from the placebo group in preventing or delaying relapse. In addition, the effects of combined medication were significantly different from the effects of either medication used alone. [From Kiefer et al. (2003), p. 96.]

therapy may be important, Mason and coworkers (2002) studied the pharmacokinetic interaction between acamprosate and naltrexone. Coadministration of the two drugs significantly increased the rate and extent of absorption of acamprosate, as indicated by an average 33 percent increase in acamprosate blood level and a 33 percent reduction in time to peak blood level. Acamprosate did not affect the pharmacokinetics of naltrexone. Thus, when using the two drugs in combination, the dose of acamprosate, although poorly absorbed orally, can be reduced by 33 percent. This pharmacokinetic interaction was not utilized in the combination study reported by Kiefer and coworkers: they used a dose of 2 grams per day with or without naltrexone. How this interaction might have affected their results is unknown.

Dopaminergic Drugs.   *Dopaminergic drugs,* such as *bupropion* (Wellbutrin), have theoretical use in maintaining abstinence because (1) the positive reinforcement associated with alcohol attractiveness appears to involve the dopaminergic reward system; (2) withdrawal may be accompanied by hypofunction of this reward system; and (3) depression is often comorbid with alcohol dependency. Since bupropion acts as an antidepressant at least partly through a dopaminergic action, individuals with comorbid depression and alcohol dependence might be candidates for treatment with this drug. Further study in this area is probably warranted.

Serotoninergic Drugs.   *Serotoninergic drugs* have been quite well studied as agents for treating alcohol dependence. The research follows from the concept that there is a relationship between serotonin function and alcohol consumption. In addition, different subtypes of alcoholics may be differentiated by the type or complexity of their serotonin dysfunction (Pettinati et al., 2003). Beyond excessive drinking, behaviors that are indicators of serotonin dysregulation include depression, anxiety, impulsiveness, and early-onset drinking. Three classes of drugs that affect serotonin function have been evaluated:

1. Selective serotonin reuptake inhibitors (SSRIs), such as *fluoxetine* (Prozac) and *sertraline* (Zoloft)
2. A serotonin 5-HT$_{1A}$ agonist, *buspirone* (BuSpar)
3. A serotonin 5-HT$_3$ antagonist, *ondansetron* (Zofran)

Currently, *selective serotonin reuptake inhibitors (SSRIs)* are FDA-approved for treating depression and anxiety disorders (Chapter 9), buspirone for treating anxiety (Chapter 6), and ondansetron for treating cancer treatment-induced and anesthesia-induced nausea and vomiting. In addition to approved indications, SSRIs have been evaluated for treating alcohol dependence, especially when alcoholic patients exhibit comorbid mood or anxiety disorders (Thase et al., 2001). In general, the results have been inconsistent. However, some progress has been made and efficacy can be differentiated in Type A and Type B alcoholics (Cornelius et al., 2000). Type B alcoholics are characterized by early-age onset of drinking (ages 13 to 14 years), high levels of premorbid vulnerability, high levels of alcohol and other drug use severity, and high levels of comorbid psychopathology. Such individuals respond poorly to treatment with SSRIs. Type A alcoholics have a later onset of heavy drinking (usually after the age of 20 years), lower levels of risk/severity of alcoholism, and lower levels of comorbid psychopathology. Type A alcoholics are relatively uncomplicated in their history and clinical presentation, despite high levels of alcohol consumption. In this population, several reports have documented the efficacy of SSRIs (Pettinati et al., 2000; Randall et al., 2001) (Figure 4.12). Both drinking behaviors and affective dysregulation may be positively affected.

The serotonin 5-HT$_{1A}$ agonist *buspirone* has been shown to be effective in improving comorbid anxiety in alcoholics, but it is much less effective in reducing alcohol consumption (Malec et al., 1996). Blood level correlations with efficacy have not been performed. Recall from Chapter 1 that buspirone is poorly absorbed (95 percent destroyed by first-pass metabolism) and that grapefruit juice greatly improves gastric absorption by reducing gastric metabolism. It would be interesting to see if buspirone administered with grapefruit juice would fare more favorably as an anticraving drug.

The serotonin 5-HT$_3$ antagonist *ondansetron* has been shown to reduce drinking behaviors (fewer drinks per day) in individuals with early-onset alcoholism. Patients with later-onset alcoholism were not benefited by the drug (Johnson et al., 2000). Ait-Daoud and coworkers (2001) reported potentiation of the action of ondansetron when it is combined with naltrexone. Much more remains to be learned about any serotoninergic involvement in various forms of alcoholism.

Cannabinoid Mechanisms.   As discussed, we are just learning about a cannabinoid mechanism underlying alcohol craving and relapse (Basavarajappa and Hungund, 2002). Perhaps cannabinoid antagonists (such as rimonabant) can effectively moderate consumption of alcohol. By the same reasoning, ingestion of tetrahydrocannabinol during periods of abstinence may lead to an *increased* propensity to drink alcohol, perhaps by increasing craving.

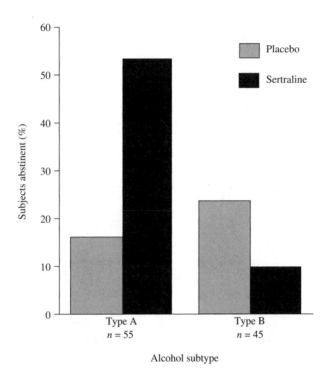

FIGURE 4.12 Proportion of alcohol-dependent persons who maintained complete abstinence over a 14-week treatment period with respect to receiving either placebo or sertraline (an SSRI-type antidepressant) in double-blind fashion. Type A persons were of the later-onset, lower-risk/severity class of alcoholics. Type B persons were of the earlier-onset, higher-risk/severity class of alcoholics. There was a significantly different response to sertraline in Type A individuals but not in those with Type B alcoholism. [From Pettinati et al. (2000), p. 1044.]

Pharmacotherapies to Help Treat Comorbid Psychological Conditions

Relapse to drinking behaviors and untreated comorbid psychological disorders are closely intertwined. Certainly addictive behaviors and cravings as well as affective psychopathology (anxiety, depression, irritability, anger, insomnia, and so on) involve complex and poorly understood interactions between the opioid, dopaminergic, and serotonergic systems. Opioid and dopaminergic systems are probably involved in mechanisms of craving, and serotonergic dysfunction is at a minimum involved in affective dysregulation. Heinz and coworkers (2001) discuss the relationship between serotonergic dysfunction, negative mood states, aggressive behavior, and excessive alcohol intake.

When alcohol abuse is in aggressive comorbidity with substance abuse, psychosocial and behavioral therapies are essential.

Pharmacological treatments are not (and probably never will be) effective without the addition of intensive psychological therapies in all their various forms. Pharmacology can assist in the treatment of cravings (perhaps dopaminergic agents, acamprosate, or an opioid antagonist), in the treatment of affective disorders (perhaps the SSRIs or the newer SNRIs; see Chapter 9), and in the control of emotional states with anger, aggression, insomnia, and emotional outbursts (perhaps anticonvulsants; see Chapter 10).

INHALANTS OF ABUSE

Inhalants are breathable chemical vapors that produce psychoactive (mind-altering) effects. A variety of products commonplace in the home and in the workplace contain substances that can be inhaled. A few were actually developed as mind-altering agents (more specifically, they were developed as anesthetics). Examples include nitrous oxide and halothane. These anesthetics were never meant to be used to achieve a "recreational" intoxicating effect. Likewise, other agents were developed for home and industrial use and were never intended to be used to affect the mind. These agents include, among many, paints and paint thinners, gasoline, polishes and polish removers, glues, cleaning and lighter fluids, and hair sprays.

Inhalant abuse, also known as *huffing,* is the intentional inhalation of a volatile substance for the purpose of achieving a euphoric state. Inhalant abuse disproportionately affects young people. Indeed, inhalants are frequently the first mind-altering drugs used by children, occasionally as young as 3 or 4 years of age. They are popular with children because of peer influence, low cost, availability, and rapid onset of effect. When inhaled, they produce euphoria, delirium, intoxication, and alterations in mental status, resembling alcohol intoxication or a "light" state of general anesthesia. Users are usually not aware of the potentially serious health consequences that can result. Especially in children, inhalant abuse is an underrecognized form of substance abuse with significant morbidity and mortality.

Inhaled substances include the following:

- Anesthetics, especially nitrous oxide and halothane
- Industrial or household solvents, including paint thinners and solvents, degreasers, and solvents in glues
- Art and office supply solvents, including typewriter correction fluid and marker pen solvents
- Gases used in household or commercial products, including butane lighters, aerosol cream dispensers, and propane tanks

- Household aerosol propellants, including paint, hair spray, and fabric protector sprays
- Aliphatic nitrites and organic solvents, including amyl nitrite capsules

Some of the substances found in these different products are listed in Table 4.2. Abused inhalants are rarely, if ever, administered by routes other than inhalation.

Why Inhalants Are Abused and Who Abuses Them

Why are inhalants used for recreational or abuse purposes, what is their attraction, and why do they have the potential for abuse? Inhalant abuse goes back at least 100 years, when ether, nitrous oxide, and chloroform were introduced into medicine as general anesthetics. Concomitant with their discovery as anesthetics was their discovery as intoxicating agents, leading to nitrous oxide and ether parties. Today, inhalant abuse is one of the most pervasive yet least recognized drug problems (Brouette and Anton, 2001). In the United States, the prevalence of inhalant abuse among adolescent youths is exceeded only by the use of marijuana, alcohol, and tobacco. More than 12 million Americans have abused inhalants at least once in their lives. The peak of inhalant abuse occurs in youths aged 14 or 15 years, with onset occurring in some youths as young as 4 to 8 years; a few users continue their abuse of inhalants into adulthood, usually as part of a polysubstance abuse pattern (Figure 4.13). Patterns of abuse resemble patterns seen in abuse of other types of substances: there are experimenters, intermittent users, and chronic inhalant abusers. Although injuries are associated with the frequency of use, the so-called sudden sniffing death syndrome can occur in first-time users. About 20 percent of youths have experience with inhalant abuse by the end of the eighth grade. Brown and coworkers (1999) reviewed deaths from inhalant abuse in the state of Virginia over the ten-year period 1987–1996. The 39 deaths accounted for 0.3 percent of all deaths in males aged 13 to 22 years. Age of death ranged from 13 to 42 years; 70 percent of deaths occurred at 22 years of age or younger. Ninety-five percent of the deaths occurred in males. Gasoline fuels accounted for 46 percent of the fatalities.

Acute Intoxication and Chronic Effects

As noted in Table 4.2, a variety of volatile substances are abused by inhalation, each with its own pharmacology and toxicology (Balster, 1998). In general, however, most inhaled vapors produce rapid onset of

TABLE 4.2 Chemicals commonly found in inhalants

	Inhalant	Chemical
Adhesives	Airplane glue	Toluene, ethyl acetate
	Other glues	Hexane, toluene, methyl chloride, acetone, methyl ethyl ketone, methyl butyl ketone
	Special cements	Trichloroethylene, tetrachloroethylene
Aerosols	Spray paint	Butane, propane (U.S.), fluorocarbons, toluene, hydrocarbons, "Texas shoe shine" (a spray containing toluene)
	Hair spray	Butane, propane (U.S.), CFCs
	Deodorant, air freshner	Butane, propane (U.S.), CFCs
	Analgesic spray	Chlorofluorocarbons (CFCs)
	Asthma spray	Chlorofluorocarbons (CFCs)
	Fabric spray	Butane, trichloroethane
	PC cleaner	Dimethyl ether, hydrofluorocarbons
Anesthetics	Gas	Nitrous oxide
	Liquid	Halothane, enflurane
	Local	Ethyl chloride
Cleaning agents	Dry cleaning	Tetrachloroethylene, trichloroethane
	Spot remover	Xylene, petroleum distillates, chlorohydrocarbons
	Degreaser	Tetrachloroethylene, trichloroethane, trichloroethylene
Solvents and gases	Nail polish remover	Acetone, ethyl acetate
	Paint remover	Toluene, methyl chloride, methanol acetone, ethyl acetate
	Paint thinner	Petroleum distillates, esters, acetone
	Correction fluid and thinner	Trichloroethylene, trichloroethane
	Fuel gas	Butane, isopropane
	Lighter	Butane, isopropane
	Fire extinguisher	Bromochlorodifluoromethane
Whipped cream	Whipped cream	Nitrous oxide
	Whippets	Nitrous oxide
"Room odorizers"	Locker Room, Rush, poppers	Isoamyl, isobutyl, isopropyl or butyl nitrate (now illegal), cyclohexyl

a state of intoxication (or "drunkenness") that resembles alcohol intoxication: the continuum of sedation with anxiolysis, disinhibition, drowsiness, light-headedness, and euphoria. With increasing intoxication, the user experiences ataxia (staggering), dizziness, delirium, and disorientation. With severe intoxication, there is muscle weakness, lethargy, and signs of light to moderate general anesthesia. With lack of oxygen (hypoxia), hallucinations and behavior changes may occur.

Toluene is a common ingredient in a number of the substances sought out for inhalant abuse, apparently for its euphorigenic, hallucinogenic, and behaviorally rewarding effects. Therefore, within the past few years several researchers have explored the effects of toluene on the brain (Bespalov et al., 2003; Gerasimov et al., 2002; Riegel and French, 2002). To summarize, toluene is taken up into and activates the central reward centers, including the mesolimbic dopaminergic reward centers and the frontal cortex, and this effect is accompanied by rewarding behaviors.

Not all inhalants exert this action on central dopaminergic reward centers, but many do. With some agents (particularly the *nitrites*), vasodilation and muscle relaxant effects appear to underlie use. With anesthetics, such as *nitrous oxide*, a state of light general anesthesia is induced, although reward activation may occur at low doses. With the *volatile solvents* and *fuels,* conclusions are difficult to draw, but their profile of acute behavioral and pharmacological effects is similar to that observed with subanesthetic concentrations of clinically used volatile anesthetics.

Although death is relatively rare during acute intoxication, when it does occur, it usually follows from lack of oxygen to the brain (anoxia), cardiac arrhythmias, aspiration of vomitus, or trauma (Kurtzman et al., 2001; Zvosec et al., 2001). In Great Britain, *sudden sniffing death syndrome* is said to account for over 50 percent of fatalities from acute intoxication. Volatile hydrocarbons sensitize the heart to serious arrhythmias when a person is startled or becomes excited during intoxication. The sudden surge of adrenaline acts on the sensitized heart to set off serious and life-threatening arrhythmias. This kind of episode can occur during initial experimentation and during any episode of abuse.

With *chronic abuse* of inhalants, serious complications can include peripheral and central nervous system dysfunction (peripheral neuropathies and encephalopathy), liver and/or kidney failure, dementia, loss of cognitive and other higher functions, gait disturbances, and loss of coordination. In a recently completed study, 55 inhalant abusers with an average 10 years of abusing were administered a battery of cognitive tests and also underwent magnetic resonance imaging (MRI) (Rosenberg et al., 2002). This group was compared with a group of 61 cocaine abusers. While both groups displayed scores below general

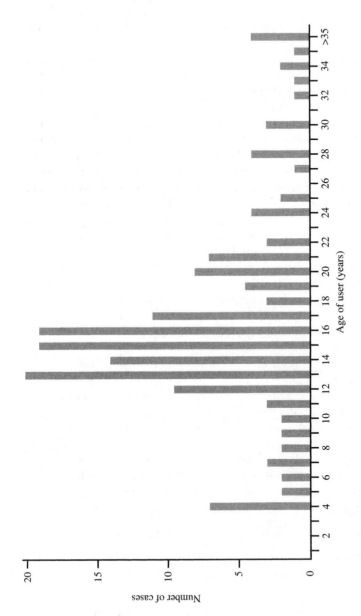

FIGURE 4.13 Bar graph of the ages of inhalant abusers who presented to the emergency room (total number = 165). The youngest inhalant abusers were age 4 years. The peak incidence was at 12 to 16 years. [From H. A. Spiller and E. P. Krenzelok, "Epidemiology of Inhalant Abuse Reported in Two Regional Poison Centers," *Journal of Toxicology-Clinical Toxicology* 35 (1997), p. 170.]

population averages on tests of cognitive functioning, inhalant abusers consistently scored even below the cocaine abusers on tests involving working memory, planning, and problem solving. Almost half of the inhalant abusers had abnormalities in their MRI scans (compared to 25 percent of the cocaine abusers). Most marked was diffuse white matter degeneration in several brain areas.

Little and colleagues (1998b) describe a fetal inhalant syndrome characterized by prenatal growth retardation (low birth weight, microcephaly), facial dysmorphism (resembling fetal alcohol syndrome), and digital malformations (short phalanges, nail hypoplasia).

Treatment of acute inhalant intoxication is primarily supportive with the administration of supplemental oxygen. Treatment of chronic inhalant abuse is much more difficult. Results of a recent survey of 550 drug treatment program directors indicate that most inhalant abusers have a pessimistic attitude about the treatment effectiveness and hopes for long-term recovery (Beauvais et al., 2002). The surveyed directors perceived that there is a great deal of neurological damage resulting from inhalant use and that there are inadequate education, preventive efforts, and treatments for these individuals.

STUDY QUESTIONS

1. Pharmacologically, what is ethyl alcohol?

2. Describe the metabolism of alcohol. What enzymes are involved? What drug blocks one of these enzymes?

3. How do women and men differ in their metabolism of alcohol?

4. How does the kinetics of alcohol metabolism differ from that of most other drugs?

5. How long does it take for an adult to metabolize the alcohol in a 1-ounce glass of 80 proof whiskey? A 4-ounce glass of wine? A 12-ounce bottle of beer? A pint of 7 percent microbrew?

6. What BAC is defined in most states as "intoxication"?

7. Describe how alcohol exerts its effects on the CNS.

8. If one has developed a physical dependence on alcohol, why might he or she be treated with a benzodiazepine as a substitute for the alcohol?

9. Summarize some of the drugs and techniques used in treating alcoholism. What medications might be used to ameliorate alcohol withdrawal? Differentiate alcohol withdrawal from alcoholism.

10. Describe the disease concept of alcoholism. Discuss the comorbidity of alcohol dependence with other psychological disorders.

11. Summarize some of the problems associated with inhalant abuse.

12. Describe some of the fetal effects of alcohol. Is there a "safe" level of drinking during pregnancy?

REFERENCES

Abbey, A., et al. (2002). "How Does Alcohol Contribute to Sexual Assault? Explanations from Laboratory and Survey Data." *Alcoholism: Clinical and Experimental Research* 26: 575–581.

Agartz, I., et al. (2003). "CSF Monoamine Metabolites and MRI Brain Volumes in Alcohol Dependence." *Psychiatry Research* 122: 21–35.

Ait-Daoud, N., et al. (2001). "Combining Ondansetron and Naltrexone Reduces Craving Among Biologically Predisposed Alcoholics: Preliminary Clinical Evidence." *Psychopharmacology* 154: 23–27.

Al-Qatari, M., et al. (1998). "Mechanism of Action of Acamprosate. Part II: Ethanol Dependence Modifies Effects of Acamprosate on NMDA Receptor Binding in Membranes from Rat Cerebral Cortex." *Alcoholism: Clinical and Experimental Research* 22: 810–814.

Autti-Ramo, I. (2000). "Twelve-Year Follow-up of Children Exposed to Alcohol in Utero." *Developmental Medicine and Child Neurology* 42: 406–411.

Baer, J. S., et al. (2003). "A 21-Year Longitudinal Analysis of the Effects of Prenatal Alcohol Exposure on Young Adult Drinking." *Archives of General Psychiatry* 60: 377–385.

Ballenger, J. C., and R. M. Post (1978). "Kindling as a Model for Alcohol Withdrawal Syndromes." *British Journal of Psychiatry* 133: 1–14.

Balster, R. L. (1998). "Neural Basis of Inhalant Abuse." *Drug and Alcohol Dependence* 51: 207–214.

Barrick, C., and G. J. Connors (2002). "Relapse Prevention and Maintaining Abstinence in Older Adults with Alcohol-Use Disorders." *Drugs and Aging* 19: 583–594.

Basavarajappa, B. S., and B. L. Hungund (2002). "Neuromodulatory Role of the Endocannaninoid Signaling System in Alcoholism: An Overview." *Prostaglandins, Leukotrienes and Essential Fatty Acids* 66: 287–299.

Beavais, F., et al. (2002). "A Survey of Attitudes Among Drug Use Treatment Providers Toward the Treatment of Inhalant Users." *Substance Use and Abuse* 37: 1391–1410.

Bespalov, A., et al. (2003). "Facilitation of Electrical Brain Self-Stimulation Behavior by Abused Solvents." *Pharmacology and Biochemistry of Behavior* 75: 199–208.

Bradley, K. A., et al. (1998). "Alcohol Screening Questionnaires in Women: A Critical Review." *Journal of the American Medical Association* 280: 166–171.

Brouette, T., and R. Anton (2001). "Clinical Review of Inhalants." *American Journal on Addictions* 10: 79–94.

Brown, M. E., et al. (1988). "Alcohol Detoxification and Withdrawal Seizures: Clinical Support for a Kindling Hypothesis." *Biological Psychiatry* 23: 507–514.

Brown, S. A., et al. (2000). "Neurocognitive Functioning of Adolescents: Effects of Protracted Alcohol Use." *Alcoholism: Clinical and Experimental Research* 24: 164–171.

Brown, S. E., et al. (1999). "Deaths Associated with Inhalant Abuse in Virginia from 1987 to 1996." *Drug and Alcohol Dependence* 53: 239–245.

Carmichael, H., et al. (1997). "Association of Prenatal Alcohol Exposure with Behavioral and Learning Problems in Early Adolescence." *Journal of the American Academy of Child and Adolescent Psychiatry* 36: 1187–1194.

Comer, S. D., et al. (2002). "Depot Naltrexone: Long-Lasting Antagonism of the Effects of Heroin in Humans." *Psychopharmacology* 159: 351–360.

Cornelius, J. R., et al. (2000). "Fluoxetine Versus Placebo in Depressed Alcoholics: A 1-Year Follow-up Study." *Addiction Behavior* 25: 307–310.

Council on Scientific Affairs, American Medical Association (1996). "Alcoholism in the Elderly." *Journal of the American Medical Association* 275: 797–801.

Daeppen, J.-P., et al. (2002). "Symptom-Triggered vs Fixed-Schedule Doses of Benzodiazepine for Alcohol Withdrawal: A Randomized Treatment Trial." *Archives of Internal Medicine* 162: 1117–1121.

Dahchour, A., and P. DeWitte (2000). "Ethanol and Amino Acids in the Central Nervous System: Assessment of the Pharmacological Actions of Acamprosate." *Progress in Neurobiology* 60: 343–362.

Day, N. L., et al. (2002). "Prenatal Alcohol Exposure Predicts Continued Deficits in Offspring Size at 14 Years of Age." *Alcoholism: Clinical and Experimental Research* 26: 1584–1591.

Djousse, L., et al. (2000). "Alcohol Consumption and Risk of Intermittent Claudication in the Framingham Heart Study." *Circulation* 102: 3092–3097.

D'Onofrio, G., et al. (1999). "Lorazepam for the Prevention of Recurrent Seizures Related to Alcohol." *New England Journal of Medicine* 340: 915–919.

Duka, T., et al. (2003). "Impairment in Cognitive Functions After Multiple Detoxifications in Alcoholic Inpatients." *Alcoholism: Clinical and Experimental Research* 27: 1563–1572.

Fadda, F., and Z. L. Rossetti (1998). "Chronic Ethanol Consumption: From Neuroadaptation to Neurodegeneration." *Progress in Neurobiology* 56: 385–431.

Feeney, G. F., et al. (2002). "Cognitive Behavioural Therapy Combined with the Relapse-Prevention Medication Acamprosate: Are Short-Term Treatment Outcomes for Alcohol Dependence Improved?" *Australian and New Zealand Journal of Psychiatry* 36: 622–628.

Feldman, R. S., J. S. Meyer, and L. F. Quenzer (1997). *Principles of Neuropsychopharmacology.* Sunderland, MA: Sinauer, p. 627.

Fillmore, M. T., et al. (2003). "Does Caffeine Counteract Alcohol-Induced Impairment? The Ironic Effects of Expectancy." *Journal of Studies on Alcohol* 63: 745–754.

Finnegan, L. P., and S. R. Kandall (1997). "Maternal and Neonatal Effects of Alcohol and Drugs." In J. H. Lowinson, P. Ruiz, R. B. Millman, and J. G. Langrod, eds., *Substance Abuse: A Comprehensive Textbook*, 3rd ed. Baltimore: Williams & Wilkins, pp. 528–529.

Frezza, M., et al. (1990). "High Blood Alcohol Levels in Women: The Role of Decreased Gastric Alcohol Dehydrogenase Activity and First-Pass Metabolism." *New England Journal of Medicine* 322: 95–99.

Frye, M. A., et al. (2003). "Gender Differences in Prevalence, Risk, and Clinical Correlates of Alcoholism Comorbidity in Bipolar Disorder." *American Journal of Psychiatry* 160: 883–889.

Fuller, R. K., and E. Gordis (2001). "Naltrexone Treatment for Alcohol Dependence." *New England Journal of Medicine* 345: 1770–1771.

Garbutt, J. C., et al. (1999). "Pharmacological Treatment of Alcohol Dependence: A Review of the Evidence." *Journal of the American Medical Association* 281: 1318–1325.

Gastpar, M., et al. (2002). "Lack of Efficacy of Naltrexone in the Prevention of Alcohol Relapse: Results from a German Multicenter Study." *Journal of Clinical Psychopharmacology* 22: 592–598.

Gerasimov, M. R., et al. (2002). "Study of Brain Uptake and Biodistribution of [11C] Toluene in Non-Human Primates and Mice." *Life Sciences* 70: 2811–2828.

Goodwin, D. W., and W. F. Gabrielli (1997). "Alcohol: Clinical Aspects." In J. H. Lowinson, P. Ruiz, R. B. Millman, and J. G. Langrod, eds., *Substance Abuse: A Comprehensive Textbook*, 3rd ed. Baltimore: Williams & Wilkins, pp.142–148.

Grant, B. F., et al. (2004). "Co-occurence of 12-Month Alcohol and Drug Use Disorders and Personality Disorders in the United States." *Archives of General Psychiatry* 61: 361–368.

Hamajima, N., et al. (2002). "Alcohol, Tobacco, and Breast Cancer—Collaborative Reanalysis of Individual Data from 53 Epidemiological Studies, Including 58,515 Women with Breast Cancer and 95,067 Women Without the Disease." *British Journal of Cancer* 87: 1234–1245.

Harty, L. C., et al. (1997). "Alcohol Dehydrogenase 3 Genotype and Risk of Oral Cavity and Pharyngeal Cancers." *Journal of the National Cancer Institute* 89: 1698–1705.

Heinz, A., et al. (1998). "In Vivo Association Between Alcohol Intoxication, Aggression, and Serotonin Transporter Availability in Nonhuman Primates." *American Journal of Psychiatry* 155: 1023–1028.

Heinz, A., et al. (2001). "Serotonergic Dysfunction, Negative Mood States, and Response to Alcohol." *Alcoholism: Clinical and Experimental Research* 25: 487–495.

Hill, K. G., et al. (2000). "Early Adult Outcomes of Adolescent Binge Drinking: Person- and Variable-Centered Analysis of Binge Drinking Trajectories." *Alcoholism: Clinical and Experimental Research* 24: 892–901.

Hindson, R., et al. (2001). "Age of Drinking Onset and Involvement in Physical Fights After Drinking." *Pediatrics* 108: 872–877.

Holbrook, A. M., et al. (1999). "Meta-Analysis of Benzodiazdepine Use in the Treatment of Acute Alcohol Withdrawal." *Canadian Medical Association Journal* 160: 649–655.

Holder, H. D., et al. (2000). "Effect of Community-Based Interventions on High-Risk Drinking and Alcohol-Related Injuries." *Journal of the American Medical Association* 284: 2341–2347.

Holdstock, L., and H. deWit (1998). "Individual Differences in the Biphasic Effect of Ethanol." *Alcoholism: Clinical and Experimental Research* 22: 1903–1911.

Hommer, D., et al. (2001). "Evidence for a Gender-Related Effect of Alcoholism on Brain Volumes." *American Journal of Psychiatry* 158: 198–204.

Hungund, B. L., and B. S. Basavarajappa (2000). "Are Anandamide and Cannabinoid Receptors Involved in Ethanol Tolerance? A Review of the Evidence." *Alcohol and Alcoholism* 35: 126–133.

Hungund, B. L., et al. (2002). "Ethanol, Endocannabinoids, and the Cannabinoidergic Signaling System." *Alcoholism: Clinical and Experimental Research* 26: 565–574.

Hungund, B. L., et al. (2003). "Cannabinoid CB1 Receptor Knockout Mice Exhibit Markedly Reduced Voluntary Alcohol Consumption and Lack Alcohol-Induced Dopamine Release in the Nucleus Accumbens." *Journal of Neurochemistry* 84: 698–704.

Ikonomidou, C., et al. (2000). "Ethanol-Induced Apoptotic Neurodegeneration and Fetal Alcohol Syndrome." *Science* 287: 1056–1060.

Johnson, B. A., et al. (2000). "Ondansetron for Reduction of Drinking Among Biologically Predisposed Alcoholic Patients: A Randomized Controlled Trial." *Journal of the American Medical Association* 284: 963–971.

Johnson, B. A., et al. (2003). "Oral Topiramate for Treatment of Alcohol Dependence: A Randomized Controlled Trial." *Lancet* 361: 1677–1685.

Kiefer, F., et al. (2003). "Comparing and Combining Naltrexone and Acamprosate in Relapse Prevention of Alcoholism: A Double-Blind, Placebo-Controlled Study." *Archives of General Psychiatry* 60: 92–99.

Komanduri, R. (2003). "Two Cases of Alcohol Craving Curbed by Topiramate." *Journal of Clinical Psychiatry* 64: 612.

Krystal, J. H., et al. (2001). "Naltrexone in the Treatment of Alcohol Dependence." *New England Journal of Medicine* 345: 1734–1739.

Kurtzman, T. L., et al. (2001). "Inhalant Abuse by Adolescents." *Journal of Adolescent Health* 28: 170–180.

Kushner, M. G., et al. (1996). "The Effects of Alcohol Consumption on Laboratory-Induced Panic and State Anxiety." *Archives of General Psychiatry* 53: 264–270.

Kushner, M. G., et al. (1999). "Prospective Analysis Between DSM-III Anxiety Disorders and Alcohol Use Disorders." *American Journal of Psychiatry* 156: 723–732.

Lapham, S. C., et al. (2001). "Prevalence of Psychiatric Disorders Among Persons Convicted of Driving While Impaired." *Archives of General Psychiatry* 58: 943–949.

Lejoyeux, M., et al. (1999). "Study of Impulse-Control Disorders Among Alcohol-Dependent Patients." *Journal of Clinical Psychiatry* 60: 302–305.

Lenz, S. K., et al. (2002). "Association Between Alcohol Consumption and Postmenopausal Breast Cancer: Results of a Case-Control Study in Montreal, Quebec, Canada." *Cancer Causes and Control* 13: 701–710.

Little, B. B., et al. (1998a). "Alcohol Use During Pregnancy and Maternal Alcoholism." In L. C. Gilstrap and B. B. Little, eds., *Drugs and Pregnancy*, 2nd ed. (pp. 395–404). New York: Chapman & Hall.

Little, B. B., et al. (1998b). "Inhalant (Organic Solvent) Abuse During Pregnancy." In L. C. Gilstrap and B. B. Little, eds., *Drugs and Pregnancy*, 2nd ed. (pp. 457–461). New York: Chapman & Hall.

Malcolm, R., et al. (2000). "Recurrent Detoxification May Elevate Alcohol Craving as Measured by the Obsessive Compulsive Drinking Scale." *Alcohol* 20: 181–185.

Malcolm, R., et al. (2001). "Update on Anticonvulsants for the Treatment of Alcohol Withdrawal." *American Journal on Addictions* 10, Supplement: 16–23.

Malcolm, R., et al. (2002). "Differential Effects of Medication on Mood, Sleep Disturbance, and Work Ability in Outpatient Alcohol Detoxifications." *American Journal on Addictions* 11: 141–150.

Malec, T. S., et al. (1996). "Efficacy of Buspirone in Alcohol Dependence: A Preview." *Alcoholism: Clinical and Experimental Research* 20(5): 853–858.

Markianos, M., et al. (2000). "Dopamine Receptor Responsivity in Alcoholic Patients Before and After Detoxification." *Drug and Alcohol Dependence* 57: 261–265.

Martin, S. E. (2001). "The Links Between Alcohol, Crime and the Criminal Justice System: Explanations, Evidence and Interventions." *American Journal on Addictions* 10: 136–158.

Martin, S. E., and K. Bryant (2001). "Gender Differences in the Association of Alcohol Intoxication and Illicit Drug Abuse Among Persons Arrested for Violent and Property Offenses." *Journal of Substance Abuse* 3: 563–581.

Mason, B. J., et al. (1999). "A Double-Blind, Placebo-Controlled Study of Oral Nalmefene for Alcohol Dependence." *Archives of General Psychiatry* 56: 719–724.

Mason, B. J., et al. (2002). "A Pharmacokinetic and Pharmacodynamic Drug Interaction Study of Acamprosate and Naltrexone." *Neuropsychopharmacology* 27: 596–606.

Matsuzawa, S., and T. Suzuki (2002). "Psychological Stress and Rewarding Effect of Alcohol." *Nihon Arukor Yakubutsu Igakkai Zasshi* 37: 143–152.

Mattson, S. N., and E. P. Riley (1998). "A Review of the Neurobehavioral Deficits in Children with Fetal Alcohol Syndrome or Prenatal Exposure to Alcohol." *Alcoholism: Clinical and Experimental Research* 22: 279–294.

McClelland, G. M., and L. A. Teplin (2001). "Alcohol Intoxication and Violent Crime: Implications for Public Policy." *American Journal on Addictions* 10: 70–85.

Morse, R. M., and D. K. Flavin (1992). "The Definition of Alcoholism." *Journal of the American Medical Association* 268: 1012–1014.

Mukamal, K. J., et al. (2003a). "Roles of Drinking Pattern and Type of Alcohol Consumed in Coronary Heart Disease in Men." *New England Journal of Medicine* 348: 109–118.

Mukamal, K. J., et al. (2003b). "Prospective Study of Alcohol Consumption and Risk of Dementia in Older Adults." *Journal of the American Medical Association* 289: 1405–1413.

Mumenthaler, J. T., et al. (2003). "Gender Differences in Moderate Drinking Effects." *Alcohol Research and Health* 23: 55–64. Published online at niaaa.nih.gov/publications/arh23-1/55-64.

Myrick, H., et al. (2001). "New Developments in the Pharmacotherapy of Alcohol Dependence." *American Journal on Addictions* 10, Supplement: 3–15.

National Institute on Alcohol and Alcoholism (1987). *Alcohol and Birth Defects: The Fetal Alcohol Syndrome and Related Disorders.* U.S. Department of Health and Human Services Publication ADM 87–1531. Washington, DC: U.S. Government Printing Office, pp. 6–10.

Noel, X., et al. (2001). "Supervisory Attentional System in Nonamnestic Alcoholic Men." *Archives of General Psychiatry* 58: 1152–1158.

Pettinati, H. M., et al. (2000). "Sertraline Treatment for Alcohol Dependence: Interactive Effects of Medication and Alcoholic Subtype." *Alcoholism: Clinical and Experimental Research* 24: 1041–1049.

Pettinati, H. M., et al. (2003). "The Status of Serotonin-Selective Pharmacotherapy in the Treatment of Alcohol Dependence." *Recent Developments in Alcoholism* 16: 247–262.

Prescott, C. A., and K. S. Kendler (1999). "Genetic and Environmental Contributions to Alcohol Abuse and Dependence on a Population-Based Sample of Male Twins." *American Journal of Psychiatry* 156: 34–40.

Randall, C. L., et al. (2001). "Paroxetine for Social Anxiety and Alcohol Use in Dual-Diagnosed Patients." *Depression and Anxiety* 14: 255–262.

Ridderinkhof, K. R., et al. (2002). "Alcohol Consumption Impairs Detection of Performance Errors in Mediofrontal Cortex." *Science* 298: 2209–2211.

Riegel, A. C., and E. D. French (2002). "Abused Inhalants and Central Reward Pathways: Electrophysiological and Behavioral Studies in the Rat." *Annals of the New York Academy of Sciences* 965: 281–291.

Roebuck, T. M., et al. (1998). "A Review of the Neuroanatomical Findings in Children with Fetal Alcohol Syndrome or Prenatal Exposure to Alcohol." *Alcoholism: Clinical and Experimental Research* 22: 339–344.

Roehrs, T., et al. (1999). "Ethanol as a Hypnotic in Insomniacs: Self-Administration and Effects on Sleep and Mood." *Neuropsychopharmacology* 20: 279–286

Rohde, P., et al. (2001). "Natural Course of Alcohol Use Disorders from Adolescence to Young Adulthood." *Journal of the American Academy of Child and Adolescent Psychiatry* 40: 83–90.

Rosenberg, N. L., et al. (2002). "Neuropsychologic Impairment and MRI Abnormalities Associated with Chronic Solvent Abuse." *Journal of Toxicology—Clinical Toxicology* 40: 21–34.

Sampson, P. D., et al. (1997). "Incidence of Fetal Alcohol Syndrome and Prevalence of Alcohol-Related Neurodevelopmental Disorder." *Teratology* 56: 317–326.

Schweier, T. A., et al. (2004). "Fast, but Error-Prone, Responses During Acute Alcohol Intoxication: Effects of Stimulus-Response Mapping Complexity." *Alcoholism: Clinical and Experimental Research* 28: 643–649.

Serra, S., et al. (2002). "Blockade by the Cannabinoid CB(1) Receptor Antagonist, SR 141716, of Alcohol Deprivation Effect in Alcohol-Preferring Rats." *European Journal of Pharmacology* 443: 95–97.

Swift, R. M. (1999). "Drug Therapy for Alcohol Dependence." *New England Journal of Medicine* 340: 1482–1490.

Thase, M. E., et al. (2001). "Comorbid Alcoholism and Depression: Treatment Issues." *Journal of Clinical Psychiatry* 62, Supplement 20: 32–41.

Tsai, G. E., et al. (1998). "Increased Glutamatergic Neurotransmission and Oxidative Stress After Alcohol Withdrawal." *American Journal of Psychiatry* 155: 726–732.

Vaillant, G. E. (1996). "A Long-Term Follow-Up of Male Alcohol Abuse." *Archives of General Psychiatry* 53: 243–249.

Wan, F.-J., et al. (1996). "Low Ethanol Concentrations Enhance GABAergic Inhibitory Postsynaptic Potentials in Hippocampal Pyramidal Neurons Only After Block of $GABA_B$ Receptors." *Proceedings of the National Academy of Sciences* 93: 5049–5054.

Wand, G. S., et al. (1998). "Family History of Alcoholism and Hypothalamic Opioidergic Activity." *Archives of General Psychiatry* 55: 1114–1119.

Wang, L., et al. (2003). "Endocannabinoid Signaling via Cannabinoid Receptor 1 is Involved in Ethanol Preference and Its Age-Dependent Decline in Mice." *Proceedings of the National Academy of Sciences of the United States of America* 100: 1393–1398.

Weinberg, N. Z. (1997). "Cognitive and Behavioral Deficits Associated with Parental Alcohol Use." *Journal of the American Academy of Child and Adolescent Psychiatry* 36: 1177–1186.

Willford, J. A., et al. (2004). "Verbal and Visuospatial Learning and Memory Function in Children with Moderate Prenatal Alcohol Exposure." *Alcoholism: Clinical and Experimental Research* 28: 497–507.

Woody, G. E. (2001). "More Reasons to Buckle Your Sear Belt." *Archives of General Psychiatry* 58: 950–951.

Zvosec, D. L., et al. (2001). "Adverse Effects, Including Death, Associated with the Use of 1,4-Butanediol." *New England Journal of Medicine* 344: 87–94.

What Is a Drink?
How Much Alcohol Is in My Drink?

One drink equivalent is the amount of alcohol that contains 10 cc (1/3 ounce) of 100% ethanol. This is the amount of ethanol that the body metabolizes in 1 hour and that reduces the blood alcohol concentration (BAC) by 0.015 grams%.

This amount of alcohol is contained in about 1 ounce of 40% (80 proof) liquor, 3 ounces of 12% wine, a 12-ounce bottle of 3.2% beer, or 7 ounces of 5% beer. Most beers currently available are in the 5% range. Currently, there are only two 3.2% beer states. All others allow higher alcohol contents.

The following beverages are converted to their calculated drink equivalents and the number of drink equivalents can be used with Figure 4.4 to estimate your BAC.

If you consume	You have consumed about
One 12-oz Budweiser (5% alcohol)	1.5 drink equivalents
One 6-pack of 12-oz Budweiser	9 drink equivalents
Short case (12 bottles) of 12-oz Budweiser	18 drink equivalents
One 16-oz Budweiser	1.9 (about 2) drink equivalents
One 24-oz Budweiser	3 drink equivalents
One 40-oz Budweiser	5 drink equivalents
One 12-oz Bud Light (4.2%)	1.25 drink equivalents
One 12-oz Bud-Ice (5.5%)	1.9 (almost 2) drink equivalents
One 16-oz Old English 800 (8%)	3.8 (almost 4) drink equivalents
One 40-oz Old English 800	9 drink equivalents
Two 40-oz Old English 800	18 drink equivalents (2/3 pint of whiskey)
One 16-oz Rainier Ale (7.2%)	3.5 drink equivalents
One 40-oz St. Ides Malt (7.3%)	8 drink equivalents
One 16-oz microbrew (5% to 7%)	2.2 to 3.4 drink equivalents
One 64-oz pitcher of microbrew	9.5 to 13 drink equivalents
One 12-oz Hornsby Draft Cider (6%)	2 drink equivalents
One 16-oz barley wine (10%)	4.8 drink equivalents
One 12-oz Zima cooler (4.6%)	1.6 drink equivalents
One 12-oz Mike's Hard Lemonade (5%)	1.8 drink equivalents

Comments

Budweiser and the other brand names are used for illustration only. Other beers are similar, with modest differences. Their alcohol concentration may or may not be listed on the label or package. Coor's beer, another popular beer, is 4.9% alcohol; Coor's Light is 4.2%. Busch beer is 4.5%; Henri Weinhard Private Reserve is 4.6%; Red Dog is 5% alcohol.

Ice beers are made by slightly freezing the brew and removing some of the ice, increasing the alcohol content. Most are 5.9% alcohol (12-oz bottle = 2 drink equivalents)

Wine coolers are classified as malt beverages and have alcohol contents from 4.6% to 7%. They are considered to be 1.5 to 2 drink equivalents per bottle.

A tavern can sell beer, ale, and malt liquor up to 14% alcohol, hard cider up to 10% alcohol, and wine to 14% alcohol. Taverns and pubs often serve beer and ales in pitchers that contain from 60 to 72 oz. If the pitcher contains regular draft beer at about 5% alcohol, a 64-oz pitcher contains about 9.5 drink equivalents of ethanol.

Chapter 5

Barbiturates, General Anesthetics, Gamma Hydroxybutyrate (GHB), and Antiepileptic Drugs

Discussion of drugs that depress the functioning of the CNS began in Chapter 4 with ethyl alcohol. We continue the discussion by introducing the barbiturates and several older nonbarbiturate sedatives, as well as gamma hydroxybutyrate, general anesthetics, and anticonvulsants. Chapter 6 covers the pharmacology of today's most widely used sedatives, the benzodiazepines.

Historical Background

From time immemorial, human beings have sought ways and means of achieving release from distressing and disabling anxiety and of inducing sleep to counteract debilitating insomnia. *Alcohol* is certainly the oldest drug used for these purposes. *Opium* (which contains *morphine* as its major active ingredient) has similarly been used to induce a somnolent stupor for relief from anxiety and to bring on sleep. The addiction potential of morphine and other "narcotics" limits this use. In the middle of the nineteenth century, *bromide* and *chloral hydrate* became available as safer, more reliable alternatives to alcohol and opium as sedative agents. Then, in 1912, *phenobarbital* was introduced into medicine as a sedative drug, the first of the structurally classified group of drugs called *barbiturates* (Figure 5.1). Between 1912 and 1950, hundreds of barbiturates were tested and approximately 50 were marketed commercially. The barbiturates so dominated the stage that few structurally different sedatives were successfully marketed before 1960, when *chlordiazepoxide* (Librium, Chapter 6)) became the first available *benzodiazepine* tranquilizer, heralding a new era in the treatment of anxiety and insomnia.

When the barbiturates were discovered, researchers had no idea of the mechanisms through which they might exert their sedative actions.

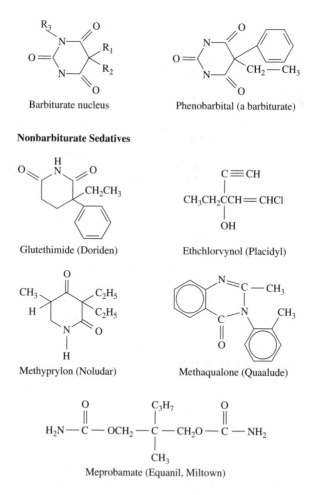

FIGURE 5.1 Chemical structures of classical sedatives. Barbiturates are defined by containing the barbiturate nucleus. Nonbarbiturate sedatives do not have this basic structure.

Therefore, they were unable to classify them by mechanisms of action; rather they were classified by their chemical structure. All drugs that share this basic structure were classified as barbiturates and all shared the same spectrum of actions.[1]

Sites and Mechanisms of Action

Historically, the sedative and hypnotic actions of the barbiturates and other sedatives have been perceived to result from a unique sensitivity of neurons in the CNS to nonselective neuronal depression that follows administration of these drugs. These compounds were presumed to depress polysynaptic, diffuse brain-stem neuronal pathways both in the brain stem and in the cerebral cortex. Brain-stem depression would continue as dosage was increased, accounting for the deep coma and death that can follow drug overdosage.

Today, the mechanisms involved in the action of the barbiturates are both complex and controversial (Dickinson et al., 2002). Barbiturates and other sedatives reduce electrical and metabolic activity of the brain, and the reductions are accompanied by decreases in whole-brain glucose metabolism. The reductions may follow from either reduction of excitatory activity or augmentation in inhibitory activity. As discussed in Chapter 3, *glutamate* is the predominant excitatory neurotransmitter in the brain, while *GABA* is the predominant inhibitory neurotransmitter.

Zhu and colleagues (1997) demonstrated that anesthetic doses of a barbiturate attenuated glutamate neurotransmission, providing not only sedation but also a degree of "brain protection" following something like head injury. Jevtovic-Todorovic and coworkers (1998) reported that the anesthetic gas *nitrous oxide* is an antagonist at glutamate-NMDA receptors, as is the psychedelic anesthetic *phencyclidine* (Chapter 19). They postulated that the amnestic properties of sedative drugs might result from glutamate antagonism, as memory formation is highly dependent on the activity of glutamate neurons. Wu and coworkers (2004) demonstrated that the anesthetic drug isoflurane depresses glutamate neurotransmission by reducing the amplitude of action potentials in the presynaptic nerve terminals of

---

[1]Before drug mechanisms were understood, virtually all drugs were classified by their chemical structures (e.g., benzodiazepines, phenothiazines, barbiturates, and so on). They were further classified by their major observable effects in animals (e.g., sedatives, antipsychotics, anticonvulsants, and so on). Today, with knowledge of mechanisms of action, we tend to classify drugs by their mechanism of action and major use (e.g., selective serotonin reuptake inhibitor antidepressants, selective noradrenaline reuptake inhibitor antidepressants, and so on). Structural classification has become less important.

glumate neurons. Veselis and coworkers (2002) demonstrated that the amnestic effects of propofol (an injectable general anesthetic) occur concomitantly with reductions in cerebral blood flow to areas of the brain associated with working memory processes (right-sided pre-frontal and posterior parietal brain regions). It is quite likely that the anxiolytic effects lie elsewhere.

That elsewhere now appears to involve augmentation of GABA neurotransmission. Recalling the discussion of the GABA$_A$ receptor in Chapter 3, barbiturates and benzodiazepines bind to this receptor, each at its own specific site, serving to facilitate binding of GABA to its receptor. Tomlin and colleagues (1999) reported the effects of three barbiturates on GABA$_A$ receptors and concluded:

> There seems to be little doubt that the barbiturates exert their effects
> by binding to specific sites on the GABA$_A$ receptor, and that these ef-
> fects play a major role in the anesthetic properties of these agents.
> (p. 1714)

The same authors (1998) reported a similar action on the GABA$_A$ receptor for the anesthetic drug *etomidate* (Amidate). Examining other anesthetics, Nishikawa and Harrison (2003) noted that several *volatile anesthetic agents* (sevoflurane, isoflurane, and desflurane) bind directly to the alpha subunit of the GABA$_A$ receptor and that the bond may underlie their general anesthetic action. In 2002, Dickinson and coworkers demonstrated that in cultured rat hippocampal neurons, *thiopental* (Pentothal, an ultrashort-acting barbiturate) specifically enhanced inhibitory GABA transmission in the absence of any action of glutaminergic neurotransmission. They concluded that inhibition of excitatory neurotransmission is not an impor-tant factor, at least in producing a state of anesthesia. Therefore, it now appears that binding to GABA receptors results in facilitation of GABA-induced neurotransmission (channel opening with in-creased influx of chloride ions and cellular hyperpolarization) and accounts for the sedative-hypnotic and anesthetic actions of bar-biturates, benzodiazepines, anesthetics, and similar "depressant" drugs.

While barbiturates bind to the GABA$_A$ receptor and facilitate GABA binding, barbiturates are also capable of opening the chloride channel in the absence of GABA. This independent action accounts for the increased toxicity of barbiturates (including fatalities in over-dosage) when compared with the relative lack of overdose toxicity seen with the benzodiazepines. As we will see in Chapter 6, the benzodi-azepines have a ceiling effect on CNS depression since they enhance only the effects of GABA; they do not open chloride ion channels inde-pendently of GABA availability.

Sedative-Induced Brain Dysfunction

Chapter 4 introduced the concept of a blackout that results from high levels of ethyl alcohol in the blood. A blackout is a state of anterograde amnesia, resulting in loss of memory for current events or actions at a certain blood level of alcohol that persists until the level of alcohol drops again below the amnestic level. More correctly, ethyl alcohol blackout is a manifestation of a *drug-induced, reversible, organic brain syndrome* (or state of dementia) that can follow use of any sedative. Therefore, any sedative, in high enough doses, can produce amnesia and a state of dementia.

This state of dementia (whether drug-induced or organic) produces characteristic behavioral, intellectual, and cognitive patterns. One way to diagnose drug-induced dementia is to perform a *mental status examination* while the patient is under the influence of the drug. This mental status examination evaluates 12 areas of mental functioning (Table 5.1). When one is in a demented state, 5 of the 12 components of the mental status examination are particularly altered (sensorium, affect, mental content, intellectual function, and insight and judgment). The sensorium becomes clouded, which causes disorientation in time and place; memory becomes impaired, which is manifested by forgetfulness and

---

TABLE 5.1 Mental status examination: Twelve areas
            of mental functioning

---

    1. General appearance
* 2. Sensorium
      a. Orientation to time, place, and person
      b. Clear vs. clouded thinking
    3. Behavior and mannerisms
    4. Stream of talk
    5. Cooperativeness
    6. Mood (inner feelings)
* 7. Affect (surface expression of feelings)
    8. Perception
      a. Illusions (misperception of reality)
      b. Hallucinations (not present in reality)
    9. Thought processes: logical vs. strange or bizarre
* 10. Mental content (fund of knowledge)
* 11. Intellectual function (ability to reason and interpret)
* 12. Insight and judgment

---

* Characteristically altered in both organic dementia and reversible, drug-induced dementia.

loss of short-term memory (the blackout); the intellect becomes depressed; judgment is altered. Affect becomes shallow and labile; that is, the person becomes extremely vulnerable to external stimuli and may be sullen and moody one moment and exhibit mock anger or rage the next. This kind of mental status is diagnosed as a brain syndrome caused by depressed nerve cell function. This state of anterograde amnesia also classifies these sedative drugs as so-called date rape drugs as the "victim" does not remember what happened during the period of intoxication.

Certain people (such as the elderly) who already have some natural loss of nerve cell function are adversely affected by these drugs; they experience increased disorientation and further clouding of consciousness. Frequently these people exhibit a state of drug-induced paradoxical excitement, which is characterized by a labile personality with marked anger, delusions, hallucinations, and confabulations, all part of the brain syndrome. Treating drug-induced dementia requires that administration of the sedative drug be stopped.

SPECIFIC DEPRESSANTS

Barbiturates

Barbiturates were the mainstays in treating anxiety and insomnia from 1912 to about 1960. During that period, they were associated with thousands of suicides, deaths from accidental ingestion, widespread dependency and abuse, and many serious interactions with other drugs and alcohol. They are now rarely used; however, they remain the classic prototype of sedative-hypnotic drugs against which newer drugs are compared.

Pharmacokinetics. Barbiturates are all of similar structure, and classification of individual drugs is by their individual pharmacokinetics. As shown in Table 5.2, their half-lives can be quite short (3-minute redistribution half-life for thiopental), longer (up to 48-hour elimination half-life for amobarbital, pentobarbital, and secobarbital), or very long (24- to 120-hour elimination half-life for phenobarbital). The hypnotic action of ultrashort-acting barbiturates (such as thiopental) is terminated by redistribution, while the action of other barbiturates is determined by their rate of metabolism by enzymes in the liver.

Taken orally, barbiturates are rapidly and completely absorbed and are well distributed to most body tissues. The ultrashort-acting barbiturates are exceedingly lipid soluble, cross the blood-brain barrier rapidly, and induce sleep within seconds. Because the longer-acting

TABLE 5.2 Half-lives and uses of some barbiturates

| Drug name | | | | | Drug name | | Uses | | |
Trade	Generic	R_1^{a}	R_2^{a}	R_3^{a}	Distribution (min)	Elimination (h)	Insomnia	Anesthesia	Epilepsy
Amytal	Amobarbital	Ethyl	Isopentyl	H		10–40	X		
Alurate	Aprobarbital	Allyl	Isopentyl	H		12–34	X		
Butisol	Butabarbital	Athyl	sec-Butyl	H		34–42	X		
Mebaral	Mephobarbital	Ethyl	Phenyl	CH_3		50–120			X
Brevital	Methohexital	Allyl	1-Methyl, 2-Pentynyl	CH_3		1–2		X	
Nembutal	Pentobarbital	Ethyl	Methyl butyl	H		15–50	X		
Luminal	Phenobarbital	Ethyl	Phenyl	H		24–120	X		X
Seconal	Secobarbital	Allyl	Methyl butyl	H		15–40	X		
Lotusate	Talbutal	Allyl	sec-Butyl	H			X		
Surital	Thiamylal	Allyl	Methyl butyl	H				X	
Pentothal	Thiopental	Ethyl	Methyl butyl	H	3	3–6		X	

[a] Symbols R_1, R_2, and R_3 refer to chemical substitution at these positions on the barbiturate nucleus shown in Figure 5.1.

barbiturates are more water soluble, they are slower to penetrate the CNS. Sleep induction with these compounds, therefore, is delayed for 20 to 30 minutes and residual hangover is prominent (since the plasma half-lives of most barbiturates vary from 10 to more than 48 hours).

Urinalysis is used to screen for the presence of barbiturates as well as other psychoactive drugs of abuse. Depending on the specific barbiturate, tests are positive for as short as 30 hours or as long as several weeks after the drug is ingested. When urinalysis is positive for barbiturates, more specific confirmation is needed to determine the exact drug that was taken.

Pharmacological Effects. Like ethyl alcohol, barbiturates have a low degree of selectivity, and it is not possible to achieve anxiolysis without evidence of sedation. Barbiturates are not analgesic; they cannot be relied on to produce sedation or sleep in the presence of even moderate pain.

Sleep patterns are markedly affected by barbiturates, with rapid eye movement (REM) sleep being markedly suppressed. Because dreaming occurs during REM sleep, barbiturates suppress dreaming. During drug withdrawal, dreaming becomes vivid and excessive. Such rebound increase in dreaming during withdrawal (termed REM rebound) is one example of a withdrawal effect following prolonged periods of barbiturate ingestion. The vivid nature of the dreams can lead to insomnia, which can be clinically relieved by restarting the drug, negating the attempt at withdrawal.

Since barbiturates are sedatives and depress memory functioning, they are *cognitive inhibitors*. Drowsiness and more subtle alterations of judgment, cognitive functioning, motor skills, and behavior may persist for hours or days until the barbiturate is completely metabolized and eliminated. Sedative doses of barbiturates have minimal effect on respiration, but overdoses (or combinations of barbiturates and alcohol) can result in death. Barbiturate-alcohol combinations have been responsible for both accidental and intentional suicides.

Barbiturates exert few significant effects on the cardiovascular system, the gastrointestinal tract, the kidneys, or other organs until toxic doses are reached. In the liver, barbiturates stimulate the synthesis of enzymes that metabolize barbiturates as well as other drugs, an effect that produces significant tolerance to the drugs.

Psychological Effects. The behavioral, motor, and cognitive inhibitions caused by barbiturates are similar to those caused by alcohol-induced inebriation and may even be indistinguishable from it. A person may respond to low doses either with relief from anxiety (the expected effect) or with withdrawal, emotional depression, or aggressive and violent behavior. Higher doses lead to more general behavioral depression and sleep. Mental set and physical or social setting can determine whether relief from anxiety, mental depression, aggression, or another unexpected or unpredictable response is experienced. Driving skills, judgment, insight, and memory all become severely impaired during the period of intoxication.

Clinical Uses.   Use of barbiturates has declined rapidly in recent years for several reasons: (1) they are lethal in overdose, (2) they have a narrow therapeutic-to-toxic range, (3) they have a high potential for inducing tolerance, dependence, and abuse, and (4) they interact dangerously with many other drugs. Despite these disadvantages, the barbiturates have occasional use as anticonvulsants, as intravenous anesthetics, to provide "brain protection" after head injury, and, in psychiatry, to sedate for an "amytal interview."

Adverse Reactions.   Drowsiness is one of the primary effects induced by barbiturates; it is an inescapable accompaniment to the anxiolytic effect and is often the effect sought if the drug is intended to produce either daytime sedation or nighttime sleep. Barbiturates significantly impair motor and intellectual performance and judgment. It should be emphasized that all sedatives are equivalent to alcohol in their effects, that all are additive in their effects with alcohol, and that their effects persist longer than might be predicted. There are no specific antidotes with which one can treat barbiturate overdosage. Treatment is aimed at supporting the respiratory and cardiovascular system until the drug is metabolized and eliminated.

Tolerance.   The barbiturates can induce tolerance by either of two mechanisms: (1) the induction of drug-metabolizing enzymes in the liver and (2) the adaptation of neurons in the brain to the presence of the drug. With the latter mechanism, tolerance develops primarily to the sedative effects, much less to the brain-stem depressant effects on respiration. Thus, the margin of safety for the person who uses the drug decreases.

Physical Dependence.   Normal clinical doses of barbiturates can induce a degree of physical dependence, usually manifested by sleep difficulties during attempts at withdrawal. Withdrawal from high doses of barbiturates may result in hallucinations, restlessness, disorientation, and even life-threatening convulsions.

Psychological Dependence.   Psychological dependence refers to a compulsion to use a drug for a pleasurable effect. All CNS depressants, including barbiturates, can have such an effect and are known to be abused compulsively. Because they can relieve anxiety, induce sedation, and produce a state of euphoria, these drugs may be used to achieve a variety of pleasurable psychological states in a variety of abuse situations.

Effects in Pregnancy. Barbiturates, like all psychoactive drugs, are freely distributed to the fetus. Data are limited on whether deleterious fetal abnormalities occur as a result of a pregnant woman taking barbiturates, although there is a suggestion that developmental abnormalities occur. This can be a concern for pregnant females who are epileptic and must take a barbiturate to prevent seizures. As reviewed by Ramin and colleagues (1998):

> The risk for the pregnant woman treated with phenobarbital and other antiseizure medications of having an infant with congenital malformations is two to three times greater than that of the general population. It is not entirely clear whether this increased risk is secondary to the anticonvulsants, genetic factors, the seizure disorder itself, or possibly a combination of these factors, although . . . evidence exists for the implication of anticonvulsants as the etiology (p. 172).

Other studies report reduced Wechsler IQ scores in adult males whose mothers used phenobarbital. All this implies that barbiturate exposure during pregnancy might result in deleterious cognitive effects in offspring. This does not imply that barbiturates might have a teratogenic potential. A conservative conclusion might be that barbiturates have the *potential* to result in adverse neonatal outcomes in offspring of mothers taking these drugs. It would be best to avoid taking them while pregnant, but they do not appear to be contraindicated (necessarily avoided) during pregnancy should they be medically necessary, for example, to prevent seizures in the mother (seizures that might also harm the fetus).

Nonbarbiturate Sedative-Hypnotic Drugs

In the early 1950s, three "nonbarbiturate" sedatives—*glutethimide* (Doriden), *ethchlorvynol* (Placidyl), and *methyprylon* (Noludar)—were introduced as anxiolytics, daytime sedatives, and hypnotics. They structurally resembled the barbiturates (see Figure 5.1), but legally they did not have the exact barbiturate nucleus and were structurally not barbiturates, despite being pharmacologically interchangeable. These drugs offered no advantages over the barbiturates. Now considered obsolete, they are occasionally encountered as drugs of abuse.

Meprobamate (Equanil, Miltown) was marketed in 1955 as an alternative to the barbiturates for daytime sedation and anxiolysis. Around it developed the term *tranquilizer* in a marketing attempt to distinguish it from the barbiturates, a distinction that was not borne out in reality. Like barbiturates, meprobamate produces long-lasting daytime sedation, mild euphoria, and relief from anxiety. Meprobamate is not as potent a respiratory depressant as the barbiturates; attempted suicides from overdosage are seldom successful unless the drug is mixed with opioid narcotics such as morphine or oxycodone (Chapter 15). Despite a continuing reduction in clinical use, abuse and dependency continue and are difficult to treat. There is a possibility that use of meprobamate during pregnancy may be associated with an increased frequency of congenital malformations.

Carisoprodol (Soma) is a precursor molecule to meprobamate; after it is absorbed, it is rapidly metabolized to meprobamate, which is the active form of the drug. Currently, carisoprodol, as an intoxicant, is increasingly encountered as a drug of abuse.

Methaqualone (Quaalude) was another nonbarbiturate sedative that had little to justify its widespread use. During the late 1970s and early 1980s, its popularity rivaled that of marijuana and alcohol in its level of abuse. Such attention was due to an undeserved reputation as an aphrodisiac (as a sedative, it was actually an *an*aphrodisiac, much like alcohol). It was, however, a "date rape" drug. Extensive illicit use and numerous deaths led to its ban from sale in the United States in 1984, although illicit supplies occasionally emerge as a drug of abuse. Far from being a "love drug," methaqualone was merely one of several nonselective depressants that were thought to affect the user favorably when they were taken in the right setting and with a particular set of expectations.

Chloral hydrate (Noctec) is yet another drug of largely historical interest, having been available clinically since the late 1800s. It is rapidly metabolized to *trichlorethanol* (a derivative of ethyl alcohol), which is a nonselective CNS depressant and the active form of chloral hydrate. The drug is an effective sedative-hypnotic, with a plasma half-life of about 4 to 8 hours. Next-day hangover is less likely to occur than with compounds having longer half-lives. Its liability in producing tolerance and dependence is similar to that of the barbiturates. Withdrawal of the drug may be associated with disrupted sleep and intense nightmares. One interesting aside is that the combination of chloral hydrate with alcohol can produce increased intoxication, stupor, and amnesia. This mixture was called a *Mickey Finn* and was an early example of a "date rape" drug or drug combination.

Paraldehyde, introduced into medicine before the barbiturates, is a polymer of acetaldehyde, an intermediate by-product in the body's metabolism of ethyl alcohol. Administered either rectally or orally, paraldehyde was historically used to treat delirium tremens (DTs) in alcoholics undergoing detoxification. Paraldehyde is rapidly absorbed (from both rectal and oral routes), sleep ensues within 10 to 15 minutes after hypnotic doses, and the drug is metabolized in the liver to acetaldehyde and eventually to carbon dioxide and water. Some paraldehyde is eliminated through the lungs, producing a characteristic breath odor. People dependent on paraldehyde (usually people who received paraldehyde as a treatment for alcoholism) suffer a variety of toxicities, primarily to the stomach, liver, and kidneys.

GENERAL ANESTHETICS

General anesthetics are potent CNS depressants that produce unconsciousness for the conduct of surgical procedures. General anesthesia is therefore the most severe state of intentional drug-induced CNS depression. The agents that are used as general anesthetics are of two types: (1) those that are administered by inhalation through the lungs and (2) those that are injected directly into a vein.

The inhalation anesthetics in current use include one gas (nitrous oxide) and five volatile liquids (isoflurane, halothane, desflurane, enflurane, and sevoflurane). These drugs produce a dose-related depression of all functions of the CNS—an initial period of sedation followed by the onset of sleep. As anesthesia deepens, the patient's reflexes become progressively depressed and both amnesia and unconsciousness are induced. Adding an opioid narcotic (such as morphine) to a volatile anesthetic induces a state of unconsciousness and analgesia.

Occasionally, the inhaled anesthetic agents are subject to misuse. *Nitrous oxide*, a gas of low anesthetic potency, is an example. Currently used not only in anesthesia but also as a carrier gas in cans of whipped cream (for example, Whippets), nitrous oxide induces a state of behavioral disinhibition, analgesia, and mild euphoria. Since the inhalation of nitrous oxide dilutes the air that a person is breathing, extreme caution must be exercised to prevent hypoxia. If the nitrous oxide were mixed only with room air, hypoxia would result, which could produce irreversible brain damage. Other inhaled anesthetics are similarly abused, presuming that the drug abuser can find a supply. Inhaled as vapors, these drugs produce intoxication, delirium, and eventually unconsciousness, which can be fatal should one lose the ability to breath while under the influence of the drug. Other forms of inhalant abuse were discussed in Chapter 4.

Several *injectable anesthetics* are available. *Thiopental* (Pentothal) and *methohexital* (Brevital) are ultrashort-acting barbiturates. *Propofol* (Diprovan) and *etomidate* (Amidate) are structurally unique; propofol structurally resembles the neurotransmitter GABA (Figure 5.2). The mechanism of action of all these anesthetics probably involves intense CNS depression produced secondary both to facilitation of GABA$_A$ receptor activity and perhaps to depression of excitatory glutamate synaptic transmission. These drugs have little or no analgesic or euphoriant activity because their onset of unconsciousness and amnesia is immediate.

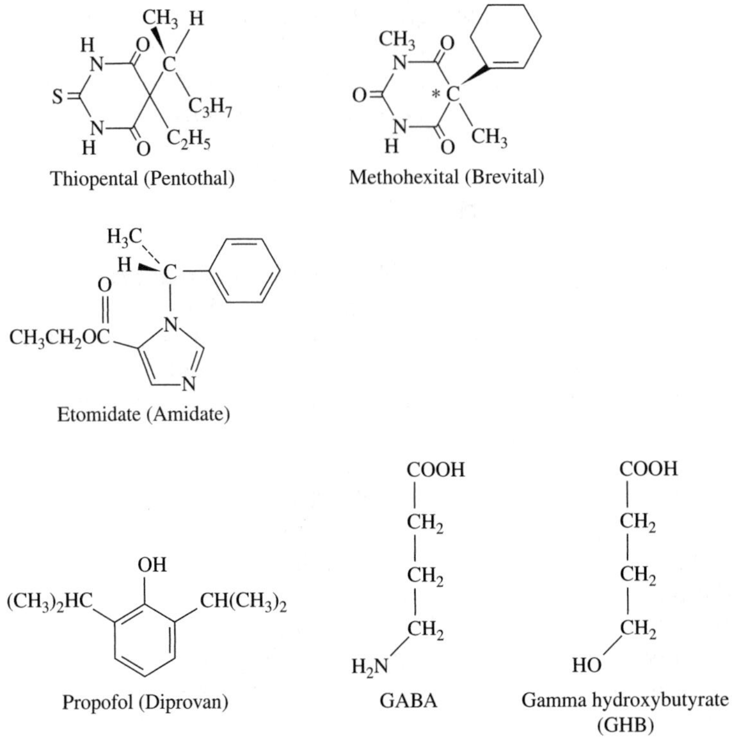

FIGURE 5.2 Chemical structures of intravenously administered "induction" anesthetics. Illustrated are two barbiturates (thiopental and methohexital) and two newer agents. Also illustrated are the structures of GABA and GHB. Propofol is structurally similar to GABA, as is GHB.

A final injectable anesthetic, *ketamine,* is discussed in Chapter 19. Ketamine is unique as an anesthetic drug because it can induce unconsciousness and amnesia along with analgesia and psychedelic hallucinations. Because of the latter property, it is frequently encountered as a drug of abuse. In anesthesia, ketamine is occasionally used because it induces amnesia and unconsciousness in the absence of reductions in blood pressure. This is important when one must conduct anesthesia in critically ill surgical patients.

GAMMA HYDROXYBUTYRATE

Gamma hydroxybutyric acid (gamma hydroxybutyrate, GHB, sodium oxybate, Xyrem) is a potent CNS depressant, used in some countries (but not the United States) as an intravenous general anesthetic. It is also a popular drug of abuse (Miotto et al., 2001; Nicholson and Balster, 2001). GHB is a naturally occurring four-carbon molecule (see Figure 5.2) with a structure similar to GABA. GHB is an endogenous constituent of mammalian brains, synthesized locally from GABA. It freely crosses the blood-brain barrier and has been used in anesthesia, in treating certain sleep disorders, in alcohol detoxification, and in treating opioid dependence.

Since it is a sedative-hypnotic drug, it has euphoriant properties and has been purported (like ethanol) to have use for sexual enhancement. Therefore, it has significant abuse potential as an aphrodisiac and as a euphoriant. It has been available from foreign sources through a variety of venues and can be made at home. It has been sold under such names as RenewTrient, Revivarant, Blue Nitro, Remiforce, GH Revitalize, and Gamma G. It has been called "Nature's Quaalude," among a variety of other names.

GHB has been widely implicated as a "date rape" drug, similar to chloral hydrate, methaqualone, and the various benzodiazepines (such as Rohypnol). Often one of these drugs is added to alcohol in order to potentiate the sedative/intoxicant/amnestic actions of the alcohol. There is no evidence that GHB aids sexual performance: it is a potent sedative and depressant. Like any depressant, it can produce a state of disinhibition, excitement, drunkenness, and amnesia. Schmidt-Mutter and coworkers (1999) reported that GHB increases dopamine levels in the brain, perhaps activating the central dopaminergic reward system by increasing the expression of dopamine receptor mRNA (a cocainelike action). It is, however, a poor reinforcer in animals (Woolverton et al., 1999).

Because of GHB's notorious reputation and abuse, the FDA scheduled GHB as a Schedule I controlled substance, implying high propensity for abuse and no therapeutic use. (The FDA also classifies heroin and marijuana as Schedule I drugs.) In 2003, although the drug was still scheduled in this manner, it was also FDA scheduled as Schedule III because it had a new clinical indication for the treatment of narcolepsy. This was the first time that one drug had been FDA scheduled under two categories of control, depending on the intent for use and the manner in which it is used or abused.

Pharmacokinetics. Available only in liquid form, GHB is rapidly absorbed after oral administration. Plasma level reaches a peak in about 30 to 75 minutes, longer if taken with a high-fat meal. The drug is rapidly metabolized to inactive metabolites and ultimately to carbon dioxide and water. The elimination half-life is about 30 minutes to an hour. Virtually no GHB is detectable in urine. Food in the stomach markedly affects the rate of drug absorption, but nocturnal administration several hours after the last meal of the day offsets this effect (Borgen et al., 2003).

Adverse Effects. GHB overdoses are characterized by stupor, delirium, unconsciousness, coma, and death (Zvosec et al., 2001). Seizures, respiratory depression, and vomiting are common. Combined with alcohol, the toxic potential is greatly magnified. Nonfatal overdoses are characterized by an unarousable coma that lasts 1 to 2 hours. There are no antidotes for treating overdoses: treatment is "supportive" until the drug is eliminated. Acute withdrawal in GHB-dependent persons results in rapid onset of a withdrawal syndrome including insomnia, anxiety, and tremors. Withdrawal symptoms usually resolve in about 3 to 10 days.

Uses. In past years, GHD has been used in the treatment of alcohol withdrawal and narcolepsy and for the induction of anesthesia. Its toxicity and the state of physical dependence it can produce have eliminated its use in alcohol withdrawal and in anesthesia. As discussed, its use in treating narcolepsy remains (Medical Letter, 2002). Narcolepsy is a lifelong disorder characterized by fragmented sleep during the night, altered sleep patterns, and excessive sleepiness during the day. One bothersome daytime symptom is cataplexy (sudden loss of muscle tone) during the day. Cataplexy occurs in 60 to 75 percent of patients with narcolepsy, often precipitated by laughter, anger, surprise, or excitement. GHB is taken at bedtime and then 2.5 to 4 hours later, even if the patient has to be wakened to take the medicine. Taken in this fashion, the drug improves sleep and markedly reduces the number of daytime cataplexy attacks. Currently, because of its abuse potential, a registry and other restrictions are placed on its availability and distribution.

ANTIEPILEPTIC DRUGS

Seizures are manifestations of electrical disturbances in the brain. The term *epilepsy* refers to CNS disorders characterized by relatively brief, chronically recurring seizures that have a rapid onset. Epileptic seizures are often associated with focal (or localized) lesions in the brain. In laboratory animals, epileptic seizures can be induced by a variety of techniques, including "kindling" (repeated low-voltage electrical stimulation of the amygdala or hippocampus to increase the sensitivity of neurons therein). Post and Weiss (1989) associate kindling not only with antiepileptic drug action but also with the treatment of *bipolar disorders*. Indeed, in recent years, antiepileptic drugs have become a mainstay for the treatment of bipolar disorder (Chapter 10). In addition, certain of the antiepileptic drugs have been reported to be efficacious in treating a variety of *explosive behavioral disorders* in children, adolescents, and adults, in managing alcohol withdrawal and cravings, and in treating certain *pain* states, including *peripheral neuropathies* that result from injury to peripheral nerves. This variety of uses of anticonvulsants is discussed throughout this text, especially in Chapter 10, where their use in the treatment of bipolar disorder is discussed. Perhaps this multitude of actions necessitates a new term for these agents, a term such as *neuromodulators* (Myrick et al., 2001b).[2] Here these drugs are introduced for their original indication: antiseizure agents or anticonvulsants. The plasma half-lives and therapeutic blood levels of available antiepileptic drugs are listed in Table 5.3. LaRoche and Helmers (2004) review the newer antiepileptic drugs.

Relationships Between Structure and Activity

The original antiepileptic drugs belong to one of two chemically similar classes, *barbiturates* or *hydantoins* (Figure 5.3). More recently introduced drugs do not bear structural resemblance to classic drugs; rather, they were developed for antiepileptic potential because they either resembled GABA (Figure 5.4) or acted on GABA receptors to potentiate GABA neurotransmission. Development of newer drugs began in about 1980 with the introduction of *carbamazepine* (Tegretol) and *valproic acid* (Depakine) and has continued since with the introduction of several other agents that have multiple clinical uses in addition to use as anticonvulsants.

Specific Agents

Among the *barbiturates*, phenobarbital was the first widely effective antiepileptic drug, replacing the more toxic agent, *bromide,* which had been used during the nineteenth century. *Mephobarbital* (Mebaral) is a second barbiturate occasionally used for treating epilepsy. Because of their sedative effects, these two barbiturates are rarely used; equally effective, more specific, and less sedating antiepileptic agents are available. Epileptic children given barbiturates can display adverse neuropsychological reactions (behavioral hyperactivity and interference with learning ability). *Primidone* (Mysoline), an antiepileptic agent structurally similar to phenobarbital, is metabolized to phenobarbital, which might well be the major active form of the drug.

Phenytoin (Dilantin) remains a commonly used *hydantoin* anticonvulsant, producing less sedation than do the barbiturates. Phenytoin

---

[2]This term removes the implication that a person with mania, behavioral disorders, alcohol dependence, or chronic pain is being treated as if he/she had a seizure disorder. N*euromodulators* act to "stabilize" neuronal membranes either by facilitating inhibition or by limiting excitation. The mechanism of neuronal stabilization is not known, although Suzuki and coworkers (2002) postulate that the effect might be exerted through drug-induced modulation of the genetic expression of an enzyme (type II nitric oxide synthetase) that controls the levels of nitric oxide in the brain.

TABLE 5.3 Antiepileptic drugs available in the United States

Year introduced	Generic name	Trade name	Half-life (hours)	Therapeutic blood level (mcg/ml) [a]
1912	Phenobarbital	Luminal	50+	15–40
1935	Mephobarbital	Mebaral	—[b]	—
1938	Phenytoin	Dilantin	18+	5–20
1946	Trimethadione	Tridione	6–13	>700
1947	Mephenytoin	Mesantoin	95	—
1949	Paramethadione	Paradione	—	—
1951	Phenacemide	Phenurone	—	—
1952	Metharbital	Gemonil	—	—
1953	Phensuximide	Milontin	8	—
1954	Primidone	Mysoline	5–20	5–40
1957	Methsuximide	Celontin	2–40	
1957	Ethotoin	Peganone	4–9	15–50
1960	Ethosuximide	Zarontin	30+	40–400
1968	Diazepam	Valium	20–50	—
1974	Carbamazepine	Tegretol	18–50	4–12
1975	Clonazepam	Klonopin	18–60	20–80
1978	Valproic acid	Depakene	5–20	50–150
1981	Clorazepate	Tranxene	30–100	—
1981	Lorazepam	Ativan	14	—
1993	Felbamate	Felbatol	22	—
1994	Gabapentin	Neurontin	5–7	—
1995	Lamotrigine	Lamictal	33	—
1998	Topiramate	Topamax	19–23	—
1998	Tiagabine	Gabatril	6–9	—
1999	Levetiracetam	Keppra	7	10
2000	Zonisamide	Zonegran	60	—

[a]mcg/ml = micrograms of drug per milliliter of blood
[b]— = data not available

has a half-life of about 24 hours; thus, daytime sedation can be minimized if the patient takes the full daily dose at bedtime. Many bothersome side effects currently limit its use.

All *benzodiazepines* (Chapter 6) possess antiepileptic properties, and a few are still occasionally used for this purpose, including *clonazepam* (Klonopin) and *clorazepate* (Tranxene). When benzodiazepines are used in children, drug-induced personality changes and learning disabilities

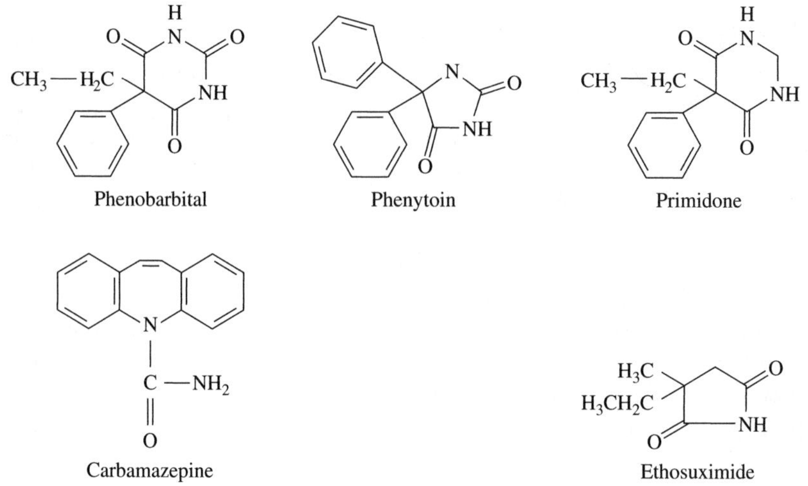

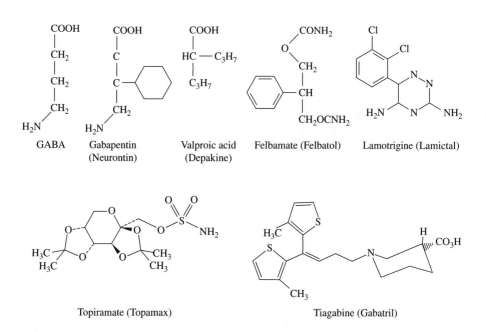

FIGURE 5.3 Chemical structures of several classic drugs used to treat epilepsy.

FIGURE 5.4 Chemical structures of several "GABAergic" drugs used to treat epilepsy. Most are also effective in treating bipolar disorder.

must be carefully monitored. Both drugs have psychiatric applications that include the treatment of acute mania and other agitated psychotic conditions, usually in combination with other "mood stabilizers."

Valproic acid (valproate, divalproex, Depakene, Depakote, Depacon) is effective and widely used in treating seizure disorders in children. It acts by augmenting the postsynaptic action of GABA. Valproic acid has a short half-life (about 6 to 12 hours); it must be administered several times a day. About 75 percent of epileptic patients receiving valproic acid respond favorably. Serious side effects are rare, but liver failure has been reported.

Like many of the newer anticonvulsants, valproic acid possesses GABAergic actions, so it is not surprising that the drug is highly effective in individuals with bipolar disorder, posttraumatic stress disorder, pathologic aggression, schizophrenia, and alcohol and cocaine dependence.

Carbamazepine (Tegretol) is an antiepileptic drug with a sedative effect that is perhaps less intense than that of the other antiepileptic agents. The primary limitations of carbamazepine include rare but potentially serious alterations in the cellular composition of blood (reduced numbers of white blood cells), presumably secondary to a depressant effect on bone marrow. For nonepileptic use, carbamazepine is used in the treatment of bipolar disorder, explosive behavioral disorders, pain syndromes, and alcohol withdrawal (Malcolm et al., 2002).

Felbamate (Felbatol) structurally resembles meprobamate, an anxiolytic discussed earlier. To date, nonepileptic, psychological uses of felbamate have not been reported, although the structural resemblance to meprobamate implies an anxiolytic effect. Although it was at first thought to be free of serious side effects, felbamate's use was drastically curtailed in late 1994 because of serious hematological reactions. Felbamate is currently used only when the drug is absolutely necessary and irreplaceable as an antiepileptic. A practice advisory offering guidelines for the safe use of felbamate has been published (French et al., 1999).

Gabapentin (Neurontin), a structural analogue of GABA (see Figure 5.4), was synthesized as a specific GABA-mimetic antiepileptic drug. Gabapentin appears to act by promoting the release of GABA from presynaptic nerve terminals. In 1995, gabapentin was reported effective in treating both an anxiety disorder (phobia) and pain (reflex sympathetic dystrophy). Since then, gabapentin has been tried in a variety of chronic pain states and psychiatric disorders, including bipolar disorder, and in the demented elderly to treat agitation and aggressive behavior. Gabapentin has also been reported to be effective in treating alcohol withdrawal (Bonnet et al., 1999) and cocaine dependence

(Myrick et al., 2001a), although topiramate may be equally or more effective.

Lamotrigine (Lamictal), introduced into medicine in 1995, acts by inhibiting ion fluxes through sodium channels, thereby stabilizing neuronal membranes and inhibiting the presynaptic release of neuro-transmitters, principally glutamate (Conroy et al., 1999). First intro-duced as an antiepileptic drug, it was reported in 1997 to improve mood, alertness, and social interactions in some epilepsy patients (Post et al., 1997). Since then, many case reports have attested to an antidepressant and antimanic action. Yatham and coworkers (2002) and Ernst and Goldberg (2003) review this use of lamotrigine and other anticonvulsants in the treatment of bipolar disorder.

Interestingly, in the treatment of head injury, release of glutamate has been associated with permanent neuronal damage. Lamotrigine and some other (but not all) anticonvulsants have been reported to in-hibit hypoxia-induced or ischemia-induced release of glutamate; per-haps the drug may be clinically useful in providing brain protection following hypoxic insult (Rekling, 2003).

Oxcarbazapine (Trileptal) is a structural derivative of carba-mazepine. It differs in two ways: first, it is rapidly metabolized by a process called *reduction* to an active molecule, and second, it has not been associated with the white blood cell toxicity associated with car-bamazepine. Oxcarbazepine has long been used in Europe for the treatment of epilepsy. It was recently introduced into the United States for that purpose. It is also being increasingly used to treat bipolar ill-ness (Hellewell, 2002) and other disorders for which carbamazepine is also effective (Gentry et al., 2002). It can be appropriately referred to as a "safer carbamazepine."

Tiagabine (Gabitril) became clinically available in 1998 as another new antiepileptic drug. The drug acts by inhibiting neuronal and glial uptake of GABA, secondary to its irreversibly inhibiting one of the GABA reuptake transporters located on the presynaptic nerve termi-nals of GABA-releasing neurons. This action serves to prolong GABA's synaptic action. Tiagabine appears to be less useful in the treatment of bipolar illness than are other antiepileptic neuromodulators.

Several other new antiepileptic drugs have found use in the treat-ment of bipolar illness. These include *topiramate* (Topamax) (Marcotte, 1998), *levetiracetam* (Keppra) (Grunze and Walden, 2002; Lamberty et al., 2001) and zonisamide (Zonegran) (Tidwell and Swims, 2003). Topiramate was discussed in Chapter 4 for its use in treating alcoholism. Zonisamide has been shown to be effective as an antiobesity agent when combined with a balanced low-calorie diet (Gadde et al., 2003). It has also been used to treat binge-eating disorder (McElroy et al., 2004).

Finally, several novel classes of drugs are being evaluated for clinical usefulness as antiepileptic agents. One class is steroid derivatives called *epalons*. These drugs bind to a specific steroid-sensitive site on the GABA receptor, facilitating GABA activity. *Ganoxalone* is an epalon that is currently in clinical trial.

Antiepileptic Drugs in Pregnancy

Rates of stillbirth and infant mortality are higher for mothers with epilepsy. Children of epileptic mothers who received antiseizure medication during the early months of pregnancy have an increased incidence of a variety of birth defects. The risk is approximately 7 percent, compared with 2 to 3 percent for the general population. Pitting this fact against the obvious necessity to control seizures is a therapeutic dilemma in treating pregnant women who have epilepsy. In general, women with epilepsy of childbearing age should be advised of teratogenic potential. Before a woman becomes pregnant, it should be determined whether drugs can be tapered off and discontinued. If termination cannot be done safely, one approach is to use a single medication at the lowest possible dose that will control seizures. Divided daily doses may decrease the peak levels in plasma while maintaining an adequate steady-state level of the drug in the blood. Cantrell and colleagues (1998) concluded: "With proper management, 90 percent of women with epilepsy can anticipate uneventful pregnancies and normal children."

STUDY QUESTIONS

1. List the various classes of CNS depressants and give examples of each class. What are common terms for CNS depressants?

2. What are the consequences of the drug blockade of glutamate receptors? Of GABA receptors?

3. Describe the gradation of action that occurs in a person as a result of taking progressively increasing doses of a nonselective CNS depressant.

4. What is meant by cross-tolerance of CNS depressants? By cross-dependence?

5. Describe what is meant by *supra-additive CNS depression.* How does potentiation work?

6. What is meant by the term *drug-induced, reversible brain syndrome*?

7. What mechanisms are responsible for the differing durations of action of various barbiturates?

8. What are the oldest CNS depressants? The newest?

9. Describe the effects of barbiturates on sleep patterns both acutely and during drug withdrawal.

10. Compare the effects of barbiturates and chloral hydrate on the elderly.

11. How does paraldehyde resemble ethyl alcohol?

12. What are the particular dangers of use of CNS depressants in the elderly? In the young?

13. Describe the use and abuse of GHB.

14. Can GHB be used in the treatment of alcohol dependence? What are the disadvantages?

15. Which antiepileptic drugs are also used in the treatment of bipolar disorder? Why might they work?

16. Why might antiepileptic drugs be considered for use in nonepileptic, psychological disorders?

17. What are some of the disorders for which antiepileptic "neuromodulators" might be used?

REFERENCES

Bonnet, U., et al. (1999). "Treatment of Alcohol Withdrawal Syndrome with Gabapentin." *Pharmacopsychiatry* 32: 107–109.

Borgen, L., et al. (2003). "The Influence of Gender and Food on the Pharmacokinetics of Sodium Oxybate Oral Solution in Healthy Subjects." *Journal of Clinical Pharmacology* 43: 59–65.

Cantrell, D. T. C., et al. (1998). "Anticonvulsant Drugs During Pregnancy." In L. C. Gilstrap and B. B. Little, eds., *Drugs and Pregnancy*, 2nd ed. (pp. 137–147). New York: Chapman & Hall.

Conroy, B. P., et al. (1999). "Lamotrigine Attenuates Cortical Glutamate Release During Global Cerebral Ischemia in Pigs on Cardiopulmonary Bypass." *Anesthesiology* 90: 844–854.

Dickinson, R., et al. (2002). "Selective Synaptic Actions of Thiopental and Its Enantiomers." *Anesthesiology* 96: 884–892.

Ernst, C. L., and J. F. Goldberg (2003). "Antidepressant Properties of Anticonvulsant Drugs for Bipolar Disorder." *Journal of Clinical Psychopharmacology* 23: 182–192.

French, J., et al. (1999). "Practice Advisory: The Use of Felbamate in Treatment of Patients with Intractable Epilepsy: Report of the Quality Standards Subcommittee of the American Academy of Neurology and the American Epilepsy Society." *Neurology* 52: 1540–1545

Gadde, K. M., et al. (2003). "Zonisamide for Weight Loss in Obese Adults: A Randomized Controlled Trial." *Journal of the American Medical Association* 289: 1820–1825.

Gentry, J. R., et al. (2002). "New Anticonvulsants: A Review of Applications for the Management of Substance Abuse Disorders." *Annals of Clinical Psychiatry* 14: 233–245.

Grunze, H., and J. Walden (2002). "Relevance of New and Recently Discovered Anticonvulsants for Atypical Forms of Bipolar Disorder." *Journal of Affective Disorders* 72, Supplement: S15–S21.

Hellewell, J. S. (2002). "Oxcarbazepine (Trileptal) in the Treatment of Bipolar Disorders: Review of Efficacy and Tolerability." *Journal of Affective Disorders* 72, Supplement: S23–S34.

Jevtovic-Todorovic, V., et al. (1998). "Nitrous Oxide (Laughing Gas) Is an NMDA Antagonist, Neuroprotectant and Neurotoxin." *Nature Medicine* 4: 460–463.

Lamberty, Y., et al. (2001). "Effect of the New Antiepileptic Drug Levetiracetam in an Animal Model of Mania." *Epilepsy Behavior* 2: 454–459.

LaRoche, S. M., and S. L. Helmers (2004). "The new Antiepileptic Drugs." *Journal of the American Medical Association* 291: 605–620.

Malcolm, R., et al. (2002). "The Effects of Carbamazepine and Lorazepam on Single Versus Multiple Previous Alcohol Withdrawals in an Outpatient Randomized Trial." *Journal of General and Internal Medicine* 17: 349–355.

Marcotte, D. (1998). "Use of Topiramate, a New Anti-Epileptic, as a Mood Stabilizer." *Journal of Affective Disorders* 50: 245–251.

McElroy, S. L., et al. (2004). "Zonisamide in the Treatment of Binge-Eating Disorder: An Open-Label, Prospective Trial." *Journal of Clinical Psychiatry* 65: 50–56.

Medical Letter on Drugs and Therapeutics (2002). "Gamma Hydroxybutyrate (Xyrem) for Narcolepsy." *Medical Letter* 44: 103–105.

Miotto, K., et al. (2001). "Gamma-Hydroxybutyric Acid: Patterns of Use, Effects, and Withdrawal." *American Journal of Addictions* 10: 232–241.

Myrick, H., et al. (2001a). "Gabapentin in the Treatment of Cocaine Dependence: A Case Series." *Journal of Clinical Psychiatry* 62: 19–23.

Myrick, H., et al. (2001b). "New Developments in the Pharmacology of Alcohol Dependence." *American Journal of Addictions* 10, Supplement: 3–15.

Nicholson K. L., and R. L. Balster (2001). "GHB: A New and Novel Drug of Abuse." *Drug and Alcohol Dependence* 63: 1–22.

Nishikawa, K., and N. L. Harrison (2003). "The Actions of Sevoflurane and Desflurane on the *Gamma*-Aminobutyric Acid Receptor Type A: Effects of TM2 Mutations in the *Alpha* and *Beta* Subunits." *Anesthesiology* 99: 678–684.

Post, R. M., and S. R. B. Weiss (1989). "Sensitization, Kindling, and Anticonvulsants in Mania." *Journal of Clinical Psychiatry* 50, Supplement 12: 23–30.

Post, R. M., et al. (1997). "Drug-Induced Switching in Bipolar Disorder: Epidemiology and Therapeutic Implications." *CNS Drugs* 8: 352–365.

Ramin, S. M., et al. (1998). "Psychotropics in Pregnancy." In L. C. Gilstrap and B. B. Little, eds., *Drugs and Pregnancy*, 2nd ed. New York: Chapman & Hall, pp. 172–175.

Rekling, J. C. (2003). "Neuroprotective Effects of Anticonvulsants in Rat Hippocampal Slice Cultures Exposed to Oxygen/Glucose Deprivation." *Neuroscience Letters* 335: 167–170.

Schmidt-Mutter, C., et al. (1999). "Gamma-Hydroxybutyrate and Cocaine Administration Increases mRNA Expression of Dopamine D_1 and D_2 Receptors in Rat Brain." *Neuropsychopharmacology* 21: 662–669.

Suzuki, E., et al. (2002). "Antipsychotic, Antidepressant, Anxiolytic, and Anticonvulsant Drugs Induce Type II Nitric Oxide Synthetase mRNA in Rat Brain." *Neuroscience Letters* 333: 217–219.

Tidwell, A., and M. Swims (2003). "Review of the Newer Antiepileptic Drugs." *American Journal of Managed Care* 9: 253–276.

Tomlin, S. L., et al. (1998). "Stereoselective Effects of Etomidate Optical Isomers on Gamma-Aminobutyric Acid Type A Receptors and Animals." *Anesthesiology* 88: 708–717.

Tomlin, S. L., et al. (1999). "Preparation of Barbiturate Optical Isomers and Their Effects on GABA$_A$ Receptors." *Anesthesiology* 90: 1714–1722.

Veselis, R. A., et al. (2002). "A Neuroanatomical Construct for the Amnestic Effects of Propofol." *Anesthesiology* 97: 329–337.

Woolverton, W. L., et al. (1999). "Evaluation of the Reinforcing and Discriminative Stimulus Effects of Gamma-Hydroxybutyrate in Rhesus Monkeys." *Drug and Alcohol Dependence* 54: 137–143.

Wu, X.-S., et al. (2004). "Isoflurane Inhibits Transmitter Release and the Presynaptic Action Potential." *Anesthesiology* 100: 663–670.

Yatham, L. N., et al. (2002). "Third Generation Anticonvulsants in Bipolar Disorder: A Review of Efficacy and Summary of Clinical Recommendations." *Journal of Clinical Psychiatry* 63: 275–283.

Zhu, H., et al. (1997). "The Effect of Thiopental and Propofol on NMDA- and AMPA-mediated Glutamate Excitotoxicity." *Anesthesiology* 87: 944–951.

Zvosec, D. L., et al. (2001). "Adverse Events, Including Death, Associated with the Use of 1,4-Butanediol" *New England Journal of Medicine* 344: 87–94.

Chapter 6

Benzodiazepines and Second-Generation Anxiolytics

BENZODIAZEPINES

Introduced in the early 1960s, benzodiazepines have anxiolytic (anti-anxiety), sedative, anticonvulsant, amnestic, and relaxant properties. Soon after their introduction, they became the most widely used class of psychotherapeutic drugs. Diazepam (Valium) and chlordiazepoxide (Librium) are the classic benzodiazepines. Alprazolam (Xanax), clonazepam (Klonopin), lorazepam (Ativan), and triazoplam (Halcion) are also popular.

In the 1960s, the term *anxiolytic* became synonymous with the benzodiazepines. Even today, their use continues, although more modern drugs have replaced the benzodiazepines for many of their former uses (Bruce et al., 2003; Stocci et al., 2003). The newer drugs are often as effective as the benzodiazepines as anxiolytics, without the long-term dependency problems that are associated with the use of anxiolytics. For example, certain of the antidepressant drugs (for example, the SSRI-type antidepressants; Chapter 9) are largely replacing the benzodiazepines for the treatment of a variety of types of anxiety disorders.

What Is a Benzodiazepine?

First, a benzodiazepine is a drug of a specific chemical structure (Figure 6.1). The classification is therefore *structural,* not mechanistic. Back in 1960, before we understood the concept of drug interaction with specific protein receptors on neuronal surfaces, drugs were synthesized in the laboratory and their clinical effects were determined by testing them both in animals and in humans. The chemical structure that provided the clinical effects was then named and all drugs of similar structure that produced similar clinical effects were given a group name based on the commonality in their chemical structure. In that era, drug manufacturers would make slight modifications to the structure to market competing and possibly better drugs either by changing side chain substituents (making a different compound of the same class) or slightly modifying the basic structure (creating a different chemical class but leaving the same biological action).

Today, with understanding of specific neurochemical receptor-drug interactions, drugs are usually named by the receptors they affect

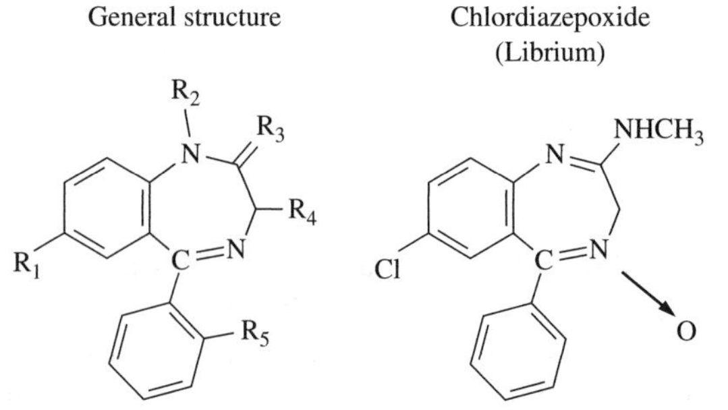

Drug	R_1	R_2	R_3	R_4	R_5
Diazepam	Cl	CH_3	$=O$	H_2	H
Nitrazepam	NO_2	H	$=O$	H_2	H
Flurazepam	Cl	$(CH_2)_2N(C_2H_5)_2$	$=O$	H_2	H
Flunitrazepam	NO_2	H	$=O$	H_2	F
Oxazepam	Cl	H	$=O$	OH	H
Temazepam	Cl	CH_3	$=O$	H_2	H
Clonazepam	NO_2	H	$=O$	H_2	Cl
Lorazepam	Cl	H	$=O$	OH	Cl
Clorazepate	Cl	H	$=O$	COOH	H
Nordiazepam	Cl	H	$=O$	H_2	H

FIGURE 6.1 Structures of some benzodiazepines. The basic "benzodiazepine" nucleus, which structurally defines this class of drugs, is shown on the left; chlordiazepoxide (the first marketed benzodiazepine) is shown on the right. Variations to the basic structure are located at the R_1–R_5 positions on the basic structure.

or that underlie their major clinical action (for example, an SSRI, a serotonin-1A agonist, a serotonin-3 antagonist, and so on). If discovered today, benzodiazepines probably would be known not by that name but as GABA agonists.

Mechanism of Action: Benzodiazepine-GABA Receptor

The benzodiazepines are agonists of the GABA-benzodiazepine-chloride receptor complex; they facilitate the binding of GABA (Figure 6.2). That action, in turn, facilitates influx of chloride ions, causing hyperpolarization of the postsynaptic neuron, depressing its excitability. Benzodiazepines exert their anxiolytic properties by acting at limbic centers. Their actions at other regions (for example, cerebral cortex and brain stem) produce side effects such as sedation, increased seizure threshold, cognitive impairment, and muscle relaxation.

Neuroanatomically, the *amygdala, orbitofrontal cortex,* and *insula* are associated with the production of behavioral responses to fearful stimuli and the central mediation of anxiety and panic. Electrical stimulation of these structures evokes behavioral and physiological responses that are associated with fear and anxiety. Electrical lesions of the amygdala in animals result in an anxiolytic effect. PET scanning of the brain demonstrates increased amygdala blood flow concomitant with anxiety responses; MRI scanning of the brain demonstrates amygdala abnormalities in panic disorder patients. Also, patients with panic disorder (compared with matched controls) have a global decrease in benzodiazepine binding; the largest decreases occur in the orbitofrontal cortex and insula. The decrease is consistent with the notion that anxiety and panic disorders may be due to defective brain inhibition that leads to or allows paroxysmal elevations in anxiety during panic attacks (Malizia et al., 1998).

Blockade of GABAergic function can elicit anxiogeniclike effects, with both behavioral and physiologic alterations similar to symptoms of human anxiety states. Saunders and colleagues (1995) "primed" or "kindled" the amygdala of rats by chronically blocking the function of a subtype of GABA receptors, namely the $GABA_A$ receptor. Results indicated that increased activity of amygdala function (with lowered GABAergic inhibition of function) produced anxiogenic responses as measured both in animal models of anxiety and by increases in heart rate and blood pressure. Thus, hypofunctional $GABA_A$ receptor activity may sensitize the amygdala to anxiogenic responses to what might otherwise be considered nondistressing stimuli. This could be one potential mechanism for developing pathological emotional responses, such as chronic, high levels of anxiety. The benzodiazepines may reset

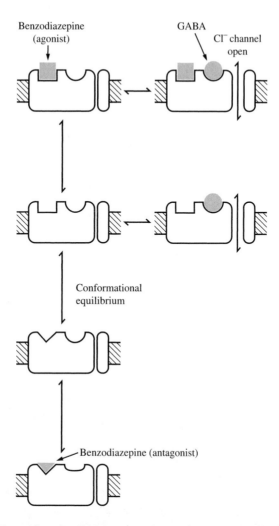

FIGURE 6.2 Benzodiazepine-GABA receptor interactions. BZD agonists (for example, diazepam) and antagonists (flumazenil) bind to a site on the GABA receptor that is distinct from the GABA-binding site. A conformational equilibrium exists between states in which the BZD receptor exists in its agonist-binding conformation *(top)* and its antagonist-binding conformation *(bottom)*. In the latter state, the GABA receptor has a much-reduced affinity for GABA, so the chloride channel remains closed. [Modified from Rang and Dale, 1991, Figure 25.6.]

the threshold of the amygdala to a more normal level of responsiveness. Sigel (2002) details the molecular biology of the interaction between benzodiazepines and GABA$_A$ receptor function. Mohler and coworkers (2002) apply this knowledge to the development of new anxiolytic drugs. Wolf and coworkers (2003) demonstrated the anxiolytic effects of low doses of alprazolam (Xanax) in oral surgery patients. Here, modest effects were seen at 0.25 mg of drug, and additional effects were not seen as the dose was increased.

Pharmacokinetics

Fifteen benzodiazepine derivatives are currently available in the United States (Table 6.1) and still more are available in other countries. They differ from each other mainly in their pharmacokinetic parameters, which include rates of metabolism to pharmacologically active intermediates and plasma half-lives of both the parent drug and any active metabolites. Of the benzodiazepines commercially available in the United States, 14 are available in a dosage form for oral ingestion, and 3 (diazepam, lorazepam, and midazolam) are available for parenteral use. These agents are marketed for use as sedatives, anxiolytics, muscle relaxants, intravenous anesthetics, and anticonvulsants.

Absorption and Distribution. Benzodiazepines are well absorbed when they are taken orally; peak plasma concentrations are achieved in about 1 hour. Some (for example, oxazepam and lorazepam) are absorbed more slowly, while others (for example, triazolam) are absorbed more rapidly. Clorazepate is metabolized in gastric juice to an active metabolite (nordiazepam), which is completely absorbed.

Metabolism and Excretion. Usually, psychoactive drugs are metabolized to pharmacologically inactive products, which are then excreted in urine (Chapter 1). Although this holds true for some benzodiazepines, several are first biotransformed to intermediate, pharmacologically active, products; these, in turn, are detoxified by further metabolism before they are excreted (Figure 6.3). As can be seen from Table 6.1 and Figure 6.3, several benzodiazepines are metabolized into long-lasting, pharmacologically active metabolites, primarily nordiazepam, the half-life of which is about 60 hours. Figure 6.4 illustrates the buildup and slow metabolism of nordiazepam in a human volunteer who was given diazepam (Valium) daily for 14 days. Thus, the long-acting benzodiazepines are so because of the long half-lives of both the parent (original) drug and its pharmacologically active, long-half-life metabolite. In contrast, the short-acting benzodiazepines are short acting because they are metabolized directly into inactive products.

The elderly have a reduced ability to metabolize long-acting benzodiazepines and their active metabolites. In this population, the elimination half-life for diazepam and its active metabolite is about 7 to 10 days. Since it takes about six half-lives to rid the body completely of a drug (Chapter 1), it may take an elderly patient 6 weeks or

TABLE 6.1 Benzodiazepines

Drug name		Dosage form		Active metab-olite	Active compounds in blood	Mean elimination half-life in hours (range)
Generic	Trade	Oral	Paren-teral			
LONG-ACTING AGENTS						
Diazepam	Valium	X	X	Yes	Diazepam	24 (20–50)
					Nordiazepam	60 (50–100)
Chlordiazepoxide	Librium	X		Yes	Chlordiaze-poxide	10 (8–24)
					Nordiazepam	60 (50–100)
Flurazepam	Dalmane	X		Yes	Desalkylfluraz-epam	80 (70–160)
Halazepam	Paxipam	X		Yes	Halazepam	14 (10–20)
					Nordiazepam	60 (50–100)
Prazepam	Centrax	X		Yes	Nordiazepam	60 (50–100)
Chlorazepate	Tranxene	X		Yes	Nordiazepam	60 (50–100)
INTERMEDIATE-ACTING AGENTS						
Lorazepam	Ativan	X	X	No	Lorazepam	15 (10–24)
Clonazepam	Klonopin	X		No	Clonazepam	30 (18–50)
Quazepam	Dormalin	X		Yes	Quazepam	35 (25–50)
					Desalkylfluraz-epam	80 (70–160)
Estazolam	ProSom	X		Yes	Hydroxyestaz-olam	18 (13–35)
SHORT-ACTING AGENTS						
Midazolam	Versed		X	No	Midazolam	2.5 (1.5–4.5)
Oxazepam	Serax	X		No	Oxazepam	8 (5–15)
Temazepam	Restoril	X		No	Temazepam	12 (8–35)
Triazolam	Halcion	X		No	Triazolam	2.5 (1.5–5)
Alprazolam	Xanax	X		No	Alprazolam	12 (11–18)

longer to become drug-free after stopping the drug. With short-acting benzodiazepines, such as midazolam, pharmacokinetics are not so drastically altered, but the dose necessary to achieve effect is reduced by about 50 percent (Albrecht et al., 1999) (Figure 6.5).

Because all benzodiazepines can produce cognitive dysfunction, elderly patients can become clinically demented as a result (Hanlon

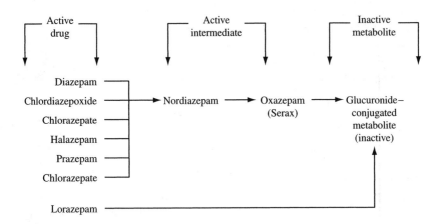

FIGURE 6.3 Metabolism of benzodiazepines. The intermediate metabolite nordiazepam is formed from many agents. Oxazepam (Serax) is commercially available and is also an active metabolite in the metabolism of nordiazepam to its inactive products.

et al., 1998). In general, benzodiazepines should be used only with great caution (if at all) for the elderly. Rang and Dale (1991) stated some years ago:

> At the age of 91, the grandmother of one of the authors was growing increasingly forgetful and mildly dotty, having been taking nitrazepam for insomnia regularly for years. To the author's lasting shame, it took a canny general practitioner to diagnose the problem. Cancellation of the nitrazepam prescription produced a dramatic improvement. (p. 637)

While it might have been expected that the elderly would exhibit cognitive dysfunction while continuously taking benzodiazepines, it had not been documented. Recently, Paterniti and coworkers (2002) followed over 130 benzodiazepine-using elderly people for up to 4 years. Even periodic use was associated with prolonged decreases in cognitive performance, compared with non-drug-taking elderly.

Another significant problem with benzodiazepines in the elderly is an increased incidence of falls and bone fractures (Wang et al., 2001). However, even intensive physician education about the dangers of benzodiazepine use in the elderly is relatively ineffective in reducing their prescription and use (Pimlott et al., 2003). Probably the drugs are in continuing demand by patients taking them as well as their families and caregivers who are not able or willing to address complications of long-term use.

A

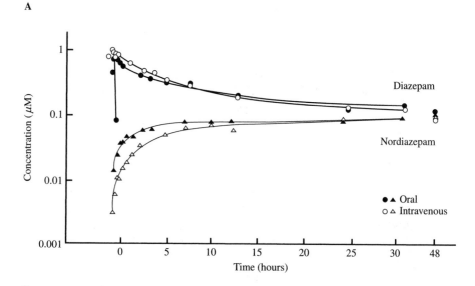

B

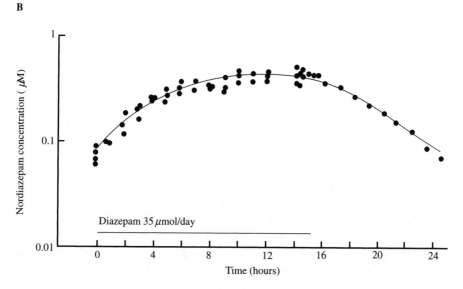

FIGURE 6.4 Pharmacokinetics of diazepam in humans. **A**. Concentrations of diazepam and its active metabolite, nordiazepam, following a single oral or intravenous dose. Note the negligible disappearance of both diazepam and noridiazepam after the first 20 hours. **B**. The accumulation of nordiazepam during 2 weeks of daily administration of diazepam is followed by a slow decline (half-life about 3 days) after the cessation of diazepam administration. [From Rang and Dale (1991), Figure 25.8.]

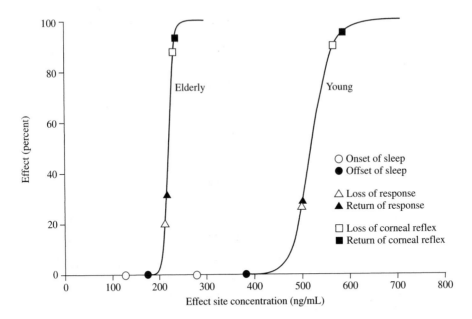

FIGURE 6.5 Concentration (effective dose-response) curve and clinical end points for young (24 to 28 years old) and elderly (67 to 81 years old) male volunteers receiving continuous infusion of midazolam (Versed) until the desired end points were attained. Plasma concentrations of drug were measured at the time of attainment of each clinical end point. In general, younger subjects required an effective site concentration about double that required in the elderly subjects. [From Albrecht et al. (1999), Figure 4.]

Pharmacological Effects

The clinical and behavioral effects of the benzodiazepines occur as a result of facilitation of GABA-induced neuronal inhibition at the various locations of GABA$_A$ receptors throughout the CNS. All benzodiazepines that exert actions similar to those exerted by diazepam are termed *complete agonists* because they faithfully facilitate GABA binding. Low doses of complete agonist benzodiazepines moderate anxiety, agitation, and fear by their actions on receptors located in the amygdala, orbitofrontal cortex, and insula. Mental confusion and amnesia follow action on GABA neurons located in the cerebral cortex and the hippocampus. The mild muscle relaxant effects of the benzodiazepines are probably caused both by their anxiolytic actions and by effects on GABA receptors located in the spinal cord, cerebellum, and brain stem. The antiepileptic actions seem to follow from actions on GABA receptors located in the cerebellum and the hippocampus. The behavioral rewarding effects, drug abuse potential, and psychological dependency probably result from actions on GABA receptors that modulate the discharge of neurons located in the ventral tegmentum and the nucleus accumbens.

Given a number of subgroups of $GABA_A$ receptors, benzodiazepine derivatives may be found that bind to various substituents of different types of $GABA_A$ receptors, perhaps with less than complete agonistic action. These drugs would be called *partial agonists,* and hopefully, some might have specificity of action (for example, anxiolysis without sedation). One such drug is clinically available: *zolpidem* (Ambien), marketed in the mid-1990s, is structurally not a benzodiazepine, but it binds to the $GABA_{1A}$ receptor and exhibits primarily a hypnotic effect rather than an anxiolytic one. Other $GABA_A$ partial agonists are discussed later in this chapter.

Clinical Uses and Limitations

For almost 40 years, the benzodiazepines have been the drugs of choice for the short-term pharmacological treatment of stress-related anxiety and insomnia. They are easy to use, they have relatively low toxicity, and they are effective in producing a "tranquil" state with reductions in anxiety. The benzodiazepines relieve the psychological distress and the dysphoria associated with anxiety. However, their adverse effects and their potential for producing dependency is generally conceded to limit their therapeutic use to relatively short periods of time, perhaps a few days to as long as 3 to 4 weeks, and only for conditions where short-term therapy is beneficial (Holbrook et al., 2000). For longer-term treatment of such disorders as insomnia, generalized anxiety, phobias, panic disorder, and posttraumatic stress disorder, behavioral treatments and antidepressant drugs are now preferred over benzodiazepine therapy. In instances where a combination of cognitive-behavioral therapies and benzodiazepines are used together to treat anxiety, the benzodiazepine interferes with the cognitive therapy, significantly reducing its efficacy (Figure 6.6). Certainly, a cognitive inhibitor should be expected to block cognitive therapy (Westra et al., 2002).

Benzodiazepines are generally not utilized for chronic anxiety or for treating depression. They should be avoided in situations requiring fine motor or cognitive skills or mental alertness or in situations where alcohol or other central nervous system (CNS) depressants are used. They should be used only with great caution in the elderly, in children or adolescents, or in individuals with a history of drug misuse or ongoing abuse.

The major indication for benzodiazepine therapy is anxiety that is so debilitating that the patient's life-style, work, and interpersonal relationships are severely hampered. A benzodiazepine may alleviate the symptoms of nervousness, dysphoria, and psychological distress without necessarily blocking the physiological correlates accompanying the state of anxiety. Usually, resolution of the psychological distress is

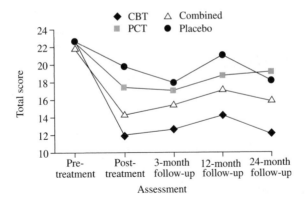

FIGURE 6.6 Effects of cognitive-behavioral therapy (CBT), pharmacotherapy (PCT), combination of CBT and PCT, and a placebo condition on late-life insomnia (as measured by changes in total score for the patient version of the Sleep Impairment Index) in 78 adults ages 65 or older with chronic and primary insomnia. PCT consisted of a benzodiazepine—temazepam (Restoril)—administered in a dose of 7.5 to 30 milligrams I hour before bedtime. Pretreatment, posttreatment, and 3-, 12-, and 24-month follow-up assessments are illustrated. CBT was most effective, followed by combination treatment, PCT alone, and placebo. Benzodiazepine medication reduced the effectiveness of CBT. [Data from C. M. Morin et al., "Behavioural and Pharmacological Therapies for Late-Life Insomnia: A Randomized Controlled Trial," *Journal of the American Medical Association* 281 (1999), p. 997.]

accompanied by amelioration of the physiological symptoms. In cases of behavioral emergencies in mania, oral or intravenous benzodiazepines, alone or in combination with an antipsychotic drug (Chapter 11), are recommended as treatment for the termination of the episode (Alderfer and Allen, 2003).

As sedatives, the benzodiazepines possess many of the characteristics of the barbiturates. Thus, they are used as hypnotics for the treatment of insomnia. Agents with rapid onset, a 2- to 3-hour half-life, and no active metabolites may be preferred to minimize daytime sedation. However, when daytime sedation or next-day anxiolysis is desired, the long-acting drugs with active metabolites might be preferred. Use in treating insomnia, however, is limited by the development of dependence as reflected by rebound increases in insomnia on discontinuation.

Because increased GABA activity inhibits neuronal function, the benzodiazepines have been used as muscle relaxants both to directly reduce states associated with increased muscle tension and to reduce the psychological distress that can predispose to muscle tension. However, they do not directly relax muscles. They relieve only the distress associated with muscle tension (much like alcohol).

Benzodiazepines are exceedingly effective in producing anterograde amnesia (amnesia that starts at the time of drug administration and ends when the blood level of drug has decreased to a point where memory function is regained). For this use, either of two injectable benzodiazepines is perhaps most reliable—lorazepam, when lasting amnesia is desirable, and midazolam, when shorter periods of amnesia are desirable. An example of a situation where amnesia might be a therapeutic goal is surgery, either during or before surgical procedures. Usually, an amnestic effect is undesirable. For example, concern has been expressed about an illegally imported "date rape" drug, which turned out to be a benzodiazepine that is commercially marketed outside the United States. This drug, *flunitrazepam* (Rohypnol), is very similar to *triazolam* (Halcion; see Table 6.1); it produces anxiolysis, sedation, and amnesia, especially when taken with alcohol. When the drug and alcohol are ingested by an unknowing victim, the effect closely resembles the effect of a Mickey Finn (chloral hydrate in alcohol) or GHB (Chapter 5).

Panic attacks and phobias can be treated with benzodiazepines such as *alprazolam* (Xanax), although the efficacy of benzodiazepines may be less than that of the serotonin-type antidepressants, which may actually be more specific anxiolytics (Stocchi et al., 2003). As discussed in Chapter 9, paroxetine (as well as other SSRIs) markedly reduces anxiety. Moreover, unlike the benzodiazepines, cessation of use is not accompanied by rebound increases in anxiety. Davidson (1997) reviewed the use of benzodiazepines, recognizing the advantages of rapid onset, anxiolysis, low-level side effects, and good patient acceptance. However, he also recognized the disadvantages: impaired psychomotor performance, impaired learning and cognition, reduced alertness, and the potential for dependence and abuse.

Because benzodiazepines can substitute for alcohol, they are used both in treating acute alcohol withdrawal and in long-term therapy to reduce the rate of relapse to previous drinking habits. As was discussed in Chapter 5, several of the antiepileptic neuromodulators appear to be viable alternatives to benzodiazepines for treating alcohol withdrawal and relapse. All benzodiazepines exert antiepileptic actions because they raise the threshold for generating seizures. In general, however, benzodiazepines are used as secondary drugs or as adjuvants to other, more specific anticonvulsants.

In summary, perhaps the only well-accepted situation in which benzodiazepines cannot readily be replaced by other drugs is the intentional production of anterograde amnesia, for example, in hospital situations where it is desirable to block the memory of certain unpleasant or painful procedures. The newer agents (the second-generation anxiolytics) should reduce benzodiazepine use for anxiety disorders and insomnia. Undoubtedly, the twenty-first century will be accompanied by continued progress in the development of potentially superior anxiolytic and hypnotic agents.

Side Effects and Toxicity

Common acute side effects associated with benzodiazepine therapy are usually dose-related extensions of the intended actions, including sedation, drowsiness, ataxia, lethargy, mental confusion, motor and cognitive impairments, disorientation, slurred speech, amnesia, and induction or extension of the symptoms of dementia. At higher doses, mental and psychomotor dysfunction progress to hypnosis. Used for the treatment of insomnia, benzodiazepines are especially controversial; drugs can cause the expected sedation, or they can induce paradoxical agitation (anxiety, aggression, hostility, and behavioral disinhibition). The excitatory, or disinhibitory, effects resemble those produced by alcohol. In addition, cessation of use results in rebound increases in insomnia and anxiety.

Respiration is not seriously depressed, even at high doses. Indeed, attempted suicides by overdose are rarely successful unless the benzodiazepine is taken along with another CNS depressant, such as alcohol. This combination can cause a serious and potentially fatal drug interaction. Sleep patterns can be altered markedly. When short-acting agents are taken at bedtime, both early-morning wakening and rebound insomnia for the next night are common. When long-acting agents (or agents with active metabolites) are taken at bedtime, daytime sedation can be a problem.

Impairment of motor abilities—especially a person's ability to drive an automobile—is common (Bramness et al., 2002). Verster and coworkers (2002a) demonstrated that low doses of alprazolam (Xanax) markedly impaired real-world driving abilities, equivalent to a 0.15 grams% blood level of alcohol. This impairment is compounded by the drug-induced suppression of the ability to assess one's own level of physical and mental impairment.

The cognitive deficits associated with benzodiazepine use are significant. In both children and adults, benzodiazepines can significantly interfere with learning behaviors, academic performance, and psychomotor functioning. Cognitive and generalized intellectual impairments can persist even long after the benzodiazepine is discontinued, although cognitive improvements after discontinuation are the norm.

> Patients who had evidence of impaired cognitive functions while on long-term benzodiazepine therapy did improve in these functions when therapy was discontinued. . . . Further, . . . patients who were able to discontinue their benzodiazepine intake after many years of use became more alert, more relaxed, and less anxious, and this change was accompanied by improved psychomotor functions. (Rickels et al., 1999)

Tolerance and Dependence

When benzodiazepines are taken for prolonged periods of time, a pattern of dependence can develop. Early withdrawal signs include a return (and possible intensification) of the anxiety state for which the drug was originally given. Rebound increases in insomnia, restlessness, agitation, irritability, and unpleasant dreams gradually appear. In rare instances, hallucinations, psychoses, and seizures have been reported. Most of these withdrawal symptoms subside within 1 to 4 weeks. Spiegel (1999) discusses psychological strategies to assist in benzodiazepine withdrawal and prevention of relapse. Rickels and coworkers (2000b) studied the use of antidepressant drugs (buspirone and imipramine, Chapter 9) in benzodiazepine withdrawal. Morin and coworkers (2004) used cognitive-behavioral therapy to facilitate benzodiazepine withdrawal in elderly people with insomnia and benzodiazepine dependence.

Zitman and Couvee (2001) studied a large group of patients for whom benzodiazepines had been (inappropriately) prescribed for the treatment of depression. They were withdrawn from their benzodiazepine either with or without administration of concomitant paroxetine. While two-thirds of the patients were successfully withdrawn, by 2 or 3 years after original discontinuation only 13 percent remained benzodiazepine free. This illustrates the attractiveness of the benzodiazepines and the inability of certain persons to refrain from their use. Patients who have histories of drug or alcohol abuse are most apt to use these agents inappropriately, and abuse of benzodiazepines usually occurs as part of a pattern of abuse of multiple drugs.

Effects in Pregnancy

During pregnancy, benzodiazepines and their metabolites freely cross the placenta and accumulate in the fetal circulation (Ramin et al., 1998). Benzodiazepines administered during the first trimester of pregnancy have been reported to cause fetal abnormalities, although the risk is probably very small. Near the time of delivery, should a mother be on high doses of benzodiazepines, a fetus can develop benzodiazepine dependence or even a "floppy-infant syndrome," followed after delivery by signs of withdrawal. Because benzodiazepines are excreted in breast milk and because they can accumulate in nursing infants, taking benzodiazepines while breast-feeding is not recommended.

FLUMAZENIL: A GABA$_A$ ANTAGONIST

Flumazenil (Romazicon) is a benzodiazepine that binds with high affinity to benzodiazepine receptors on the GABA$_A$ complex (see Figure 6.2), but after binding, it exhibits no intrinsic activity. As a consequence, it competitively blocks the access of pharmacologically active benzodiazepines to the receptor, effectively reversing the anti-anxiety and sedative effects of any benzodiazepines administered before flumazenil.

Flumazenil is metabolized quite rapidly in the liver and has a short half-life (about 1 hour). Because this half-life is much shorter than that of most benzodiazepines, the benzodiazepine effects can reappear as flumazenil is lost, thus necessitating reinjection. Flumazenil is utilized as an antidote when benzodiazepine overdosage is suspected.

SECOND-GENERATION ANXIOLYTICS

Zolpidem

Zolpidem (Ambien; Figure 6.7) is a nonbenzodiazepine that was marketed in 1993 for the short-term treatment of insomnia. Although structurally unrelated to the benzodiazepines, zolpidem acts similarly, binding to a specific subtype (type 1) of the $GABA_A$ receptor. It displays most of the actions of all the other benzodiazepine agonists: it is primarily a sedative rather than an anxiolytic, and its sedative actions overwhelm any anxiolytic effects. With a half-life of about 2 to 2.5 hours, zolpidem is often compared to triazolam (Halcion), a benzodiazepine with similar pharmacokinetics; at comparable doses, there appears to be little to differentiate the two drugs (Lobo and Greene, 1997).

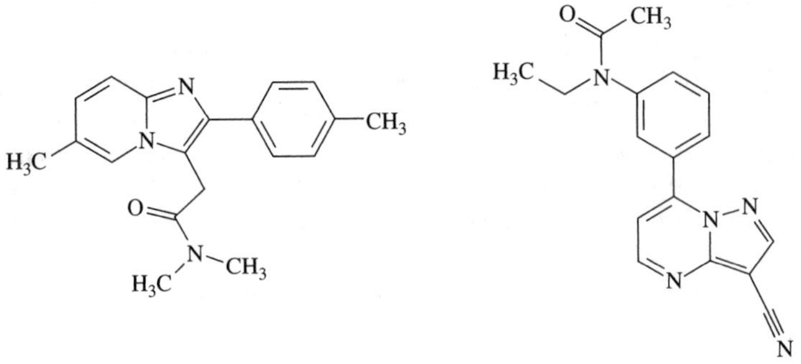

Zolpidem (Ambien)   Zaleplon (Sonata)

FIGURE 6.7 Structural formulas of zolpidem (Ambien) and zaleplon (Sonata). Note the close (but dissimilar) relationship of their basic three-ring structures to the benzodiazepine nucleus (Figure 6.1). Thus, these two compounds are nonbenzodiazepines despite similar GABAergic actions and clinical effects.

Pharmacokinetics. Zolpidem is rapidly absorbed from the gastroin-testinal tract after oral administration, with about 75 percent of the ad-ministered drug reaching the plasma. Only a small amount (about 20 percent) is metabolized by first-pass metabolism. Peak plasma levels are reached in about 1 hour. Following metabolism in the liver, the kid-neys excrete the products. The calculated half-life is prolonged in the elderly.

Pharmacodynamics. At doses of 5 to 10 milligrams, zolpidem pro-duces sedation and promotes a physiological pattern of sleep in the ab-sence of anxiolytic, anticonvulsant, or muscle relaxant effects. Memory is affected as it is by benzodiazepines. Flumazenil effectively reverses any memory impairments or overdosage induced by zolpidem.

Adverse Effects. Dose-related adverse effects of zolpidem include drowsiness, dizziness, and nausea. In the elderly who take 20 mil-ligrams or more, confusion, falls, memory loss, and psychotic reac-tions have been reported. Zolpidem, in doses of 10 milligrams, exhibits minimal effects on memory or psychomotor performance in healthy volunteers participating in a driving-performance study; however, doses of 20 milligrams significantly impair performance and memory even 4 hours after taking the drug (Verster et al., 2002b). A high-dose incidence of nausea and vomiting tends to limit overdosage in suicide attempts. Overdoses to 400 milligrams (40 times the therapeutic dose) have not been fatal.

Zaleplon and Zopiclone

Zaleplon (Sonata; see Figure 6.7) is a nonbenzodiazepine agonist that binds to the GABA$_{1A}$ receptor. In general, it exerts actions similar to those of the benzodiazepines (Patat et al., 2001). It was released in late 1999 for clinical use as a hypnotic agent. Zaleplon is unique among hypnotic drugs because its half-life is very short (less than 1 hour) and only about 30 percent of the dose reaches the bloodstream; most un-dergoes first-pass metabolism in the liver. Orally, it is half as potent as zolpidem; perhaps this difference would disappear should zaleplon be taken with grapefruit juice.

Zaleplon, since it is so short acting, does not require that an indi-vidual predict whether he or she will have insomnia on a particular night. Instead, if the person cannot fall asleep and stay asleep without pharmacological assistance, he or she has the option of taking this very short-acting agent without fear of detrimental effects the next morning.

Sleep is quite rapidly induced with zaleplon at doses of 5 to 10 mil-ligrams, and sleep quality is improved without rebound insomnia. Zaleplon appears particularly noteworthy in its lack of deleterious effects on psychomotor function and driving ability the morning following use (Verster et al., 2002b). Allowing at least 4 hours from drug intake to driving results in no adverse effects (Patat et al., 2001). Indeed, at 4 hours after oral administration, most of the drug is eliminated from the body. Dependence is unlikely to develop because of the short half-life: by morning the drug is metabolized. In essence, a person taking the drug withdraws daily, and drug does not persist in the body. At extremely high doses (25 to 75 milligrams), an abuse potential comparable to that seen for triazolam (Halcion) is seen.

Zopiclone (Imovane) is another nonbenzodiazepine that shares all the actions of zolpidem and traditional benzodiazepines. At a dosage of 7.5 milligrams, it is equal to zaleplon in clinical efficacy as a hypnotic. It may have slightly more effect on next-morning psychomotor performance, but the differences are probably minimal. Hajak (1999) and Noble and coworkers (1998) reviewed the pharmacology and clinical experience with zopiclone in Europe. Rebound insomnia, daytime sedation, and dependence liability have been minimal.

Partial Agonists at GABA$_A$ Receptors

"Full" GABA agonists such as the benzodiazepines are effective anxiolytics; however, their use is limited by rebound anxiety (on discontinuation), physical dependence (with extended use), abuse potential, and side effects that include ataxia, sedation, and memory and cognitive disturbances. Therefore, attempts have been made to identify "partial" agonists of GABA receptors in the hope of providing anxiolytics that may be equally as effective without the side effects that limit the use of the benzodiazepines. To date, several have been examined, although zolpidem is the only GABA partial agonist currently available in the United States, and it is indicated not for anxiolysis but for the treatment of insomnia. Other GABA partial agonists are being studied as anxiolytics. The best studied of these agents are alpidem (marketed in Europe), etizolam, imidazenil, abecarnil, and bretazenil. Each of these partial agonists is in various stages of experimentation or trial.

Alpidem is a partial agonist at GABA$_A$ receptors, is more anxiolytic than full GABA agonists, produces little sedation, and appears not to interact with ethanol. Unfortunately, reports of drug-induced hepatitis have tempered the enthusiasm for the drug.

Etizolam is a potent anxiolytic with a profile similar to classical benzodiazepines; it is claimed to have a lower incidence of side effects at comparable efficacy (Sanna et al., 1999).

Imidazenil is an effective anxiolytic with minimal disruptive effects on cognition and memory, and it appears to have only minimal side effects (Costa et al., 2002).

Abecarnil has a rapid onset of anxiolytic action and a low incidence of physical dependence. Rickels and coworkers (2000a) demonstrated the safety and efficacy of abercarnil in the treatment of generalized anxiety disorder with only minimal discontinuation symptoms.

Bretazenil has anxiolytic action and presumed lower incidence of side effects and dependence liability (Richards and Martin, 1998). Bretazenil also exhibits modest antipsychotic efficacy (Delini-Stula and Berdah-Tordjman, 1996) and appears to increase feeding behavior in animals (Clifton and Cooper, 1996). Perhaps this partial agonist of benzodiazepine receptors will be of clinical use in anxious patients experiencing unwanted loss of appetite.

Serotoninergic Anxiolytics

Anxiety may, at least in part, result from defects in serotonin neurotransmission, and drugs that augment serotoninergic activity are useful in the treatment of anxiety disorders. Of the 15 or more subtypes of serotonin receptors, most interest in anxiolytic effects has focused on the presynaptic serotonin transporter and on postsynaptic serotonin 5-HT_{1A} receptors.

Serotonin 5-HT_{1A} Receptors and Anxiolytics

Serotonin 5-HT_{1A} receptors are found in high density in the hippocampus, the septum, parts of the amygdala, and the dorsal raphe nucleus, areas all presumed to be involved in fear and anxiety responses. Activity in the 5-HT_{1A} receptor is thought to diminish neuronal activity. Mice selectively bred without 5-HT_{1A} receptors display increased fear responses, suggesting that reductions in 5-HT_{1A} receptor activity or density (presumably due to genetic deficits or environmental stressors) result in heightened anxiety (Rambos et al., 1998).

Buspirone. Clinical interest in serotonin anxiolytics began 20 years ago with demonstration of the anxiolytic action of *buspirone,* a selective serotonin 5-HT_{1A} agonist. In 1986 the drug was approved for clinical use, and it is marketed under the trade name *BuSpar.* Thereafter, other related agents were identified, but they have not yet been marketed. Such drugs include gepirone, ipsapirone, and alnespirone. Buspirone (BuSpar) is a 5-HT_{1A} agonist with demonstrable anxiolytic properties. It relieves anxiety in a unique fashion:

- Its anxiolysis occurs without significant sedation or hypnotic action, even in overdosage.

- Amnesia, mental confusion, and psychomotor impairment are minimal or absent.

- It does not potentiate the CNS depressant effects of alcohol, benzodiazepines, or other CNS sedatives (synergism does not occur).
- It does not substitute for benzodiazepines in treating anxiety or benzodiazepine withdrawal.
- It does not exhibit cross-tolerance or cross-dependence with benzodiazepines.
- It exhibits little potential for addiction or abuse.
- It exhibits an antidepressant effect in addition to its anxiolytic effect, making it potentially useful in depressive disorders with accompanying anxiety.
- Its effect has a gradual onset rather than the immediate onset of the action of the benzodiazepines.
- It is ineffective as a hypnotic to promote the onset of sleep.

Buspirone is a weak agonist at 5-HT_{1A} receptors. As a result, it exerts both an anxiolytic action and an antidepressant action (the antidepressant role of 5-HT_{1A} receptors is discussed in Chapter 9). Buspirone is effective in the treatment of generalized anxiety disorder. It has also been recommended for patients who suffer from mixed symptoms of anxiety and depression, as well as for elderly people with agitated dementia.

Buspirone is most helpful in anxious patients who do not demand immediate gratification or the immediate response they associate with the benzodiazepine response. Slower and more gradual onset of anxiety relief is balanced by the increased safety and lack of dependency-producing aspects of buspirone. To see clinical effects takes several weeks of continuous treatment. Patients who have previously been taking benzodiazepines do poorly on buspirone.

Harvey and Balon (1995) summarized the efficacy of buspirone in several psychological disorders, including depression, panic disorder, obsessive compulsive disorder, schizophrenia, and anxiety. They conclude that the major usefulness of buspirone in treating these disorders may be for the augmentation of the beneficial effects of other psychotropic medications. Chapter 1 presents a likely reason why the effects of buspirone are so subtle: most of the drug is detoxified by first-pass metabolism; only about 5 percent of orally administered drug reaches the bloodstream. Inhibition of metabolism (for example, by concurrent drinking of grapefruit juice) improves its efficacy by increasing its absorption.

Gepirone.   *Gepirone* is another 5-HT_{1A} agonist currently in clinical trial. Rickels and co-workers (1997) compared diazepam and gepirone in the treatment of generalized anxiety disorder. Gepirone's anxiolytic response was delayed, differing from placebo only after 6 weeks of treatment (diazepam's response began by the end of the first week). Diazepam was also statistically more effective as an anxiolytic (Figure 6.8). On drug withdrawal, diazepam caused a temporary worsening of anxiety symptoms, while gepirone did not.

Recently, a gepirone extended-release preparation was shown to be effective in the treatment of major depression (Feiger et al., 2003). In fact, as will be shown in Chapter 9, the serotonin-1 receptor has been implicated in brain mechanisms related to both anxiety and depression. The ability of an anxiolytic capable of relieving depression (Figure 6.9) offers advantages over both the benzodiazepines and the SSRI-type antidepressants that have significant adverse effects (such as depression of sexual libido).

Alnespirone. *Alnespirone* exhibits anxiolytic and antiaggressive properties similar to those of gepirone, also mediated by 5-HT$_{1A}$ receptor agonism (Cervo et al., 2000). The drug also has antidepressant properties (Munoz and Papp, 1999). Some components of anxiety and depression may be related to defects in the serotonin transporter protein (Katsuragi et al., 1999). Also, the clinical usefulness of SSRIs (fluoxetine, Prozac) in treating various anxiety disorders results from increased availability of serotonin at the 5-HT$_1$ receptor (Chapter 9). In comparative trials, both the SSRIs and the 5-HT$_{1A}$ receptor agonists are as effective as are the benzodiazepines in treating anxiety disorders, with less likelihood of dependence. Use of SSRIs is limited by a slow onset of action; the specific 5-HT$_{1A}$ agonists may be of similar efficacy with a faster onset of action and a more desirable spectrum of side effects.

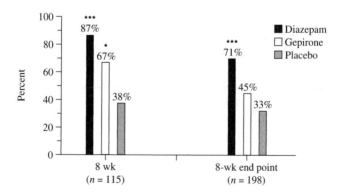

FIGURE 6.8 Percentage of patients experiencing marked or moderate global improvement (in symptoms of generalized anxiety disorder) after 8 weeks of drug treatment (diazepam or gepirone) or placebo capsule. Drug/placebo differences: *$p < 0.05$; ***$p < 0.001$. Statistical difference between diazepam and gepirone responses were not presented. [From Rickels et al. (1997), Figure 3.]

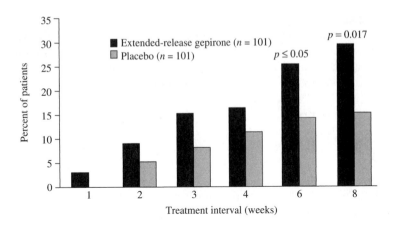

FIGURE 6.9 Percentage of patients achieving a remission 17-item Hamilton Rating Scale for Depression. [Adapted from Feiger et al. (2003), p. 247, Figure 5.]

Repinotan. Repinotan is yet another 5-HT_1 agonist being investigated for clinical use (Lutsep, 2002). Currently in clinical trials, it is showing efficacy not only as an anxiolytic but also as a brain-protective agent for ischemic stroke and traumatic brain injury. The drug is still a few years away from clinical availability.

Serotonin 5-HT_2 Receptor Antagonist and Anxiolysis

Deramciclane is a new nonbenzodiazepine anxiolytic currently in the final phases of clinical trials in Europe (Koks and Vasar, 2002). The drug is unusual in that it is a selective serotonin 5-HT_{2A} receptor antagonist and a 5-HT_{2C} *inverse agonist* (very similar to a receptor antagonist). It is the first molecule of this type to be extensively developed as an anxiolytic compound. More research is forthcoming on this promising compound.

Anticonvulsants as Anxiolytics

Pande and coworkers (2003, 2004) reported that the neuromodulator *pregabalin* was effective in the treatment of both generalized anxiety disorder and social anxiety disorder. In early 2005, pregabalin was approved under the trade name *Lyrica* for use in treating painful neuropathies; approval for treating anxiety disorders has not yet been granted by the FDA. Such use would be "off-label." Pregabalin is a derivative of gabapentin (Neurontin; Chapter 5). In the Pande studies, pregabalin was as effective as the benzodiazepine lorazepam (Ativan), was of rapid onset, and patients taking pregabalin did not experience withdrawal symptoms on discontinuation (in sharp contrast to that seen in patients stopping lorazepam). Pregabalin may be a viable alternative to benzodiazepines. (Pregabalin is discussed further in Chapter 10.)

STUDY QUESTIONS

1. What are the advantages of benzodiazepines over barbiturates?

2. Describe the mechanism of action of benzodiazepines.

3. Describe evidence for and against a natural anxiolytic in the brain.

4. Describe the structure and function of the benzodiazepine receptor.

5. How might you describe anxiety or panic in terms of receptors or neurochemicals (at this point)?

6. List some of the clinical uses of benzodiazepines.

7. List three processes that might prolong the half-life of a benzodiazepine.

8. Why should the elderly avoid using long-acting benzodiazepines?

9. Describe the most clinically significant drug interaction that involves benzodiazepines.

10. Discuss benzodiazepine withdrawal and its treatment.

11. What is flumazenil and for what purpose can it be used?

12. Compare and contrast the mechanisms of action and clinical uses of benzodiazepines and buspirone.

13. To what benzodiazepine is zolpidem most often compared? Why?

14. Compare and contrast zolpidem and zaleplon.

15. Discuss the future treatment of anxiety disorders with either benzodiazepines or serotonin agonists.

REFERENCES

Albrecht, S., et al. (1999). "The Effects of Age on the Pharmacokinetics and Pharmacodynamics of Midazolam." *Clinical Pharmacology and Therapeutics* 65: 630–639.

Alderfer, B. S., and M. H. Allen (2003). "Treatment of Agitation in Bipolar Disorder Across the Life Cycle." *Journal of Clinical Psychiatry* 64, Supplement 4: 3–9.

Bramness, J. G., et al. (2002). "Clinical Impairment of Benzodiazepines—Relation Between Benzodiazepine Concentrations and Impairment in Apprehended Drivers." *Drug and Alcohol Dependence* 68: 131–141.

Bruce, S. E., et al. (2003). "Are Benzodiazepines Still the Medication of Choice for Patients with Panic Disorder with or without Agoraphobia?" *American Journal of Psychiatry* 160: 1432–1438.

Cervo, L., et al. (2000). "Alnespirone and Buspirone Have Anxiolytic-Like Effects in a Conflict Procedure in Rats by Stimulating 5-HT(1A) Receptors." *Behavioral Pharmacology* 11: 153–160.

Clifton, P. G., and S. J. Cooper (1996). "The Benzodiazepine Partial Agonist, Bretazenil, Provokes a Strong Hyperphagic Response: A Meal Pattern Analysis in Freely-Feeding Rats." *Behavioral Pharmacology* 7: 454–461.

Costa, E., et al. (2002). "GABA(A) Receptors and Benzodiazepines: A Role for Dendritic Resident Subunit mRNAs(1)." *Neuropharmacology* 43: 925–937.

Davidson, J. R. T. (1997). "Use of Benzodiazepines in Panic Disorder." *Journal of Clinical Psychiatry* 58, Supplement 2: 26–28.

Delini-Stula, A., and D. Berdah-Tordjman (1996). "Antipsychotic Effects of Bretazenil, a Partial Benzodiazepine Agonist, in Acute Schizophrenia—A Study Group Report." *Journal of Psychiatric Research* 30: 239–250.

Feiger, A. D., et al. (2003). "Gepirone Extended Release: New Evidence for Efficacy in the Treatment of Major Depressive Disorder." *Journal of Clinical Psychiatry* 4: 243–249.

Hajak, G. (1999). "A Comparative Assessment of the Risks and Benefits of Zopiclone: Review of 15 Years' Clinical Experience." *Drug Safety* 21: 457–469.

Hanlon, J. T., et al. (1998). "Benzodiazepine Use and Cognitive Function Among Community-Dwelling Elderly." *Clinical Pharmacology and Therapeutics* 64: 684–692.

Harvey, K. V., and R. Balon (1995). "Augmentation with Buspirone: A Review." *Annals of Clinical Psychiatry* 7: 143–147.

Holbrook, A. M., et al. (2000). "Meta-Analysis of Benzodiazepine Use in the Treatment of Insomnia." *Canadian Medical Association Journal* 162: 225–233.

Katsuragi, S., et al. (1999). "Association Between Serotonin Transporter Gene Polymorphism and Anxiety-Related Traits." *Biological Psychiatry* 45: 368–370.

Koks, S., and E. Vasar (2002). "Deramciclane." *Current Opinion in Investigational Drugs* 3: 289–294.

Lobo, B. L., and W. L. Greene (1997). "Zolpidem: Distinct from Triazolam?" *Annals of Pharmacotherapy* 31: 625–632.

Lutsep, H. L. (2002). "Repinotan, Bayer." *Current Opinions in Investigational Drugs* 3: 924–927.

Malizia, A. L., et al. (1998). "Decreased Brain GABA$_A$-Benzodiazepine Receptor Binding in Panic Disorder: Preliminary Results from a Quantitative PET Study." *Archives of General Psychiatry* 55: 715–720.

Mohler, H., et al. (2002). "A New Benzodiazepine Pharmacology." *Journal of Pharmacology and Experimental Therapeutics* 300: 2–8.

Morin, C. M., et al. (2004). "Randomized Clinical Trial of Supervised Tapering and Cognitive Behavior Therapy to Facilitate Benzodiazepine Discontinuation in Older Adults with Chronic Insomnia." *American Journal of Psychiatry* 161: 332–342.

Munoz, C., and M. Papp (1999). "Alnespirone (S 20499), an Agonist of 5-HT1A Receptors, and Imipramine Have Similar Activity in a Chronic Mild Stress Model of Depression." *Pharmacology of Biochemistry and Behavior* 63: 647–653.

Noble, S., et al. (1998). "Zopiclone. An Update of Its Pharmacology, Clinical Efficacy and Tolerability of Insomnia." *Drugs* 55: 277–302.

Pande, A. C., et al. (2003). "Pregabalin in Generalized Anxiety Disorder: A Placebo-Controlled Trial." *American Journal of Psychiatry* 160: 533–540.

Pande, A. C., et al. (2004). "Efficacy of the Novel Anxiolytic Pregabalin on Social Anxiety Disorder: A Placebo-Controlled, Multicenter Trial." *Journal of Clinical Psychopharmacology* 24: 141–149.

Patat, A., et al. (2001). "Pharmacodynamic Profile of Zaleplon: A New Non-Benzodiazepine Hypnotic Agent." *Human Psychopharmacology* 16: 369–392.

Paterniti, S., et al. (2002). "Long-Term Benzodiazepine Use and Cognitive Decline in the Elderly: The Epidemiology of Vascular Aging Study." *Journal of Clinical Psychopharmacology* 22: 285–293.

Pimlott, N. J., et al. (2003). "Educating Physicians to Reduce Benzodiazepine Use by Elderly: A Randomized Controlled Trial." *Canadian Medical Association Journal* 168: 835–839.

Rambos, S., et al. (1998). "Serotonin Receptor 1A Knockout: An Animal Model of Anxiety-Related Disorder." *Proceedings of the National Academy of Sciences* 95: 14476–14481.

Ramin, S. M., et al. (1998). "Psychotropics in Pregnancy." In L. C. Gilstrap and B. B. Little, eds., *Drugs and Pregnancy*, 2nd ed. New York: Chapman & Hall.

Rang, H. P., and M. M. Dale (1991). *Pharmacology*, 2nd ed. Edinburgh: Churchill Livingstone.

Richards, J. G., and J. R. Martin (1998). "Binding Profiles and Physical Dependence Liabilities of Selected Benzodiazepine Receptor Ligands." *Brain Research Bulletin* 45: 381–387.

Rickels, K., et al. (1999). "Psychomotor Performance of Long-Term Benzodiazepine Users Before, During, and After Benzodiazepine Discontinuation." *Journal of Clinical Psychopharmacology* 19: 107–113.

Rickels, K., et al. (1997). "Gepirone and Diazepam in Generalized Anxiety Disorder: A Placebo-Controlled Trial." *Journal of Clinical Psychopharmacology* 17: 272–277.

Rickels, K., et al. (2000a). "A Double-Blind, Placebo-Controlled Trial of Abercarnil and Diazepam in the Treatment of Patients with Generalized Anxiety Disorder." *Journal of Clinical Psychopharmacology* 20: 12–18.

Rickels, K., et al. (2000b). "Imipramine and Buspirone in Treatment of Patients with Generalized Anxiety Disorder Who Are Discontinuing Long-Term Benzodiazepine Therapy." *American Journal of Psychiatry* 157: 1973–1979.

Sanna, E., et al. (1999). "Molecular and Neurochemical Evaluation of the Effects of Etizolam on $GABA_A$ Receptors Under Normal and Stress Conditions." *Arzneimittel-Forschung* 49: 88–95.

Saunders, S. K., et al. (1995). "Priming of Experimental Anxiety by Repeated Subthreshold GABA Blockade in the Rat Hippocampus." *Brain Research* 699: 250–259.

Sigel, E. (2002). "Mapping of the Benzodiazepine Recognition Site on GABA(A) Receptors." *Current Topics in Medicinal Chemistry* 2: 833–839.

Spiegel, D. A. (1999). "Psychological Strategies for Discontinuing Benzodiazepine Treatment." *Journal of Clinical Psychopharmacology* 19, Supplement 2: 17S–22S.

Stocchi, F., et al. (2003). "Efficacy and Tolerability of Paroxetine for the Long-Term Treatment of Generalized Anxiety Disorder." *Journal of Clinical Psychiatry* 64: 250–258.

Verster, J. C., et al. (2002a). "Effects of Alprazolam on Driving Ability, Memory Functioning, and Psychomotor Performance: A Randomized, Placebo-Controlled Study." *Neuropsychopharmacology* 27: 260–269.

Verster, J. C., et al. (2002b). "Residual Effects of Middle-of-the-Night Administration of Zaleplon and Zolpidem on Driving Ability, Memory Functions, and Psychomotor Performance." *Journal of Clinical Psychopharmacology* 22: 576–583.

Wang, P. S., et al. (2001). "Hazardous Benzodiazepine Regimens in the Elderly: Effects of Half-Life, Dosage, and Duration on Risk of Hip Fracture." *American Journal of Psychiatry* 158: 892–898.

Westra, H. A., et al. (2002). "Naturalistic Manner of Benzodiazepine Use and Cognitive Behavioral Therapy Outcome in Panic Disorder with Agoraphobia." *Journal of Anxiety Disorders* 16: 233–246.

Wolf, D. L., et al. (2003). "Anticipatory Anxiety in Moderately to Highly-Anxious Oral Surgery Patients as a Screening Model for Anxiolytics: Evaluation of Alprazolam." *Journal of Clinical Psychopharmacology* 23: 51–57.

Zitman F. G., and J. E. Couvee (2001). "Chronic Benzodiazepine Use in General Practice Patients with Depression: An Evaluation of Controlled Treatment and Taper-Off." *British Journal of Psychiatry* 178: 317–324.

Drugs That Stimulate Brain Function: Psychostimulants

Classically, psychostimulant drugs were defined by their behavioral effects in animals; they increased the behavioral activity of animals. In human beings, psychostimulants elevate mood, increase motor activity, increase alertness, allay sleep, and increase the brain's metabolic activity. As a behavioral description, the term *psychostimulant* does not specify neurotransmitter or receptor processes. The term says little about therapeutic usefulness, just as it says little about abuse and dependency liabilities. Each psychostimulant must be described individually—its pharmacology, its mechanism of action, any therapeutic properties or potential, and its abuse and dependency issues.

The psychostimulants are discussed in two chapters. Chapter 7 describes the psychostimulants classically thought to act through potentiation of dopaminergic neurotransmission, thus directly activating the reward system involving the nucleus accumbens and the limbic and frontal cortex. These drugs include cocaine and the amphetamines. They have historical and continuing uses in medicine and also have significant abuse issues as well. Chapter 8 details the pharmacology of caffeine and nicotine, the most widely used recreational drugs. Neither drug has much therapeutic value, but both are attractive to users because of their psychostimulant properties. Their overuse can result in moderate to extreme degrees of habituation or dependence.

Cocaine and the Amphetamines

Cocaine and the amphetamines are powerful psychostimulants that markedly affect one's mental functioning and behavior. These drugs act through various synaptic mechanisms to augment the action of several neurotransmitters, most importantly dopamine. Cocaine and the amphetamines, in addition to other actions, increase dopaminergic activity on the nucleus accumbens and other limbic structures associated with behavioral reinforcement, compulsive abuse, drug dependency, and cue-induced drug craving (Kilts et al., 2001). Cocaine and the amphetamines are therefore widely recognized as important drugs of compulsive abuse. Paradoxically, these drugs also have a variety of therapeutic uses, although today, reasonable alternatives are available for most of them. All psychostimulants have significant side effects, toxicities, and patterns of abuse.

In low doses, cocaine and other psychostimulants evoke an alerting, arousing, or behavior-activating response that is not unlike a normal reaction to an emergency or stress. Physiologically, blood pressure and heart rate increase, pupils dilate, blood flow shifts from skin and internal organs to muscle, and oxygen levels rise, as does the level of glucose in the blood. In the CNS, psychostimulants produce positive and attractive effects that include an elevation of mood, induction of euphoria, increased alertness, reduced fatigue, a sense of increased energy, decreased appetite, improved task performance, and relief from boredom.

These positive effects, however, are offset by many negatives. Anxiety, insomnia, and irritability are common side effects. As doses increase, irritability and anxiety become more intense, and a pattern of psychotic behavior may appear. Eventually, intense dependence develops, a dependence that so far has resisted widely successful treatment and rehabilitation.

COCAINE

The leaves of *Erythroxylon coca* have been used since ancient times in their native South America for religious, mystical, social, euphoriant, and medicinal purposes—most notably to increase endurance, promote a sense of well-being, reduce fatigue, increase stamina, induce euphoria, and alleviate hunger (Calatayud and Gonzalez, 2003). Chewing the leaves as an endurant produced a usual total daily dose of cocaine of up to about 200 milligrams, a point that will become more important later in this discussion. Today, the relevant clinical issues related to cocaine's history have to do largely with the changes over time in dosage, route of administration, patterns of use, and technology of production.

The active alkaloid in *E. coca* was isolated in 1855 and purified and named cocaine in 1860. At the same time, the introduction of the syringe and hypodermic needle led to many attempts to use cocaine to produce local anesthesia for surgery. Perhaps the first medical report of cocaine's local anesthetic action[1] was made in 1880. Further identification of cocaine's local anesthetic properties were made by several surgeons, and cocaine became widely used for topical anesthesia, spinal anesthesia, and nerve blocks from about 1884 until about 1918, when procaine (Novocaine) was developed as the first synthetic local anesthetic. Procaine is devoid of psychological and dependence-producing effects (Calatayud and Gonzalez, 2003).

In 1884, Sigmund Freud obtained cocaine, studied its psychological effects, used it himself, and prescribed it for his patients. Freud advocated the use of cocaine to treat depression and to alleviate chronic fatigue. He described cocaine as a "magical" and marvelous drug with the ability even to cure opioid (morphine and heroin) addiction (Boghdadi and Henning, 1997). While using cocaine to relieve his own depression, Freud described the drug as inducing exhilaration and lasting euphoria, which in no way differs from the normal euphoria of the healthy person. However, he did not immediately perceive its side effects—tolerance, dependence, a state of psychosis, and withdrawal depression. In his later writings, Freud called cocaine the "third scourge" of humanity, after alcohol and heroin. This is perhaps an appropriate description.

---

[1]At that time, no other anesthetics (general or local) had been discovered. Surgical procedures were limited to brief procedures conducted without anesthetic or with the patient under alcohol intoxication.

In the United States, around the end of the nineteenth century, there were no restrictions regarding the sale or consumption of cocaine. Thus, the drug was incorporated in numerous patent medicines and the beverage Coca-Cola, which contained approximately 60 milligrams of cocaine per 8-ounce serving. In the late 1800s, however, concern about cocaine's toxicities increased, with several hundred reports of cocaine intoxication and several reported deaths. About 1910, President Taft proclaimed cocaine as Public Enemy Number 1, and in 1914 the Harrison Narcotic Act banned the incorporation of cocaine in patent medicines and beverages. With enforcement of the Narcotic Act, cocaine use decreased during the 1930s and cocaine was largely replaced by the newly available amphetamines, which were cheaper and produced longer-lasting yet similar effects. Cocaine all but disappeared until the late 1960s, when tight federal restrictions on amphetamine distribution raised the cost of amphetamines, once again making cocaine attractive.[2]

In the late 1970s and early 1980s, a new epidemic of cocaine use began with the widespread availability of "crack" cocaine intended for use by inhalation (smoking) rather than by injection. This cocaine epidemic continues today, although relatively inexpensive and widely available methamphetamine is currently more widely encountered. Cocaine users today are characterized by three patterns of use:

- Occasional users usually nasally "snort" lines of powder containing cocaine hydrochloride; each line usually contains about 25 milligrams of the drug.
- Frequent, heavy users either snort the drug or smoke the free-base form for a recreational high.
- Regular users have developed tolerance to cocaine and either inject water-soluble solutions of cocaine hydrochloride in doses of 100 milligrams to 1 gram or more or smoke the base form of cocaine in similar doses. These users usually continue a drug use "run" until their money runs out.

The use of high doses of either cocaine hydrochloride or the base form of cocaine is characterized by high-dose, rapid-onset effects and the rapid development of both toxicity and dependency. One of the most addictive and reinforcing of the abused drugs, cocaine has been used at some time by about 25 million people in the United States. With the increased availability of methamphetamine, the numbers of users of

---

[2]Because their net effects are nearly indistinguishable, cocaine and the amphetamines can be used almost interchangeably as euphoriants. Availability, price, and sociocultural considerations now largely determine their comparative popularity.

cocaine has now rapidly declined. In 2002, an estimated 2 million persons were current cocaine users, 567,000 of whom used "crack" cocaine during the same time period. The percentage of young adults (ages 18 to 25 years) who had ever used cocaine rose steadily from below 1 percent in the 1960s to 17.9 percent in 1984. By 1996, the rate had dropped to 10.1 percent, but it climbed to 15.4 percent in 2002 (Substance Abuse and Mental Health Services Administration, 2003).

Cocaine use is associated with a range of violent premature deaths, including homicides, suicides, and accidents. Although cocaine dependence occurs more commonly in males than in females, smoked cocaine abuse is particularly common in women of childbearing years, certainly a risk factor for harm to both the mother and the fetus should the smoker become pregnant.

Forms of Cocaine

The leaf of *E. coca* contains about 1 percent cocaine. When the leaves are soaked and mashed, cocaine is extracted in the form of coca paste (60 to 80 percent cocaine). Coca paste is usually treated with hydrochloric acid to form the less potent, water-soluble salt *cocaine hydrochloride* before it is exported. The powdered hydrochloride salt can be absorbed through the nasal mucosa (snorted) and, because this salt form is water soluble, it can be injected intravenously. However, in the hydrochloride form, cocaine decomposes when it is heated and is destroyed at the temperature of smoke, making it unsuitable for use by inhalation. In contrast, cocaine base, also known as *freebase* or *crack cocaine*, is insoluble in water but is soluble in alcohol, acetone, or ether. Heating the freebase converts cocaine to a stable vapor that can be inhaled. The name *crack* is derived from the sound of cocaine crystals popping when smoked. Crack cocaine is readily available and is the most popular form of cocaine.

Cocaine hydrochloride ("crystal" or "snow"), when snorted as a "line" of drug, provides a dose of about 25 milligrams; a user might sniff about 50 to 100 milligrams of drug at a time. The smoking of crack cocaine yields average doses in the range of 250 milligrams to 1 gram (Table 7.1). The consequences of these higher doses are severe and are discussed later in this chapter.

Pharmacokinetics

Absorption

Cocaine is absorbed from all sites of application, including mucous membranes, the stomach, and the lungs. Thus, cocaine can be snorted, smoked, taken orally, or injected intravenously. Table 7.1 presents some pharmacokinetic data for common methods of administration.

TABLE 7.1 Effects of cocaine administration

Administration		Initial onset of action (s)	Duration of "high" (min)	Average acute dose (mg)	Peak plasma levels (ng/ml)	Purity (%)	Bioavailability (% absorbed)
Route	Mode						
Oral	Coca leaf chewing	300–600	45–90	20–50	150	0.5–1	25
Oral	Cocaine HCl	600–1800		100–200	150–200	20–80	20–30
Intranasal	Snorting cocaine HCl	120–180	30–45	5×30	150	20–80	20–30
Intravenous	Cocaine HCl	30–45	10–20	25–50	300–400	$7\text{–}100 \times 58$	100
				>200	1000–1500		
Smoking	Coca paste	8–10	5–10	60–250	300–800	40–85	6–32
	Free base	8–10	5–10	250–1000	800–900	90–100	6–32
	Crack	8–10	5–10	250–1000	?	50–95	6–32

From M. S. Gold, "Cocaine (and Crack): Clinical Aspects," in J. H. Lowinson, P. Ruiz, R. B. Millman, and J. G. Langrod, eds., *Substance Abuse: A Comprehensive Textbook*, 3rd ed. (Baltimore: Williams & Wilkins, 1997), p. 185.

Snorted intranasally, cocaine hydrochloride poorly crosses the mucosal membranes since the drug is a potent *vasoconstrictor* (one of its defining pharmacologic actions), constricting blood vessels and limiting its own absorption. As a consequence, only about 20 to 30 percent of the snorted drug is absorbed through the nasal mucosa into blood, with plasma levels not peaking for 30 to 60 minutes. The time course of the pharmacological effects (the subjective "high") parallels the plasma levels as well as the amount of drug actually in brain tissue. With nasal inhalation, the euphoric effect is prolonged (because the drug is absorbed slowly) and the drug may persist in plasma for up to 6 hours.

When cocaine base is vaporized and smoked, drug molecules pass through the pharynx into the trachea and onto lung surfaces, from which absorption is rapid and quite complete. Onset of effects is within seconds, peaks at 5 minutes, and persists for about 30 minutes. Only about 6 to 32 percent of the initial amount vaporized ever reaches plasma.

Intravenous injection of cocaine hydrochloride bypasses all the barriers to absorption, placing the total dose of drug immediately into the bloodstream. The 30- to 60-second delay in onset of action simply reflects the time it takes the drug to travel from the site of injection through the pulmonary circulation and into the brain.

Distribution

Cocaine penetrates the brain rapidly; initial brain concentrations far exceed the concentrations in plasma. After it penetrates the brain, cocaine is rapidly redistributed to other tissues. Cocaine freely crosses the placental barrier, achieving levels in the unborn equal to those in the mother.

Metabolism and Excretion

Cocaine has a biological half-life in plasma of only about 50 minutes; it is rapidly and almost completely metabolized by enzymes located both in plasma and in the liver. Although it is rapidly removed from plasma, it is more slowly removed from the brain, in which it can be detected for 8 or more hours after initial use. Urine can test positive for cocaine for up to 12 hours. The major metabolite of cocaine is the inactive compound *benzoylecgonine* (Figure 7.1), which can be detected in the urine for about 48 hours and much longer (up to 2 weeks) in chronic users. Urine detection of benzoylecgonine forms the basis of drug testing for cocaine use. The persistence of the metabolite in urine implies that high-dose, long-term users might accumulate drug in their body tissues.

The metabolic interaction between cocaine and ethanol is interesting and important. In individuals who use cocaine and concurrently drink alcohol, a unique ethyl ester of benzoylecgonine is produced by the liver enzymes that metabolize the two drugs. This metabolite (called *cocaethylene*) is pharmacologically as active as cocaine in block-

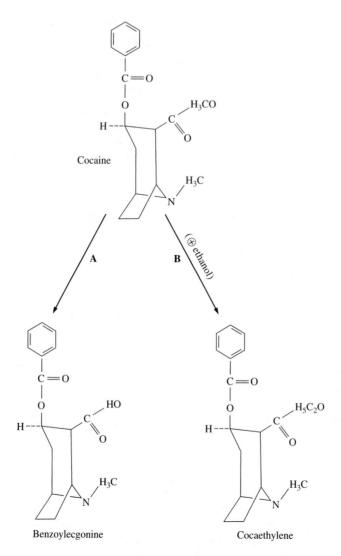

FIGURE 7.1 Structures of cocaine and the products of cocaine metabolism.
A. Normal metabolism to benzoylecognine. **B.** Metabolism to the abnormal, active metabolite cocaethylene, formed from the interaction between cocaine and alcohol. Cocaethylene is the ethyl ester of benzoylecognine.

ing the presynaptic dopamine reuptake transporter, potentiating the euphoric effect of cocaine, increasing the risk of dual dependency, and increasing the severity of withdrawal with chronic patterns of use (Bunney et al., 2001). The cocaethylene metabolite is actually more toxic than cocaine and exacerbates cocaine's toxicity (Wilson et al., 2001). The half-life of cocaethylene is about 150 minutes, outlasting cocaine in the body.

Mechanism of Action

Pharmacologically, cocaine has three prominent actions that account for virtually all its physiological and psychological effects. Indeed, cocaine is the only drug that possesses these three characteristics.

1. It is a potent *local anesthetic*.
2. It is a *vasoconstrictor*, strongly constricting blood vessels.
3. It is a powerful *psychostimulant* with strong reinforcing qualities.

The psychostimulant property leads to compulsive abuse of the drug. Therefore, this section focuses on the actions that lead to its psychostimulation and its behavior-reinforcing properties. Its vasoconstrictive and local anesthetic actions contribute to severe cardiovascular toxicities.

Dopaminergic Actions

For 25 years, cocaine has been known to potentiate the synaptic actions of dopamine, norepinephrine, and serotonin. Such potentiation occurs as a result of cocaine's ability to block the active reuptake of these three transmitters into the presynaptic nerve terminals from which they were released (Figure 7.2). Currently, most focus is on cocaine's blockade of the presynaptic transporter for dopamine as being crucial to its behavior-reinforcing and psychostimulant properties, although blockade of serotonin reuptake is being reexamined. Blockade of the dopamine transporter markedly increases the levels of dopamine within the synaptic cleft, an observation well documented in animal and human studies. Increased dopamine levels in the nucleus accumbens and other components of the dopaminergic reward system seem to be responsible for the euphoric/addictive effects of the drug (Wise, 1998). Dopamine, cocaine, and cocaethylene all decrease the discharge rate of neurons located in both the ventral tegmental area and the nucleus accumbens, indicating that dopamine exerts inhibitory effects on the postsynaptic receptors (i.e., dopamine is primarily an inhibitory neurotransmitter). Cocaine markedly potentiates this dopamine-induced decrease in discharge rate: such potentiation occurs secondary to blockade of dopamine reuptake, potentiating its inhibitory action on postsynaptic receptors.

In 1991, the presynaptic transporter protein for dopamine, which is blocked by cocaine, was cloned and characterized. This transporter protein is a 619-amino-acid protein with 12 putative membrane-spanning regions; both termini of the protein are located in the intracellular cytoplasm of the presynaptic neuron (refer to Figure 2.7 in Chapter 2). Cocaine competes with dopamine for this receptor; the cocaine blocks the binding of dopamine and prolongs its presence in the synaptic cleft.

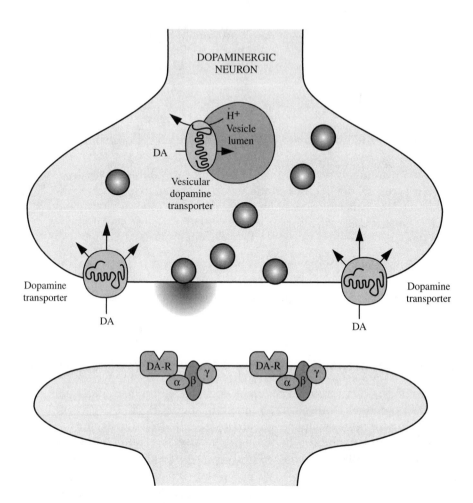

FIGURE 7.2 Transporter proteins involved in the active uptake of dopamine (DA). Two transporters are shown. The first is a vesicular DA transporter located in the cytoplasm of the presynaptic neuron, bound to DA-containing storage vesicles. This transporter carries DA from the cytoplasm into storage. The second type of DA transporter is found on the synaptic membrane of the presynaptic neuron and functions to transport DA from the synaptic cleft into the presynaptic nerve terminal, recycling the transmitter and ending the process of synaptic transmission. It is the second transporter that is blocked by cocaine, prolonging the action of DA in the synaptic cleft. Amphetamines function to induce the release of increased amounts of DA from the storage vesicles into the synaptic cleft. The result is the same: increased amounts of DA at the postsynaptic receptor (DA-R). [From S. G. Amara and M. S. Sonders, "Neurotransmitter Transporters as Molecular Targets for Addictive Drugs," *Drug and Alcohol Dependence* 51 (1998), Figure 1.]

Serotoninergic Actions

Augmentation of dopaminergic neurotransmission as a basis for euphoria/reward/dependency had gone nearly unchallenged for many years. Rocha and coworkers (1998) studied cocaine effects in mice that genetically lacked either the presynaptic dopamine transporter or the postsynaptic serotonin 5-HT_{1B} receptor. In mice lacking the dopamine transporter, dopamine would not be expected to serve as a positive reinforcer; contrary to expectations, the drug was indeed a reinforcer! Thus, other pathways must be involved, pathways that involve binding of cocaine to the serotonin transporter, supporting the reinforcing effects of cocaine. The researchers concluded:

> The serotonin system may provide an additional component of reinforcement, which in the case of dopamine-transporter-deficient mice seems to be sufficient to initiate the self-administration behavior. (p. 175)

Also, in mice genetically breed to lack the serotonin 5-HT_{1B} receptor, cocaine's effects were greater than those in normal control mice. In addition, the genetically altered mice were even more motivated to self-administer cocaine. Thus, serotonin 5-HT_{1B} receptors may put the brake on or antagonize the reinforcing effects of cocaine.

Perhaps individuals with altered serotonin receptor function may have increased susceptibility to cocaine dependence (White, 1998). K. Y. Little and coworkers (1998) tested the hypothesis that alterations in brain serotonin transporter exist in chronic users of cocaine and alcohol. Their results lent support to the hypothesis of genetically defective transporter function in drug dependence. Sora and coworkers (2001) studied mice without either transporter (dopamine or serotonin) and concluded that (1) cocaine may normally work to provide rewarding actions at both transporters and/or (2) either dopamine or serotonin transporters can modulate cocaine reward in the lifelong absence of the other transporter.

Pharmacological Effects in Human Beings

Effects of Short-Term, Low-Dose Use

Low-dose (25 to 75 milligrams) nontoxic *physiological responses* to cocaine include increased alertness, motor hyperactivity, tachycardia, vasoconstriction, hypertension, bronchodilation, increased body temperature, pupillary dilation, increased glucose availability, and shifts in blood flow from the internal organs to the muscles. *Psychological effects* of low doses include an immediate euphoria, giddiness, enhanced self-consciousness, and forceful boastfulness that last only about

30 minutes. This period is followed by one of milder euphoria mixed with anxiety, which can last for 60 to 90 minutes, followed by a more protracted anxious state that spans hours. During acute and subacute intoxication, thoughts typically race, and speech becomes talkative and rapid, often pressured, even garrulous, and sometimes tangential and incoherent. Appetite is markedly suppressed but later rebounds. Sleep is delayed; fatigue is postponed but later rebounds. Conscious awareness and mental acuity are increased but are followed by depression. Motor activity is increased, with agitation, restlessness, and a feeling of constant motion. Perhaps most important, cocaine promotes one's desire to take more cocaine, even instead of such important reinforcers as food.

Low-dose acute effects of cocaine are difficult to maintain because either (1) the perceived effects promote increased use or (2) tolerance develops and higher doses must be taken to perceive continued effects or avoid withdrawal. Thus, a person "graduates" rapidly to the use of higher doses and the onset of increased risks and toxicities.

Cocaine has long been known to function as a discriminative stimulus in several species of animals, a fundamental mechanism by which a drug can control behavior. Also, cocaine use can be followed by an increase in cocaine craving, an effect that may, like its positive reinforcing effect, increase the likelihood of additional cocaine consumption (Woolverton and Johnson, 1992). Extinction training (a form of behavioral conditioning that removes the reward associated with a learned behavior) can reduce the tendency toward relapse. Sutton and coworkers (2003) demonstrated that extinction training during cocaine withdrawal induces increases of subunits of AMPA-type glutamate receptors in the nucleus accumbens. The authors conclude that "extinction-induced plasticity in AMPA receptors may facilitate control over cocaine seeking by restoring glutaminergic tone in the nucleus accumbens, and may reduce the propensity for relapse under stressful situations in prolonged abstinence" (p. 70).

Effects of Moderate-Dose Use

As the dose or duration of use of cocaine increases, all the effects are intensified, and a rebound depression follows. There is a progressive loss of coordination, followed by tremors and eventually seizures. CNS activation is followed by depression, dysphoria, anxiety, somnolence, and drug craving. Although sexual interest may be heightened by using cocaine, and high doses (injected or smoked) are some-times described as orgasmic, cocaine is not an aphrodisiac. Sexual dysfunction is common in heavy users, as they lose interest in interpersonal and sexual interactions. Further, when dysfunction is combined with the isolation that cocaine-dependent individuals experience, normal interpersonal, sensual, and sexual interactions are markedly compromised.

Organ-specific medical and physiological risks and complications of cocaine use are listed in Table 7.2. In the CNS, acute use of cocaine may cause local depletions of oxygen (cerebral ischemia), vascular thrombosis, intracranial hemorrhage and hemorrhagic strokes, cerebral atrophy, seizures, and movement disorders.

Cardiac complications associated with moderate use include hypertensive crises, cardiac ischemia (lack of oxygen), heart attacks, cardiac arrhythmias, sudden death, heart failure, infected heart tissue or valves, and rupture of the aorta. Complications can occur during prolonged use or with single use.

Nasal and pulmonary complications include nasal-septal perforation, pulmonary lesions, hemorrhage, edema, and infections. Gastrointestinal and renal complications can also be seen (see Table 7.2).

Finally, cocaine, with or without alcohol, plays a role in fatal automobile crashes (Dussault et al., 2001). The mechanisms are unclear but likely involve visual deficits, alterations in judgment, incoordination, and feeling of power.

Effects of Long-Term, High-Dose Use

Although low doses of cocaine can cause CNS stimulation that is pleasurable and euphoric, higher doses produce toxic symptoms, including anxiety, sleep deprivation, hypervigilance, suspiciousness, paranoia, and persecutory fears. A person taking cocaine may become hyperreactive, paranoid, and impulsive and may display a repetitive, compulsive pattern of behavior. The person can have a markedly altered perception of reality and become aggressive or homicidal in response to imagined persecution. These behaviors make up what is called a *toxic paranoid psychosis.*

Other high-dose, long-term effects of cocaine use include interpersonal conflicts (resulting from the sense of isolation and paranoia), depression, dysphoria, and bizarre and violent psychotic disorders that can last days or weeks after a person stops using the drug. In its most extreme form, a cocaine psychosis is characterized by paranoia, impaired reality testing, anxiety, a stereotyped compulsive repetitive pattern of behavior, and vivid visual, auditory, and tactile hallucinations. More subtle changes in behavior may include irritability, hypervigilance, extreme psychomotor activation, paranoid thinking, impaired interpersonal relations, and disturbances of eating and sleeping.

An acutely toxic dose of cocaine has been estimated to be about 2 milligrams per kilogram of body weight. Thus, 150 milligrams of cocaine is a toxic one-time dose for a 150-pound (70-kilogram) person. Serious physiological toxicity follows higher doses.

TABLE 7.2 Organ-specific medical and physiological risks and complications of cocaine use

Central nervous system
   Ischemic or hemorrhagic strokes
   Seizures
   Movement disorders
   Intracranial hemorrhage

Cardiac complications
   Acute myocardial infarction (heart attack)
   Cardiac arrhythmias
   Sudden cardiac arrest and death
   Heart failure
   Myocarditis (infections of the heart)
   Ruptured aorta

Pulmonary complications
   Nasal-septal perforations
   Inhalation injuries
   Immunity-related diseases
   Pulmonary edema, hemorrhage
   Bronchiolitis (inflamation of the bronchial tree)

Gastrointestinal complications
   Ulcers, perforations of the stomach and upper intestine
   Bowel ischemia (lack of oxygen)
   Intestinal infarction

Renal complications
   Renal failure
   Renal ischemia

Maternal, fetal, and neonatal complications
   Maternal
      Spontaneous abortion, abruptio placentae
      Placenta previa, stillbirth
   Fetal
      Growth retardation, premature delivery
      Congenital anomalies
      Cerebral infarction and/or hemorrhage
   Neonatal
      Drug withdrawal, seizure disorders
      Cardiovascular system complications

Modified from Boghdadi and Henning (1997).

Comorbidity

Cocaine-dependent people are typically young (12 to 39 years of age), dependent on at least three drugs, and male (75 percent). They tend to have coexisting psychopathology (30 percent have anxiety disorders, 67 percent suffer from clinical depression, and 25 percent exhibit paranoia). About 85 to 90 percent are alcohol dependent.

Chronic cocaine use produces virtually every psychiatric syndrome: affective disorders (mania and depression), schizophrenialike syndromes, personality disorders, and so on. Rounsaville and colleagues (1991) studied 300 cocaine abusers: 56 percent met current criteria and 73 percent met lifetime criteria for the presence of a neuropsychological disorder (major depression, anxiety disorder, bipolar affective disorder, antisocial personality disorder, posttraumatic stress disorder, or attention deficit hyperactivity disorder). Thus, toxicities or withdrawal complications may indicate either high-dose drug toxicities or the onset of symptoms of a coexisting neuropsychological disorder (or both). Most cocaine-dependent people also have problems with other drugs of abuse. Like alcoholics and heroin addicts, cocaine addicts often show a certain profile on personality tests—they are reckless, rebellious, and have a low tolerance for frustration and a craving for excitement. In fact, most of them have been or will be alcoholics or heroin addicts as well. They use opiates and alcohol either to enhance the effects of cocaine or to medicate themselves for unwanted side effects—calming jitters, dulling perceptions, and reducing paranoia to indifference. Intravenous drug users often take cocaine and heroin together in a mixture known as a speedball. Probably more than half of people treated for cocaine abuse are also alcoholic, and the rate of alcoholism in the families of cocaine addicts is high. Comorbidity of cocaine dependence with other psychological or drug-dependency disorders is discussed further in the section on treatment of cocaine dependence.

Cocaine and Pregnancy

One of the tragedies of the late twentieth century was the birth of thousands of infants who are thought to have been injured in utero by cocaine taken by their mothers while pregnant. Figure 7.3 outlines the effects of cocaine on the fetus. Indirect effects result from cocaine's vasoconstrictive action on the mother's blood vessels, decreasing blood flow to the uterus and placenta and reducing oxygen delivery to the fetus. Adverse consequences of blood flow decrease include placental detachment, placental insufficiency, preterm or precipitous labor, fetal death (stillbirth), low birth weight, intrauterine growth retardation, small head size (microcephaly), and possible aberrations in

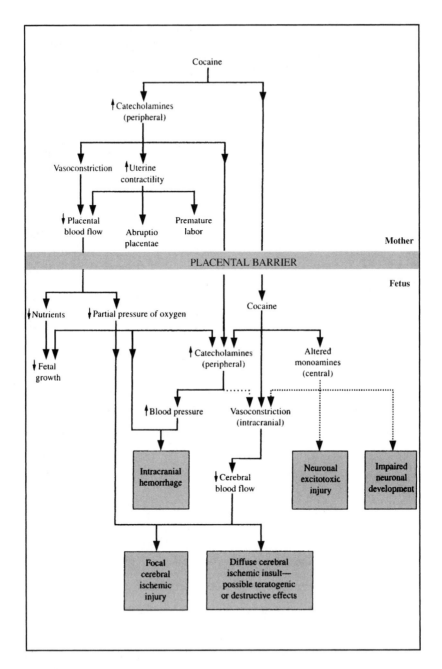

FIGURE 7.3 Deleterious effects of maternal cocaine use on fetuses. Effects that appear plausible on the basis of current information but whose confirmation requires more supporting evidence are indicated by dotted lines. ↑ denotes increase and ↓ denotes decrease. [From Volpe (1992), p. 401].

nervous system development. Virtually any body organ of the neonate can be adversely affected if blood flow to the organ is restricted during development (Volpe, 1992). B. B. Little and coworkers (1998) stated that cocaine use during pregnancy should be considered teratogenic and fetotoxic. The exact mechanism of cocaine-induced congenital anomalies may be related to placental vasoconstriction and fetal hypoxia produced by the drug, with the resulting intermittent vascular disruptions and ischemia in the embryo and fetus actually causing congenital anomalies.

In Figure 7.4, note that cocaine also exerts adverse direct effects on the fetus. Cocaine easily crosses the placental barrier, and fetal concentrations can equal those in the mother. Direct organ toxicity can involve the heart, the CNS, the urinary system, and the GI tract. Vasoconstriction in either the mother or the fetus can increase blood pressure in the fetus, leading to intracerebral hemorrhage, thickening of heart muscle, and various vascular and structural abnormalities (Konkol and Olsen, 1996). Volpe (1992), reviewing the direct fetotoxic effects of cocaine, notes that, as the brain develops, exposure of the fetus to cocaine may promote serious destructive lesions, leading to a neonatal neurological syndrome typified by abnormal sleep patterns, tremors, poor feeding, irritability, occasional seizures, and an increased risk or incidence of sudden infant death syndrome (SIDS).

Some have tried to define a fetal cocaine syndrome. However, because of the wide spectrum of indirect and direct effects on the fetus, any such syndrome is not as clearly defined as the fetal alcohol

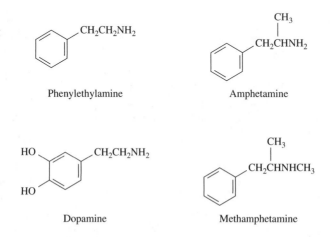

FIGURE 7.4 The basic sympathomimetic amine nucleus (phenylethylamine), the neurotransmitter dopamine (di-hydroxy-phenylethylamine), and the structures of amphetamine and methamphetamine.

syndrome, and cocaine use by the mother is usually only one of many undesirable influences in the children's lives. Babies born into a drug-using environment and possibly into poverty experience little physical or emotional nurturing, so bonding is incomplete or absent. Cocaine's effects on the unborn and newborn may also be related to poor nutrition, poor hygiene, and neglect. Cocaine compromises the mother or any caregiver's ability to respond to the baby through talking, eye contact, and tactile stimulation. The specific interactional behavior of cocaine-using mothers is still under investigation.

Does use of cocaine during pregnancy result in a "crack baby"? The answer is far from clear. On the one hand, Singer and coworkers (2002) reported that cocaine-exposed children had significant cognitive deficits and a doubling of the rate of developmental delay during their first 2 years of life. Because 2-year outcomes predict later cognitive outcomes, the authors proposed that cocaine-exposed children will continue to have learning difficulties at school age. On the other hand, Frank and coworkers (2001) performed a meta-analysis of studies assessing possible links between cocaine use by a pregnant mother and childhood difficulties in the offspring. The authors concluded that crack/cocaine exposure in utero has not been demonstrated to affect physical growth, developmental scores, or motor development. Difficulties in offspring in these areas seemed to be more related to prenatal exposure to tobacco, marijuana, or alcohol and to the quality of the child's environment.

Neurotoxicity of Cocaine

The possible neurotoxic effects of *cocaine* are difficult to measure by the persistence of neurological abnormalities for a period following cessation of drug use. Cocaine is a short-acting drug and is not present in the body if the drug is not repeatedly ingested, smoked, or injected. Toomey and coworkers (2003) conducted a twin study (all males) in which only one member had had heavy stimulant abuse (cocaine and/or methamphetamine) that ended at least one year before the evaluation. Subjects underwent a comprehensive neuropsychological battery of tests. Timed tests demonstrated evidence of long-term residual neuropsychological impairments in the abusers, consistent with persistent psychomotor slowing and slowed reactions associated with cocaine abuse. In contrast, abusers (abstinent for at least one year) exhibited improved performance on attentional tests, suggesting that the positive effects of stimulants on attentional measures (such as ADHD) may persist after drug discontinuation.

Drug-abstinent users may show persistent detrimental changes in their brains (Chang et al., 1999) with associated alterations in memory function (Van Gorp et al., 1999). Bartzokis and colleagues (1999) demonstrated that, in men who are cocaine dependent, doses of cocaine usually caused a "subclinical" form of brain damage of the kind usually caused by vascular insufficiency. It is possible that this kind of injury could predispose to early-onset dementia and other neurological syndromes as subtle brain damage accumulates and adds to normal aging. Little and coworkers (2003) demonstrated in humans that cocaine users lose a specific protein in the brain, which might reflect damage to dopaminergic neurons. This, they speculate, "could play a role in causing disordered mood and motivational processes in more severely dependent patients" (p. 47).

Pharmacological Treatment of Cocaine Dependency

A variety of pharmacological approaches have been suggested for treating cocaine abuse, but as yet there is no consensus regarding any generally accepted successful treatment (Lavori et al., 1999). Kilts and coworkers (2004) noted cue-induced craving differences in male and female cocaine addicts and suggested that different approaches may be needed for dependent males and females. Several problems complicate attempts at therapy. First is the intensity of both the drug effect and the intense behavior-reinforcing action of cocaine. Second is the pronounced tendency toward relapse, with cocaine-related activities acting as a cue to an increased craving for the drug. Third, most cocaine addicts have a coexisting disorder involving drug dependencies and/or psychiatric disorders, including major depression, an anxiety disorder, bipolar disorder, borderline personality disorder, and/or antisocial personality disorder. Given these complications, there appear to be several areas of potential pharmacologic intervention:

1. *Aversive agents,* similar to disulfiram for alcohol dependence.

2. *Dopaminergic agents* intended both to assist in the treatment of withdrawal and to restore or enhance the dopaminergic tone of hypoactive limbic system regions. Such agents, perhaps including the antidepressant *bupropion* and the psychostimulant *methylphenidate,* might be beneficial to ameliorate withdrawal depression and the hypodopaminergic state.

3. *Anticraving agents,* perhaps including *topiramate, gabapentin, vigabatrin,* and other anticonvulsant neuromodulators (Chapter 10), as well as the as-yet-experimental cannabinoid antagonists (Chapter 18) that may prevent relapse to cocaine use following detoxification. These drugs might either reduce cue-induced craving or blunt the euphoric effect of subsequently administered cocaine.

4. *Drug-substitution agents* that would provide much the same dopaminergic effect as does cocaine yet without the abuse potential. Such a drug would be used like methadone is used in opioid dependence programs (Chapter 15).

5. *Agents for comorbid disorders* might assist in treating comorbid psychological disorders and help reduce the drive that propels a person to self-medicate with cocaine to ameliorate psychological distress.

To date, there are no clearly identified aversive agents (item 1 in the list) that induce illness when cocaine is taken. Similarly, there are no clearly defined agents that work through a process of substitution, as methadone can substitute for heroin or benzodiazepines can substitute for alcohol (item 4). However, progress is being made in the other three areas. Prolonged cocaine use is associated with a down regulation of dopamine receptors and a reduction in the absolute number of such receptors. Thus, cocaine withdrawal leads to a hypofunctional dopaminergic system, a state that probably persists for weeks or months after drug abstinence. Perhaps an alternate cocainelike agent (item 2) with less abuse potential might help maintain receptor activity until new receptors are generated. Methylphenidate (Ritalin) and bupropion (Wellbutrin) are two example of such drugs. With both, however, even though positive results can be demonstrated, the results are not clinically robust (Roache et al., 2000).

Anticraving or antirelapse agents (item 3) are an area of intense study. Studies are currently focusing on two areas: antiepileptic neuro-modulators and cannabinoid antagonists. Gabapentin (Neurontin; Chapter 10), a neuromodulator, has been reported to be effective in the treatment of cocaine dependence (Myrick et al., 2001; Raby and Coomaraswamy, 2004). Vigabatrin (*gamma-vinyl-GABA*, an antiepileptic drug available in Europe and in clinical trial in the United States) exhibits anticraving effects against alcohol, heroin, nicotine, and cocaine (Brodie et al., 2003; Gardner et al., 2002). Vigabatrin is an irreversible inhibitor of the enzyme *GABA transaminase*; it increases GABA activity and attenuates drug-induced increases in extracellular nucleus accumbens dopamine as well as the behaviors associated with this dopamine increase (Gerasimov et al., 1999; Schiffer et al., 2003). Vigabatrin is being studied for use in treating cocaine dependence; its use is limited by a drug-induced loss of some portion of visual field (peripheral vision) in about 10 to 30 percent of people taking the drug (McDonagh et al., 2003). The visual field damage may be a result of vigabatrin-induced atrophy of the optic nerve (Frisen and Malmgren, 2003). It remains to be determined how significant this side effect will be and how its occurrence rate can be reduced.

As discussed in Chapter 18, cannabinoid antagonists (blockers of anandamide receptors) can be demonstrated to be remarkably effective anticraving agents. The next few years should clarify the usefulness of antiepileptics and cannabinoid antagonists in the treatment of cocaine (and other drug) cravings.

Currently most amenable to treatment are disorders that co-occur with cocaine dependency. The majority of people who abuse cocaine have a history of depression and a positive family history for affective illness (Brown et al., 1998). Because cocaine blocks the presynaptic dopamine transporter, it resembles mechanistically the pharmacologic actions of the antidepressant *bupropion* (Welbutrin; Chapter 9). Margolin and colleagues (1995), however, reported that bupropion was only minimally effective. A few studies have reported favorable effects of tricyclic antidepressants, such as *desipramine* and *imipramine*, in improving mood and prolonging abstinence in patients (with coexisting depression) who have withdrawn from cocaine. Similarly, the SSRI antidepressant *fluoxetine* (Prozac; Chapter 9) has been reported to alleviate comorbid depression and reduce cocaine use, although Mendelson and Mello (1996) found fluoxetine to be of minimal use.

Levin and coworkers (1998) note that 35 percent of cocaine abusers seeking treatment have a history of childhood attention deficit hyperactivity disorder (ADHD), and approximately 15 percent of cocaine abusers seeking treatment may have adult ADHD. They evaluated the efficacy of long-acting *methylphenidate* (Ritalin SR) on 12 patients with comorbid cocaine dependence abuse and adult ADHD, noting that the combined intervention of the drug plus relapse prevention therapy reduced both the ADHD and the cocaine dependency.

Psychosocial Interventions for Cocaine Dependence

With the (to date) failure of successful pharmacological approaches to the treatment of cocaine dependence, psychosocial interventions offer the most promise. Approaches to treatment are many, from classic 12-step recovery programs resembling that of Alcoholics Anonymous to interventions utilizing individual and/or group drug counseling, cognitive-behavioral therapy, supportive-expressive psychodynamic therapy (Crits-Christoph et al., 1999), or behavioral reinforcement approaches (Silverman et al., 1996). Compared with professional psychotherapy, a manual-guided combination of intensive individual drug counseling and group drug counseling certainly has promise for the treatment of cocaine dependence.

AMPHETAMINES

The amphetamines (see Figure 7.4) are a structurally defined group of drugs, all of which produce a variety of effects on both the CNS and the autonomic nervous system.[3] Amphetamines are also called *sympathomimetic agents* because they mimic the actions of adrenaline (epinephrine, one of the transmitters of our "sympathetic" nervous system). Amphetamines produce vasoconstriction, hypertension, tachycardia, and other signs and symptoms of our normal alerting response. These drugs also stimulate the CNS, producing tremor, restlessness, increased motor activity, agitation, insomnia, and loss of appetite. These actions result from an indirect action involving the presynaptic release of dopamine and norepinephrine and, to a lesser extent, direct stimulation of postsynaptic catecholamine receptors. Representative amphetamines include amphetamine (sold as *Adderall* for the treatment of ADHD), dextroamphetamine (*Dexedrine*), and methamphetamine (*Methadrine*).

Amphetamines have long been used to treat a variety of disorders. Between 1935 and 1946, a list of 39 conditions for which amphetamine could be used in treatment was developed. The list included schizophrenia, morphine addiction, tobacco smoking, heart block, head injury, radiation sickness, hypotension, seasickness, severe hiccups, and caffeine dependence. During World War II, amphetamines were used to fight fatigue and enhance the performance of people in the armed services. In the 1960s, amphetamines were used as diet pills. Today, use is largely restricted to the clinical treatment of childhood, adolescent, and adult ADHD (Chapter 12). Spencer and coworkers (2004) discuss psychostimulants in adult ADHD.

In some individuals, therapeutic use has led to compulsive abuse. Large-scale abuse (usually oral ingestion of amphetamine tablets) began in the late 1940s, primarily by students and truck drivers in efforts to maintain wakefulness, temporarily increase alertness, and delay sleep. Amphetamines continued to be used (and abused) as appetite suppressants, despite the fact that the anorectic effect persists only over the first two weeks of treatment, after which time it diminishes. In the

---

[3]The *autonomic nervous system* (ANS) is frequently called the visceral nervous system because it regulates and maintains the homeostasis of the body's internal organs. It controls the function of the heart, the flow of blood, and the functioning of the digestive tract, and it regulates other internal functions that are essential for maintaining the balance necessary for life. The ANS is divided into two subdivisions—the *sympathetic* and the *parasympathetic*. The latter can be viewed as maintaining our "vegetative" functions, while the former handles the body's response to stress, fright, fear, and other responses that demand an immediate alerting response. Neurotransmitters in the sympathetic division of the ANS include epinephrine (adrenaline), norepinephrine, and dopamine.

late 1960s, the abuse pattern of amphetamines changed with the advent of injectable forms of amphetamine. These injectable products (by legitimate manufacturers) have been discontinued. Use by injection today involves the illicit injection of methamphetamine. Therefore, today, interest in the amphetamines involves two areas:

- Therapeutic use in the treatment of narcolepsy and attention-deficit/hyperactivity disorder. Although efficacy can be demonstrated and wide use in treating ADHD continues, new alternatives are becoming clinically available.
- Compulsive misuse and drug dependency, especially with the amphetamine derivative *methamphetamine* in its various illicit forms and routes of administration (including the smoking of freebase methamphetamine).

Mechanism of Action

The amphetamines exert virtually all their physical and psychological effects by causing the release of norepinephrine and dopamine from presynaptic storage sites in nerve terminals (King and Ellinwood, 1997). The behavioral stimulation and increased psychomotor activity appear to follow from the resulting stimulation of the dopamine receptors in the mesolimbic system, including the nucleus accumbens (Solanto, 1998). The high-dose stereotypical behavior (including constant repetition of meaningless acts) appears to involve dopamine neurons in the caudate nucleus and putamen of the basal ganglia.

The actions leading to an increase in aggressive behavior are complex. Clinically, this behavioral stimulant action is seen primarily in adults suffering from psychostimulant toxicity and consists of increases in stereotypical, repetitive behaviors. In children, low doses of amphetamines are used therapeutically to reduce aggressive behavior and activities characteristic of ADHD; in adults with a history of ADHD, behavioral calming can also occur.

Pharmacological Effects

As stated, amphetamines exert their peripheral and central actions largely by causing the release of norepinephrine and dopamine from presynaptic nerve terminals (see Figure 7.2). All the physical and behavioral effects of the amphetamines appear to follow from this action. Note that the release of dopamine increases the amount of dopamine available to the postsynaptic receptor, much as does cocaine. Both drugs have the net effect of increasing the amount of dopamine available (although through two different mechanisms). Indeed, cocaine abusers have difficulty distinguishing between the subjective effects of 8 to 10 milligrams of cocaine and 10 milligrams of dextroamphetamine when both are administered intravenously.

The pharmacological responses to amphetamines vary with the specific drug, the dose, and the route of administration. In general, with amphetamine itself, effects may be categorized as those observed at low to moderate doses (5 to 50 milligrams), usually administered orally, and those observed at high doses (more than approximately 100 milligrams), often administered intravenously. These dose ranges are not the same for all amphetamines. For example, dextroamphetamine is three to four times more potent than amphetamine. Low to moderate doses of dextroamphetamine range from 2.5 to 20 milligrams, while high doses are 50 milligrams or more. Because methamphetamine is even more potent, dose ranges must be lowered even more.

At low doses, all amphetamines increase blood pressure, slow heart rate, relax bronchial muscle, and produce a variety of other responses that follow from the body's alerting response. In the CNS, amphetamine is a potent psychomotor stimulant, producing increased alertness, euphoria, excitement, wakefulness, a reduced sense of fatigue, loss of appetite, mood elevation, increased motor and speech activity, and a feeling of power. Although task performance is improved, dexterity may deteriorate. When short-duration, high-intensity energy output is desired, such as during an athletic competition, a user's performance may be enhanced, despite the fact that his or her dexterity and fine motor skills may be impaired. Amphetamine metabolites are excreted in the urine and are detectable for up to 48 hours.

At moderate doses (20 to 50 milligrams), additional effects of amphetamine include stimulation of respiration, slight tremors, restlessness, a greater increase in motor activity, insomnia, and agitation. In addition, amphetamines prevent fatigue, suppress appetite, promote wakefulness, and cause sleep deprivation.

A person who chronically uses high doses of amphetamine suffers from a different set of drug effects. Stereotypical behaviors include continual, purposeless, repetitive acts, sudden outbursts of aggression and violence, paranoid delusions, and severe anorexia. The harmful effects that are seen in the high-dose user include psychosis and abnormal mental conditions, weight loss, skin sores, infections resulting from neglected health care, and a variety of other consequences that occur both because of the actions of the drug itself and because of poor eating habits, lack of sleep, or the use of unsterile equipment for intravenous injections. Most high-dose users show a progressive deterioration in their social, personal, and occupational affairs. Also seen is amphetamine psychosis with paranoid ideation; many addicts must be hospitalized intermittently for treatment of episodes of psychosis. Today, psychosis is especially seen in people who abuse methamphetamine.

The toxic dose of amphetamine varies widely. Severe reactions can occur from low doses (20 to 30 milligrams). On the other hand, people who have not developed tolerance have survived doses of 400 to 500 milligrams. Even larger doses are tolerated by chronic users. The slogan "Speed kills" refers not only to a direct fatal effect of single doses of amphetamine but also to the deteriorating mental and physical condition that occurs in the addicted user.

The possibility of adverse effects of amphetamines taken either licitly or illicitly during pregnancy have been little studied. There is no clear-cut pattern of congenital anomalies, although there is some consensus that infants born of amphetamine-using mothers have a degree of growth retardation and lower birth weights. An increased rate of intracerebral hemorrhage can be observed, probably brought on by drug-induced increases in blood pressure in both the mother and the fetus. In the long term, there is evidence of psychometric deficits, poor academic performance, behavioral problems, cognitive slowing, and general maladjustment.

Dependence and Tolerance

As potent psychomotor stimulants and behavior-reinforcing agents, the amphetamines are prone to compulsive abuse. Physical dependence is readily induced in both humans and laboratory animals and follows a classical positive conditioning model (the positive reward leads to further drug use). Once drug use is stopped, the individual experiences a withdrawal syndrome, although it is less dramatic than the withdrawal associated with either opioids (Chapter 15) or barbiturates (Chapter 5). As Bernstein (1995) stated:

> Withdrawal symptoms associated with the amphetamines include increased appetite, weight gain, decreased energy, and increased need for sleep. Patients may develop a voracious appetite and sleep for several days after amphetamines are discontinued. Paranoid symptoms may persist during drug withdrawal, but generally do not develop as a result of withdrawal. The patient suddenly discontinuing amphetamine use may develop severe depression and become suicidal. Management of amphetamine withdrawal does not require detoxification, but does require appropriate and cautious clinical observation of the patient, recognition of depression, and treatment with an appropriate antidepressant drug if clinically necessary. . . . High-potency antipsychotic drugs, such as haloperidol, may be necessary [to treat paranoid reactions]. (p. 495)

Tolerance rapidly develops and can necessitate higher and higher doses, which starts a vicious circle of drug use and withdrawal. At this point, tolerance to the euphoriant effects develops, and periods of prolonged binge drug use begin. This tolerance combined with the memory of drug-induced highs leads to further drug intake, social withdrawal, and a focus on procuring drugs. Comer and coworkers (2001) studied the effects of 5 and 10 milligrams of methamphetamine twice daily on nonusers in a controlled setting. Positive feelings toward the drug were experienced only on day 1; on subsequent days the subjects felt a loss of positive effects and increases in negative feelings (dizziness, nausea, depression, and so on). This rapid development of tolerance to the positive effects may lead to the psychotic consequences in long-term use.

Ice: A Free-Base Form of Methamphetamine

Methamphetamine is a more potent drug than dextroamphetamine. Generally considered to be an illicit drug, manufactured in clandestine laboratories, methamphetamine was actually a licit drug, effective in the treatment of ADHD. Today, however, after so much negative publicity, it is rarely used legitimately and illicit use dominates. Methamphetamine is easily synthesized from readily obtainable chemicals. In animals, methamphetamine has been implicated as a neurotoxic agent, and toxicity has now been demonstrated in humans. As a drug of abuse, methamphetamine is also known as "speed," "crystal," "crank," "go," and "ice," with considerable overlap in nomenclature with other amphetamines except for ice, which refers to the smokable form of methamphetamine.

Like cocaine hydrochloride, methamphetamine (the hydrochloride salt) is broken down at the temperatures that must be achieved for it to be vaporized for smoking. However, when converted to its base, methamphetamine can be effectively vaporized and inhaled in smoke. Methamphetamine hydrochloride is used orally, by intravenous injection, and by snorting; the base form (ice) is administered by smoking. The speed of ice's absorption through the lungs and mucous membranes is as rapid or even more rapid than intravenous injection of methamphetamine hydrochloride. Thus, ice is to methamphetamine as crack is to cocaine: the free-base, concentrated, smokable form of the parent compound. Unlike crack, methamphetamine has an extremely long half-life (about 12 hours), resulting in an intense, persistent drug action. As a form of methamphetamine, ice is between 90 and 100 percent pure. Chronic use can result in serious and persistent psychiatric, cardiovascular, metabolic, and neuromuscular changes.

Pharmacokinetics

Smoking ice results in its near-immediate absorption into plasma, with additional absorption continuing over the next 4 hours. The blood level then progressively declines. The biological half-life of methamphetamine is more than 11 hours. After distribution to the brain, about 60 percent of the methamphetamine is slowly metabolized in the liver, and the end products are excreted through the kidneys, along with unmetabolized methamphetamine (about 40 percent is excreted unchanged) and small amounts of its pharmacologically active metabolite, amphetamine.

Pharmacological Effects

The effects of methamphetamine closely resemble those produced by cocaine. Both are potent psychomotor stimulants and positive reinforcers; self-administration is extremely difficult to control and modify, especially in abusers who use the drug either by injection or by smoking. Repeated high doses of methamphetamine are associated with violent behavior and paranoid psychosis. Such doses cause long-lasting decreases in dopamine and serotonin in the brain. These changes appear to be persistent, at best. Just as prolonged cocaine use can result in psychoses resembling paranoid schizophrenia, smoking ice produces a pattern of acute delusional and psychotic behavior. However, unlike that of cocaine, ice-induced psychosis can persist for days or weeks. Fatalities have resulted from cardiac toxicity.

Methamphetamine Neurotoxicity

As noted, prolonged use of methamphetamine is associated with a variety of toxicities, including psychosis. Sato noted in 1992 that behavioral and mental changes appear to persist long after the cessation of methamphetamine use. This conclusion led to speculation that methamphetamine may cause some sort of long-lasting or persistent injury to the brain. Laboratory studies in the 1990s noted evidence of neuronal death (loss of both dopaminergic and serotonergic neurons) in rodents treated with large doses of methamphetamine. In rhesus monkeys, neurotoxic effects were seen for as long as 4 years after the last drug exposure. There was speculation that methamphetamine abuse might be associated with reductions in the functioning of the presynaptic dopamine transporter.

Ernst and coworkers (2000) studied 26 abstinent methamphetamine abusers with a history of methamphetamine dependence. The abusers were "clean," had no history of alcohol abuse or dependence, and had used methamphetamine for at least 12 months at least 5 days per week and took at least 0.5 gram per day. Routes of former drug use had been by snorting, smoking, and intravenous injection. The test instrument was magnetic resonance spectroscopy and MRI. Measured were the brain concentrations of a neuronal marker, N-acetylaspartate, reductions of which are associated with neuronal damage. The subjects displayed metabolic abnormalities in frontal cortex, frontal white matter, and basal ganglia. Neuronal reductions averaged about 6 percent and indicated reduced neuronal density or neuronal content, primarily in frontal lobes. This study related the first in vivo evidence for neuronal injury as a result of methamphetamine use.

The researchers concluded that the abnormalities "may be related to persistent abnormal behaviors, such as violence, psychosis, and personality changes, which are observed in some individuals months or even years after their last drug use" (p. 1348). This conclusion can explain the alterations seen in frontal lobe "executive functioning" observed in long-time methamphetamine users, even during periods of abstinence. To allay fears of neuronal damage with low doses of amphetamines, the authors stated that low doses of methamphetamine may be preferential for serotonin neurons and that the dopamine neurotoxicity may not occur with the low-dose regimens used to treat ADHD.

Volkow and coworkers (2001a,b) demonstrated in detoxified methamphetamine abusers that dopamine transporter function was reduced in the basal ganglia for at least 11 months after drug cessation. Further, these reductions were associated with persistent motor slowing and memory impairments. Glucose metabolism was also reduced in the basal ganglia, indicating reduced neuronal activity even long after cessation of drug use. Sekine and coworkers (2001) extended this work and demonstrated a dose-dependent and duration of use-dependent reduction in dopamine transporter density and function in the basal ganglia and (even more) in the frontal cortex and the nucleus accumbens (executive and reward centers). These alterations persisted long after cessation of drug use. The reductions were associated with persistent neuropsychiatric symptoms. Volkow and coworkers (2001c) correlated this reduction in transporter density with reductions in dopamine-2 receptors and with reductions in brain metabolism in dopamine-innervated areas of brain. Therefore, methamphetamine selectively injures dopamine neurons, generally without inducing cell death.

Larsen and coworkers (2002) examined the mechanism leading to methamphetamine-caused neurotoxicity. They started with the hypothesis that methamphetamine induces redistribution of dopamine from the intracellular nerve terminal vesicular storage pool into the cytoplasm, where the dopamine can be oxidized to produce reactive oxygen species that, in turn, cause the neurotoxic damage. In their studies in rodents, methamphetamine promoted the synthesis of dopamine via "up regulation" of the activity of the enzyme *tyrosine hydroxylase*. This activity elevated the dopamine levels in the cytoplasm and promoted the formation of "autophagic granules," particularly in neuronal terminals and ultimately in the cell bodies of dopamine neurons. They proposed that "methamphetamine neurotoxicity results from the induction of a specific cellular pathway that is activated when DA cannot be effectively sequestered in synaptic vesicles, thereby producing oxyradical stress, autophagy, and neurite degeneration" (p. 8951).

Wang and coworkers (2004) compared brain glucose metabolism, motor tests, and verbal memory tests in three groups of patients: a control group of people who were not drug dependent, methamphetamine abusers evaluated after a short period (< 6 months) of abstinence, and methamphetamine abusers evaluated after a long period (12 to 17 months) of abstinence. After both short-term and long-term abstinence, abusers exhibited persistent decreases in glucose metabolism both in the basal ganglia and in the nucleus accumbens, implying long-lasting changes in dopamine cell activity as well as the "persistence of amotivation and anhedonia observe in detoxified methamphetamine abusers" (p. 242).

These data indicate that long-term methamphetamine abuse leads to persistent reductions in striatal, frontal cortical, and nucleus accumbens dopamine function, activity, and numbers. The reductions are associated with persistent positive psychotic symptom ratings. Thus, methamphetamine abuse leads both to neurotoxic injury in humans (actual structural damage) and to a chronic psychotic state that may be difficult to treat. These permanent or at least persistent neurobehavioral alterations may be expressed as alterations in sleep or sexual function, depression, movement disorders, frontal lobe "executive" functioning, or schizophrenia.

Nonamphetamine Behavioral Stimulants

An amphetamine is any drug with the basic amphetamine nucleus (see Figure 7.4). A *nonamphetamine behavioral stimulant* does not have this basic nucleus (Figure 7.5), but it shares the same action of potentiating the sympathomimetic actions of the dopamine. Nonamphetamine stimulants include *ephedrine* (found in nature in the Chinese herb ma-huang), *methylphenidate, pemoline,* and *sibutramine.* The latter three drugs are used in the medical treatment of ADHD, narcolepsy, and obesity, among other medical disorders.

Ephedrine today has little use in medicine; most use has been in herbal medicine (Chapter 16). It acts by transiently releasing body epinephrine, a normal adrenal hormone that causes elevations in blood pressure and heart rate, and increases one's level of alertness. Ephedrine also transiently reduces appetite. It has been incorporated into numerous herbal and dietary supplements for both energy and weight loss. Unfortunately, the drug can be toxic or even fatal when combined with other stimulant drugs such as caffeine.

Methylphenidate (Ritalin) is a nonamphetamine behavioral stimulant in which the regular-release formulation has a half-life of 2 to 4 hours (see Table 7.1). Its primary medical use is in the treatment of

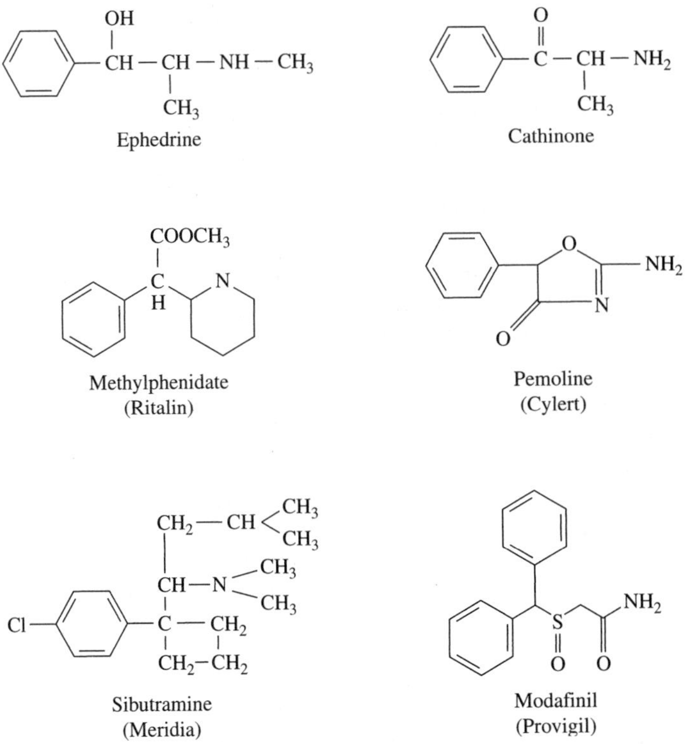

FIGURE 7.5 Structures of two naturally occurring catecholamine psychostimulants—ephedrine (from *Ephedra,* or ma-huang) and cathinone (from *Catha edulis,* or khat)]—and four synthetic noncatecholamine psychostimulants used in medicine—methylphenidate (Ritalin), pemoline (Cylert), sibutramine (Meridia), and modafinil (Provigil).

ADHD. (This use is discussed at length in Chapter 12.) Mechanistically, methylphenidate increases the synaptic concentration of dopamine by blocking the presynaptic dopamine transporter (a cocainelike action) and also perhaps by slightly increasing the release of dopamine (an amphetaminelike or ephedrinelike action). When these drugs are injected intravenously, experienced cocaine users can perceive a cocainelike or amphetaminelike rush, an action not usually experienced with oral dosage. Volkow and coworkers (1998) demonstrated that at clinically relevant doses, methylphenidate blocked more than 50 percent of the dopamine transporters 60 minutes after oral administration (Figure 7.6). They postulated that the slow uptake of methylphenidate into the brain after oral administration accounts for the low rate of positive reinforcement effects seen with use of the drug.

Although this clinical action of methylphenidate is thought to be exerted through dopaminergic increases, Gainetdinov and coworkers

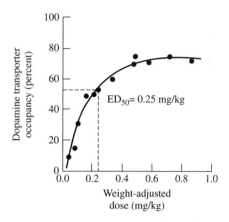

FIGURE 7.6 Levels of dopamine transporter occupancy for weight-adjusted doses of methylphenidate. Also shown is the dose required to occupy 50 percent of the dopamine transporters (ED_{50}). [From Volkow et al. (1998), p. 1327.]

(1999) demonstrated in mice that lacked the gene for the dopamine transporter that methylphenidate still calmed hyperactivity in a novel environment, presumably by raising serotonin levels to balance the animal's high brain dopamine level. In these animals, *fluoxetine* (Prozac; Chapter 9) exerted a methylphenidatelike action, presumably by also blocking the presynaptic serotonin transporter. Thus, at least in some people, ADHD may represent an imbalance between dopamine and serotonin systems.

Pemoline (Cylert) is a CNS stimulant structurally dissimilar to either methylphenidate or amphetamine (see Figure 7.5). Pemoline is presumed to reduce ADHD symptoms by potentiating CNS dopaminergic transmission. It is thought to have a lower abuse potential than does either methylphenidate or amphetamines. Its use is limited by reports of rare instances of hepatitis, necessitating close monitoring of liver function. If pemoline is used to treat ADHD, patients (or their parents) sign a consent form, and liver function tests are recommended at 2-week intervals.

Sibutramine (Meridia) is a serotonin, norepinephrine, and (to a lesser extent) dopamine reuptake inhibitor (it blocks their presynaptic transporter proteins). Sibutramine is currently marketed as an anti-obesity agent (Berkowitz et al., 2003; Leung et al., 2003). Sibutramine is structurally related to amphetamine (see Figure 7.5), but it is not literally an amphetamine. Sibutramine is rapidly metabolized in the liver to active metabolites that are responsible for the drug's pharmacologic actions. These metabolites reach a peak concentration in plasma in 3 to 4 hours; their half-life is 14 to 16 hours (Cole et al., 1998). Modest weight losses for up to one year have been reported, and the drug does not appear to have a potential for compulsive misuse. Significant increases in heart rate and blood pressure have been reported and may limit the use of the drug. Appolinario and coworkers (2002) reported that sibutramine produced complete resolution of binge eating in obese patients.

Modafinil is a nonamphetamine psychostimulant whose exact mechanism of psychostimulant action remains unclear but is thought to be unique. Modifinil may potentiate excitatory glutamate neurotransmission and inhibit the activity of GABA neurons in the cerebral cortex and the nucleus accumbens, altering the balance between glutamate and GABA transmission. It may not be associated with dependence or compulsive abuse.

Modafinil is used clinically to maintain daytime wakefulness in the treatment of narcolepsy, an inherited disorder of sleep (U.S. Modafinil in Narcolepsy Multicenter Study Group, 1998). Chapter 6 discussed the use of gamma hydroxybuyrate (GHB) to improve sleep patterns in people with narcolepsy. Note that modafinil and GHB act through vastly different mechanisms and therapeutic approaches.

Potential uses of modafinil include cognitive improvement in patients with Alzheimer's disease, use in the treatment of ADHD (Chapter 12), and potentiation of the action of antidepressant drugs (Chapter 9). The drug appears to have only minimal peripheral side effects such as drug-induced hypertension. Modafinil is an important addition to the pharmacologic treatment of narcolepsy as well as an interesting stimulant for evaluation for use in the treatment of other CNS disorders amenable to treatment with a psychostimulant.

STUDY QUESTIONS

1. Compare and contrast cocaine and amphetamine.

2. What is crack? What is ice?

3. Describe the three major actions of cocaine.

4. Discuss the effects of cocaine on the fetus.

5. What are some of the issues and therapeutic approaches to treating cocaine dependence?

6. Describe the behavioral states that are observed in high-dose amphetamine users.

7. Describe the effects of amphetamine on neurotransmission, neurotransmitters, and the CNS reward system.

8. Discuss the evidence for and against methamphetamine neuro-toxicity.

9. Compare and contrast psychostimulants with clinical antidepressants.

10. What is meant by the phrase "Speed kills"?

11. What is modafinil? How does it differ from amphetamine? What are its potential uses?

REFERENCES

Appolinario, J. C., et al. (2002). "An Open-Label Trial of Sibutramine in Obese Patients with Binge-Eating Disorder." *Journal of Clinical Psychiatry* 63: 28–30.

Bartzokis, G., et al. (1999). "Magnetic Resonance Imaging Evidence of 'Silent' Cerebrovascular Toxicity in Cocaine Dependence." *Biological Psychiatry* 45: 1203–1211.

Berkowitz, R. I., et al. (2003). "Behavioral Therapy and Sibutramine for the Treatment of Adolescent Obesity: A Randomized Controlled Trial." *Journal of the American Medical Association* 289: 1851–1853.

Bernstein, J. G. (1995). *Drug Therapy in Psychiatry*, 3rd ed. St. Louis: Mosby.

Boghdadi, M. S., and R. J. Henning (1997). "Cocaine: Pathophysiology and Clinical Toxicology." *Heart and Lung* 26: 466–483.

Brodie, J. D., et al. (2003). "Treating Cocaine Addiction: From Preclinical to Clinical Trial Experience with Gamma-Vinyl GABA." *Synapse* 50: 261–265.

Brown, R. A., et al. (1998). "Depression Among Cocaine Abusers in Treatment: Relation to Cocaine and Alcohol Use and Treatment Outcome." *American Journal of Psychiatry* 155: 220–225.

Bunney, E. B., et al. (2001). "Electrophysiological Effects of Cocaethylene, Cocaine, and Ethanol on Dopaminergic Neurons of the Ventral Tegmental Area." *Journal of Pharmacology and Experimental Therapeutics* 297: 696–703.

Calatayud, J., and A. Gonzalez (2003). "History of the Development and Evolution of Local Anesthesia Since the Coca Leaf." *Anesthesiology* 98: 1503–1508.

Chang, L., et al. (1999). "Gender Effects on Persistent Cerebral Metabolic Changes in the Frontal Lobes of Abstinent Cocaine Users." *American Journal of Psychiatry* 156: 716–722.

Cole, J. O., et al. (1998). "Sibutramine: A New Weight Loss Agent Without Evidence of the Abuse Potential Associated with Amphetamines." *Journal of Clinical Psychopharmacology* 18: 231–236.

Comer, S. D., et al. (2001). "Effects of Repeated Oral Methamphetamine Administration in Humans." *Psychopharmacology* 155: 397–404.

Crits-Christoph, P., et al. (1999). "Psychosocial Treatments for Cocaine Dependence: National Institute on Drug Abuse Collaborative Treatment Study." *Archives of General Psychiatry* 56: 493–502.

Dussault, C., et al. (2001). "The Role of Cocaine in Fatal Crashes: First Results of the Quebec Drug Study." *Annals of the Proceedings of the Association for the Advancement of Automotive Medicine* 45: 125–137.

Ernst, T., et al. (2000). "Evidence for Long-Term Neurotoxicity Associated with Methamphetamine Abuse: A ^{1}H MRS Study." *Neurology* 54: 1344–1349.

Frank, D. A., et al. (2001). "Growth, Development, and Behavior in Early Childhood Following Prenatal Cocaine Exposure: A Systematic Review." *Journal of the American Medical Association* 285: 1613–1625.

Frisen, L., and K. Malmgren (2003). "Characterization of Vigabatrin-Associated Optic Atrophy." *Acta Ophthalmologica Scandinavica* 81: 466–473.

Gainetdinov, R. R., et al. (1999). "Role of Serotonin in the Paradoxical Calming Effect of Psychostimulants on Hyperactivity." *Science* 283: 397–401.

Gardner, E. L., et al. (2002). "Gamma-Vinyl-GABA, an Irreversible Inhibitor of GABA Transaminase, Alters the Acquisition and Expression of Cocaine-Induced Sensitization in Male Rats." *Synapse* 46: 240–250.

Gerasimov, M. R., et al. (1999). "Gamma-Vinyl GABA Inhibits Methamphetamine, Heroin, or Ethanol-Induced Increases in Nucleus Accumbens Dopamine." *Synapse* 34: 11–19.

Kilts, C. D., et al. (2001). "Neural Activity Related to Drug Craving in Cocaine Addiction." *Archives of General Psychiatry* 58: 334–341.

Kilts, C. D., et al. (2004). "The Neural Correlates of Cue-Induced Craving in Cocaine-Dependent Women." *American Journal of Psychiatry* 161: 233–241.

King, G. R., and E. H. Ellinwood, Jr. (1997). "Amphetamines and Other Stimulants." In J. H. Lowinson, P. Ruiz, R. B. Millman, and J. G. Langrod, eds., *Substance Abuse: A Comprehensive Textbook*, 3rd ed. (pp. 207–223). Baltimore: Williams & Wilkins.

Konkol, R. J., and G. D. Olsen. (1996). *Prenatal Cocaine Exposure*. Boca Raton, FL: CRC Press.

Larsen, K. E., et al. (2002). "Methamphetamine-Induced Degeneration of Dopaminergic Neurons Involves Autophagy and Upregulation of Dopamine Synthesis." *Journal of Neuroscience* 22: 8951–8960.

Lavori, P. W., et al. (1999). "Plans, Designs, and Analyses for Clinical Trials of Anti-Cocaine Medications: Where We Are Today." *Journal of Clinical Psychopharmacology* 19: 246–256.

Leung, W. Y., et al. (2003). "Weight Management and Current Options in Pharmacotherapy: Orlistat and Sibutramine." *Clinical Therapeutics* 25: 58–80.

Levin, F. R., et al. (1998). "Methylphenidate Treatment for Cocaine Abusers with Adult Attention-Deficit/Hyperactivity Disorder: A Pilot Study." *Journal of Clinical Psychiatry* 59: 300–305.

Little, B. B., et al. (1998). "Cocaine Abuse During Pregnancy." In L. C. Gilstrap and B. B. Little, eds., *Drugs and Pregnancy*, 2nd ed. (pp. 419–444). New York: Chapman & Hall.

Little, K. Y., et al. (1998). "Cocaine, Ethanol, and Genotype Effects on Human Midbrain Serotonin Transporter Binding Sites and mRNA Levels." *American Journal of Psychiatry* 155: 207–213.

Little, K. Y., et al. (2003). "Loss of Striatal Vesicular Monoamine Transporter Protein (VMAT2) in Human Cocaine Users." *American Journal of Psychiatry* 160: 47–55.

Margolin, A., et al. (1995). "A Multicenter Trial of Bupropion for Cocaine Dependence in Methadone-Maintained Patients." *Drug and Alcohol Dependence* 40: 125–131.

McDonagh, J., et al. (2003). "Peripheral Retinal Dysfunction in Patients Taking Vigabatrin." *Neurology* 61: 1690–1694.

Mendelson, J. H., and N. K. Mello (1996). "Management of Cocaine Abuse and Dependence." *New England Journal of Medicine* 334: 965–972.

Myrick, H., et al. (2001). "Gabapentin in the Treatment of Cocaine Dependence: A Case Series." *Journal of Clinical Psychiatry* 62: 19–23.

Raby, W. N., and S. Coomaraswamy (2004). "Gabapentin Reduces Cocaine Use Among Addicts from a Community Clinic Sample." *Journal of Clinical Psychiatry* 65: 84–86.

Roache, J. D., et al. (2000). "Laboratory Measures of Methylphenidate Effects in Cocaine-Dependent Patients Receiving Treatment." *Journal of Clinical Psychopharmacology* 20: 61–68.

Rocha, B. A., et al. (1998). "Increased Vulnerability to Cocaine in Mice Lacking the Serotonin-1B Receptor." *Nature* 393: 175–178.

Rounsaville, B. J., et al. (1991). "Psychiatric Diagnoses of Treatment-Seeking Cocaine Abusers." *Archives of General Psychiatry* 48: 43–51.

Sato, M. (1992). "A Lasting Vulnerability to Psychosis in Patients with Previous Methamphetamine Psychosis." *Annals of the New York Academy of Sciences* 654: 160–170.

Schiffer, W. K., et al. (2003). "Sub-Chronic Low Dose Gamma-Vinyl GABA (Vigabatrin) Inhibits Cocaine-Induced Increases in Nucleus Accumbens Dopamine." *Psychopharmacology* 168: 339–343.

Sekine, Y., et al. (2001). "Methamphetamine-Related Psychiatric Symptoms and Reduced Brain Dopamine Transporters Studied with PET." *American Journal of Psychiatry* 158: 1206–1214.

Silverman, K., et al. (1996). "Sustained Cocaine Abstinence in Methadone Patients Through Voucher-Based Reinforcement Therapy." *Archives of General Psychiatry* 53: 409–415.

Singer, L. T., et al. (2002). "Cognitive and Motor Outcomes of Cocaine-Exposed Infants." *Journal of the American Medical Association* 287: 1952–1960.

Solanto, M. V. (1998). "Neuropsychopharmacological Mechanisms of Stimulant Drug Action in Attention-Deficit Hyperactivity Disorder: A Review and Integration," *Behavioral Brain Research* 94: 127–152.

Sora, I., et al. (2001). "Molecular Mechanisms of Cocaine Reward: Combined Dopamine and Serotonin Transporter Knockouts Eliminate Cocaine Place Preference." *Proceedings of the National Academy of Sciences* 98: 5300–5305.

Spencer, T., et al. (2004). "Stimulant Treatment of Adult Attention-Deficit/ Hyperactivity Disorder." *Psychiatric Clinics of North America* 27: 361–372.

Substance Abuse and Mental Health Services Administration (2003). *Results from the 2002 National Survey on Drug Use and Health: National Findings.* Rockville, MD: Office of Applied Studies, NHSDA Series H-22, DHHS Publication number SMA 03-3836.

Sutton, M. A., et al. (2003). "Extinction-Induced Upregulation in AMPA Receptors Reduces Cocaine-Seeking Behaviour." *Nature* 421: 70–75.

Toomey, R., et al. (2003). "A Twin Study of the Neuropsychological Consequences of Stimulant Abuse." *Archives of General Psychiatry* 60: 303–310.

U.S. Modafinil in Narcolepsy Multicenter Study Group (1998). "Randomized Trial of Modafinil for the Treatment of Pathological Somnolence in Narcolepsy." *Annals of Neurology* 43: 88–97.

Van Gorp, W. G., et al. (1999). "Declarative and Procedural Memory Functioning in Abstinent Cocaine Abusers." *Archives of General Psychiatry* 56: 85–89.

Volkow, N. D., et al. (1998). "Dopamine Transporter Occupancies in the Human Brain Induced by Therapeutic Doses of Oral Methylphenidate." *American Journal of Psychiatry* 155: 1325–1331.

Volkow, N. D., et al. (2001a). "Association of Dopamine Transporter Reduction with Psychomotor Impairment in Methamphetamine Abusers." *American Journal of Psychiatry* 158: 377–382.

Volkow, N. D., et al. (2001b). "Higher Cortical and Lower Subcortical Metabolism in Detoxified Methamphetamine Abusers." *American Journal of Psychiatry* 158: 383–389.

Volkow, N. D., et al. (2001c). "Low Level of Brain Dopamine D_2 Receptors in Methamphetamine Abusers: Association with Metabolism in the Orbitofrontal Cortex." *American Journal of Psychiatry* 158: 2015–2021.

Volpe, J. J. (1992). "Effects of Cocaine Use on the Fetus." *New England Journal of Medicine* 327 :399–407.

Wang, G.-J., et al. (2004). "Partial Recovery of Brain Metabolism in Methamphetamine Abusers After Protracted Abstinence." *American Journal of Psychiatry* 161: 242–248.

White, F. J. (1998). "Cocaine and the Serotonin Saga." *Nature* 393: 118–119.

Wilson, L. D., et al. (2001). "Cocaine, Ethanol, and Cocaethylene Cardiotoxicity in an Animal Model of Cocaine and Ethanol Abuse." *Academic Emergency Medicine* 8: 211–222

Wise, R. A. (1998). "Drug Activation of Brain Reward Pathways." *Drug and Alcohol Dependence* 51: 13–22.

Woolverton, W. L., and K. M. Johnson (1992). "Neurobiology of Cocaine Abuse." *Trends in Pharmacological Sciences* 13: 193–200.

Caffeine and Nicotine

CAFFEINE

Caffeine is the most commonly consumed psychoactive drug in the world; in the United States it is consumed daily by up to 80 percent of the adult population. Caffeine is found in significant concentrations in coffee, tea, cola drinks, chocolate candies and ice creams, fortified waters, and cocoa. As shown in the Chapter 8 Appendix on page 252, the average cup of coffee contains about 100 milligrams of caffeine.[1] A 12-ounce bottle of cola contains about 40 milligrams. The caffeine content of chocolate may be as high as 25 milligrams per ounce. Over-the-counter (OTC) wakefulness-promoting drugs (for example, NoDoz, Vivarin) contain as much as 200 milligrams of caffeine per tablet. Excedrin contains 75 milligrams of caffeine per tablet, Anacin about half that amount, and NoDoz 100 milligrams (the same as a cup of brewed coffee). Many herbal-based OTC products contain fairly large amounts of caffeine. Among regular caffeine ingesters, daily intake averages between 200 and 500 milligrams, correlating with two to five

---

[1]The caffeine content of coffee varies widely. One hundred milligrams is often used as an average. However, among locally popular "gourmet" coffees, one company's coffee averages 200 milligrams per 8 fluid ounces. Thus, a 12-ounce cup of black coffee has 300 milligrams; the 16-ounce "grande" has 400 milligrams. Mixed coffee drinks have less caffeine because of added milk or flavorings. Another company's coffee averages 80 to 90 milligrams; a third's has 100 to 125 milligrams of caffeine per 8 ounces. McCusker and coworkers (2003) found wide variances in caffeine content (260 to 564 milligrams) in the same 16-ounce beverage at the same outlet on 6 consecutive days.

cups of coffee daily. Regulatory agencies impose no restrictions on the sale or use of caffeine, nor is the human consumption of caffeine-containing beverages commonly considered to be drug abuse.

Pharmacokinetics

Taken orally, caffeine is rapidly and completely absorbed. Significant blood levels of caffeine are reached in 30 to 45 minutes; complete absorption occurs over the next 90 minutes. Levels in plasma peak at about 2 hours and decrease thereafter.

Caffeine is freely and equally distributed throughout the total body water. Thus, caffeine is found in almost equal concentrations in all parts of the body and the brain. Like all psychoactive drugs, caffeine freely crosses the placenta to the fetus.

The liver metabolizes most caffeine before the kidneys excrete it. Only about 10 percent of the drug is excreted unchanged. The structure and metabolism of caffeine are shown in Figure 8.1. The two major metabolites of caffeine, theophylline and paraxanthine, behave similarly to caffeine; a third metabolite, theobromine, does not.

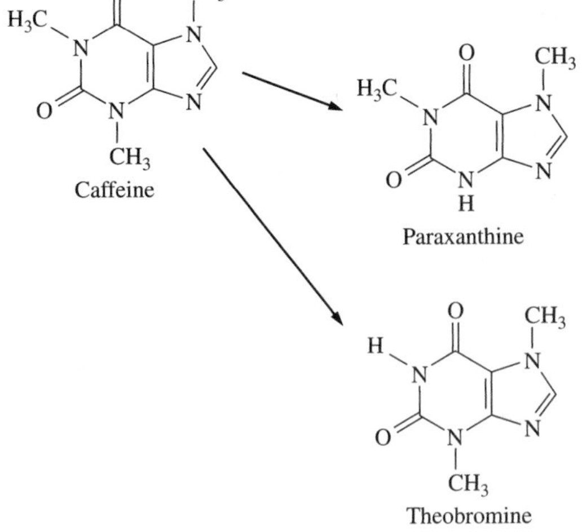

FIGURE 8.1 Metabolism of caffeine to three end products.

Caffeine is metabolized by the CYP1A2 subgroup of hepatic drug-metabolizing enzymes. Interestingly, certain SSRI-type antidepressants such as fluvoxamine (Chapter 9) are potent inhibitors of CYP1A2, and people taking these antidepressants can exhibit unexpected toxicity or intolerance to caffeine as plasma levels of caffeine rise (Rasmussen et al., 1998). Antidepressants that do not inhibit CYP1A2 (for example, venlafaxine) do not alter caffeine's metabolism (Amchin et al., 1999).

The half-life of caffeine is about 3.5 to 5 hours in most adults, which accounts for nighttime wakefulness in some people. Caffeine's half-life is extended in infants, in pregnant women, and in the elderly. During the latter part of pregnancy, the half-life of caffeine increases from 3 to 10 hours.

In cigarette smokers, caffeine's half-life is shortened; however, when smoking is terminated, caffeine's half-life increases. This reduced metabolism of caffeine when smoking ceases can result in an increase in plasma caffeine levels and may contribute to cigarette withdrawal symptoms in heavy coffee drinkers, particularly since caffeine induces anxiety at high doses (Feldman et al., 1997).

Pharmacological Effects

The CNS-stimulant, cardiac, respiratory, and diuretic effects of caffeine have been known for many years. Therapeutically, these effects have been used to treat a variety of disorders including asthma, narcolepsy, and migraine, and as an adjunct to aspirin or other analgesics in treating headache and other pain syndromes.

Caffeine is an effective psychostimulant, ingested to obtain a rewarding effect, usually described as feeling more alert and competent. Behavioral effects seen at the lower doses of caffeine include increased mental alertness, a faster and clearer flow of thought, and wakefulness. Fatigue is reduced and the need for sleep is delayed. This increased mental awareness results in sustained intellectual effort for prolonged periods of time without significant disruption of coordinated intellectual or motor activity. Tasks that involve delicate muscular coordination and accurate timing or arithmetic skills may be adversely affected. These effects occur after oral doses as small as 100 or 200 milligrams, that is, one to two cups of coffee. Most individuals adjust, or titrate, their intake of caffeine to achieve these beneficial effects while minimizing undesirable effects. Heavy consumption of coffee (12 or more cups per day, or 1.5 grams of caffeine) can cause agitation, anxiety, tremors, rapid breathing, and insomnia. The lethal dose of caffeine is about 10 grams, which is equivalent to 100 cups of coffee.

People with anxiety disorders tend to be quite sensitive to the anxiogenic properties of caffeine, especially if they usually avoid caffeinated products and do not develop a tolerance to this effect. In general, individuals with anxiety disorders are wise to totally avoid caffeinated products. *Caffeinism* is a clinical syndrome, characterized by both CNS and peripheral symptoms, produced by the overuse or overdoses of caffeine. CNS symptoms include increases in anxiety, agitation, insomnia, and mood changes. Peripheral symptoms include tachycardia, hypertension, cardiac arrhythmias, and gastrointestinal disturbances. Caffeinism is usually dose related, with doses higher than about 500 to 1000 milligrams (1 gram, or 5 to 10 cups of coffee) causing the most unpleasant effects. Cessation of caffeine ingestion resolves these symptoms. Much lower doses of caffeine produce this syndrome in sensitive individuals, such as those with an underlying anxiety disorder. The usually ingested doses of caffeine do not induce panic attacks in normal individuals. However, in people predisposed to panic disorders, the peripheral and the CNS effects of caffeine are exaggerated.

Outside the CNS, caffeine exerts significant effects, some beneficial and some adverse. Caffeine has a slight stimulant action on the heart. It increases both cardiac contractility (increases the workload of the heart) and cardiac output. While this might predispose a person to hypertension (caffeine does raise blood pressure in adults prone to hypertension), caffeine also dilates the coronary arteries, providing more oxygen to a harder-working heart (Rachima-Maoz et al., 1998). Thus, it remains controversial whether or not caffeine increases the incidence of heart disease and deaths due to cardiac disease. Certainly, individuals with hypertension or heart disease might do well to minimize exposure to caffeinated products.

It should be noted that caffeine exerts an opposite effect on cerebral blood vessels; it constricts these vessels, thus decreasing blood flow to the brain by about 30 percent and reducing pressure within the brain. This action can effect striking relief from headaches, especially migraines (Lipton et al., 1998). Other physical actions of caffeine include bronchial relaxation (an antiasthmatic effect), increased secretion of gastric acid, and increased urine output.

Mechanism of Action

Caffeine exerts a variety of effects on the CNS. In Figure 8.2, note the close structural resemblance of caffeine and a naturally occurring substance in the brain called *adenosine*. It should therefore not be surprising that caffeine might bind to any receptors to which adenosine binds. Caffeine does have a strong affinity for adenosine receptors, but binding is not accompanied by adenosinelike action; caffeine blocks access of adenosine to its receptors, and thus caffeine is classified as

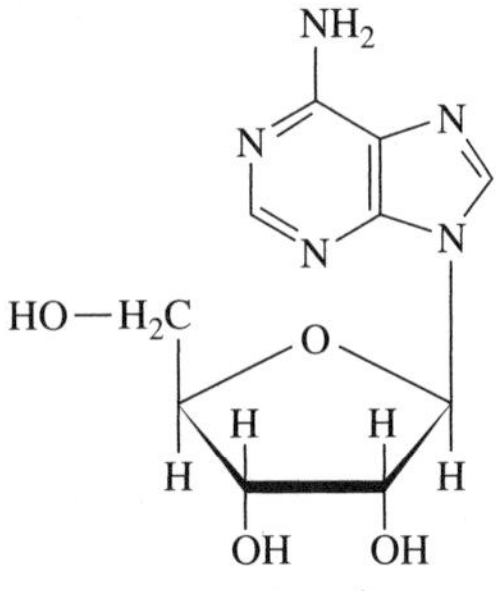

FIGURE 8.2 Structure of adenosine. Note the similarity of adenosine to caffeine (shown in Figure 8.1).

an *adenosine antagonist* at physiological concentrations comparable to one or more cups of coffee (Figure 8.3). In mice lacking a specific subtype of adenosine receptor, caffeine has only depressant (not stimulant) effects on behavioral activity (Ledent et al., 1997).

Since caffeine is an adenosine antagonist, a pharmacological effect of caffeine would not be expected unless adenosine receptors were tonically active under stimulation by adenosine. Adenosine is a *neuromodulator* that influences the release of several neurotransmitters in the CNS. There do not appear to be discrete adenosinergic pathways in the CNS; rather, adenosinergic neurons form a diffuse and important system sometimes labeled a depressant. Adenosine appears to exert sedative, depressant, and anticonvulsant actions; blockade of adenosine receptors produces actions considered to be stimulating or anxiogenic. Adenosine receptors decrease the discharge rate of many central neurons, increasing the activity of dopaminergic, cholinergic, glutaminergic, and noradrenergic neurons. Blockade of these receptors accounts for the modest reward and the increased vigilance and mental acuity actions of caffeine. Adenosine also limits the release of acetylcholine, inhibition of which by caffeine accounts for the behavioral arousal effects of caffeine.

The positive stimulatory effects of caffeine appear in large measure to be due to blockade of the adenosine receptors that stimulate GABAergic neurons of inhibitory pathways to the dopaminergic reward system of the striatum. Thus, caffeine may produce its behavioral effects by removing the negative modulatory effects of adenosine from dopamine receptors, thus indirectly stimulating dopaminergic activity (Garrett and Griffiths, 1997). Caffeine does not induce a release of dopamine in the nucleus accumbens; it leads to a release of dopamine in the prefrontal cortex, which is consistent with caffeine's alerting effects with only mild behavioral reinforcing properties. Nehlig (1999) concluded that caffeine appears to fulfill some of the criteria for drug dependence and shares with amphetamines

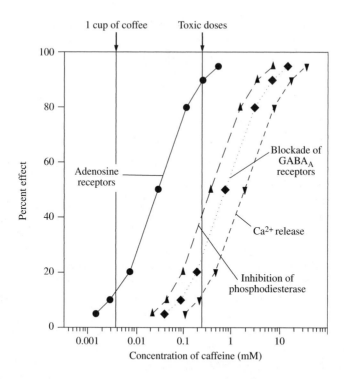

FIGURE 8.3 Adenosine receptors as site of action of caffeine. Concentration-dependent effects of caffeine to block adenosine receptors, to block GABA receptors, to inhibit calcium ion release (Ca^{2+}), and to inhibit the activity of the enzyme phosphodiesterase. At concentrations approximating one cup of coffee and continuing through to a toxic dose, only the adenosine receptors are affected. [From J. W. Daly and B. B. Fredholm, "Caffeine–An Atypical Drug of Dependence," *Drug and Alcohol Dependence* 51 (1998), p.201.]

and cocaine a certain specificity of action on the cerebral dopaminergic system. However, it does not act on the dopaminergic structures related to reward, motivation, and addiction.

Reproductive Effects

Is caffeine safe during pregnancy? Caffeine, the most widely used psychotropic drug, is consumed by at least 75 percent of pregnant women via caffeinated beverages. Despite its widespread use, the safety of this habit during pregnancy is unresolved. As early as 1980, the U.S. Food and Drug Administration cautioned pregnant women to minimize their intake of caffeine. On the other hand, D'Ambrosio (1994) concluded that it is difficult to implicate caffeine, even at the highest levels of daily consumption, as a genotoxin to humans.

A 1999 study by Klebanoff and coworkers concluded that the consumption of large amounts of caffeine (perhaps more than 6 to 10 cups of coffee per day) is associated with an increased risk of spontaneous abortion but that moderate consumption does not increase the risk. Recently, Wisborg and coworkers (2003) reported a prospective study of over 18,000 pregnancies in Denmark, asking whether there was an association between coffee consumption during pregnancy and the risks of either stillbirth or infant death in the first year of life. Pregnant women who drank eight or more cups of coffee per day during pregnancy had an increased risk of having a stillbirth compared with women who did not consume caffeine. Adjusting for smoking habits and alcohol consumption modestly reduced the risk. There was no association between caffeine consumption and infant deaths during the first year of life. The overall risk of stillbirth increased from 4 per 1000 births in nonusers of caffeine to 12 per 1000 in drinkers of 8 or more cups of coffee per day. At 4 to 7 cups per day, the risk was 7 per 1000 births. It does not appear that caffeine itself is a human teratogen, and caffeine does not appear to affect the course of normal labor and delivery.

Tolerance and Dependence

Chronic use of caffeine, even in regular daily doses as low as 100 milligrams, is associated with habituation and tolerance, and discontinuation may produce a withdrawal syndrome (Evans and Griffiths, 1999). People who drink the most coffee complain of headache (the most common symptom), drowsiness, fatigue, and a generally negative mood state on withdrawal from caffeine. Withdrawal symptoms typically begin slowly, maximize after 1 or 2 days, and cease within a few days; readministering caffeine rapidly relieves withdrawal symptoms. These symptoms certainly indicate the development of a state of mild dependency. Other reported withdrawal signs include impaired intellectual and motor performance, difficulty with concentration, drug (caffeine) craving, and other psychological complaints. Greden and Walters (1997) wrote:

> Caffeine . . . will continue to be the norm in most people. However, caffeinism and caffeine withdrawal also continue to be common and clinically important but unrecognized, underdiagnosed even when recognized, and untreated in many treatment settings. . . . Clinicians who actively consider the diagnosis of caffeinism in their patients will be surprised at how many afflicted subjects are identified, impressed at how many are helped by removal of the offending agent, and pleased to know that almost all are grateful. (p. 305)

NICOTINE

Nicotine is one of the three most widely used psychoactive drugs in our society; the others are caffeine and ethyl alcohol. Despite the fact that nicotine has no therapeutic applications in medicine, its potency, its widespread use, and its toxicity give it immense importance. Nicotine and the other ingredients in tobacco are responsible for a wide variety of health problems, including the deaths of more than 1100 Americans every day. Every year, 4.3 million persons die prematurely worldwide as a result of cigarette smoking (Ezzati and Lopez, 2003). Half these deaths occur in developing countries and half occur in rich nations.

Prior to about the mid-1960s, cigarette smoking was considered chic. Today, after more than 40 years of U.S. government reports on the adverse health consequences of cigarettes, cigarette smoking is being increasingly shunned as unhealthy and unwise. Nevertheless, each day 6000 American teenagers try their first cigarette and 3000 children become regular smokers; almost 1000 of them will eventually die from diseases related to smoking. Also, 9 in 10 smokers become addicted before age 21. Today, in the United States, 3 million adolescents are smokers. Advertisements for cigarettes still appeal to children, and, in subtle ways, the depiction of smoking as okay continues.

On the positive side, half of all persons who have ever smoked cigarettes have quit, and the proportion of American adults who smoke fell from 50 percent in 1965 to 25 percent in 1998. About 1 million potential deaths have been averted or postponed by persons who have quit smoking. Millions more deaths will be avoided or postponed in the twenty-first century. Even 30 years ago, the Surgeon General of the United States identified smoking as the major *preventable* cause of death and disability, and this finding will probably continue to be the case. In this discussion, it is important to note the following:

- Nicotine is the primary active ingredient in tobacco.

- Nicotine is only 1 of about 4000 compounds released by the burning of cigarette tobacco.

- Nicotine accounts only for the acute pharmacological effects of smoking and for the dependence on cigarettes. The adverse, long-term cardiovascular, pulmonary, and carcinogenic effects of cigarettes are related to other compounds contained in the product.

- While nicotine itself may have some adverse effects, its delivery device (the tobacco cigarette) is responsible for much of its toxicity.

Pharmacokinetics

Nicotine is readily absorbed from every site on or in the body, including the lungs, buccal and nasal mucosa, skin, and gastrointestinal tract. Easy and complete absorption forms the basis for the recreational abuse of smoked or chewed tobacco, as well as the medical use of nicotine (in treating nicotine dependency) in chewing gums, nasal sprays, transdermal skin patches, and smokeless inhalers.

Nicotine is suspended in cigarette smoke in the form of minute particles (tars), and it is quickly absorbed into the bloodstream from the lungs when the smoke is inhaled, although absorption is much slower than once thought and arterial concentrations of nicotine rise rather slowly (Rose et al., 1999). It is likely that blood rapidly saturates with nicotine, and blood leaving the lungs (to the left side of the heart) can carry only a modest amount of drug. Thus, the arterial concentration rises slowly, even though blood carried to the brain at the initiation of smoking is near-saturated with nicotine, accounting for the early "rush" perceived with the first cigarette.

Most cigarettes contain between 0.5 and 2.0 milligrams of nicotine, depending on the brand. Only about 20 percent (between 0.1 and 0.4 milligram) of the nicotine in a cigarette is actually inhaled and absorbed into the smoker's bloodstream; the hepatic enzyme CYP2A6 rapidly metabolizes the remainder. Individuals in whom the CYP2A6 enzyme is absent (or inhibited by certain drugs) have higher blood levels of nicotine and lower levels of its metabolite (Nakajima et al., 2000).

A smoker can readily avoid acute toxicity, because inhalation as a route of administration offers exceptional controllability of the dose. The user-controlled frequency of breaths, the depth of inhalation, the time the smoke is held in the lungs, and the total number of cigarettes smoked all allow the smoker to regulate the rate of drug intake and thus control the blood level of nicotine. The pharmacokinetic goals of nicotine administration were summarized by Sellers (1998):

> Tobacco smoking is a complex but highly regulated behavior that has as its goal the maintenance of steady-state brain levels of the highly addictive psychoactive agent nicotine. Smokers "self-regulate" the level of nicotine in their system to produce desired effects (e.g., relaxation, increased concentration) and to avoid unpleasant adverse effects associated with too high (e.g., dizziness) or too low concentrations (e.g., desire to smoke or withdrawal). (p. 179)

Smokers wake in the morning in a state of nicotine deficiency. Characteristically, they will smoke one or more cigarettes fairly rapidly to achieve a blood level of about 15 ng/ml and continue smoking through the day to maintain this level. The smoker does not behave this way consciously, but the behavior occurs nevertheless. The elimination half-life of nicotine in a chronic smoker is about 2 hours, necessitating frequent administration of the drug to avoid withdrawal symptoms or drug craving. When nicotine is administered orally in the form of snuff, chewing tobacco, or gum, blood levels of nicotine are comparable to those achieved by smoking.

Nicotine is quickly and thoroughly distributed throughout the body, rapidly penetrating the brain, crossing the placental barrier, and appearing in all bodily fluids, including breast milk. There are no barriers in the body to the distribution of nicotine.

The liver metabolizes approximately 80 to 90 percent of the nicotine administered to a person either orally or by smoking before the kidneys excrete it. The primary metabolite of nicotine is *cotinine* (Figure 8.4), and this substance serves as a marker of both tobacco use and exposure to environmental smoke. Interestingly, black smokers may have higher cotinine levels than do white smokers, "indicating either slower elimination of cotinine or higher intake of nicotine per cigarette in blacks" (Perez-Stable et al., 1998, p. 155). It may also "explain why blacks find it harder to quit and are more likely to experience higher rates of lung cancer than white smokers" (Caraballo et al., 1998).

Pharmacological Effects

Nicotine is the only pharmacologically active drug in tobacco smoke apart from carcinogenic tars. It exerts powerful effects on the brain, the spinal cord, the peripheral nervous system, the heart, and various other body structures.

Effects on the Brain

In the early stages of smoking, nicotine causes nausea and vomiting by stimulating both the vomiting center in the brain stem and the sensory receptors in the stomach. Tolerance to this effect develops rapidly. Nicotine stimulates the hypothalamus to release a hormone, antidiuretic hormone (ADH), that causes fluid retention. Nicotine reduces

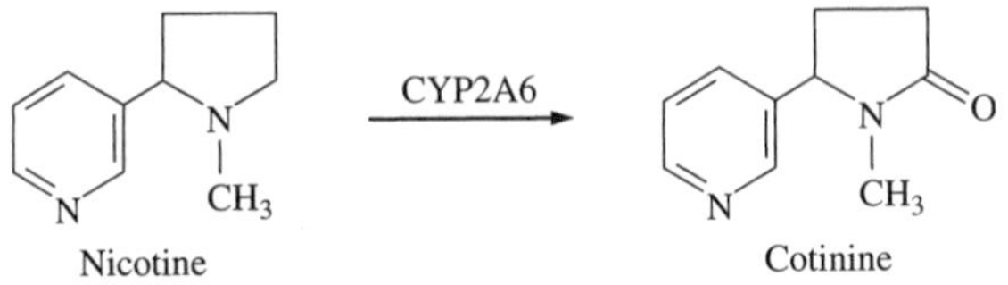

FIGURE 8.4 Structures of nicotine and its metabolite cotinine.

the activity of afferent nerve fibers coming from the muscles, leading to a reduction in muscle tone. This action may be involved (at least partially) in the relaxation a person may experience as a result of smoking. Nicotine also reduces weight gain, probably by reducing appetite.

Nicotine produces multiple actions in the CNS, resulting in increases in psychomotor activity, cognitive functioning, sensorimotor performance, attention, and memory consolidation. Rose and coworkers (2003) reported that nicotine increases blood flow to the CNS structures that mediate arousal and reward, suggesting a link between activation of these structures and the positive motivational effects of nicotine. At higher doses, nicotine can induce nervousness and tremors and, in toxic overdosage, seizures. Cigarette smoking is also associated with an increased occurrence of panic attacks and panic disorder (Breslau and Klein, 1999).

Nicotine improves performance in a variety of cognitive tasks, such as vigilance and rapid information processing (Picciotto, 1998), probably a reflection of activation of frontal cortical executive functioning (Rose et al., 2003). The beneficial effects of nicotine seem to be greatest for tasks requiring working memory rather than long-term memory. Smokers often state that they will smoke a cigarette before doing a complex task that requires attention and arousal, perhaps combining the drug's anxiolytic action with its stimulant action. The brain regions activated by nicotine include areas involved in cognition, working memory, attention, motivation, mood and emotion (frontal lobes and cingulate cortex), and behavioral arousal and vigilance (locus coeruleus).

Several reports note an antidepressant effect of nicotine as well as the comorbidity of depression and cigarette use. Salin-Pascual and coworkers (1996), noting a high frequency of cigarette smoking among individuals with major depression, found that, in nonsmokers, transdermal nicotine patches produced remarkable improvements in depression (Figure 8.5). They postulated that the high rate of smoking among depressed individuals might, in part, represent an attempt at self-medication to assist in dealing with some of their depressive symptoms. In agreement with this concept, Fergusson and colleagues (1996), in a study of 16-year-olds, reported:

> There was evidence of clear comorbidity between depressive disorders and nicotine dependence in this cohort of 16-year-olds; subjects with depression had odds of nicotine dependence that were more than 4.5 times the odds for those without depression. This relationship was similar for male and female subjects. These results suggest that comorbidities between nicotine dependence and depression are well established by the age of 16 years. (p. 1047)

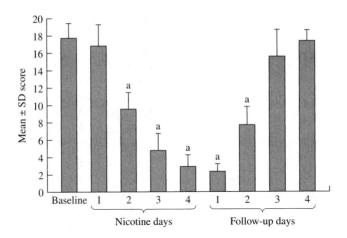

FIGURE 8.5 Hamilton Rating Scale for Depression ratings of 10 depressed patients before, during, and after administration of nicotine patches. A significant reduction was observed on the second day of nicotine patches and continued until the second follow-up day. [From Salin-Pascual et al. (1996), p.388.]

Riggs and coworkers (1999) noted that most of the risk for adolescent smoking, as well as the subsequent development of nontobacco substance involvement, is mediated through the presence of conduct disorder. Additional comorbidity, such as ADHD and depression, adds to the already high risk of smoking imparted by conduct disorder. This study highlights the contribution of comorbidity to smoking initiation and the need for coordinated assessment and treatment of smoking cessation along with concurrent treatment of other drug use and psychiatric comorbidity such as ADHD and major depression in such youths.

Anda and coworkers (1999), in a retrospective survey of over 9000 adults, found a strong relationship between smoking behaviors and adverse childhood experiences, including emotional, physical, and sexual abuse; spouse abuse; parental separation or divorce; and growing up with a substance-abusing, mentally ill, or incarcerated household member. At least one of these experiences was listed by 63 percent of respondents. As the number of adverse experiences increased, the likelihood of being an early and a current smoker increased, as did the likelihood of being currently depressed. The authors speculated that for these people cigarette smoking may provide a mood-elevating effect and that "unconscious selection of cigarette use could occur in situations of chronic distress, such as depression" (p. 1657). How conduct disorder and adult ADHD fit into this pattern was not addressed.

Klimek and coworkers (2001) compared postmortem brains of smokers with those of nonsmokers. Brains of long-term smokers were characterized by 50 percent reductions in receptor densities in the locus coeruleus, an effect that is the opposite of that in the brains of depressed or suicidal patients. Dierker and coworkers (2002) reported evidence for a shared association between dysthymia and cigarette smoking. These reports reinforce the idea of an antidepressant action of nicotine and that smoking by depressed people may be a form of self-medication.

Since depression and a propensity to smoke nicotine-containing cigarettes may be closely linked, does cessation of smoking in patients with a history of depression lead to relapse to depressive episodes? Tsoh and coworkers (2000) and Glassman and coworkers (2001) addressed this issue and noted that cessation of smoking placed depressed patients at risk of relapse, at least over a one-year period postcessation (Figure 8.6). This certainly needs to be kept in mind during treatment for smoking cessation in patients with a history of depression or dysthymia. Treatment of cigarette dependence is discussed later in this chapter.

Nicotine exerts a potent behavioral-reinforcing action, especially in the early phases of drug use. The reinforcing action of nicotine involves indirect activation of midbrain dopamine neurons. In the veteran smoker, this reinforcing action diminishes, and the user smokes primarily to relieve or avoid withdrawal symptoms. Spring and coworkers (2003) studied the rewarding effects of cigarette smoking in schizophrenic

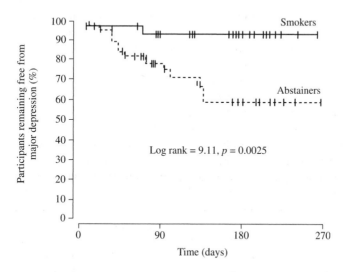

FIGURE 8.6 Time (in days) for individuals who both were smokers and had a history of major depression to relapse to an episode of depression. Two groups of depressed patients were studied. One group (solid line) of 34 smokers continued to smoke and few relapsed. The second group of 42 patients (dashed line) abstained from smoking, and almost 50 percent experienced a depressive episode within 4 months of smoking cessation. [From Glassman et al. (2001), p.1931.]

patients, depressed patients, and patients with no psychiatric history. While all three groups of patients recognized the drawbacks associated with smoking, schizophrenic and depressed smokers perceived more benefits than did nonpatients and found cigarettes more appealing than alternative rewards. Thus, these two groups of patients found that smoking offered ongoing rewards while patients without a mental health history did not. This may be important for the tailoring of smoking withdrawal programs to different patient populations.

Some of the acute effects and motivational responses elicited by nicotine can be modulated by the endogenous cannabinoid system (Chapter 18), which supports the existence of a physiological interaction between these two systems (Castane et al., 2002; Gonzalez et al., 2002). Much remains to be learned about this interaction. Also, people with a lifetime history of mental illness (including drug and alcohol abuse disorders) smoke 44 percent of the cigarettes smoked yearly in the United States and are twice as likely to smoke as are those without a history of mental illness (Haustein et al., 2002).

Effects on the Body

In addition to its effects on the CNS, normal doses of nicotine can increase heart rate, blood pressure, and cardiac contractility. In nonatherosclerotic coronary arteries, nicotine initiates vasodilation, increasing blood flow to meet the increased oxygen demand of the heart muscle. In atherosclerotic coronary arteries (which cannot dilate), however, cardiac ischemia can result when the oxygen supply fails to meet the oxygen demand created by the drug's cardiac stimulation. This occurrence can precipitate angina or myocardial infarction (a heart attack).

Mechanism of Action

Nicotine exerts virtually all its CNS and peripheral effects by activating certain specific acetylcholine receptors (nicotinic receptors). In the peripheral nervous system, activation of these receptors causes an increase in blood pressure and heart rate, causes release of epinephrine (adrenaline) from the adrenal glands, and increases the tone, secretions, and activity of the gastrointestinal tract.

In the CNS, the nicotine-sensitive acetylcholine receptors are widely distributed and may be located on the presynaptic nerve terminals of dopamine-, acetylcholine-, and glutamine-secreting neurons. Activation of nicotinic receptors by nicotine facilitates the release of these transmitters and increases their actions in the brain.

Nicotine increases dopamine levels in the mesocortico-limbic system involving the ventral tegmentum, nucleus accumbens, and forebrain. This increase accounts for the behavioral reinforcement, stimulant, antidepressant, and addictive properties of the drug.

The increased acetylcholine resulting from nicotine administration contributes to the cognitive potentiation and memory facilitation properties of the drug. It may also be responsible for the arousal effects commonly seen with smoking. It is at least theoretically possible that nicotine (if administered other than by cigarette smoking) might have some use in delaying the onset of some of the cognitive deficits seen in Alzheimer's disease. Finally, the facilitation of glutaminergic neurotransmission might contribute to the improvement in memory functioning seen in nicotine users.

Tolerance and Dependence

Nicotine does not appear to induce any pronounced degree of biological tolerance. On the other hand, nicotine clearly induces both physiological and psychological dependence in a majority of smokers (Breslau et al., 2001; Hughes, 2001). Only a minority appears capable of abrupt cessation of smoking without abstinence symptoms, and even they are prone to craving and relapse. As early as 1988, the Surgeon General of the United States made the following conclusions:

- Cigarettes and other forms of tobacco are addicting.
- Nicotine is the drug in tobacco that causes addiction.
- The pharmacologic and behavioral processes that determine tobacco addiction are similar to those that determine addiction to drugs such as heroin and cocaine.
- More than 300,000 cigarette-addicted Americans die yearly as a consequence of their addiction. (Today this number approaches 440,000 per year.)

Despite all the verbal exchanges between public, regulatory, medical, political, and industry sources, the scientific case that nicotine is addictive is overwhelming:

> Patterns of use by smokers and the remarkable intractability of the smoking habit point to compulsive use as the norm. Studies in both animal and human subjects have shown that nicotine can function as a reinforcer, albeit under a more limited range of conditions than with some other drugs of abuse. In drug discrimination paradigms, there is some cross-generalization between nicotine on the one hand, and amphetamine and cocaine on the other. A well-defined withdrawal syndrome has been delineated which is alleviated by nicotine replacement. Nicotine replacement also enhances outcomes in smoking cessation, roughly doubling success rates. In total, the evidence clearly identifies nicotine as a powerful drug of addiction, comparable to heroin, cocaine, and alcohol. (Stolerman and Jarvis, 1995, p. 2)

Withdrawal from cigarettes is characterized by an abstinence syndrome that is usually not life threatening. Abstinence symptoms include a severe craving for nicotine, irritability, anxiety, anger, difficulty in concentrating, restlessness, impatience, increased appetite, weight gain, and insomnia. The period of withdrawal may be intense and persistent, often lasting for many months. The difficulty in handling cigarette dependence is illustrated by the fact that cigarette smokers who seek treatment for other drug and alcohol problems often find it harder to quit cigarette smoking than to give up the other drugs. Even Sigmund Freud continued his cigar habit (20 per day) until death, in spite of an endless series of operations for mouth and jaw cancer (the jaw was eventually totally removed), persistent heart problems that were exacerbated by smoking, and numerous attempts at quitting.

Abstinent smokers displaying signs of withdrawal often tend to increase their caffeine (coffee) consumption; blood caffeine levels increase and remain elevated for as long as six months. The symptoms of nicotine withdrawal, caffeine withdrawal, and caffeine toxicity are similar enough to be confused; symptoms of nicotine withdrawal may be a mixture of nicotine withdrawal and caffeine toxicity (Swanson et al., 1994).

Toxicity

As discussed, both the acute pharmacologic effects and the withdrawal signs seen on cessation of smoking result from the nicotine in tobacco. The *tar* in tobacco is mainly responsible for the diseases associated with long-term tobacco use. Of the 440,000 deaths of people in the United States who die prematurely each year from tobacco use, 82,000 are caused by noncancerous lung diseases, 115,000 are caused by lung cancer, 30,000 are caused by cancers of other body organs, and more than 200,000 result from heart and vascular diseases. A person's life is shortened 14 minutes for every cigarette smoked. In other words, a person who smokes two packs of cigarettes a day for 20 years loses an estimated 8 years of his or her life. More than 50 million people (one out of every five Americans) alive today will die prematurely from the effects of smoking cigarettes. Cigarette smoking, the nation's greatest public health hazard, is the nation's most preventable cause of premature death, illness, and disability. For each of the approximately 22 billion packs of cigarettes sold yearly in the United States, $3.45 was spent on medical care attributable to smoking, and $3.73 in productivity losses were incurred, for a total cost of *$7.18 for each and every pack smoked* (Centers for Disease Control and Prevention, 2002).

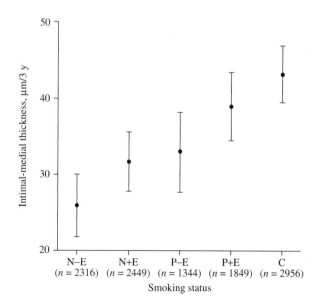

FIGURE 8.7 Mean and 95 percent confidence intervals of three-year progression in the wall thickness of the carotid artery, shown by smoking status category, after adjustment for demographic characteristics, cardiovascular risk factors, and life-style variables. N = nonsmoker. P = past smoker. C = current smoker. +E = with exposure to environmental tobacco smoke. −E = without exposure to environmental tobacco smoke. [From G. Howard et al., "Cigarette Smoking and Progression of Atherosclerosis: The Atherosclerosis Risk in Communities (ARIC) Study," *Journal of the American Medical Association* 279 (1998), p. 122.]

Cardiovascular Disease

The carbon monoxide in smoke decreases the amount of oxygen delivered to the heart muscle, while nicotine increases the amount of work the heart must do (by increasing the heart rate and blood pressure). Both carbon monoxide and nicotine increase the incidence of atherosclerosis (narrowing) and thrombosis (clotting) in the coronary arteries.[2] These three actions (and others as well) seem to underlie the dramatic increase in the risk of death from coronary heart disease in smokers compared to nonsmokers. Cigarette smokers manifest a 50 percent increase in the progression of atherosclerosis when compared with people who have never smoked (Figure 8.7).

[2]Atherosclerosis first appears as fatty deposits inside large arteries and progresses to occlusion of the arteries throughout the body; the result is clinically manifested as strokes or peripheral vascular ischemic disease. Atherosclerosis is not a disease of the elderly; it begins in youth and is readily apparent during the 15- to 34-year age span.

Finally, besides occurring in the coronary arteries, atherosclerosis occurs in other arteries as well, most notably the aorta (in the abdomen), the carotid arteries (in the neck), and the femoral and other arteries of the legs. Cigarette-induced occlusion of these vessels blocks the blood flow to important body organs and results in ischemic damage, strokes, and other disorders, causing great discomfort and disability and necessitating continuing and often futile surgical interventions.

Pulmonary Disease

In the lungs, chronic smoking results in a smoker's syndrome, characterized by difficulty in breathing, wheezing, chest pain, lung congestion, and increased susceptibility to infections of the respiratory tract. Cigarette smoking impairs ventilation and greatly increases the risk of emphysema (a form of irreversible lung damage). Smoke exposure also reduces the efficacy of the immune defense mechanisms in the lungs. About 9 million Americans suffer from cigarette-induced chronic bronchitis and emphysema. In fact, 70 percent of pulmonary diseases and deaths are tobacco related; 57,000 deaths per year result from emphysema alone.

Cancer

Although nicotine itself is not carcinogenic, the relationship between smoking and cancer is now beyond question. Cigarette smoking is the major cause of lung cancer in both men and women, causing approximately 112,000 deaths in the United States every year. More women today die from cigarette-induced lung cancer than die from breast cancer, a remarkable testament to the carcinogenicity of cigarettes. Recently, Harris and coworkers (2004) followed 940,000 male and female smokers and nonsmokers for 6 years and concluded that the risk of dying from lung cancer was the same for smokers of very low-tar, low-tar, and medium-tar cigarettes. Risk increased only in smokers of very high-tar, nonfiltered cigarettes. Only smokers who quit smoking and people who never smoked had a significantly lower risk of lung cancer.

Smoking is also a major cause of cancers of the mouth, voice box, and throat. Concomitant alcohol ingestion greatly increases the incidence of these problems. In addition, cigarette smoking is a primary cause of more than 50 percent of the nearly 10,000 deaths every year that result from bladder cancer; it is a primary cause of pancreatic cancer, and it increases the risk of cancer of the uterine cervix twofold. Of all cancer deaths in the United States, 30 percent (154,000 annually) would be prevented if no one smoked.

Effects of Passive Smoke

In addition to the direct effects of cigarettes on smokers, the environmental pollution caused by smokers can have adverse consequences for nonsmokers. About 4000 Americans die annually from lung cancer caused by other persons' smoking (so-called passive smoke), and an additional 37,000 deaths every year follow from heart disease contracted as a result of inhaling passive smoke. Nonsmokers exposed to passive smoking have a coronary death rate 20 to 70 percent higher than nonsmokers not exposed to passive smoking. Cornelius and Day (2000) demonstrated that smoking during pregnancy is associated with a number of adverse effects on the growth, cognitive development, and behavior of children. In addition, even nonsmoking mothers can place their child at risk through their own environmental exposure to tobacco smoke.

Effects During Pregnancy

Cigarette smoking adversely affects the developing fetus, leading to increases in the rates of spontaneous abortion, stillbirth, early postpartum death, and preterm deliveries (Cnattingius et al., 1999). The risk of intrauterine growth retardation is increased 40 percent, and low birth weights are common, although the weight of smoker's low-birth-weight offspring usually rises to normal at about 18 months of age (Little and Gilstrap, 1998). Even women exposed to passive smoke inhalation have low-birth-weight children. More than 2000 infant deaths per year are attributed to maternal smoking.

Cigarette smoking reduces oxygen delivery to the developing fetus, causing a variable degree of fetal hypoxia, which can result in long-term, irreversible intellectual and physical deficiencies. Milberger and coworkers (1996) presented evidence that school-age children born of mothers who smoked during pregnancy have lower intelligence quotients (IQs) and an increased prevalence of ADHD when compared with children born of nonsmoking mothers. Thus, maternal smoking may well cause neurobehavioral deficits that persist for a prolonged period of time, even decades. Indeed, maternal smoking results in offspring at increased risk of developing later childhood externalizing problems, including ADHD, oppositional defiant behavior, substance abuse, and conduct disorder (Weissman et al. 1999).

Therapy for Nicotine Dependence

The late 1990s saw dramatic advances in the recognition of nicotine dependence as a biological reality and in its treatment. Perhaps the most important advance was the development and clinical application of nicotine replacement therapies, specifically nicotine-containing gum, transdermal nicotine-containing patches, and nicotine-containing nasal sprays and inhalers. Besides nicotine replacement therapies, additional efforts have been made to identify agents that reduce cigarette cravings, relieve the distress of comorbid psychiatric illnesses, or relieve withdrawal symptoms.

Efforts began in 1996 with the publication of the first clinical practice guidelines for the treatment of nicotine-dependent individuals. Since then, several additional guidelines have been published, including a year-2000 guideline titled "A Clinical Practice Guideline for Treating Tobacco Use and Dependence, A U.S. Public Health Service Report" (Tobacco Use and Dependence Clinical Practice Guideline Panel, 2000). This report concluded:

- Tobacco dependence is a chronic condition that warrants repeated treatment until long-term or permanent abstinence is achieved.

- Effective treatments for tobacco dependence exist and all tobacco users should be offered those treatments.

- Clinicians and health care delivery systems must institutionalize the consistent identification, documentation, and treatment of every tobacco user at every visit.

- Brief tobacco dependence treatment is effective and every tobacco user should be offered at least brief treatments.

- There is a strong dose-response relationship between the intensity of tobacco dependence counseling and its effectiveness.

- Three types of counseling were found to be especially effective: practical counseling, social support as part of treatment, and social support arranged outside treatment.

- Tobacco dependence treatments are cost effective relative to other medical and disease prevention interventions; as such, all health insurance plans should include as a reimbursed benefit the counseling and pharmacotherapeutic treatments identified as being effective.

- Five first-line pharmacotherapies for tobacco dependence are effective: sustained-release bupropion, nicotine gum, nicotine inhaler, nicotine nasal spray, and nicotine patch. At least one of these medications should be prescribed in the absence of contraindications.

Rigotti (2002) reviewed the efficacy of these five pharmacotherapeutic regimes. She noted that combining pharmacotherapy and counseling was more effective than either alone. In nicotine replacement therapy, each has demonstrable efficacy in randomized, controlled trials.

Nicotine-containing patches double the long-term smoking cessation rate, while nicotine gum increases cessation rates by 50 to 70 percent. For heavy smokers, gum containing 4 milligrams of nicotine per piece is more effective than gum containing 2 milligrams. Few studies have assessed the nasal spray and the vapor inhaler, but evidence indicates that both are effective. All forms of replacement therapy indicate similar efficacy at 12 weeks; compliance is highest for the patch, intermediate for the gum, and lowest for the vapor inhaler and nasal spray. Figure 8.8 illustrates the plasma nicotine levels achieved after a smoker has smoked a cigarette, received nicotine nasal spray, begun chewing nicotine gum, or applied a nicotine patch.

Regarding sustained-release bupropion (Zyban), Rigotti concludes that, when combined with counseling, it doubles smoking cessation rates as compared with placebo. Bupropion delays smoking relapse and also results in less weight gain (Hays et al., 2001). The tricyclic antidepressant nortriptyline also seems to be efficacious. It will be interesting to see whether or not the new norepinephrine reuptake inhibitors (Chapter 9) will be efficacious. Figure 8.9 offers a smoking cessation strategy that may be used by health care workers in compliance with the recommendations of the U.S. Public Health Service. Coleman (2004) and Fiore and coworkers (2004) discuss the effectiveness of even very brief interventions and advice.

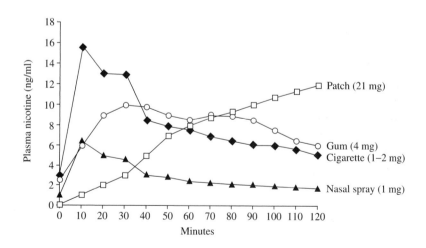

FIGURE 8.8 Plasma nicotine levels after a smoker has smoked a cigarette, received nicotine nasal spray, begun chewing nicotine gum, or applied a nicotine patch. The amount of nicotine in each product is shown in parentheses. The pattern produced by use of a nicotine inhaler (not shown) is similar to that for nicotine gum. [From Rigotti (2002), p. 510.]

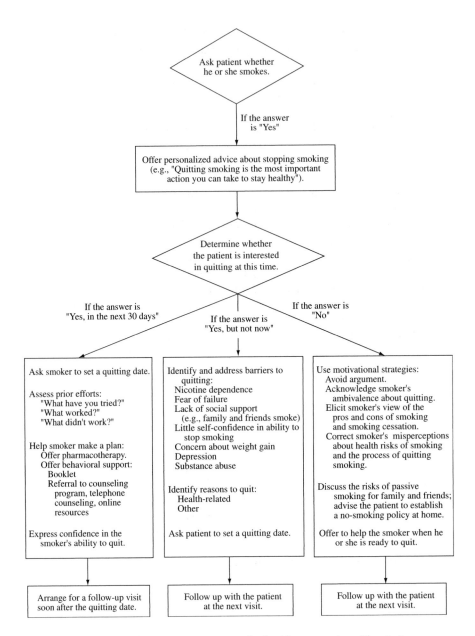

FIGURE 8.9 Smoking cessation strategy for health care workers. The strategy uses the steps recommended in Public Health Service guidelines: ask, advise, assess, assist, and arrange follow-up. [From Rigotti (2002), p. 508.]

Cromwell and coworkers (1997) estimated the cost effectiveness of implementing smoking cessation guidelines, calculating that society could expect to gain 1.7 million new quitters (of smoking) at an average cost of $3779 per quitter, $2587 per life-year saved, and $1915 for every quality-adjusted life-year saved. Discouragingly, in the majority of instances, the daily practices of health care workers fall far short of the listed national health objectives: they are not meeting the published practice guidelines either in offering counseling or in prescribing or monitoring nicotine replacement programs. Most practitioners are poorly prepared to treat nicotine dependence. For example, although 70 percent of smokers visit a physician each year, most are not advised or assisted in an attempt to quit.

Tyndale and coworkers (1999) reported that administration of a blocker of nicotine metabolism (recall that nicotine is metabolized to cotinine by CYP2A6) allows for effective oral absorption of nicotine; this might provide a new approach to treatment of tobacco dependence by making an oral nicotine replacement therapy feasible. Sellers and coworkers (2003) discuss efforts to decrease smoking behaviors through drug-induced inhibition of CYP2A6 enzyme activity.

What else might be an effective deterrent to cigarette smoking? Certainly, reducing availability and sales of cigarettes to children and adolescents is necessary. Programs oriented to reducing the attractiveness of smoking by children are effective (Bauer et al., 2000). Kobus (2003) addresses the contribution that peers have in adolescents' use of tobacco, sometimes promoting use, sometimes deterring use. These are usually extremely subtle influences, but they need addressing.

Blum and coworkers (2004) review the ongoing problems involved in integrating the many reports of the Surgeon Generals to curtail smoking. Finally, in 2003, Richard Carmona, Surgeon General of the United States, publicly supported the banning of tobacco products in the United States. This was the first time that America's top doctor and public health advocate made such a strong statement about this historically contentious and politically sensitive subject. He reportedly stated, "I see no need for any tobacco products in society"—a valid statement and opinion.

STUDY QUESTIONS

1. Differentiate the CNS stimulant actions of caffeine from those of amphetamine and cocaine.

2. Describe the mechanism of action of caffeine. How does this mechanism explain the clinical effects of the drug?

3. What is the relationship between panic attacks and caffeine?

4. Discuss the effects of caffeine in the cardiovascular system.

5. What evidence is there for and against the use of caffeine by women who are pregnant or breast-feeding?

6. Discuss the political, health, and economic issues related to tobacco. Should the FDA regulate nicotine as a drug?

7. List some of the statistics that are relevant to the health effects of cigarettes.

8. Discuss the antidepressant property of nicotine. Might this contribute to cigarette dependence? Why?

9. Are cigarettes addicting or are they merely habit forming? Defend your position.

10. Discuss the clinical uses and limitations of nicotine replacement devices. How might their efficacy be boosted?

11. If nicotine exerts an antidepressant action, what drugs or therapies might assist in withdrawal and relapse prevention?

12. Should tobacco products be banned in our society? Defend your views.

REFERENCES

Amchin, J., et al. (1999). "Effect of Venlafaxine on CYP1A2-Dependent Pharmacokinetics and Metabolism of Caffeine." *Journal of Clinical Pharmacology* 39: 252–259.

Anda, R. F., et al. (1999). "Adverse Childhood Experiences and Smoking During Adolescence and Adulthood." *Journal of the American Medical Association* 282: 1652–1658.

Bauer, U. E., et al. (2000). "Changes in Youth Cigarette Use and Intentions Following Implementation of a Tobacco Control Program: Findings from the Florida Youth Tobacco Survey, 1998–2000." *Journal of the American Medical Association* 284: 723–728.

Blum, A., et al. (2004). "The Surgeon General's Report on Smoking and Health 40 Years Later: Still Wandering in the Desert." *Lancet* 363: 97–98.

Breslau, N., and D. F. Klein (1999). "Smoking and Panic Attacks." *Archives of General Psychiatry* 56: 1141–1147.

Breslau, N., et al. (2001). "Nicotine Dependence in the United States: Prevalence, Trends, and Smoking Persistence." *Archives of General Psychiatry* 58: 810–816.

Caraballo, R. S., et al. (1998). "Racial and Ethnic Differences in Serum Cotinine Levels of Cigarette Smokers." *Journal of the American Medical Association* 280: 135–139.

Castane, A., et al. (2002). "Lack of CB1 Cannabinoid Receptors Modifies Nicotine Behavioral Responses, but Not Nicotine Abstinence." *Neuropharmacology* 43: 857–867.

Centers for Disease Control and Prevention (2002). "Annual Smoking-Attributable Mortality, Years of Potential Life Lost, and Economic Costs—United States, 1995–1999." *Journal of the American Medical Association* 287: 2355–2356.

Cnattingius, S., et al. (1999). "The Influence of Gestational Age and Smoking Habits on the Risk of Subsequent Preterm Deliveries." *New England Journal of Medicine* 341: 943–948.

Coleman, T. (2004). "Use of Simple Advice and Behavioural Support." *British Medical Journal* 328: 397–399.

Cornelius, M. D., and N. L. Day (2000). "The Effects of Tobacco Use During and After Pregnancy on Exposed Children: Relevance of Findings for Alcohol Research." *Alcohol Research and Health* 224: 242a-249.

Cromwell J., et al. (1997). "Cost-Effectiveness of the Clinical Practice Recommendations in the AHCPR Guideline for Smoking Cessation." *Journal of the American Medical Association* 278: 1759–1766.

D'Ambrosio, S. M. (1994). "Evaluation of the Genotoxicity Data on Caffeine." *Regulatory Toxicology and Pharmacology* 19: 243–281.

Dierker, L. C., et al. (2002). "Smoking and Depression: An Examination of Mechanisms of Comorbidity." *American Journal of Psychiatry* 159: 947–953.

Evans, S. M. and R. R. Griffiths. (1999). "Caffeine Withdrawal: A Parametric Analysis of Caffeine Dosing Conditions." *Journal of Pharmacology and Experimental Therapeutics* 289: 285–294.

Ezzati, M., and A. D. Lopez (2003). "Estimates of Global Mortality Attributable to Smoking in 2000." *Lancet* 362: 847–852.

Feldman, R. S., et al., (1997). *Principles of Neuropsychopharmacology.* Sunderland, MA: Sinauer.

Fergusson, D. M., et al. (1996). "Comorbidity Between Depressive Disorders and Nicotine Dependence in a Cohort of 16-Year-Olds." *Archives of General Psychiatry* 53: 1043–1047.

Fiore, M. C., et al. (2004). "Preventing 3 Million Premature Deaths and Helping 5 Million Smokers Quit: A National Action Plan for Tobacco Cessation." *American Journal of Public Health* 94: 205–210. Entire February 2004 issue is devoted to tobacco.

Garrett, B. E., and R. R. Griffiths (1997). "The Role of Dopamine in the Behavioral Effects of Caffeine in Animals and Humans." *Pharmacology, Biochemistry and Behavior* 57: 533–541.

Glassman, A. H., et al. (2001). "Smoking Cessation and the Course of Major Depression: A Follow-up Study." *Lancet* 357: 1929–1932.

Gonzalez, S., et al. (2002). "Changes in Endocannabinoid Contents in the Brain of Rats Chronically Exposed to Nicotine." *Brain Research* 954: 73–81.

Greden, J. F., and A. Walters (1997). "Caffeine." In J. H. Lowinson, P. Ruiz, R. B. Millman, and J. G. Langrod, eds., *Substance Abuse: A Comprehensive Textbook,* 3rd ed. (pp. 294–307). Baltimore: Williams & Wilkins.

Harris, J. E., et al. (2004). "Cigarette Tar Yields in Relation to Mortality from Lung Cancer in the Cancer Prevention Study II Prospective Cohort, 1982-8."*British Medical Journal* 328: 72–76.

Haustein, K. O., et al. (2002). "A Review of the Pharmacological and Psychopharmacological Aspects of Smoking and Smoking Cessation in Psychiatric Patients." *International Journal of Clinical Pharmacology and Therapeutics* 40 (2002): 404–418.

Hays, J. T., et al. (2001). "Sustained-Release Bupropion for Pharmacologic Relapse Prevention After Smoking Cessation: A Randomized, Controlled Trial." *Annals of Internal Medicine* 135: 423–433.

Hughes, J. R. (2001). "Distinguishing Nicotine Dependence from Smoking: Why It Matters to Tobacco Control and Psychiatry." *Archives of General Psychiatry* 58: 817–818.

Klebanoff, M. A., et al. (1999). "Maternal Serum Paraxanthine, a Caffeine Metabolite, and the Risk of Spontaneous Abortion." *New England Journal of Medicine* 341: 1639–1644.

Klimek, V., et al. (2001). "Effects of Long-Term Cigarette Smoking on the Human Locus Coeruleus." *Archives of General Psychiatry* 58: 821–827.

Kobus, K. (2003). "Peers and Adolescent Smoking." *Addiction* 98, Supplement 1: 37–55.

Ledent, C., et al. (1997). "Aggressiveness, Hypoalgesia, and High Blood Pressure in Mice Lacking the Adenosine A_{2A} Receptor." *Nature* 388: 674–678.

Lipton, R. B., et al. (1998). "Efficacy and Safety of Acetaminophen, Aspirin, and Caffeine in Alleviating Migraine Headache Pain: Three Double-Blind, Randomized, Placebo-Controlled Trials." *Archives of Neurology* 55: 210–217.

Little, B. B., and L. C. Gilstrap (1998). "Tobacco Use in Pregnancy." In L. C. Gilstrap and B. B. Little, eds., *Drugs and Pregnancy*, 2nd ed. (pp. 443–472). New York: Chapman & Hall.

McCusker, R. R., et al. (2003). "Caffeine Content of Specialty Coffees." *Journal of Analytical Toxicology* 27: 520–522.

Milberger, S., et al. (1996). "Is Maternal Smoking During Pregnancy a Risk Factor for Attention Deficit Hyperactivity Disorder in Children?" *American Journal of Psychiatry* 153: 1138–1142.

Nakajima, M., et al. (2000). "Deficient Cotinine Formation from Nicotine Is Attributed to the Whole Deletion of the CYP2A6 Gene in Humans." *Clinical Pharmacology and Therapeutics* 67: 57–69.

Nehlig, A. (1999). "Are We Dependent upon Coffee and Caffeine? A Review of Human and Animal Data." *Neuroscience and Biobehavioral Reviews* 23: 563–576.

Perez-Stable, E. M., et al. (1998). "Nicotine Metabolism and Intake in Black and White Smokers." *Journal of the American Medical Association* 280: 152–156.

Picciotto, M. R. (1998). "Common Aspects of the Action of Nicotine and Other Drugs of Abuse." *Drug and Alcohol Dependence* 51: 165–172.

Rachima-Maoz, C., et al. (1998). "The Effect of Caffeine on Ambulatory Blood Pressure in Hypertensive Patients." *American Journal of Hypertension* 11: 1426–1432.

Rasmussen, B. B., et al. (1998). "Fluvoxamine Is a Potent Inhibitor of the Metabolism of Caffeine in Vitro." *Pharmacology and Toxicology* 83: 240–245.

Riggs, P. D., et al. (1999). "Relationship of ADHD, Depression, and Non-Tobacco Substance Use Disorders to Nicotine Dependence in Substance-Dependent Delinquents." *Drug and Alcohol Dependence* 54: 195–205.

Rigotti, N. A. (2002). "Treatment of Tobacco Use and Dependence." *New England Journal of Medicine* 346: 506–512.

Rose, J. E., et al. (1999). "Arterial Nicotine Kinetics During Cigarette Smoking and Intravenous Nicotine Administration: Implications for Addiction." *Drug and Alcohol Dependence* 56: 99–107.

Rose, J. E., et al. (2003). "PET Studies of the Influence of Nicotine on Neural Systems in Cigarette Smokers." *American Journal of Psychiatry* 160: 323–333.

Salin-Pascual, R. J., et al. (1996). "Antidepressant Effect of Transdermal Nicotine Patches in Nonsmoking Patients with Major Depression." *Journal of Clinical Psychiatry* 57: 387–389.

Sellers, E. M. (1998). "Pharmacogenetics and Ethnoracial Differences in Smoking." *Journal of the American Medical Association* 280: 179–180.

Sellers, E. M., et al. (2003). "Decreasing Smoking Behavior and Risk Through CYP2A6 Inhibition." *Drug Discovery Today* 8: 487–493.

Spring, B., et al. (2003). "Reward Value of Cigarette Smoking for Comparably Heavy Smoking Schizophrenic, Depressed, and Nonpatient Smokers." *American Journal of Psychiatry* 160: 316–322.

Stolerman, I. P., and M. J. Jarvis (1995). "The Scientific Case That Nicotine Is Addictive." *Psychopharmacology* 117: 2–10.

Swanson, J. A., et al. (1994). "Caffeine and Nicotine: A Review of Their Joint Use and Possible Interactive Effects in Tobacco Withdrawal." *Addictive Behaviors* 19: 229–256.

Tobacco Use and Dependence Clinical Practice Guideline Panel, Staff, and Consortium Representatives (2000). "A Clinical Practice Guideline for Treating Tobacco Use and Dependence, A U.S. Public Health Service Report." *Journal of the American Medical Association* 283: 3244-3254.

Tsoh, J. Y., et al. (2000). "Development of Major Depression After Treatment for Smoking Cessation." *American Journal of Psychiatry* 157: 368–374.

Tyndale, R. F., et al. (1999). "Inhibition of Nicotine's Metabolism: A Potential New Treatment for Tobacco Dependence." *Clinical Pharmacology and Therapeutics* 65: 145.

Weissman, M. M., et al. (1999). "Maternal Smoking During Pregnancy and Psychopathology in Offspring Followed to Adulthood." *Journal of the American Academy of Child and Adolescent Psychiatry* 38: 892–899.

Wisborg, K. et al. (2003). "Maternal Consumption of Coffee During Pregnancy and Stillbirth and Infant Death in the First Year of Life: Prospective Study." *British Medical Journal* 326: 420–422.

Caffeine Content in Beverages, Foods, and Medicines

Item	Caffeine content Average (mg)	Range
Coffee (5-ounce cup)	100	50–150
Tea (5-ounce cup)	50	25–90
Cocoa (5-ounce cup)	5	2–20
Chocolate (semisweet, baking) (1 ounce)	25	15–30
Chocolate milk (1 ounce)	5	1–10
Cola drink (12 ounces)	40	35–55
OTC stimulants (No Doz, Vivarin)[a]	100+	
OTC analgesics (Excedrin)	65	
(Anacin, Midol, Vanquish)	33	
OTC cold remedies (Coryban-D, Triaminic)	30	
OTC diuretics (Aqua-ban)	100	

[a]OTC = over the counter.

Drugs That Are Used to Treat Psychological Disorders

The chapters in this part introduce drugs that are used to treat psychological disorders, including major depression (Chapter 9), bipolar disorder (Chapter 10), schizophrenia (Chapter 11), Alzheimer's disease and parkinsonism (Chapter 12), and disorders of children and adolescents (Chapter 13). Today, remarkable advances are being made in the pharmacotherapeutics of these disorders, allowing affected people to lead much more "normal" lives than they have ever been able to before in human history. More remarkable advances are constantly occurring, with even more hope and promise of relief from frequently disabling disorders. The goals of these chapters are to impart a sense of the historical development of therapeutics of each disorder, to cover the pharmacology of drugs currently being used to treat these disorders, and to convey a sense of excitement about the promise of even better therapies.

The drugs are neatly compartmentalized in these chapters under descriptive headings (antidepressants, mood stabilizers, antipsychotics, and so forth), but the headings do not adequately describe or define the drugs. For example, besides relieving major depression, antidepressants are used as antianxiety drugs, as analgesics, and as antidysthymic agents. Many of the mood stabilizers, besides being used to treat bipolar disorder, are used to treat chronic pain syndromes, psychological disorders associated with agitation and aggression, and even substance abuse. Antipsychotic drugs, besides being used to treat schizophrenia, are now being used to treat bipolar disorder, explosive and aggressive disorders, autism, and other pervasive developmental disorders. Newer antipsychotic agents are even being used to treat depression and dysthymia. Nevertheless, these artificial distinctions are maintained in order to present the pharmacology of these drugs in a logical manner.

Chapter 14 integrates pharmacological therapy of the disorders with psychological and behavioral interventions. In some situations (for example, depression), behavioral therapies are as effective as drug therapies, and the combination offers additive clinical efficacy. In other situations (bipolar disorder and schizophrenia, for example), pharmacological therapy is essential; psychological and behavioral therapies add to clinical efficacy and provide insights, behavioral changes, and support. This chapter provides an important perspective for both medical practitioners and the nonprescribing therapists who need to understand the balance between drug and nondrug therapies.

Chapter 9

Antidepressant Drugs

Depression

Depression is an *affective disorder* characterized by loss of interest or pleasure in almost all usual activities or pastimes. Accompanying this condition are feelings of intense sadness and despair; diminished energy; decreased sexual drive; mental slowing and loss of concentration; pessimism; feelings of worthlessness or self-reproach; inappropriate guilt; recurrent thoughts of death, suicide, and hopelessness; blunted affect; fatigue; and insomnia. Depression is a common psychiatric disorder. About 6.6 percent of Americans (13 to 14 million U.S. adults) suffer from a depressive disorder in any given year (Kessler et al., 2003). If left untreated, perhaps 25 to 30 percent of adult depressives attempt or commit suicide. Interestingly, most cases of major depression have another comorbid psychological disorder, with the depressive disease only rarely primary (Zimmerman et al., 2002). About 50 percent of the yearly cases of depression receive medical treatment, but treatment is considered adequate in only about 42 percent of the cases. Therefore, only 21 percent of the yearly cases of depression are adequately treated (Kessler et al., 2003). The costs of untreated or undertreated depression are substantial, including significant costs in lost productive work time (Stewart et al., 2003).

Antidepressant medications and psychological therapies (cognitive-behavioral and interpersonal psychotherapies) are both effective treatments for depressive disorders, although both therapies require improvement (Gilbody et al., 2003; Horvitz-Lennon et al., 2003; Leon et al., 2003). In one survey, over a one-year period, 83 percent of adults with a probable depressive or anxiety disorder did see a health care provider. Of these, 30 percent received some measure of appropriate treatment; discouragingly, of the patients who visited a primary care physician, only 19 percent received appropriate care (Young et al., 2001). Adherence to published guidelines for treatment improves therapeutic outcome (increases the number of depression-free days). However, appropriate care occurs at a cost of $50 per depression-free day. Melfi and colleagues (2000) compared rates of office visits, depression diagnosis, and antidepressant pharmacology among whites, African Americans, and Hispanics. Rates of diagnosis of a depressive disorder and prescription of an antidepressant were comparable among African Americans and Hispanics but less than half the rate for whites.

When antidepressant drugs were introduced 40 years ago, depression was the sole indication for their use. Today, treatment with antidepressants is recognized for anxiety disorders,[1] dysthymia, and certain chronic pain syndromes. Although many of the anxiety disorders have historically been treated with benzodiazepine anxiolytics (Chapter 6), they are today most often treated with antidepressants. The newer combined antidepressant-anxiolytic drugs are equally or more efficacious, they are less prone to compulsive abuse, and they impair learning, memory, and concentration to a lesser degree than do the benzodiazepines. Stahl (1999a and b) analyzes this largely historical progression of treatment of major depression and anxiety disorders (Figure 9.1).

In addition, individuals formerly regarded as having *anxiety neurosis* (historically treated with benzodiazepines) have now been reconceptualized as having *dysthymia,* an affective disorder responsive to antidepressant medications. The need for pharmacotherapy for dysthymia was articulated by Shelton and coworkers (1997):

> Dysthymia . . . affects 3% to 6% of the adult population of the United States and as many as 36% of patients who seek treatment at psychiatric outpatient clinics. The symptoms of dysthymia are less severe than those observed in patients with major depression, and hence dysthymia is often considered to be a disorder of subsyndromal intensity. Nevertheless, patients with this disorder experience considerable social dysfunction and disability. Dysthymics . . . are more likely to take nonspecific psychotropic drugs, such as minor tranquilizers (benzodiazepines) and sedatives . . . . More than 75% of dysthymics have coexisting psychiatric disorders, including anxiety disorders and substance abuse. Approximately 40% of dysthymics have coexisting major depression—a combination termed *double depression.* Untreated dysthymia rarely improves spontaneously over time. Dysthymia has historically been underrecognized and undertreated.

---

[1]According to current diagnostic criteria, anxiety disorders include panic disorder (PD), obsessive compulsive disorder (OCD), posttraumatic stress disorder (PTSD), social phobia, and generalized anxiety disorder (GAD).

A. Treatment of Depression and Anxiety in the 1960s

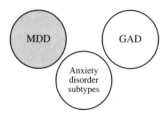

The earliest antidepressants were tricyclic anti-depressants (TCAs) and monoamine oxidase inhibitors (MAOIs) and were conceptualized as targeting an entirely different syndrome (major depressive disorder [MDD]) than did the earliest anxiolytics, namely, benzodiazepines. At that time, benzodiazepines targeted anxiety disorders as a whole including generalized anxiety disorder (GAD) or anxiety neurosis, which was much more broadly defined at that time, as well as anxiety disorder subtypes.

◯ First-line treatments with antidepressants.
◯ First-line treatments with anxiolytics.

B. Treatment of Depression and Anxiety in the 1970s and 1980s

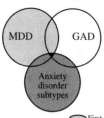

As the TCA/MAOI era matured, mixtures of anxiety and depression were increasingly recognized and treated both with these antidepressants and with buspirone as well as benzodiazepines. Benzodiazepines along with TCAs and MAOIs began to make inroads into treating anxiety disorder subtypes such as panic disorder, and in the case of the TCA clomipramine, obsessive-compulsive disorder (OCD).

◯ First-line treatments with antidepressants.
◯ First-line treatments with anxiolytics.
⬤ First-line treatments with either antidepressants or anxiolytics.

C. Treatment of Depression and Anxiety in the 1990s

Once the selective serotonin reuptake inhibitor (SRRI) era came into full swing, these agents eventually took over as first-line treatment choices not only of MDD but also of numerous anxiety disorder subtypes, from panic disorder and OCD to social phobia and posttraumatic stress disorder, but not GAD. Benzodiazepines became progressively second-line treatments of anxiety disorder, although buspirone continued as a first-line treatment of GAD.

◯ First-line treatments with antidepressants.
◯ First-line treatments with anxiolytics.

D. Treatment of Depression and Anxiety in the Twenty-First Century

When is an antidepressant an antidepressant, and when is an antidepressant an anxiolytic? Recently, the first antidepressant was approved for the treatment of GAD, namely, venlafaxine XR. Venlafaxine XR, as well as nefazodone and mirtazapine, has preliminary evidence of efficacy for some anxiety disorder subtypes, such as panic disorder, social phobia, and posttraumatic stress disorder. SSRIs, nefazodone, and mirtazapine have preliminary evidence of efficacy in generalized anxiety disorder. Virtually all forms of anxiety can now be treated by an antidepressant, with the documentation of efficacy of some antidepressants better than that of others. Perhaps the distinction between an antidepressant and an anxiolytic will cease to exist in the twenty-first century.

◯ First-line treatments with antidepressants.

FIGURE 9.1 Progression in the treatment of major depressive disorder (MDD), generalized anxiety disorder (GAD), and anxiety disorder subtypes from 1960 to 2000. [From Stahl (1999a), pp. 356–357.]

Pathophysiology of Depression

Depression is not just a behavioral state; *depression is a reversible disease of the brain* with distinct neuronal pathology that includes structural and neurochemical changes in specific regions of the brain, especially the hippocampus (Benninghoff et al., 2002; Glitz et al., 2002) and frontal cortex (Bremner et al., 2003). More specifically, depression can now be considered as a *stress-induced, reversible, structural disorder of the brain, involving neuronal atrophy and neuronal loss secondary to reduced expression of certain neurotrophic factors that are essential to maintenance of neuronal health and survival.*

Classically, depression has been conceptualized as a problem or deficiencies involving neurotransmitters such as norepinephrine, dopamine, and serotonin. Restoring these neurotransmitters (usually by prolonging their presence in the synaptic cleft) restored the state of normality. We are now learning that depression is not just a synaptic transmitter deficiency but also an intracellular illness that involves deficiencies in certain tropic hormones (proteins) that act normally to maintain cell survival and health (Manji and Duman, 2001). In essence, depression is now viewed as a disorder of cellular plasticity and survival, especially in hippocampal neurons, resulting in loss of neurons and impairment of neuronal health and survivability (Duman, 2002; Lee et al., 2002; Sheline et al., 2003; Vaidya and Duman, 2001).

Antidepressants and psychotherapeutic interventions seem to exert their effects by stimulating appropriate adaptive changes in neuronal systems that have lost their cellular plasticity (Garcia, 2002; Manji et al., 2003; Santarelli et al., 2003). How might neurons lose their cellular plasticity? Duman and coworkers (1997) proposed that stress-induced vulnerability to depression and other types of neuronal insult occur "via intracellular mechanisms that decrease neurotropic factors necessary for the survival and function of particular neurons" (p. 597). Indeed, stress and other insults decrease the expression of "brain-derived neurotropic factors (BDNF) and lead to atrophy of vulnerable neurons in the hippocampus and cerebral cortex." The authors also proposed that the "transcription factor cyclic 3′, 5′-monophosphate response element-binding protein (CREB) is one intracellular target of long-term antidepressant drug treatment and that brain-derived neurotropic factor is one target gene of CREB" (Figures 9.2 and 9.3). Conti and coworkers (2002), Bierhaus and coworkers (2003), and Matthew and coworkers (2003) expand on this concept of stress and cellular dysfunction. Caspi and coworkers (2003) attribute this stress-induced susceptibility to depression to an abnormality on the gene responsible for the encoding of the serotonin transporter. They propose that there is a genetic-environmental interaction that occurs in susceptible persons exposed to life-stress. Russo-Neustadt and coworkers (1999)

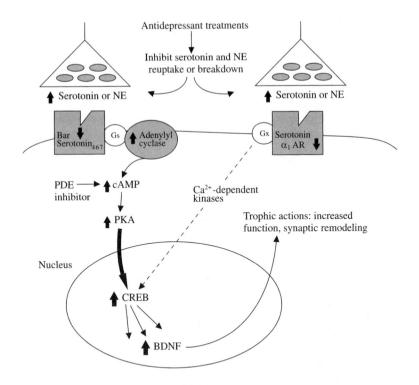

FIGURE 9.2 A model for the molecular mechanism of action of long-term antidepressant treatments. Antidepressants induce short-term increases in 5-HT and NE. Longer-term use decreases the function and expression of their receptors, but the cAMP signal transduction pathway is increased, including increased levels of adenyl cyclase and cAMP-dependent protein kinase (PKA), as well as translocation of PKA to the cell nucleus. Antidepressants increase expression and function of the transcription factor cAMP response element-binding protein (CREB), suggesting that CREB is a common postreceptor target for antidepressants. Brain-derived neurotrophic factor is also increased by antidepressant treatment; up regulation of CREB and BDNF could influence the function of hippocampal neurons or neurons innervating this brain region, increasing neuronal survival, function, and remodeling of synaptic or cellular architecture. [From Duman et al., (1997), p. 600.]

reported that, in rat studies, combined antidepressant treatment (either a monoamine-oxidase inhibitor or a tricyclic agent) and physical activity have an additive, potentiating effect on BDNF mRNA expression within several areas of rat hippocampus. Russo-Neustadt (2003) reviewed BDNF and concluded that it is a member of a family of neurotropic cell survival-promoting molecules that plays an important part in the growth, development, maintenance, and function of neuronal systems as well as in normal cognitive and emotional functioning. Maintenance of normal BDNF function (and perhaps that of other trophic protein hormones) is necessary for a normal emotional state as

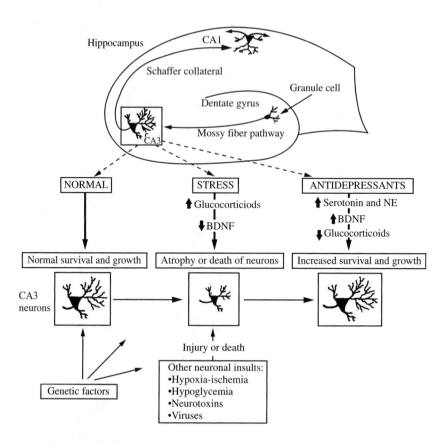

FIGURE 9.3 A molecular and cellular model for the action of antidepressants and the pathophysiology of stress-related disorders. Chronic stress decreases the expression of BDNF in the hippocampus, contributing to atrophy or death of neurons in the hippocampus. Elevated levels of glucocorticoids also decrease survival of these neurons, as do many other insults. Antidepressants increase the expression of BDNF and prevent the down regulation of BDNF elicited by stress, increasing neuronal survival or helping repair or protect neurons from further damage. See Figure 9.2. [From Duman et al. (1997), p. 603.]

well as for memory formation (Tokuyama et al., 2000; Shors et al., 2001; Tyler et al., 2002). Stress-induced deficiencies in BDNF formation occur as a result of reduced transcription of BDNF from its mRNA as a result of reductions in its regulatory factor, CREB (Garcia, 2002). Reduced BDNF then leads to a state of depression as well as altered memory formation. Up regulation in BDNF restores neuronal plasticity and is ultimately responsible for the therapeutic action of antidepressants (Okamoto et al., 2003; Popoli et al., 2002; Reid and Stewart,

2001; Sheldon, 2000; Shimizu et al., 2003). Saarelainen and coworkers (2003) extended this work, implicating the role of the BDNF receptor, TrkB, which is up regulated by antidepressant treatment. They conclude, "Neurotrophin signaling increased by antidepressants may induce formation and stabilization of synaptic connectivity, which gradually leads to clinical antidepressant effects and mood recovery" (p. 349). Dwivedi and coworkers (2003) demonstrated reduced expression of frontal cortical and hippocampal BDNF in brains of humans who successfully committed suicide (Figure 9.4), suggesting that BDNF "may play an important role in the pathophysiological aspects of suicidal behavior" (p. 804).

Altar and coworkers (2003) demonstrated in rats that electroconvulsive therapy (ECT) produced rapid, large, and widespread elevations in BDNF in the brain. Again this finding is consistent with BDNF augmentation as a target and as a substrate for depression. Thomas and Peterson (2003) review this new neurogenic theory of depression. In summary, as stated by Sheldon (2000):

> Depression is a disorder of the stress response and adaptation (sometimes referred to as *neural plasticity*). It begins with cellular mechanisms related to antidepressant drug actions, including transductional and transcriptional factors, culminating in the regulation of the expression of specific genes related to the stress-response system more broadly. . . . . Ultimately, antidepressants produce their therapeutic effects by altering the expression of specific target genes. . . . Antidepressants activate cascades involved in the expression of genes encoding the expression of CREB, BDNF, and its receptor trkB. . . . By modulating transcriptional mechanisms and gene expression, effective antidepressant therapies normalize the state of depression (p. 715).

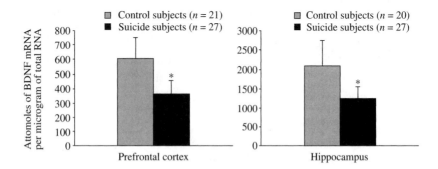

FIGURE 9.4 Reductions in brain-derived neurotrophic factor (BDNF) messenger RNA (mRNA) in prefrontal cortex (*left*) and hippocampus (*right*) in control subjects and in subjects who died by suicide. 95% confidence intervals shown. Differences significant P<0.001. [From Dwivedi et al., 2003, p. 807.]

This new definition of depression as a cellular dysfunction reversible by antidepressant drugs (and probably also by psychotherapeutic interventions) leads to the conclusion that although different antidepressant drugs act via different synaptic mechanisms, all are therapeutically effective and usually equivalent. Therefore, choice of a specific antidepressant drug for a particular patient is not by efficacy, but by a specific side effect profile appropriate for the individual patient.

Evolution of Antidepressant Drug Therapy

Forty years ago, the antidepressant properties of *imipramine* were accidentally discovered. Since then, it has been learned that imipramine and similar *tricyclic antidepressants* (Table 9.1) block the presynaptic transporter protein receptors for the neurotransmitters norepinephrine and serotonin. Note that the term *tricyclic antidepressant* refers to a commonality in basic *structure*, in contrast to newer antidepressants, which are defined by their mechanism of action. When the antidepressant action of imipramine was discovered almost 50 years ago, its mechanism of action was unknown; thus, a structural classification had to suffice and persists today.

At about the same time the TCAs were discovered, another class of early antidepressant drugs called the *monoamine oxidase inhibitors* (MAOIs) were identified; three orally administered MAOIs remain commercially available for the treatment of depression and an MAOI-containing skin patch was introduced in the year 2003. Both the TCIs and the MAOIs are effective in the treatment of major depression, but both possess considerable disadvantages because of adverse side effect profiles. TCAs carry a high incidence of anticholinergic effects and cardiotoxicity, extremely important in (suicidal) overdoses; orally administered MAOIs may cause hypertensive crises if sympathomimetic agents (for example, certain other drugs or tyramine in foodstuffs) are additionally taken. Together, we refer to these two classes of drugs as "first-generation" antidepressants.

Many problems with the first-generation agents prompted the search for new antidepressants that were equally effective, better tolerated, and less toxic. First came the development of several drugs that were slight modifications of the basic tricyclic structure but that still exhibited antidepressant efficacy. These drugs were termed *second-generation* or *atypical antidepressants*. Several are available clinically (see Table 9.1) and some—for example, venlafaxine (Effexor) and bupropion (Wellbutrin)— remain popular today.

During the late 1980s and continuing through the 1990s, the *selective serotonin reuptake inhibitors* (SSRIs) were developed and introduced clinically; the first of these was fluoxetine (Prozac). Several additional agents are also clinically available (see Table 9.1). Today, recognizing the limitations and side effects of the SSRIs, antidepressant drug research is progressing to identify compounds that act by different mechanisms. One approach combines SSRI activity with postsynaptic serotonin-type 2 receptor (5-HT$_2$) antagonism—two drugs that do so are nefazodone (Serzone) and mirtazapine (Remeron). These drugs are not necessarily more clinically efficacious than the older TCAs, but they may have a more favorable profile of toxicity or side effects. Another approach is to develop drugs that are specific blockers of serotonin and norepinephrine reuptake—for example, duloxetine (Cymbalta) and milnacipram (Ixel)— or a specific blocker of just norepinephrine reuptake—for example, atomoxetine (Strattera) and reboxetine (Vestra, Edronax). Experimental drugs under development include drugs that are classified as substance P antagonists and other novel agents such as tianepine.

The availability of the newer drugs has not yet reduced the number of treatment-resistant individuals with major depression: the new drugs have only altered the profile of side effects, including a reduction in overdose cardiotoxicity. Three main therapeutic needs have still to be met: (1) superior efficacy to tricyclic antidepressants, (2) faster onset of action, and (3) reliable effectiveness in the treatment of therapy-resistant depression. In essence, the development of new antidepressants has always been a progression, and the end is nowhere in sight.

The following discussion of specific antidepressant drugs is subdivided into categories according to their chronology and the neurotransmitters upon which each group is thought to act.

First-Generation Antidepressants

The first antidepressants were introduced into medicine in the late 1950s and early 1960s. They were of two classes, one named for the similar chemical structures of the drugs (*tricyclic antidepressants*) and the other for the mechanism of action of the drugs (*monoamine oxidase inhibitors*). Drugs of both classes increased the levels of norepinephrine and serotonin in the brain, leading to a concept that depression resulted from a relative deficiency of these neurotransmitters in the brain. Conversely, excesses in the amounts of these transmitters were thought to lead to a state of mania. This concept was called the *catecholamine concept of mania and depression* and held until more recent demonstrations that depression appears to result from neuronal injury. Regardless, these first-generation agents are still quite frequently used as psychopharmacological agents.

TABLE 9.1 Drugs used to treat depression

Drug name: Generic (trade)	Sedative activity	Anticholinergic activity[a]	Elimination half-life (h)	Reuptake inhibition		
				Norepinephrine	Serotonin	Dopamine
TRICYCLIC COMPOUNDS						
Imipramine (Tofranil)	Moderate	Moderate	10–20	++	++	0
Desipramine (Norpramin)	Low	Low	12–75	+++	+	0
Trimipramine (Surmontil)	High	Moderate	8–20	+	+	0
Protriptyline (Vivactil)	Low	Moderate	55–125	+++	+	0
Nortriptyline (Pamelor, Aventil)	Moderate	Low	15–35	++	++	0
Amitriptyline (Elavil)	High	High	20–35	++	++	0
Doxepin (Adapin, Sinequan)	High	High	8–24	++	++	0
Clomipramine (Anafranil)	Low	Low	19–37	++	++++	0
SECOND-GENERATION (ATYPICAL) COMPOUNDS						
Amoxapine (Asendin)[b]	Low	Moderate	8–10	++	+	0
Maprotiline (Ludiomil)	Moderate	Moderate	27–58	+++	0	0
Trazodone (Desyrel)	Moderate	Low	6–13	0	++	0
Bupropion (Wellbutrin)	Low	Low	8–14	0/+	0/+	++
Venlafaxine (Effexor)	None	None	3–11	++	++++	0

[a]Anticholinergic side effects include dry mouth, blurred vision, tachycardia, urinary retention, and constipation.
[b]Also has antipsychotic effects due to blockage of dopamine receptors (Chapter 7).
0 = no effect; + = mild effect; ++ = moderate effect; +++ = strong effect; ++++ = maximal effect.

TABLE 9.1 Drugs used to treat depression *(continued)*

Drug name: Generic (trade)	Sedative activity	Anticholinergic activity[a]	Elimination half-life (h)	Reuptake inhibition		
				Norepinephrine	Serotonin	Dopamine
SELECTIVE SEROTONIN REUPTAKE INHIBITORS						
Fluoxetine (Prozac)	None	None	24–96	0	++++	0
Sertraline (Zoloft)	None	None	26	0	++++	0
Paroxetine (Paxil)	None	None	24	+	++++	0
Citalopram (Celexa)	None	None	33	0	++++	0
Fluvoxamine (Luvox)	None	None	15	0	++++	0
Escitalopram (Lexapro)	None	None	2–5	0	++++	0
DUAL-ACTION ANTIDEPRESSANTS						
Nefazodone (Serzone)	Low	None	3–4	0	++++	0
Mirtazapine (Remeron)	High	Low	20–40	++	++++	0
Duloxetine (Cymbalta)	Low	Low	11–16	+++	+++	0
MAO INHIBITORS: IRREVERSIBLE						
Phenelzine (Nardil)	Low	None	2–4[c]	0	0	0
Isocarboxazid (Marplan)	None	None	1–3[c]	0	0	0
Tranylcypromine (Parnate)	None	None	1–3[c]	0	0	0
SELECTIVE NOREPINEPHRINE REUPTAKE INHIBITORS						
Reboxetine (Edronax)	None	Low	13	++++	0	0
Atomoxetine (Strattera)	None	Low	5	++++	0	0

[c]Half-life does not correlate with clinical effect (see text).
0 = no effect; + = mild effect; ++ = moderate effect; +++ = strong effect; ++++ = maximal effect.

Tricyclic Antidepressants

The term *tricyclic antidepressant* (TCA) describes a class of drugs that all have a characteristic three-ring molecular core (Figure 9.5). TCAs effectively relieve depression in people who experience major depressive illness. They also possess significant anxiolytic and analgesic actions. Mavissakalian and Perel (2000) demonstrated the efficacy of *imipramine* in the treatment of panic disorder with agoraphobia, with only a modest side effect burden. Imipramine's efficacy and tolerability was not very inferior to the efficacy and tolaerability of SSRIs in treating panic disorder. Since most of these older drugs are available in less expensive generic form, manufacturers are less willing to fund research and seek FDA approval for their use in treating anxiety. Therefore, despite efficacy, TCAs are not likely to be promoted for use as anxiolytics.[2]

Historically, the TCAs were drugs of first choice for the treatment of major depression. The SSRIs, which today are widely prescribed, are no more effective and are considerably more expensive; they may, however, be less toxic, and their use may be associated with a higher rate of patient comfort and compliance. TCAs, however, remain the standard against which other antidepressants are compared; no other group of antidepressants has yet been demonstrated to be either more clinically effective or capable of exerting a more rapid onset of antidepressant effect than the TCAs, although alternative agents may be better tolerated (McGrath and coworkers, 2000).

Imipramine (Tofranil) is the prototype TCA, but another clinically available TCA, *desipramine* (Norpramin), is the pharmacologically active intermediate metabolite of imipramine. Likewise, *amitriptyline* (Elavil) has an active intermediate metabolite, *nortriptyline* (Pamelor, Aventil). In fact, these active intermediates may actually be responsible for much of the antidepressant effect of both imipramine and amitriptyline.

---

[2]FDA approval does not mean that a drug is any more effective than any other drug for the treatment of a given medical symptom or disorder. It means that the manufacturer submitted sufficient research data, applied for approval to advertise the indication, and demonstrated sufficient efficacy and safety to justify the formal approval by the FDA. If a similar drug is not approved for a use that another drug is approved for, it does not necessarily mean that the nonapproved drug is ineffective; the manufacturer just had not conducted the research and applied for approval. If any drug is over about 17 years old, it goes "generic," and any other manufacturer can sell it. Therefore, one manufacturer probably will not commit to the research and go through the approval process when anyone can then sell the drug for that use. Therefore, a new use for an old drug is "off-label," meaning that there is no FDA approval for that specific use. Off-label use is not illegal, but it must be defensible by the prescribing physician.

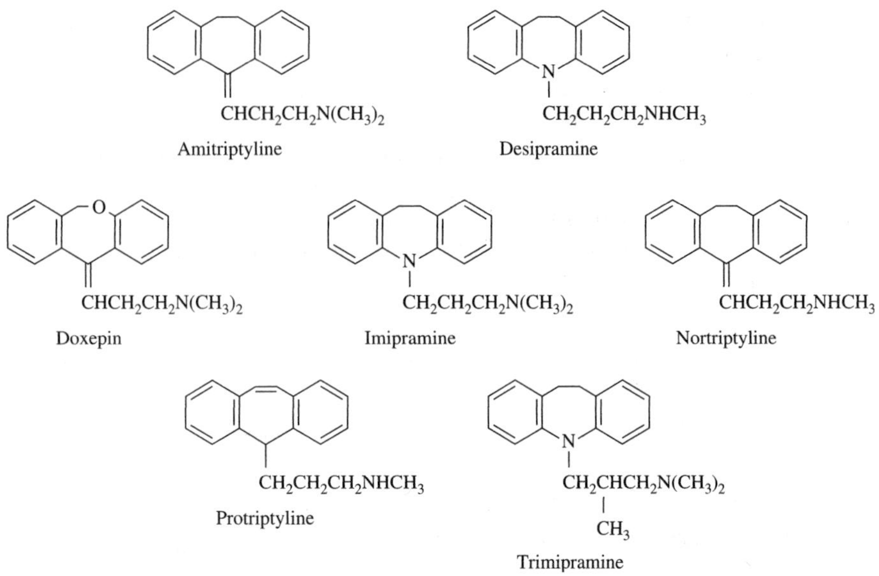

FIGURE 9.5 Chemical structures of seven tricyclic antidepressants.

Mechanism of Action. TCAs exert four significant pharmacologic actions that account for both the therapeutic actions and the side effects of these drugs:

1. They block the presynaptic norepinephrine reuptake transporter.
2. They block the presynaptic serotonin reuptake transporter.
3. They block postsynaptic histamine receptors.
4. They block postsynaptic acetylcholine receptors.

The therapeutic effects of the TCAs result from drug-induced blockade of presynaptic serotonin and norepinephrine receptors. Blockade of acetylcholine receptors results in dry mouth, confusion, memory and cognitive impairments, blurred vision, dry mouth, increased heart rate, and urinary retention. Blockade of histamine receptors results in drowsiness and sedation, an effect similar to the sedation seen after administration of the classic antihistamine diphenhydramine (Benadryl). In general, nortriptyline and desipramine are preferred TCAs in a patient without a history of favorable response to a specific antidepressant (in other words, they are good drugs of first choice for initial treatment of depression when therapy with a TCA is chosen). These two TCAs cause less sedation and cognitive impairment and exert fewer anticholinergic side effects than most other TCAs.

Pharmacokinetics. The TCAs are well absorbed when they are administered orally. Because most of them have relatively long half-lives (see Table 9.1), taking them at bedtime minimizes unwanted side effects, especially persistent sedation. The TCAs are metabolized in the liver, and, as discussed earlier, two TCAs are converted into pharmacologically active intermediates that are detoxified later (Figure 9.6). This combination of a pharmacologically active drug and active metabolite results in a clinical effect lasting up to 4 days, even longer in elderly patients.

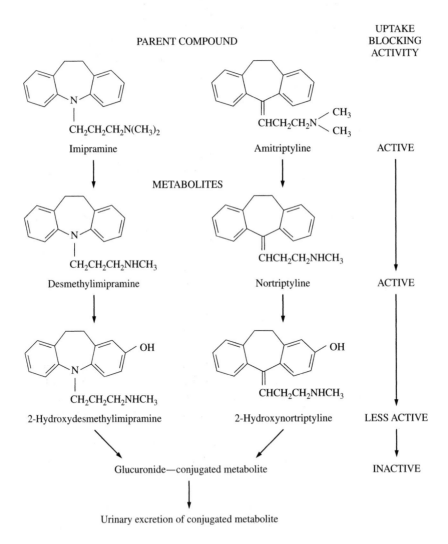

FIGURE 9.6 Metabolism of imipramine (Tofranil) and amitriptyline (Elavil). Note that the two active intermediates (desmethylimipramine and nortriptyline) are marketed commercially as Norpramin and Pamelor or Aventil, respectively.

TCAs readily cross the placental barrier. However, in utero expo-sure does not affect global IQ, language development, or behavioral de-velopment in preschool children. No fetal abnormalities from these drugs have yet been reported.

Pharmacological Effects. All the TCAs attach to and inhibit (to varying degrees) the presynaptic transporter proteins for both norepinephrine and serotonin, accounting for therapeutic efficacy. The TCAs, however, have three clinical limitations. First, they are claimed to have a slow onset of action, although overall, TCAs seem to start acting as fast as any other antidepressant drug, provided that comparable dosage strategies can be tolerated. Second, the TCAs exert a wide variety of ef-fects on the CNS, causing a variety of bothersome side effects that the SSRIs do not. Third, in overdosage (as in suicide attempts), TCAs are cardiotoxic and potentially fatal.

Nelson and coworkers (1999) studied 81 patients with depression and ischemic heart disease. The authors administered either a TCA (nortriptyline) or an SSRI (paroxetine); the two drugs were equally ef-fective (averaging a 50 percent improvement on the Hamilton Depression Rating Scale), but paroxetine was better tolerated than nortriptyline and less likely to produce cardiovascular side effects.

Because TCAs do not produce euphoria in normal individuals, they have no recreational or behavior-reinforcing value. Therefore, abuse and psychological dependence are not concerns. Similarly, in contrast to withdrawal from SSRIs (discussed later), withdrawal from TCAs is not usually a cause for undue concern. The clinical choice of TCA is determined by effectiveness, tolerance of side effects, and dura-tion of action of the particular TCA.

In depressed patients, TCAs elevate mood, increase physical activ-ity, improve appetite and sleep patterns, and reduce morbid preoccu-pation, even in the elderly (Gasto et al., 2003). They are useful in treat-ing acute episodes of major depression as well as in preventing relapses. About one-third of patients resistant to other antidepressants respond favorably to a TCA (Nierenberg et al., 2003). In addition, TCAs are clinically effective in the long-term therapy of dysthymia (Hellerstein et al., 2000), although SSRIs may be equally effective and better tolerated. TCAs are as effective as SSRIs in treating bipolar de-pression (as an adjunct to a mood stabilizer), although the SSRIs are better tolerated (Nemeroff et al., 2001).

TCAs are effective analgesics in a variety of clinical pain syn-dromes; they are consistently superior to a placebo in the treatment of chronic pain (Godfrey, 1996). Uses have included diabetes-associated peripheral neuropathies, postherpetic neuralgia, migraine headache, fibromyalgia, myofascial pain, chronic fatigue, and so on. In addition to a direct analgesic action, the antidepressant action no doubt adds a feeling of well-being to the analgesic action, improving the affect as well as reducing physical discomfort. This combined analgesic-antidepressant action will be expanded upon in the discussion of dualoxetine.

Side Effects. Side effects result from the anticholinergic and antihistaminic actions listed above. In the patient on long-term therapy with TCAs, tolerance develops to many of these side effects, but some will persist and must be tolerated. Often, choosing a particular TCA with an awareness of its side effects can turn a disadvantage into a therapeutic advantage. For example, amitriptyline and doxepin are the most sedating of the TCAs, making them useful in treating people with agitation as well as depression or where improved sleep is desirable. Administering one of these drugs at bedtime would provide both the antidepressant effect as well as the needed sedation.

The effects of TCAs on memory and cognitive function are important. The direct adverse effects on cognition are related to the anticholinergic and antihistaminic properties of TCAs; more positive, indirect effects result from the improvement in mood. TCAs can directly impair attention, motor speed, dexterity, and memory. Relatively nonsedating compounds with low degrees of anticholinergic side effects cause very little direct impairment of psychomotor or memory functions. The young and the elderly may be more susceptible to the anticholinergic-induced impairment of memory. Individuals at the extremes of age, if treated with TCAs, should probably receive a drug with low degrees of antihistaminic and anticholinergic effects.

TCAs cause both cardiac depression and increased electrical irritability (as shown by cardiac arrhythmias). Cardiac depression can be life-threatening when an overdose is taken, as in suicide attempts. The patient commonly exhibits excitement, delirium, and convulsions, followed by respiratory depression and coma, which can persist for several days. Cardiac arrhythmias can lead to ventricular fibrillation, cardiac arrest, and death. Arrhythmias are extremely difficult to treat. Thus, all TCAs can be lethal in doses that are commonly available to depressed patients. For this reason, it is unwise to dispense more than a week's supply of an antidepressant to an acutely depressed patient.

There have been reports of about 12 cases of sudden death in children receiving desipramine for the treatment of ADHD or depression. These deaths are certainly cause for concern in using TCAs to treat depression in children, and the therapeutic efficacy of TCAs in treating major depression in children is questionable anyway (Chapter 13). In cases where efficacy is more demonstrable—enuresis (bed-wetting), obsessive-compulsive disorder (OCD), and ADHD—use may be appropriate, but caution is warranted.

Monoamine Oxidase Inhibitors

Several monoamine oxidase inhibitors (MAOIs) have been used since the late 1950s for treating major depressive illnesses. Their use was and continues to be limited by serious side effects involving potentially fatal interactions when taken with certain foods and medicines. The drugs include adrenalinelike drugs found in nasal sprays, antiasthma medications, and cold medicines. The foods include those that contain tyramine, a by-product of fermentation, such as many cheeses, wines, beers, liver, and some beans. As a result of the interaction, blood pressure increases severely, occasionally enough to be fatal. During the checkered and controversial history of MAOIs, it was learned that, although they are potentially dangerous, they could be used safely with strict dietary restrictions. Gardner and colleagues (1996) discuss the MAOI diet and its appropriate presentation to patients. Today, the MAOIs are experiencing resurgence in use because of the availability of a new formulation (an MAOI in a transdermal skin patch) that is effective yet devoid of the food and drug interactions. Interest in MAOIs has continued because (1) they can be as safe as TCAs, (2) they can work in many patients who respond poorly to both TCAs and SSRIs, and (3) they are excellent drugs for the treatment of atypical depression, which presents primarily with anxiety and phobic symptoms, masked depression (such as hypochondriasis), anorexia nervosa, bulimia, bipolar depression, dysthymia, depression in the elderly, panic disorder, and phobias.

Monoamine oxidase (MAO) is one of two enzymes that break down normal neurotransmitters in the body, including norepinephrine, dopamine, and serotonin. There are two types of the enzyme: MAO-A ("good" MAO) is found in norepinephrine and serotonin nerve terminals; MAO-B ("bad" MAO) is found in dopamine-secreting neurons. Pharmacologically, drug-induced inhibition of MAO-A is presumably responsible for the antidepressant activity, while inhibition of MAO-B is responsible for the side effects, including serious drug interactions. A few years ago, a specific MAO-A inhibitor (moclobomide) was developed and marketed in Canada and European countries. It was not released in the United States.

Three orally administered MAOIs are available in the United States: *phenelzine* (Nardil), *tranylcypromine* (Parnate), and *isocarboxazid* (Marplan). These three are "irreversible" in their effect, since they form a chemical bond with part of the MAO enzyme, a bond that cannot be broken; enzyme function returns only as new enzyme is biosynthesized. Because of this irreversibility in action and because of their many food and drug interactions, they are rarely used, despite their efficacy.

In 2003, the nonselective MAOI *selegiline* (Eldapril) became commercially available as a transdermal skin patch that allows for slow, continuous absorption. At the low doses absorbed across the skin, food and drug interactions are not observed. As reported by Amsterdam (2003), selegiline is robustly effective, with onset of effect in only a few days. Sexual functioning is not impaired, and compliance is excellent. Skin irritation seems to be the only significant side effect. Certainly more will be written about this new method of delivering an effective antidepressant medication.

Second-Generation (Atypical) Antidepressants

Efforts from the late 1970s to the mid-1980s to find structurally different agents that might overcome some of the disadvantages of the TCAs (slow onset of action, limited efficacy, and significant side effects) produced the so-called second-generation (or atypical) antidepressants (Figure 9.7). Their pharmacokinetic data and a comparison with standard TCAs are listed in Tables 9.1 and 9.2, respectively.

Maprotiline (Ludiomil) was one of the first clinically available antidepressants (other than the MAOIs) that modified the basic tricyclic structure (see Figure 9.7). It has a long half-life, blocks norepinephrine reuptake, and is as efficacious as imipramine (the "gold standard" of

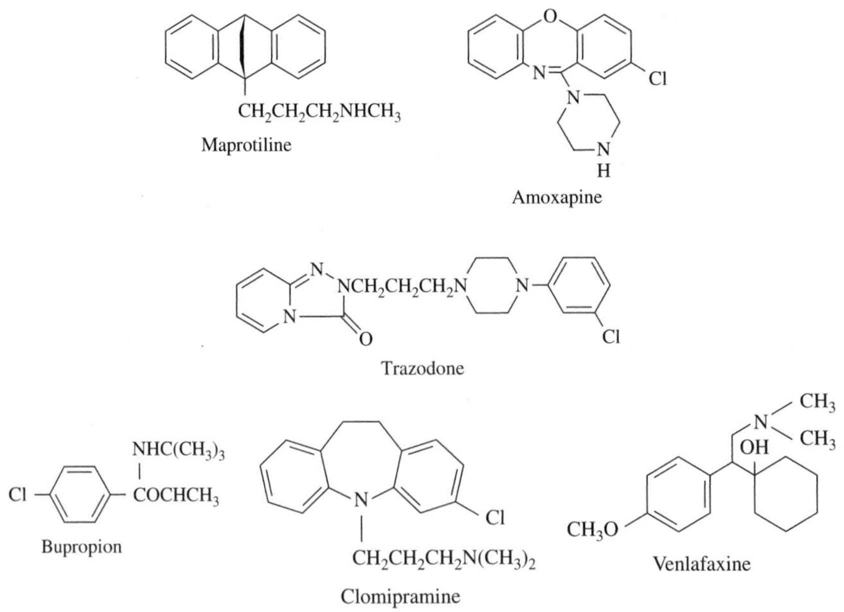

FIGURE 9.7 Chemical structures of six second-generation "atypical" antidepressants.

TABLE 9.2 Advantages and disadvantages of second-generation antidepressants compared to tricyclic antidepressants

Drug	Advantages	Disadvantages
Maprotiline	Sedating and may be useful for agitation Does not antagonize antihypertensive effects of clonidine Minimal cognitive impairment	Increased incidence of seizures Increased lethality in overdose Has long half-life; therefore accumulates Increased incidence of rashes
Amoxapine	Low in sedative effects Low in anticholinergic effects Possibly effective for monotherapy for psychotic depression Has possible rapid onset Relieves anxiety and agitation Toxic in overdose	Can promote parkinsonian side effects and tardive dyskinesia Cannot separate antidepressant from "antipsychotic" effect Increased lethality in overdose
Trazodone	Relatively safe in overdose Sedating (may be useful in controlling agitation and hostility in geriatric patients) Useful as a hypnotic in conjunction with MAO inhibitors	Efficacy not clearly established May induce or exacerbate ventricular arrhythmia Can promote priapism Drowsiness is common
Bupropion	Low in sedative, hypotensive, and anticholinergic side effects Does not promote weight gain Lack of ECG changes May assist with weight loss May be "anticraving"	Tends to "overstimulate," with insomnia, terror Not effective for panic; unknown effectiveness for obsessive compulsive disorders Increased incidence of seizures in bulimia May induce perceptual abnormalities and psychosis Causes increase in prolactin
Venlafaxine	Low in anticholinergic and antihistaminic effects Improves psychomotor and cognitive function Few drug interactions	Can increase blood pressure May cause anxiety, nervousness, and insomnia
Clomipramine	Indicated in OCD Long half-life	Toxicity limits therapy Increased risk of seizures May increase risk of psychotic episodes May activate mania/hypomania Can promote weight gain Can decrease libido

TCAs). However, it offers few, if any, therapeutic advantages. A major limitation of maprotiline is that it can (although rarely) cause seizures, presumably because of the accumulation of active metabolites that excite the CNS. Maprotiline does not appear to cause deterioration in cognitive functions. It is generally not an antidepressant of first choice.

Amoxapine (Asendin) is another atypical antidepressant, structurally different from the TCAs (see Figure 9.7). Amoxapine is primarily a norepinephrine reuptake inhibitor, clinically as effective an antidepressant as imipramine, although it may be slightly more effective in relieving accompanying anxiety and agitation. The use of amoxapine can be associated with parkinsonianlike neuroleptic side effects (it blocks postsynaptic dopamine receptors). The drug is metabolized to an active intermediate, 8-hydroxy-amoxapine, which may be responsible for the dopamine receptor blockade and neuroleptic effects. Like TCAs, overdosage can result in fatalities. Again, it is not generally an antidepressant of first choice.

Trazodone (Desyrel) is yet another chemically unique antidepressant (see Figure 9.7), therapeutically as efficacious as the TCAs. Its mechanism of antidepressant action is unclear because it is not a potent reuptake blocker of either norepinephrine or serotonin. However, it (or its active metabolite) does block a subclass of serotonin receptors (the serotonin-2, or 5-HT$_2$, receptors), and it appears to down regulate serotonin receptors. Trazodone has a shorter onset of action (about a week), but 2 to 5 weeks are still required to produce an optimal effect. Drowsiness is the most common side effect, and the drug's main use is as an antidepressant sleeping pill. The drug is taken at bedtime to promote a good night's sleep. Its main side effect can be serious: in rare instances, priapism (prolonged and painful penile erections) limits its use in males. This side effect requires prompt attention as it can lead to permanent impotence and infertility. The detrimental effects of trazodone on cognitive functioning appear modest. Trazodone has less anticholinergic activity than the TCAs and causes fewer problems than TCAs when taken in overdose.

Bupropion (Wellbutrin, Zyban; see Figure 9.7) is an effective antidepressant that is used both for its antidepressant action and as an anticraving agent in the treatment of nicotine dependence. Its antidepressant effect is similar to that seen with SSRIs, and the use of bupropion is associated with less nausea, diarrhea, somnolence, and sexual dysfunction (Niewstraten and Dolovich, 2001). Bupropion is also useful as add-on, or augmenting, therapy in patients only partially responsive or nonresponsive to SSRIs (DeBattista et al., 2003; Kennedy et al., 2002) and in patients with difficult-to-treat bipolar depression (Erfurth et al., 2002). In treating depressed patients, bupropion, unlike SSRIs, exhibits evidence of enhanced sexual functioning or minimal sexual dysfunction (Clayton et al., 2002; Fava and Rankin, 2002). It can be combined with SSRIs to antagonize the sexual dysfunction caused by the SSRI (Clayton et al. 2004). Short-term treatment with long-acting bupropion (Wellbutrin SR) can result in weight loss, an advantage in patients in whom weight gain is a problem. Tolerance appears to develop to this action, however, and weight loss is limited.

As an anticraving drug, bupropion is widely used as part of nicotine replacement therapies for smoking cessation (Ferry and Johnston, 2003; Haustein, 2003; West, 2003). Treatment of nicotine dependence is discussed further in Chapter 8.

Mechanistically, bupropion is unique as an antidepressant in that it selectively inhibits *dopamine* and, to a lesser degree, *norepinephrine* reuptake (Horst and Preskorn, 1998). It is without effect on serotonin neurons. Bupropion does not exert a reinforcing or dependency-inducing action. Because of its potentiation of dopamine, it has been used to treat children with ADHD (Chapter 13), although this effect is not very robust. While not commonly used as an anxiolytic, Zisook and coworkers (2001) reported that bupropion was effective in treating grief following the death of a loved one.

Side effects of bupropion include anxiety, restlessness, tremor, and insomnia. More serious side effects include the induction of psychosis de novo and generalized seizures. Bupropion is not effective in the treatment of panic disorder, and it may even exacerbate or precipitate panic in susceptible individuals. Higher-than-recommended doses of bupropion may cause a manic switch in patients with bipolar depression.

Clomipramine (Anafranil) is structurally a TCA (see Figure 9.7), but unlike TCAs, it exerts inhibitory effects on serotonin reuptake (Suhara et al., 2003). In addition, it and its active metabolite, desmethylclomipramine, also inhibit norepinephrine reuptake. Thus, it is classified as a *mixed serotonin-norepineprine reuptake inhibitor,* similar to venlafaxine (discussed next). Clomipramine has long been used to treat OCD; about 40 to 75 percent of patients with OCD respond favorably. The drug has also been used in the treatment of depression, panic disorder, and phobic disorders. Clomipramine is approximately equal to the TCAs in both its efficacy and its profile of side effects.

Clinically, clomipramine is one of the older antidepressants. It has strong antidepressant and antipanic efficacy, equaling or surpassing that of many other antidepressants. Its efficacy, however, is limited by a high dropout rate due to adverse side effects. Papp and coworkers (1997) concluded that clomipramine should not be used as a first-line antipanic medication.

Venlafaxine (Effexor; see Figure 15.7) is also classified as a mixed *serotonin-norepinephrine reuptake inhibitor.* The serotonin blockade occurs at lower doses than does the norepinephrine blockade (Horst and

Preskorn, 1998). To a far lesser degree, venlafaxine also inhibits the re-uptake of dopamine. Venlafaxine lacks anticholinergic or antihista-minic effects, a distinct advantage. The primary metabolite of ven-lafaxine is pharmacologically active; the half-lives of the parent compound and the primary metabolite are 5 hours and 11 hours, re-spectively. Its clinical effectiveness compares favorably with that of SSRIs, even in depressed elderly patients (Gasto et al., 2003; *Medical Letter*, 2004). Venlafaxine produces improvements in psychomotor and cognitive function, probably because of the relief of depression and the absence of detrimental sedative and anticholinergic effects. In high doses, venlafaxine can cause modest increases in blood pressure. Venlafaxine has comparable efficacy to clomipramine in treating OCD, with fewer adverse effects. In an extended-release formulation (Effexor ER), venlafaxine is widely used in the treatment of generalized anxiety disorder (Gelenberg et al., 2000; Rickels et al., 2000).

Venlafaxine appears to have only minimal effects on drug-metabo-lizing enzymes, and drug interactions are few. Einarson and coworkers (1999) conducted a meta-analysis review of venlafaxine, SSRIs, and TCAs in the treatment of depression and concluded that venlafaxine may be clinically superior to other classes of antidepressants in treating adults with major depression. Venlafaxine has analgesic properties superior to those of the SSRIs, and this action may be beneficial when combined with its anxiolytic and antidepressant properties. Venlafaxine is useful in treating patients with fibromyalgia and chronic pain syn-dromes with comorbid anxiety and depression.

Selective Serotonin Reuptake Inhibitors

Selective serotonin reuptake inhibitors (SSRIs) have now been used to treat depression for more than 15 years. Six SSRIs are currently avail-able: fluoxetine (Prozac), paroxetine (Paxil), sertraline (Zoloft), fluvox-amine (Luvox), citalopram (Celexa), and escitalopram (Lexapro). These drugs all block the function of the presynaptic transporter for serotonin reuptake; they do not appear to block reuptake of other neu-rotransmitters to any significant degree, nor do they block postsynap-tic serotonin receptors of any subtype. Therefore, more serotonin is available in the synaptic cleft to activate any or all of the many postsy-naptic receptors for serotonin. Such "purity" of effect has led to both the popularity and the side effects of SSRIs.

The only known common final effect of antidepressant treatments is an enhancement of 5-HT neurotransmission in the CNS. Increased serotonin availability at 5-HT_1-type receptors is associated with anti-depressant and anxiolytic effects. Increased serotonin availability at 5-HT_2- and 5-HT_3-type receptors is related to adverse effects. Increased

$5-HT_2$ receptor activity is associated with insomnia, anxiety, agitation, sexual dysfunction, and the production of a "serotonin syndrome" in higher doses. Increased $5-HT_3$ receptor activity is responsible for the nausea that these drugs can cause.

As a general statement, there are only minimal differences between individual SSRIs; all are equally effective (Kroenke et al., 2001). However, they are not necessarily interchangeable: patients who discontinue one SSRI for lack of tolerability or response can sometimes be treated effectively with another. Differences lie in individual pharmacokinetics and in effects that inhibit particular drug-metabolizing enzymes in the liver (Table 9.3), thus adversely and possibly dangerously interacting with other medicines that the patient may be taking.

Therapeutic indications for SSRI therapy are primarily for major depression, dysthymia, and the anxiety disorders (panic disorder, OCD, GAD, PTSD, phobias). SSRIs have also been tried in many other clinical situations. Before discussing individual SSRIs, we address four concerns associated with SSRI therapy: (1) the serotonin syndrome, (2) the serotonin withdrawal syndrome, (3) SSRI-induced sexual dysfunction, and (4) possible fetal effects if the mother takes the SSRI during pregnancy or periods of breast-feeding.

Serotonin Syndrome

At high doses or when combined with other drugs, a disturbing situation termed *serotonin syndrome* can occur. Increased central accumulation of serotonin leads to an exaggerated response, characterized by alterations in cognition (disorientation, confusion, hypomania), behavior (agitation, restlessness), autonomic nervous system functions (fever, shivering, chills, sweating, diarrhea, hypertension, tachycardia), and neuromuscular activity (ataxia, increased reflexes, myoclonus) (Lane and Baldwin, 1997). Visual hallucinations have even been

TABLE 9.3 Ability of SSRIs to inhibit CYP liver enzymes of various subtypes

Drug	CYP450 1A2	CYP450 2C9	CYP450 2C19	CYP450 2D6	CYP450 3A4
Citalopram (Celexa)	0	0	0	+	0
Escitalopram (Lexapro)	0	0	0	+	0
Fluoxetine (Prozac)	+	++	+/++	+++	+/++
Paroxetine (Paxil)	+	+	+	+++	+
Sertraline (Zoloft)	+	+	+	+/++	+
Fluvoxamine (Luvox)	+	++	++	+++	++

reported. Some of these symptoms might result from excess serotonin at 5-HT$_2$ receptors, the site of action of the psychedelic drug LSD (Chapter 19). The higher the serotonin specificity, the higher the potential for producing serotonin syndrome. For example, paroxetine (Paxil) is one of the most specific SSRIs, and it is perhaps the SSRI most implicated in causing serotonin syndrome.

In theory, any drug that has a net effect of increasing serotonin function can produce the syndrome; usually, however, it results from the combination of an SSRI and other serotonergic drugs, especially since these drugs can inhibit each other's metabolic detoxification and potentiate each other's effects (Hamilton and Malone, 2000). The syndrome can even occur when SSRIs are combined with with herbal substances such as St. John's wort or valerian (Chapter 16). Once drugs are discontinued, the syndrome usually resolves within 24 to 48 hours; during this time, support is the primary treatment.

Serotonin Withdrawal Syndrome

If drug dependence is defined as a change in physiology or behavior following drug discontinuation, a person can become dependent on SSRIs, even though they are not considered to be "addicting" drugs. A serotonin withdrawal syndrome occurs in perhaps 60 percent of SSRI-treated patients following drug removal. The syndrome was originally associated with withdrawal from paroxetine, but it can occur following discontinuation of any SSRI. Onset is usually within a few days and persists perhaps three to four weeks. The exception is fluoxetine, whose long half-life results in a slow onset of symptomatology (perhaps one to two weeks) with persistence for several weeks thereafter. Schatzberg and coworkers (1997) describe five core somatic sets of symptoms:

- Disequilibria (dizziness, vertigo, ataxia)
- Gastrointestinal symptoms (nausea, vomiting, diarrhea)
- Flulike symptoms (fatigue, lethargy, myalgias, chills)
- Sensory disturbances (paresthesia, sensation of electric shocks)
- Sleep disturbances (insomnia, vivid dreams)

Psychological symptoms include anxiety, agitation, crying spells, and irritability. Other less frequently reported symptoms include overactivity, depersonalization, depressed mood, memory problems, confusion, decreased concentration, and slowed thinking. All these somatic and psychological phenomena abate over time and rapidly disappear when the SSRI is reintroduced. It is felt that the syndrome results from a relative deficiency of serotonin when the SSRI is stopped; however, the etiology of the exact mechanism may be more complex.

SSRI-Induced Sexual Dysfunction

Sexual dysfunction is often associated with major depressive disorder and SSRI medications can further compound it. Up to 80 percent of depressed patients treated with SSRIs exhibit sexual dysfunction, including problems with orgasm, erection, sexual interest, desire, and psychological arousal (Michelson et al., 2000). In males, ejaculatory dysfunction seems most prominent. Loss of desire and sexual dysfunction can affect medication compliance and impair interpersonal relationships. Treatment of sexual dysfunction may involve discontinuation of the SSRI and switching to an antidepressant in another class (for example, bupropion). The use of sildenafil (Viagra) may relieve males with erectile dysfunction (Nurnberg et al., 2001; Seidman et al., 2001).

Effects in Pregnancy and Breast-Feeding

Taken during pregnancy, no SSRI introduced through 1998 (fluoxetine, fluvoxamine, paroxetine, or sertraline) increased the incidence of major malformations, live births, teratogenicity, or low birth weights or led to higher rates of miscarriage, stillbirths, or prematurity. Data with citalopram are somewhat controversial, but that drug appears to be relatively safe during pregnancy and periods of breast-feeding. Heikkinen and coworkers (2002) observed no complications from citalopram in children of 10 pregnant women; infant concentrations at the time of delivery were 65 percent of the mother's plasma concentration. During breast-feeding, while concentrations of citalopram were high in mother's milk, concentrations in the infants were very low or undetectable.

Whether or not SSRIs taken during pregnancy might have subtle effects on the newborn is controversial. On the one hand, Heikkinen and coworkers (2003) noted that, despite newborns having fluoxetine levels 65 percent of those of the mother, growth and development of all infants up to 1 year of age were normal. On the other hand, Laine and coworkers (2003) observed signs of serotonin withdrawal syndrome in infants exposed to SSRIs administered to the mother in the late stages of pregnancy. Casper and coworkers (2003) reported that at birth, newborns of mothers exposed to SSRIs during pregnancy had lower APGAR scores than did infants of nontreated mothers. In addition, some children exhibited subtle effects on motor development and motor control to age 40 months. Nonetheless, it is felt that depression in women who happen to be pregnant needs to be treated, although perhaps alternatives to the use of SSRIs should be sought.

After delivery, any postpartum depression should be treated and the SSRIs are drugs of choice because of well-documented safety. The effects of drugs on the breast-feeding infant must be considered, but levels of drug in breast-feeding infants are extremely low—about 1 to 3 percent of the maternal concentration (Heikkinen et al., 2002, 2003).

Specific SSRIs

Fluoxetine. Fluoxetine (Prozac; Figure 9.8) became clinically available in the United States in 1988 as the first SSRI-type antidepressant and the first non-TCA that could be considered a first-line antidepressant (not just for patients who have failed therapy with TCAs). Fluoxetine's efficacy is comparable to that of the TCAs; more important, it is not fatal in overdosage because it is devoid of the TCA-caused cardiac toxicity (as are all SSRIs). Because of its selectivity, fluoxetine (and other SSRIs) demonstrate few anticholinergic or antihistaminic side effects. Thus, SSRIs cause little or no sedation and little impairment of learning, memory, or cognition.

Besides use in treating major depression, fluoxetine has been used in the treatment of dysthymia, alcohol withdrawal, and virtually all the

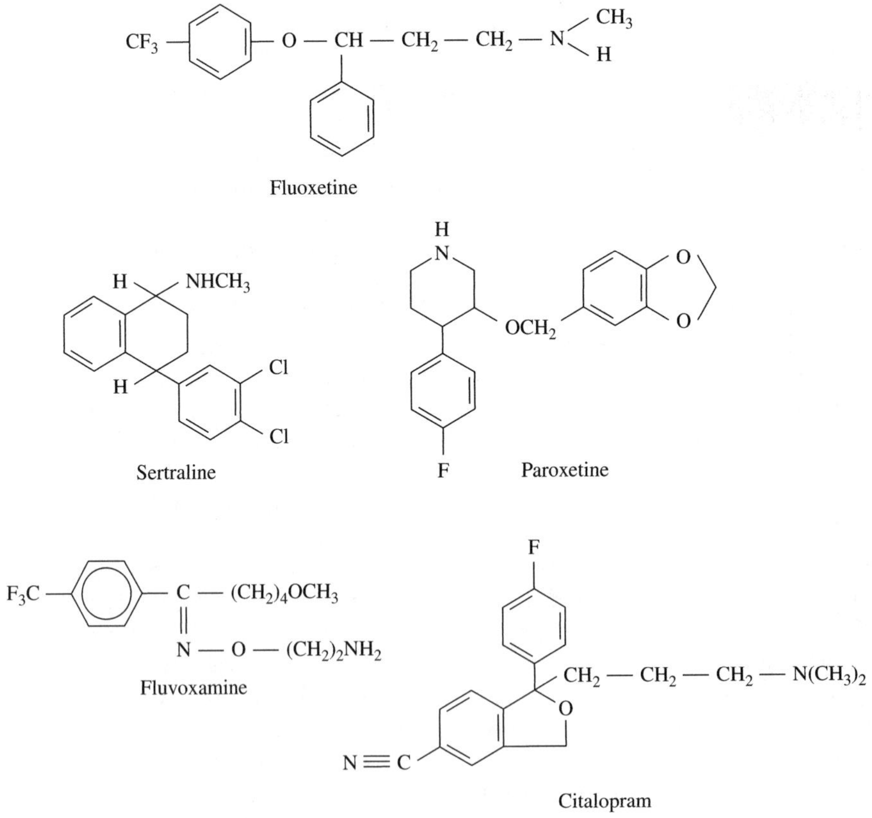

FIGURE 9.8 Chemical structures of five selective serotonin reuptake inhibitor (SSRI) antidepressants. The sixth SSRI, escitalopram, is the active isomer of citalopram and is therefore not shown.

various subtypes of anxiety disorders. In treatment of comorbid anxiety and depression, fluoxetine is effective but not quite as effective as venlafaxine (Davidson et al., 2002). More recently, fluoxetine (and sertraline) has been shown to be effective in relieving the symptoms of a syndrome termed "premenstrual dysphoric disorder" (Pearlson, 2002). For this use, the manufacturer of Prozac marketed fluoxetine under an additional and new trade name, *Serafem*. Pearlson and coworkers (2003) demonstrated that symptoms of premenstrual dysphoric disorder recur when fluoxetine administration is stopped. They claim that this finding "supports the view of premenstrual dysphoric disorder as a clinical entity distinct from depression" (p. 887).

Fluoxetine has a half-life of about 2 to 3 days, but its active metabolite (*norfluoxetine,* which is even a stronger reuptake inhibitor than fluoxetine) has a half-life of about 6 to 10 days. This prolonged action distinguishes fluoxetine from other SSRIs, which have half-lives of about 1 day and no active intermediates. Also because of its long half-life, fluoxetine need not be administered every day; it can be taken as infrequently as once a week (Schmidt et al., 2000). A once-weekly oral formulation of fluoxetine is commercially available under the trade name *Prozac Weekly.*

Like all SSRIs, fluoxetine's antidepressant action is of slow onset (about 4 to 6 weeks), and the drug and its metabolite thus tend to build with repeated doses over about 2 months, presumably because both compounds continue to accumulate. This action can explain not only the slow onset of peak therapeutic effect but the late onset of side effects and the prolonged duration of action following drug discontinuation. Therapeutic trials with fluoxetine should continue for at least 8 weeks before the drug is determined to be ineffective (Quitkin et al., 2003). If therapy needs to be stopped and the patient switched to another antidepressant, a 5-week drug-free interval is recommended between the two events.

Significant and important side effects of fluoxetine include anxiety, agitation, and insomnia, which at the extreme can result in the serotonin syndrome. At the extreme, SSRIs (including fluoxetine) may have been implicated in new-onset manic or psychotic attacks, especially in patients with either a family history of schizophrenia or a personal history of either mania or psychosis (Henry et al., 2001). As discussed, sexual dysfunction is common, as is serotonin withdrawal syndrome, on discontinuation. However, the long half-life of fluoxetine limits the intensity of the syndrome and prolongs it over a period of several weeks.

Garland and Baerg (2001) reported on five adolescents, previously well treated with fluoxetine or paroxetine (discussed later), who developed a dose-dependent, reversible, frontal lobe amotivational syndrome characterized by apathy, lack of motivation, indifference, loss of initiative, and/or behavioral disinhibition. Perhaps this induced state of detachment, apathy, and indifference explains the usefulness of SSRIs in treating obsessive compulsive disorder.

Fluoxetine and the other SSRIs (except citalopram) inhibit certain of the drug-metabolizing enzymes in the liver (see Table 9.3). Therefore, coadministration of fluoxetine can increase the level of other drugs that the patient might be taking, even doubling the blood levels of caffeine after drinking usual doses of caffeine-containing beverages.

Finally, in 2004, the FDA approved a novel combination of fluoxetine and olanzapine (discussed in Chapter 11) for the treatment of depressive episodes associated with bipolar disorder (Chapter 10). The combination product is trade named Symbyax, and it is the first FDA-approved treatment for this phase of bipolar disorder (Tohen et al., 2003). The rationale for this use will become more apparent following discussion of bipolar disorder (Chapter 10) and the pharmacology of olanzapine (Chapter 11).

Sertraline. Sertraline (Zoloft; see Figure 9.8) was the second SSRI approved for clinical use in the United States. Clinically, like all SSRIs, it is as effective as TCAs in the treatment of major depression and dysthymia, with fewer side effects and improved patient compliance (Ravindram et al., 2000; Williams et al., 2000). It has also been approved by the FDA for use in treating premenstrual dysphoric disorder. Compared with desipramine (a TCA), sertraline is more effective in reducing major depressive disorder and OCD symptoms. Further, more patients receiving a TCA discontinue treatment because of adverse effects. Sertraline is also effective in anxiety disorder subtypes such as social phobias, panic disorder, OCD, and posttraumatic stress disorder (PTSD) (Davidson et al., 2001). In elderly people with cognitive impairments, sertraline can alleviate depression and improve measures of attention and executive functioning (Devan et al., 2003).

Sertraline is four to five times more potent than fluoxetine in blocking serotonin reuptake and is more selective. Because of this increased serotonin selectivity, serotonin-associated side effects (serotonin syndrome and serotonin withdrawal syndrome) may be more intense than with fluoxetine. Steady-state levels of the drug in plasma are achieved within 4 to 7 days, and its metabolites are less cumulative and less pharmacologically active. Like all SSRIs, sertraline has few anticholinergic, antihistaminic, and adverse cardiovascular effects, as well as a low risk of toxicity in overdose.

Paroxetine. Paroxetine (Paxil, Pexeva) was the third SSRI available for clinical use in treating major depression, dysthymia, and the various anxiety disorders. Therapeutically, it is comparable to the TCAs in efficacy and clearly superior to placebo (Wagstaff et al., 2002). It is highly effective in reducing anxiety, a common symptom in depressive illness. It is effective in PTSD (Marshall et al., 2001) and generalized anxiety disorder (Rickels et al., 2003; Stocchi et al., 2003). Similar data indicate usefulness in OCD, panic disorder, social phobia, social anxiety disorder, and premenstrual dysphoric disorder (Green, 2003). Like sertraline, paroxetine is more selective than fluoxetine in blocking serotonin reuptake. Also, paroxetine's metabolites are relatively inactive, and steady state is achieved in about 7 days. The metabolic half-life is about 24 hours.

Paroxetine is perhaps the SSRI most associated with serotonin syndrome, serotonin withdrawal syndrome, new-onset or precipitation of psychosis, paranoid ideations, temper dyscontrol, delusional convictions, and even visual hallucinations. These effects all may be the result of its being the most selective SSRI and perhaps selective to abnormal 5-HT_2 receptor stimulation.

Fluvoxamine. In 1995 fluvoxamine (Luvox), a structural derivative of fluoxetine (see Figure 9.8) became available for the treatment of OCD. Like all SSRIs, fluvoxamine has well-described antidepressant properties, comparable in efficacy to the TCA imipramine, but fewer serious side effects and superior patient compliance. Fluvoxamine, like all SSRIs, has a variety of clinical uses, including treatment of PTSD, OCD (Hollander et al., 2003), dysphoria, panic disorder, and social phobia. It is effective in the treatment of mixed anxiety and depression (Rausch et al., 2001). Fluvoxamine, like other SSRIs, is useful in the treatment of anxiety disorders in children and adolescents (Cheer and Figgitt, 2002). This topic and the ongoing controversy over the use of SSRIs in this population are discussed further in Chapter 13.

Citalopram. (Celexa; see Figure 9.8) is an SSRI available in Europe since 1989 and introduced into the United States in 1998 as the fifth SSRI. It is effective in the treatment of major depression, social phobia, panic disorder, and OCD. In treating all these disorders, it is equal in efficacy to other drug therapies, including all other SSRIs (Pollock, 2001). Citalopram is claimed to have a more rapid onset of action than does fluoxetine, but this speed is probably related to differences in half-life and therefore to different times to peak plasma levels with continued dosing. Extremely large doses of citalopram have been associated with ECG irregularities, seizures, and rare fatalities. It has a lower incidence of inhibition of drug-metabolizing hepatic enzymes, so it might be better for patients who are taking multiple medications (Brosen and Naranjo, 2001).

Citalopram is well absorbed orally; peak plasma levels are reached in about 4 hours. Steady state is achieved in about 1 week, and maximal effects are seen in about 5 to 6 weeks. Citalopram is metabolized in the liver to three metabolites with SSRI activity; however, these metabolites are less selective and less potent than the parent drug and they are present in only low levels in plasma. The elimination half-life is about 33 hours, enabling once-per-day dosing. The elderly have a reduced ability to metabolize citalopram and a 33 to 50 percent reduction in dose is necessary.

Citalopram has been reported to moderately reduce alcohol consumption in problem alcoholics. It would be expected that citalopram would exert anxiolytic effects similar to those exerted by other SSRIs. Adverse effects of citalopram resemble those of other SSRIs.

Escitalopram. Escitalopram (Lexapro) was released in the United States in 2002 for the treatment of major depression (Burke et al., 2002). It is also effective in the treatment of GAD, panic disorder, OCD, and social anxiety disorders. The drug is the therapeutically active isomer of citalopram. As an active isomer, the only difference is potency: escitalopram is twice as potent as citalopram, so the prescribed dose is 50 percent of the dose of citalopram. In other words, 10 milligrams of escitaloprame is equivalent to 20 milligrams of citalopram.

Dual-Action Antidepressants

In many respects, the TCAs were the first dual-action antidepressants: they block the presynaptic reuptake of both norepinephrine and serotonin. Side effects due to histamine and acetylcholine receptors limited their widespread use. Similarly, venlafaxine is a dual-action antidepressant, and its utility is becoming increasingly appreciated. The unitary action of the SSRIs, while associated with efficacy against a wide variety of anxiety and depressive disorders, is limited by side effects common to serotonin overactivity, especially at $5\text{-}HT_2$ and $5\text{-}HT_3$ receptors. Therefore, attempts have been made to expand on the concept that actions at two different synaptic sites may improve or maintain efficacy while limiting side effects. Kent (2000) and Tran and coworkers (2003) reviewed the pharmacology of several of these drugs. Four of them are discussed here.

Nefazodone

Nefazodone (Serzone; Figure 9.9) is a dual-action antidepressant chemically related to trazodone but with some important pharmacological distinctions (DeVane et al., 2002). Nefazadone's strongest pharmacological action is $5\text{-}HT_2$ receptor blockade, an action that distinguishes it from the SSRIs. Nefazodone also inhibits both serotonin and norepinephrine reuptake at its therapeutic dose. With chronic administration, nefazodone ultimately down regulates both

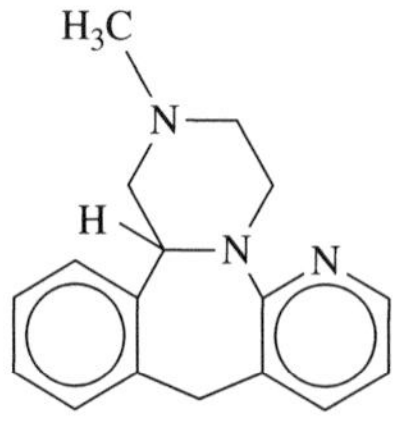

Mirtazepine (Remeron)

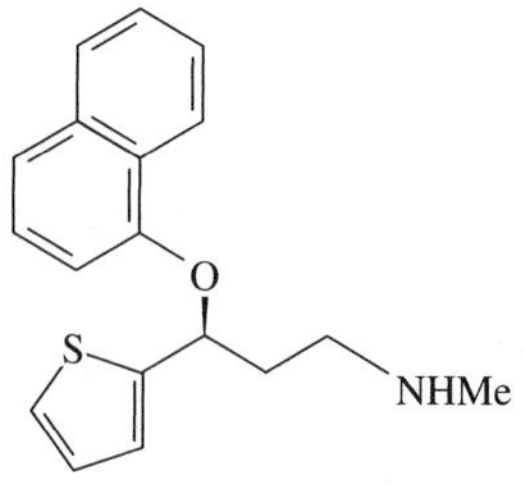

Duloxetine (Cymbalta)

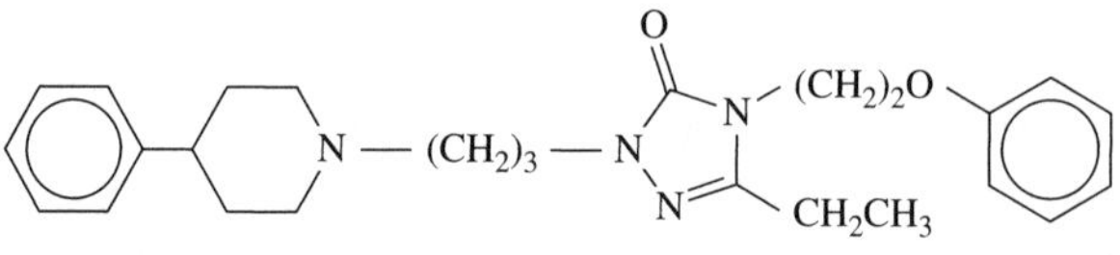

Nefazodone (Serzone)

FIGURE 9.9 Chemical structures of three dual-action antidepressants.

norepinephrine and serotonin receptors. Blockade of reuptake is thought to be responsible for its antidepressant activity, and the 5-HT_2 blockade is thought to be responsible for the absence of SSRI-type side effects as well as relief of the sleep disturbances and comorbid anxiety symptoms often seen in depressed patients (Horst and Preskorn, 1998). Comorbid panic and phobic symptoms in depressed patients respond favorably to nefazodone. Serotonin 5-HT_2 receptor blockade also accounts for the relative absence of drug-induced sexual dysfunction with ongoing treatment.

Sedation can be bothersome, as can nausea, dry mouth, dizziness, and light-headedness. The sedative effects can often be advantageous in the treatment of depression-related insomnia and nighttime awakenings. In treating depression, nefazodone has not been shown to have therapeutic superiority over TCAs or SSRIs or faster onset of action. However, absence of weight gain and sexual dysfunction make it a good alternative in patients who are unresponsive to or intolerant of other antidepressants.

Other reported uses of nefazodone include use in alcoholics with comorbid depression (it relieves depression but does not reduce alcohol consumption) (Roy-Byrne et al., 2000), in pathological gamblers (Pallanti et al., 2002), and in relieving the distress of PTSD in combat veterans who are treatment resistant (Zisook et al., 2000).

In 2003, a new "black box" warning concerning liver failure that may result in death or necessitate liver transplantation was added to the information literature about nefazodone. Analysis of over

7 million patients taking the drug noted an incidence of liver failure in 1 case per 250,000 to 300,000 patient-years of nefazodone treatment. (1 patient-year is equal to one patient taking the drug for one year, two patients taking the drug for 6 months each, and so on.) This rate is about three to four times greater than that in the general population. Although the rate is low, caution is warranted. The drug was removed from the market in Canada in 2004 but currently remains available in the United States.

Mirtazepine

Mirtazepine (Remeron; see Figure 9.9) was introduced into clinical use in the United States in 1997. Mirtazepine is as effective and as well tolerated as fluoxetine in treating depression. It relieves depression, anxiety, somatization, and sleep disturbances associated with depression. According to Kasper (1996):

> In line with the concept that severe depression may respond better to drugs with a dual rather than a single mode of action, mirtazepine is a noradrenergic and specific serotonergic antidepressant. It has a different mode of action from TCAs, SSRIs, and MAOIs, because it increases noradrenergic and serotonergic neurotransmission via a blockade of the central alpha$_2$-autoreceptors and heteroreceptors. The increased release of serotonin, via increased cell firings of 5-HT neurons, stimulates only the 5-HT$_1$ type receptors, because 5-HT$_2$ and 5-HT$_3$ type receptors are specifically blocked by mirtazepine. (p. 556)

Although this explanation is complicated, it explains how mirtazepine enhances both norepinephrine and serotonin neurotransmission and ultimately down regulates receptor activity. Holm and Markham (1999) reviewed the pharmacology of mirtazepine.

Mirtazepine is a potent antagonist of postsynaptic 5-HT$_2$ and 5-HT$_3$ receptors (Figure 9.10), so it does not produce the side effects of SSRIs (especially anxiety, insomnia, agitation, nausea, and sexual dysfunction). Mirtazepine is also a potent blocker of histamine receptors, and drowsiness is a prominent and often therapeutically limiting side effect. Sedation may be advantageous in depressed patients with symptoms of anxiety and insomnia, a common occurrence. Because of the drowsiness, the drug should not be combined with alcohol or other CNS depressants. Other side effects of mirtazepine include increased appetite and weight gain.

Mirtazepine is rapidly absorbed orally; peak blood levels occur 2 hours after administration. The elimination half-life is 20 to 40 hours, allowing once-a-day administration, usually at bedtime to maximize sleep and minimize daytime sedation.

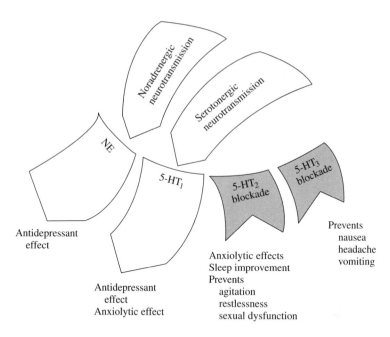

FIGURE 9.10 Pharmacological profile of mirtazapine. Note that the drug potentiates noradrenergic and serotoninergic neurotransmission and blocks serotonin 5-HT$_2$ and 5-HT$_3$ receptors. The consequences of each action are shown at the bottom of the figure. [From R. M. Pinder, "The Pharmacologic Rationale for the Clinical Use of Antidepressants," *Journal of Clinical Psychiatry* 58 (1997), p. 502.]

Duloxetine

Duloxetine (Cymbalta) is a dual-action antidepressant that was approved for clinical use in the United States in late 2004. Duloxetine binds to and blocks the reuptake transporters for norepinephrine and serotonin (Karpa et al., 2002). The blockade seems to be more complete than that of venlafaxine (Bymaster et al., 2001). The manufacturer that markets Prozac also developed duloxetine. Now that fluoxetine is available in generic form, Cymbalta is being promoted as a replacement. As a medical director of the manufacturer once stated, "It is well known that depression is a disease involving multiple transmitters; patients get therapeutic benefit from both mechanisms of action."[3]

Duloxetine is clinically effective in the treatment of both depression (Detke et al., 2002; Goldstein et al., 2002) and anxiety (Dunner et al., 2003). In these studies, duloxetine significantly reduced physical symptoms of pain—such as backaches, headache, muscle and joint

[3]Quotation taken from an interview with the medical director of the dualoxetine antidepressant research team at Lilly Research Laboratories. It appeared in *Psychopharmacology Update* 12 (July 2001): 1.

pain, and back and shoulder pain—reduced interference with daily activities, and reduced time in pain while awake. There is a close association between pain and the development of depressive symptoms (Bair et al., 2003), and it seems likely that duloxetine will be useful for the treatment of syndromes with comorbid pain and depression (fibromyalgia, chronic fatigue syndrome, and so on). Duloxetine is also being tested for the treatment of urinary stress incontinence (Norton et al., 2002). The mechanism underlying this action is unclear.

The half-life of duloxetine is about 12 hours, allowing once-daily dosing. Nausea is the most common side effect. Weight gain and sexual dysfunction have not yet been problems with the drug. Elevations in blood pressure (hypertension), thought to be possible with duloxetine, have not yet been a major problem in clinical studies.

Milnacipran

Milnacipran (Ixel) is a new drug in clinical development as a dual-action antidepressant. Like duloxetine, it is a blocker of norepinephrine and serotonin reuptake (Tran et al., 2003). In the treatment of major depression in hospitalized patients, milnacipran was equivalent in efficacy to imipramine and superior to SSRIs (Clerk, 2001). Onset of action appears to be shorter than with other agents, perhaps as short as 2 weeks. A timetable for availability of this agent is not yet set.

Selective Norepinephrine Reuptake Inhibitors

Recently, drugs have been identified that are specific blockers of the presynaptic transporter that captures norepinephrine present in the synaptic cleft and transports the norepinephrine back into the presynaptic nerve terminal. These drugs are referred to as selective norepinephrine reuptake inhibitors (SNRIs). The first SNRI (atomoxetine) has been marketed, and a second (reboxetine) is awaiting FDA approval. Both drugs have potential for a wide variety of clinical uses.

Atomoxetine

Until recently, no antidepressant exhibited specific NE reuptake blockade in the absence of dopamine or serotonin reuptake blockade. *Reboxetine* (Vestra, Edronax) and *atomoxetine* (Strattera) are two agents now pharmacologically classified as SNRIs (Figure 9.11). Atomoxetine became commercially available in 2003 for the treatment of ADHD in children, adolescents, and adults (Michelson et al., 2003); It was the first nonstimulant drug to be approved by the FDA for the treatment of ADHD. It is claimed to be as effective as methylphenidate (Kratochvil et al., 2002), probably without abuse potential (Heil et al.,

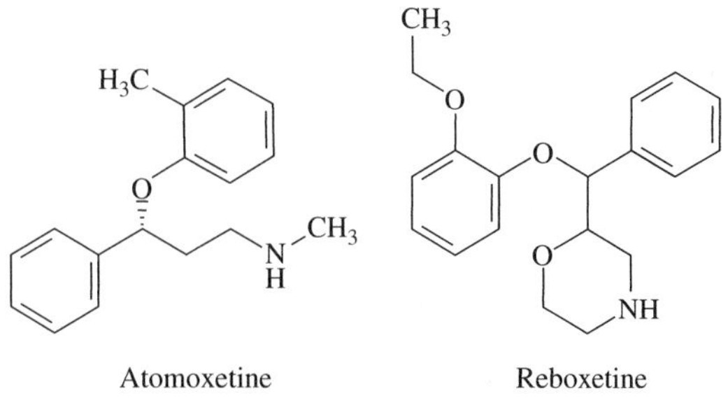

FIGURE 9.11 Structures of atomoxetine and reboxetine.

2002). The use of atomoxetine in children and adolescents is discussed in Chapter 13. Simpson and Plosker (2004) and Spencer and coworkers (2004) review the use of atomoxetine in adult ADHD.

Mechanistically, as stated, atomoxetine is an inhibitor of presynaptic norepinephrine reuptake. Bymaster and coworkers (2002) reported that atomoxetine increases norepinephrine and dopamine release threefold in the prefrontal cortex without changing dopamine amounts in the striatum or nucleus accumbens, as do stimulants. Methylphenidate increases striatal and nucleus accumbens dopamine and increases prefrontal cortical norepinephrine and dopamine levels only 1.5 times. The absence of dopamine effects in the striatum and nucleus accumbens implies that atomoxetine is unlikely to have abuse potential and also differentiates it from methylphenidate (Stahl, 2003).

In addition to positive effects on mood and attention, atomoxetine exerts positive effects on social functioning, improving patient motivation, energy, and self-perception (Keller, 2001): "These results indicate that antidepressant therapy can achieve more than symptom relief in depression. It is speculated that there may be a difference in the roles played by serotonin and noradrenaline in social functioning" (p. 15). The same effects on social functioning seem also to apply to reboxetine (Kasper et al., 2000).

Reboxetine

Reboxetine (Vestra, Edronax) was the first SNRI developed for clinical use specifically as an antidepressant drug (atomoxetine is indicated for the treatment of ADHD). Reboxetine has little or no effect on serotonin or dopamine neurotransmission, as well as little or no effect on acetylcholine or histamine neurotransmission or receptors. Therefore, it is virtually devoid of the side effects associated with these transmitters. Montgomery and coworkers (2003) reviewed four prospective, double-blind studies involving reboxetine. The results of the four studies are summarized in Figure 9.12. Overall, the responder rate with reboxetine ranged from 56 percent to 74 percent (mean 63 percent) while that of placebo ranged from 20 to 52 percent (mean 36 percent). Beneficial effects were seen as early as 1 week after starting therapy, considerably sooner than the effects of SSRIs. Indeed, reboxetine is as effective an antidepressant as is fluoxetine, perhaps with beneficial differences in time to onset of action and improvements in social functioning, psychological well-being, and self-motivation.

Ferguson and coworkers (2003) examined the effects of reboxetine, paroxetine, and placebo on cognitive functioning in depressed patients. Results demonstrated that, in comparison with placebo and paroxetine, reboxetine improved the ability to sustain attention and

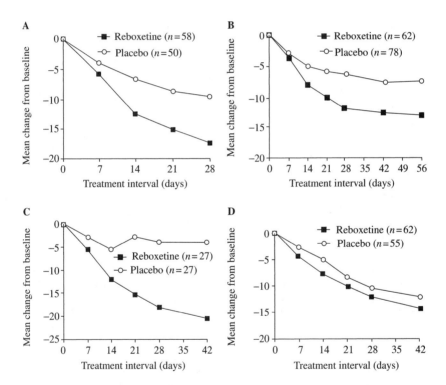

FIGURE 9.12 Reboxetine-induced reductions in Hamilton Depression Rating Scale scores (measured as mean change from baseline values) in four clinical trials as reviewed by Montgomery and coworkers (2003). In three of the four studies (A–C), the response rate (decrease in HAM-D score of at least 50 percent from baseline) was significantly better with reboxetine than with placebo. In the fourth study (D), the responder rate was similar with reboxetine to that seen in the other three studies, but the difference from placebo was not statistically significant because of a high response rate to placebo. Overall, the response rate with reboxetine ranged from 56 to 74 percent (mean 63 percent) and that of placebo ranged from 20 to 52 percent (mean 36 percent).

improved the speed of cognitive functioning. It therefore appears that reboxetine favorably affects cognitive processes in depressed patients, probably independently of its effects on depression. Fava and coworkers (2003) note that reboxetine may be effective in the treatment of depression in patients unresponsive to fluoxetine. In addition, the switch to reboxetine was well tolerated.

Side effects are mainly cholinergic in nature and usually are quite mild: increased heart rate and blood pressure, dry mouth, sweating, and urinary retention (beneficial in treatment of urinary incontinence). The half-life of reboxetine is about 12 hours, allowing once-daily dosing. The drug is well absorbed orally and is metabolized in the liver by the CYP3A4 system of enzymes: there are no significant enzyme interactions. Plasma concentrations are increased in the elderly and in patients with liver dysfunction.

Aside from use in depression, reboxetine has been shown to be effective in seasonal affective disorder, often producing full remission (Hilger et al., 2001). Dannon and coworkers (2002) and Versiani and coworkers (2002) reported on its efficacy in treating panic disorder: "The favorable tolerability profile of reboxetine will prove to be a valuable alternative therapy for treatment of this debilitating condition" (p. 35). Reboxetine has also been used as adjuvant therapy in the treatment of schizophrenia with atypical antipsychotics. It also serves to attenuate the weight gain caused by such antipsychotics as olanzapine (Poyurovsky et al., 2003). A year-2000 symposium discusses reboxetine and the role of norepinephrine in the treatment of depression. It is expected that reboxetine will become available for clinical use in 2004.

Antidepressants of the Future

The history of antidepressant drugs now encompasses almost 50 years. Scientists are still seeking the "perfect" antidepressant, one that is widely effective in causing remission of acute episodes and preventing future relapses in the absence of significant side effects. As is apparent in the descriptions of current drugs, this goal has yet to be achieved. Therefore, the search continues for potentially superior antidepressant drugs (Holden, 2003). In this section, potential agents of the future are briefly examined.

Modafinil

Modafinil (Provigil) is a nonstimulant wakefulness-promoting drug used to combat daytime fatigue in patients with narcolepsy. In narcoleptic patients, Modafinil may also improve perceived psychological well-being, fatigue, and concentration. Typical psychostimulant-induced side effects (Chapter 7) are not seen with modafinil. Three reports (DeBattista et al., 2004; Markovitz and Wagner, 2003; Menza et al., 2000) have investigated the use of modafinil as an augmenting agent for patients with only partial response to traditional antidepressant drugs. Efficacy and safety were well documented.

Other agents that may well serve as augmenting agents to supplement antidepressant medications in partially responsive patients include mood stabilizers such as *lamotrigine* (Ernst and Goldberg, 2003; Rocha and Hara, 2003) (Chapter 10), the newer atypical antipsychotic drugs such as *quetiapine* and *aripiprazole* (Chapter 11), and certain of the omega-3 fatty acids (discussed at the end of this chapter).

Serotonin 5-HT$_1$ Agonists

Chapter 6 introduced *buspirone* (BuSpar) as an anxiolytic agent and noted that it exerts its effects secondary to weak stimulation of serotonin 5-HT$_{1A}$ receptors. Its poor absorption could be modified but remains a clinical limitation. Since stimulation of 5-HT$_1$ receptors results in antidepressant and anxiolytic effects, it would be logical that specific stimulation of 5-HT$_1$ receptors would provide antidepressant and anxiolytic efficacy. These agents might be most effective in combination with an SSRI, although Feiger and coworkers (2003) reported efficacy of *gepirone-ER* as monotherapy for depression. Gepirone and other similar drugs are in the late stages of development. They are discussed as anxiolytics in Chapter 6.

Substance P Antagonists

Substance P antagonists (SPAs) are a new class of promising compounds for the treatment of depression and associated anxiety (Kramer et al., 2004; Krishnan, 2002; Mantyh, 2002). Substance P is also physiologically involved in such disorders as asthma, inflammatory bowel disease, emesis, and psoriasis, as well as in a variety of pain syndromes including migraine headache and fibromyalgia (Herpfer and Lieb, 2003; Russell, 2002).

Substance P is a naturally occurring, 11-amino-acid protein that belongs to the neurokinin (NK) family of proteins and reacts with the NK$_1$ receptor. Substance P regulates affective behavior and the perception of pain. Substance P is released in response to stress and pain; it increases their perception. Substance P neurons occur in many regions of the brain implicated in the pathogenesis of depression (midbrain, hypothalamus, amygdala, and hippocampus). It is associated with other neurotransmitters implicated in the pathogenesis of depression (Rupniak, 2002), and the adverse effects of this protein are attenuated by SPAs (van der Hart et al., 2002). Therefore, SPAs (also called NK$_1$ antagonists) might be expected to reduce stress, pain, and depression. One such agent, *aprepitant*, is currently under investigation. In early studies, aprepitant appears to be as effective as is paroxetine in treating depression (Rupniak and Kramer, 1999). More research in this most interesting area will be forthcoming.

Tianeptine

Tianeptine is a novel antidepressant compound. In contrast to SSRIs, it *increases* the presynaptic neuronal uptake of serotonin in the brain and thus decreases serotonin neurotransmission. However, tianeptine appears to reduce stress-induced atrophy of neuronal dendrites, exerting a neuronal protective effect against stress (Czeh et al., 2001; Nickel et al., 2003; Wagstaff et al., 2001). Tianeptine appears to restore intracellur mechanisms adversely affected by stress and other insults (Dziedzicka-Wasylewska et al., 2002; Kole et al., 2002; Shakesby et al., 2002).

Its efficacy against major depression is well documented (Dalery et al., 2001; Loo et al., 2001). Its use does not appear to be associated with adverse cognitive, psychomotor, sleep, cardiovascular, body weight, or sexual side effects. Tianeptine is also effective in bipolar depression, dysthymia, and anxiety. It appears quite useful in the elderly and in patients with chronic alcoholism. This fascinating new compound offers both an alternative medication to standard antidepressants and exciting new insights into the pathophysiology of depression and anxiety.

Dehydroepiandrosterone (DHEA)

DHEA is a glucocorticoid hormone secreted by the adrenal glands, but its physiological role is unclear. Sold as a food supplement, DHEA is a precursor of both estrogen and testosterone. Secretion of the hormone peaks at 20 to 25 years of age and declines by about 90 percent by age 70. Low levels of DHEA have been associated with increased incidence of cardiovascular disease. DHEA has been promoted to prevent heart disease, cancer, diabetes, obesity, dementia, aging, multiple sclerosis, and lupus; it increases feelings of physical and psychological well-being. There probably is some truth and much exaggeration in these claims of efficacy. Perhaps the most enduring claim has been that DHEA may delay the aging process, improve mood, and delay the cognitive decline that occurs with age.

Bloch and coworkers (1999) and Wolkowitz and coworkers (1999) conducted double-blind, randomized studies of DHEA on objective measurements of depression, dysthymia, and cognitive functioning. DHEA, but not placebo, exerted a robust effect on mood, improving depression ratings on all measurement scales (Figure 9.13). Symptoms that improved after 6 weeks of DHEA compared with baseline or placebo were as follows: low energy, anhedonia, lack of motivation,

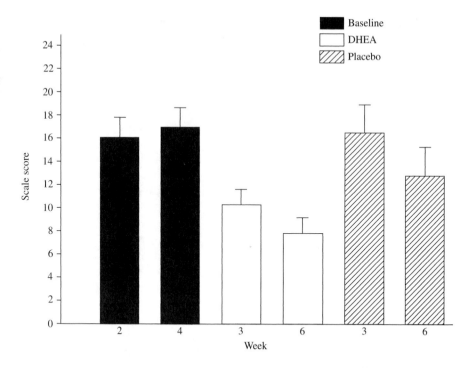

FIGURE 9.13 Reduction of Beck Depression Inventory (BDI) scores during DHEA but not placebo treatment in midlife-onset dysthymia. Fifteen men and women with midlife dysthymia experienced significant reduction in BDI during DHEA treatment compared to both their baseline scores and their scores after placebo treatment. [From Bloch et al. (1999).]

emotional flattening (numbness), sadness, excessive worry, and inability to cope. Response rates (60 percent) were comparable to those seen with standard antidepressants. DHEA had no effect on cognitive function or sleep disturbances. Wolkowitz and coworkers stated:

> DHEA had statistically significant antidepressant effects; nearly half of the DHEA-treated subjects showed clinically meaningful improvement. . . . This finding adds to the growing literature indicating that hormonal dysregulation may be causally related to depressive illness and that certain hormonal treatments can have antidepressant effects. Larger scale controlled trials with DHEA are clearly warranted (p. 648).

Bloch and coworkers concluded by stating: "DHEA may represent a new therapeutic option for mid-life dysthymia" (p. 1533). Strous and coworkers (2003) reported on the efficacy of DHEA to moderate the negative, depressive, and anxiety symptoms of schizophrenia. This effect was especially prominent in women and was independent of improvements in depression. There were no effects on positive symptomatology.

DHEA is usually classified as an androgen because one of its metabolites is testosterone. Therefore, it would not be surprising to see its use accompanied by side effects characteristic of androgens: acne, male-pattern baldness, hirsutism, voice changes, and so on. More serious effects include the theoretical potential for causing breast or prostate cancer and liver damage. The degree to which this damage might happen is unknown.

S-adenosyl-methionine (SAM; SAMe)

S-adenosyl-methionine is a ubiquitous molecule located throughout the body. It plays a key role in metabolic reactions that involve the transfer of methyl groups between molecules. It is not commonly present in the diet, but it is formed in the body by the combination of the amino acid methionine and adenosine triphosphate (ATP). SAMe functions by donating its methyl group to any of a wide range of molecules that are subsequently transformed to homocysteine. Ultimately, the homocysteine is transformed to methionine and the process repeats.

Almost all European trials of the drug have involved parenteral injection. Administered intravenously, SAMe appears to be effective in reducing depression. Trials utilizing oral SAMe have produced poor results. SAMe became available in oral formulation in the United States in 1999. It is marketed as a dietary supplement to promote emotional well-being. Orally administered, less than 1 percent of the ingested drug reaches the bloodstream. Because oral absorption is poor, efficacy by that route is unlikely; it is not valid to extrapolate data from studies that used the parenteral formulation of SAMe to the oral formulations that are available in the United States.

The *Medical Letter* (1999) reviewed the reported clinical trials with SAMe and reported that in short-term trials (usually less than 3 weeks), SAMe (about 200 mg/day parenterally) was more effective than placebo in relieving depression and about as effective as several comparison tricyclic antidepressants. Adversely, the *Medical Letter* noted that many different formulations are available in the United States, all of which are oral, none of which are regulated by the FDA, and many of which contain no SAMe at all.

As a result of intravenous administration (in Europe), mania has been observed. Since SAMe is metabolized to homocysteine and because elevated homocysteine levels have been associated with early onset of atherosclerosis and coronary artery disease, there is concern that overuse of SAMe may predispose to these diseases. It is not known whether SAMe raises homocysteine levels in blood or whether SAMe has any adverse effects on coronary artery disease, although caution is certainly advised. No reports of safety in pregnancy or breast-feeding are available.

Omega-3 Fatty Acids

Chapter 10 discusses the results of trials of omega-3 fatty acids in the treatment of bipolar illness, trials first made in 1999. More recently, researchers have studied the possible effectiveness of certain of these fatty acids in the treatment of unipolar depression. The family of omega-3 fatty acids includes two main substances: (1) eicosapentaenoic acid (EPA) and (2) docosahexaenoic acid (DHA). Marangell and coworkers (2003) studied the effects of DHA on 35 depressed adults, noting a 28 percent positive response in the treated group versus 24 percent in the placebo-treated group. This trial failed to demonstrate a significant effect of DHA as monotherapy in patients with major depression.

In contrast, Peet and Horrobin (2002) and Nemets and coworkers (2002) reported that EPA could be effective as an augmenting agent in patients not fully responsive to standard antidepressant drugs. Of note, Zanarini and Frankenburg (2003) reported efficacy of EPA in treating aggressive and depressive symptoms in a group of females with borderline personality disorder. The role of EPA in psychological disorders such as depression and borderline personality disorder is unclear. Additional research should help clarify the role of omega-3 fatty acids in unipolar depression and other psychological disorders.

STUDY QUESTIONS

1. Differentiate between major depression and bipolar disorder.

2. What is the correlation between depression and the biological amine transmitters in the brain?

3. Describe the probable mechanism of both acute and ultimate effects of antidepressant drugs. What might account for the delay in clinical effect?

4. Differentiate cocaine and the amphetamines from clinical antidepressants. Include acute effects, psychological effects, and liabilities for misuse.

5. List and differentiate the major classes of antidepressants.

6. Compare and contrast imipramine and fluoxetine.

7. Discuss what happens when a patient overdoses on a tricyclic antidepressant. Who is at risk?

8. Discuss the side effects of SSRIs. What is the serotonin syndrome? What is the serotonin withdrawal syndrome? Discuss the effects of these drugs on sexual function.

9. Which drug or class of drugs do you think is the "best" antidepressant? Defend your position.

10. Which antidepressants are used in the treatment of anxiety disorders? Why? How do these drugs differ from the benzodiazepine-type anxiolytics?

11. What can be done if a formerly depressed patient becomes manic on antidepressant medication? Which antidepressants are most likely to bring on such an effect? To which drug can the patient be switched? Why?

12. What is DHEA? What is its therapeutic potential? Its potential complications?

13. Discuss the possible role of omega-3 fatty acids in depression.

REFERENCES

Altar, C. A., et al. (2003). "Effects of Electroconvulsive Seizures and Antidepressant Drugs on Brain-Derived Neurotrophic Factor Protein in Rat Brain." *Biological Psychiatry* 54: 703–709.

Amsterdam, J. D. (2003). "A Double-Blind, Placebo-Controlled Trial of the Safety and Efficacy of Selegiline Transdermal System Without Dietary Restrictions in Patients with Major Depressive Disorder." *Journal of Clinical Psychiatry* 64: 208–214.

Bair, M. J., et al. (2003). "Depression and Pain Comorbidity." *Archives of Internal Medicine* 163: 2433–2445.

Benninghoff, J., et al. (2002). "When Cells Become Depressed: Focus on Neural Stem Cells in Novel Treatment Strategies Against Depression." *Journal of Neural Transmission* 109: 947–962.

Bierhaus, A., et al. (2003). "A Mechanism Converting Psychosocial Stress into Mononuclear Cell Activation." *Proceedings of the National Academy of Sciences of the United States of America* 100: 1920–1925.

Bloch, M., et al. (1999). "Dehydroepiandrosterone Treatment of Midlife Dysthymia." *Biological Psychiatry* 45: 1533–1541.

Bremner, J. D., et al. (2003). "Regional Brain Metabolic Correlates of Alpha-Methyl-Paratyrosine-Induced Depressive Symptoms: Implications for the Neural Circuitry of Depression." *Journal of the American Medical Association* 289: 3125–3134.

Brosen, K., and C. A. Naranjo (2001). "Review of Pharmacokinetic and Pharmacodynamic Interaction Studies with Citalopram." *European Neuropsychopharmacology* 11: 275–283.

Burke, W. J., et al. (2002). "Fixed-Dose Trial of the Single Isomer SSRI Escitalopram in Depressed Outpatients." *Journal of Clinical Psychiatry* 63: 331–336.

Bymaster, F. P., et al. (2001). "Comparative Affinity of Duloxetine and Venlafaxine for Serotonin and Norepinephrine Transporters in Vitro and in Vivo, Human

Serotonin Receptor Subtypes, and Other Neuronal Receptors." *Neuropsychopharmacology* 25: 871–880.

Bymaster, F. P., et al. (2002). "Atomoxetine Increases Extracellular Levels of Norepinephrine and Dopamine in Prefrontal Cortex of Rat: A Potential Mechanism for Efficacy in Attention Deficit/Hyperactivity Disorder." *Neuropsychopharmacology* 27: 699–711.

Casper, R. C., et al. (2003). "Follow-Up of Children of Depressed Mothers Exposed or Not Exposed to Antidepressant Drugs During Pregnancy." *Journal of Pediatrics* 142: 402–408.

Caspi, A., et al. (2003). "Influence of Life Stress on Depression: Moderation by a Polymorphism in the 5-HTT Gene." *Science* 301: 386–389.

Cheer, S. M., and D. P. Figgitt (2002). "Spotlight on Fluvoxamine in Anxiety Disorders in Children and Adolescents." *CNS Drugs* 16: 139–144.

Clayton, A. H., et al. (2002). "Prevalence of Sexual Dysfunction Among Newer Antidepressants." *Journal of Clinical Psychiatry* 63: 357–366.

Clayton, A. H., et al. (2004). "A Placebo-Controlled Trial of Bupropion SR as an Antidote for Selective Serotonin Reuptake Inhibitor-Induced Sexual Dysfunction." *Journal of Clinical Psychiatry* 65: 62–67.

Clerk, G. (2001). "Antidepressant Efficacy and Tolerability of Milnacipran, a Dual Serotonin and Norepinephrine Reuptake Inhibitor: A Comparison with Fluvoxamine." *International Clinical Psychopharmacology* 16: 145–151.

Conti, A. C., et al. (2002). "cAmp Response Element-Binding Protein Is Essential for the Upregulation of Brain-Derived Neurotrophic Factor Transcription but Not the Behavioral or Endocrine Responses to Antidepressant Drugs." *Journal of Neuroscience* 22: 3262–3268.

Czeh, B., et al. (2001). "Stress-Induced Changes in Cerebral Metabolites, Hippocampal Volume, and Cell Proliferation Are Prevented by Antidepressant Treatment with Tianeptine." *Proceedings of the National Academy of Sciences of the United States of America* 22: 12796–12801.

Dalery, J., et al. (2001). "Efficacy of Tianeptine vs Placebo in the Long-Term Treatment (16 Months) of Unipolar Major Recurrent Depression." *Human Psychopharmacology* 16: S39–S47.

Dannon, P. N., et al. (2002). "The Efficacy of Reboxetine in the Treatment-Refractory Patients with Panic Disorder: An Open-Label Study." *Human Psychopharmacology* 17: 329–333.

Davidson, J., et al. (2001). "Efficacy of Sertraline in Preventing Relapse of Posttraumatic Stress Disorder: Results of a 28-Week Double-Blind, Placebo-Controlled Study." *American Journal of Psychiatry* 158: 1974–1981.

Davidson, J. R. T., et al. (2002). "Achieving Remission with Venlafaxine and Fluoxetine in Major Depression: Its Relationship to Anxiety Symptoms." *Depression and Anxiety* 16: 4–13.

DeBattista, C., et al. (2003). "A Prospective Trial of Bupropion-SR Augmentation of Partial and Non-Responders to Serotonergic Antidepressants." *Journal of Clinical Psychopharmacology* 23: 27–30.

DeBattista, C., et al. (2004). "A Prospective Trial of Modafinil as an Adjunctive Treatment of Major Depression." *Journal of Clinical Psychopharmacology* 24: 87–90.

Detke, M. J., et al. (2002). "Duloxetine, 60 Mg Once Daily, for Major Depressive Disorder: A Randomized Double-Blind Placebo-Controlled Trial." *Journal of Clinical Psychiatry* 63: 308–315.

Devan, D., et al. (2003). "Sertraline Treatment of Elderly Patients with Depression and Cognitive Impairment." *International Journal of Geriatric Psychiatry* 18: 123–130.

DeVane, C. L., et al. (2002). "Pharmacology of Antidepressants: Focus on Nefazodone." *Journal of Clinical Psychiatry* 63: 10–17.

Duman, R. S. (2002). "Synaptic Plasticity and Mood Disorders." *Molecular Psychiatry* 7, Supplement 1: S29–S34.

Duman, R. S., et al. (1997). "A Molecular and Cellular Theory of Depression." *Archives of General Psychiatry* 54: 597–606.

Dunner, D., et al. (2003). "Duloxetine in Treatment of Anxiety Symptoms Associated with Depression." *Depression and Anxiety* 18: 53–61.

Dwivedi, Y., et al. (2003). "Altered Gene Expression of Brain-Derived Neurotropic Factor and Receptor Tyrosine Kinase B in Postmortem Brain of Suicide Subjects." *Archives of General Psychiatry* 60: 804–815.

Dziedzicka-Wasylewska, M., et al. (2002). "Effect of Tianeptine and Fluoxetine on the Levels of Met-Enkephalin and mRNA Encoding Proenkephalin in the Rat." *Journal of Physiology and Pharmacology* 53: 117–125.

Einarson, T., et al. (1999). "Meta-Analysis of Venlafaxine, SSRIs, and TCAs in the Treatment of Major Depressive Disorder." *Canadian Journal of Clinical Pharmacology* 5: 205–216.

Erfurth, A., et al. (2002). "Bupropion as Add-On Strategy in Difficult-to-Treat Bipolar Depressive Patients." *Neuropsychobiology* 45, Supplement 1: 33–36.

Ernst, C. L., and J. F. Goldberg (2003). "Antidepressant Properties of Anticonvulsant Drugs for Bipolar Disorder." *Journal of Clinical Psychopharmacology* 23: 182–192.

Fava, M., and M. Rankin (2002). "Sexual Functioning and SSRIs." *Journal of Clinical Psychiatry* 63, Supplement 5: 13–16.

Fava, M., et al. (2003). "Switching to Reboxetine: An Efficacy and Safety Study in Patients with Major Depressive Disorder Unresponsive to Fluoxetine." *Journal of Clinical Psychopharmacology* 23: 365–369.

Feiger, A. D., et al. (2003). "Gepirone Extended Release: New Evidence for Efficacy in the Treatment of Major Depressive Disorder." *Journal of Clinical Psychiatry* 64: 243–249.

Ferguson, J. M., et al. (2003). "Reboxetine Versus Paroxetine Versus Placebo: Effects on Cognitive Functioning in Depressed Patients." *International Clinical Psychopharmacology* 18: 9–14.

Ferry, L., and J. A. Johnston (2003). "Efficacy and Safety of Bupropion SR for Smoking Cessation: Data from Clinical Trials and Five Years of Postmarketing Experience." *International Journal of Clinical Practice* 57: 224–230.

Garcia, R. (2002). "Stress, Metaplasticity, and Antidepressants." *Current Molecular Medicine* 2: 629–638.

Gardner, D. M., et al. (1996). "The Making of a User-Friendly MAOI Diet." *Journal of Clinical Psychiatry* 57: 99–104.

Garland, E. J., and E. A. Baerg (2001). "Amotivational Syndrome Associated with Selective Serotonin Reuptake Inhibitors in Children and Adolescents." *Journal of Child and Adolescent Psychopharmacology* 11: 181–186.

Gasto, C., et al. (2003). "Single-Blind Comparison of Venlafaxine and Nortriptyline in Elderly Major Depression." *Journal of Clinical Psychopharmacology* 23 (2003): 21–26.

Gelenberg, A. J., et al. (2000). "Efficacy of Venlafaxine Extended-Release Capsules in Nondepressed Outpatients with Generalized Anxiety Disorder." *Journal of the American Medical Association* 283: 3082–3088.

Gilbody, S., et al. (2003). "Educational and Organizational Interventions to Improve the Management of Depression in Primary Care: A Systematic Review." *Journal of the American Medical Association* 289: 3145–3151.

Glitz, D. A., et al. (2002). "Mood Disorders: Treatment-Induced Changes in Brain Neurochemistry and Structure." *Seminars in Clinical Neuropsychiatry* 7: 269–280.

Godfrey, R. G. (1996). "A Guide to the Understanding and Use of Tricyclic Antidepressants in the Overall Management of Fibromyalgia and Other Chronic Pain Syndromes." *Archives of Internal Medicine* 156: 1047–1052.

Goldstein, D. J., et al. (2002). "Duloxetine in the Treatment of Major Depressive Disorder: A Double-Blind Clinical Trial." *Journal of Clinical Psychiatry* 63: 225–231.

Green, B. (2003). "Focus on Paroxetine." *Current Medical Research and Opinion* 19: 13–21.

Hamilton, S., and K. Malone. (2000). "Serotonin Syndrome During Treatment with Paroxetine and Risperidone." *Journal of Clinical Psychopharmacology* 20: 103–105.

Haustein, K. O. (2003). "Bupropion: Pharmacological and Clinical Profile in Smoking Cessation." *International Journal of Clinical Pharmacology and Therapeutics* 41: 56–66.

Heikkinen, T., et al. (2002). "Citalopram in Pregnancy and Lactation." *Clinical Pharmacology and Therapeutics* 72: 184–191.

Heikkinen, T., et al. (2003). "Pharmacokinetics of Fluoxetine and Norfluoxetine in Pregnancy and Lactation." *Clinical Pharmacology and Therapeutics* 73: 330–337.

Heil, S. H., et al. (2002). "Comparison of the Subjective, Physiological, and Psychomotor Effects of Atomoxetine and Methylphenidate in Light Drug Users." *Drug and Alcohol Dependence* 67: 149–156.

Hellerstein, D. J., et al. (2000). "Double-Blind Comparison of Sertraline, Imipramine, and Placebo in the Treatment of Dysthymia: Effects on Personality." *American Journal of Psychiatry* 157: 1436–1444.

Henry, C., et al. (2001). "Antidepressant-Induced Mania in Bipolar Patients: Identification of Risk Factors." *Journal of Clinical Psychiatry* 62: 249–255.

Herpfer, I., and K. Lieb (2003). "Substance P and Substance P Receptor Antagonists in the Pathogenesis and Treatment of Affective Disorders." *World Journal of Biological Psychiatry* 4: 56–63.

Hilger, E., et al. (2001). "Reboxetine in Seasonal Affective Disorder: An Open Trial." *European Neuropsychopharmacology* 11: 1–5.

Holden, C. (2003). "Future Brightening for Depression Treatments." *Science* 302: 810–813.

Hollander, E., et al. (2003). "A Double-Blind, Placebo-Controlled Study of the Efficacy and Safety of Controlled-Release Fluvoxamine in Patients with Obsessive-Compulsive Disorder." *Journal of Clinical Psychiatry* 64: 640–647.

Holm, K. J., and A. Markham (1999). "Mirtazapine: A Review of Its Use in Major Depression." *Drugs* 57: 607–631.

Horst, W. D., and S. H. Preskorn (1998). "Mechanisms of Action and Clinical Characteristics of Three Atypical Antidepressants: Venlafaxine, Nefazodone, Bupropion." *Journal of Affective Disorders* 51: 237–254.

Horvitz-Lennon, M., et al. (2003). "Usual Care for Major Depression in the 1990s: Characteristics and Expert-Estimated Outcomes." *American Journal of Psychiatry* 160: 720–726.

Karpa, K. D., et al. (2002). "Duloxetine Pharmacology: Profile of a Dual Monoamine Modulator." *CNS Drug Reviews* 8: 361–376.

Kasper, S. (1996). "Treatment Options in Severe Depression," in "Controversies in the Diagnosis and Treatment of Severe Depression." *Journal of Clinical Psychiatry* 57: 554–561.

Kasper, S., et al. (2000). "Reboxetine: The First Selective Noradrenaline Re-Uptake Inhibitor." *Expert Opinion on Pharmacotherapy* 1: 771–782.

Keller, M. (2001). "Role of Serotonin and Noradrenalin in Social Dysfunction: A Review of Data on Reboxetine and the Social Adaptation Self-Evaluation Scale (SASS)." *General Hospital Psychiatry* 23: 15–19.

Kennedy, S. H., et al. (2002). "Combining Bupropion-SR with Venlafaxine, Paroxetine, or Fluoxetine: A Preliminary Report on Pharmacokinetic, Therapeutic, and Sexual Dysfunction Effects." *Journal of Clinical Psychiatry* 63: 181–186.

Kent, J. M. (2000). "SnaRIs, NaSSAs, and NaRIs: New Agents for the Treatment of Depression." *Lancet* 355: 911–918.

Kessler, R. C., et al. (2003). "The Epidemiology of Major Depressive Disorder: Results from the National Comorbidity Survey Replication (NCS-R)." *Journal of the American Medical Association* 289: 3095–3105.

Kole, M. H., et al. (2002). "The Antidepressant Tianeptine Persistently Modulates Glutamate Receptor Currents of the Hippocampus CA3 Commissural Associated Synapse in Chronically Stressed Rats." *European Journal of Neuroscience* 16: 807–816.

Kramer, M. S., et al. (2004). "Demonstration of the Efficacy and Safety of a Novel Substance P (NK$_1$) Receptor Antagonist in Major Depression." *Neuropsychopharmacology* 29: 385–392.

Kratochvil, C. J., et al. (2002). "Atomoxetine and Methylphenidate Treatment in Children with ADHD: A Prospective, Randomized, Open-Label Trial." *Journal of the American Academy of Child and Adolescent Psychiatry* 41: 776–784.

Krishnan, K. R. R. (2002). "Pathophysiology of Depression: The Emerging Role of Substance P." *Journal of Clinical Psychiatry* 63, Supplement 11: 4–5.

Kroenke, K., et al. (2001). "Similar Effectiveness of Paroxetine, Fluoxetine, and Sertraline in Primary Care: A Randomized Trial." *Journal of the American Medical Association* 286: 2947–2955.

Laine, K., et al. (2003). "Effects of Exposure to Selective Serotonin Reuptake Inhibitors During Pregnancy on Serotonergic Symptoms in Newborns and Cord Blood Monoamine and Prolactin Concentrations." *Archives of General Psychiatry* 60: 720–726.

Lane, R., and D. Baldwin. (1997). "Selective Serotonin Reuptake Inhibitor-Induced Serotonin Syndrome: Review." *Journal of Clinical Psychopharmacology* 17: 208–221.

Lee, A. L., et al. (2002). "Stress and Depression: Possible Links to Neuron Death in the Hippocampus." *Bipolar Disorders* 4: 117–128.

Leon, A. C., et al. (2003). "A 20-Year Longitudinal Observational Study of Somatic Antidepressant Treatment Effectiveness." *American Journal of Psychiatry* 160: 727–733.

Loo, H., et al. (2001). "Efficacy and Safety of Tianeptine in the Treatment of Depressive Disorders in Comparison with Fluoxetine." *Human Psychopharmacology* 16: S31–S38.

Manji, H. K., and R. S. Duman (2001). "Impairments of Neuroplasticity and Cellular Resilience in Severe Mood Disorders: Implications for the Development of Novel Therapies." *Psychopharmacology Bulletin* 35: 5–49.

Manji, H. K., et al. (2003). "Enhancing Neuronal Plasticity and Cellular Resilience to Develop Novel, Improved Therapies for Difficult-to-Treat Depression." *Biological Psychiatry* 53: 707–742.

Mantyh, P. W. (2002). "Neurobiology of Substance P and the NK-1 Receptor." *Journal of Clinical Psychiatry* 63, Supplement 11: 6–10.

Marangell, L. B., et al. (2003). "A Double-Blind, Placebo-Controlled Study of the Omega-3 Fatty Acid Docosahexaenoic Acid in the Treatment of Major Depression." *American Journal of Psychiatry* 160: 996–998.

Markovitz, P. J., and S. Wagner. (2003). "An Open-Label Trial of Modafinil in Patients with Partial Response to Antidepressant Therapy." *Journal of Clinical Psychopharmacology* 23: 207–209.

Marshall, R. D., et al. (2001). "Efficacy and Safety of Paroxetine Treatment for Chronic PTSD: A Fixed-Dose, Placebo-Controlled Study." *American Journal of Psychiatry* 158: 1982–1988.

Matthew, S. J., et al. (2003). "A Magnetic Resonance Spectroscopic Imaging Study of Adult Nonhuman Primates Exposed to Early-Life Stressors." *Biological Psychiatry* 54: 727–735.

Mavissakalian, M. R., and J. M. Perel (2000). "The Side Effects Burden of Extended Imipramine Treatment of Panic Disorder." *Journal of Clinical Psychopharmacology* 20: 547–555.

McGrath, P. J., et al. (2000). "A Placebo-Controlled Study of Fluoxetine Versus Imipramine in the Acute Treatment of Atypical Depression." *American Journal of Psychiatry* 157: 344–350.

Medical Letter on Drugs and Therapeutics (1999). "SAMe for Depression," *Medical Letter* 41 (November 5): 107–108.

Medical Letter on Drugs and Therapeutics (2004). "Is Effexor More Effective for Depression Than an SSRI?" *Medical Letter* 46 (February 16): 15–16.

Melfi, C. A., et al. (2000). "Racial Variation in Antidepressant Treatment in a Medicaid Population." *Journal of Clinical Psychiatry* 61: 16–21.

Menza, M. A., et al. (2000). "Modafinil Augmentation of Antidepressant Treatment in Depression." *Journal of Clinical Psychiatry* 61: 378–381.

Michelson, D., et al. (2000). "Female Sexual Dysfunction Associated with Antidepressant Administration: A Randomized, Placebo-Controlled Study of Pharmacologic Intervention." *American Journal of Psychiatry* 157: 239–243.

Michelson, D., et al. (2003). "Atomoxetine in Adults with ADHD: Two Randomized, Placebo-Controlled Studies." *Biological Psychiatry* 15: 112–120.

Montgomery, S., et al. (2003). "The Antidepressant Efficacy of Reboxetine in Patients with Severe Depression." *Journal of Clinical Psychopharmacology* 23: 45–50.

Nelson, J. C., et al. (1999). "Treatment of Major Depression with Nortriptyline and Paroxetine in Patients with Ischemic Heart Disease." *American Journal of Psychiatry* 156: 1024–1028.

Nemeroff, C. B., et al. (2001). "Double-Blind, Placebo-Controlled Comparison of Imipramine and Paroxetine in the Treatment of Bipolar Depression." *American Journal of Psychiatry* 158: 906–912.

Nemets, B., et al. (2002). "Addition of Omega-3 Fatty Acid to Maintenance Medication Treatment for Recurrent Unipolar Depressive Disorder." *American Journal of Psychiatry* 159: 477–479.

Nickel, T., et al. (2003). "Clinical and Neurobiological Effects of Tianeptine and Paroxetine in Major Depression." *Journal of Clinical Psychopharmacology* 23: 155–168.

Nierenberg, A. A., et al. (2003). "Nortriptyline for Treatment-Resistant Depression." *Journal of Clinical Psychiatry* 64: 35–39.

Niewstraten, C. E., and L. R. Dolovich. (2001). "Bupropion versus Selective Serotonin-Reuptake Inhibitors for Treatment of Depression." *Annals of Pharmacotherapy* 35: 1608–1613.

Norton, P. A., et al. (2002). "Duloxetine versus Placebo in the Treatment of Stress Urinary Incontinence." *American Journal of Obstetrics and Gynecology* 187: 40–48.

Nurnberg, H. G., et al. (2001). "Efficacy of Sildenafil Citrate for the Treatment of Erectile Dysfunction in Men Taking Serotonin Reuptake Inhibitors." *American Journal of Psychiatry* 158: 1926–1928.

Okamoto, H., et al. (2003). "Dynamic Changes in AP-1 Transcription Factor DNA Binding Activity in Rat Brain Following Administration of Antidepressant Amitryptiline and Brain-Derived Neurotrophic Factor." *Neuropharmacology* 45: 251–259.

Pallanti, S., et al. (2002). "Nefazodone Treatment of Pathological Gambling: A Prospective Open-Label Controlled Trial." *Journal of Clinical Psychiatry* 63: 1034–1039.

Papp, L. A., et al. (1997). "Clomipramine Treatment of Panic Disorder: Pros and Cons." *Journal of Clinical Psychiatry* 58: 423–425.

Pearlson, T. (2002). "Selective Serotonin Reuptake Inhibitors for Premenstrual Dysphoric Disorder: The Emerging Gold Standard?" *Drugs* 62: 1869–1885.

Pearlson, T., et al. (2003). "Recurrence of Symptoms of Premenstrual Dysphoric Disorder After the Cessation of Luteal-Phase Fluoxetine Treatment." *Journal of Obstetrics and Gynecology* 188: 887–895.

Peet, M., and D. F. Horrobin (2002). "A Dose-Ranging Study of the Effects of Ethyl-Eicosapentaenoate in Patients with Ongoing Depression Despite Apparently Adequate Treatment with Standard Drugs." *Archives of General Psychiatry* 59: 913–919.

Pollock, B. G. (2001). "Citalopram: A Comprehensive Review." *Expert Opinion on Pharmacotherapy* 2: 681–698.

Popoli, M., et al. (2002). "Modulation of Synaptic Plasticity by Stress and Antidepressants." *Bipolar Disorders* 4: 166–182.

Poyurovsky, M., et al. (2003). "Attenuation of Olanzapine-Induced Weight Gain with Reboxetine in Patients with Schizophrenia: A Double-Blind, Placebo-Controlled Study." *American Journal of Psychiatry* 160: 297–302.

Quitkin, F. M., et al. (2003). "When Should a Trial of Fluoxetine for Major Depression Be Declared Failed?" *American Journal of Psychiatry* 160: 734–740.

Rausch, J. L., et al. (2001). "Fluvoxamine Treatment of Mixed Anxiety and Depression: Evidence of Serotonergically Mediated Anxiolysis." *Journal of Clinical Psychopharmacology* 21: 139-142.

Ravindran, A. V., et al. (2000). "Treatment of Dysthymia with Sertraline: A Double-Blind, Placebo-Controlled Trial in Dysthymic Patients Without Major Depression." *Journal of Clinical Psychiatry* 61: 821-827.

Reid, I. C., and C. A. Stewart (2001). "How Antidepressants Work: New Perspectives on the Pathophysiology of Depressive Disorder." *British Journal of Psychiatry* 179: 559–560.

Rickels, K., et al. (2000). "Efficacy of Extended-Release Venlafaxine in Nondepressed Outpatients with Generalized Anxiety Disorder." *American Journal of Psychiatry* 157: 968–974.

Rickels, K., et al. (2003). "Paroxetine Treatment of Generalized Anxiety Disorder: A Double-Blind, Placebo-Controlled Study." *American Journal of Psychiatry* 160: 749–756.

Rocha, F., and C. Hara (2003). "Lamotrigine Augmentation in Unipolar Depression." *International Clinical Psychopharmacology* 18: 97–99.

Roy-Byrne, P. P., et al. (2000). "Nefazodone Treatment of Major Depression in Alcohol-Dependent Patients: A Double-Blind, Placebo-Controlled Trial." *Journal of Clinical Psychopharmacology* 20: 129–136.

Rupniak, N. M. (2002). "New Insights into the Antidepressant Actions of Substance P (NK1 receptor) Antagonists." *Canadian Journal of Physiology and Pharmacology* 80: 489–494.

Rupniak, N. M., and M. S. Kramer. (1999). "Discovery of the Antidepressant and Anti-Emetic Efficacy of Substance P Receptor (NK-1) Antagonists." *Trends in Pharmacological Sciences* 20: 485–490.

Russell, I. J. (2002). "The Promise of Substance P Inhibitors in Fibromyalgia." *Rheumatic Diseases Clinics of North America* 28: 329–342.

Russo-Neustadt, A. (2003). "Brain-Derived Neurotrophic Factor, Behavior, and New Directions for the Treatment of Mental Disorders." *Seminars in Clinical Neuropsychiatry* 8: 109–118.

Russo-Neustadt, A., et al. (1999). "Exercise, Antidepressant Medications, and Enhanced Brain-Derived Neurotrophic Factor Expression." *Neuropsychopharmacology* 21: 679–682.

Santarelli, L., et al. (2003). "Requirement of Hippocampal Neurogenesis for the Behavioral Effect of Antidepressants." *Science* 301: 805–809.

Saarelainen, T., et al. (2003). "Activation of the TrkB Neurotrophin Receptor Is Induced by Antidepressant Drugs and Is Required for Antidepressant-Induced Behavioral Effects." *Journal of Neuroscience* 23: 349–357.

Schatzberg, A. F., et al. (1997). "Serotonin Reuptake Inhibitor Discontinuation Syndrome: A Hypothetical Definition." *Journal of Clinical Psychiatry* 58, Supplement 7: 5–10. (See also the other articles in Supplement 7.)

Schmidt, M. E., et al. (2000). "The Efficacy and Safety of a New Enteric-Coated Formulation of Fluoxetine Given Once Weekly During the Continuation Treatment of Major Depressive Disorder." *Journal of Clinical Psychiatry* 61: 851–857.

Seidman, S. N., et al. (2001). "Treatment of Erectile Dysfunction in Men with Depressive Symptoms: Results of a Placebo-Controlled Trial with Sildenafil Citrate." *American Journal of Psychiatry* 158: 1623–1630.

Shakesby, A. C., et al. (2002). "Overcoming the Effects of Stress on Synaptic Plasticity in the Rat Hippocampus: Rapid Actions of Serotoninergic and Antidepressant Agents." *Journal of Neuroscience* 22: 3638–3644.

Sheldon, R. C. (2000). "Cellular Mechanisms in the Vulnerability to Depression and Response to Antidepressants." *Psychiatric Clinics of North America* 23: 713–729.

Sheline, Y. I., et al. (2003). "Untreated Depression and Hippocampal Volume Loss." *American Journal of Psychiatry* 160 (2003): 1516–1518.

Shelton, R. C., et al. (1997). "The Undertreatment of Dysthymia." *Journal of Clinical Psychiatry* 58: 59–65.

Shimizu, E., et al. (2003). "Alterations of Serum Levels of Brain-Derived Neurotrophic Factor (BDNF) in Depressed Patients with or Without Antidepressants." *Biological Psychiatry* 54: 70–75.

Shors, T. J., et al. (2001). "Neurogenesis in the Adult Is Involved in the Formation of Trace Memories." *Nature* 410: 372–376.

Simpson, D., and Plosker, G. L. (2004). "Atomoxetine: A Review of Its Use in Adults with Attention Deficit Hyperactivity Disorder." *Drugs* 64: 205–222.

Spencer, T., et al. (2004). "Nonstimulant Treatment of Adult Attention-Deficit/Hyperactivity Disorder." *Psychiatric Clinics of North Ameerica* 27: 373–383.

Stahl, S. M. (1999a). "Antidepressants: The Blue-Chip Psychotropic for the Modern Treatment of Anxiety Disorders." *Journal of Clinical Psychiatry* 60: 356–357.

Stahl, S. M. (1999b). "Mergers and Acquisitions Among Psychotropics: Antidepressant Takeover of Anxiety May Now Be Complete." *Journal of Clinical Psychiatry* 60: 282–283.

Stahl, S. M., (2003). "Mechanism of Action of Selective NRIs: Both Dopamine and Norepinephrine Increase in Prefrontal Cortex." *Journal of Clinical Psychiatry* 64: 230–231.

Stewart, W. F., et al. (2003). "Cost of Lost Productive Work Time Among US Workers with Depression." *Journal of the American Medical Association* 289: 3135–3144.

Stocchi, F., et al. (2003). "Efficacy and Tolerability of Paroxetine for the Long-Term Treatment of Generalized Anxiety Disorder." *Journal of Clinical Psychiatry* 64: 250–258.

Strous, R. D., et al. (2003). "Dehydroepiandrosterone Augmentation in the Management of Negative, Depressive, and Anxiety Symptoms in Schizophrenia." *Archives of General Psychiatry* 60: 133–141.

Suhara, T., et al. (2003). "High Levels of Serotonin Transporter Occupancy with Low-Dose Clomipramine in Comparative Occupancy Study with Fluvoxamine Using Positron Emission Tomography." *Archives of General Psychiatry* 60: 386–391.

Symposium (2000). "Norepinephrine: Neurotransmitter for the Millennium." *Journal of Clinical Psychiatry* 61, Supplement 10.

Thomas, R. M., and Peterson, D. A. (2003). "A Neurogenic Theory of Depression Gains Momentum." *Molecular Interventions* 3: 441–444.

Tohen, M., et al. (2003). "Efficacy of Olanzapine and Olanzapine-Fluoxetine Combination in the Treatment of Bipolar I Depression." *Archives of General Psychiatry* 60: 1079–1088.

Tokuyama, W., et al. (2000). "BDNF Upregulation During Declarative Memory Formation in Monkey Inferior Temporal Cortex." *Nature Neuroscience* 3: 1134–1142.

Tran, P. V., et al. (2003). "Dual Monoamine Modulation for Improved Treatment of Major Depressive Disorder." *Journal of Clinical Psychopharmacology* 23: 78–86.

Tyler, W. J., et al. (2002). "From Acquisition to Consolidation: On the Role of Brain-Derived Neurotrophic Factor Signaling in Hippocampal-Dependent Learning." *Learning and Memory* 9: 224–237.

Vaidya, V. A., and R. S. Duman (2001). "Depression—Emerging Insights from Neurobiology." *British Medical Bulletin* 57: 61–79.

van der Hart, M. G., et al. (2002). "Substance P Receptor Antagonists and Clomipramine Prevent Stress-Induced Alterations in Cerebral Metabolites, Cytogenesis in the Dentate Gyrus, and Hippocampal Volume." *Molecular Psychiatry* 7: 933–941.

Versiani, M., et al. (2002). "Reboxetine, a Selective Norepinephrine Reuptake Inhibitor, Is an Effective and Well-Tolerated Treatment for Panic Disorder." *Journal of Clinical Psychiatry* 63: 31–37.

Wagstaff, A. J., et al. (2001). "Tianeptine: A Review of Its Use in Depressive Disorders." *CNS Drugs* 15 (2001): 231–259.

Wagstaff, A. J., et al. (2002). "Spotlight on Paroxetine in Psychiatric Disorders in Adults." *CNS Drugs* 16: 425–434.

West, R. (2003). "Bupropion SR for Smoking Cessation." *Expert Opinions in Pharmacotherapy* 4: 533–540.

Williams, J. W., et al. (2000). "A Systematic Review of Newer Pharmacotherapies for Depression in Adults: Evidence Report Summary." *Annals of Internal Medicine* 132: 743–756.

Wolkowitz, O. M., et al. (1999). "Double-Blind Treatment of Major Depression with Dehydroepiandrosterone." *American Journal of Psychiatry* 156: 646–649.

Young, A. S., et al. (2001). "The Quality of Care for Depression and Anxiety in the United States." *Archives of General Psychiatry* 58: 55–61.

Zanarini, M., and F. Frankenburg (2003). "Omega-3 Fatty Acid Treatment of Women with Borderline Personality Disorder: A Double-Blind, Placebo-Controlled Pilot Study." *American Journal of Psychiatry* 160: 167–169.

Zimmerman, M., et al. (2002). "Major Depressive Disorder and Axis I Diagnostic Comorbidity." *Journal of Clinical Psychiatry* 63: 187–193.

Zisook, S., et al. (2000). "Nefazodone in Patients with Treatment-Refractory Posttraumatic Stress Disorder." *Journal of Clinical Psychiatry* 61: 203–208.

Zisook, S., et al. (2001). "Bupropion Sustained Release for Bereavement: Results of an Open Trial." *Journal of Clinical Psychiatry* 62: 227–230.

Chapter 10

Drugs Used to Treat Bipolar Disorder (Mood Stabilizers)

Bipolar Disorder

Bipolar disorder (manic-depressive disorder) is characterized by recurrent episodes of mania and depression. The disorder is also associated with widespread cognitive deficits, especially when individuals are acutely symptomatic (Quraishi and Frangou, 2002). Bipolar disorder requires therapeutic intervention when the mood changes are severe enough to disrupt the patient's life or the lives of people associated with the patient. It is a major medical disorder, and it occurs in up to 5 percent of the population; a bipolar patient is defined as having suffered at least one manic, hypomanic, or mixed episode. If the episode was severe enough to require hospitalization or to seriously interfere with normal functioning, the disorder is classified as bipolar I; if the manic episode was less severe, the disorder is classified as bipolar II. *Cyclothymia* is defined as recurrent mood swings between depression and elation but of lower severity than bipolar II. Bipolar patients who have had four illness episodes in a 12-month period are termed "rapid cyclers." Rapid cycling may not be permanent; it may appear and disappear during the course of the illness. Bipolar I disorder can lead to the destruction of a patient's livelihood, marriage, social relationships, or even life. The course of the illness is usually episodic, with periods of mania and/or depression alternating with intervening well periods of varying duration. The great majority of patients experience several episodes during the course of their lives and the risk of recurrence is ever present. Even today, despite intensive care and treatment, outpatients with bipolar disorder have a considerable degree of residual illness-related morbidity, including a threefold greater amount of time spent depressed versus time spent manic (Post et al., 2003).

A person who experiences onset of bipolar disorder at age 25 and remains untreated will lose about 9 years of life, 14 years of effective activity, and 12 years of normal health. It is estimated that one of every four or five untreated or inadequately treated patients commits suicide during the course of the illness, a rate ten times that of the general population (Osby et al., 2001). An increase in deaths secondary to accidents or intercurrent illnesses (especially substance abuse) also contributes to the greater mortality rate seen in this disorder. Unfortunately, epidemiological studies have indicated that only one-third of bipolar patients are in active treatment despite the availability of effective therapies. It is generally agreed that a patient who exhibits at least two episodes of mania is a candidate for long-term treatment with an antimanic (mood-stabilizing) drug.

Treatment Issues

A patient with bipolar disorder can present initially with either mania or depression. Depending on the presentation (manic or depressive) and its severity (mild to severe), pharmacological treatment differs in the choice of agents for initial control of the acute situation. Despite the initial presentation, use of a *mood stabilizer* best accomplishes successful long-term management of bipolar disorder (Bauer and Mitchner, 2004). An ideal mood stabilizer can be defined as a medicine that does the following:

- Stabilizes acute mania, mixed, and depressive symptoms

- Does not induce the alternate mood symptom (for instance, does not cause a switch from mania into depression or depression into mania)

- Prevents future relapses into mania, mixed, or depressive symptoms or episodes (Keck and Susman, 2003)

Concerning pharmacological management of bipolar disorder, medications are used to treat acute manic states, mixed states (rapid alternation between mania and depression), acute bipolar depression, and for the prophylactic prevention of recurrent episodes (mood stabilizer prophylaxis). Sachs (2003) presents a decision tree for choosing appropriate medications for therapy in specific situations. He also offers a "quality of evidence" table, reflecting the relative usefulness of various mood stabilizers in bipolar disorder (Table 10.1). Drugs in this table include lithium ion, several anticonvulsant "neuromodulators," several

TABLE 10.1 Quality of Evidence for the Use of Mood Stabilizers in Bipolar Disorder

A Double-blind placebo-controlled trials with adequate samples
B Double-blind comparator studies with adequate samples
C Open trials with adequate samples
D Uncontrolled observation or controlled study with ambiguous result
E No published evidence
F Available evidence negative

	Acute mania/Mixed	Mood stabilizer prophylaxis	Acute bipolar depression
Lithium	A+	A+	A
Divalproex	A+	A−	D
Carbamazepine	A	B−	D
Lamotrigine	F	A+	A
Gabapenntin	F	E	D
Topiramate	D	E	D
Aripiprazole	A	E	E
Haloperidol	A	E	E
Olanzapine	A+	E	A
Risperidone	A	E	D
Quetiapine	A	E	E
Ziprasidone	A	E	E
Omega-3	E	D	E

A+ is reserved for those instances when fewer than 40 studies have been reported and more than one double-blind placebo-controlled study supports the same finding. A− indicates positive outcomes on some but not all relevant measures. From Sachs (2003), p. 37.

"atypical" antipsychotics, and a dietary supplement, omega-3 fatty acids. This chapter will describe the pharmacology of these medications as they are used in treating bipolar disorder. The atypical antipsychotics are further discussed in Chapter 11.

The classic mood stabilizer is *lithium*. This substance effectively controls manic symptoms and reduces the rate of recurrence. However, its many bothersome and serious side effects and toxicities have necessitated a search for an equally effective and safer agent. Today, the focus is on the variety of medications shown in Table 10.1. Often combination treatment using two or more medications is necessary (Fawcett, 2003; Mondimore et al., 2003), and the essential role of psychosocial interventions as adjuncts to medical therapies cannot be overlooked.

In 1996, the American Psychiatric Association published its first clin-ical practice guideline for the treatment of patients with bipolar disorder. In April 2002, a revision of this guideline was published (American Psychiatric Association, 2002). As the revised guideline states, the major objectives of pharmacologic intervention are to treat acute episodes of mania and to reduce the frequency of recurrence of these episodes. Additional goals are to maintain compliance with therapy, treat accompa-nying depression, psychosis, and substance abuse, establish and main-tain a therapeutic alliance, promote regular patterns of activity and sleep, anticipate stressors; and minimize functional impairment.

Drug therapy is a cornerstone of this overall treatment plan. To this end, the guideline recommends using lithium or valproic acid plus an atypical antipsychotic for severe manic or mixed episodes, monotherapy with lithium, an anticonvulsant, or an atypical antipsy-chotic for less severe situations, and carbamazepine or oxcarbazepine as alternatives to lithium or valproate. Lamotrigine (a "third-genera-tion" neuromodulator anticonvulsant) and a new (in 2004) combina-tion product containing olanzapine and fluoxetine (the trade name is Symbyax) are drugs of choice for treating bipolar depression. In Symbyax, the fluoxetine (Chapter 9) is antidepressant while the olan-zapine (discussed later in this chapter and also in Chapter 11) is anti-manic. The treatment of bipolar disorder in children and adolescents is discussed in Chapter 12.

Neuronal Injury and Mechanisms of Drug Action

Chapter 9 discussed neuronal injuries in clinical depression; the litera-ture is now well established. Bipolar disorder, like depression, has clas-sically been conceptualized as a neurochemical disorder. However, evidence is now beginning to accumulate that bipolar disorder is ac-companied by regional differences in neuronal density and specific re-ductions in the numbers of neurons and the functioning of remaining neurons in discrete brain areas. Bipolar disorder is a progressive ill-ness with multiple recurrences and a deteriorating course if left un-treated; changes in cognition and brain function are evident early in the course of the disease. Recently, Bertolino and coworkers (2003) identified hippocampal neuronal pathology in bipolar patients, while Blumberg and coworkers (2003) identified left prefrontal cortex abnor-malities in similar patients. Gray and coworkers (2003) reviewed the body of evidence supporting the importance of altered states of neu-ronal plasticity and cellular resilience in the pathophysiology of bipo-lar illness. Antimanic drugs such as lithium and valproic acid increase the levels of a cellular-protective protein, and use of these drugs is as-sociated not only with a variety of clinical improvements (in bipolar disorder, aggressive disorders, pain, and so on), but reduction of brain damage and facilitation of neurological recovery after brain injury (Ren et al., 2003). More will undoubtedly be forthcoming to clearly identify neuronal deficiencies specific to bipolar disorder as well as the reversal of these dysfunctions by therapeutically effective medications.

Lithium

Lithium has historically been the most recommended drug for treating bipolar disorder and reducing its rate of relapse.[1] Unfortunately, its clinical effectiveness is less than that predicted by clinical trials; relapse often occurs because of patient noncompliance with therapy. Therefore, the pharmacology of lithium and reasons for patient noncompliance with lithium therapy must be clearly understood and alternative drug therapies closely examined.

Lithium (Li^+) is the lightest of the alkali metals (Figure 10.1) and shares some characteristics with sodium (Na^+). In nature, lithium is abundant in some alkaline mineral spring waters. Devoid of psychotropic effects in normal individuals, lithium is effective in treating 60 to 80 percent of acute hypomanic and manic episodes, although in recent years, the limitations, side effects, relapse, toxicities, and compliance issues associated with its use have become increasingly appreciated.

History

Lithium was used in the 1920s as a sedative-hypnotic compound and as an anticonvulsant drug. During the late 1940s, lithium chloride was employed as a salt substitute for patients with heart disease. Wide use for this purpose resulted in cases of severe toxicity and death, causing medicine to abandon use of the drug. In 1949, however, an Australian scientist (J. Cade) noted that when lithium was administered to guinea pigs, the animals became lethargic. Taking an intuitive leap, Cade administered lithium to patients with acute mania and noted remarkable improvement. However, because of the earlier problems with lithium as a salt substitute, the medical community took more than 20 years to accept this agent as an effective treatment for mania. Clinical research in the 1970s found lithium to be clearly superior to placebo in the prophylaxis of bipolar disorder; fewer than a third of lithium-treated patients relapsed, compared with 80 percent of placebo-treated patients.

Today, lithium's use appears to be decreasing, not from a lack of efficacy, but from the prevalence of bothersome side effects, the difficulty in controlling blood levels of the drug, and its serious toxicities. Many controlled studies demonstrate the efficacy of lithium for acute

[1]For a historical overview of lithium therapy and commentaries on lithium, see four related letters in *Archives of General Psychiatry* 54 (1997): 9–23.

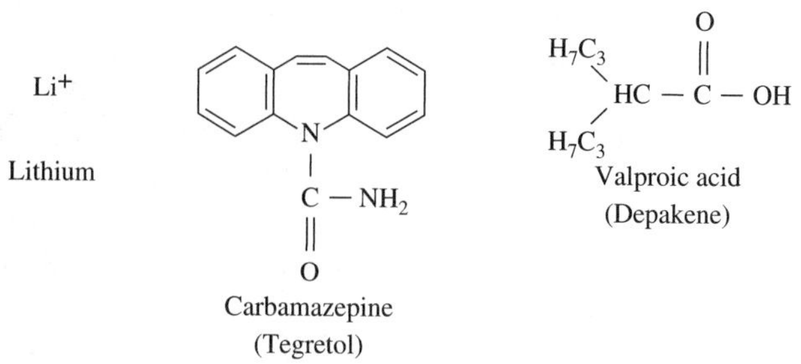

FIGURE 10.1 Drugs classically used in the treatment of bipolar disorder. Structures of newer anticonvulsants used in bipolar disorder are shown in Figure 5.4

mania and mixed episodes as well as acute depressive episodes (see Table 10.1). Baldessarini and Tondo (2000) recommended lithium as a drug of first choice for both the treatment of acute manic attacks and the long-term management of bipolar disorder:

> We suggest that the growing American urge to abandon lithium maintenance therapy as ineffective, excessively toxic, or complicated is unwarranted. No other proposed mood-stabilizing treatment has such substantial research evidence of long-term efficacy in both type I and type II bipolar disorders, as well as yielding a substantial reduction of mortality risk. (p.190)

Lithium has therefore been referred to as the "gold standard" of bipolar treatment. However, fewer clinicians are prescribing lithium in favor of neuromodulator anticonvulsants and atypical antipsychotics. To demonstrate poor lithium compliance, Maj and coworkers (1998) concluded that long-term "real-world" studies are reporting poorer results than expected; 28 percent of patients discontinue the drug, 38 percent take the drug but experience recurrences of the disorder, and only 23 percent taking the drug did not have recurrent episodes.

Pharmacokinetics

Lithium is absorbed rapidly and completely when it is administered orally. Peak blood levels are reached within 3 hours, complete absorption by 8 hours. The therapeutic efficacy of lithium is directly correlated to its level in the blood. Lithium crosses the blood-brain barrier slowly and incompletely. There also can be a twofold variation in the concentration of lithium in the brain when compared with its concentration in plasma. The clinical significance of this observation is unclear.

Lithium is not metabolized before excretion; most is excreted unchanged by the kidneys, with only small amounts excreted through the skin. About half an oral dose is excreted within 18 to 24 hours and the rest (which represents the amount of lithium that is taken up by the body's cells) is excreted over the next 1 to 2 weeks. Thus, when therapy is initiated, lithium accumulates slowly over about 2 weeks until a steady state is reached. With this long half-life, once-daily dosage is appropriate for many individuals.

The therapeutic dose of lithium is determined by closely monitoring blood levels of the drug. Lithium has a very narrow therapeutic range, below which the drug fails to have therapeutic effect and above which side effects and toxicity dominate. In the 1980s and early 1990s, a therapeutic goal was to maintain a plasma level of lithium between 0.75 to 1.0 milliequivalents per liter (mEq/l) of blood. Today, levels of about 0.5 to 0.7 mEq/l are recommended, although some guidelines allow up to a level of 1.2 mEq/l. Unfortunately, many patients do not receive appropriate testing. More adverse effects, leading to an increased risk of noncompliance, accompany lithium levels over about 1.5 mEq/l. Because lithium closely resembles table salt, when a patient lowers his or her salt intake or loses excessive amounts of salt (such as through sweating), lithium blood levels rise and intoxication may inadvertently follow. Consequently, patients taking lithium should avoid marked changes in sodium intake or excretion.

Pharmacodynamics

In therapeutic concentrations, lithium has almost no discernible psychotropic effect in normal persons. It does not induce sedation, depression, or euphoria, which differentiates it from other psychoactive drugs. Indeed, it exhibits few effects on the brain other than its specific action on mania.

The mechanism through which lithium exerts its antimanic effect is a matter of ongoing research. In general, a consensus is developing that regulation of intracellular second-messenger signaling pathways ultimately modulating the levels of several genes may play a major part in the long-term actions of lithium. Certainly intracellular protein kinase enzyme pathways are modulated (Li et al., 2002). Manji and coworkers (2001) demonstrated a lithium-induced elevation in the intracellular levels of a cellular protective protein termed *bcl-2*. This finding implies that mood stabilizers may exert underappreciated neuroprotective effects through positive effects on neuroplasticity and neurotrophic actions involving CREB and BDNF, similar in many ways to those exerted by the antidepressants (Hashimoto et al., 2002; Kopnisky et al., 2003). An extrapolation is that optimal long-term treatment for bipolar illness may best be achieved by early use of mood stabilizers (lithium or anticonvulsants) with positive neuropro-tective/neurotropic effects, regardless of the primary, symptomatic treatment (Manji et al., 2000).

Side Effects and Toxicity

Because lithium has an extremely narrow therapeutic range, blood lev-els of the drug must be closely monitored. The occurrence and inten-sity of side effects are, in most cases, directly related to plasma concen-trations of lithium. When levels in plasma fall below 0.5 to 0.6 mEq/l, side effects are usually minimal; they become much more bothersome at levels of 1.0 mEq/l or higher. At levels above 2.0 mEq/l, toxicity is severe and potentially fatal.

The main toxic effects involve the gastrointestinal tract, the kid-neys, the thyroid, the cardiovascular system, the skin, and the nervous system. At plasma levels of 1.5 to 2.0 mEq/l (and sometimes at lower levels), most reactions involve the gastrointestinal tract, resulting in nausea, vomiting, diarrhea, and abdominal pain. Neurological side ef-fects commonly seen at this level of lithium include a slight tremor, lethargy, impaired concentration, dizziness, slurred speech, ataxia, muscle weakness, and nystagmus. Difficulty with memory is another frequent complaint, as is weight gain with continued treatment. In long-term therapy, up to 30 percent of patients became frankly obese, a prevalence of obesity three times greater than in the general popula-tion. Elmslie and coworkers (2000) and Chengappa and coworkers (2002) reviewed the subject of drug-induced obesity in treating bipolar illness. Chronic treatment with either lithium or valproate results in weight gain of over 8 percent of baseline body weight. Weight gain can profoundly affect compliance with therapy (Keck and McElroy, 2003).

With long-term lithium therapy, the thyroid may become enlarged, and rashes or some other kind of skin eruption may occur. In addition, about 60 percent of patients taking lithium experience an increase in urine output (due to an impairment of renal concentrating ability), along with increased thirst and water intake. Although kidney function should be assessed periodically, permanent damage is rare.

Adverse effects on memory and cognitive functioning accompany chronic lithium therapy. Some researchers report improvements in motor performance, cognition, and creative ability after lithium with-drawal, implying detrimental effects of lithium in these areas during drug therapy. Severe cognitive deficits are seen with lithium intoxica-tion (Bartha et al., 2002).

At plasma levels of lithium above 2.0 mEq/l, more severe side ef-fects include fatigue, muscle weakness, slurred speech, and worsening tremors. Thyroid gland function becomes depressed, and the thyroid gland may enlarge further, resulting in goiter. Muscle fasciculations, increased reflexes, abnormal motor movements, psychosis, and stupor may occur. At plasma levels exceeding 2.5 mEq/l, toxicity includes muscle rigidity, coma, renal failure, cardiac arrhythmias, and death.

Treatment of poisoning or overdosage is nonspecific; there is no antidote to lithium. Usually drug administration is halted and sodium-containing fluids are infused immediately. If toxic signs are serious, hemodialysis, gastric lavage, diuretic therapy, antiepileptic medication, and other supports may be urgently needed. Complete recovery from intoxication may be prolonged, with full renal and neurological recovery taking weeks or months.

Effects in Pregnancy

Lithium possesses a degree of teratogenic potential, especially to the heart of the developing fetus. In general, lithium is not advised during pregnancy, particularly in the first trimester, as the risk of fetal malformation of the cardiovascular system is increased (Ernst and Goldberg, 2002). If mood stabilization treatment is necessary during pregnancy, other agents should be employed if possible. When a pregnant woman is on lithium therapy, the drug should be discontinued for several days before delivery, because the newborn will have difficulty excreting the drug. On the other hand, restarting lithium within 24 hours of delivery is important to reduce the risk of relapse. Viguera and coworkers (2000) addressed this issue in a study of 42 pregnant and 59 nonpregnant females with bipolar disorder. Discontinuation of lithium during pregnancy was followed by a recurrence rate similar to that seen in nonpregnant females. However, following delivery, postpartum females demonstrated a threefold increase in the rate of recurrence compared with that in nonpregnant females. The researchers concluded:

> Treatment planning for potentially pregnant women with bipolar disorder should consider the relative risks of fetal exposure to mood stabilizers versus the high recurrence risks after discontinuing lithium. (p. 179)

The same researchers ascertained family planning decisions by 116 women with bipolar disorder (Viguera et al., 2002). Breast-feeding is contraindicated during maternal lithium therapy. Lithium passes easily into breast milk, with milk levels approaching one-third to one-half that in plasma. Infant levels are about equivalent to milk levels. Neonatal toxicity has occurred. If mood-stabilizing therapy is necessary during breast-feeding, Piontek and coworkers (2000) recommend valproic acid because little valproate gets to the infant (only about 1 to 3 percent of maternal levels). Yonkers and coworkers (2004) review complications involved in medicating pregnant bipolar patients.

Noncompliance

In clinical use, up to 50 percent of patients taking lithium stop taking the drug against medical advice. Noncompliance is associated with significant morbidity, recurrent manic episodes, and greatly increased suicide risk. Some years ago it was felt that the illness course after stopping lithium treatment could actually be worse than would be predicted from the natural history of bipolar disease. Thus, treatment followed by medication discontinuation might be harmful to bipolar patients. Today, it is felt that discontinuation of lithium therapy does not appear to result in treatment resistance when therapy is resumed.

Noncompliance seems to result largely from intolerance of side effects, particularly memory impairment and cognitive slowing, weight gain, and the subjective feeling of reduced energy and productivity. Other reasons include missing the manic "highs," feelings that the disorder has resolved and the drug is unnecessary, and feelings of stigmatism of chronic illness. Psychological support, family therapy, and other treatments and encouragements can help the patient stay on the drug.

Baldessarini and coworkers (1999) reported that lithium therapy in bipolar patients reduced suicidal behaviors by 77 percent. Unfortunately, when patients stopped taking lithium, the rate of suicide attempts increased fourteenfold, and the rate of completed suicides increased thirteenfold. These data reinforce the necessity for long-term, even lifelong therapy once the decision is made to initiate drug therapy. It is currently not known whether the same decision-making process applies to other antimanic drugs.

Combination Therapy

Combination therapy (often lithium plus an antiepileptic drug) can offer both greater therapeutic efficacy and greater protection against relapse than lithium therapy alone. Indeed, combination therapy has become the rule rather than the exception (Geddes et al., 2004). Bauer and coworkers (2000) reported that lithium was effective in augmenting antidepressant medication in depressed patients only partially responsive to their antidepressant. Goodwin and coworkers (2004) concluded:

> Lamotrigine and lithium stabilized mood by delaying the time to treatment for a mood episode. Lamotrigine was effective against depression and mania, with more robust activity against depression. Lithium was effective against mania. (p. 432)

Substance Abuse

It is disturbing to note that more than 55 percent of bipolar patients have a history of substance abuse. Substances involved include alcohol (82 percent), cocaine (30 percent), marijuana (29 percent), sedatives or amphetamines (21 percent), and opioids (13 percent). In some individuals, substance abuse predated the first bipolar episode, and in others the abuse postdated the affective diagnosis (Tohen et al., 1998). Perhaps in both instances, it may at least initially represent an attempt at self-medication for the symptoms accompanying the affective disorder. Regardless, this comorbidity of disease complicates treatment and outcomes and needs to be recognized and addressed during treatment.

Neuromodulator Anticonvulsants

About 40 percent of bipolar patients either are resistant to lithium treatment or develop side effects that limit its effectiveness. Only about 60 percent to 70 percent of patients with bipolar disorder can be adequately controlled on lithium alone (for maintenance/prevention therapy), and the drug is even less effective in controlling episodes of acute or rapid-cycling mania. Therefore, there is a need for alternative agents, effective in patients for whom lithium is inadequate, patients who are noncompliant with lithium therapy, and patients who are intolerant of lithium's side effects. One alternative is anticonvulsants.

The basic pharmacology of the anticonvulsants was elucidated in Chapter 5. In Chapter 4, their use in alcohol detoxification and prevention of relapse was detailed. In Chapter 12, the use of anticonvulsants in treating aggressive and explosive behavioral disorders in children and adolescents is presented. These drugs are also useful in the treatment of anxiety disorders (Stahl, 2004) and the control of emotional outbursts in disorders such as PTSD (Chapter 9) and borderline personality disorder. Here we focus on the use of the drugs in the treatment of bipolar illness, now one of their primary uses. Such diversity of action and clinical utility obviously encompasses more than the name "anticonvulsant" and an antiepileptic action. To treat any of these varieties of disorders with an antiepileptic drug may give the wrong impression that they are somehow "epileptic." To avoid this misconception, we introduce the broader term *neuromodulator* (used interchangeably with *anticonvulsant*), reflecting the variety of uses of the drugs.

First-generation anticonvulsants included phenobarbital, other barbiturates, phenytoin, and derivatives of phenytoin. These drugs were used to treat epilepsy and had little efficacy in treating bipolar illness. Second-generation anticonvulsants included valproic acid (Divalproex, Depakote) and carbamazepine (Tegretol). These agents have significant side effects that can limit their use. At present, "third-generation" neuromodulators are being increasingly used (Yatham et al., 2002). These agents include gabapentin (Neurontin), pregabalin (Lyrica), oxcarbazepine (Trileptal), topiramate (Topamax), and tiagabine (Gabitril). They are listed in Table 10.1.

Carbamazepine

Studies conducted in the early 1990s indicated that carbamazepine (Tegretol; see Figure 10.1) might be as effective as lithium in preventing the recurrence of mania. However, Hartong and coworkers (2003) reported that lithium was superior in prophylactic efficacy to carbamazepine in bipolar patients not previously treated with mood stabilizers. Despite this, some patients who do not respond adequately to either lithium or carbamazepine alone responded to the two drugs used in combination (Keck and McElroy, 2002).

Patients who fail to respond to carbamazepine often have taken an amount of the drug that is inadequate in plasma. There is correlation between therapeutic effectiveness and the plasma level of the drug; the therapeutic level of carbamazepine is estimated to be between 5 and 10 micrograms per milliliter, the same as the range for antiepileptic effectiveness.

Adverse effects of carbamazepine include gastrointestinal upset, sedation, ataxia, visual disturbances, and dermatological reactions. Carbamazepine may also have modest detrimental effects on cognitive functioning, but any negative effect on higher-order cognitive functioning appears rather limited. Nevertheless, some patients may be particularly sensitive to the cognitive side effects of the drug. More serious reactions involve the blood, ranging from a relatively benign reduction in white blood cell count (leukopenia) to, on rare occasions, severe aplastic anemia. For this reason blood must be analyzed periodically.

Drug interactions involving carbamazepine are common and result from drug-induced stimulation of drug-metabolizing enzymes (especially CYP3A4) in the liver. As a result, tolerance to the drug develops and more drug is needed to maintain a therapeutic blood level; this tolerance also extends to other drugs metabolized by the same enzyme family. Because carbamazepine is potentially teratogenic (it produces a neural tube defect in 1 percent of offspring), it should not be administered during pregnancy if at all possible.

Valproic Acid

Valproate (valproic acid, divalproex, Depakene, Depakote; see Figure 10.1) is the second neuromodulator that was systematically studied for use in bipolar illness. From its introduction in 1994 to the present, valproate has been used to treat bipolar disease. It is felt that valproate acts by augmenting the postsynaptic action of GABA at its receptors, although the exact mechanisms responsible for its antimanic action have not been elucidated. Chen and coworkers (1999) studied the effects of valproate on gene expression in vitro and concluded that valproate-induced mediation of gene expression in critical brain circuits may underlie its antiepileptic, antimanic, and antiaggression effectiveness. This conclusion is in agreement with the studies of Manji and coworkers discussed earlier.

Valproate is particularly effective in the treatment of acute mania, mixed states, schizoaffective disorder, and rapid-cycling bipolar disorder. It is as effective as and less toxic than lithium when used in low doses as an alternative to lithium in the treatment of cyclothymia. It is also more effective than lithium in patients with comorbid depression, although lamotrigine may be superior in this regard. Muller-Oerlinghausen and coworkers (2000) demonstrated the added efficacy of a valproate-olanzapine combination in reducing the symptoms of acute mania.

In acute mania in lithium-resistant patients, valproate therapy results in positive response in up to 71 percent of patients. Also, the therapeutic combination of valproate and lithium is more efficacious then is either agent used alone. Therapeutic blood levels of valproate range between 50 and 100 micrograms per milliliter. Revicki and coworkers (2003) compared valproate against olanzapine (Zyprexa) in patients with acute mania. The drugs were equally effective and valproate is much less expensive.

Grunze and coworkers (1999) described an intravenous loading technique with valproate to control acute mania; this was the first reported use of an intravenously administered antimanic drug. It was thought to overcome the slow (3- to 10-day) period normally required to control manic symptoms with orally administered drug. In a more recent study, Phrolov and coworkers (2004) reported that previously nonmedicated persons with mania failed to respond to intravenous valproate over at least a two-hour period following drug injection. They conclude: "Slow-evolving biochemical changes, perhaps at the gene level, may be required for the antimanic effect of anticonvulsants" (p. 68).

Valproic acid has traditionally been administered in divided doses through the day. A new extended-release preparation allows once-daily dosing, usually at bedtime to improve compliance and help alleviate daytime sedation and memory impairments (Horne and Cunanan, 2003).

Side effects associated with valproate include GI upset, sedation, lethargy, hand tremor, alopecia (loss of hair), and some metabolic changes in the liver. In females starting valproate before the age of 20 years, the drug has been associated with an 8 percent prevalence of marked obesity, polycystic ovaries, and markedly increased levels of serum androgens (increased testosterone levels). Valproate may be slightly more detrimental to cognitive function than is carbamazepine. Like lithium and carbamazepine, valproate can be teratogenic, and caution must be exercised in using this agent in women who might become pregnant during drug therapy. Unlike lithium, little valproate is secreted in breast milk (Piontek et al., 2000). Valproate therefore may be a preferred drug for use by nursing mothers who must take an antimanic drug. Serious side effects associated with valproate include hepatotoxicity (liver damage), teratogenicity (fetal damage), and pancreatitis (inflammation of the pancreas).

In addition to its uses as an antiepileptic and an antimanic drug, valproate has been used in the treatment of alcoholism (Chapter 4), borderline personality disorder (Frankenburg and Zanarini, 2002), and disorders associated with behavioral dyscontrol (agitation, aggression, temper outbursts) (Hollander et al., 2003). It has even been reported to be effective in the treatment of pathological gambling. These uses are probably not unique to valproic acid but are shared by several neuromodulators.

Gabapentin

The efficacy in bipolar disorder of other several other anticonvulsants has been investigated and several deserve discussion. Gabapentin (Neurontin; see Figure 5.4) was introduced in the United States in 1993 for use as an anticonvulsant. In addition to this use, it is used for the treatment of bipolar disorder, to alleviate anxiety disorders, as an analgesic to relieve certain pain states, to treat behavioral dyscontrol disorders, and to treat substance dependency disorders. This spectrum of uses is similar to that seen for valproate, with the exception that gabapentin appears to be a superior analgesic while valproate is superior in the treatment of bipolar disorder.

Mechanistically, gabapentin is a GABA analogue and may have some effects on GABA neurotransmission; it functions to increase intracellular and brain GABA. In addition, gabapentin has an excellent pharmacokinetic profile: it is not bound to plasma proteins, is not metabolized, is excreted unchanged through the kidneys, and has few pharmacokinetic drug interactions. Its elimination half-life is 5 to 7 hours. Gabapentin is absorbed by a saturable active transport mechanism from intestine to plasma, so doses to only 1500 mg can be given at any one time. Gabapentin does not alter the kinetics of lithium, implying that it may turn out to be an excellent choice for combination therapy with lithium.

In 1997, McElroy and coworkers conducted an open trial of gabapentin in nine patients unresponsive to lithium therapy. Doses were advanced to as much as 4800 milligrams per day, in divided doses. Seven patients were moderately or markedly improved after a month of treatment and an eighth was improved at 3 months. Side effects were tolerable, consisting of sleepiness, dizziness, ataxia, nystagmus, and double vision. Frye and coworkers (2000) compared gabapentin to lamotrigine and placebo as monotherapy in refractory unipolar depression and bipolar disorder. Gabapentin was slightly better than placebo and only half as effective as lamotrigine. There is now developing consensus that gabapentin is most effective as an adjunctive medication in patients resistant to another, more effective mood stabilizer such as lithium, valproate, or lamotrigine (Perugi et al., 2002).

Pande and coworkers (1999) noted positive results of gabapentin on 69 patients with social phobia. Side effects included dizziness, dry mouth, somnolence, nausea, flatulence, and reduced libido. Preliminary data with gabapentin indicate that it improves depression and anxiety in female patients with borderline personality disorder. In addition, gabapentin is analgesic and anxiolytic, "which may also provide a greater therapeutic yield in mood disorders complicated by comorbid pain syndromes, social phobia, anxiety, or insomnia" (Frye et al., 2000, p. 612). Also, "the utility of gabapentin in resistant bipolar disorder resides in its effectiveness against comorbid panic disorder and alcohol abuse" (Perugi et al., 2002, p. 584).

Gabapentin holds a special place for the treatment of certain pain states, including peripheral neuropathy (as can occur in diabetes), sympathetic dystrophy (which may follow peripheral nerve injury), postradiation myopathy, phantom limb pain, postsurgical pain, and other difficult-to-treat pain situations (Backonja and Glanzman 2003; Dirks et al., 2002; Feng et al., 2003; Gilron et al., 2003; Hurley et al., 2002; Matthews and Dickenson, 2002). Analgesic action occurs secondary to a direct spinal cord action of gabapentin on pain-processing circuits involving glutamate and substance P neurotransmission.

Recently, Bonnet and coworkers (2003) reported that gabapentin was of little use in treating symptoms associated with acute alcohol withdrawal.

Pregabalin

Pregabalin (Lyrica), a derivative of gabapentin, was approved for use in the United States in 2005 for the treatment of diabetic peripheral neuropathies, post-herpes neuralgia, and as adjunctive therapy in the treatment of partial seizures in adults. Although reportedly effective, it was not formally approved for the treatment of generalized anxiety disorder. FDA approval has not yet been sought for use in bipolar disorder, even though the drug is effective for that use, probably as an adjunctive agent with anxiolytic, antidepressant, and analgesic properties. As an anxiolytic for generalized anxiety disorder, pregabalin is as effective as the benzodiazepines lorazepam (Ativan) and alprazolam (Xanax) (Pande et al., 2003).

Lamotrigine

As a third-generation anticonvulsant neuromodulator, lamotrigine (Lamictal; See Figure 5.4) has gained rapid acceptance as an important monotherapeutic drug for treatment of acute bipolar depression and rapid-cycling bipolar II disorder, as well as the prevention of recurrent bipolar depressive episodes. Lamotrigine is poorly effective in treating acute manic episodes. In all studies, lamotrigine was noted to produce antidepressant effects and improve the quality of life, including positive effects on mood, alertness, and cognition (Sokolenko and Kutcher,

2001). Figure 10.2 illustrates the beneficial effect of lamotrigine on depression in bipolar illness. In patients with monopolar depression unresponsive to antidepressant drugs, lamotrigine may significantly improve the response (Rocha et al., 2003). Compared with antidepressants, lamotrigine is less likely to produce a shift from depression to mania (Keck et al., 2003). In combination therapy, valproate doubles and carbamazepine halves the half-life of lamotrigine (Hurley, 2002).

In a study by Bowden and coworkers (2003), lamotrigine was as effective as lithium in preventing relapse to any manic episode over an 18-month period. It was superior to lithium in preventing relapse to any depressive episode. Headache was the most frequently reported side effect. Lamotrigine has also been reported to be effective in the treatment of borderline personality disorder, posttraumatic stress disorder, and schizoaffective disorder. In 2003, lamotrigine was approved for the long-term maintenance of adults with bipolar I disorder.

Following oral administration, lamotrigine is rapidly and completely absorbed, with little first-pass metabolism. Peak plasma concentrations occur in 1 to 5 hours. Lamotrigine is metabolized before excretion and its half-life is about 26 hours, decreasing to 7.4 hours when used with phenytoin (as an anticonvulsant) or carbamazepine (requiring increased doses of lamotrigine). Its half-life is lengthened to 60 hours when used with valproate, necessitating greatly reduced doses of lamotrigine (Hurley, 2002).

Mechanistically, lamotrigine inhibits the release of the excitatory neurotransmitter glutamate in the cortex and hippocampus, an action that accounts for the antiepileptic, antimanic, and analgesic actions of the drug (Arguelles et al., 2002). It therefore inhibits neuronal excitability, produces analgesia, and modifies synaptic plasticity (Ketter et al., 2003). Because of this glutamate-inhibiting action, it may be effective in people who suffer traumatic brain injuries (Pachet et al., 2003).

Side effects associated with lamotrigine therapy include dizziness, tremor, somnolence, headache, nausea, and rash. The most serious of these is rash, which initially was thought to occur in about 10 percent of patients and could be so severe that hospitalization is necessary. In fact, the rash has been fatal in some cases. Adolescents were initially thought to be more prone to serious rashes, so, at this time, lamotrigine is not indicated for persons below the age of 16 years. The incidence of rash is now thought to be about 1 in 500 patients; a slow titration of dose over about 6 weeks is thought to reduce the incidence. Indeed, in more recent studies, rashes have not been a major problem. Sokolenko and Kutcher (2001) summarize an approach to minimizing the occurrence of rash:

> Low initial doses, very slow titration, and diligent conformation to the guidelines for concurrent use of valproate and lamotrigine have decreased the incidence of this adverse effect. (p. 4)

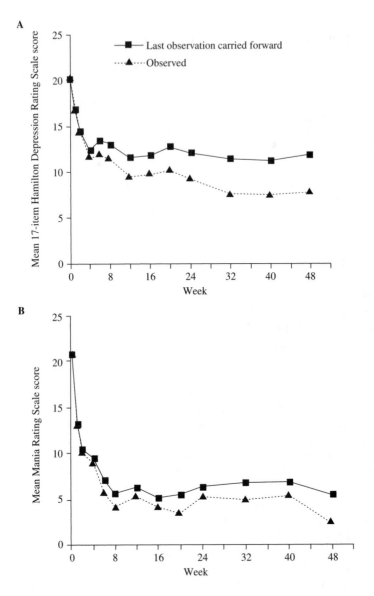

FIGURE 10.2 A. Mean scores on the Hamilton Depression Rating Scale (HDRS) for the reduction in depression in 40 patients with bipolar disorder who presented with depression. Among them, 48 percent exhibited a marked response and 20 percent exhibited a moderate response to lamotrigine as measured by the HDRS. **B.** Mean scores on the Mania Rating Scale of 31 patients with bipolar disorder presenting in hypomanic, manic, or mixed states during lamotrigine treatment. Of the patients, 81 percent exhibited a marked response and 3 percent exhibited a moderate response on the Mania Rating Scale. [From J. R. Calabrese et al., "Spectrum of Activity of Lamotrigine in Treatment-Refractory Bipolar Disorder," *American Journal of Psychiatry* 156 (1999), p. 1020.]

Calabrese and coworkers (2002) reviewed the incidence of rash over many studies and concluded:

> Serious drug eruptions associated with lamotrigine were rare. . . . The risk of serious rash due to lamotrigine should be weighed against the more common risks associated with untreated or undertreated bipolar depression. (p. 1012)

Lamotrigine easily crosses the placenta, although fetal effects have been incompletely studied. At this time, it is thought that the drug should not be used during the first trimester of pregnancy (Ohman et al., 2000). In breast milk, lamotrigine occurs at a level about 60 percent of that in maternal blood; serum levels in breast-feeding infants are about 23 to 50 percent of the mother's serum concentration.

Oxcarbazepine

Oxcarbazepine (Trileptal) can be considered as a new, safer carbamazepine, capable of replacing carbamazepine for all its uses with comparable efficacy and greatly improved safety. This difference follows from the small structural difference in the two drugs (Figure 10.3). Oxcarbazepine is essentially carbamazepine with an oxygen molecule attached to one of the rings. This allows the liver to easily metabolize the drug by a process called hydroxylation. In fact, this process occurs within 5 minutes after drug absorption, and the monohydroxy derivative is the active form of the drug (oxcarbazepine is therefore an inactive "pro-drug"). Because of this easy metabolic process, there is no enzyme induction, no alterations in liver enzymes, no white blood cell problems, no required blood monitoring, and few drug interactions.

Oxcarbazepine is approved for use in epilepsy, and it is becoming widely used to treat bipolar disorder and other disorders treatable by carbamazepine (Ghaemi et al., 2003; Hellewell, 2002; Hummel et al., 2002). Centorrino and coworkers (2003) concluded that oxcarbazepine is well tolerated and simpler to use clinically than is carbamazepine. At this time, oxcarbazepine still has needs:

- Better documentation in the treatment of bipolar disorder
- Investigations of potential usefulness in aggressive and behavioral disorders in children and adolescents
- Studies of usefulness in alcohol withdrawal, craving, and relapse
- Studies of potential usefulness in relapse to other drugs of abuse
- Investigations into possible analgesic effects

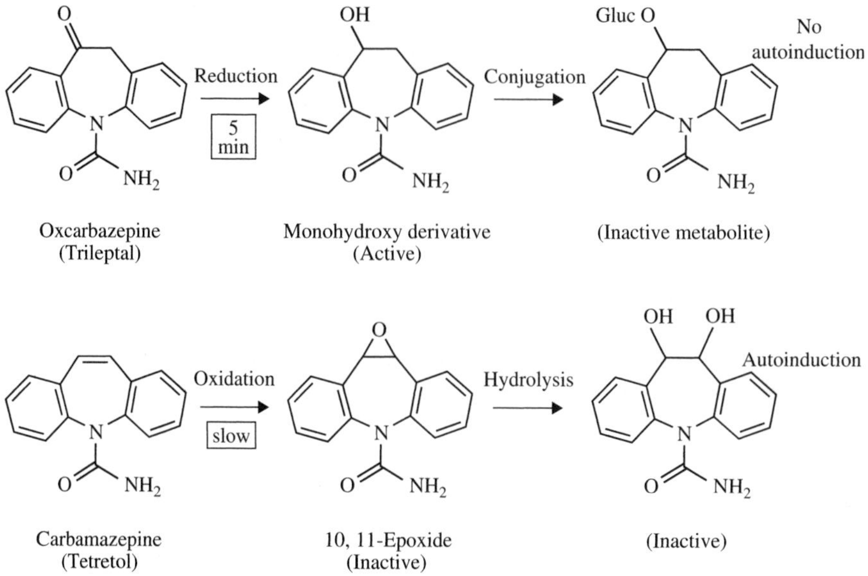

FIGURE 10.3 Metabolic pathways for the metabolism of oxcarbazepine and carbamazepine. Oxcarbazepine is "reduced" to its active metabolite (monohydroxy oxcarbazepine) and then to glucuronide, which is conjugated to an inactive metabolite that is excreted. Carbamazepine is slowly "oxidized" to an inactive epoxide and then to a metabolite that is excreted.

Topiramate

Chapter 4 discussed the use of the antiepileptic drug topiramate (Topamax) as an antirelapse drug in the treatment of alcoholism. Open-label studies indicate that topiramate is potentially useful as an anti-manic agent: about 50 percent of bipolar patients who have been treated with the drug improved (Suppes, 2002). The main advantage of topiramate is that use of the drug is associated with weight loss, rather than weight gain (Chengappa et al., 2002). This characteristic may make the drug useful as an adjunctive agent to offset the weight gain associated with the use of other antimanic drugs, such as lithium and valproate. Topiramate may be especially useful in the treatment of bipolar disorder in children and adolescents (DelBello et al., 2002; Pavuluri et al., 2002). It may be useful as a mood stabilizer in obese patients with either unipolar depression or bipolar disorder who want to lose weight (Carpenter et al., 2002). It will be interesting to see whether or not topiramate will be useful in individuals with either bulimia nervosa or anorexia, with or without bipolar disorder. Preliminary evidence indicates positive effects in comorbid bipolar disorder and bulimia (Felstrom and Blackshaw, 2002). Unfortunately, the cognitive depressant effects of topiramate are greater than those of gabapentin or lamotrigine (Lee et al., 2003; Martin et al., 1999). Side effects include tingling in the extremities, irritability, anxiety, and depression.

Topiramate is excreted unchanged by the kidneys and therefore has a reduced likelihood of being involved in drug interactions involving the liver. However, topiramate has the potential to increase the plasma levels of other drugs excreted by the kidneys (for example, lithium). Increasingly, topiramate is being used as an adjunct, with goals both to improve therapeutic response and to reduce the weight gain caused by other agents.

Berlant and vanKammen (2002) reported that topiramate was effective in the treatment of PTSD, with the drug decreasing nightmares in 79 percent of patients and flashbacks in 86 percent. Janowsky and coworkers (2003) noted the usefulness of topiramate to reduce aggressive, self-injurious, and destructive behaviors in developmentally disabled adults. Topiramate was used as an adjunct to the patients' other psychoactive medications. The researchers concluded: "Topiramate may have a role in the treatment of challenging/maladaptive behaviors in intellectually disabled individuals" (p. 500). Finally, topiramate has been useful in the treatment of OCD, binge-eating, and PTSD.

Tiagabine

To date, there have been no blinded, controlled, or comparative trials of tiagabine in the treatment of bipolar disorder. In 1998, it was reported to effectively treat both bipolar disorder and schizoaffective disorder in three patients. This spurred interest in the drug. However, subsequent open trials demonstrated that tiagabine has limited efficacy; the majority of patients experience either no change or else worsening of symptoms (Schaffer et al., 2002).

The mechanism of action of tiagabine as an anticonvulsant involves selective inhibition of the active reuptake of GABA by inhibiting the GABA transporter in the hippocampus and cerebral cortex. Its utility in the treatment of pain states has not been reported.

Zonisamide

Zonisamide (Zonegran) is an antiepileptic drug long available in Japan that became available in the United States in mid-2000 for the treatment of epilepsy. Preliminary studies in small numbers of patients indicate that zonisamide may have use in the treatment of bipolar disorder: 80 percent of the patients showed at least moderate improvement and 33 percent showed marked improvement (Evins, 2003). Side effects included sedation, reduced white blood cell counts, and elevated liver enzymes. Other, more severe side effects also occurred as well as several drug interactions. Interestingly, zonisamide is being studied for weight loss in obese patients (Gadde et al., 2003).

Atypical Antipsychotics

For decades, traditional antipsychotic drugs, such as haloperidol (Chapter 11), have been used to help control the symptoms and behaviors associated with acute mania. Indeed, the use of antipsychotic drugs to treat bipolar disorder predated the use of lithium by 20 years. Antipsychotic drugs were not without problems, including the production of extrapyramidal signs that included akathesia and tardive dyskinesia (Chapter 11). They also were of little use against depressive symptoms, and they were not very effective in preventing recurrent episodes of the disorder.

The newer "atypical" antipsychotics (Chapter 11) do not share this profile. They demonstrate efficacy against acute mania and prevent relapse in the absence of extrapyramidal side effects. Frye and coworkers (1998) reviewed the use of clozapine, risperidone, and olanzapine in bipolar disorder. Clozapine appeared more antimanic than antidepressant. Risperidone (Risperdal) appeared more antidepressant than antimanic, potentially aggravating mania. While clozapine is efficacious, potentially serious side effects limit its use. If it were not for the serious blood cell reactions it can cause, clozapine might well be a drug of first choice for the treatment of bipolar disorder.

Olanzapine (Zyprexa) has now been evaluated in several studies and its efficacy is well documented. It is useful both as monotherapy for acute mania (Dennehy et al., 2003; Sanger et al., 2003) and in combination with mood stabilizers (Gonzalez-Pinto et al., 2002). It is now considered to be as effective as lithium or valproic acid (Tohen et al., 2002). In mid-2000, the FDA formally approved olanzapine for the short-term treatment of acute mania, the first such approval for an antipsychotic drug. In addition, olanzapine augments the antidepressant effect of fluoxetine in depressed patients only partially responsive to fluoxetine (Shelton et al., 2001). The combination of these two drugs became available in 2004 (as Symbyax).

Frazier and coworkers (1999) studied *risperidone* (Risperdal) in 28 youths with juvenile bipolar disorder and concluded that the drug is effective. Yatham and coworkers (2003) reported that risperidone was superior to placebo when used as an augmenting agent in combination with either lithium or valproate.

Quetiapine (Seroquel) also has been reported to be very effective as a treatment option in the management of bipolar disorder (Kasper, 2002; Brown et al., 2002). In addition, *ziprasidone* (Geodon) and *aripiprazole* (Abilify) may eventually be reported to be effective in the treatment of bipolar disorder. What are needed are comparative studies of atypical antipsychotics either as monotherapeutic agents or as augmenting agents (to either mood stabilizers or antidepressants) in bipolar disorder (Malhi and Berk, 2002).

Acetylcholinesterase Inhibitors

Despite best efforts, many patients are unresponsive to or intolerant of the antimanic drugs heretofore discussed. Therefore, a need exists for additional alternative agents, especially those with unique mechanisms of action. One such drug is *donepezil* (Aricept), an acetylcholinesterase inhibitor used in the treatment of Alzheimer's disease (Chapter 13). Study of the psychedelic drug *scopolamine* (Chapter 19) reveals that blockade of the action of acetylcholine produces clinical effects that include euphoria, talkativeness, difficulties in concentration, and flight of ideas, all resembling symptoms seen in manic disorder. Therefore, perhaps potentiating the action of acetylcholine might exert the opposite effect: relief from mania. *Donepezil* inhibits the enzyme acetylcholine esterase (AChE) and therefore can be postulated to be therapeutically effective in bipolar disorder.

Burt and colleagues (1999) administered donepezil to eleven patients with bipolar disorder who were treatment resistant to other medications. Six patients demonstrated marked improvement, and three additional patients demonstrated slight improvement. Side effects were minor. Although this unusual paper indicates efficacy in treatment-resistant patients, it is too early to tell whether or not donepezil will become a useful alternative or adjunctive therapy (Gnanadesikan et al., 2003).

Omega-3 Fatty Acids

In countries where the diet is rich in fish oils, the incidence of bipolar disorder is quite low (Noaghiul and Hibbeln, 2003). Therefore, it is possible that fish oils prevent bipolar disorder, perhaps offering the necessary neuronal protection to prevent the neuronal injuries now being identified in bipolar disorder. As we know, the mechanisms of action of antimanic drugs involve inhibitory effects on neuronal signaling transduction systems. Omega-3 fatty acids, obtained from marine or plant sources, are known to damp these signal transduction pathways in a variety of cell systems.

Stoll and coworkers (1999) hypothesized that omega-3 fatty acids might be therapeutically useful in bipolar disorder. They administered the acids (under double-blind, placebo-controlled conditions) to 30 patients with bipolar disorder for 4 months. Patients received the fatty acids in addition to their normal antimanic medications (if any). The researchers concluded that the omega-3 fatty acid patient group had a much longer period of remission than the placebo group (Figure 10.4). Results were impressive even for individuals who were not taking concurrent medication for their disorder (Figure 10.5). In addition, for nearly every other outcome measure, the omega-3 group performed

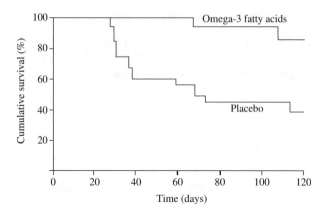

FIGURE 10.4 Effect of omega-3 fatty acids on mean time to recurrence of a bipolar episode compared to placebo (olive oil) therapy. Note the 50 percent recurrence rate at about 75 days with placebo therapy and the prolonged efficacy observed in omega-3-treated patients. [From Stoll et al. (1999), p. 409.]

better than the placebo group (which also received their normal medications). These pilot results are certainly intriguing and merit further study. As discussed in Chapter 9, omega-3 fatty acids include docosahexaenoid acid and eicosapentaenoic acid. These individual fatty acids have not yet been tried in bipolar disorder.

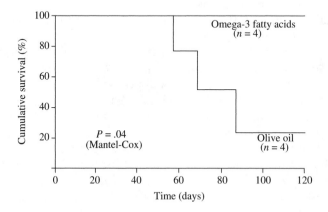

FIGURE 10.5 Effect of omega-3 fatty acids on mean time to recurrence of a bipolar episode. Four patients received only omega-3 fatty acids monotherapy (no other antimanic drugs were taken). These four had no recurrences over the 120-day study period. Four patients received only placebo therapy (olive oil) and no other antimanic drugs: recurrences began at 60 days and all had a recurrence by 90 days. [From Stoll et al. (1999), p. 409.]

Miscellaneous Agents

In Chapter 6, the pharmacology of the *benzodiazepines* was presented. Two such drugs (*clonazepam* and *lorazepam*) can be used to treat symptoms and behaviors associated with acute mania. The pharmacology of *antidepressant drugs* was presented in Chapter 9. Some patients with bipolar disorder with recurrent depressive episodes may require continuous treatment with one of these agents. However, therapy with antidepressants is undertaken with the knowledge that antidepressants may precipitate a manic episode. As stated earlier, a combination product of olanzapine and fluoxetine is available as Symbyax. The Practice Guideline of the American Psychiatric Association (2002) states:

> As some bipolar patients continue to develop depression despite optimal use of mood stabilizers, antidepressants are often necessary for acute and/or prophylactic treatment. Patients who require antidepressant treatment should receive the lowest effective dose for the shortest time necessary. (p. 4)

Because lithium interferes with membrane ion function, *verapamil* and other *calcium channel blockers* have been tried in bipolar disorder. Despite early reports, their effectiveness remains questionable.

Clonidine, an antihypertensive drug, has been tried in treatment-refractory patients with bipolar disorder. Because clonidine decreases the release of norepinephrine, it was hypothesized that the decrease might lead to a reduction in manic episodes. Despite initial positive results, effectiveness remains unproven.

Psychotherapeutic and Psychosocial Treatments

While not widely appreciated, a combination of drug therapy and psychotherapeutic interventions is the most effective treatment modality for bipolar illness:

> The increasing evidence of efficacy of the pharmacologic treatment of bipolar disorders has sometimes led clinicians to forget psychological interventions as an adjunctive treatment. (Colom et al., 2003, p. 402)

Goals of psychotherapy and psychosocial treatments are to improve clinical outcomes, functional outcomes, and disease management skills (Bauer, 2001). Patients with bipolar disorder suffer from the psychosocial consequences of past episodes, the ongoing vulnerability to future episodes, and the burdens of adhering to a long-term treatment plan that may involve some unpleasant side effects. In addition, many patients have clinically significant mood instability between episodes. Successful treatment involves a social network primed to recognize the early symptoms of an episode, to seek help for patients who lack insight into their condition, and to assist with recognition of side effects and toxicities, thus aiding in compliance with therapy. Issues of importance include the following:

- Emotional consequences of periods of major mood disorder and diagnosis of a chronic mental illness
- Developmental deviations and delays caused by past episodes
- Problems associated with stigmatization
- Problems regulating self-esteem
- Fears of recurrence and consequent inhibition of normal psychosocial functioning
- Interpersonal difficulties
- Marriage, family, childbearing, and parenting issues
- Academic and occupational problems
- Other legal, social, and emotional problems that arise from reckless, violent, withdrawn, or bizarre behavior that may occur during episodes

It is also important to ensure that the manic state is not being caused by medications, such as antidepressants, caffeine, herbals containing ephedrine, behavioral stimulants (including illegal drugs such as cocaine), corticosteroids (cortisone), anabolic steroids, antiparkinsonian drugs, over-the-counter cough and cold preparations, and diet aids. One must also rule out thyroid disease because mania secondary to thyroid hyperactivity is common.

Psychotherapy interventions used concomitantly with pharmacotherapy include group psychoeducation (Colom et al., 2003), cognitive-behavioral therapy (Lam et al., 2003; Otto et al., 2003), psychodynamically oriented therapy, family therapy, couples therapy, interpersonal psychotherapy, and self-help groups. For complete treatment, a practitioner well versed in the pharmacological management of poorly responsive bipolar patients is necessary. Other personnel are required to monitor the effectiveness of treatment, side effects, other causative factors, and compliance with therapy.

To date, it has been demonstrated that psychosocial and cognitive-behavioral therapies added to mood stabilizer treatment can result in fewer relapses, fewer days in a bipolar episode, reduced admissions for inpatient treatment, and other positive outcomes. Larger trials are needed to further delineate to exact role and efficacy of these adjunctive therapies. Currently there is an ongoing, multisite, federally funded Systematic Treatment Enhancement Program (STEP), which aims to randomize up to 1000 bipolar patients in a controlled investigation of these treatments (Otto et al., 2003).

STUDY QUESTIONS

1. Outline the pharmacological agents useful in the treatment of bipolar disorder. What are the major drugs in each category?

2. List the clinical uses of lithium.

3. Describe the correlations between plasma levels of lithium and the therapeutic and side effects of the drug.

4. How does lithium exert its antimanic effect?

5. List the major organ systems affected by lithium. What are the drug's major side effects on each system?

6. Discuss the effects of the various antimanic drugs on memory and cognitive behaviors.

7. Discuss the use of antimanic drugs in pregnancy and in the potentially pregnant female with bipolar disorder.

8. Discuss the comorbidity of bipolar disorder with other psychological disorders.

9. Which antiepileptic drugs are used in the treatment of bipolar disorder? List the advantages and disadvantages of each.

10. What intrudes on patient compliance with mood-stabilizing medication? What can be done to improve compliance?

11. What medications or diseases might precipitate or worsen bipolar illness?

12. How can a health care professional who is not the prescribing physician contribute to the well-being of the bipolar patient?

13. Describe the possible role of omega-3 fatty acids in bipolar illness.

REFERENCES

American Psychiatric Association (2002). "Practice Guideline for the Treatment of Patients with Bipolar Disorder (Revision)." *American Journal of Psychiatry* 159, Supplement (April).

Arguelles, C. F., et al. (2002). "Peripheral Antinociceptive Action of Morphine and the Synergistic Interaction with Lamotrigine." *Anesthesiology* 96: 921–925.

Backonja, M., and R. L. Glanzman (2003). "Gabapentin Dosing for Neuropathic Pain: Evidence from Randomized, Placebo-Controlled Clinical Trials." *Clinical Therapeutics* 25: 81–104.

Baldessarini, R. J., and L. Tondo (2000). "Does Lithium Treatment Still Work? Evidence of Stable Responses over Three Decades." *Archives of General Psychiatry* 57: 187–190.

Baldessarini, R. J., et al. (1999). "Effects of Lithium Treatment and Its Discontinuation on Suicidal Behavior in Bipolar Manic Depressive Disorders." *Journal of Clinical Psychiatry* 60, Supplement 2: 77–84.

Bartha, L., et al. (2002). "Persistent Cognitive Deficits Associated with Lithium Intoxication: A Neuropsychological Case Description." *Cortex* 38: 743–752.

Bauer, M. S. (2001). "An Evidence-Based Review of Psychosocial Treatments for Bipolar Disorder." *Psychopharmacology Bulletin* 35: 109–134.

Bauer, M. S., and L. Mitchner (2004). "What Is a 'Mood Stabilizer'? An Evidence-Based Response." *American Journal of Psychiatry* 161: 3–18.

Bauer, M. S., et al. (2000). "Double-Blind, Placebo-Controlled Trial of the Use of Lithium to Augment Antidepressant Medication in Continuation Treatment of Unipolar Major Depression." *American Journal of Psychiatry* 157: 1429–1435.

Berlant, J., and D. P. vanKammen (2002). "Open-Label Topiramate as Primary or Adjunctive Therapy in Chronic Civilian Posttraumatic Stress Disorder: A Preliminary Report." *Journal of Clinical Psychiatry* 63: 15–20.

Bertolino, A., et al. (2003). "Neuronal Pathology in the Hippocampal Area of Patients with Bipolar Disorder: A Study with Proton Magnetic Resonance Spectroscopic Imaging." *Biological Psychiatry* 53: 906–913.

Blumberg, H. P., et al. (2003). "A Functional Magnetic Resonance Imaging Study of Bipolar Disorder: State- and Trait-Related Dysfunction in Ventral Prefrontal Cortex." *Archives of General Psychiatry* 60: 601–609.

Bonnet, U., et al. (2003). "Treatment of Acute Alcohol Withdrawal with Gabapentin: Results from a Controlled Two-Center Trial." *Journal of Clinical Psychopharmacology* 23: 514–519.

Bowden, C. L., et al. (2003). "A Placebo-Controlled 18-Month Trial of Lamotrigine and Lithium Maintenance Treatment in Recently Manic or Hypomanic Patients with Bipolar I Disorder." *Archives of General Psychiatry* 60: 392–400.

Brown, E. S., et al. (2002). "Quetiapine in Bipolar Disorder and Cocaine Dependence." *Bipolar Disorders* 4: 406–411.

Burt, T., et al. (1999). "Donepezil in Treatment-Resistant Bipolar Disorder." *Biological Psychiatry* 45: 959–964.

Calabrese, J. R., et al. (2002). "Rash in Multicenter Trials of Lamotrigine in Mood Disorders: Clinical Relevance and Management." *Journal of Clinical Psychiatry* 63: 1012–1019.

Carpenter, L. L., et al. (2002). "Do Obese Depressed Patients Respond to Topiramate? A Retrospective Chart Review." *Journal of Affective Disorders* 69: 251–255.

Centorrino, F., et al. (2003). "Oxcarbazepine: Clinical Experience with Hospitalized Psychiatric Patients." *Bipolar Disorders* 5: 370–374.

Chen, G., et al. (1999). "Valproate Robustly Enhances AP-1 Mediated Gene Expression." *Brain Research: Molecular Brain Research* 64: 52–58.

Chengappa, K. N., et al. (2002). "Changes in Body Weight and Body Mass Index Among Psychiatric Patients Receiving Lithium, Valproate, or Topiramate: An Open-Label, Nonrandomized Chart Review." *Clinical Therapeutics* 24: 1576–1584.

Colom, F., et al. (2003). "A Randomized Trial on the Efficacy of Group Psycho-education in the Prophylaxis of Recurrences in Bipolar Patients Whose Disease Is in Remission." *Archives of General Psychiatry* 60: 402–407.

DelBello, M. P., et al. (2002). "Adjunctive Topiramate Treatment for Pediatric Bipolar Disorder: A Retrospective Chart Review." *Journal of Child and Adolescent Psychopharmacology* 12: 323–330.

Dennehy, E. B., et al. (2003). "The Efficacy of Olanzapine Monotherapy for Acute Hypomania or Mania in an Outpatient Setting." *International Clinical Psychopharmacology* 18: 143–145.

Dirks, J., et al. (2002). "A Randomized Study of the Effects of Single-Dose Gabapentin Versus Placebo on Postoperative Pain and Morphine Consumption After Mastectomy." *Anesthesiology* 96: 560–564.

Elmslie, J. L., et al. (2000). "Prevalence of Overweight and Obesity in Bipolar Patients." *Journal of Clinical Psychiatry* 61: 179–184.

Ernst, C. L., and J. F. Goldberg (2002). "The Reproductive Safety Profile of Mood Stabilizers, Atypical Antipsychotics, and Broad-Spectrum Psychotropics." *Journal of Clinical Psychiatry* 63, Supplement 4: 42–55.

Evins, A. E. (2003). "Efficacy of Newer Anticonvulsant Medications in Bipolar Disorder Spectrum Mood Disorders." *Journal of Clinical Psychiatry* 64, Supplement 8: 9–14.

Fawcett, J. A. (2003). "Lithium Combinations in Acute and Maintenance Treatment of Unipolar and Bipolar Depression." *Journal of Clinical Psychiatry* 64, Supplement 5: 32–37.

Felstrom, A., and S. Blackshaw (2002). "Topiramate for Bulimia Nervosa with Bipolar II Disorder." *American Journal of Psychiatry* 159: 1246–1247.

Feng, Y., et al. (2003). "Gabapentin Markedly Reduces Acetic Acid-Induced Visceral Nociception." *Anesthesiology* 98: 729–733.

Frankenburg, F. R., and M. C. Zanarini (2002). "Divalproex Sodium Treatment of Women with Borderline Personality Disorder and Bipolar II Disorder: A Double-Blind, Placebo-Controlled Pilot Study." *Journal of Clinical Psychiatry* 63: 442–446.

Frazier, J. A., et al. (1999). "Risperidone Treatment for Juvenile Bipolar Disorder: A Retrospective Chart Review." *Journal of the American Academy of Child and Adolescent Psychiatry* 38: 960–965.

Frye, M. A., et al. (1998). "Clozapine in Bipolar Disorder: Treatment Implications for Other Atypical Antipsychotics." *Journal of Affective Disorders* 48: 91–104.

Frye, M. A., et al. (2000). "A Placebo-Controlled Study of Lamotrigine and Gabapentin Monotherapy in Refractory Mood Disorders." *Journal of Clinical Psychopharmacology* 20: 607–614.

Gadde, K. M. M., et al. (2003). "Zonisamide for Weight Loss in Obese Adults: A Randomized Controlled Trial." *Journal of the American Medical Society* 289: 1820–1825.

Geddes, J. R., et al. (2004). "Long-Term Lithium Therapy for Bipolar Disorder: Systematic Review and Meta-Analysis of Randomized Controlled Trials." *American Journal of Psychiatry* 161: 217–222.

Ghaemi, S. N., et al. (2003). "Oxcarbazepine Treatment of Bipolar Disorder." *Journal of Clinical Psychiatry* 64: 943–945.

Gilron, I., et al. (2003). "Gabapentin Blocks and Reverses Antinociceptive Morphine Tolerance in the Rat Paw-Pressure and Tail-Flick Tests." *Anesthesiology* 98: 1288–1292.

Gnanadesikan, M., et al. (2003). "Alternatives to Lithium and Divalproex in the Maintenance Treatment of Bipolar Disorder." *Bipolar Disorders* 5: 203–216.

Gonzalez-Pinto, A., et al. (2002). "Treatment of Bipolar I Rapid Cycling Patients During Dysphoric Mania with Olanzapine." *Journal of Clinical Psychopharmacology* 22: 450–454.

Goodwin, G. M., et al. (2004). "A Pooled Analysis of Two Placebo-Controlled 18-Month Trails of Lamotrigine and Lithium Maintenance in Bipolar I Disorder." *Journal of Clinical Psychiatry* 64: 432–441.

Gray, N. A., et al. (2003). "The Use of Mood Stabilizers as Plasticity Enhancers in the Treatment of Neuropsychiatric Disorders." *Journal of Clinical Psychiatry* 64, Supplement 5: 3–17.

Grunze, H., et al. (1999). "Intravenous Valproate Loading in Acutely Manic and Depressed Bipolar I Patients." *Journal of Clinical Psychopharmacology* 19: 303–309.

Hartong, E. G., et al. (2003). "Prophylactic Efficacy of Lithium Versus Carbamazepine in Treatment-Naïve Bipolar Patients." *Journal of Clinical Psychiatry* 64: 144–151.

Hashimoto, R., et al. (2002). "Lithium Induces Brain-Derived Neurotrophic Factor and Activates TrkB in Rodent Cortical Neurons: An Essential Step for Neuroprotection Against Glutamate Excitotoxicity." *Neuropharmacology* 43: 1173–1179.

Hellewell, J. S. (2002). "Oxcarbazepine (Trileptal) in the Treatment of Bipolar Disorders: Review of Efficacy and Tolerability." *Journal of Affective Disorders* 72, Supplement (December): S23–S34.

Hollander, E., et al. (2003). "Divalproex in the Treatment of Impulsive Aggression: Efficacy in Cluster B Personality Disorders." *Neuropsychopharmacology* 28: 1186–1197.

Horne, R. L., and C. Cunanan (2003). "Safety and Efficacy of Switching Psychiatric Patients from a Delayed-Release to an Extended-Release Formulation of Divalproex Sodium." *Journal of Clinical Psychopharmacology* 23: 176–181.

Hummel, B., et al. (2002). "Acute Antimanic Efficacy and Safety of Oxcarbazepine in an Open Trial with an On-Off-On Design." *Bipolar Disorders* 4: 412–417.

Hurley, R. W., et al. (2002). "Gabapentin and Pregabalin Can Interact Synergistically with Naproxen to Produce Antihyperalgesia." *Anesthesiology* 97: 1263–1273.

Hurley, S. C. (2002). "Lamotrigine Update and Its Use in Bipolar Disorders." *Annals of Pharmacotherapy* 36: 860–873.

Janowsky, D. S., et al. (2003). "Effects of Topiramate on Aggressive, Self-Injurious, and Disruptive/Destructive Behaviors in the Intellectually Disabled: An Open-Label Retrospective Study." *Journal of Clinical Psychopharmacology* 23: 500–504.

Kasper, S., et al. (2002). "Atypical Antidepressants in Mood Disorders," *International Clinical Psychopharmacology* 17, Supplement 3: S1–S10.

Keck, P. E., and S. L. McElroy (2002). "Carbamazepine and Valproate in the Maintenance Treatment of Bipolar Disorder." *Journal of Clinical Psychiatry* 63, Supplement 10: 13–17.

Keck, P. E., and S. L. McElroy (2003). "Bipolar Disorder, Obesity, and Pharmacotherapy-Associated Weight Gain." *Journal of Clinical Psychiatry* 64: 1426–1435.

Keck, P. E., and J. Susman (2003). "Introduction: Foundational Treatment for Bipolar Disorder." *Journal of Family Practice* Supplement (March): 4–5.

Keck, P. E., et al. (2003). "Advances in the Pharmacological Treatment of Bipolar Depression." *Biological Psychiatry* 53: 671–679.

Ketter, T. A., et al. (2003). "Potential Mechanisms of Action of Lamotrigine in the Treatment of Bipolar Disorders." *Journal of Clinical Psychopharmacology* 23: 484–495.

Kopnisky, K. L., et al. (2003). "Chronic Lithium Treatment Antagonizes Glutamate-Induced Decrease of Phosphorylated CREB in Neurons via Reducing Protein Phosphorylase 1 and Increasing MEK Activities." *Neuroscience* 116: 425–435.

Lam, D. H., et al. (2003). "A Randomized Controlled Study of Cognitive Therapy for Relapse Prevention for Bipolar Affective Disorder: Outcome of the First Year." *Archives of General Psychiatry* 60: 145–152.

Lee, S., et al. (2003). "The Effects of Adjunctive Topiramate on Cognitive Function in Patients with Epilepsy." *Epilepsia* 44: 339–347.

Li, X., et al. (2002). "Synaptic, Intracellular, and Neuroprotective Mechanisms of Anticonvulsants: Are They Relevant for the Treatment and Course of Bipolar Disorders?" *Journal of Affective Disorders* 69: 1-14.

Maj, M., et al. (1998). "Long-Term Outcome of Lithium Prophylaxis in Bipolar Disorder: A Five-Year Prospective Study of 402 Patients at a Lithium Clinic." *American Journal of Psychiatry* 155: 30–35.

Malhi, G. S., and M. Berk (2002). "Pharmacotherapy of Bipolar Disorder: The Role of Atypical Antipsychotics and Experimental Strategies." *Human Psychopharmacology* 17: 407–412.

Manji, H. K., et al. (2000). "Clinical and Preclinical Evidence for the Neurotrophic Effects of Mood Stabilizers: Implications for the Pathophysiology and Treatment of Manic-Depressive Illness." *Biological Psychiatry* 48: 740–754.

Manji, H. K., et al. (2001). "Bipolar Disorder: Leads from the Molecular and Cellular Mechanisms of Action of Mood Stabilizers." *British Journal of Psychiatry* 178, Supplementum 41: S107–S119.

Martin, R., et al. (1999). "Cognitive Effects of Topiramate, Gabapentin, and Lamotrigine in Healthy Young Adults." *Neurology* 52: 321–327.

Matthews, E. A., and A. H. Dickenson (2002). "A Combination of Gabapentin and Morphine Mediates Enhanced Inhibitory Effects on Dorsal Horn Neuronal Responses in a Rat Model of Neuropathy." *Anesthesiology* 96: 633–640.

McElroy, S. L., et al. (1997). "A Pilot Trial of Adjunctive Gabapentin in the Treatment of Bipolar Disorder." *Annals of Clinical Psychiatry* 9: 99–103.

Mondimore, F. M., et al. (2003). "Drug Combinations for Mania." *Journal of Clinical Psychiatry* 64, Supplement 5: 25–31.

Muller-Oerlinghausen, B., et al. (2000). "Valproate as an Adjunct to Neuroleptic Medication for the Treatment of Acute Episodes of Mania: A Prospective, Randomized, Double-Blind, Placebo-Controlled, Multicenter Study." *Journal of Clinical Psychopharmacology* 20: 195–203.

Noaghiul, S., and J. R. Hibbeln (2003). "Cross-National Comparisons of Seafood Consumption and Rates of Bipolar Disorder." *American Journal of Psychiatry* 160: 2222–2227.

Ohman, I., et al. (2000). "Lamotrigine in Pregnancy: Pharmacokinetics During Delivery, in the Neonate, and During Lactation." *Epilepsia* 41: 709–713.

Osby, U., et al. (2001). "Excess Mortality in Bipolar and Unipolar Disorder in Sweden." *Archives of General Psychiatry* 58: 844–850.

Otto, M. W., et al. (2003). "Psychoeducational and Cognitive-Behavioral Strategies in the Management of Bipolar Disorder." *Journal of Affective Disorders* 73: 171–181.

Pachet, A., et al. (2003). "Beneficial Behavioural Effects of Lamotrigine in Traumatic Brain Injury." *Brain Injury* 17: 715–722.

Pande, A. C., et al. (1999). "Treatment of Social Phobia with Gabapentin: A Placebo-Controlled Study." *Journal of Clinical Psychopharmacology* 19: 341–348.

Pande, A. C., et al. (2003). "Pregabalin in Generalized Anxiety Disorder: A Placebo-Controlled Trial." *American Journal of Psychiatry* 160: 533–540.

Pavuluri, M. N., et al. (2002). "Topiramate plus Risperidone for Controlling Weight Gain and Symptoms in Preschool Mania." *Journal of Child and Adolescent Psychopharmacology* 12: 271–273.

Perugi, G., et al. (2002). "Effectiveness of Adjunctive Gabapentin in Resistant Bipolar Disorders: Is It Due to Anxious-Alcohol Abuse Comorbidity?" *Journal of Clinical Psychopharmacology* 22: 584–591.

Piontek, C. M., et al. (2000). "Serum Valproate Levels in 6 Breastfeeding Mother-Infant Pairs." *Journal of Clinical Psychiatry* 61: 170–172.

Post, R. M., et al. (2003). "Morbidity in 258 Bipolar Outpatients Followed for 1 Year with Daily Prospective Ratings on the NIMH Life Chart Method." *Journal of Clinical Psychiatry* 64: 680–690.

Quraishi, S., and S. Frangou (2002). "Neuropsychology of Bipolar Disorder: A Review." *Journal of Affective Disorders* 72: 209–226.

Ren, M., et al. (2003). "Postinsult Treatment with Lithium Reduces Brain Damage and Facilitates Neurological Recovery in a Rat Ischemia/Reperfusion Model." *Proceeding of the National Academy of Sciences* 100: 6210–6215.

Revicki, D. A., et al. (2003). "Divalproex Sodium Versus Olanzapine in the Treatment of Acute Mania in Bipolar Disorder: Health-Related Quality of Life and Medical Cost Outcomes." *Journal of Clinical Psychiatry* 64: 288–294.

Rocha, F., and C. Hara (2003). "Lamotrigine Augmentation in Unipolar Depression." *International Clinical Psychopharmacology* 18: 97–99.

Sachs, G. S. (2003). "Decision Tree for the Treatment of Bipolar Disorder." *Journal of Clinical Psychiatry* 64, Supplement 8: 35–40.

Sanger, T. M., et al. (2003). "Olanzapine in the Acute Treatment of Bipolar I Disorder with a History of Rapid Cycling." *Journal of Affective Disorders* 73: 155–161.

Schaffer, L. C., et al. (2002). "An Open Case Series on the Utility of Tiagabine as an Augmentation in Refractory Bipolar Outpatients." *Journal of Affective Disorders* 71: 259–263.

Shelton, R. C., et al. (2001). "A Novel Augmentation Strategy for Treating Resistant Major Depression." *American Journal of Psychiatry* 158: 131–134.

Sokolenko, M., and S. Kutcher (2001). "Lamotrigine." *Child and Adolescent Psychopharmacology News* 6 (August): 1–5.

Stahl, S. M. (2004). "Anticonvulsants as Anxiolytics, Part I: Tiagabine and Other Anticonvulsants with Actions on GABA." *Journal of Clinical Psychiatry* 65: 291–292.

Stoll, A. L., et al. (1999). "Omega-3 Fatty Acids in Bipolar Disorder: A Preliminary Double-Blind, Placebo-Controlled Trial." *Archives of General Psychiatry* 56: 407–412.

Suppes, T., et al. (2002). "Tiagabine in Treatment Refractory Bipolar Disorders: A Clinical Case Series." *Bipolar Disorders* 4: 283–289.

Tohen, M., et al. (1998). "The Effect of Comorbid Substance Abuse Disorders on the Course of Bipolar Disorder: A Review." *Harvard Review of Psychiatry* 6: 133–141.

Tohen, M., et al. (2002). "Efficacy of Olanzapine in Combination with Valproate or Lithium in the Treatment of mania in Patients Partially Nonresponsive to Valproate or Lithium Monotherapy." *Archives of General Psychiatry* 59: 62–69.

Viguera, A. C., et al. (2000). "Risk of Recurrence of Bipolar Disorder in Pregnant and Nonpregnant Women After Discontinuing Lithium Maintenance." *American Journal of Psychiatry* 157: 179–184.

Viguera, A. C., et al. (2002). "Reproductive Decisions by Women with Bipolar Disorder After Psychiatric Consultants." *American Journal of Psychiatry* 159: 2102–2104.

Yatham, L. N., et al. (2002). "Third-Generation Anticonvulsants in Bipolar Disorder: A Review of Efficacy and Summary of Clinical Recommendations." *Journal of Clinical Psychiatry* 63: 275–283.

Yatham, L. N., et al. (2003). "Mood Stabilizers plus Risperidone or Placebo in the Treatment of Acute Mania: International, Double-Blind, Randomized Controlled Trial." *British Journal of Psychiatry* 182: 141–147.

Yonkers, K. A., et al. (2004). "Management of Bipolar Disorder During Pregnancy and the Postpartum Period." *American Journal of Psychiatry* 161: 608–620.

Chapter 11

Antipsychotic Drugs

Schizophrenia

Schizophrenia is a debilitating neuropsychiatric illness that typically strikes young people just when they are maturing into adulthood (Freedman, 2003). The disorder is associated with marked social and/or occupational dysfunction, and its course and outcome vary greatly (Buckley, 2003). Approximately 1 percent of the population suffers from schizophrenia; many are unemployed, and family costs (lost work time and treatment expenses) are enormous. Schizophrenia is associated with an increased risk of suicide; approximately 10 to 15 percent of individuals with schizophrenia take their own lives, usually within the first 10 years of developing the disorder. In the premorbid phase of the illness, subtle motor, social, or cognitive impairments are often observed, but these differences generally fail to place affected people outside the normal range of functioning. In the prodromal phase, mood symptoms, cognitive symptoms, social withdrawal, or obsessive behaviors may occur. After the onset of the full syndrome, symptoms lead to substantial functional deterioration (work, interpersonal relationships, self-care), especially during the first 5 to 10 years, after which clinical deterioration reaches a plateau. Schizophrenia is further defined by characteristic but nonspecific disturbances in the form and content of thought, perception, emotion, cognition, sense of self, volition, social relationships, and psychomotor behavior (Lieberman et al., 2001). Jarbin and coworkers (2003) reviewed the poor prognosis in 80 percent of individuals with early-onset schizophrenia (onset before age 19 years).

Until recently, treatment of patients with schizophrenia with *antipsychotic drugs* was reserved for seriously ill patients because of the numerous and serious side effects associated with their use. Symptom relief (especially relief from the delusions and hallucinations) was originally the most essential outcome parameter (Karow and Naber, 2002). Today, the development of new agents has revolutionized antipsychotic drug use (Lohr and Braff, 2003). There is now hope of raising patients' functioning to levels that truly can facilitate reintegration into the community. In the late 1990s and continuing into the twenty-first century, pharmacologic breakthroughs occurred that offer patients a real chance of leading more normal lives. This revolution, however, occurred in an atmosphere of reduced social services and support. The current challenge may not be so much the discovery of additional agents to improve functional levels but the preparation of social services, family, and counselors to help patients develop their newly found skills and abilities. Only through multilevel interventions can patients with severe and persistent mental illness successfully reintegrate into the community. While continuous drug therapy is indispensable in most cases, nonpharmacological interventions, the cooperation of several professions, and regard for the views of patients and relatives are essential. Atypical antipsychotics can improve the quality of therapy and can also improve and support other aspects of treatment (Krausz, 2002). In this chapter, of course, the focus is on the pharmacology of the medications used to treat schizophrenia. In 2004, the American Psychiatric Association published a revised and updated guideline for the treatment of patients with schizophrenia (American Psychiatric Association, 2004).

Schizophrenia is a disease of the brain that is expressed clinically as a disease of the mind. It is associated with significant abnormalities in brain structure and function, even in schizophrenic individuals who have never been treated with antipsychotic medications (Torrey, 2002). Therefore, brain abnormalities in schizophrenia are inherent in the disease and not medication related. Schizophrenia is a disease of neural connectivity (Figure 11.1) caused by many factors that affect brain development (Miyamoto et al., 2003). Schizophrenia is a misconnection syndrome that reflects a basic disorder in neural circuits (Andreasen, 1999).

Neurochemically, schizophrenia appears to be a neurodevelopmental and progressive disorder with multiple biochemical abnormalities involving the dopaminergic, serotonin, glutamate, and GABA systems (Javitt and Coyle, 2004; Miyamoto et al., 2003). Therefore, if several chemical transmitter systems are involved, therapy involves drugs that affect a variety of transmitter systems. From the late 1950s until about 1990, the primary dysfunction in schizophrenia was thought to involve an overactivity of dopaminergic neurotransmission.

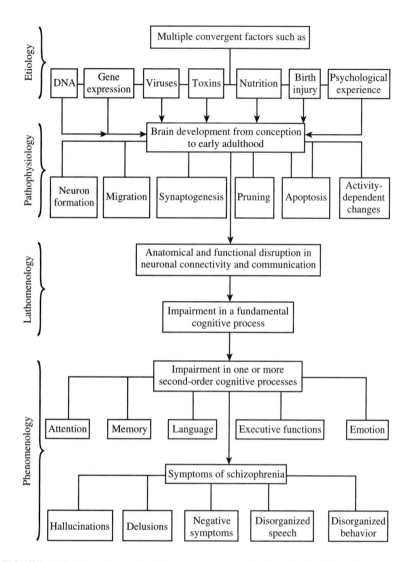

FIGURE 11.1 General model of the development of schizophrenia. [From Andreasen (1999), p. 783.]

The *traditional* (or *typical*) antipsychotic drugs blocked a specific sub-type of dopamine receptor (the dopamine-2 receptor) and effectively ameliorated the symptoms of schizophrenia. People treated with these drugs, however, suffered significant side effects, some of which were serious and often irreversible. Newer drugs typically block more than one receptor type, are associated with fewer serious side effects, and now may be more broadly utilized. Since they have fewer serious side effects, therapy can now be initiated at a much earlier stage of the schizophrenic process, even in the prodromal phase (Cannon et al., 2002; Woods et al., 2003).

Ideally, drug therapy should be aimed at ameliorating most if not all of the symptoms of schizophrenia as well as producing improvements in the patient's quality of life. The degree to which each drug accomplishes this goal is covered in this chapter. The signs and symptoms that require amelioration encompass the entire range of human mental activity and include abnormalities in perception (hallucinations), inferential thinking (delusions), language (disorganized speech), social and motor behavior (disorganized behavior and abnormal or stereotyped movements), and initiation of goal-directed activity (avolition), as well as impoverishment of speech and mental creativity (alogia), blunting of emotional expression (flattened affect), and loss of the ability to experience pleasure (anhedonia). Patients with schizophrenia also have impairments in many different cognitive systems such as memory, attention, and executive function. Therefore, treatment of schizophrenia is now aimed at more than control of behaviors and thought processes; attention is being focused on life improvements, including improvements in cognitive functioning (Sharma, 2002; Weickert et al., 2003).

Classically, the symptoms of schizophrenia have been classified as either *positive* or *negative*. The positive symptoms are those typical of psychosis and include delusions and hallucinations, bizarre behaviors, dissociated or fragmented thoughts, incoherence, and illogicality. The negative symptoms include blunted affect, impaired emotional responsiveness, apathy, loss of motivation and interest, and social withdrawal. This differentiation of symptomatology is important in the pharmacology of antipsychotic drugs because the classic agents affect primarily the positive symptoms, while the atypical antipsychotic drugs tend to relieve both the positive and the negative symptoms. Some of the newer agents are also effective in relieving the depressive mood states that can accompany schizophrenia.

Dopamine Involvement

Early scientific evidence favored a pure *dopamine theory* of schizophrenia: the disorder arises from dysregulation in certain brain regions of the dopamine system, resulting in a relative surplus of dopamine in the brain (McGowan et al., 2004). Antipsychotic drugs therefore work by blocking dopamine receptors, an action that qualifies them as *dopamine receptor antagonists*.

In the 1990s, molecular cloning studies identified several genes that code for dopamine receptors. There are now at least two subtypes of dopamine-1 receptors and three subtypes of dopamine-2 receptors (called D_2, D_3, and D_4). The D-1 and D-2 receptors exert opposite effects on intracellular mechanisms. All antipsychotic drugs (typical as well as atypical) have relative affinities for the dopamine-2 receptors. In fact, the affinity of a drug for a dopamine-2 receptor remains the single best predictor of its dose in a clinical situation (Figure 11.2) (Kapur and Remington, 2001).

Until the 1990s, dopamine-2 receptor blockade was thought to be the sole mechanism responsible for producing antipsychotic actions. The parkinsonian side effects and even the production of permanent tardive dyskinesias were thought to be unavoidable consequences of drug therapy. Given these limitations, alternative antipsychotics were and continue to be sought and developed. These new drugs, the so-called *atypical antipsychotics*, exhibit antipsychotic efficacy with fewer undesirable side effects.

There is no consensus concerning the biological mechanisms that might impart and define an atypical antipsychotic (Kapur and

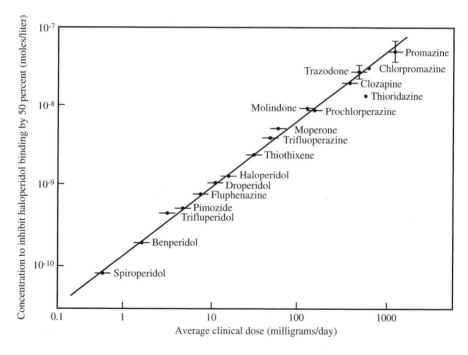

FIGURE 11.2 Correlation between the clinical potency and receptor-binding activities of neuroleptic drugs. Clinical potency is expressed as the daily dose used in treating schizophrenia, and binding activity is expressed as the concentration needed to produce 50 percent inhibition of haloperidol binding. Haloperidol binds to dopamine-2 receptors; other antipsychotic drugs compete for the same receptors. Thus, measuring the competitive inhibition of haloperidol binding correlates with potency as an antipsychotic drug.

Remington, 2001; Marder and Goldman-Rakic, 1999). Atypical antipsychotics display more than one mechanism for achieving atypicality. Almost all of these drugs are antagonists at dopamine-2 receptors and have a second action, usually antagonism of the serotonin 5-HT$_2$ receptors. One of the newest agents, aripiprazole (Abilify), is thought to exert a stabilizing action on dopamine receptors, not just a simple antagonism of the receptor (Grunder et al., 2003). Some (Kapur and Seeman, 2001) suggest that fast dissociation of drug from dopamine-2 receptors can account for atypical action without invoking serotonin involvement.

Serotonin Involvement

Early investigations into alternative mechanisms besides dopamine receptor blockade followed from observations on the actions of psychedelic drugs (Vollenweider, 1998). The serotonin psychedelic drug LSD (Chapter 19) produces a state similar in many respects to the clinical syndrome seen in schizophrenia. Some hallucinogenic drugs are thought to exert their psychedelic actions because they are agonists of 5-HT$_2$ receptors; thus *5-HT$_2$ receptor antagonism* may be beneficial in antipsychotic efficacy.

Sprouse and coworkers (1999) studied ziprasidone (an atypical antipsychotic) and noted that it functions as an agonist at 5-HT$_{1A}$ receptors and an antagonist at both 5-HT$_2$ and dopamine-2 receptors. The 5-HT$_{1A}$ agonistic action distinguishes this atypical agent, possibly endowing it with an antidepressant-anxiolytic action similar to that exerted by buspirone (BuSpar; Chapter 6), the prototype 5-HT$_{1A}$ agonist. The researchers concluded that serotoninergic activity might be a complementary action to dopaminergic blockade, reducing negative symptomatology and blocking the production of drug-induced abnormal motor problems. The early atypical antipsychotics (clozapine, risperidone, and olanzapine) indeed were characterized by a dual action of dopamine-2 blockage and 5-HT$_2$ blockade. More recent studies have demonstrated that for such drugs to be termed *atypical*, the serotonin 5-HT$_2$ blockade must be greater and occur at lower doses than does the dopamine-2 receptor blockade (Figure 11.3). Newer atypical antipsychotics (a *third generation* of antipsychotic drugs, following traditional agents and atypical agents) exhibit a more complicated pattern of receptor interactions.

To cloud the issue further, Aghajanian and Marek (1999) proposed that several atypical antipsychotics are capable of blocking serotonin 5-HT$_2$ receptors and that the physiological role of these receptors is to induce the release of glutamate. Thus, there may be an interaction of serotonin and glutamate whereby drug-induced serotonin blockade functions to modulate glutamate release.

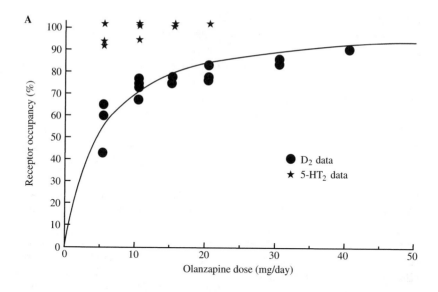

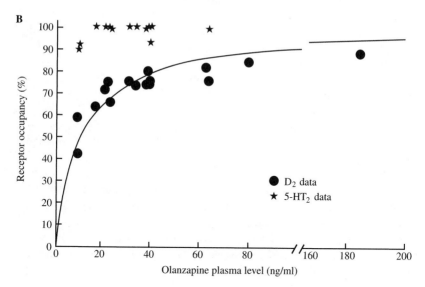

FIGURE 11.3 Relationship between dopamine D_2 and serotonin 5-HT$_2$ receptor occupancy and (**A**) olanzapine dose and (**B**) plasma level. [From Kapur et al. (1999), p. 290.]

Glutamate Involvement

For many years we have known that the two psychedelics drugs *phencyclidine* (PCP) and *ketamine* (Chapter 19) produce a schizophrenialike state with hallucinations, out-of-body experiences, negative symptomatology, and cognitive deficits. The mechanism responsible for these effects is a potent blockade of NMDA-type glutamate receptors. This correlation suggests that there may be an involvement of glutamate receptor dysfunction in the etiology of schizophrenia. In other words, NMDA antagonism results in schizophrenialike behaviors. Goff and Coyle (2001) reviewed the role of glutamate in the pathophysiology and the treatment of schizophrenia.

Thus, there is an increasingly popular glutamate-NMDA receptor hypofunction hypothesis of schizophrenia (Tamminga and Frost, 2001; Volk et al., 2000). NMDA hypofunction is proposed to result in excessive release of excitatory neurotransmitters (glutamate and acetylcholine) in the frontal cortex, damaging cortical neurons and triggering the deterioration seen in patients with schizophrenia. A protracted NMDA-hypofunctional state could trigger neuronal injury throughout many corticolimbic brain regions.

To tie all these influences together into an integrated hypothesis, hyperdopaminergic activity could be relevant for positive symptoms, whereas a glutamate-NMDA receptor deficiency could explain the negative symptoms and cognitive dysfunction seen in the disease. Two atypical antipsychotic drugs (clozapine and quetiapine) reduce the mRNA expression for NMDA-forming subunits in the nucleus accumbens (Tascedda et al., 1999). Quetiapine also increases the mRNA expression of a second type of glutamate receptor, the AMPA receptor (Chapter 3), further evidence that glutamate receptors can be a target for antipsychotic drug action as well as a potential site of receptor dysfunction in schizophrenia.

As further evidence that glutaminergic NMDA receptor dysfunction may be involved in schizophrenia, Mohn and colleagues (1999) studied genetically altered mice in which NMDA receptors were reduced by 95 percent. These mice exhibited behavioral homologies remarkably similar to schizophrenia, unrelated to dopaminergic dysfunction and sensitive to antipsychotic drugs. Once again, this finding is consistent with a glutaminergic dysfunction in schizophrenic symptomatology. Finally, to complicate matters further, Wassef and coworkers (2003) discuss a possible role of GABA in the pathogenesis of schizophrenia.

Overview of Antipsychotic Drugs

The clinical efficacy of traditional antipsychotic drugs is, as was stated, highly correlated with their ability to competitively block dopamine receptors (see Figure 11.2). This purity of action of the traditional agents accounts for efficacy against positive symptoms as well as many undesirable side effects. With the atypical agents, dopaminergic blockade is balanced by other actions on serotonin receptors, adding beneficial effects to relieve negative symptoms and improve cognitive deficits

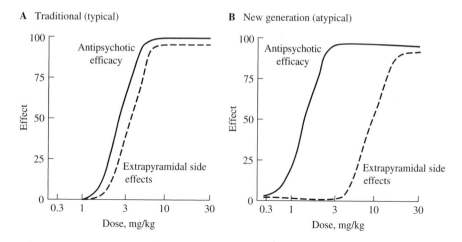

A Traditional (typical) **B** New generation (atypical)

FIGURE 11.4 Dose-response curves for antipsychotic efficacy (*solid lines*) and extrapyramidal symptoms (*dashed lines*) for (**A**) traditional antipsychotic neuroleptics and (**B**) new-generation antipsychotics. [From D. E. Casey, "Motor and Mental Aspects of EPS," *International Journal of Psychopharmacology* 10 (1995): p. 107.]

while reducing the incidence of abnormal movement-generating side effects.

The extent of binding to dopamine-2 receptors predicts efficacy, daily dosage, and likelihood of causing extrapyramidal side effects. Studies demonstrate that the therapeutic effects of many *neuroleptics*[1] are achieved beginning at about 70 percent dopamine-2 receptor occupancy, while extrapyramidal side effects are generally seen at higher dopamine-2 receptor occupancies. As Figure 11.4 illustrates, it is now possible to separate antipsychotic efficacy from extrapyramidal side effects. Drugs that exhibit this pattern do so through a variety of receptor mechanisms, but in general, this separation is vitally important. The antipsychotic compounds being developed today all have demonstrable antipsychotic efficacy combined with encouragingly low extrapyramidal profiles at therapeutic doses. Improvements in negative symptomatology and cognitive deficits are added benefits.

[1]The word *neuroleptic* means "to take control of the neuron." Some 70 years ago, the antipsychotic and extrapyramidal (motor) effects of classical antipsychotics (for example, chlorpromazine) were thought to be linked and inseparable. This led to the *neuroleptic threshold concept*, which held that the neuroleptic dose was gradually increased to the level that produced extrapyramidal side effects. Thus, the "right" dose was the one that caused some degree of motor side effects. Atypical antipsychotics, in general, have a better therapeutic ratio, with antipsychotic effects seen at doses that do not produce motor side effects (see Figure 11.4B).

Thus, while the terms *classical, traditional,* or *neuroleptic antipsychotic* apply to the drugs with inseparable therapeutic and extrapyramidal effects (see Figure 11.4A), the term *atypical* applies to agents that do separate the two (see Figure 11.4B). These new drugs are as revolutionary today as chlorpromazine and other "phenothiazines" (traditional antipsychotics) were in the 1950s.

Clozapine (Clozaril) was the first atypical antipsychotic (early 1990s), and it was followed by *risperidone* (Risperdal). Clozapine is a relatively weak blocker of dopamine-2 receptors; it is a much more effective blocker of serotonin 5-HT$_2$ receptors. Risperidone exhibits high levels of dopamine-2 receptor blockade and a very high affinity for 5-HT$_2$ receptors.

Olanzapine (Zyprexa), introduced in 1996, acts much like clozapine, except for a higher affinity for the D$_2$ receptor subtype of dopamine-2 receptors and a slightly lower affinity for 5-HT$_2$ receptors. Only about 40 percent of D$_2$ receptors are blocked by either clozapine or olanzapine. A fourth atypical antipsychotic, *sertindole* (Serlect), was introduced in 1997. It affects a variety of dopamine receptors as well as serotonin receptors. Unfortunately, a serious side effect led to its being removed from the market.

The fifth and sixth atypical antipsychotics, *quetiapine* (Seroquel) and *ziprasidone* (Geodon), were introduced in 1999 and 2000; they also serve as antagonists at several neurotransmitter receptors including 5-HT$_{1A}$, 5-HT$_2$, D$_1$, D$_2$, histamine, and adrenergic. The combination of D$_2$ and 5-HT$_2$ blockade probably underlies most of quetiapine's and ziprasidone's therapeutic actions.

Finally, in 2003, aripiprazole (Abilify) was introduced as the seventh atypical antipsychotic. Because of the uniqueness of its synaptic actions, it may also be the first of a third generation of antipsychotic drugs. Aripiprazole is not an antagonist at dopamine receptors; it is a *partial agonist*, serving to "stabilize" both hyperactive and hypoactive activity at dopamine-2 receptors. It is also an antagonist at serotonin 5-HT$_2$ receptors and a partial agonist at 5-HT$_{1A}$ receptors. The clinical implications of all these actions of newer drugs are discussed later. Miyamoto and coworkers (2003) review several additional antipsychotic drugs that are currently under development. Davis and Chen (2004) review the dose-response and dose-equivalence relationships between the many antipsychotic drugs.

Historical Background

Prior to 1950, effective drugs for treating psychotic patients were virtually nonexistent, and psychotic patients were usually permanently or semipermanently hospitalized; by 1955, more than half a million psychotic persons in the United States were residing in mental hospitals.

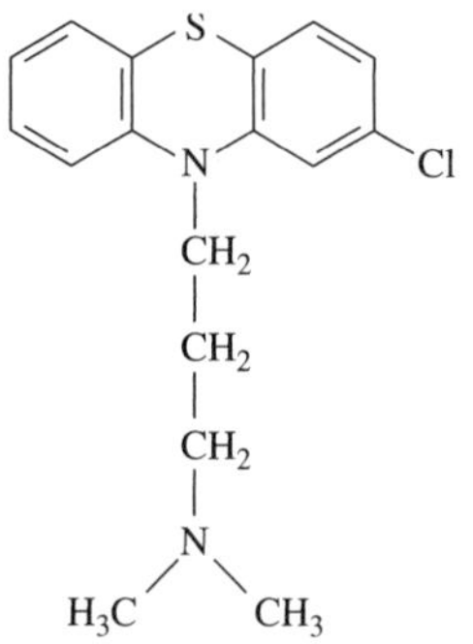

Chlorpromazine (Thorazine)

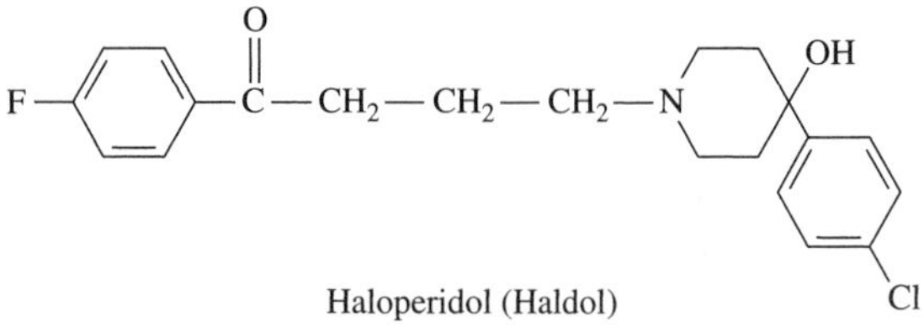

Haloperidol (Haldol)

FIGURE 11.5 Structural formulas of a phenothiazine (chlorpromazine) and a butyrophenone (haloperidol). Both are traditional antipsychotic drugs.

In 1956, a dramatic and steady reversal in this trend began. By 1983, fewer than 220,000 were institutionalized. This decline occurred despite a doubling in the numbers of admissions to state hospitals. By the early 1990s, people with schizophrenia were routinely stabilized on medication and discharged from institutions quite rapidly.[2] What accounted for the dramatic shift was a class of drugs called the *phenothiazines*.

In 1952, the French researcher H. Laborit used *promethazine* (the first of the phenothiazines) to deepen anesthesia. Later that year, other French researchers studied a second phenothiazine, *chlorpromazine* (Thorazine). This drug was administered in a "cocktail" to patients the night before surgery to allay their fears and anxieties. Chlorpromazine (Figure 11.5) was found to lower the amount of anesthetic drugs that a patient needed without making the patient unconscious; instead,

---

[2]Although the discharge rate of schizophrenics from institutions is high, there is concern about their ultimate functioning in society. Many patients who were discharged on phenothiazines failed to continue their medication, and they functioned poorly as a result. It has been estimated that about 50 percent of the adult homeless population in the United States may suffer from inadequately controlled schizophrenia.

treatment with chlorpromazine produced a state characterized by calmness, conscious sedation, and disinterest in and detachment from external stimuli. This condition was termed a *neuroleptic state,* and chlorpromazine was the first neuroleptic drug. Because of these behavioral calming effects, chlorpromazine was found to be remarkably effective in alleviating the clinical manifestations of the psychotic process. Although chlorpromazine did not provide a permanent cure, its use in conjunction with supportive therapy allowed thousands of patients who otherwise would have been hospitalized permanently to return to their communities, although in a less than satisfactory state.

In the continuing search for more effective and less bothersome drugs, alternatives to the phenothiazines have been (and are continuing to be) developed. *Reserpine* (Serpasil) was a late 1950s alternative, but significant side effects have today rendered the drug obsolete. The second class of alternative agents was the *butyrophenones,* developed in Belgium in the mid-1960s. Two butyrophenones are currently available—*haloperidol* (Haldol; see Figure 11.5) and *droperidol* (Inapsine). Neither drug seems to have significant advantages over the phenothiazines, but haloperidol is occasionally used for patients who cannot tolerate the phenothiazines. During the 1970s, other agents became available, including *loxapine* (Loxitane) and *molindone* (Moban).

The early twenty-first century has ushered in a new era of treatment goals for the patient with schizophrenia. Treatment of the positive symptoms of schizophrenia may make a patient more manageable, but it leads to an important question: how do these changes actually benefit the person with schizophrenia? Previously peripheral concerns, such as quality of life, are now being addressed. The new-generation atypical antipsychotics—clozapine, risperidone, olanzapine, quetiapine, zirasidone, and aripiprazole—are providing the means to address these vital issues. These new drugs have vast implications for how health care is delivered to patients with schizophrenia, challenging the "system" as never before. The documented savings in hospitalization (and rehospitalization) costs associated with the new generation of drugs can occur only by committing increased funds for the new drugs as well as increased commitment to social and community services for outpatient treatment of patients who may "waken" from their prior incapacitation.

"Major" versus "Minor" Tranquilizers

The benzodiazepines (Chapter 6) are often called *tranquilizers* because they reduce anxiety states and neurotic behavior and produce a state of calmness or tranquility. They are, however, not effective in treating psychosis. The antipsychotic drugs discussed in this chapter are sometimes also referred to as tranquilizers. To distinguish these two very different classes of drugs, the benzodiazepines are sometimes called *minor tranquilizers* and the antipsychotic drugs *major tranquilizers*. Although these terms are less commonly used today, they are occasionally encountered. Thus, the terms *major tranquilizer, neuroleptic, antipsychotic,* and *antischizophrenic* can all be used interchangeably.

Note that the word *tranquilizer* implies an agent that induces a peaceful, tranquil, calm, or pleasant state. Such a state can be produced by a minor tranquilizer, such as diazepam. However, the psychological effects produced by the major tranquilizers are neither pleasant nor euphoric. They may cause unpleasant or dysphoric feelings, especially when administered to nonpsychotic persons. Hence, these drugs do not cause positive behavioral reinforcement and are not encountered as drugs of abuse. Whenever one hears the term *tranquilizer,* clear distinction needs to be made between these two classes of drugs

Classification of Antipsychotic Drugs

Antipsychotic drugs can now be broadly classified into three groups: (1) *traditional antipsychotics,* (2) *atypical (or second-generation) antipsychotics,* and, most recently, (3) *third-generation antipsychotics.* The latter differentiates the dopamine partial agonist aripiprazole (Abilify) from dopamine receptor antagonists. The phenothiazines are the prototypical agents of the traditional antipsychotics, and clozapine, risperidone, olanzapine, sertindole, quetiapine, and ziprazadone are the currently available agents of the second class.

With the traditional antipsychotics, it has not been possible to separate the therapeutic effects on the positive symptoms from their prominent side effects involving the extrapyramidal motor system (see Figure 11.4). These side effects closely resemble the motor alterations observed in patients who have Parkinson's disease: rigidity, tremor, slowed movements, and restlessness (discussed in Chapter 13). Some of these symptoms disappear when the medication is discontinued, but persistent or permanent motor disorders (for example, tardive dyskinesia) also occur. Atypical agents have two advantages: (1) they are therapeutically effective without necessarily causing this neuroleptic syndrome or extrapyramidal side effects, and (2) they help relieve the negative symptoms and cognitive dysfunctions associated with schizophrenia (Weickert et al., 2003). Whether or not the atypical agents are more effective than traditional agents (at least against positive symptomatology) remains controversial (Leucht et al., 2003), although most researchers are beginning to believe that the atypical agents are a heterogeneous group and at least some are more effective than traditional agents such as the phenothiazines (Davis et al., 2003).

Phenothiazines

Historically, the phenothiazines were the most widely used drugs for treating schizophrenia. The phenothiazines were also used for other purposes, such as to treat nausea and vomiting, to sedate patients before anesthesia, to delay ejaculation, to relieve severe itching, to manage the psychotic component that may accompany acute manic attacks, to treat alcoholic hallucinosis, and to manage the hallucinations caused by psychedelic agents. Today's treatment of most of these disorders now involves the use of newer agents. Table 11.1 lists the phenothiazines still available for clinical use.

Pharmacokinetics

The phenothiazines are absorbed erratically and unpredictably from the gastrointestinal tract. However, because patients usually take these drugs for long periods of time, the oral route of administration is effective and commonly used. Intramuscular injection of phenothiazines is even more effective; it increases the effectiveness of the drug to about four to ten times that achieved with oral administration. Once these drugs are in the bloodstream, they are rapidly distributed throughout the body. The levels of phenothiazines that are found in the brain are low compared with the levels found in other body tissues; the highest concentrations are found in the lungs, liver, adrenal glands, and spleen.

The phenothiazines have half-lives of 24 to 48 hours, and they are slowly metabolized in the liver. The clinical effects of a single dose persist for at least 24 hours. Thus, taking the daily dose at bedtime often minimizes certain side effects (such as excessive sedation). The phenothiazines become extensively bound to body tissues, which partially accounts for their slow rate of elimination. Metabolites of some of the phenothiazines can be detected for several months after the drug has been discontinued. Such slow elimination may also contribute to the slow rate of recurrence of psychotic episodes following the cessation of drug therapy.

Pharmacological Effects

In addition to blocking the dopamine-2 receptors, the phenothiazines also block acetylcholine, histamine, and norepinephrine receptors. Blockade of acetylcholine receptors results in dry mouth, dilated pupils, blurred vision, constipation, urinary retention, and tachycardia. Blockade of norepinephrine receptors can result in hypotension and sedation. Blockade of histamine receptors has sedating as well as antiemetic effects.

TABLE 11.1 Antipsychotic drugs

Chemical classification	Drug name: Generic (Trade)	Dose equivalent (mg)	Sedation	Autonomic side effects[a]	Involuntary movement
Phenothiazine	Chlorpromazine (Thorazine)	100	High	High	Moderate
	Prochlorperazine (Compazine)	15	Moderate	Low	High
	Fluphenazine (Prolixin)	2	Low	Low	High
	Trifluoperazine (Stelazine)	5	Moderate	Low	High
	Perphenazine (Trilafon)	8	Low	Low	High
	Acetophenazine (Tindal)	20	Moderate	Low	High
	Carphenazine (Proketazine)	25	Moderate	Low	High
	Triflupromazine (Vesprin)	25	High	Moderate	Moderate
	Mesoridazine (Serentil)	50	High	Moderate	Low
	Thioridazine (Mellaril)	100	High	Moderate	Low
Thioxanthene	Thiothixene (Navane)	4	Low	Low	High
	Chlorprothixene (Taractan)	100	High	High	Moderate
Butyrophenone	Haloperidol (Haldol)	2	Low	Low	Very high
Miscellaneous	Loxapine (Loxitane)	10	Moderate	Low	Moderate
	Molindone (Moban)	10	Moderate	Moderate	Moderate
	Pimozide (Orap)	2	Low	Low	Moderate
New generation	Clozapine (Clozapil)	50	Moderate	Moderate	Low
	Risperidone (Risperdal)	1	Low	Low	Low-Moderate
	Olanzapine (Zyprexa)	1.5	Moderate	Low	Low
	Quetiapine (Seroquel)	40	Low	Low	Low
	Ziprasidone (Geodon)	15	Low	Low	Low
	Aripiprazole (Abilify)	3	Low	Low	Low
	Amisulpride (NA)[b]	NA	low	Low	Low

[a]Autonomic side effects include dry mouth, blurred vision, constipation, urinary retention, and reduced blood pressure.

[b]Not available

Limbic System. Dopamine-secreting neurons located in the central midbrain portion of the brain stem send axonal projections to the parts of the limbic system that regulate emotional expression as well as to the limbic forebrain areas, where thought and emotions are integrated. An increased sensitivity of dopamine receptors in those areas may be responsible for the positive symptomatology of schizophrenia. Thus, a phenothiazine decreases paranoia, fear, hostility, and agitation; it also reduces the intensity of schizophrenic delusions and hallucinations. In addition, phenothiazines dramatically relieve the agitation, restlessness, and hyperactivity associated with an acute schizophrenic attack. The delusions and hallucinations are particularly sensitive to treatment.

Brain Stem. Through actions on the brain stem, phenothiazines suppress the centers involved in behavioral arousal (the ascending reticular activating center) and vomiting (the chemoreceptor trigger zone). By suppressing activity in the reticular formation, the phenothiazines induce an indifference to external stimuli, reducing the inflow of sensory stimuli that would otherwise reach higher brain centers.

Basal Ganglia. The phenothiazines produce two main kinds of motor disturbances, which comprise both the most bothersome and the most serious side effects associated with the use of these agents. The two syndromes are (1) acute extrapyramidal reactions, which develop early in treatment in up to 90 percent of patients, and (2) tardive (late) dyskinesia, which occurs much later, during and even after cessation of chronic neuroleptic therapy. Acute extrapyramidal side effects are threefold:

1. Akathesia, a syndrome of the subjective feeling of anxiety, accompanied by restlessness, pacing, constant rocking back and forth, and other repetitive, purposeless actions

2. Dystonia, characterized by involuntary muscle spasms and sustained abnormal, bizarre postures of the limbs, trunk, face, and tongue

3. Neuroleptic-induced parkinsonism, which resembles idiopathic (of unknown etiology) Parkinson's disease (drugs used to treat parkinsonism are discussed in Chapter 13)

Neuroleptic-induced parkinsonism is characterized by tremor at rest, rigidity of the limbs, and slowing of movement with a reduction in spontaneous activity. In idiopathic parkinsonism, these symptoms occur when the concentration of dopamine in the nuclei of the basal ganglia (caudate nucleus, putamen, and globus pallidus) decreases to about 20 percent of normal. Here neuroleptic drug-induced blockade of dopamine receptors in excess of 80 percent occupancy produces the parkinsonismlike symptoms.

Tardive dyskinesia is a much more puzzling and serious form of movement disorder. Victims exhibit involuntary hyperkinetic movements, often of the face and tongue but also of the trunk and limbs, which can be severely disabling. More characteristic are sucking and smacking of the lips, lateral jaw movements, and darting, pushing, or twisting of the tongue. Choreiform movements of the extremities are frequent. The syndrome appears a few months to several years after the beginning of neuroleptic treatment (hence the description "tardive") and is often irreversible. The incidence of tardive dyskinesia has been estimated at more than 10 percent of patients who are treated with phenothiazines, but this side effect depends greatly on the dosage, the age of the patient (it is most common in patients older than 50), and the particular drug used. Adequately controlling dyskinesia may necessitate restarting the phenothiazine or increasing the dosage, which is a problem if parkinsonian side effects are troublesome.

Hypothalamus-Pituitary.   Pathways of dopamine-secreting neurons extend from the hypothalamus to the pituitary gland. The hypothalamus is intimately involved in the emotions, eating and drinking, sexual behavior, and the secretion of some pituitary hormones. By suppressing the function of the hypothalamus, phenothiazines interrupt these functions. By suppressing the appetite, food intake may be reduced. By suppressing the temperature-regulating centers of the hypothalamus, body temperature fluctuates widely with changes in room temperature. In addition, several body hormones are affected. This can result in breast enlargement in males and lactation in females. Phenothiazines also reduce the release of hormones from the pituitary gland, which regulates the secretion of sex hormones. Thus, in men ejaculation may be blocked; in women libido may be decreased, ovulation may be blocked, and normal menstrual cycles may be suppressed, resulting in infertility.

Side Effects and Toxicity

The therapeutic use of the phenothiazines invariably leads to many side effects. Much of the art of managing schizophrenic patients being treated with a phenothiazine lies in diagnosing and managing side effects. In general, the high-potency phenothiazines (fluphenazine, trifluoperazine, and perphenazine; Table 11.2) cause less sedation, fewer anticholinergic side effects, less postural hypotension, and more extrapyramidal side effects than the low-potency pheno-thiazines (chlorpromazine and thioridazine). Where sedation is desirable, either a

> **TABLE 11.2** Possible therapeutic and adverse effects of receptor blockade by neuroleptics

Blockade of dopamine D_2 receptors
  Therapeutic effects
    Amelioration of the positive signs and symptoms of psychosis
  Adverse effects
    Extrapyramidal movement disorders: dystonia, parkinsonism, akathisia, tardive dyskinesia, rabbit syndrome
    Endocrine effects: prolactin elevation (galactorrhea, gynecomastia, menstrual changes, sexual dysfunction in males)
Blockade of muscarinic receptors
  Therapeutic effects
    Mitigation of extrapyramidal side effects
  Adverse effects
    Blurred vision
    Attack or exacerbation of narrow-angle glaucoma
    Dry mouth
    Sinus tachycardia
    Constipation
    Urinary retention
    Memory dysfunction
Blockade of serotonin $5-HT_{2A}$ receptors
  Therapeutic effects
    Amelioration of the negative signs and symptoms of psychosis
    Mitigation of extrapyramidal side effects
  Adverse effects
    Unknown
Blockade of histamine H_1 receptors
  Therapeutic effects
    Sedation
  Adverse effects
    Sedation
    Drowsiness
    Weight gain
    Potentiation of central depressant drugs
Blockade of α_1-adrenoceptors
  Therapeutic effects
    Unknown
  Adverse effects
    Potentiation of the antihypertensive effects of prazosin, terazosin, doxazosin, and labetalol
    Postural hypotension, dizziness
    Reflex tachycardia
Blockade of α_2-adrenoceptors
  Therapeutic effects
    Unknown
  Adverse effects
    Blockade of the antihypertensive effects of clonidine and methyldopa

low-potency phenothiazine used alone or a high-potency drug combined with a benzodiazepine has the desired therapeutic effect. Where the anticholinergic side effects limit drug compliance, a high-potency drug is desirable, and the drug-induced movement disorders must be controlled with other medications (anticholinergic, antihistaminic, antiadrenergic, or antiparkinsonian drugs), discussed in Chapter 13.

In patients who are at risk for developing extrapyramidal side effects, who cannot tolerate phenothiazines, or who are treatment resistant, two options are available: (1) they can be prophylactically medicated with anticholinergic, antiparkinsonian, or antiadrenergic drugs, or (2) the phenothiazine can be discontinued and treatment continued with an atypical antipsychotic agent. Marder (1996) stated that there are three categories of treatment-resistant patients:

> The first category includes patients who continue to demonstrate positive psychotic symptoms when they receive adequate trials of an antipsychotic. . . . The second category of poor responders consists of patients who are unable to tolerate the side effects of antipsychotics. . . . The third category includes patients who have persistent negative symptoms while they are treated with an antipsychotic. (p. 26)

Marder concludes by stating:

> There is substantial evidence that these patients will demonstrate improvement . . . when they receive clozapine and risperidone as well as newer antipsychotics including olanzapine and quetiapine. (p. 26)

Other potentially serious but much less common side effects of phenothiazines include altered pigmentation of the skin, pigment deposits in the retina, permanently impaired vision, decreased pituitary function, menstrual dysfunction, and allergic (hypersensitivity) reactions, which include liver dysfunction and blood disorders.

It has long been recognized that cognitive disturbances are evident in 40 to 60 percent of patients with schizophrenia. Tests show deficits in attention, language, memory, problem solving, judgment, concentration, planning, concept formation, and other "executive" functions. Neurochemical assays suggest that serotonin, dopamine, and glutamate all play significant roles in schizophrenia-induced cognitive impairments. These impairments impede psychosocial performance and eventual reintegration into society. Although there is general agreement that antipsychotic drugs improve the psychopathology of schizophrenia, there is continued debate concerning the impact of these drugs on cognitive functioning (Sharma, 2002). Phenothiazines impair cognitive functioning. In contrast, atypical agents may improve cognition (Bilder et al.,

2002; Purdon et al., 2000; Weiss et al., 2002). Since phenothiazines have, as side actions, blockade of cholinergic receptors (an anticholinergic action) and histamine receptors (an antihistaminic effect), these actions may contribute to cognitive decline as histamine blockade produces sedation and cholinergic blockade results in interference with memory (see the discussion of scopolamine in Chapter 19).

Ichikawa and coworkers (2002) demonstrated an additional, possibly important, difference between typical and atypical antipsychotics, again relating to effects on cognition. The atypical agents improved cerebral cortical acetylcholine function by inducing acetylcholine release from neurons. Since acetylcholine is necessary for the formation of memory, this action may contribute to positive effects on cognition.

Tolerance and Dependence

One of the positive attributes of the phenothiazines is that they are not prone to compulsive abuse. They do not produce tolerance, physical dependence, or psychological dependence. Psychotic patients may take phenothiazines for years without increasing their dose because of tolerance; if a dose is increased, it is usually done to increase the control of psychotic episodes.

Older Alternatives to Phenothiazines

Following the introduction of chlorpromazine and the other phenothiazines in the late 1950s and early 1960s, it rapidly became apparent that their use was associated with significant side effects, including the movement disorders described earlier. Pharmaceutical manufacturers therefore attempted to find drugs of novel chemical structure that might exert antipsychotic efficacy without the accompanying motor side effects. In general, between the late 1960s and the late 1980s, the attempts were largely unsuccessful. However, some of these structurally novel agents were made available clinically and are briefly described here.

Haloperidol

In 1967, haloperidol (Haldol) was introduced as the first therapeutic alternative to the phenothiazines. A related compound, *droperidol* (Inapsine), was subsequently introduced into anesthesia for the treatment of postoperative nausea and vomiting. Pharmacologically, although haloperidol is structurally different from the phenothiazines, its pharamacological effects and its side effects are remarkably similar to the effects of phenothiazines. It produces sedation and an indifference to external stimuli and reduces initiative, anxiety, and activity. It is well absorbed orally and has a moderately slow rate of metabolism and excretion; stable blood levels can be seen for up to three days following discontinuation of the drug. It takes approximately five days for 40 percent of a single dose to be excreted by the kidneys.

The mechanism of the antipsychotic action of haloperidol is like that of the phenothiazines—it occupies and competitively blocks dopamine-2 receptors. Haloperidol does not produce many of the serious side effects occasionally observed in patients who are taking phenothiazines (jaundice, blood abnormalities, and so on), but it causes parkinsonian motor movements that are of the same or greater intensity as those induced by the high-potency phenothiazines. Prophylactic antiparkinsonian medication may be needed. In general, however, haloperidol is an effective drug for treating acutely psychotic patients, as it is of rapid onset (especially when given parenterally).

Molindone

Until the 1990s, most attempts at finding alternative agents to the phenothiazines and haloperidol met with little success. For example, the two alternative medications molindone and loxapine were introduced in the early 1970s. Molindone (Moban) is a structurally unique molecule (Figure 11.6) with antipsychotic properties, resembling the neurotransmitter serotonin. Whether this resemblance is related to its antipsychotic action is unknown. Molindone resembles the traditional antipsychotic drugs in therapeutic efficacy, occupancy of dopamine receptors, and side effects. It produces moderate sedation, increased motor activity, and possibly euphoria. It can also lead to abnormal motor (parkinsonian) movements that resemble those observed in patients taking phenothiazines. Clinical effects following a single dose of molindone persist for about 24 to 36 hours.

Loxapine

Loxapine (Loxitane) structurally resembles the atypical antipsychotic clozapine (see Figure 11.6). Despite this resemblance, however, its actions differ little from those of the traditional antipsychotic drugs. It has antipsychotic, antiemetic, and sedative properties and causes abnormal motor movements. It lowers convulsive thresholds somewhat more than the phenothiazines. Taken orally, loxapine is well absorbed, and it is metabolized and excreted within about 24 hours.

Loxapine binds strongly to both dopaminergic and serotoninergic receptors. Kapur and coworkers (1999) explained loxapine's unique status as a clozapinelike yet traditional neuroleptic drug: it differs

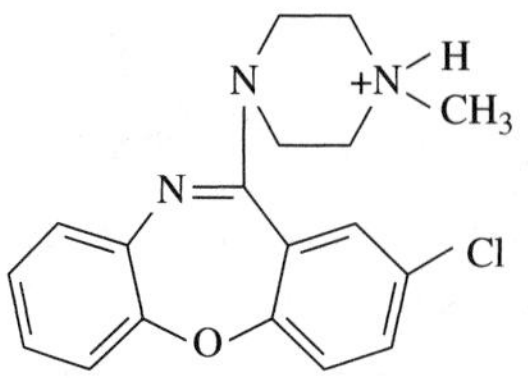

Loxapine (Loxitane)

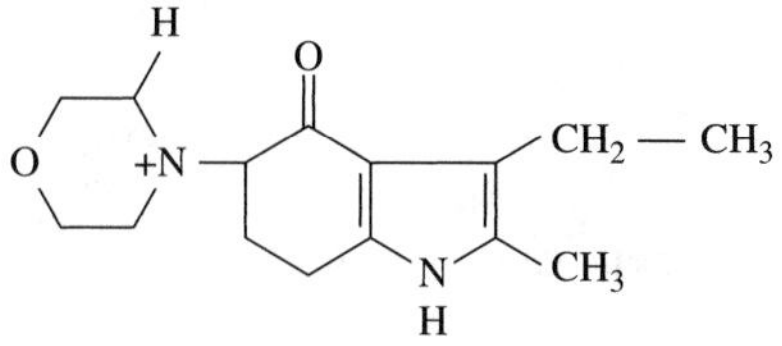

Molindone (Moban)

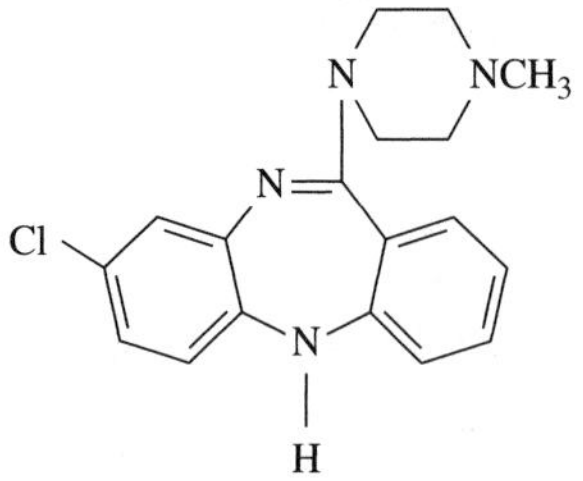

Clozapine (Clozaril)

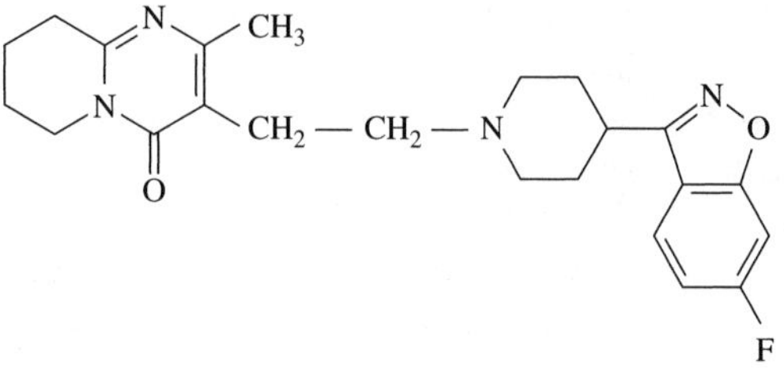

Risperidone (Risperdal)

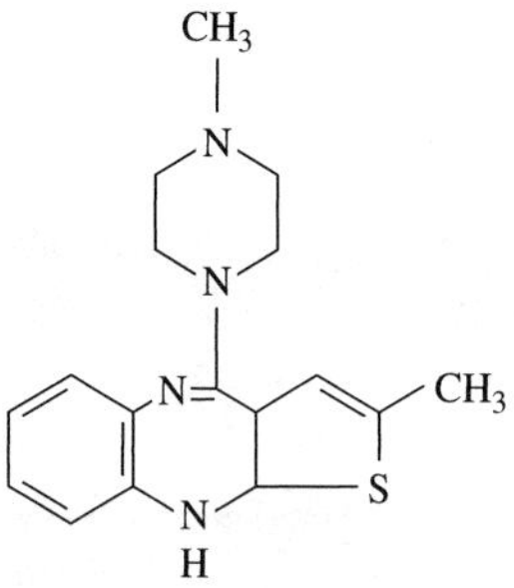

Olanzapine (Zyprexa)

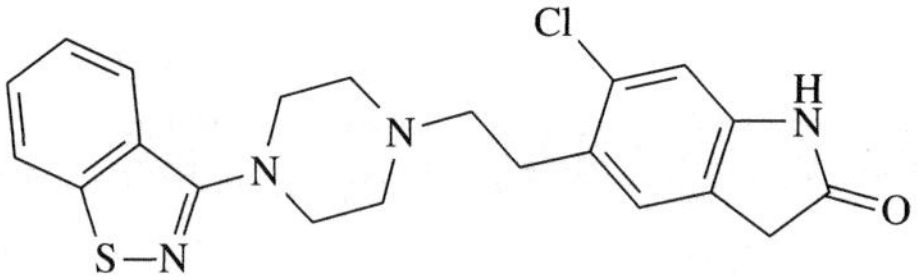

Ziprasidone (Geodon)

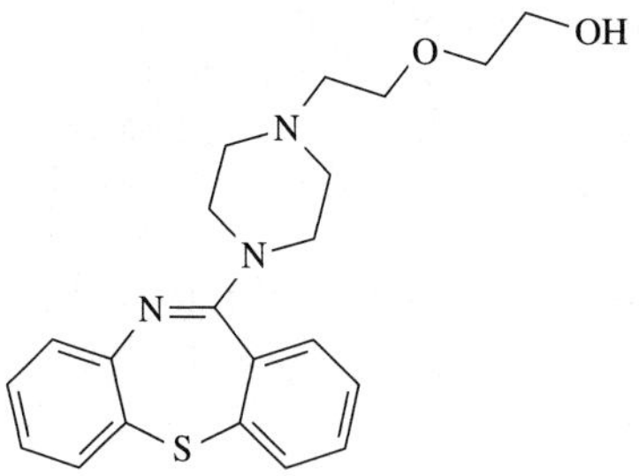

Quetiapine (Seroquel)

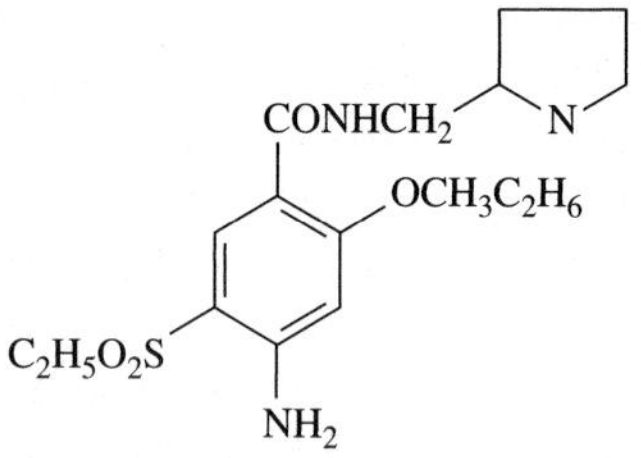

Amisulpride

FIGURE 11.6 Structural formulas of new-generation, atypical antipsychotic drugs.

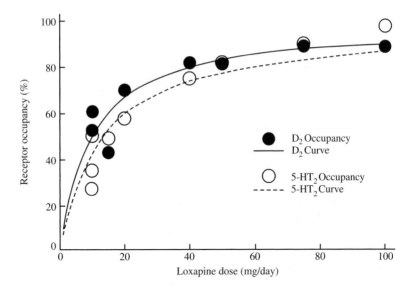

FIGURE 11.7 Dopamine D_2 receptor occupancy and serotonin 5-HT_2 occupancy in PET studies of 10 subjects taking loxapine. Fifty percent of D_2 receptors were occupied at a dose of 9.6 mg/day and 50 percent of the 5-HT_2 receptors were occupied at a dose of 13.6 mg/day. See text for details. [From Kapur et al. (1999), p. 290.]

from traditional antipsychotics in that it has a high degree of 5-HT_2 receptor occupancy; it is not atypical since its 5-HT_2 occupancy is not higher than its D_2 occupancy (Figure 11.7).[3]

Pimozide

Pimozide (Orap) is an antipsychotic drug that also blocks dopamine receptors. Currently, the drug is marketed in the United States for the treatment of motor and phonic tics in patients with Tourette's disorder who are unresponsive to other medications. In Europe and South America, pimozide is more widely used as a neuroleptic antipsychotic drug. The side effects that most limit use of pimozide (besides the usual movement disorders and tardive dyskinesia) are electrocardiographic abnormalities (called QT prolongation) that are potentially severe.

[3]A high level of 5-HT_2 occupancy is not a sufficient condition for atypicality. If atypical antipsychotic action is predicated on a combination of 5-HT_2 and D_2 effects, then it requires >80 percent 5-HT_2 occupancy in conjunction with <80 percent D_2 occupancy (Kapur and coworkers, 1999).

Atypical Antipsychotic Agents

From 1975 to 1989, not a single new antipsychotic was marketed in the United States. Since 1990, clozapine (1990), risperidone (1994), olanzapine (1996), sertindole (1997), quetiapine (1999), ziprasidone (2000), and aripiprazole (2003) have been introduced. Additional drugs, such as amisulpride, are on the horizon. Each atypical antipsychotic is unique in its actions as well in its side effects.

Clozapine

Clozapine (Clozaril) was the first atypical antipsychotic introduced into medicine. Its structure is closely related to that of loxapine (see Figure 11.6). Clozapine has been demonstrated to be clinically superior to traditional antipsychotics; it relieves both the positive and the negative symptomatology of schizophrenia, it lacks the extrapyramidal side effects associated with the traditional neuroleptics (Volavka et al., 2002), and it is much less of a cognitive inhibitor (Bilder et al., 2002). There is evidence that clozapine may improve the core deficits of schizophrenia, improving psychomotor speed, verbal fluency, verbal learning, and memory.

In contrast to phenothiazines, for patients with primary parkinsonism who demonstrate psychotic symptoms (such as visual hallucinations and delusions), clozapine can effectively treat their psychosis without aggravating the movement disorder (Parkinson Study Group, 1999).

Background. Synthesized in 1959, clozapine was introduced into clinical practice in Europe in the early 1970s. Its lack of extrapyramidal side effects was appreciated immediately. However, in 1975 several schizophrenic patients in Finland died of severe infectious diseases after developing agranulocytosis (loss of white cells in the blood) while taking clozapine. As a result, clinical testing ceased, and the drug was withdrawn from unrestricted use in Europe. Later, clozapine was reexamined for two major reasons: (1) the agranulocytosis was found to be reversible when the drug was discontinued, and (2) the drug was found to be therapeutically beneficial in patients with schizophrenia who failed to respond to the traditional neuroleptic compounds.

In 1986 a large, multicenter trial of the drug in the United States found a 30 percent improvement among 318 severely psychotic patients with schizophrenia who were unresponsive to other drugs; only 1 to 2 percent developed agranulocytosis. More recent studies show that the rate of improvement may approach 60 percent with longer therapy. In some patients who appear hopelessly lost in a psychotic world, the improvements in both positive and negative symptoms result in striking changes; the patients emerge as individuals who can be discharged from hospitals or participate meaningfully in rehabilitation programs. The phenomenon has been called *wakening*. Other clozapine responders do not improve substantially in their positive symptoms but report that their mood and sense of well-being are much improved; the deficits associated with schizophrenia do not improve, but the quality of life is better.

Pharmacokinetics. Clozapine is well absorbed orally and plasma levels of the drug peak in about 1 to 4 hours. Clozapine is metabolized into two major metabolites, both of which are fairly inactive pharmacologically. The metabolic half-life of clozapine varies from 9 to 30 hours. In some patients, monitoring blood levels of clozapine may aid in optimizing treatment. The optimal plasma level of clozapine is 200 to 350 ng/ml, corresponding to a daily dose of 200 to 400 mg, although dosage must be individualized. Monitoring plasma levels might be useful, for example, when psychotic symptoms recur during clozapine therapy, indicating either noncompliance with therapy or abrupt discontinuation of the drug (Tollefson et al., 1999).

Pharmacodynamics. As reviewed by Brunello and coworkers some years ago (1995):

> If schizophrenia is in some way related to morphological abnormalities, it becomes hard to believe that a *curative* treatment will ever be possible. Considering this scenario, treatment of schizophrenia will be restricted to symptomatic and preventive therapy and therefore, more effective and better tolerated antipsychotics are necessary. . . . Clozapine constitutes a major advance in particular for patients not responding to conventional neuroleptics. (p. 177)

Clozapine has high binding affinity for dopamine-4, serotonin-1C, serotonin-2, alpha-1 (an adrenergic receptor), muscarine (an acetylcholine receptor), and histamine receptors; moderate affinity is seen for many other receptor subtypes. Clozapine has a low rate of binding to D_2 receptors and has greater $5\text{-}HT_2$ blockade at therapeutic doses; this binding ratio defines an atypical antipsychotic, providing therapeutic efficacy with only minimal production of extrapyramidal symptoms.

Side Effects and Toxicity. Clozapine's efficacy is well documented. Its use is severely limited by its side effects and potential for serious toxicity. Common side effects include sedation, extreme weight gain, constipation, and rare instances of agranulocytosis.

Sedation occurs in about 40 percent of patients taking clozapine; it may be dose limiting and have a negative impact on compliance. It appears to be an antihistaminic effect of the drug. Taking the drug at bedtime may help improve compliance.

Weight gain is a problem for up to 80 percent of patients; it can be severe, with gains of 20 pounds or more not unusual.

Discontinuation of clozapine can be followed by a syndrome characterized by delusions, hallucinations, hostility, and paranoid reactions. Other less severe withdrawal signs include nausea, vomiting, diarrhea, headache, restlessness, agitation, confusion, and sweating. Olanzapine (Zyprexa) has a structure and receptor-blocking profile similar to that of clozapine, so it has been tried in efforts to block this withdrawal syndrome: direct substitution appears to greatly minimize the syndrome, and olanzapine is the only other atypical antipsychotic that does so (Tollefson et al., 1999). Gradual tapering of the dose may also be beneficial.

Constipation occurs in about 30 percent of patients and can be quite bothersome. Education and stool softeners can help.

As discussed, the greatest concern with clozapine is the risk of developing severe, life-threatening (although reversible) *agranulocytosis.* White blood cell counts must be monitored weekly or biweekly for the first four to five months of therapy and monthly thereafter, with more frequent monitoring if the white blood cell count decreases. Other drugs that can cause reductions in white blood cell count (most notably carbamazepine; see Chapter 10) should not be taken concomitantly. The incidence of this side effect has been estimated at 1 to 2 percent (Tschen et al., 1999). The etiology of clozapine-induced agranulocytosis appears to involve an unusual cellular-toxic mechanism. Eutrecht (1992) demonstrated that clozapine could be metabolized not only in the liver but also by the white blood cells themselves (an extremely unusual situation). An intermediate compound in this metabolic process is reactive and is toxic to the cell, possibly destroying the white cells that formed the metabolite.

Risperidone

Risperidone (Risperdal; see Figure 11.6) was introduced in 1993 as the second atypical antipsychotic drug. Risperidone acts as a potent inhibitor of both D_2 and $5\text{-}HT_2$ receptors, particularly the latter, resulting in improved control of psychotic symptoms with only a minimum of neuroleptic-induced extrapyramidal side effects.

Pharmacokinetics. Risperidone is well absorbed when taken orally, is highly bound to plasma proteins, and is metabolized to an active intermediate (9-hydroxy-risperidone). The metabolic half-life of risperidone is about 3 hours; that of the metabolite (which accounts for much of the action of risperidone) is about 22 hours.

Pharmacodynamics. Several studies and reviews have concluded that risperidone is as effective as haloperidol in reducing the positive symptomatology of schizophrenia without producing a high incidence of extrapyramidal side effects (Marder et al., 2003). Risperidone may not be quite as effective as clozapine for relieving the positive symptoms of schizophrenia and the parkinsonan side effects, but it is equal to clozapine in relieving negative symptoms (Azorin et al., 2001). Although not quite as efficacious as clozapine, the safety profile of risperidone can make it a first-line agent in treating schizophrenia. Csernansky and coworkers (2002) demonstrated that adults with stable schizophrenia or schizoaffective disorder have a lower risk of relapse if they are treated with risperidone than if they are treated with haloperidol. Risperidone is also an effective augmenter of clozapine in patients only partially responsive to the latter drug (Freudenreich and Goff, 2002).

Risperidone is effective in treating symptoms of autism and other pervasive developmental disorders in both children and adults (McCracken et al., 2002; McDougle, 1998) (Figure 11.8). It also reduces

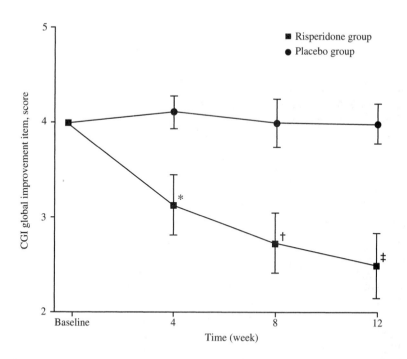

FIGURE 11.8 Global improvement in patients with autism or pervasive development disorder who were given risperidone or placebo for 12 weeks, as measured on the Clinical Global Impression Scale global improvement item. * = <.006; † = <.004; ‡ = <.001 (risperidone vs placebo). [From McDougle (1998), p. 638.]

aggression in youths with conduct disorder. These uses in children are discussed further in Chapter 12. Rocca and coworkers (2002) reported that risperidone could reduce aggression, reduce depressive symptomatology, and increase energy and global functioning in patients with borderline personality disorder. A long-acting injectable form of risperidone (Risperdal Consta) has been shown to be effective in controlling both the positive and negative symptomatology of schizophrenia (Fleishhacker et al., 2003; Kane et al., 2003). In novel technology, the risperidone is encapsulated in biodegradable polymer microspheres suspended in a water-based solution. A single intramuscular injection can last up to two weeks.

Side Effects. Common side effects of risperidone include somnolence, agitation, anxiety, insomnia, headache, extrapyramidal effects (at high doses), and nausea. Weight gain occurs but is only about 50 percent of that seen with either clozapine or olanzapine. Extrapyramidal symptoms are minimal at doses below 8 mg/day and increase with doses above 8 mg/day. However, in newly diagnosed patients with schizophrenia with no previous exposure to antipsychotic drugs, extrapyramidal symptoms were identical to those produced by haloperidol, even at low doses of risperidone (Rosebush and Mazurek, 1999). Risperidone may be most useful in patients whose symptoms can be controlled by lower doses of the drug. Risperidone is considered to be safe in breast-fed infants; infant levels of risperidone are only about 4 percent of those attained in the mother (Ilett et al., 2004).

In 2004, the manufacturer of risperidone advised of an increased incidence of strokes and CNS ischemic attacks in elderly patients taking risperidone for dementia-related psychosis.

Olanzapine

Introduced in 1996, olanzapine (Zyprexa) structurally and pharmacologically resembles clozapine, without clozapine's toxicity on white blood cells. Kapur and coworkers (1998) reported that olanzapine completely blocked 5-HT$_2$ receptors at low doses (5 mg/day); D$_2$ blockade increased (43 to 80 percent) with increasing doses (5 to 20 mg/day; see Figure 11.3). Effective antipsychotic control appears to occur at a dopamine-2 receptor occupancy between 60 percent and 70 percent (de Haan et al., 2003). The greater serotonin blockade accounts for a low incidence of extrapyramidal side effects.

Pharmacokinetics. Olanzapine is well absorbed orally. Peak plasma levels occur in about 5 to 8 hours. Metabolized in the liver, olanzapine has an elimination half-life in the range of 27 to 38 hours. This half-life is similar in both adults and children (Grothe et al., 2000). Gardiner and coworkers (2003) and Ambresin and coworkers (2004) studied the levels of olanzapine in infants of breast-feeding mothers who were tak-ing olanzapine. They noted that infants received doses of only about 1 to 4 percent of that given the mother. Plasma levels in the infants were about 38 percent of those found in the mothers (Figure 11.9). No adverse effects were noted in the infants.

Pharmacodynamics.   Reports from the late 1990s to the present demonstrated the superiority of olanzapine over haloperidol (Breier and Hamilton, 1999; Lieberman et al., 2003), although one recent, large study (Rosenheck et al., 2003) failed to confirm superiority over haloperidol. In this study, outcomes were comparable: olanzapine was associated with greater expense and more weight gain. The drug is comparable in efficacy to clozapine. Extrapyramidal side effects are only rarely observed. However, in more severely impaired patients, tra-ditional antipsychotic agents may be more effective against positive symptomatology. To this end, Raskin and coworkers (2000) demon-strated the additive effect of administering a traditional neuroleptic with low-dose olanzapine therapy in treatment-resistant schizophren-ics. Olanzapine has not been reported to cause agranulocytosis, and once-daily dosing is possible. The absence of agranulocytosis elimi-nates the need for blood count examinations and may improve patient compliance. Early trials in adolescents demonstrate significant effec-tiveness, with reductions in both positive and negative symptoms, oc-casional extrapyramidal side effects, increases in appetite and weight gain, and mild sedation (Findling et al., 2003).

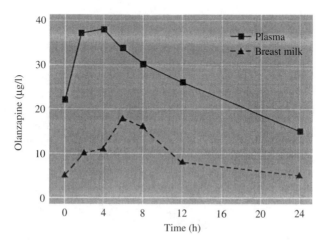

FIGURE 11.9 Plasma and breast milk olanzapine concentration following a dose of olanzapine to a mother who was taking olanzapine chronically. The dose was taken at time zero. [From Gardiner et al. (2003), p. 1430.]

Other Uses. As discussed in Chapter 10, olanzapine is approved for the treatment of *bipolar disorder.* Olanzapine therapy results in a 50 percent improvement in about half of bipolar patients, compared with about a 25 percent response rate in placebo-treated patients. Somnolence, dizziness, dry mouth, and weight gain are the major side effects. Combining olanzapine with either valproate or lithium in patients poorly responsive to valproate or lithium monotherapy results in improved control. As was noted in Chapter 10, a combination product containing olanzapine and fluoxetine is indicated for treating bipolar depression.

Potenza and coworkers (1999) studied olanzapine in four adolescents and four adults with *pervasive developmental disorder.* Seven of the eight demonstrated marked improvement in most of the symptoms associated with their disorder. Increased appetite and weight gain (almost 20 pounds per patient) were the major side effects.

Schur and coworkers (2003) reviewed the use of antipsychotic drugs in the management of *agitation* and *aggression* in youth. This topic is covered in more detail in Chapter 12, where the use of antipsychotic drugs for aggression is compared with other agents.

In April 2004, a new formulation of olanzapine was marketed. Zyprexa IntraMuscular, like intramuscular formulations of risperidone and ziprasidone, is for the acute treatment of severe agitation associated with bipolar mania and schizophrenia. Side effects were modest, and drug-induced motor abnormalities were not seen. Efficacy was superior to that of either haloperidol or lorazepam given intramuscularly.

Sertindole

Sertindole (Serlect) was released in 1997 as the fourth atypical antipsychotic. It is primarily a 5-HT$_2$ antagonist, binding (in decreasing order of affinity) to serotonin 5-HT$_2$, alpha-1 adrenoreceptors, and D$_2$ receptors. It therefore possessed the requisite dual action of blocking D$_2$ and 5-HT$_2$, thought to define the second-generation antipsychotics. This dual action predicted therapeutic efficacy in ameliorating both the positive and the negative symptoms of schizophrenia, with a low incidence of extrapyramidal side effects. Unlike risperidone and clozapine, sertindole had no affinity for histamine receptors; therefore it was much less sedative.

Several studies demonstrated the efficacy and relative absence of extrapyramidal side effects of sertindole; the drug compared favorably with other atypical antipsychotics. However, a major complication with sertindole arose: the drug can adversely affect the electrocardiogram, prolonging the QT interval, an effect that can lead to severe cardiac arrhythmias. For this reason, sertindole was removed from commercial availability.

Quetiapine

Quetiapine (Seroquel), the fifth atypical, 5-HT$_2$/D$_2$ receptor-blocking agent, was introduced in 1998. It is structurally related to both loxapine and clozapine (see Figure 11.6). Like clozapine, quetiapine has greater affinity for 5-HT$_2$ receptors than for D$_2$ receptors, separating antipsychotic action from extrapyramidal side effects. Arvanitis and Miller (1997) noted that quetiapine is effective, superior to placebo, and comparable to haloperidol in reducing positive symptoms; relief from negative symptoms was less consistent; extrapyramidal symptoms were few. In its pharmacology, quetiapine appears to closely resemble clozapine (without the hemodynamic problems with white blood cells). Quetiapine may exert beneficial effects on cognitive functioning, an important advantage (Velligan et al., 2003). Like clozapine, quetiapine reduces the expression of glutamate receptor mRNA, an action consistent with a glutaminergic involvement in schizophrenia. Side effects include nausea, sedation, and dizziness. Weight gain did not differ in patients treated with quetiapine and those treated with placebo.

Quetiapine is useful in treating disorders besides schizophrenia (Adityanjee, 2002). For example, it reduces psychosis in individuals with Parkinson's disease (Reddy et al., 2002). The drug is also useful in patients with bipolar disorder (Altamura et al., 2003) and in patients with schizoaffective disorders (Zarate et al., 2000). Added to therapy with selective serotonin reuptake inhibitors, quetiapine is effective in reducing symptoms of obsessive compulsive disorder (Denys et al., 2002; Mohr et al., 2002). Walker and coworkers (2003) reported that quetiapine was effective against target symptoms of severe aggression and impulsivity in four criminals offenders with antisocial personality disorder.

Ziprasidone

Ziprasidone (Geodon; see Figure 11.6) is the sixth of the available atypical antipsychotic agents. The drug is very effective in treating schizophrenia, with low liability for causing extrapyramidal side effects (Arato et al., 2002; Gunasekara et al., 2002). Perhaps its major clinical advantage is that unwanted weight gain is negligible. The drug also appears to enhance cognition (Abdul-Monim et al., 2003; Harvey, 2003). Ziprasidone is poorly absorbed orally, but the drug that is absorbed is extensively metabolized to a variety of inactive by-products. Its half-life appears to be short, in the range of 6 hours.

The receptor actions of ziprasidone are unique. In addition to blocking 5-HT$_2$ and D$_2$ receptors, it is an agonist at 5-HT$_{1A}$ receptors, a buspironelike action, and it is a moderate inhibitor of serotonin and norepinephrine reuptake. These receptor actions contribute an antidepressant effect to the drug; it improves depressive symptoms, anergia, negative symptoms, and cognition. For example, ziprasidone reduced both the depressive symptoms and the psychotic symptoms in people with schizoaffective disorder (Keck et al., 2001). Like other atypical antipsychotics, ziprasidone is effective in the treatment of bipolar disorder (Keck et al., 2003b). An injectable form of ziprasidone was approved in 2003 for intramuscular use to rapidly control agitated behavior and psychotic symptoms such as hallucinations and delusions in patients with schizophrenia. Ziprasidone was the first atypical antipsychotic drug approved for intramuscular use. Its use in the treatment of bipolar mania has not been reported.

The efficacy of ziprasidone is unquestioned. Relief of both negative and positive symptoms is impressive, as is the absence of weight gain. Its antidepressant action may be important. The limiting factor to the wide use of ziprasidone is its effects on the heart. The drug prolongs the QT interval, causing concern but as yet few or no fatal results. In children and adolescents, QT prolongation may be a greater problem (Blair et al., 2005).

Aripiprazole

Aripiprazole (Abilify; see Figure 11.6) was introduced in 2003 as the sixth atypical antipsychotic agent. The drug is extolled as a new, "third generation" of antipsychotic drugs, effective in ameliorating acute exacerbations of schizophrenia (Potkin et al., 2003). Aripiprazole is a partial agonist at dopamine-2 receptors and at serotonin-1A receptors, and it is also an antagonist at serotonin-2 receptors (Jordan et al., 2002). These receptor actions account for the actions of aripiprazole to ameliorate positive and negative symptomatology and to relieve anxiety, depression, and cognitive symptoms. It has been termed a "dopamine-serotonin system stabilizer" (Jordan et al., 2002).

By "dopaminergic partial agonism" is meant a stabilization or activation of dopaminergic receptors at low doses and receptor blockade at higher doses, enhancing dopamine functions that mediate negative and cognitive symptoms and reducing hyperactive dopamine neurons that mediate positive symptomatology (Stahl, 2002). To date, use of aripiprazole has not yet been associated with serious side effects. It does not cause QT prolongation, it is not associated with weight gain, and no extrapyramidal side effects have been reported, even at higher doses. One editorial headline claimed that aripiprazole is emerging as the next great hope for schizophrenia.

Keck and coworkers (2003a) reported aripiprazole to be effective in bipolar mania. Aripiprazole is currently being studied in children for the treatment of psychotic symptoms, bipolar disorder, and conduct disorder.

Amisulpride

Amisulpride (Solian) is likely to be the atypical antipsychotic drug released next (see Figure 11.6). Amisulpride has a unique and interesting neurochemical and psychopharmacological profile: it has high selectivity for blocking D_2 and D_3 receptor subtypes in the limbic system (but not the basal ganglia), and it blocks functional responses mediated by those receptors. At low doses, it releases dopamine (an antidepressant action); dopamine-2 blockade is seen at higher doses. The drug lacks serotonin-2 blocking action (the first atypical agent that does not block serotonin-2 receptors). This dual action results in increased dopamine activity in the mesolimbic system at low doses and an antipsychotic action at higher doses, with a low incidence of extrapyramidal side effects (Bressan et al., 2003).

Clinically, at low doses amisulpride has been shown to be effective in the treatment of dysthymia and depression and as effective as olanzapine in the treatment of schizophrenia (Martin et al., 2002). It may be rather selective for the treatment of negative symptomatology in schizophrenic patients (Storosum et al., 2002). In higher doses, it relieves psychosis, with perhaps more efficacy against negative symptoms than against positive ones (Leucht et al., 2002; Muller et al., 2002). Green (2002) speculated on the possible use of amisulpride in affective psychosis and chronic fatigue syndrome. In combination with olanzapine, its effects are additive in efficacy; it may be an "olanzapine augmenter." Amisulpride is well tolerated, exhibits few extrapyramidal side effects, and has a half-life of about 12 hours, 16 hours in elderly people.

Additional Information About Atypical Antipsychotics

Weight Gain. Weight gain as a result of taking antipsychotic drugs has been suggested to contribute to patient noncompliance with treatment and may adversely affect clinical outcome (Poyurovsky et al., 2003). Olanzapine and clozapine have the greatest propensity to induce weight gain, often of severe magnitude. Allison and Casey (2001) noted ziprasidone to cause the least weight gain (Figure 11.10). Weight gain occurs in 20 to 30 percent of persons taking risperidone, quetiapine, and olanzapine. The gain with risperidone is about half that seen with the other two drugs. Weight gain in adolescents is even higher than that reported in adults (Figure 11.11) (Ratzoni et al., 2002).

The mechanism responsible for this weight gain is still being elucidated. Fadel and coworkers (2002) studied rat lateral hypothalamic neurons that express *orexins* (proteins involved in feeding stimulation and weight regulation). They found that clozapine, risperidone, and olanzapine increased orexin expression; haloperidol, ziprasidone, and

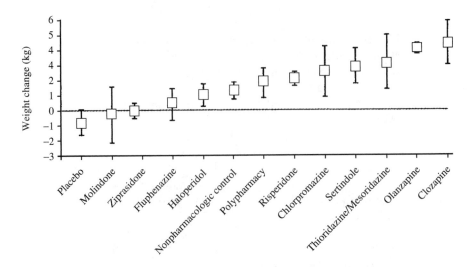

FIGURE 11.10 Estimated weight change after 10 weeks of treatment with standard drug doses. Shown are mean values and 95 percent confidence intervals. [From Allison and Casey (2001), p. 24.]

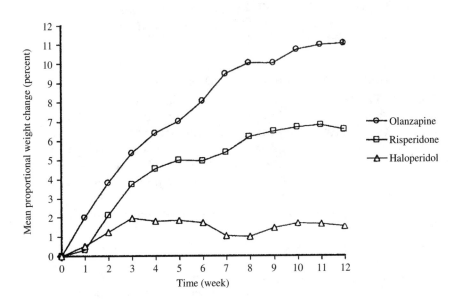

FIGURE 11.11 Mean proportional weekly weight gain (percent of increase from baseline body weight) during the 12 weeks of study in adolescents taking olanzapine, risperidone, or haloperidol. [From Ratzoni et al. (2002), p. 341.]

amphetamine did not, suggesting that orexin secretion may underlie weight and appetite gains associated with certain atypical antipsychotics. It also suggests orexin receptor antagonists as future weight reduction (antiobesity) drugs. Finally, McIntyre and coworkers (2003) correlated weight gain while taking atypical antipsychotics with elevations in plasma levels of *leptin*, a similar protein that modulates energy intake, energy expenditure, and various obesity hormones (Figure 11.12).

Diabetes and Hyperglycemia. Patients who receives atypical antipsychotic drugs are 9 to 14 percent more likely to develop adult-onset (Type II) diabetes than patients who receive traditional antipsychotic drugs (Lindenmayer et al., 2003; Sernyak et al., 2002). Increases are seen in patients over 40 years of age who were taking clozapine, olanzapine, and quetiapine but not risperidone (Gianfrancesco et al.,

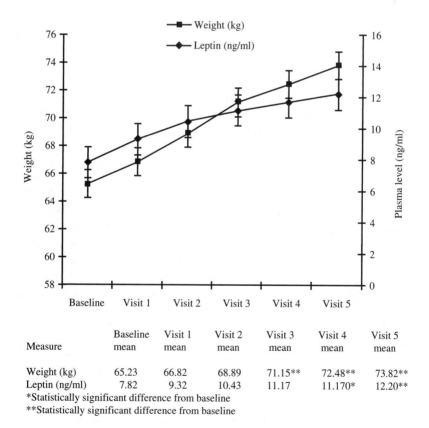

Measure	Baseline mean	Visit 1 mean	Visit 2 mean	Visit 3 mean	Visit 4 mean	Visit 5 mean
Weight (kg)	65.23	66.82	68.89	71.15**	72.48**	73.82**
Leptin (ng/ml)	7.82	9.32	10.43	11.17	11.170*	12.20**

*Statistically significant difference from baseline
**Statistically significant difference from baseline

FIGURE 11.12 Average body weight and plasma leptin levels in patients taking olanzapine or risperidone for 6 months. Olanzapine and risperidone results were pooled. [From McIntyre et al. (2003), p. 325].

2003). In patients less than 40 years old, all agents increase the incidence of diabetes. These changes are independent of weight gain induced by these drugs and seem to reflect a hastening effect of onset of diabetes. Newcomer and coworkers (2002) demonstrated that olanzapine and clozapine increased mean glucose levels as well as glucose and insulin levels after a glucose load. Both drugs induce a state of insulin resistance (Ebenbichler et al., 2003). Koller and Doraiswamy (2002) noted that this hyperglycemic effect could frequently be quite severe, leading to diabetic ketoacidosis and even death. Patients placed on clozapine or olanzapine should probably undergo monthly glucose monitoring for the first 6 months of treatment, with periodic study thereafter. The long-term medical consequences of small elevations in blood glucose are unknown at this time but may include increased risk of cardiovascular disease (Wirshing et al., 2002).

Electrocardiographic Abnormalities. The "pacemaker" of the heart is the sinoatrial (SA) node, located in the right atrium of the heart. An electrical signal from this pacemaker flows over the atria and into the ventricles through the atrioventricular (AV) node. The ventricles then contract, propelling blood forward into the aorta and the arteries. Following depolarization and mechanical contraction, the ventricles repolarize to be ready for the next depolarization. Figure 11.13 illustrates the electrocardiogram (ECG) for one electrical cycle. The QT interval is the time period from the start of spread of electricity to the ventricles to the end of ventricular repolarization. In essence, if this time period is prolonged about 500 milliseconds (0.5 second), the patient is at significant risk of developing the arrhythmia *torsades de pointes* (Figure 11.14), which can result in sudden death. The normal range for the QT interval for men below the age of 55 years is 350 to 430 milliseconds. For women, the comparable value is 350 to 450 milliseconds. Concern should arise when the QT interval is between 450 and 500 milliseconds. Besides drug-induced QT interval prolongation, *torsades de pointes* arrhythmias may, at least partly, be involved in sudden death in athletes and in sudden death in infants (SIDS).

Many psychotropic medications, including neuroleptics, antidepressants, stimulants, and antianxiety drugs, may cause alterations of the ECG, manifest as prolongation of the QT interval, an action that can result in the severe arrhythmia of *torsades de pointes* (Al-Khatib et al., 2003; Witchel et al., 2003). Even nonpsychotropic drugs have caused this and some have been removed from the market for this reason (for example, the antihistamine Seldane and the gastric stimulant Propulsid). Of the antipsychotic drugs, thioridazine is most associated and is rarely prescribed. The butyrophenones (haloperidol and droperidol) are also implicated and use is restricted. Of the atypical

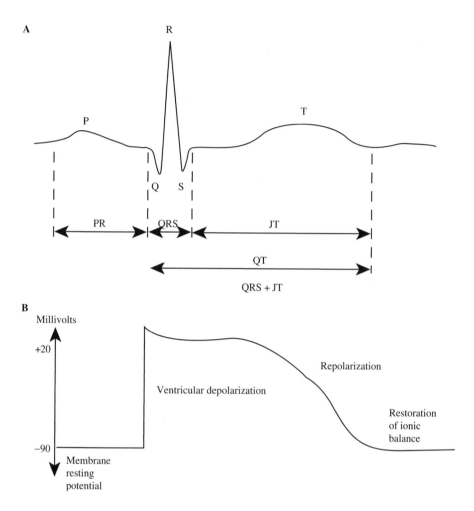

FIGURE 11.13 A. Normal electrocardiogram (ECG) in sinus rhythm. P wave is atrial electrical depolarization and leads to muscular contraction of the right and left ventricles. QRS complex is ventricular electrical depolarization and leads to muscular contraction of the right and left ventricles. JT is the time period from the end of ventricular depolarization (QRS) to the end of ventricular repolarization. The QT interval includes both ventricular depolarization (QRS) and ventricular repolarization. **B**. Rapid ventricular depolarization and slower repolarization. Most of the QT interval duration represents ventricular repolarization.

agents, sertindole has been removed from the market for this reason and ziprasidone (Geodon), initially withdrawn for this reason, has now been reapproved and made available after further examination of available safety data. Quetiapine, risperidone, and olanzapine cause lesser prolongations of the QT interval, aripiprazole none at all.

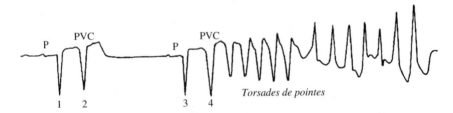

FIGURE 11.14 Characteristic development of *torsades de pointes* type of ventricular arrhythmia. Sinus beat with normal ventricular complex (1) followed by a premature ventricular contraction (PVC; 2) closely coupled to the sinus beat. After a long pause (2–3), this paired complex is repeated (3–4). The second PVC initiates a bizarre ventricular arrhythmia consistent with *torsades de pointes*. This ventricular arrhythmia is accompanied by poor contraction of ventricular muscle and therefore loss of contractility and output of blood from the heart, leading to a cardiac arrest.

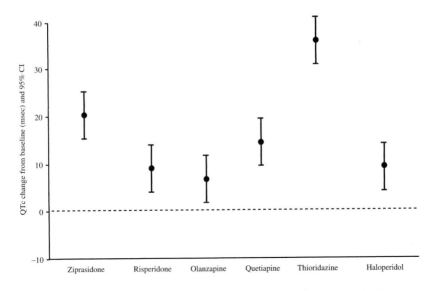

FIGURE 11.15 Results of studies showing QT interval changes associated with therapeutic doses of various antipsychotic drugs.

It appears that the risk of *torsades de pointes* increases with QT interval prolongation of 20 milliseconds or more. Thioridazine increases it well beyond this point. Ziprasidone prolongs the interval about 10 or 15 milliseconds, other antipsychotics somewhat less (Figure 11.15). Curently, the use of ziprasidone is controversial. As of October 1, 2002, the number of patients treated with ziprasidone exceeded 150,000, and no cases of sudden death or cardiac arrhythmias due to the drug were reported. The current consensus is that, although ziprasidone modestly prolongs the QT interval, this event has not been associated with either *torsades de pointes* or sudden death (Kelly and Love, 2001; Taylor, 2003). Even so, patients considered to be at risk (recent heart attack, heart disease, renal disease, and so on) should be medically evaluated, including obtaining a premedication ECG. Combining drugs that all prolong the QT interval probably should be avoided. Glassman and Bigger (2001) and Ray and coworkers (2001) review this topic. Whether ziprasidone should be a first-line or a second-line drug, based on its potential to prolong the QT interval, is a clinical decision.

STUDY QUESTIONS

1. What are the positive and negative symptoms of schizophrenia? Why are these symptoms important in drug therapy and in rehabilitation?

2. Which neurotransmitters are most involved in the pathogenesis of schizophrenia?

3. Are all antipsychotics neuroleptic? Are all neuroleptics antipsychotic?

4. What are the primary clinical differences between traditional and atypical antipsychotic drugs?

5. Discuss the meaning of the word *tranquilizer.*

6. Discuss the mechanisms of action of traditional antipsychotics and atypical antipsychotics.

7. Discuss the side effects of phenothiazines.

8. Discuss the consequences of reducing the numbers of institutionalized schizophrenic patients.

9. Compare and contrast clozapine and chlorpromazine, clozapine and olanzapine.

10. Name the currently available atypical antipsychotic drugs. How are they alike? How do they differ?

11. What appears unique about ziprasidone, aripiprazole, and amisulpride?

12. What is the QT interval and how is it involved with psychotropic drugs?

13. Why might antipsychotic drugs induce weight gain and/or diabetes?

14. Compare and contrast the newer atypical antipsychotics in terms of their efficacy, diabetes potential, weight gain, QT effects, and other side effects.

REFERENCES

Abdul-Monim, Z., et al. (2003). "The Atypical Antipsychotic Ziprasidone, but Not Haloperidol, Improves Phencyclidine-Induced Cognitive Deficits in a Reversal Learning Task in the Rat." *Journal of Psychopharmacology* 17: 57–65.

Adityanjee, S. C. (2002). "Clinical Use of Quetiapine in Disease States Other Than Schizophrenia." *Journal of Clinical Psychiatry* 63, Supplement 13: 32–38.

Aghajanian, G. K., and G. J. Marek (1999). "Serotonin-Glutamate Interactions: A New Target for Antipsychotic Drugs." *Neuropsychopharmcology* 21: S122–S133.

Al-Khatib, S. M., et al. (2003). "What Clinicians Should Know About the QT Interval." *Journal of the American Medical Association* 289: 2120–2127.

Allison, D. B., and D. E. Casey (2001). "Antipsychotic-Induced Weight Gain: A Review of the Literature." *Journal of Clinical Psychiatry* 62, Supplement 7: 22–31.

Altamura, A., et al. (2003). "Efficacy and Tolerability of Quetiapine in the Treatment of Bipolar Disorder: Preliminary Evidence from a 12-Month, Open-Label Study." *Journal of Affective Disorders* 76: 267–271.

Ambresin, G., et al. (2004). "Olanzapine Excretion into Breast Milk: A Case Report." *Journal of Clinical Psychopharmacology* 24: 93–95.

American Psychiatric Association (2004). "Practice Guideline for the Treatment of Patients with Schizophrenia, Second Edition." *American Journal of Psychiatry* 161 (February Supplement).

Andreasen, N. C. (1999). "A Unitary Model of Schizophrenia: Bleuler's 'Fragmented Phrene' as Schizencephaly." *Archives of General Psychiatry* 56: 781–787.

Arato, M., et al. (2002). "A 1-Year, Double-Blind, Placebo-Controlled Trial of Ziprasidone 40, 80 and 160 mg/day in Chronic Schizophrenia: The Ziprasidone Extended Use in Schizophrenia (ZEUS) Study." *International Clinical Psychopharmacology* 17: 207–215.

Arvanitis, L. A., and B. G. Miller (1997). "Multiple Fixed Doses of 'Seroquel' (Quetiapine) in Patients with Acute Exacerbation of Schizophrenia: A Comparison with Haloperidol and Placebo. The Seroquel Trial 13 Study Group." *Biological Psychiatry* 42: 233–246.

Azorin, J.-M., et al. (2001). "A Double-Blind Comparative Study of Clozapine and Risperidone in the Management of Severe Chronic Schizophrenia." *American Journal of Psychiatry* 158: 1305–1313.

Bilder, R. M., et al. (2002). "Neurocognitive Effects of Clozapine, Olanzapine, Risperidone, and Haloperidol in Patients with Chronic Schizophrenia or Schizoaffective Disorder." *American Journal of Psychiatry* 159: 1018–1028.

Blair, J., et al. (2005). "Electrocardiographic Changes in Children and Adolescents Treated with Ziprasidone: A Prospective Study." *Journal of the American Academy of Child and Adolescent Psychiatry* 44: 73–79.

Breier, A., and S. H. Hamilton (1999). "Comparative Efficacy of Olanzapine and Haloperidol for Patients with Treatment-Resistant Schizophrenia." *Biological Psychiatry* 45: 403–411.

Bressan, R. A., et al. (2003). "Is Regionally Selective D_2/D_3 Dopamine Occupancy Sufficient for Atypical Antipsychotic Effect? An In Vivo Quantitative [^{123}I]Epidepride SPET Study of Amisulpride-Treated Patients." *American Journal of Psychiatry* 160: 1413–1420.

Brunello, N., et al. (1995). "New Insights into the Biology of Schizophrenia Through the Mechanism of Action of Clozapine." *Neuropsychopharmacology* 13: 177–213.

Buckley, P. F. (2003). "Schizophrenia: Contemporary Clinical Perspectives." *Psychiatric Clinics of North America* 26 (March): xv–xvii.

Cannon, T. D., et al. (2002). "Antipsychotic Drug Treatment in the Prodromal Phase of Schizophrenia." *American Journal of Psychiatry* 159: 1230–1232.

Csernansky, J. G., et al. (2002). "A Comparison of Risperidone and Haloperidol for the Prevention of Relapse in Patients with Schizophrenia." *New England Journal of Medicine* 346: 16–22.

Davis, J. M., and N. Chen (2004). "Dose Response and Dose Equivalence of Antipsychotics." *Journal of Clinical Psychopharmacology* 24: 192–208.

Davis, J. M., et al. (2003). "A Meta-Analysis of the Efficacy of Second-Generation Antipsychotics." *Archives of General Psychiatry* 60: 553–564.

de Haan, L., et al. (2003). "Subjective Experience and D-2 Receptor Occupancy in Patients with Recent-Onset Schizophrenia Treated with Low-Dose Olanzapine or Haloperidol: A Randomized, Double-Blind Study." *American Journal of Psychiatry* 160: 303–309.

Denys, D., et al. (2002). "Quetiapine Addition to Serotonin Reuptake Inhibitor Treatment in Patients with Treatment-Refractory Obsessive-Compulsive Disorder: An Open-Label Study." *Journal of Clinical Psychiatry* 63: 700–703.

Ebenbichler, C. F., et al. (2003). "Olanzapine Induces Insulin Resistance: Results from a Prospective Study." *Journal of Clinical Psychiatry* 64: 1436–1439.

Eutrecht, J. P. (1992). "Metabolism of Clozapine by Neutrophils: Possible Implications for Clozapine-Induced Agranulocytosis." *Drug Safety* 7, Supplement 1: 51–56.

Fadel, J., et al. (2002). "Differential Activation of Orexin Neurons by Antipsychotic Drugs Associated with Weight Gain." *Journal of Neuroscience* 22: 6742–6746.

Findling, R. L., et al. (2003). "A Prospective, Open-Label Trial of Olanzapine in Adolescents with Schizophrenia." *Journal of the American Academy of Child and Adolescent Psychiatry* 42: 170–175.

Fleishhacker, W. W., et al. (2003). "Treatment of Schizophrenia with Long-Acting Injectable Risperidone: A 12-Month Open-Label Trial of the First Long-Acting, Second-Generation Antipsychotic." *Journal of Clinical Psychiatry* 64: 1250–1257.

Freedman, R. (2003). "Schizophrenia." *New England Journal of Medicine* 349: 1738–1749.

Freudenreich, O., and D. C. Goff (2002). "Antipsychotic Combination Therapy in Schizophrenia: A Review of Efficacy and Risks of Current Combinations." *Acta Psychiatrica Scandinavica* 106: 323–330.

Gardiner, S. J., et al. (2003). "Transfer of Olanzapine into Breast Milk, Calculation of Infant Drug Dose, and Effect on Breast-Fed Infants." *American Journal of Psychiatry* 160: 1428–1431.

Gianfrancesco, F., et al. (2003). "Antipsychotic-Induced Type 2 Diabetes: Evidence from a Large Health Plan Database." *Journal of Clinical Psychopharmacology* 23: 328–335.

Glassman, A. H., and J. T. Bigger (2001). "Antipsychotic Drugs: Prolonged QTc Interval, *torsade de Pointes*, and Sudden Death." *American Journal of Psychiatry* 158: 1774-1782

Goff, D. C., and J. T. Coyle (2001). "The Emerging Role of Glutamate in the Pathophysiology and Treatment of Schizophrenia." *American Journal of Psychiatry* 158: 1367–1377.

Green, B. (2002). "Focus on Amisulpride." *Current Medical Research and Opinions* 18: 113–117.

Grothe, D. R., et al. (2000). "Olanzapine Pharmacokinetics in Pediatric and Adolescent Inpatients with Schizophrenia." *Journal of Clinical Psychopharmacology* 20: 220–225.

Grunder, G., et al. (2003). "Mechanism of New Antipsychotic Medications: Occupancy Is Not Just Antagonism." *Archives of General Psychiatry* 60: 974–977.

Gunasekara, N. S., et al. (2002). "Ziprasidone: A Review of Its Use in Schizophrenia and Schizoaffective Disorder." *Drugs* 62: 1217–1251.

Harvey, P. D. (2003). "Ziprasidone and Cognition: The Evolving Story." *Journal of Clinical Psychiatry* 64, Supplement 19: 33–39.

Ichikawa, J., et al. (2002). "Atypical, but Not Typical, Antipsychotic Drugs Increase Cortical Acetylcholine Release Without an Effect in the Nucleus Accumbens or Striatum." *Neuropsychopharmacology* 26: 325–339.

Ilett, K,. et al. (2004). "Transfer of Risperidone and 9-Hydroxyrisperidone into Human Milk." *Annals of Pharmacotherapy* 38: 273–276.

Jarbin, H., et al. (2003). "Adult Outcome of Social Function in Adolescent-Onset Schizophrenia and Affective Psychosis." *Journal of the American Academy of Child and Adolescent Psychiatry* 42: 176–183.

Javitt, D. C., and J. T. Coyle (2004). "Decoding Schizophrenia: A Fuller Understanding for Signaling in the Brain of People with This Disorder Offers a New Hope for Improved Therapy." *Scientific American* 290: 48–56.

Jordan, S., et al. (2002). "The Antipsychotic Aripiprazole Is a Potent, Partial Agonist at the Human 5-HT1A Receptor." *European Journal of Pharmacology* 441: 137–140.

Kane, J. M., et al. (2003). "Long-Acting Injectable Risperidone: Efficacy and Safety of the First Long-Acting Atypical Antipsychotic." *American Journal of Psychiatry* 160: 1125–1132.

Kapur, S., and G. Remington (2001). "Atypical Antipsychotics: New Directions and New Challenges in the Treatment of Schizophrenia." *Annual Reviews of Medicine* 52: 503–517.

Kapur, S., and P. Seeman (2001). "Does Fast Dissociation from the Dopamine D2 Receptor Explain the Action of Atypical Antipsychotics? A New Hypothesis." *American Journal of Psychiatry* 158: 360–369.

Kapur, S., et al. (1998). "5-HT$_2$ and D$_2$ Receptor Occupancy of Olanzapine in Schizophrenia: A PET Investigation." *American Journal of Psychiatry* 155: 921–928.

Kapur, S., et al (1999). "Clinical and Theoretical Implications of 5-HT2 and D2 Receptor Occupancy of Clozapine, Risperidone, and Olanzapine in Schizophrenia." *American Journal of Psychiatry* 156: 286–293.

Karow, A., and D. Naber (2002). "Subjective Well-Being and Quality of Life Under Atypical Antipsychotic Treatment." *Psychopharmacology* 162: 3–10.

Keck, P. E., et al. (2001). "Ziprasidone in the Short-Term Treatment of Patients with Schizoaffective Disorder: Results from Two Double-Blind, Placebo-Controlled, Multicenter Studies." *Journal of Clinical Psychopharmacology* 21: 27–35.

Keck, P. E., et al. (2003a). "A Placebo-Controlled, Double-Blind Study of the Efficacy and Safety of Aripiprazole in Patients with Acute Bipolar Disorder." *American Journal of Psychiatry* 160: 1651–1658.

Keck, P. E., et al. (2003b). "Ziprasidone in the Treatment of Acute Bipolar Mania: A Three-Week, Placebo-Controlled, Double-Blind, Randomized Trial." *American Journal of Psychiatry* 160: 741–748.

Kelly, D. L., and R. C. Love (2001). "Ziprasidone and the QTc Interval: Pharmacokinetic and Pharmacodynamic Considerations." *Psychopharmacology Bulletin* 35: 66–79.

Koller, E. A., and P. M. Duraiswamy (2002). "Olanzapine-Associated Diabetes Mellitus." *Pharmacotherapy* 22: 841–852.

Krausz, M. (2002). "Efficacy Review of Antipsychotics." *Current Medical Research and Opinion* 18, Supplement 3: S8–S12.

Leucht, S., et al. (2002). "Amisulpride, an Unusual "Atypical" Antipsychotic: A Meta-Analysis of Randomized Controlled Trials." *American Journal of Psychiatry* 159: 180–190.

Leucht, S., et al. (2003). "New Generation Antipsychotics Versus Low-Potency Conventional Antipsychotics: A Systematic Review and Meta-Analysis." *Lancet* 361: 1581–1589.

Lieberman, J. A., et al. (2001). "The Early Stages of Schizophrenia: Speculations on Pathogenesis, Pathophysiology, and Therapeutic Approaches." *Biological Psychiatry* 50: 884–897.

Lieberman, J. A., et al. (2003). "Comparative Efficacy and Safety of Atypical and Conventional Antipsychotic Drugs in First-Episode Psychosis: A Randomized Double-Blind Trial of Olanzapine Versus Haloperidol." *American Journal of Psychiatry* 160: 1396–1404.

Lindenmayer, J.-P., et al. (2003). "Changes in Glucose and Cholesterol in Patients with Schizophrenia Treated with Typical or Atypical Antipsychotics." *American Journal of Psychiatry* 160: 290–296.

Lohr, J. B., and D. L. Braff (2003). "The Value of Referring to Recently Introduced Antipsychotics as 'Second Generation.'" *American Journal of Psychiatry* 160: 1371–1372.

Marder, S. R. (1996). "Management of Treatment-Resistant Patients with Schizophrenia." *Journal of Clinical Psychiatry* 57, Supplement 11: 26–30.

Marder, S. R., and P. S. Goldman-Rakic, editors (1999) "Special Supplement Issue: Is D_2 Antagonism Required for Antipsychotic Activity?" *Neuropsychopharmacology* 21, Supplement 6 (December): S117–S224.

Marder, S. R., et al. (2003). "Maintenance Treatment of Schizophrenia with Risperidone or Haloperidol: 2-Year Outcomes." *American Journal of Psychiatry* 160: 1405–1412.

Martin, S., et al. (2002). "A Double-Blind, Randomized Comparative Trial of Amisulpride Versus Olanzapine in the Treatment of Schizophrenia: Short-Term Results at Two Months." *Current Medical Research and Opinions* 18: 355–362.

McCracken, J. T., et al. (2002). "Risperidone in Children with Autism and Serious Behavioral Problems." *New England Journal of Medicine* 347: 314–321.

McDougle, C. J. (1998). "A Double-Blind, Placebo-Controlled Study of Risperidone in Adults with Autistic Disorder and Other Pervasive Developmental Disorders." *Archives of General Psychiatry* 55: 633–641.

McGowan, S., et al. (2004). "Presynaptic Dopaminergic Dysfunction in Schizophrenia: A Positron Emission Tomographic [^{18}F] Fluorodopa Study." *Archives of General Psychiatry* 61: 134–142.

McIntyre, R. S., et al. (2003). "Antipsychotic-Induced Weight Gain: Bipolar Disorder and Leptin." *Journal of Clinical Psychopharmacology* 23: 323–327.

Miyamoto, S., et al. (2003). "Recent Advances in the Neurobiology of Schizophrenia." *Molecular Interventions* 3: 27–39.

Mohn, A. R., et al. (1999). "Mice with Reduced NMDA Receptor Expression Display Behaviors Related to Schizophrenia." *Cell* 98: 427–436.

Mohr, N., et al. (2002). "Quetiapine Augmentation of Serotonin Reuptake Inhibitors in Obsessive-Compulsive Disorder." *International Clinical Psychopharmacology* 17: 37–40.

Muller, M. J., et al. (2002). "Dose-Related Effects of Amisulpride on Five Dimensions of Psychopathology in Patients with Acute Exacerbations of Schizophrenia." *Journal of Clinical Psychopharmacology* 22: 554–560.

Newcomer, J. W., et al. (2002). "Abnormalities in Glucose Regulation During Antipsychotic Treatment of Schizophrenia." *Archives of General Psychiatry* 59: 337–345.

Parkinson Study Group (1999). "Low-Dose Clozapine for the Treatment of Drug-Induced Psychosis in Parkinson's Disease." *New England Journal of Medicine* 340: 757–763.

Potenza, M. N., et al. (1999). "Olanzapine Treatment of Children, Adolescents, and Adults with Pervasive Developmental Disorders: An Open-Label Pilot Study." *Journal of Clinical Psychopharmacology* 19: 37–44.

Potkin, S. G., et al. (2003). "Aripiprazole: An Antipsychotic with a Novel Mechanism of Action, and Risperidone vs. Placebo in Patients with Schizophrenia and Schizoaffective Disorder." *Archives of General Psychiatry* 60: 681–690.

Poyurovsky, M., et al. (2003). "Attenuation of Olanzapine-Induced Weight Gain with Reboxetine in Patients with Schizophrenia: A Double-Blind, Placebo-Controlled Study." *American Journal of Psychiatry* 160: 297–302.

Purdon, S. E., et al. (2000). "Neuropsychological Changes in Early-Phase Schizophrenia During 12 Months of Treatment with Olanzapine, Risperidone, or Haloperidol." *Archives of General Psychiatry* 57: 249–258.

Raskin, S., et al. (2000). "Olanzapine and Sulpride: A Preliminary Study of Combination/Augmentation in Patients with Treatment-Resistant Schizophrenia." *Journal of Clinical Psychiatry* 20: 500–503.

Ratzoni, G., et al. (2002). "Weight Gain Associated with Olanzapine and Risperidone in Adolescent Patients: A Comparative Prospective Study." *Journal of the American Academy of Child and Adolescent Psychiatry* 41: 337–343.

Ray, W. A., et al. (2001). "Antipsychotics and the Risk of Sudden Cardiac Death." *Archives of General Psychiatry* 58: 1161–1167.

Reddy, S., et al. (2002). "The Effect of Quetiapine on Psychosis and Motor Function in Parkinsonian Patients With and Without Dementia." *Movement Disorders* 17: 676–681.

Rocca, P., et al. (2002). "Treatment of Borderline Personality Disorder with Risperidone." *Journal of Clinical Psychiatry* 63: 241–244.

Rosebush, P. I., and M. F. Mazurek (1999). "Neurologic Side Effects in Neuroleptic-Naive Patients Treated with Haloperidol or Risperidone." *Neurology* 52: 782–785.

Rosenheck, R., et al. (2003). "Effectiveness and Cost of Olanzapine and Haloperidol in the Treatment of Schizophrenia: A Randomized Controlled Trial." *Journal of the American Medical Association* 290: 2693–2702.

Schur, S. B., et al. (2003). "Treatment Recommendations for the Use of Antipsychotics for Aggressive Youth (TRAAY). Part I: A Review." *Journal of the American Academy of Child and Adolescent Psychiatry* 42: 132–144.

Sernyak, M. J., et al. (2002). "Association of Diabetes Mellitus with Use of Atypical Neuroleptics in the Treatment of Schizophrenia." *American Journal of Psychiatry* 159: 561–566.

Sharma, T. (2002). "Impact on Cognition of the Use of Antipsychotics." *Current Medical Research and Opinions* 18, Supplement 3: S13–S17.

Sprouse, J. S., et al. (1999). "Comparison of the Novel Antipsychotic Ziprasidone with Clozapine and Olanzapine: Inhibition of Dorsal Raphe Cell Firing and the Role of 5-HT$_{1A}$ Receptor Activation." *Neuropsychopharmacology* 21: 622–631.

Stahl, S. M. (2002). "Dopamine System Stabilizers, Aripiprazole, and the Next Generation of Antipsychotics. Part 1: Goldilocks Actions at Dopamine Receptors; Part 2: Illustrating Their Mechanism of Action." *Journal of Clinical Psychiatry* 62: 841–842 and 923–924.

Storosum, J. G., et al. (2002). "Amisulpride: Is There a Treatment for Negative Symptoms in Schizophrenia Patients?" *Schizophrenia Bulletin* 28: 193–201.

Tamminga, C. A., and D. O. Frost (2001). "Changing Concepts in the Neurochemistry of Schizophrenia." *American Journal of Psychiatry* 158: 1365–1366.

Tascedda, F., et al. (1999). "Regulation of Ionotropic Glutamate Receptors in the Rat Brain in Response to the Atypical Antipsychotic Seroquel (Quetiapine Fumarate)." *Neuropsychopharmacology* 221: 211–217.

Taylor, D. (2003). "Ziprasidone in the Management of Schizophrenia: The QT Interval Issue in Context." *CNS Drugs* 17: 423–430.

Tollefson, G. D., et al. (1999). "Controlled, Double-Blind Investigation of the Clozapine Discontinuation Symptoms with Conversion to Either Olanzapine or Placebo." *Journal of Clinical Psychopharmacology* 19: 435-443.

Torrey, E. F. (2002). "Studies of Individuals with Schizophrenia Never Treated with Antipsychotic Medications: A Review." *Schizophrenia Research* 58: 101-115.

Tschen, A. C., et al. (1999). "The Cytotoxicity of Clozapine Metabolites: Implications for Predicting Clozapine-Induced Agranulocytosis." *Clinical Pharmacology and Therapeutics* 65: 526–532.

Velligan, D. I., et al. (2003). "The Effectiveness of Quetiapine Versus Conventional Antipsychotics in Improving Cognitive and Functional Outcomes in Standard Treatment Settings." *Journal of Clinical Psychiatry* 64: 524–531.

Volavka, J., et al. (2002). "Clozapine, Olanzapine, Risperidone, and Haloperidol in the Treatment of Patients with Chronic Schizophrenia and Schizoaffective Disorder." *American Journal of Psychiatry* 159: 255–262.

Volk, D. W., et al. (2000). "Decreased Glutamic Acid Decarboxylase$_{67}$ Messenger RNA Expression in a Subset of Prefrontal Cortical Gamma-Aminobutyric Acid Neurons in Subjects with Schizophrenia." *Archives of General Psychiatry* 57: 237–245.

Vollenweider, F. X. (1998). "Advances and Pathophysiological Models of Hallucinogenic Drug Actions in Humans: A Preamble to Schizophrenia Research." *Pharmacopsychiatry* 31, Supplement 2: 92–103.

Walker, C. et al. (2003). "Treating Impulsivity, Irritability, and Aggression of Antisocial Personality Disorder with Quetiapine." *International Journal of Offender Therapy and Comparative Criminology.* 47: 556–567.

Wassef, A., et al. (2003). "GABA and Schizophrenia: A Review of Basic Science and Clinical Studies." *Journal of Clinical Psychopharmacology* 23 (2003): 601–640.

Weickert, T., et al. (2003). "Comparison of Cognitive Performance During a Placebo Period and an Atypical Antipsychotic Treatment Period in Schizophrenia: Critical Examination of Confounds." *Neuropsychopharmacology* 28: 1491–1500.

Weiss, E. M., et al. (2002). "The Effects of Second-Generation Atypical Antipsychotics on Cognitive Functioning and Psychosocial Outcomes in Schizophrenia." *Psychopharmacology* 162: 11–17.

Wirshing, D. A., et al. (2002). "The Effects of Novel Antipsychotics on Glucose and Lipid Levels." *Journal of Clinical Psychiatry* 63: 856–865.

Witchel, H. J., et al. (2003). "Psychotropic Drugs, Cardiac Arrhythmia, and Sudden Death." *Journal of Clinical Psychopharmacology* 23: 58–77.

Woods, S. W., et al. (2003). "Randomized Trial of Olanzapine Versus Placebo in the Symptomatic Acute Treatment of the Schizophrenic Prodrome." *Biological Psychiatry* 54: 453–464.

Zarate, C. A., et al. (2000). "Clinical Predictors of Acute Response with Quetiapine in Psychotic Mood Disorders." *Journal of Clinical Psychiatry* 61: 185–189.

Chapter 12

Child and Adolescent Psychopharmacology

The numbers of prescriptions written for psychoactive medication for youth (ranging from preschooler through adolescence) has risen markedly; total prescriptions have increased two- to threefold over the last 10 years (Figure 12.1), nearly reaching adult utilization patterns (Zito et al., 2003). The vast majority of psychotropic medications prescribed for youth are prescribed "off-label," which means that the drug prescribed was approved by the FDA either for another use or for another population. Usually, published research has demonstrated efficacy of the drug in studies in children, but the manufacturer of the medicine has not sought FDA approval for use in children. Sometimes the medication is prescribed without demonstrated efficacy in children but in hopes that it will be effective, especially since it probably was shown to be effective in populations of adults. Only recently have large studies been designed to evaluate medication results in children and adolescent populations. Until the results of these studies are published, results from studies in adults must be extrapolated to pediatric populations.

The large increase in the prescription of psychotropic medications in children and adolescents in the absence of adequate evidence for safety and efficacy in that population can nonetheless be a cause for concern. After all, we do not want to damage a developing brain. On the other hand, the possibility that early use of certain medications can head off long-term disorders may be extremely appealing. Ideally, one would not prescribe any psychotropic medication to *any* person (young or old) in

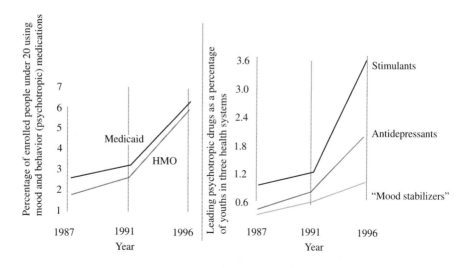

FIGURE 12.1 Increases in prescribed psychotropic medications over a 10-year period in youths. Two populations were studied: children of HMO enrollees and children of Medicaid enrollees in two states. Leading psychotropics studied included stimulants, antidepressants, and mood stabilizers. [Modified from Zito et al. (2003), p. 20.]

the absence of demonstrated efficacy and safety. This is especially true for a young person with a still developing nervous system. On the other hand, recent literature clearly demonstrates the long-term adverse consequences of untreated childhood and adolescent disorders persisting into adulthood as even more severe psychological disorders. Whether or not early intervention will prevent this progression is unknown. Regardless, even in the absence of demonstrated efficacy, these long-term consequences of untreated adverse or abnormal behaviors may lead to intervention (either pharmacological or psychotherapeutic) in an attempt to prevent the progression of the disorder into adult psychopathology.

What are some of the psychological disorders that occur in children and adolescents that might be amenable to pharmacological treatment? In essence, they are the same disorders commonly seen in adults (anxiety disorders, depression, bipolar disorder, schizophrenia, substance abuse) as well as attention deficit hyperactivity disorder (ADHD), pervasive developmental disorders, and various aggressive and behavioral outburst disorders. Costello and coworkers (2003) studied the prevalence of psychiatric disorders in youth aged 9 through 16 years. Remarkably, during that period of life, 36.7 percent of youths (31 percent of girls and 42 percent of boys) had at least one psychiatric disorder!

Pharmacological treatment of childhood and adolescent disorders is not new. In the 1930s, amphetamines were used to treat ADHD. In the

1960s, tricyclic antidepressants were tried in young people, usually without demonstrated efficacy. In the 1970s, benzodiazepines were used to treat anxiety disorders in children. Significantly, in 1997, Emslie and colleagues demonstrated the efficacy of fluoxetine (Prozac) in reducing depression in adolescents (Figure 12.2). While the effect was not robust and was not much greater than that achieved with psychological therapies (except at the 8-week end point), the demonstration led to the widespread prescription of selective serotonin reuptake inhibitors (SSRIs) for the treatment of childhood and adolescent depression. As we will discuss, this use of SSRIs has recently come under much scrutiny. Finally, many research reports have recently appeared that have documented drug efficacy and have described the long-term consequences of untreated mental and behavioral disorders in children and adolescents.

Behavioral and Aggressive Disorders

Aggressive and antisocial behaviors include a variety of acts such as fighting, lying, stealing, fire setting, property destruction, vandalism, truancy, and rule breaking more generally. The term *conduct disorder* is used to encompass these acts, and it refers to actions that are sufficiently intense,

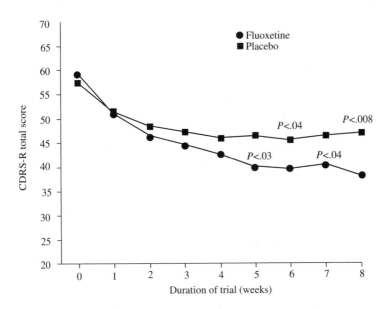

FIGURE 12.2 Weekly Children's Depression Rating Scale in 96 child and adolescent outpatients (aged 7 to 17 years) with nonpsychotic major depressive disorder treated with fluoxetine or placebo and evaluated weekly for 8 consecutive weeks. [From Emslie et al. (1997), p. 1035.]

frequent, or chronic to cause impairment and to warrant intervention (Kazdin, 2000). Children referred for treatment for these disorders are likely to show several other problems (for example, hyperactivity, depression, drug use) that raise their own challenges. Parents and families of children referred for therapy for conduct disorder often themselves show significant impairment (psychiatric disorder, marital discord, family stress, dysfunctional relationships, abusive parenting, and so on).

Cavell (2000) addressed working with parents of aggressive children. Children who have aggressive behavior and antisocial behaviors before age 12 are at greater risk of exhibiting adult criminality than children who become aggressive at an older age. Childhood aggression is stable over time and is a factor in the emergence of school failure, peer rejection, and delinquency. The prognosis for aggressive children is poor: as time goes by, these youths become less responsive to treatment interventions. Children do not "grow out of it."

Nansel and coworkers (2001) studied 15,700 students in grades 6 through 10. Twenty-nine percent of those studied reported moderate or frequent involvement in bullying: as a bully (13 percent), as an object of bullying (10.6 percent), or both (13 percent). There were more males than females in the latter group. The frequency of occurrence was greatest in the lower grades. Extrapolating these numbers to the nation at large, bullying affects many millions of youth. Bullies and their objects all demonstrate poorer social/emotional adjustments (versus those not involved in bullying) and problem behaviors. Bullies have higher levels of conduct problems and dislike of school. Those bullied show higher levels of insecurity, anxiety, depression, loneliness, unhappiness, physical and mental symptoms, and low self-esteem. Those who both bullied and were themselves bullied exhibited the poorest psychosocial functioning overall.

The long-term consequences of being a bully, being the object of bullying, or both are significant and persist into adulthood. Former bullies have a fourfold increase in criminal behavior by age 24 years; 60 percent of former bullies have at least one conviction and 35 to 40 percent have three or more convictions. Bullying seems to limit the learning of socially acceptable ways of negotiating with others. Those bullied have higher levels of depression and poor self-esteem at the age of 23 years, even though harassment did not persist into adulthood. Spivak and Prothrow-Stith (2001) commented on this report:

> Bullying and being bullied appear to be important indicators that something is wrong, and children who experience either or both need help. Furthermore, the primary prevention of bullying/being bullied involves eliminating factors that promote such behaviors (risk reduction) and teaching children the skills for more prosocial interpersonal interactions (resiliency development). . . . European school-based interventions report up to 50% reductions in reported bullying. (p. 2131)

This report has resulted in the beginning of efforts in the United States to address bullying/being bullied as detrimental to youth and as a disorder that has dire consequences (Juvonen et al., 2003).

Older literature associated conduct disorder in children with psychopathology in adulthood: 50 percent of conduct-discordered children progressed to antisocial personality disorder as adults. Certainly externalizing disruptive symptoms in childhood seems to be a marker for more pervasive psychopathology as adults. Lavigne and coworkers (2001) followed 510 preschool children with oppositional defiant disorder (ODD) for 5 years. The onset of ODD that presented in grammar school at ages 6 to 11 years was much more likely to have been in preschool than in later years. The presence of ODD in preschool was a strong predictor of later diagnosis of ODD (with or without comorbid ADHD) at ages 6 to 11 years. ODD exhibits a "developmental progression" to diverse outcomes (ODD or ADHD). Later depressive disorders or anxiety disorders occur comorbidly with ODD.

Pine and Cohen (1999) and Steiner and coworkers (2003) reviewed the state of pharmacological treatment of aggression in children as of the late 1990s. They stated that medication is a part of complete therapy of aggression:

- *Psychostimulants* are useful for aggressive and conduct disorder, even in the absence of ADHD (Connor et al., 2002).

- Chronically aggressive children have a high risk of developing a substance abuse disorder.

- It is not known whether psychostimulants promote or reduce the likelihood of developing a substance use disorder. (Today, we know that psychostimulants reduce subsequent substance abuse.)

- Antisocial behaviors, such as stealing and lying, can be reduced by psychostimulants.

The researchers also reviewed other drugs:

- *Lithium* exhibits little consistency of efficacy, even though it has been reported to reduce pathological aggression and conduct disorder in children with explosive behaviors.

- *Typical antipsychotic drugs* (haloperidol, for example) are effective but have significant and often severe side effects.

- Studies of newer, second-generation *atypical antipsychotic drugs* (such as olanzapine) are needed, although evidence is now accumulating that they are useful in treating aggressive and violent children.

- *SSRIs* (for example, fluoxetine) can be effective in some adults, but there are too few studies in children to warrant conclusions.

- There is some evidence for efficacy of *clonidine* in pediatric hyperactivity and aggression (Hazell and Stuart, 2003) and perhaps in pervasive developmental disorders, but the evidence for efficacy is weak.
- *Benzodiazepines*—for example, clonazepam (Klonopin) and alprazolam (Xanax)—can reduce agitation and irritability, but they can induce behavioral disinhibition. They must be used with care in children with pathologic aggression.
- Open trials suggest efficacy of the *anticonvulsant neuromodulators*. Valproic acid and carbamazepine (Tegretol) are effective for children with rage outbursts and pathologic aggression. Controlled trials are needed. Carbamazepine and valproic acid can be toxic and better drugs are needed, including gabapentin (Neurontin), oxcarbazepine (Trileptal), and perhaps pregabalin. Kim (2002) reviewed the use of the newer anticonvulsants in the management of neuropsychiatric disorders, particularly aggression and agitation.

Of all these agents, perhaps the most hope for the treatment of aggressive behaviors in children and adolescents lies in two classes of drugs: (1) neuromodulator anticonvulsants and (2) newer atypical antipsychotic drugs.

Donovan and coworkers (2000) administered valproic acid (Depakote) to 20 youths (10 to18 years old, 80 percent male) with conduct or oppositional defiant disorder as well as explosive temper and mood lability. Each youth received 6 weeks of valproic acid or placebo. Eight of 10 on valproic acid responded positively; none in 10 responded to placebo. Reeves and coworkers (2003) and Hollander and coworkers (2003) also report the usefulness of valproic acid in aggressive behaviors associated with certain personality disorders.

Schur and coworkers (2003) reviewed the use of newer antipsychotic drugs for treatment of aggressive youth. They concluded that atypical antipsychotics (risperidone, clozapine, olanzapine, quetiapine, and ziprasidone) appear to be safe and effective, although controlled trials are still lacking. The current consensus of opinion is the following:

> Psychosocial interventions and atypical antipsychotics are promising treatments for aggression in youths. Double-blinded studies should examine the safety and efficacy of atypical antipsychotics compared to each other and to medications from other classes, the efficacy of specific medications for different subgroups of aggression, combining various psychotropic medications, optimal dosages, and long-term safety. (p. 132)

Pappadopulos and coworkers (2003) expanded on this article and made 14 treatment recommendations on the use of atypical antipsychotics for aggression in youth.

In summary, the pharmacological treatment of behavioral and aggressive disorders of children and adolescents is in its infancy. Whether psychostimulants, atypical antipsychotics, or neuromodulators will be preferred is open to study. Perhaps all three classes of drugs will have their place in therapy in differing circumstances, individuals, situations, and combinations.

Autism and Other Pervasive Developmental Disorders

Autism is a complex disorder whose core features are deficits in social interaction and speech/communication skills, repetitive behaviors, and restricted interests. Associated abnormalities include seizures, electroencephalographic (EEG) abnormalities, affective instability, impulsivity, and aggression. A recent survey indicated an incidence of 3.4 cases per 1000 children (Yeargin-Allsopp et al., 2003). Rates generally increase up to about age 5 years and are three to four times higher in boys than in girls. Cognitive impairment is seen in 68 percent of children, and 8 percent have comorbid epilepsy. Extrapolation to the broad population of the United States would translate to about 425,000 children under 18 years of age with autism.

McDougle and coworkers (2003) reviewed the use of drugs for amelioration of behavioral symptoms of autism and other pervasive developmental disorders (PDDs):

- Haloperidol and other traditional antipsychotic agents were the most studied drugs and the most effective. Their use was limited by all the limitations common to this group of drugs (Chapter 11).

- Risperidone, olanzapine, and newer atypical antipsychotic agents have efficacy and are better tolerated than haloperidol. Of these drugs, ziprasidone exhibits efficacy without unwanted weight gain.

- Selective serotonin reuptake inhibitor antidepressants appear favorable in adult populations, but there have been no studies in children.

- Naltrexone (Traxan), once thought to be effective, had minimal efficacy.

- Clonidine, although effective in clinical trials, was limited by a high rate of relapse.

- Psychostimulants reduced hyperactivity and irritability. However, they could also exacerbate irritability, produce insomnia, and precipitate aggression.
- Buspirone (BuSpar) and neuromodulator mood stabilizers are worthy of study.

New reports have addressed the use of risperidone for autism. Masi and colleagues (2003) and Findling and coworkers (2004) noted that risperidone improved disruptive/hyperactive behavior and affective dysregulation. Malone and coworkers (2002) reported that risperidone reduced disruptive symptoms such as hyperactivity, fighting, anger, labile affect, negativity, and uncooperativeness. After 6 months of treatment, 91 percent of the children and adolescents on risperidone scored "very much improved" and "much improved." Discontinuation of risperidone was associated with worsening of clinical symptoms, further demonstrating the efficacy of the medication. McDougle and coworkers (2003) summarized the experiences with risperidone (Figure 12.3).

A similar atypical antipsychotic medication, olanzapine (Zyprexa), also reduced irritability, hyperactivity, and excessive speech patterns. However, overall ratings were improved less with olanzapine than with

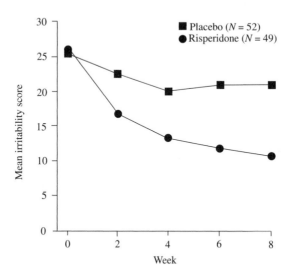

FIGURE 12.3 Mean score for irritability in risperidone- and placebo-treated children with autism. Total number of subjects studied = 101. Higher scores on the irritability subscale of the Aberrant Behavior Checklist indicate greater irritability. Data from the Research Units on Pediatric Psychopharmacology Autism Network. [From McDougle et al. (2003), p. 17.]

risperidone, and weight gain was greater with olanzapine (Kemner et al., 2002).

Hollander and colleagues (2001) reported results of an open trial of valproic acid in 14 patients with autism and PDD for up to 45 months. There were 12 males and 2 females in the study. Ten were children/adolescents and 4 were adults. Of the 14, 10 had a sustained response to all three core dimensions of autism and associated features. Reductions were most marked in affective instability and aggression. Most interestingly, all patients who had an abnormal EEG prior to initiation of drug therapy were responders! Although this was a pilot study, its results were consistent with the demonstrated efficacy of valproic acid for the treatment of target symptoms of impulsivity, aggression, and mood instability within a broad range of psychiatric disorders. It will be interesting to see whether a pretreatment EEG can be a predictor of responsiveness to valproate or risperidone.

In conclusion, autism and other pervasive developmental disorders may be most responsive to agents from either (or both) of two classes: atypical antipsychotic agents (for example, risperidone) and the anti-convulsant, mood-stabilizing neuromodulators (for example, valproic acid). Remaining to be determined is which of the newer neuro-modulators are of equal or greater efficacy with a wider safety margin. Other pharmacological treatments remain experimental. One agent, *ampalex*, is currently under study. This drug is hoped to improve cognitive deficits by enhancing glutamate neurotransmission in the brain, most probably through activation of the AMPA-type glutaminergic receptor (Knapp et al., 2002). Johnson and Hollander (2003) report on the successful use of eicosapentaenoic acid (an omega-3 fatty acid) in an 11-year-old boy with autism and associated aggression and anti-social behaviors.

Attention Deficit Hyperactivity Disorder

Attention deficit hyperactivity disorder (ADHD) is the most common psychological disorder of childhood, affecting 3 to 10 percent of school-age children (Rowland et al., 2002). Anywhere from 15 to 70 percent of these children are being treated with stimulant medication, depending on the population studied. Age-inappropriate problems with attention, learning, impulse control, and (usually) hyperactivity characterize ADHD. ADHD has been thought to be more prevalent and more severe in boys than in girls. However, Biederman and colleagues (1999) reported that girls with ADHD share with boys the same cluster-ing and intensity of core symptoms of the disorder (Figure 12.4), the same comorbidity profile (Figure 12.5), and the same dysfunction in multiple domains.

A. Symptom profile

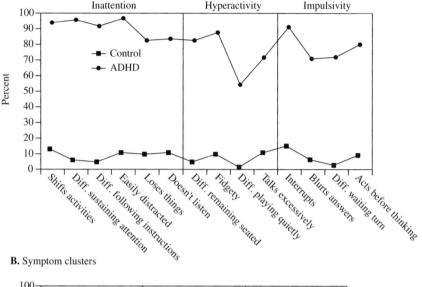

B. Symptom clusters

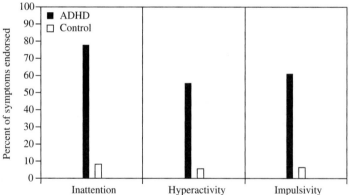

FIGURE 12.4 DSM-III-R symptom profile (**A**) and symptom clusters (**B**) in 140 girls aged 6 to 18 years diagnosed with ADHD and 122 non-ADHD controls. Diff = difficulty. From Biederman et al. (1999), p. 969.]

ADHD persists beyond childhood and into adulthood in about 40 to 60 percent of affected individuals. In adults, it is associated with a tenfold increase of antisocial personality disorder, up to a fivefold increased risk of drug abuse, a twenty-fivefold increase in risk for institutionalization for delinquency, and up to a ninefold increased risk for incarceration. A recent symposium discusses the treatment of adult ADHD (Biederman, 2004).

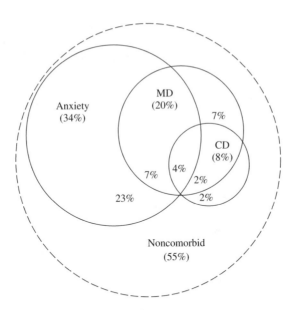

FIGURE 12.5 Psychiatric comorbidity in 140 girls aged 6 to 18 years with ADHD. MD = mood disorder; CD = conduct disorder. Other disorders that aggregated significantly included tics and enuresis. Statistical trends suggested increased risk for panic disorder, obsessive-compulsive disorder, language disorders, alcohol and drug abuse, and cigarette smoking. [From Biederman et al. (1999), p. 971.]

It is now recognized that childhood ADHD is associated with measured rates of maternal and paternal childhood ADHD (Chronis et al., 2003). Children with ADHD frequently have mothers with mood disorder, anxiety disorder, and stimulant/cocaine dependence and fathers with a history of childhood disruptive behavioral disorder. Chronis and colleagues state:

> Many young children with ADHD, particularly those with comorbid ODD/CD, require comprehensive services to address both their ADHD and the mental health needs of their parents. (p. 1424)

A remarkable incidence of comorbid or concomitant disease occurs in children affected with ADHD. As many as two-thirds of elementary school-age children with ADHD who are referred for clinical evaluation have at least one other diagnosable psychiatric disorder. Concomitant diseases include conduct disorder, oppositional defiant disorder, learning disorders, anxiety disorders, mood disorders (especially depression), and substance abuse.

The genetic involvement in ADHD has recently become the subject of interesting research, although much remains to be done. Family studies, twin studies, adoption studies, segregation analysis studies, and molecular genetic studies all contribute to this growing literature. All are consistent in showing genes to influence susceptibility to ADHD. Many of the molecular data focus on the dopamine D_4 receptor gene, which encodes a protein receptor that mediates the postsynaptic action of dopamine (McCracken et al., 2000). The situation is undoubtedly more complex, probably involving the combined actions of several genes. Moreover, environment almost certainly plays a role. Smalley and coworkers (2002) demonstrated a genetic lineage deficit in a chromosomal region that also may contain an autism susceptibility gene. Such demonstration of commonality in clinically distinct disorders may help explain overlapping features such as maladaptive social functioning and a deficit in executive functioning.

Stimulant Treatment

Stimulant drugs improve behavior and learning ability in 60 to 80 percent of children who are correctly diagnosed. The treatment of ADHD with psychostimulants has become one of the most broadly effective drug therapies of the twenty-first century (Rapport et al., 2002). In December 1999, a long-awaited result of the Multimodal Treatment Study of Children with Attention-Deficit/Hyperactivity Disorder (MTA Cooperative Group, 1999) was published. In the study, a cohort of 579 children with ADHD was assigned to 14 months of medication management, intensive behavioral treatment, and the two combined, or standard community care. Carefully structured medication management resulted in better outcome than intensive behavioral treatment, and combined treatment yielded outcome that was better than behavioral treatment but equivalent to medication management. Thus,

> carefully crafted medication management was superior to behavioral treatment and to routine community care that included medication. Combined treatment did not yield significantly greater benefits than medication management for core ADHD symptoms, but it may have provided modest advantages for non-ADHD symptoms and positive functioning outcomes. (p. 1073)

Since this study covered a period of only 14 months, longer term efficacy remained unknown. A 24-month follow-up of the MTA study (MTA Cooperative Group, 2004) revealed that cessation of drug therapy was associated with clinical deterioration, continued drug therapy was associated with only mild deterioration, and stimulant initiation (in the group not receiving stimulants in the early study) was associated with clinical improvements. The follow-up concluded: "Consistent use of stimulant medication was associated with maintenance of effectiveness but continued mild growth suppression" (p. 762). What is now clear is that stimulants improve behavioral symptoms of ADHD as well as cognitive functioning, academic performance, and social functioning. Short and coworkers (2004) report on the successful use of stimulants in preschool children with ADHD.

A persistent question involved whether or not there is any association between the use of stimulants during childhood and the later use of drug of abuse. The answer is now quite clear: childhood and adolescent use of stimulant medication for ADHD *is not* associated with later substance abuse. In fact, stimulant therapy for ADHD results in a nearly twofold *reduction* in the risk for later substance abuse (Barkley et al., 2003; Wilens et al., 2003b).

In children who have ADHD comorbid with other psychological disorders, more than one medication may be needed. In ADHD comorbid with depression, treatment may involve a combination of serotonin reuptake-blocking antidepressants as well as a stimulant. In cases of ADHD comorbid with bipolar illness, treatment may begin with a mood stabilizer, as the stimulant might precipitate a manic episode. ADHD with ODD/CD responds well to stimulant therapy. ADHD with a comorbid anxiety disorder appears to respond to a combination of stimulant medication combined with psychosocial therapies. ADHD with comorbid substance abuse requires treatment for both conditions, beginning with substance abuse therapy. Long-term treatment may involve use of stimulants and antidepressants (Hechtman, 2001).

The primary stimulants used in the treatment of ADHD are methylphenidate and various formulations of amphetamines. Secondary agents include buspirone (BuSpar) and bupropion (Wellbutrin), especially in refractory cases. Newer agents of interest as viable alternatives to psychostimulants include modafinil (Provigil) and atomoxetine (Strattera). Atomoxetine is the first of a new class of drugs known as selective norepinephrine reuptake inhibitors (SNRIs; Chapter 9).

Methylphenidate.   Currently, methylphenidate accounts for 90 percent of the prescribed medication for ADHD. Methylphenidate is of rapid onset and short duration; thus, it must be administered two or three times daily. It is not administered in the evening to permit the blood level to drop, allowing normal sleep. The short half-life is a problem in some children who experience an end-of-dose rebound in dysfunctional behavior. Early sustained-release preparations of methylphenidate were disappointing. Recently, however, more dependable extended-release preparations have become available. The first of these was Concerta, a formulation consisting of a plastic shell coated with a layer of immediate-release methylphenidate and filled with methylphenidate in an osmotic medium that slowly releases the drug over a 10-hour period, providing gradually increasing plasma concentrations of the drug. The empty shell is then excreted in the feces. One daily dose of Concerta yields about the same plasma concentrations as three daily doses of immediate-release methylphenidate with essentially equal efficacy (Swanson et al., 2003; Wilens et al., 2003a).

Other new formulations of methylphenidate include Metadate CD, Methylin ER, Metadate ER, and Ritalin LA. Lopez and coworkers (2003) compared Ritalin LA and Concerta, noting potentially important differences. Ritalin LA resulted in increased effect (in reducing ADHD symptoms) in the first 4 hours after drug administration, but Concerta's effects persisted longer later in the day, at 8 to 12 hours after administration.

Newly available is dexmethylphenidate (Focalin), the active D isomer of methylphenidate. This isomer has twice the potency of methylphenidate, so the dose of dexmethylphenidate is one-half the dose of methylphenidate.

In a series of reports, Volkow and coworkers addressed the question of why methylphenidate is not an "addicting" drug when taken orally, especially since its mechanism of action is essentially the same as that of cocaine, a highly "addicting" drug (Chapter 7) (Volkow et al., 1998, 2002a, 2002b). Both methylphenidate and cocaine block the presynaptic dopamine transporter and, as a result, increase the amount of dopamine in the synaptic cleft. Orally administered methylphenidate, however, slowly enters the brain, reaching maximal concentrations after 60 to 90 minutes (Figure 12.6). Once in the brain and attached to the dopamine transporter, it releases slowly, preventing further release of dopamine. In contrast, inhaled or injected cocaine rapidly reaches peak concentrations in the brain; the concentrations are of short duration, allowing for repeated "highs." Therefore, the abuse potential (with oral administration) of methylphenidate is low and those to whom the drug is prescribed seldom abuse the drug.

Amphetamines. Since the 1930s, *amphetamines* have been prescribed for the treatment of ADHD. Available amphetamines include *dextroamphetamine* (Dexedrine), a mixture of *amphetamine salts* (Adderall), and a new extended-release formulation of Adderall (Adderall XR) (McCracken et al., 2003; McGough et al., 2003). Manos and colleagues (1999) stated:

> Single-dose treatments of Adderall appear to be as effective as two daily doses of methylphenidate and therefore increase the possibility of managing treatment without involving the school in medication administration. In addition, youths who have previously been unsuccessfully treated with methylphenidate because of adverse side effects or poor response may be successfully treated with Adderall. (p. 813)

Pliszka and coworkers (2000), who concluded that once-daily Adderall is similar to twice-daily methylphenidate, reiterated this conclusion.

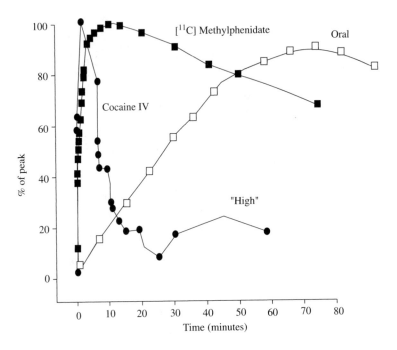

FIGURE 12.6 Peak concentrations of cocaine and methylphenidate in three situations. Cocaine was administered intravenously, reaching a peak within a few minutes. The "high" correlated with plasma levels of the drug. Methylphenidate was administered either intravenously (solid squares) or orally (open squares). A "high" was achieved only initially after the intravenous dose, paralleling the cocaine high. With oral administration, peak blood level was reached only after 70 minutes and no "high" was perceived. [Adapted from Volkow and coworkers (1998, 2002a, 2002b).]

Rapport and coworkers (2002) conducted a meta-analysis of methylphenidate and Adderall. They concluded:

> Adderall is therapeutically equivalent or even superior to generic methylphenidate for improving a relatively wide range of behavior problems commonly displayed by children with ADHD. (p. 4)

They also stated:

> Collectively, our review suggests that Adderall holds clear promise as an effective treatment for children with ADHD, but that it is premature to conclude therapeutic equivalence to methylphenidate based on parent and teacher ratings alone. Reductions in maladaptive behaviors are insufficient to conclude that a drug is a therapeutic equivalent for children with ADHD and must be accompanied by clear evidence of increased adaptive behavior and cognitive functioning. (p. 4)

Alternative Medications

Although methylphenidate and amphetamines are currently the drugs of choice in the treatment of ADHD, about 10 to 30 percent of ADHD patients do not respond adequately and are considered to be treatment resistant. In addition, some children and their parents may desire that stimulants not be used. Therefore, there is a need for treatment alternatives.

Tricyclic antidepressants (especially *nortriptyline;* Chapter 9) have been studied and have been reported to be effective (Spencer et al., 2002a). However, rare cases of potentially fatal cardiac toxicities associated with tricyclic antidepressant use in children and adolescents pose a considerable limitation (Gutgesell et al., 1999).

Initial reports on other antidepressants indicate some usefulness of *fluoxetine* (Prozac) and *buspirone* (Buspar), although the effects were not robust. Of more interest is the dopaminergic antidepressant *bupropion SR* (Wellbutrin); Daviss and colleagues (2001) reported efficacy in adolescents with comorbid ADHD and either depression or dysthymia. Upadhyaya and coworkers (2004) discuss the use of bupropion for adolescents with comorbid ADHD and nicotine dependence.

Other nonstimulants reported to have positive effects in the treatment of ADHD include *carbamazepine* (Tegretol) and two CNS-acting antihypertensive (blood pressure-lowering) dopaminergic agonists—*clonidine* (Catapres) and *guanfacine* (Tenex) (Taylor and Russo, 2001). To date, no homeopathic or herbal medications have been demonstrated to possess the necessary combination of safety and efficacy in treating ADHD.

Pemoline (Cylert) is an older drug for the treatment of ADHD. Recently, concerns have arisen over pemoline-induced liver toxicity that necessitates liver transplantation. This finding caused a shift in the use of the drug from a first-line to a second- or third-line drug. Baseline and biweekly follow-up liver testing are required when using the drug.

Modafinil (Provigil) is a nonstimulant drug currently indicated to maintain daytime wakefulness in the treatment of narcolepsy, an inherited neurological disorder involving excess daytime sedation. Modafinil is similar to, yet distinct from, amphetamine in that its abuse potential is minimal. Small studies (Rugino and Copley, 2001) have demonstrated efficacy, especially against hyperactive/impulsive features, with minimal weight loss and little decrease in appetite.

In 2003 *atomoxetine* (Strattera), the first of a series of selective norepinephrine reuptake inhibitors, was approved by the FDA for use in treating ADHD in adolescents and adults (Wernicke and Kratochvil, 2002). Spencer and coworkers (2002b) reported the efficacy of the drug in reducing both the inattentive and the hyperactive/impulse subscales of the ADHD rating scale. Adverse effects can include reduced appetite, weight loss, increased heart rate, and increased blood pressure. Wernicke and coworkers (2003) noted atomoxetine-caused increases in pulse rate of 5 to 9 beats per minute during the first week of therapy. This increase did not persist past the first week. Blood pressure increases were minimal. Atomoxetine had no effect on QT interval on the ECG. As with other SNRI antidepressants (Chapter 9), not only were ADHD symptoms reduced, but the drug also improved social and family functioning.

Atomoxetine has a short half-life (about 4 hours), initially necessitating twice-daily administration. Michelson and coworkers (2002) reported that once-daily administration (mean dose = 1.3 mg/kg/day) was effective. Parent ratings demonstrated positive effects of atomoxetine persisting until late in the day with fewer inattentive symptoms in the late afternoon and early evening and with less difficulty settling at bedtime. Modest increases in systolic blood pressure and pulse rate were seen along with a 2-pound average weight loss. Biederman and coworkers (2002) demonstrated efficacy in school-age girls comparable to that seen in boys.

Another SNRI agent being studied is *reboxetine* (Chapter 9). Several SNRI-type antidepressants will undoubtedly become commercially available for treatment of depression, ADHD, and perhaps chronic pain conditions.

Recently, a clinical practice parameter has been published to guide treatment of ADHD (American Academy of Child and Adolescent Psychiatry, 2002). Among other topics, this report addresses comorbidity of ADHD, conduct disorder, and aggression. It notes that severe outbursts are seen in some children with ADHD. Stimulant treatment may help some. If aggression remains a problem after stimulant treatment, an anticonvulsant neuromodulator or an alpha agonist may be added. If aggression is pervasive, severe, and persistent and is an acute danger, risperidone can be justified. The guideline does not address the use of either modafinil or atomoxetine. Finally, an algorhithm for the treatment of ADHD has been proposed (Pliszka et al., 2003). Again, neither modafinal nor atomoxetine are included.

Depression in Children and Adolescents

The prevalence of depression is estimated at 8 percent of adolescents and 2 percent of children, some as young as 3 years of age. An estimated 20 percent of adolescents have had at least one episode of major depression by age 18 years, and 65 percent report transient, less severe depressive symptoms (Varley, 2003). In recognition, during the 1990s the use of antidepressants increased fivefold (Zito et al., 2002). In preschoolers, anhedonia appears to be a specific marker for future development of depression (Luby et al., 2003). The stability of the diagnosis over 6 months indicates that the illness is not transient, and the social impairment already evident shows that preschool children who meet diagnostic criteria have reached a threshold that requires intervention (Luby et al., 2002). In grade school-age children, the diagnosis can be well established with equal numbers of boys and girls (Brent and Birmaher, 2003). By adolescence, girls with depression outnumber boys by 2:1 (Hoffman et al., 2003). Family history is positive for affective disorders in 50 to 80 percent of cases of childhood depression. In such instances, a family-based intervention reduces internalizing symptoms and improves the child's understanding of parental illness (Beardslee et al., 2003).

About 3 million youths in the United States suffer from symptoms of depression, yet most fail to receive treatment. Without treatment, there is a high risk of school failure, social isolation, promiscuity, self-medication with drugs and alcohol, and suicide. From 1952 to 1995, a period of over 40 years prior to the widespread use of antidepressant medications in child/adolescent depression, the incidence of suicide among adolescents nearly tripled. Suicide is now the third leading cause of death in 10- to 24-year-olds; 19 percent of high school students have had suicidal thoughts and perhaps 2 million of those actually began planning to take their life. Early onset of depression is associated with poor education, risk of adult depression, and bipolar and personality disorders. Not only does depression exist in adolescence, but adolescence is the period of greatest risk for the onset of depression. Lifetime rates range from 15 to 20 percent by late adolescence. Depressive episodes often have a protracted course and a high tendency for recurrence and onset of bipolar disorder. It is hoped that treatment of depressed youth with antidepressants may help prevent the onset of neuropsychological disorders that can eventually develop when depression remains untreated (Voelker, 2003).

Kasen and coworkers (2001) followed 700 depressed children into their twenties. They found that childhood depression was a strong predictor of personality disorders in adult life: antisocial, histrionic, dependent, and passive-aggressive personality disorders were increased tenfold, threefold, thirteenfold, and sevenfold respectively. Similarly, Giaconia and coworkers (2001) followed 365 children from age 5 to age 21 years. They assessed major depression and drug disorders at age 18 and subsequent psychological functioning at age 21. Depressed adolescents later experienced multiple internalizing problems, interpersonal difficulties, poor psychological well-being, career dissatisfaction, and active depression. Drug-disordered adolescents were less likely to finish secondary education and more likely to be fired, and they experienced active drug disorders. Adolescents with both experienced lower global functioning, externalizing behavioral problems, and suicide. Adolescent depression persists into adulthood with ongoing disruption of interpersonal relationships, risk for substance abuse and early pregnancy, low educational attainment, poor occupational functioning, unemployment, and increased risk of suicide as adults.

These data argue for early and aggressive approaches to treating depression in children (whether pharmacologically or through psychological interventions). The consequences of untreated adolescent depression are so dire that they argue for treatment in the absence of definitive research conclusions.

Treatment

The general goals of treatment of childhood and adolescent depression are to (1) shorten the acute episode of depression, (2) limit the dysfunction caused by the episode, (3) prevent recurrence, (4) treat comorbid conditions, and (5) prevent future problems resulting from preadulthood depression. Specific psychotherapies (primarily cognitive, cognitive-behavioral, and interpersonal therapies) are effective, especially in adolescents. Such therapies are probably of equal efficacy to drug therapy in mild to moderate depression. If chosen, pharmacological therapies remain controversial because specific data about the efficacy of drugs are limited in the pediatric age group. Nevertheless, antidepressants are widely prescribed for children and adolescents, action that may be appropriate: depression is a serious disorder, and we probably should not wait for long-term longitudinal studies of drug efficacy in reducing adulthood consequences of untreated depression. Therefore, strategies and algorithms are necessary to combine available data and clinical consensus. The first step is to choose between psychological therapy, drug therapy, and a combination of both. This is a joint decision of the professionals, the child, and the parents or guardians. Important factors include the severity of depression, family history, recurrence, chronicity, nonresponsiveness to psychological therapies, convenience, and stressors. If drug therapy is chosen, the next step is to decide which medication to use. Obviously, a medicine with a favorable side effect profile, high safety, and low toxicity is desirable, but all of these features are not necessarily available in a single drug. Medication selection usually involves an SSRI as the first choice; fluoxetine is perhaps the most appropriate (Whittington et al., 2004). Uncontrolled clinical trials show 65 to 75 percent efficacy; more controlled trials show efficacy at about 50 to 60 percent, compared with 35 to 40 percent efficacy of placebo therapy. The efficacy of other classes of drugs is too little studied in children and adolescents to merit conclusions.

Antidepressants

Selective Serotonin Reuptake Inhibitors. The SSRIs have been widely used for the treatment of child and adolescent depression, relieving depression in about 50 to 60 percent of takers (leaving 40 percent as non-responders.). Even in responders, however, residual symptomatology and functional impairments can persist. Garland and Berg (2001) described five 14- to 17-year-old patients who developed a reversible, dose-dependent frontal lobe amotivational syndrome after taking fluoxetine (Prozac) and paroxetine (Paxil). The syndrome was characterized by masklike apathy, indifference, and loss of initiative and/or disinhibition. Each adolescent became indifferent to work performance and exhibited impulsive and disinhibited behaviors, poor concentration, and forgetfulness. The onset appeared to be after a month of good functioning as a result of drug therapy. This state of apparent apathy and indifference may be one reason why the SSRIs are excellent choices for treatment of obsessive compulsive behaviors.

Which specific SSRI might be more effective than other SSRIs in treating childhood and adolescent depression is controversial. In 1997, Emslie and coworkers reported results of the first randomized, controlled trial examining the effectiveness of fluoxetine (Prozac) in the treatment of major depression in adolescents. Burke and coworkers (2002) reported on the efficacy of escitalopram (Lexapro). Baumgartner and colleagues (2002) reported on the effectiveness of citalopram (Celexa) in pediatric depression and anxiety. Ravindram and colleagues (2000) demonstrated effectiveness of sertraline (Zoloft) in the treatment of dysthymia in adults, suggesting usefulness against both depression and dysthymia in children and adolescents.

In 2003, Wagner and coworkers demonstrated that sertraline was effective in short-term trials (10 weeks) of major depression. In unpublished studies, paroxetine (Paxil) fared no better than placebo, and its use was associated with emotional lability, which included crying, mood fluctuations, thoughts of suicide, and rare attempts at suicide. In response, in 2003 the U.S. Food and Drug Administration (FDA) warned against the use of paroxetine for the treatment of depression in adolescents under the age of 18 years. The warning followed British observations of suicidal thinking and suicide attempts in pediatric patients taking paroxetine for depression. The incidence of episodes was 1.5 to 3.2 times that seen with placebo therapy.

Chapter 9 discusses the pharmacology and side effects of the various SSRIs at length. Side effects include nausea, insomnia, behavioral activation, anxiety, restlessness, and reduced libido. The activating effects in children and adolescents may be greater than those seen in adults and have been thought perhaps to be related to the future development of bipolar illness in this population. Wilens and coworkers (2003c) discuss these SSRI-related adverse psychiatric events.

Of additional concern are recent reports of serotonin withdrawal syndrome in children and adolescents who abruptly discontinue the SSRI (Diler and Avci, 2002) as well as a report of cases of growth attenuation and growth hormone deficiency associated with SSRI therapy in children (Weintrob et al., 2002).

As indicated, controversy has recently arisen over the possibility that use of SSRIs (and other antidepressants as well) may be associated with an increased frequency of suicides. This possibility flies in the face of data that report an *inverse* relationship between antidepressant use and suicide rates (Olfson et al., 2003). In December 2003, the British government responded to the concerns over possible drug-related suicides with SSRIs and recommended cessation of use of all SSRI-type antidepressants, with the exception of fluoxetine, for depressed youths under the age of 18 years (Whittington et al., 2004). In 2004, Canada took up this recommendation. In the United States, the FDA in 2004 urged stronger warnings on the labels of antidepressants, warning against drug-induced agitation, anxiety, irritability, and restlessness. The FDA acknowledged suicidal-related behaviors, but as yet they cannot determine whether or not the medicine (not the disease) was the cause.

So what should the responsible response be? First, the increase in suicidal behavior that has occurred in adolescents over the last 40 years was not related to antidepressant drug therapy; the increase occurred before the drugs were marketed. Second, the only antidepressant well documented and approved by the FDA for treating major depression in children and adolescents is fluoxetine. This makes fluoxetine the drug of choice, the more so because it is available in an inexpensive generic formulation. Third, psychological therapies are as effective as fluoxetine. Pharmacological therapy with fluoxetine should probably be initiated only in combination with psychological therapy.

Why might SSRI-type antidepressants be associated with suicidal thought or actions, especially considering their efficacy in many cases in relieving depression? First, as psychologists recognize, relief from depression might provide a person with the energy to attempt an act that the person formerly did not have the energy to even contemplate. Second, increased serotonin at the 5-HT$_2$ receptors (Chapter 9) may be responsible for the adverse psychological events that lead to suicidal ideations. Third, if a dose of short-acting antidepressants is missed (all but fluoxetine have half-lives of about 20 hours), a state of serotonin withdrawal can occur within 16 to 24 hours and can lead not only to serotonin withdrawal syndrome but to relapse to depression and thoughts of suicide. Regardless, today, fluoxetine combined with psychological therapies is the treatment of choice for child/adolescent depressive disorder.

Other Antidepressants. In brief, *tricyclic antidepressants* are no more effective than placebo in treating depression in children and adolescents. Significant side effects, higher patient attrition rates, and high toxicity (including fatalities) are limitations. The older *monoamine oxidase inhibitors* (MAOIs) are effective in treating adolescent depression, but their serious toxicities limit clinical use. The new transdermal preparation (skin patch) of an MAOI (*selegiline*) may necessitate reevaluation of this form of treatment (see Chapter 9), although no trials of transdermal selegiline have been conducted in children or adolescents. Other antidepressants shown to be effective in adults have not yet been studied in children. Garland (2003) reviews the use of venlafaxine in children and adolescents. She noted that, in limited studies, venlafaxine has seldom been superior to placebo therapy, relegating it to second- or third-line therapy.

The pharmacology and use of tricyclic agents in treating depression in adults is discussed in Chapter 9. Also, the new class of SNRI-type antidepressants (for example, *atomoxetine, reboxetine*) has not yet been studied in adolescent depression. These drugs may be effective and may herald a new option for treating this disorder. These agents are likely to be as effective as fluoxetine and may be better in increasing social functioning; they may improve patient motivation, energy, and self-perception.

The use of "alternative medicines" to treat ADHD has been poorly studied, generally with demonstration of little or no effect. Recently, Findling and coworkers (2003b) studied extracts of *Hypericum perforatum* (St. John's wort) for possible efficacy in juvenile depression. Figure 12.7 illustrates the improvements on the Children's Depression Rating Scale—Revised during 8 weeks of therapy with 150 milligrams of the extract three times daily, increased to 300 milligrams three times daily after 4 weeks if the patient did not respond to the lower dose. Thirty-three youths started the trial and the dose of 22 was increased at 4 weeks. Depression scores slowly reduced over the 8 weeks, indicating positive response. However, note that this was an open-label, noncontrolled, nonblinded trial. There was no way to ascertain what a placebo response might have been. Placebo-controlled studies appear indicated.

In 2003, the National Institute of Mental Health funded the Treatment for Adolescents with Depression Study (TADS) as a multicenter, randomized, blinded trial designed to evaluate the short-term (12 weeks) and long-term (36 weeks) effectiveness of four treatments for adolescents with major depression: fluoxetine, cognitive-behavioral therapy, a combination of the two, and placebo (Treatment for Adolescents with Depression Study Team, 2005). When completed, TADS will improve our understanding of how best to initiate treatment for adolescents with depression.

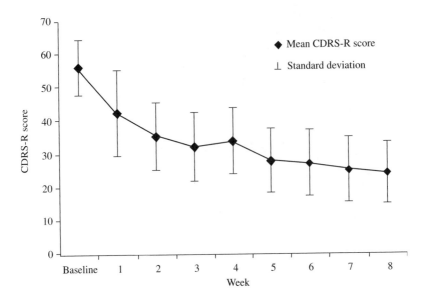

FIGURE 12.7 Mean score and standard deviations on the Children's Depression Rating Scale–Revised for 33 youths treated with St. John's wort. Note the absence of control patients. [From Findling et al. (2003b), p. 911.]

Depression and Psychiatric Comorbidity

Common psychiatric comorbidities with child and adolescent depression include anxiety disorders, ADHD, and behavioral disorders. In a study of 130 children and adolescents referred with depression, 46 percent had a comorbid anxiety disorder, 35 percent had ADHD, and 31 percent had oppositional defiant disorder or conduct disorder.

Anxiety disorders commonly seen with depression include generalized anxiety disorder, panic disorder, and social phobias. For these disorders, psychological therapies are strongly indicated. Monotherapy with an SSRI is first-line treatment if drug therapy is chosen.

If both depression and ADHD are thought to be present, first-line treatment is a stimulant with reassessment in 2 or 3 weeks. If both improve, continue the stimulant. If ADHD improves but depression continues, consider adding an SSRI. If neither improves, consider stopping the stimulant and treating the depression. Once depression improves, assess the ADHD and consider adding a stimulant.

Children are often taken to therapy for treatment of a behavioral disorder. Depression may then be diagnosed. Of importance, bipolar disorder often masks itself in children and adolescents as oppositional defiant disorder and conduct disorder. Thus, hypomania and mania must be sought and ruled out. A practitioner in this situation often begins by treating the depression; first-line therapy is fluoxetine. If behavioral problems persist, an anticonvulsant neuromodulator such as gabapentin (Neurontin) might be added.

Anxiety Disorders in Children and Adolescents

The prevalence of any anxiety disorder in children and adolescents ranges in various studies from 5.7 percent to as high as 17.7 percent. A reasonable estimate is that about 10 percent of 15-year-olds meet diagnostic criteria for having an anxiety disorder. The rate of specific anxiety disorders varies from 6 percent having overanxious disorder (or generalized anxiety disorder, GAD), to between 1 and 2 percent having social phobia and separation anxiety disorder. Obsessive compulsive disorder (OCD) occurs in about 0.5 to 1.5 percent of children and adolescents. We now recognize that these are adolescents at risk. Woodward and Fergusson (2001), conducting a 21-year study of a birth cohort of 1265 New Zealand children, assessed the presence of any anxiety disorder in adolescence and the presence of psychological dysfunction as young adults. There was a linear association between the number of persistent anxiety disorders in adolescence and later persistent anxiety disorders, major depression, nicotine, alcohol and illicit drug dependence, suicidal behavior, educational underachievement, and early parenthood. Sociofamilial and personal disadvantages accounted for some of this association, and correction for them still left anxiety-induced association strongly associated with elevated rates of anxiety and depressive disorders. Similarly, Stein and coworkers (2001) noted that social anxiety disorder (SAD) during adolescence or young adulthood is an important predictor of subsequent depressive disorders. The presence of both SAD and depression in adolescence leads to "a more malignant course and character of subsequent depressive illness" (p. 251).

Generalized Anxiety Disorder

Wagner (2001) reviewed the pharmacological treatment of GAD in children and adolescents, in whom GAD is characterized by excessive anxiety, worry, restlessness, fatigue, concentration difficulty, irritability, muscle tension, or sleep disturbances of 6 months duration or causing functional disturbances. The child may experience tension, apprehension, need for reassurance, and negative self-image and have physical complaints. He or she may appear overly mature, perfectionistic, and sensitive to criticism. He or she may tend to seek reassurance for worries and self-doubt. Over 50 percent of children and adolescents with GAD have another anxiety disorder (social phobia, avoidance disorder, separation anxiety disorder, and/or panic disorder). Over 50 percent have a comorbid depressive disorder (the converse is also true). Evidence shows a high familial association; 40 percent of parents of children with GAD have had the disorder themselves during their childhood. There are currently no studies of possible association of GAD in children and adolescents with development of a substance abuse disorder. In youth with GAD, 47 percent continue to have the disorder 8 years later and many have the onset of a new anxiety disorder or depression. Adolescent GAD is associated with poor societal functioning as adults ("psychosocial adversity"). The two- or threefold increased risk for anxiety-depressive disorders in adulthood argues for early and aggressive intervention—psychological, pharmacological, or both. Intervention should probably be multifaceted, involving psychological therapy, psychoeducation, and interactive therapy with parents and teachers. Combined therapy can reduce the disorder by threefold, with positive effects persisting long after cessation of treatment. Cognitive-behavioral therapy with family anxiety management appears to be somewhat effective (Leger et al., 2003).

The use of *benzodiazepines* (Chapter 6) may seem intuitively appropriate as a treatment for GAD in youth, but these drugs are clinically ineffective. Nonetheless, clonazepam (Klonopin) and alprazolam (Xanax) continue to be prescribed for this purpose. Behavioral activation (irritability, aggression, tantrums), sleepiness, cognitive dysfunction, and addictive potential all must be considered as side effects of the use of benzodiazepines.

Tricyclic antidepressants have been tried, but there are no published reports of efficacy in children or adolescents. In addition, side effects are considerable (Chapter 9), and potentially fatal cardiovascular toxicities must be considered.

Buspirone (BuSpar, Chapter 6) has been effective in open trials. The drug is safe to use and more controlled trials are needed to further assess efficacy. It is unknown whether or not taking the drug with grapefruit juice will improve therapeutic efficacy in this age population (Chapter 1).

SSRIs appear to be effective in the treatment of child and adolescent GAD, although studies are still incomplete. In 37 patients, Birmaher and coworkers (2003) reported that fluoxetine reduced GAD and other anxieties in 61 percent compared with a 35 percent reduction in 37 matched patients taking placebo (Figure 12.8). Despite this response, a substantial number of improved patients remained symptomatic. Rynn and coworkers (2001) reported on 22 children and adolescents (5 to 17 years) with GAD who were treated with *sertraline* (Zoloft) for 9 weeks. The drug was reported to be both safe and efficacious. Baumgartner and coworkers (2002) reported on a small number of adolescents with GAD who were medicated with *citalopram*

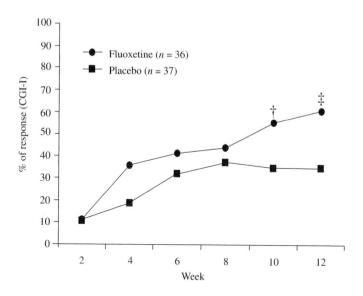

FIGURE 12.8 Effect of 12 weeks of treatment with fluoxetine, compared with control, in 37 patients with generalized anxiety disorder. Note the 8–10 week delay in onset of statistically significant response. CGI-I = Clinical Global Impression—Improvement; $^\dagger p =.02$; $^\ddagger p =.008$. [From Birmaher et al. (2003), p. 420.]

(Celexa). Again the drug was reported to be effective with only minor and transient side effects. The Pediatric Psychopharmacology Anxiety Study Group (2001) reported on the efficacy of *fluvoxamine* (Luvox). Anxiety rating scales were significantly improved over the 8 weeks of the study. Cheer and Figgitt (2002) also reported on the efficacy of fluvoxamine in the management of anxiety disorders (including GAD) in children and adolescents. They stated:

> Reductions in symptoms of anxiety with fluvoxamine have been observed for up to one year in children and adolescents. However, there are currently no comparative trials of fluvoxamine with other pharmacological agents. In the absence of such trials, current consensus opinion recommends that when pharmacotherapy is indicated, fluvoxamine, like other SSRIs, can be used as first-line treatment for anxiety disorders, particularly OCD, in pediatric patients. However, direct comparisons are required to assess the relative efficacy and tolerability of pharmacological agents in order to make firm recommendations for the treatment of anxiety disorders in this patient group. (p. 139)

Venlafaxine ER was very robust against GAD in a large study of over 500 18- to 86-year-old patients (Allgulander et al., 2001). Garland (2003) reviews the effectiveness of venlafaxine over placebo in treating GAD in children and adolescents, concluding, "Venlafaxine can be considered as a potential alternative to SSRIs for GAD in young people" (p. 4).

Atypical neuroleptic agents (for example, olanzapine, Zyprexa) have not been studied as a treatment for GAD in children or adolescents and probably are rarely indicated as therapy for GAD.

There are as yet no reports on the usefulness of *nefazadone, bupropion,* or *mirtazepine* (see Chapter 9) for GAD in children or adolescents. Similarly, any usefulness of *atomoxetine* (Strattera) or other SNRIs has not been reported, although drugs of this class may be useful and appropriate for study.

In summary, GAD in children and adolescents is a chronic problem that may require chronic therapy; whether or not drug therapy must be prolonged and which drugs are effective remains unclear. At present, either venlafaxine or an SSRI may be a reasonable and appropriate choice.

Social Anxiety Disorder

Within the past few years, social anxiety disorder has been separated from other anxiety disorders. It appears to be closely related to both GAD and avoidance personality disorder (Moutier and Stein, 1999). It is a common anxiety disorder with a one-year prevalence estimated at 7 to 8 percent and a lifetime prevalence of 13 to 14 percent in patients aged between 15 and 54 years (Sareen and Stein, 2000). It is certainly underrecognized and undertreated. Regardless, social anxiety disorder has a chronic course and is associated with significant morbidity. It is critical that patients receive an accurate diagnosis and appropriate treatment. Treatment of social anxiety disorder usually involves a combination of pharmacotherapy and psychotherapy (cognitive-behavioral therapy, social skills training, and exposure in vivo therapy).

Many pharmacotherapies have been proposed for various subtypes of social anxiety disorder. Beta-adrenergic blockers (propranolol, for example) are useful in treating performance anxieties because they reduce the physical symptoms. SSRIs, MAOIs, and benzodiazepines all have been proposed. Lydiard and Bobes (2000) conducted a meta-analysis of three studies on the use of paroxetine (Paxil, an SSRI) for social anxiety disorder. Of a total of 861 patients treated, paroxetine reduced symptomatology by 45 to 66 percent.

Obsessive Compulsive Disorder

OCD is a disorder of early onset characterized by recurrent obsessions or compulsions that are severe enough to be time-consuming or result in marked distress or significant impairment, especially of social life. In children, the incidence of OCD is thought to be rare, but in adolescents the reported prevalence is estimated at 2 to 3.6 percent. In fact, the majority of adults with OCD had an onset of the disorder during adolescence or earlier. OCD is now estimated as the fourth most common psychiatric disorder in children and adolescents.

Pharmacotherapy is an important component of the multimodal treatment of children and adolescents with OCD. The effective and commonly used treatment of OCD is a combination of behavioral therapy and pharmacological treatment, usually with an SSRI. All SSRIs are considered to be effective, as is clomipramine (Anafranil; Chapter 9). Currently, three SSRIs (fluvoxamine, paroxetine, and sertraline) along with clomipramine are approved by the FDA for the treatment of OCD in children and adolescents (Allen and Grados, 2002). As alternatives, although the atypical neuroleptic agents (Chapter 11) may work, the serotonin 5-HT$_2$ receptor blockade caused by these drugs may exacerbate OCD symptoms in some patients. Other alternatives have little or no documentation of efficacy (Allen and Grados, 2002).

Cook and coworkers (2001) reported on the efficacy of *sertraline* (Zoloft) for OCD in children and adolescents. Of 137 patients studied during a 52-week study, 72 percent of children and 61 percent of adolescents showed marked improvement, and the improvement was maintained over the 52 weeks of study.

Thomsen and coworkers (2001) reported on the efficacy of *citalopram* (Celexa) in 30 nondepressed adolescents with OCD. Seventy percent showed a marked decrease in symptoms. Nevertheless, only 26 percent appeared to have changed sufficiently to no longer fulfill DSM criteria for OCD. Twenty percent of adolescents were considered to be nonresponders. It is possible that adolescents have a somewhat poorer response to SSRI treatment for OCD than do adults with the disorder.

Geller and coworkers (2001) and Liebowitz and coworkers (2002) reported on the efficacy of *fluoxetine* (Prozac) in childhood and adolescent OCD. The drug was variously effective in 30 to 60 percent of individuals, significant residual symptoms persisted in many patients, and the drug was of slow onset with a prolonged time to clinical response. The full effect of fluoxetine may take more than 8 weeks to develop.

Bergeron and coworkers (2002) compared *sertraline* and *fluoxetine* in a double-blind, 24-week study in 106 adults with OCD (no head-to-head comparisons of two or more SSRIs have yet been reported in the pediatric population). Overall, both drugs were of equal efficacy, with sertraline more rapid in onset and perhaps having a higher rate of remission of symptoms.

Riddle and coworkers (2001) reported on the efficacy of *fluvoxamine* (Luvox) in a 10-week study in 120 children and adolescents with OCD. Effects were highly significant from week 1 through week 10 of the study (Figure 12.9). Cheer and Figgitt (2002) reported similar results. Thus, fluvoxamine was of rapid onset, was effective, and was

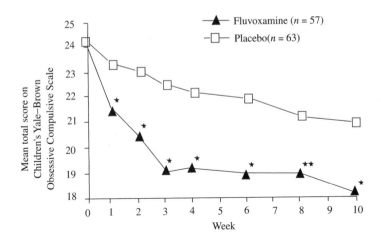

FIGURE 12.9 Mean total scores on ten items of the Children's Yale–Brown Obsessive Compulsive Scale in children and adolescents aged 8 to 17 years, at 17 study sites, administered either fluvoxamine or placebo following a 7- to 14-day washout period prior to entry into the trial. $*\ p <05;\ **p < .10$. [From Riddle et al. (2001), p. 225.]

well tolerated (similar to other SSRIs, perhaps with the exception of the slower onset of fluoxetine).

Rosenberg and coworkers (1999) and Shapiro (2002) reported on the efficacy of low-dose *paroxetine* (Paxil) in several cases of pediatric OCD. Efficacy was similar to reports on the efficacy of other SSRIs.

Bipolar Disorder in Children and Adolescents

As early as 1997, the American Academy of Child and Adolescent Psychiatry published clinical practice parameters for the assessment and treatment of bipolar disorder in children and adolescents. Today, however, bipolar disorder in juveniles is underdiagnosed and misdiagnosed according to various accounts; it is accompanied by high rates of attention deficit and disruptive disorders (Reddy and Srinath, 2000). Close association with substance abuse problems is also a significant problem. Early recognition of bipolar disorder can present a diagnostic dilemma due to overlap with symptoms of such disorders as ADHD and conduct disorder (Kim and Miklowitz, 2002). It is now clear, however, that early recognition of bipolar disorder and early treatment with antimanic drugs (Chapter 10) can reduce the severity of both the bipolar symptoms and the substance abuse. It is hoped that treatment staves off the devastating consequences of bipolar disease that occur in adult life should the disorder go unrecognized and untreated.

Perhaps earlier recognition and diagnosis of bipolar disorder in children and adolescents follows from the observations that aggressive and explosive behaviors as well as excessive elation and grandiosity can be signs of the disorder and that children who display manic symptoms when either their depression or their ADHD are treated with an antidepressant or a stimulant probably will eventually develop more classic bipolar disease.

Environment seems to play an important role, as living with an intact biological family predicts more rapid rates of recovery, and a low level of maternal warmth significantly predicts more rapid rates of relapse (Geller et al., 2004). Therefore, diagnosis and treatment of childhood and adolescent bipolar disease presents special challenges. Certainly, early psychotherapy is needed to address the larger philosophical question of what the diagnosis means for sense of self.

In the late 1990s, *lithium* became the treatment of choice for childhood and adolescent bipolar disease. It still is: large studies in adolescents aged 12 to 18 years have demonstrated efficacy (Figure 12.10) (Kafantaris et al., 2003). In addition, *valproic acid* and other antimanic anticonvulsants are becoming more widely utilized. DelBello and coworkers (2002), in a preliminary study, reported on the efficacy of topiramate (Topamax) for pediatric bipolar disorder. Topiramate may have an advantage over lithium and valproic acid in that use of topiramate is associated with weight loss rather than with

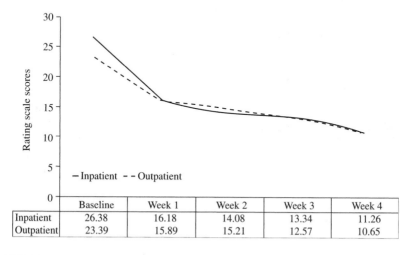

	Baseline	Week 1	Week 2	Week 3	Week 4
Inpatient	26.38	16.18	14.08	13.34	11.26
Outpatient	23.39	15.89	15.21	12.57	10.65

FIGURE 12.10 Effect of lithium carbonate on bipolar mania as measured over a 4-week study period using the Young Mania Rating Scale. The numbers at the bottom are the numeric scores from baseline to the end of week 4 in both inpatients and outpatients. There were 77 inpatients and 23 outpatients in the study, and both groups exhibited similar responsiveness. [From Kafantaris et al. (2003), p. 1043.]

weight gain (Chapter 10). Thus, neuromodulators and newer atypical antipsychotics are the mainstay of treatment of bipolar disorder in children and adolescents (Kowatch and DelBello, 2003).

As with adult-onset bipolar disease, combinations of neuromodulators and atypical antipsychotics might be superior to monotherapy with either drug alone (Findling et al., 2003a). The addition of an antipsychotic drug to the neuromodulator may be necessary as, in youth, the manic components may be more difficult to treat than the depressive symptoms that can dominate adult bipolar disorder (Kafantaris et al., 2001; Yatham et al., 2004).

Following mood stabilization, if the bipolar disorder is comorbid with ADHD, the addition of a psychostimulant may be necessary. Regardless, therapy of bipolar disorder in children and adolescents is challenging and expert assistance is essential. Adequate clinical response is difficult to achieve, relapses are frequent, side effects of drugs are considerable, and patient and family acceptance of this long-term disorder can be difficult.

Psychotic Disorders in Children and Adolescents

Schizophrenia and its related conditions are considered quite rare in children, and when it occurs it presents significant challenges to clinicians (Reimherr and McClellan, 2004). However, schizophrenia is relatively common in adolescents. About one in three patients with schizophrenia develop symptoms of psychosis between the ages of 10 and 20 years. Since both childhood and adolescent schizophrenia is generally associated with a poor long-term outcome, effective treatments are needed for children and adolescents with psychotic disorders (Jarbin et al., 2003).

The current best psychopharmacological agents for the treatment of childhood- and adolescent-onset schizophrenia are the newer atypical antipsychotic drugs (Chapter 11). While effective, haloperidol and the phenothiazines are best avoided because of their extrapyramidal side effects. Double-blinded, controlled studies have shown that clozapine (Clozaril), risperidone (Risperdal), olanzapine (Zyprexa), and quetiapine (Seroquel) are all effective for treating children and adolescents with this disorder (Findling et al., 2003; Frazier et al., 2001). In children, no single agent has been shown to be any more or less effective than another (comparative studies have not been conducted in children). However, in adults, some differences have been noted (Chapter 11). Clozaril, although effective, is probably a drug of second choice because of unique side effects (Chapter11) (Remschmidt et al., 2000). Risperidol and olanzapine are quite effective, but weight gain has been a major problem (Ross et al., 2003). Quetiapine has been reported to be effective in very limited trials (Shapiro, 2001). Use of the newer atypical antipsychotic drugs, such as ziprasidone and aripiprazole, is yet to be reported in children or adolescents. Recently, Sallee and coworkers (2003) studied the pharmacodynamics of ziprasidone in children and adolescents. They noted that the drug was a dopaminergic antagonist and, in a delayed fashion, appears to stimulate dopaminergic neurotransmission. Correlation was not made with potential efficacy in adolescent-onset schizophrenia. Certainly, agents such as ziprasidone (without weight gain) and aripiprazole (with an antidepressant action) will be interesting to study.

STUDY QUESTIONS

1. What is meant by an "off-label" use of a drug?

2. Why are psychotherapeutic drugs usually used "off-label" in children and adolescents?

3. Defend early therapeutic interventions in treating psychological disorders in children.

4. What classes of psychotherapeutic drugs might be used to treat aggressive disorders in children and adolescents? Which might be of the most benefit?

5. What classes of psychotherapeutic drugs might be useful in treating autism and other pervasive developmental disorders?

6. How might one of these classes be choosen over another?

7. Besides stimulant medication, what other classes of drugs might be considered for use in treating ADHD? Compare and contrast them with psychostimulants.

8. How does methylphenidate compare and contrast with cocaine?

9. Should depression in children be treated? Defend your answer.

10. Compare and contrast the tricyclic antidepressants and the SSRIs in childhood and adolescent depression.

11. What might be comorbid with generalized anxiety disorder in children? How might this comorbidity affect therapy?

12. Compare and contrast the benzodiazepines and the SSRIs in the treatment of anxiety disorders in children and adolescents.

13. Compare and contrast the neuromodulator mood stabilizers and the atypical antipsychotics in the treatment of bipolar disorder in children and adolescents.

14. Discuss the relevant issues in the treatment of schizophrenia, schizoaffective disorder, and the prodromal phase of schizophrenia in children and adolescents.

REFERENCES

Allen, A., and M. A. Grados. (2002). "Pharmacologic Treatment of Children and Adolescents with Obsessive-Compulsive Disorder." *Child and Adolescent Psychopharmacology News* 7 (February): 1–5.

Allgulander, C., et al. (2001). "Venlafaxine Extended Release (ER) in the Treatment of Generalized Anxiety Disorder: Twenty-Four Week, Placebo-Controlled, Dose-Ranging Study." *British Journal of Psychiatry* 179: 15–22.

American Academy of Child and Adolescent Psychiatry (2002). "Practice Parameter for the Use of Stimulant Medications in the Treatment of Children, Adolescents, and Adults." *Journal of the American Academy of Child and Adolescent Psychiatry* 41: 26S–47S.

Barkley, R. A. (2003). "Does the Treatment of Attention-Deficit/Hyperactivity Disorder with Stimulants Contribute to Drug Use/Abuse?" *Pediatrics* 111: 97–109.

Baumgartner, J. L., et al. (2002). "Citalopram in Children and Adolescents with Depression or Anxiety." *Annals of Pharmacotherapy* 36: 1692–1697.

Beardslee, W., et al. (2003). "A Family-Based Approach to the Prevention of Depressive Symptoms in Children at Risk: Evidence of Parental and Child Change." *Pediatrics* 112: e119–e131.

Bergeron, R., et al. (2002). "Sertraline and Fluoxetine Treatment of Obsessive-Compulsive Disorder: Results of a Double-Blind, 6-Month Treatment Study." *Journal of Clinical Psychopharmacology* 22: 148–154.

Biederman, J., et al. (1999). "Clinical Correlates of ADHD in Females: Findings from a Large Group of Girls Ascertained from Pediatric and Psychiatric Referral Sources." *Journal of the American Academy of Child and Adolescent Psychiatry* 38: 966–975.

Biederman, J., et al. (2002). "Efficacy of Atomoxetine Versus Placebo in School-Age Girls with Attention-Deficit/Hyperactivity Disorder." *Pediatrics* 110: e75.

Biederman, J., ed. (2004). "Diagnosing and Treating ADHD in Adults." *Journal of Clinical Psychiatry* 65, Supplement 3: 3–44.

Birmaher, B., et al. (2003). "Fluoxetine for the Treatment of Childhood Anxiety Disorders." *Journal of the American Academy of Child and Adolescent Psychiatry* 42: 415–423.

Brent, D. A., and B. Birmaher (2003). "Adolescent Depression." *New England Journal of Medicine* 347: 667–671.

Burke, W., et al. (2002). "Fixed Trial of the Single Isomer SSRI Escitalopram in Depressed Outpatients." *Journal of Clinical Psychiatry* 63: 331–336.

Cavell, T. A. (2000). *Working with Parents of Aggressive Children: A Practitioner's Guide.* Washington, DC: American Psychological Asssociation.

Cheer, S. M., and D. P. Figgitt (2002). "Spotlight on Fluvoxamine in Anxiety Disorders in Children and Adolescents." *CNS Drugs* 16: 139–144.

Chronis, A., et al. (2003). "Psychopathology and Substance Abuse in Parents of Young Children with Attention-Deficit/Hyperactivity Disorder." *Journal of the American Academy of Child and Adolescent Psychiatry* 42: 1424–1432.

Connor, D. F., et al. (2002). "Psychopharmacology and Aggression: I. A Meta-Analysis of Stimulant Effects on Overt/Covert Aggression-Related Behaviors in

ADHD." *Journal of the American Academy of Child and Adolescent Psychiatry* 41: 253–261.

Cook, E. H., et al. (2001). "Long-Term Sertraline Treatment of Children and Adolescents with Obsessive-Compulsive Disorder." *Journal of the American Academy of Child and Adolescent Psychiatry* 40: 1175–1181.

Costello, E. J., et al. (2003). "Prevalence and Development of Psychiatric Disorders in Childhood and Adolescence." *Archives of General Psychiatry* 60: 837–844.

Daviss, W. B., et al. (2001). "Bupropion Sustained Release in Adolescents with Comorbid Attention-Deficit/Hyperactivity Disorder and Depression." *Journal of the American Academy of Child and Adolescent Psychiatry* 40: 307–314.

DelBello, M. P., et al. (2002). "Adjunctive Topiramate Treatment for Pediatric Bipolar Disorder: Retrospective Chart Review." *Journal of Child and Adolescent Psychopharmacology* 12: 323–330.

Diler, R. S., and A. Avci (2002). "Selective Serotonin Reuptake Inhibitor Discontinuation Syndrome in Children: Six Case Reports." *Current Therapeutic Research and Clinical Experimentation* 63: 188–197.

Donovan, S. J., et al. (2000). "Divalproex Treatment for Youth with Explosive Temper and Mood Lability: A Double-Blind, Placebo-Controlled Crossover Study." *American Journal of Psychiatry* 157: 818–820.

Emslie, G. J., et al. (1997). "A Double-Blind, Randomized, Placebo-Controlled Trial of Fluoxetine in Children and Adolescents with Depression." *Archives of General Psychiatry* 54: 1031–1037.

Emslie, G. J., et al. (2000). "Updates on the Pharmacological Treatment of Childhood Depression." *Psychiatric Clinics of North America* 23: 813–835.

Findling, R. L., et al. (2003a). "Combination Lithium and Divalproex Sodium in Pediatric Bipolarity." *Journal of the American Academy of Child and Adolescent Psychiatry* 42: 895–901.

Findling, R. L., et al. (2003b). "An Open-Label Pilot Study of St. John's Wort in Juvenile Depression." *Journal of the American Academy of Child and Adolescent Psychiatry* 42: 908–914.

Findling, R. L., et al. (2003c). "A Prospective, Open-Label Trial of Olanzapine in Adolescents with Schizophrenia." *Journal of the American Academy of Child and Adolescent Psychiatry* 42: 170–175.

Findling, R. L., et al. (2004). "Long-Term, Open-Label Study of Risperidone in Children with Severe Disruptive Behaviors and Below-Average IQ." *American Journal of Psychiatry* 161: 677–684.

Frazier, J. A., et al. (2001). "A Prospective, Open-Label Treatment Trial of Olanzapine Monotherapy in Children and Adolescents with Bipolar Disorder." *Journal of Child and Adolescent Psychopharmacology* 11: 239–250.

Garland, E. J. (2003). "Use of Venlafaxine in Child and Adolescent Psychiatry." *Child and Adolescent Psychopharmacology News* 8 (August): 1–4.

Garland, E. J., and E. A. Berg. (2001). "Amotivational Syndrome Associated with Selective Serotonin Reuptake Inhibitors in Children and Adolescents." *Journal of Child and Adolescent Psychopharmacology* 11: 181–186.

Geller, B., et al. (2004). "Four-Year Prospective Outcome and Natural History of Mania in Children with a Prepubertal and Early Adolescent Bipolar Disorder Phenotype." *Archives of General Psychiatry* 61: 459–467.

Geller, D. A., et al. (2001). "Fluoxetine Treatment for Obsessive-Compulsive Disorder in Children and Adolescents: A Placebo-Controlled Clinical Trial." *Journal of the American Academy of Child and Adolescent Psychiatry* 40: 773–779.

Giaconia, A., et al. (2001). "Major Depression and Drug Disorders in Adolescence: General and Specific Impairments in Early Adulthood." *Journal of the American Academy of Child and Adolescent Psychiatry* 40: 1426–1433.

Gutgesell, H., et al. (1999). "AHA Scientific Statement: Cardiovascular Monitoring of Children and Adolescents Receiving Psychotropic Drugs." *Journal of the American Academy of Child and Adolescent Psychiatry* 38: 1047–1050.

Hazell, P. L., and J. E. Stuart (2003). "A Randomized Controlled Trial of Clonidine Added to Psychostimulant Medication for Hyperactive and Aggressive Children." *Journal of the American Academy of Child and Adolescent Psychiatry* 42: 886–894.

Hoffman, J. P., et al. (2003). "Onset of Major Depressive Disorder Among Adolescents." *Journal of the American Academy of Child and Adolescent Psychiatry* 42: 217–224

Hollander, E., et al. (2001). "An Open Trial of Divalproex Sodium in Autism Spectrum Disorders." *Journal of Clinical Psychiatry* 62: 530–534.

Hollander, E., et al. (2003). "Divalproex in the Treatment of Impulsive Aggression: Efficacy in Cluster B Personality Disorders." *Neuropsychopharmacology* 28: 1186–1197.

Jarbin, H., et al. (2003). "Adult Outcome of Social Function in Adolescent-Onset Schizophrenia and Affective Psychosis." *Journal of the American Academy of Child and Adolescent Psychiatry* 42: 176–183.

Johnson, S. M., and E. Hollander (2003). "Evidence That Eicosapentaenoic Acid Is Effective in Treating Autism." *Journal of Clinical Psychiatry* 64: 848–849.

Juvonen, J., et al. (2003). "Bullying Among Young Adolescents: The Strong, the Weak, and the Troubled." *Pediatrics* 112: 1231–1237.

Kafantaris, V., et al. (2001). "Adjunctive Antipsychotic Treatment of Adolescents with Bipolar Psychosis." *Journal of the American Academy of Child and Adolescent Psychiatry* 40: 1448–1456.

Kafantaris, V., et al. (2003). "Lithium Treatment of Acute Mania in Adolescents: A Large Open Trial." *Journal of the American Academy of Child and Adolescent Psychiatry* 42: 1038–1045.

Kasen, S., et al. (2001). "Childhood Depression and Adult Personality Disorder: Alternative Pathways of Continuity." *Archives of General Psychiatry* 58: 231–236.

Kazdin, A. E. (2000). "Treatments for Aggressive and Antisocial Children." *Child and Adolescent Psychiatric Clinics of North America* 9: 841–858.

Kemner, C., et al. (2002). "Open-Label Study of Olanzapine in Children with Pervasive Developmental Disorder." *Journal of Clinical Psychopharmacology* 22: 455–460.

Kim, E. (2002). "The Use of Newer Anticonvulsants in Neuropsychiatric Disorders." *Current Psychiatry Reports* 4: 331–337.

Kim, E. Y., and D. J. Miklowitz (2002). "Childhood Mania, Attention Deficit Hyperactivity Disorder, and Conduct Disorder: A Critical Review of Diagnostic Dilemmas." *Bipolar Disorders* 4: 215–225.

Knapp, R. J., et al. (2002). "Antidepressant Activity of Memory-Enhancing Drugs in the Reduction of Submissive Behavior Model." *European Journal of Pharmacology* 440: 27–35.

Kowatch, R. A., and M. P. DelBello (2003). "The Use of Mood Stabilizers and Atypical Antipsychotics in Children and Adolescents with Bipolar Disorders." *CNS Spectrums* 8: 273–280.

Lavigne, J. V., et al. (2001). "Oppositional Defiant Disorder with Onset in Preschool Years: Longitudinal Stability and Pathways to Other Disorders." *Journal of the American Academy of Child and Adolescent Psychiatry* 40: 1393–1400.

Leger, E., et al. (2003). "Cognitive-Behavioral Treatment of Generalized Anxiety Disorder Among Adolescents: A Case Series." *Journal of the American Academy of Child and Adolescent Psychiatry* 42: 327–330.

Liebowitz, M., et al. (2002). "Fluoxetine in Children and Adolescents with OCD: A Placebo-Controlled Trial." *Journal of the American Academy of Child and Adolescent Psychiatry* 41: 1431–1438.

Lopez, F., et al. (2003). "Comparative Efficacy of Two Once-Daily Methylphenidate Formulations (Ritalin LA and Concerta) and Placebo in Children with

Attention Deficit Hyperactivity Disorder Across the School Day." *Pediatric Drugs* 5: 545–555.

Luby, J., et al. (2002). "Preschool Major Depressive Disorder: Preliminary Validation for Developmentally Modified DSM-IV Criteria." *Journal of the American Academy of Child and Adolescent Psychiatry* 41: 928–937.

Luby, J., et al. (2003). "The Clinical Picture of Depression in Preschool Children." *Journal of the American Academy of Child and Adolescent Psychiatry* 42: 340–348.

Lydiard, R. B., and J. Bobes (2000). "Therapeutic Advances: Paroxetine for the Treatment of Social Anxiety Disorder." *Depression and Anxiety* 11: 99–104.

Malone, R. P., et al. (2002). "Risperidone Treatment in Children and Adolescents with Autism: Short- and Long-Term Safety and Effectiveness." *American Journal of the Academy of Child and Adolescent Psychiatry* 41: 140–147.

Manos, M. J., et al. (1999). "Differential Effectiveness of Methylphenidate and Adderall in School-Age Youths with Attention-Deficit/Hyperactivity Disorder." *Journal of the American Academy of Child and Adolescent Psychiatry* 38: 813–819.

Masi, G., et al. (2003). "A 3-Year Naturalistic Study of 53 Preschool Children with Pervasive Developmental Disorders Treated with Risperidone." *Journal of Clinical Psychiatry* 64: 1039–1047.

McCracken, J. T., et al. (2000). "Evidence for Linkage of a Tandem Duplication Polymorphism Upstream of the Dopamine D_4 Receptor Gene (DRD_4) with Attention Deficit Hyperactivity Disorder (ADHD)." *Molecular Psychiatry* 5: 531–536.

McCracken, J. T., et al. (2003). "Analog Classroom Assessment of a Once-Daily Mixed Amphetamine Formulation, SLI381 (ADDERALL XR), in Children with ADHD." *Journal of the American Academy of Child and Adolescent Psychiatry* 42: 673–683.

McDougle, C. J., et al. (2003). "Treatment of Aggression in Children and Adolescents with Autism and Conduct Disorder." *Journal of Clinical Psychiatry* 64, Supplement 4: 16–25.

McGough, J. J., et al. (2003). "Pharmacokinetics of SLI381 (ADDERALL XR), an Extended-Release Formulation of Adderall." *Journal of the American Academy of Child and Adolescent Psychiatry* 42: 684–691.

Michelson, D., et al. (2002). "Once-Daily Atomoxetine Treatment for Children and Adolescents with Attention Deficit/Hyperactivity Disorder: A Randomized, Placebo-Controlled Study." *American Journal of Psychiatry* 159: 1896–1901.

Moutier, C. Y., and M. B. Stein (1999). "The History, Epidemiology, and Differential Diagnosis of Social Anxiety Disorder." *Journal of Clinical Psychiatry* 60, Supplement 9: 4–8.

MTA Cooperative Group (1999). "A 14-Month Randomized Clinical Trial of Treatment Strategies for Attention-Deficit/Hyperactivity Disorder." *Archives of General Psychiatry* 56: 1073–1086.

MTA Cooperative Group (2004). "National Institute of Mental Health Multimodal Treatment Study of ADHD Follow-Up: Changes in Effectiveness and Growth After the End of Treatment." *Pediatrics* 113: 762–769.

Nansel, T. R., et al. (2001). "Bullying Behaviors Among U.S. Youth: Prevalence and Association with Psychological Adjustment." *Journal of the American Medical Association* 285: 2094–2100.

Olfson, M., et al. (2003). "Relationship Between Antidepressant Medication Treatment and Suicide in Adolescents." *Archives of General Psychiatry* 60: 978–982.

Pappadopulos, E., et al. (2003). "Treatment Recommendations for the Use of Antipsychotics for Aggressive Youth (TRAAY). Part II." *Journal of the American Academy of Child and Adolescent Psychiatry* 42: 145–161.

Pediatric Psychopharmacology Anxiety Study Group (2001). "Fluvoxamine for the Treatment of Anxiety Disorders in Children and Adolescents." *New England Journal of Medicine* 344: 1279–1285.

Pine, D. S., and E. Cohen (1999). "Therapeutics of Aggression in Children." *Paediatric Drugs* 1: 183–196.

Pliszka, S. R., et al. (2000). "A Double-Blind, Placebo-Controlled Study of Adderall and Methylphenidate in the Treatment of Attention-Deficit/Hyperactivity Disorder." *Journal of the American Academy of Child and Adolescent Psychiatry* 39: 619–626.

Pliszka, S. R., et al. (2003). "A Feasibility Study of the Children's Medication Algorithm Project (CMAP) Algorithm for the Treatment of ADHD." *Journal of the American Academy of Child and Adolescent Psychiatry* 42: 279–287.

Rapport, M. D., et al. (2002). "Methylphenidate and Adderall Treatment for Children with ADHD: Has Therapeutic Equivalence Been Demonstrated?" *Child and Adolescent Psychopharmacology News* 7 (April): 4–12.

Ravindram, A., et al. (2000). "Treatment of Dysthymia with Sertraline: A Double-Blind, Placebo-Controlled Trial in Dysthymic Patients Without Major Depression." *Journal of Clinical Psychiatry* 61: 821–827.

Reddy, Y. C., and S. Srinath (2000). "Juvenile Bipolar Disorder." *Acta Psychiatrica Scandinavica* 102: 162–170.

Reimherr, J. P., and J. M. McClellan (2004). "Diagnostic Challenges in Children and Adolescents with Psychotic Disorders." *Journal of Clinical Psychiatry* 65, Supplement 6: 5–11.

Reeves, R. R., et al. (2003). "EEG Does Not Predict Response to Valproate Treatment of Aggression in Patients with Borderline and Antisocial Personality Disorders." *Clinical Electroencephalography* 34: 84–86.

Remschmidt, H., et al. (2000). "Management of Schizophrenia in Children and Adolescents: The Role of Clozapine." *Paediatric Drugs* 2: 253–262.

Riddle, M. A., et al. (2001). "Fluvoxamine for Children and Adolescents with Obsessive-Compulsive Disorder: A Randomized, Controlled, Multicenter Trial." *Journal of the American Academy of Child and Adolescent Psychiatry* 40: 222–229.

Rosenberg, D. R., et al. (1999). "Paroxetine Open-Label Treatment of Pediatric Outpatients with Obsessive-Compulsive Disorder." *Journal of the American Academy of Child and Adolescent Psychiatry* 38: 1180–1185.

Ross, R., et al. (2003). "A 1-Year Open-Label Trial of Olanzapine in School-Age Children with Schizophrenia." *Journal of Child and Adolescent Psychopharmacology* 13: 301–309.

Rowland, A. S., et al. (2002). "Prevalence of Medication Treatment for Attention Deficit-Hyperactivity Disorder Among Elementary School Children in Johnston County, North Carolina." *American Journal of Public Health* 92: 231–234.

Rugino, T. A., and T. C. Copley (2001). "Effects of Modafinil in Children with Attention-Deficit/Hyperactivity Disorder: An Open-Label Study." *Journal of the American Academy of Child and Adolescent Psychiatry* 40: 230–235.

Rynn, M. A., et al. (2001). "Placebo-Controlled Trial of Sertraline in the Treatment of Children with Generalized Anxiety Disorder." *American Journal of Psychiatry* 158: 2008–2014.

Sallee, F. R., et al. (2003). "Pharmacodynamics of Ziprasidone in Children and Adolescents: Impact on Dopamine Transmission." *Journal of the American Academy of Child and Adolescent Psychiatry* 42: 902–907.

Sareen, L., and M. Stein (2000). "A Review of the Epidemiology and Approaches to the Treatment of Social Anxiety Disorder." *Drugs* 59: 497–509.

Schur, S. B., et al. (2003). "Treatment Recommendations for the Use of Antipsychotics for Aggressive Youth (TRAAY). Part I: A Review." *Journal of the American Academy of Child and Adolescent Psychiatry* 42: 132–144.

Shapiro, G. (2001). "Case Study: The Use of Quetiapine in Two Adolescent Inpatients with Psychosis." *Child and Adolescent Psychopharmacology News* 6 (February), 5–6.

Shapiro, G. (2002). "Low-Dose Paroxetine in the Treatment of Obsessive-Compulsive Disorder and Obsessive-Compulsive Personality Disorder in Pediatric Patients." *Child and Adolescent Psychopharmacology News* 7 (June): 4–6.

Short, E. J., et al. (2004). "A Prospective Study if Stimulant Response in Preschool Children: Insights from ROC Analyses." *Journal of the American Academy of Child and Adolescent Psychiatry* 43: 251–259.

Smalley, S., et al. (2002). "Genetic Linkage of Attention-Deficit/Hyperactivity Disorder on Chromosome 16p13, in a Region Implicated in Autism." *American Journal of Human Genetics* 71: 959–963.

Spencer, T., et al. (2002a). "A Double-Blind Comparison of Desipramine and Placebo in Children and Adolescents with Chronic Tic Disorder and Comorbid Attention Deficit/Hyperactivity Disorder." *Archives of General Psychiatry* 59: 649–656.

Spencer, T., et al. (2002b). "Results from 2 Proof-of-Concept, Placebo-Controlled Studies of Atomoxetine in Children with Attention-Deficit/Hyperactivity Disorder." *Journal of Clinical Psychiatry* 63: 1140–1147.

Spivak, H., and D. Prothrow-Stith (2001). "The Need to Address Bullying: An Important Component of Violence Prevention." *Journal of the American Medical Association* 285: 2131–2132.

Stein, M. B., et al. (2001). "Social Anxiety Disorder and the Risk of Depression: A Prospective Community Study of Adolescents and Young Adults." *Archives of General Psychiatry* 58: 251–256.

Steiner, H., et al. (2003). "Psychopharmacological Strategies for the Treatment of Aggression in Youth." *CNS* 8: 298–308.

Swanson, J., et al. (2003). "Development of a New Once-a-Day Formulation of Methylphenidate for the Treatment of Attention-Deficit/Hyperactivity Disorder: Proof-of-Concept and Proof-of-Product Studies." *Archives of General Psychiatry* 60: 204–211.

Taylor, F. B., and J. Russo (2001). "Comparing Guanfacine and Dextroamphetamine for the Treatment of Adult Attention-Deficit/Hyperactivity Disorder." *Journal of Clinical Psychopharmacology* 21: 223–228.

Thomsen, P. H., et al. (2001). "Long-Term Experience with Citalopram in the Treatment of Adolescent OCD." *Journal of the American Academy of Child and Adolescent Psychiatry* 40: 895–902.

Treatment for Adolescents with Depression Study Team (2005). "Treatment for Adolescents with Depression Study (TADS): Demographic and Clinical Characteristics." *Journal of the American Academy of Child and Adolescent Psychiatry* 44: 28–40.

Upadhyaya, H., et al. (2004). "Bupropion SR in Adolescents with Comorbid ADHD and Nicotine Dependence: A Pilot Study." *Journal of the American Academy of Child and Adolescent Psychiatry* 43: 199–205.

Varley, C. K. (2003). "Psychopharmacological Treatment of Major Depressive Disorder in Children and Adolescents." *Journal of the American Medical Association* 290: 1091–1093.

Voelker, R. (2003). "Researchers Probe Depression in Children." *Journal of the American Medical Association* 289: 3078–3079.

Volkow, N. D., et al. (1998). "Dopamine Transporter Occupancies in the Human Brain Induced by Therapeutic Doses of Oral Methylphenidate." *American Journal of Psychiatry* 155: 1325–1331.

Volkow, N. D., et al. (2002a). "Mechanism of Action of Methylphenidate: Insights from PET Imaging Studies." *Journal of Attention Disorders* 6, Supplement 1: S31–S43.

Volkow, N. D., et al. (2002b). "Relationship Between Blockade of Dopamine Transporters by Oral Methylphenidate and the Increases in Extracellular Dopamine: Therapeutic Implications." *Synapse* 43: 181–187.

Wagner, K. D. (2001). "The Pharmacological Treatment of Generalized Anxiety Disorder in Children and Adults." *Psychiatric Clinics of North America* 24: 139–153.

Wagner, K. D., et al. (2003). "Efficacy of Sertraline in the Treatment of Children and Adolescents with Major Depressive Disorder: Two Randomized Controlled Trials." *Journal of the American Medical Association* 290: 1033–1041.

Weintrob, N., et al. (2002). "Decreased Growth During Therapy with Selective Serotonin Reuptake Inhibitors." *Archives of Pediatric and Adolescent Medicine* 156: 696–701.

Wernicke, J. F., and C. J. Kratochvil (2002). "Safety Profile of Atomoxetine in the Treatment of Children and Adults with ADHD." *Journal of Clinical Psychiatry* 63, Supplement 12: 50–55.

Wernicke, J. F., et al. (2003). "Cardiovascular Effects of Atomoxetine in Children, Adolescents, and Adults." *Drug Safety* 26: 729–740.

Whittington, C. J., et al. (2004). "Selective Serotonin Reuptake Inhibitors in Childhood Depression: Systematic Review of Published and Unpublished Data." *Lancet* 363: 1341–1345.

Wilens, T. E., et al. (2003a). "ADHD Treatment with Once-Daily OROS Methylphenidate: Interim 12-Month Results from a Long-Term Open-Label Study." *Journal of the American Academy of Child and Adolescent Psychiatry* 42: 424–433.

Wilens, T. E., et al. (2003b). "Does Stimulant Therapy of Attention-Deficit/Hyperactivity Disorder Beget Later Substance Abuse?" *Pediatrics* 111: 179–185.

Wilens, T. E., et al. (2003c). "A Systematic Chart Review of the Nature of Psychiatric Adverse Events in Children and Adolescents Treated with Selective Serotonin Reuptake Inhibitors." *Journal of Child and Adolescent Psychopharmacology* 13: 143–152.

Woodward, L. J., and D. M. Fergusson (2001). "Life-Course Outcomes of Young People with Anxiety Disorders in Adolescence." *Journal of the American Academy of Child and Adolescent Psychiatry* 40: 1086–1093.

Yatham. L. N., et al. (2004). "Risperidone plus Lithium versus Risperidone plus Valproate in Acute and Continuation Treatment of Mania." *International Clinical Psychopharmacology* 19: 103–109.

Yeargin-Allsopp, M., et al. (2003). "Prevalence of Autism in a US Metropolitan Area." *Journal of the American Medical Association* 289: 49–55.

Zito, J. M., et al. (2002). "Rising Prevalence of Antidepressants Among U.S. Youths." *Pediatrics* 109: 721–727.

Zito, J. M., et al. (2003). "Psychotropic Practice Patterns for Youth: A 10-Year Perspective." *Archives of Pediatric and Adolescent Medicine* 157: 17–25.

Chapter 13

Geriatric Psychopharmacology: Drugs for Parkinsonism and Alzheimer's Disease

Earlier chapters of this book have presented several principles concerning the actions and effects of psychoactive drugs administered to elderly patients. Some of these are summarized here:

1. Lower doses of medication are often as effective in the elderly as larger doses in younger persons.

2. When initiating drug therapy in the elderly, it is wise to "start low and go slow."

3. Elimination half-lives are often prolonged in the elderly, sometimes to about twice as long as the half-lives seen in younger persons.

4. Sedative-hypnotic drugs (Chapters 4–6) can be quite "dementing" in the elderly, causing marked and often prolonged loss of the ability to form memory.

5. Sedative-hypnotic drugs can also induce psychomotor incoordination, resulting in an increased incidence of falls, altered driving behaviors, and so on.

6. Depression and combined anxiety and depression are common in the elderly and need to be addressed and treated.

7. Psychological therapies can be used effectively to treat anxiety disorders, sleep disorders, and other psychological disorders for which drugs are often prescribed.

8. As a general observation, psychoactive medications tend to be overused in the elderly rather than underused.

In this chapter, we address the pharmacology of drugs used to treat two disorders commonly seen in the elderly: Parkinson's disease (parkinsonism) and the dementias, primarily Alzheimer's disease, which is by far the most common of the dementias.

PARKINSON'S DISEASE

Chapter 11 discussed the classical neuroleptic agents used to treat schizophrenia. The most prominent side effects of those drugs are movement disorders that resemble those seen in idiopathic Parkinson's disease (parkinsonism). Mechanistically, these side effects result from drug-induced blockade of dopamine-2 receptors, resulting in a hypo-dopaminergic state.

Parkinson's disease is similarly associated with a hypodopaminergic state, characterized by a loss of dopamine neurons, most prominently in the extrapyramidal motor areas of the basal ganglia (caudate and putamen). Thus, the symptomatology of parkinsonism resembles the side effects seen with traditional neuroleptics; the goals of therapy are to replace the lost dopaminergic function and (hopefully) slow or reverse the loss of dopamine neurons.

Parkinson's disease is the second most common neurodegenerative disease, after Alzheimer's disease. Parkinsonism occurs in about 0.5 to 1 percent of people 65 to 69 years of age, rising to 1 to 3 percent of people 80 years of age and older. Although the cause of parkinsonism remains unknown, its symptoms clearly follow from a deficiency in the number and function of dopamine-secreting neurons located in the basal ganglia of the brain. Nussbaum and Ellis (2003) discuss recent progress in the genetic theories of parkinsonism. Schapira and Olanow (2004) discuss recent advances in neuroimaging techniques in parkinsonism and future neuroprotective drugs that are under development.

The clinical disease emerges when dopamine is depleted to about 20 percent of normal. In other words, the disease results when about 80 percent of dopamine neurons are lost. (Recall from Chapter 11 that the antipsychotic efficacy of neuroleptic drugs occurs when about 80 percent of dopamine-2 receptors are blocked.) The clinical syndrome of parkinsonism has four cardinal features (Colcher and Simuni, 1999;

Nussbaum and Ellis, 2003): (1) bradykinesia (slowness and poverty of movement), (2) muscle rigidity (especially a "cogwheel" rigidity), (3) resting tremor, which usually abates during voluntary movement, and (4) an impairment of postural balance leading to disturbances of gait and falling. These and other frequently seen secondary manifestations of Parkinson's disease are listed in Table 13.1.

The availability of effective treatments for the symptoms of parkinsonism has radically altered the prognosis of this disease. In most cases, good functional mobility can be maintained for many years and the life expectancy of an affected person has been greatly expanded. Replacement of the dopamine or the administration of either dopaminergic agonists or inhibitors of dopamine breakdown can restore function and ameliorate much of the symptomatology. These three approaches—dopamine replacement therapy, administration of a dopaminergic agonist, and administration of dopamine breakdown inhibitors—underlie the present-day treatment of the disease.

Levodopa

Levodopa, a precursor drug to dopamine, continues to be the mainstay of therapy for Parkinson's disease, although today it is usually used in combination therapy with other medications. Because a loss of dopamine is the primary problem in patients who have Parkinson's disease, replacement of the dopamine would be expected to ameliorate the symptoms of the disease. It does, but not by itself, because dopamine does not cross the blood-brain barrier from plasma into the CNS. In an intuitive step, the precursor compound in the biosynthesis of dopamine from the amino acid tyramine, a substance called *dihydroxyphenylalanine* or *DOPA* (Figure 13.1), crosses the blood-brain barrier and in the CNS is converted into dopamine, replacing the dopamine that is absent. Therefore, today, levodopa (the *levo* isomer being more active than the *dextro* isomer) is the most effective treatment for parkinsonian motor disability, and many practitioners consider an initial beneficial response an important diagnostic criterion for the diagnosis of parkinsonism (Hughes, 1997).

Mechanism of Action

Levodopa is itself largely inert; its therapeutic as well as its adverse effects result from its conversion to dopamine (Standaert and Young, 2001). Administered orally, levodopa is rapidly absorbed into the bloodstream, where most of it (about 95 percent) is converted to dopamine in the plasma. Although only a small amount (about 1 to 5 percent) of levodopa crosses the blood-brain barrier and is converted to dopamine in the brain, it is enough to alleviate the symptoms of

TABLE 13.1 Clinical features of Parkinson's disease

CARDINAL MANIFESTATIONS
  Resting tremor
  Bradykinesia (akinesia, hypokinesia)
  Cogwheel rigidity
  Postural reflex impairment

SECONDARY MANIFESTATIONS

  Cognitive
    Dementia
    Bradyphrenia
    Visuospatial deficits, impaired
      attention and executive function

  Psychiatric
    Depression
    Anxiety
    Sleep disturbances
    Sexual dysfunction

  Craniofacial
    Masked facies
    Decreased eye blinking
    Blurred vision (impaired
      accommodation)
    Olfactory hypofunction
    Dysarthria (soft, palilalic speech)
    Dysphagia
    Sialorrhea

  Autonomic
    Orthostatic hypotension
    Impaired gastrointestinal motility
      Constipation, dysphagia,
        sensation of fullness
    Urinary bladder dysfunction
      Urgency, frequency, loss of control
    Abnormal thermoregulation,
      increased sweating

  Sensory
    Cramps
    Paresthesia
    Pain
    Numbness, tingling

  Musculoskeletal
    Scoliosis
    Wrist and foot dystonia
    Peripheral edema

  Skin
    Seborrhea

  Other
    Micrographia
    Weight loss

From Colcher and Simuni (1999), pp. 329–330.

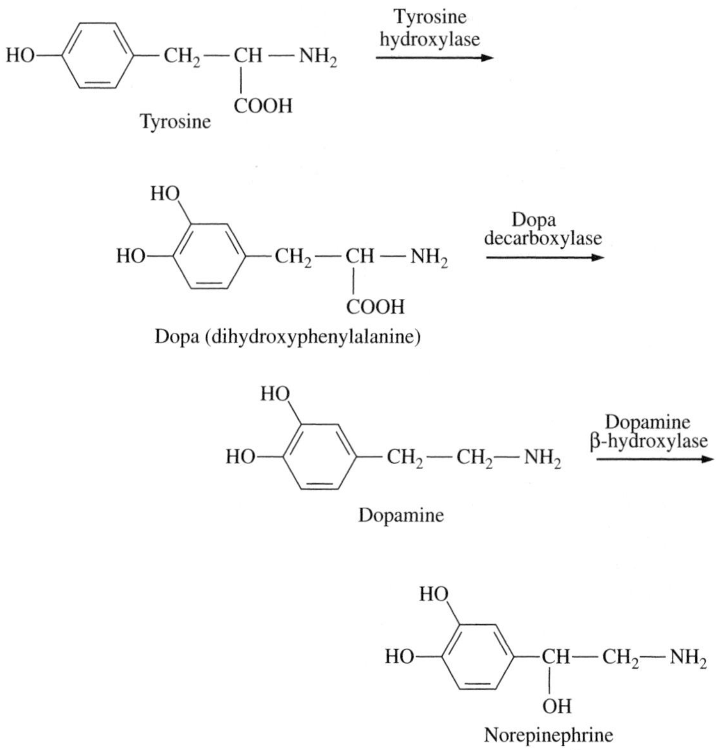

FIGURE 13.1 Synthesis of dopamine from tyrosine.

parkinsonism. In the CNS, levodopa is converted to dopamine, primarily within the presynaptic terminals of dopaminergic neurons in the basal ganglia.

One problem with this therapy is that, when levodopa is administered by itself, large amounts are destroyed by enzymes located both in the intestine and in plasma, so that little drug is available to cross the blood-brain barrier. In addition, the levodopa in the peripheral circulation is converted to dopamine in the body, resulting in undesirable side effects, such as nausea. Back to basic pharmacology. One approach to solving the problem is to reduce the high levels of dopamine in the systemic circulation while maintaining sufficient quantities in the brain. To do this, the biosynthetic pathway that leads to dopamine (see Figure 13.1) must be examined. Since the enzyme *dopa decarboxylase* is responsible for converting dopa to dopamine, by inhibiting this enzyme in the systemic circulation but not in the brain, systemic biotransformation of the drug should be reduced, with a concomitant reduction in blood levels of dopamine and therefore in side effects. The drug would need a unique characteristic: it would have to be active in the body but not cross the blood-brain barrier into the brain. Thus, the metabolic conversion would occur in the CNS but not in the periphery.

An example of such a drug is *carbidopa*, which is available in combination with levodopa (the combination is marketed as Sinemet). By combining carbidopa with levodopa, the effective dose of levodopa is reduced by 75 percent, with a concomitant reduction in side effects and no loss of CNS therapeutic effect. The current treatment of parkinsonism relies heavily on the use of Sinemet, and it is the standard of current symptomatic treatment for Parkinson's disease (Hauser and Zesiewicz, 1999). The combination of levodopa and carbidopa provides near maximal therapeutic benefit with the fewest side effects.

COMT Inhibitors

Recently, a new advance has been made in the Parkinson's therapeutic regimen. Even with the Sinemet combination, much of an oral dose of levodopa is wasted. The enzyme *catechol-o-methyltransferase (COMT)* in the vasculature of the gastrointestinal tract and liver converts levodopa to an inactive metabolite with no clinical benefit. The half-life and clinical effects of Sinemet can be increased with the addition of a COMT-inhibitory drug. In 1998, the first of these drugs—*tolcapone* (Tasmar)—was introduced; it blocks the COMT enzyme, increasing the half-life of L-dopa and prolonging its effect. Unfortunately, tolcapone has caused a few cases of serious liver toxicity, so in late 1998 it was withdrawn from the market in Canada and in Europe. In the United States, its use is restricted to cases where all other adjunctive therapies have failed. A second COMT inhibitor, *entacapone,* became available in 2001 under the trade name Comtan; entacapone has not yet been associated with liver toxicity (*Medical Letter,* 2000; Holm and Spencer, 1999). Like tolcapone, entacapone inhibits peripheral COMT; it does not alter central COMT. Inhibition of peripheral degradation of levodopa increases central levodopa and, therefore, central dopamine concentrations. Coadministration of entacapone with levodopa plus carbidopa potentiates the effects of levodopa in patients with Parkinson's disease and reduces the so-called wearing-off phenomenon (within 1 or 2 years of taking levodopa plus carbidopa—Sinemet—the beneficial effects of therapy last for progressively shorter and shorter periods of time after each dose). In 15 to 20 percent of patients, the result may be extreme and disabling: doses that originally were effective for 8 hours last for only 1 or 2 hours.

In 2004, the FDA approved a fixed combination product containing levodopa, carbidopa, and entacapone (available under the trade name Stalevo). As noted, the carbidopa increases the amounts of dopamine in the brain while the entacapone inhibits the degradation of dopamine through inhibition of its degragative enzyme COMT. The combination provides more dopamine to the brain for a longer period of time, providing more "on time" and less "wearing off" associated with each dose of the drug (Hauser, 2004).

Limitations of Levodopa Therapy

As just discussed, as time goes on, each dose of levodopa becomes less effective and the patient's symptoms fluctuate dramatically between doses, eventually developing into the wearing-off phenomenon. Part of the phenomenon is due to the short half-life of levodopa and can be minimized by increasing the dose, by decreasing the interval between doses, and by adding entacapone. This adjustment, however, risks the development of levodopa-induced movement disorders (for example, dyskinesias), which can be as uncomfortable and disabling as the rigidity and akinesia of parkinsonism.

An unanswered question with levodopa therapy is whether or not this drug adversely accelerates the course of parkinsonism. One theory of the disease is that the metabolism of dopamine produces free radicals that contribute to the death of the dopamine-releasing neurons. Oxidative stress may therefore be an important precipitating mechanism, and neuroprotective drugs might eventually be of more use in prevention of the disease. Simon and Standaert (1999) first discussed possible therapeutic strategies that might eventually be used to reduce or eliminate oxidative stress. For the present, however, there is continuing concern that ameliorating symptoms may be aggravating the disease. Thus, initiation of levodopa therapy is often delayed until the symptoms of parkinsonism actually cause an unacceptable degree of functional impairment. It leaves the clinician in a quandary about how to treat early stages of parkinsonism.

Dopamine Receptor Agonists

Between one and five years after the start of levodopa therapy, most patients gradually become less responsive. One hypothesis for this effect is that the progression of parkinsonism may be associated with a progressive inability of dopamine neurons to synthesize and store dopamine. To relieve this problem, attempts have been made to identify drugs that will directly stimulate postsynaptic dopamine receptors in the basal ganglia. These drugs do not depend on the ability of existing dopaminergic neurons to synthesize dopamine. In addition, if the free radical theory described in the previous paragraph is accepted, these drugs would avoid the biotransformation of dopamine into potentially neurotoxic metabolites. These drugs might be effective in the later stages of parkinsonism, when dopamine neurons are largely absent or nonfunctional. In addition, they are increasingly being advocated for use in early stages of parkinsonism, especially in patients younger than about 65 years.

Four dopamine receptor agonists are currently available for the treatment of parkinsonism (Figure 13.2): *bromocriptine* (Parlodel), *pergolide* (Permax), *pramipexole* (Mirapex), and *ropinirole* (Requip). Bromocriptine has been available since 1978, pergolide since 1989, and both have structures that closely resemble that of dopamine. They

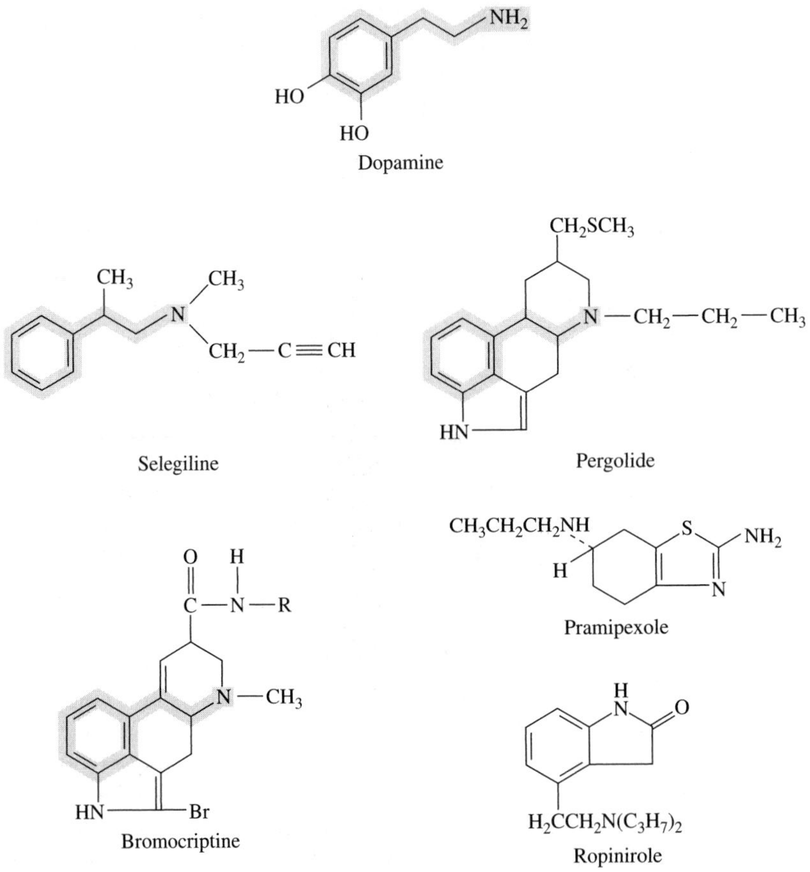

FIGURE 13.2 Structures of dopamine, selegiline, and four dopamine receptor agonists that are used to treat parkinsonism. The shaded portions, which are shared by selegiline, bromocriptine, and pergolide, resemble dopamine. The two newer dopamine receptor agonists are structurally unique and have greater affinity for dopamine-3 receptors than do older dopamine receptor agonists (which stimulate dopamine-2 receptors).

are considered to be only marginally effective, and they have a number of bothersome side effects (Factor, 1999).

Pramipexole and ropinirole were marketed in 1997. They have less affinity for dopamine-2 receptors than the older drugs; their affinity for dopamine-3 receptors is greater. The significance of the dopamine-3 receptor specificity is unclear. Also unlike the older two drugs, pramipexole and ropinirole are indicated for use in early-onset parkinsonism: their efficacy and safety profile is much better than that of the two older drugs. Both can increase quality of life in the early stages of the disease by improving motor features and decreasing fluctuations in response to levodopa (Hauser and Zesiewicz, 1999). Their long half-lives may at least partially explain the reduction in the wearing-off phenomenon seen with levodopa therapy.

Side effects of dopamine agonists include somnolence, dizziness, nausea, hallucinations, and insomnia. Frucht and coworkers (1999) described eight patients on the newer dopamine agonists who experienced sudden attacks of falling asleep at the wheel while taking the drug and driving. Sleep attacks also occurred during other activities. Modafinil (Provigil) can reduce the daytime somnolence. Alternatively, the attacks cease when the agonist is stopped. In reviewing the topic of dopamine agonists, Factor (1999) concluded:

> There is much talk about what properties are essential to an ideal antiparkinson drug. Such a drug has a central site of action, mimics dopamine, activates postsynaptic receptors, lacks potency for presynaptic receptors on dying cell terminals, and has no requirements for metabolic conversion. Dopamine agonists fulfill many of these requirements but still lack the potency of L-dopa, which for all its faults is still the best antiparkinson drug available today. Therefore, there is no ideal drug, but there is an acceptable standard of treatment, which currently is a combination of L-dopa and the dopamine agonists. As dopamine agonists are refined and improved, the medical community will move closer to providing patients with a still higher standard of care and an enhanced quality of life. (p. 439)

Selegiline

Selegiline (Eldepryl) effectively ameliorates the symptoms of parkinsonism through a unique mechanism. The enzyme monoamine oxidase (MAO) exists in two forms (isoenzymes): MAO-A and MAO-B. Both are present in the brain; MAO-A is more closely involved with norepinephrine and serotonin nerve terminals, while MAO-B has preferential affinity for dopamine neurons located in the basal ganglia (striatum). Selegiline selectively and irreversibly inhibits MAO-B. Similarly, selegiline inhibits the local breakdown of dopamine, thus preserving the small amounts of dopamine that are present. Both actions enhance the therapeutic effect of levodopa. Unlike the nonselective MAO inhibitors used as clinical antidepressants (Chapter 9), selegiline does not inhibit peripheral metabolism of levodopa; thus it can safely be taken with levodopa (Standaert and Young, 2001). Selegiline also does not have the severe interactions and dangers when combined with tyramine-containing foods. However, if doses of selegiline are increased over 10 milligrams daily, the drug inhibits MAO-A; large doses should be avoided. Standaert and Young (2001) review possible neuroprotective properties of selegiline.

Selegiline is being used increasingly in the treatment of newly diagnosed, younger patients who have Parkinson's disease because it appears to slow down the early progression of the disease and delays the need for initiating levodopa therapy. Interestingly, selegiline is metabolized to several by-products, including amphetamine and methamphetamine. These metabolic by-products may account for some of the side effects associated with the use of selegiline. Attempts are underway to find routes of delivery for selegiline that bypass intestinal absorption and first-pass metabolism; an example is the selegiline skin patch, recently approved and made available for the treatment of major depression. No reports are yet available for the use of this preparation in the treatment of Parkinson's disease (Mahmood, 2002).

Selegiline should be used with caution. A 1995 report from the United Kingdom stated that, in combination with levodopa, selegiline may be associated with a significant increase in morbidity after five years of use. A more recent analysis of these data showed that, while mortality is increased with selegiline use, the increase is only about half as large as originally thought. These data are currently quite controversial. The reason for a possible increase in mortality remains unclear. Ben-Shlomo and colleagues (1998) offer some possible explanations.

Muscarinic Receptor Antagonists

Although widely used before the introduction of levodopa, certain anticholinergic agents (muscarinic antagonists) are now used much less and are considered second-tier agents for the treatment of symptoms of parkinsonism. Their use was originally postulated on the basis of an unopposed cholinergic system after death of the dopaminergic neurons.

Occasionally, anticholinergic drugs are used as an adjunct to levodopa in patients with difficult-to-control tremors. Anticholinergic drugs relieve tremor in about 50 percent of patients, but they do not reduce rigidity or bradykinesia. Cognitive dysfunction limits their use, especially in the elderly, who may have an underlying cognitive disorder (Lu and Tune, 2003). Representative agents include *trihexyphenidyl* (Artane), *procyclidine* (Kemadrin), *biperiden* (Akineton), *ethopropazine*

(Parsidol), and *benztropine* (Cogentin). Occasionally, the antihistaminic drug *diphenhydramine* (Benadryl) is also used (Benadryl has significant anticholinergic properties).

Amantadine and Memantine

Amantadine (Symmetrel) is an antiviral agent (used to treat viral influenza) with modest antiparkinsonian actions. Its mechanism of action in parkinsonism is unclear; it might alter dopamine release or reuptake, or it might have anticholinergic properties. Amantadine and a related drug, *memantine,* are active at NMDA-type glutaminergic receptors (discussed later in the treatment of Alzheimer's disease); this action perhaps offers a degree of "brain protection" that may contribute to its antiparkinsonian effects. Side effects are usually mild and reversible.

Interestingly, as an NMDA antagonist, amantadine also exhibits analgesic activity, reducing postoperative pain and morphine consumption (Snijdelaar et al., 2004). This action requires further study and delineation.

CEP-1347

In late 2002, a two-year study involving 800 patients at 65 research sites in the United States and Canada was undertaken to evaluate the antiparkinsonian effects of a new, unique agent code named CEP-1347. This agent exhibits neuroprotective effects, enhancing the survival of brain neurons that produce dopamine. Mechanistically, dopaminergic neurons in the basal ganglia are hypothesized to undergo cell death by a process called *apoptosis.* As a neurodegenerative disease, the ultimate treatment of parkinsonism may involve the functional restoration and/or cessation of progression of cell loss, not merely replacement of lost transmitter (Saporito et al., 2002). CEP-1347 is considered as an inhibitor of the mixed linkage kinase (MLK) family of enzymes (more simply, a *kinase apoptosis inhibitor*) (Bilsland and Harper, 2003). It is hoped that its action may help protect dopaminergic neurons, offering for the first time a protective action against the progression of this neurodegenerative disease (Wang et al., 2004).

Rasagiline

Rasagiline is a novel antiparkinsonian drug currently in clinical trial. Rasagiline is a potent and irreversible inhibitor of a subtype (type B) of the enzyme *monoamine oxidase* (Finberg and Youdim, 2002). It appears to be well tolerated and effective as single-drug therapy in early parkinsonism, at least over a 26-week period of trial administration

(Parkinson Study Group, 2002). Mechanistically, rasagiline appears to possess a neuroprotective action against the progression of parkinsonism, certainly a new approach to treating this devastating disease (Bar-Am et al., 2004).

ALZHEIMER'S DISEASE

Alzeimer's disease (AD) is the most common neurodegenerative disease and it accounts for about two-thirds of all cases of dementia, with vascular causes and other rarer, neurodegenerative diseases making up the majority of the remaining cases (Nussbaum and Ellis, 2003). AD is a progressive neurodegenerative disease that results in the irreversible loss of neurons, particularly in the cerebral cortex and hippocampus. Onset occurs generally after 60 years of age but is earlier in rare cases. Its prevalence is about 1 percent among people 65 to 69 years of age and increases with age to 40 or 50 percent among persons 95 years of age and older (Figure 13.3). In essence, prevalence doubles every 5 years

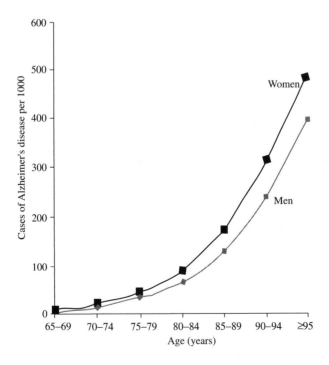

FIGURE 13.3 Prevalence of Alzheimer's disease as a function of age in men and women. [From Nussbaum and Ellis (2003), p. 1357.]

after age 65, projecting an increase of the disease from 2.32 million cases in the late 1990s to 8.64 million by the year 2047 (Figure 13.4) (Grossberg, 2003).

Time between symptom onset and death may span 8 to 10 years. The gradual and continuous decline caused by AD is characterized by cognitive deterioration, changes in behavior, loss of functional independence, and increasing requirements for care (Grossberg, 2003). Hallmarks of AD include progressive impairment in memory, judgment, decision making, orientation to physical surroundings, and language. Dementia (defined as cognitive impairment with the inability to form recent memory) is the critical feature of AD. Diagnosis is based on neurological examination and the exclusion of other causes of dementia. A definitive diagnosis can be made only at autopsy. Nussbaum and Ellis (2003) and Wenk (2003) review the neuropathological changes seen in AD.

Current treatments for mild to moderate AD involve primarily the *acetylcholinesterase inhibitors (AChE-I,* or *cholinesterase inhibitors)* (Doody, 2003). One new drug, *memantine,* was introduced in 2004 for the treatment of more severe cases of AD. The economic impact of these medications is important. It is currently estimated that the costs of informal and formal care for one patient with mild (early-onset) AD is about $1500 monthly, a patient with moderate AD $2100, and a patient with severe (advanced) AD $3100 (these costs escalate markedly when nursing home care is needed). Use of a cholinesterase inhibitor can be associated with a savings of over

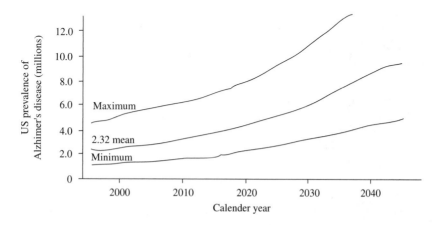

FIGURE 13.4 Projected prevalence of Alzheimer's disease from 1997 to 2047. 1997 prevalence 2.32 million. [From R. Brookmeyer et al., "Projections of Alzheimer's Disease in the United States and the Public Health Impact of Delaying Disease Onset," *American Journal of Public Health* 88 (1998), p. 1340.]

$9000 (or 7.5 percent of total expenditure) from diagnosis to death (Grossberg, 2003). Savings are attributable to reduced nursing home care because patients may remain more functional for a longer period of time before nursing home care is needed. Reducing nursing home entrance by only one year equates to enormous savings. AChE-I medications, however, only delay onset of AD; they do not cure or prevent AD. Current therapy is therefore discouraging. More encouraging is the recent introduction of medications that may offer a degree of neuroprotection.

AD is associated not only with cognitive impairments but with a myriad of bothersome mood alterations and behavioral symptoms that pose further challenges to treatment:

- Depression with AD is common and is usually treated with antidepressant medications that lack substantial anticholinergic side effects. Thus, SSRIs are used rather than the tricyclic agents (Chapter 9). An example: Lyketsos and coworkers (2003) demonstrated the beneficial effects of sertraline (Zoloft).

- Treatments for apathy may be considered. Drugs employed include psychostimulants, the antidepressant bupropion, the dopamine receptor agonist bromocriptine, and the antiparkinsonian agent amantadine. Memantine, an agent similar to amantadine, has recently been approved for AD.

- Psychosis, agitation, and other behavioral disturbances may require treatment with a newer atypical antipsychotic agent (Chapter 11). Benzodiazepines and other sedatives are associated with worsening cognition and falls and should be avoided.

- Of possible benefit in treating behavioral symptoms are the mood stabilizers (Chapter 10) (Porsteinsson et al., 2003), the sedating antidepressant trazodone (Chapter 9), and the SSRIs.

Currently, no treatment can prevent or cure AD. Cholinesterase inhibitors (of which four are approved for the treatment of AD) can delay the onset of symptoms. Estrogen replacement (for women), antioxidants (for examples, vitamin E), and nonsteroidal anti-inflammatory drugs (NSAIDs; Chapter 14) all may have some usefulness. Of these, vitamin E, either alone or in combination with an AchE-I, may prevent further cognitive decline among patients with moderate AD (Sano, 2003). Ginkgo biloba (Chapter 16) has been shown to be relatively ineffective in improving cognitive function in patients with AD (Mintzer, 2003). Selegiline (discussed in the Parkinson's section) can be as effective as vitamin E, but selegiline is associated with more side effects.

Acetylcholinesterase Inhibitors

There is now considerable evidence that deficits in the functioning of acetylcholine-secreting neurons (cholinergic deficits) are strongly correlated with cognitive impairments seen in AD (Giacobini, 2003). Patients with severe AD show AChE (cholinesterase enzyme) levels that are 60 to 85 percent lower than normal, which implies very little residual AChE in the cortex—a condition that is still compatible with life but no longer optimal for brain function (Giacobini, 2003). Today, a cholinergic dysfunction hypothesis of AD suggests that the disease results from a selective loss in cholinergic neurons, accounting for the decrease in AChE levels (Jones, 2003).

The most successful effort to increase cholinergic functioning has been to target the AChE enzyme, inhibition of which increases levels of acetylcholine in the brain. Trinh and coworkers (2003) suggest a trial of acetylcholinesterase inhibitors (AChE-Is) in patients with mild to moderate AD who exhibit neuropsychiatric and/or functional impairments.

Four drugs have been approved by the FDA for the treatment of AD: *tacrine* (Cognex), *donepezil* (Aricept), *rivastigmine* (Excelon), and *galantamine* (Reminyl). Each improves cholinergic neurotransmission by preventing the synaptic breakdown of acetylcholine in the brain. These drugs can produce modest improvements in cognition, but their side effects include nausea, diarrhea, abdominal cramping, and anorexia. These side effects result from inhibition of AChE in the periphery (in the body), not from the elevations of acetylcholine in the brain. In small numbers of patients receiving AChE-I medication, drug-induced, reversible increases in aggressive behaviors may be seen; these are reversible with drug discontinuation (or dosage reductions), and treatment with antipsychotic drugs (without stopping the AChE-I) is inappropriate (Bianchetti et al., 2003). The modest efficacy combined with these side effects tends to limit therapeutic usefulness of these agents.

Tacrine was the first of these agents to be approved; it is now the least used of the four, primarily because it needs frequent administration and can cause a reversible toxicity in the liver (elevates liver enzymes in up to 50 percent of patients taking the drug). Donepezil, rivastigmine, and galantamine are not associated with the liver toxicity that limits the use of tacrine (Standaert and Young, 2001).

Donepezil appears to be more selective for AChE in the brain rather than in the periphery. It has a long half-life and produces fewer gastrointestinal side effects. It is much more tolerable than tacrine. Wilkinson and coworkers (2003) reported very modest efficacy of donepezil in 616 patients with vascular dementia; the results were of dubious clinical significance.

Rivastigmine is clinically effective, producing modest improvements in cognitive functioning. It is better tolerated than tacrine but somewhat less so than donepezil. In contrast to the other three agents, rivastigmine causes a very slowly reversible inhibition of AChE, prolonging its therapeutic action (Darreh-Shori et al., 2002).

Galantamine appears to have a safety and efficacy profile similar to that of rivastigmine in measures of both cognitive functioning and functional ability. Doody (2003) critically reviews the research results with these four drugs and their effectiveness in treating AD. She concludes:

> Cholinesterase inhibitors have positive effects compared with placebo in the treatment of AD—affecting cognition, function, and behavioral outcomes. They are effective in mild to moderate disease, and preliminary data suggest that this effect is mirrored in severe disease as well. . . .
>
> There are limitations to these medications, however, because although stabilization occurs, there is typically only a modest improvement from baseline. Additionally, the effects are not sustained indefinitely, and the disease continues to progress even while patients are receiving treatment with cholinesterase inhibitors. Adverse effects are manageable, and with careful titration, patients can tolerate increases quite well; however, side effects can include diarrhea, nausea, vomiting, dyspepsia, asthenia, dizziness, headache, weight loss, and even anorexia—sometimes to such an extreme that patients must discontinue treatment. Additional therapies for AD need to be developed that include highly tolerable agents with alternative mechanisms of action and broader efficacy to delay disease onset, arrest the disease, and even reverse the progression of the disease entirely. Until these new therapies are developed, the cholinesterase inhibitors will remain important treatments for AD. (p. 17)

Memantine

As discussed in Chapter 3, *glutamate* is the principal excitatory neurotransmitter in the brain. Glutaminergic overactivity may result in neuronal damage, a phenomenon termed *excitotoxicity*. Excitotoxicity ultimately leads to neuronal calcium overload and has been implicated in neurodegenerative disorders. In addition, glutaminergic NMDA receptor activity appears to be important in memory processes, dementia, and the pathogenesis of AD (Reisberg et al., 2003). Glutaminergic overstimulation at NMDA receptors is thought to be toxic to neurons, and prevention of this neurotoxicity affords a degree of brain protection to limit further deterioration.

Memantine (Namenda) is a new "moderate-affinity" noncompetitive NMDA receptor antagonist that has been shown to reduce clinical deterioration in patients with moderate to severe AD, a phase associated with significant distress for patients and caregivers alike and for which no other treatments are available (Reisberg et al., 2003). It appears to have therapeutic potential without the undesirable side effects associated with "high-affinity" NMDA antagonists such as ketamine (Chapter 19). Available in Germany since 1982, it became available for use in the United States in 2004.

Like other NMDA antagonists, high brain concentrations of memantine can inhibit glutaminergic mechanisms of synaptic plasticity that are believed to underlie learning and memory (Chapter 3). In other words, at high doses, memantine can produce the same amnestic effects as does ketamine. However, at lower, clinically relevant doses, memantine can promote cellular plasticity and can preserve or enhance memory (Danysz and Parsons, 2003). In adults, low doses can protect against the excitotoxic destruction of cholinergic neurons. Rogawski and Wenk (2003) postulate that memantine could theoretically confer disease-modifying activity in AD by inhibiting the "weak" NMDA receptor-dependent excitotoxicity that has been hypothesized to play a role in the progressive neuronal loss that underlies the evolving dementia.

These researchers also discuss other potential actions that may further differentiate memantine from the stronger NMDA antagonists-psychedelics-amnestics such as ketamine. As a "weak" NMDA antagonist, memantine may reduce overactive NMDA receptor activity that would be neurotoxic, while sparing synaptic responsiveness required for normal behavioral functioning, cognition, and memory.

Several clinical studies have now shown that in moderate to severe AD (and in vascular dementia), memantine consistently (yet modestly) improves cognition in the absence of significant side effects (example studies: Mobius, 2003; Orgogozo et al., 2002; Reisberg et al., 2003; Wilcock et al., 2002). The *Medical Letter* (2003) summarized:

> Memantine has been modestly effective in some U.S. studies in improving performance in patients with moderate-to-severe AD. There is no evidence that memantine has any effect in earlier stages of AD, or that it alters the course of the disease. (p. 74)

Wimo and coworkers (2003) delineated the considerable cost savings of using memantine, reflected as reductions in caretaker time in treated versus placebo-treated patients. It appears that memantine may safely be combined with cholinesterase inhibitors; the combination is safe, effective, and well tolerated (Hartman and Mobius, 2003; Tariot et al., 2004). As concluded by Tariot and coworkers:

> In patients with moderate to severe Alzheimer's disease receiving stable doses of donepezil (a cholinesterase inhibitor), memantine resulted in significantly better outcomes than placebo on measures of cognition, activities of daily living, global outcome, and behavior and was well tolerated. These results, together with previous studies, suggest that memantine represents a new approach for the treatment of patients with moderate to severe Alzheimer's disease. (p. 317)

Investigational Drugs

Alzhemed, a potential new treatment for AD, is currently in clinical trial. Alzhemed is designed to prevent and stop the formation and depositing of beta amyloid fibrils in the brain and to prevent the inflammatory response associated with this amyloid buildup. In mice, alzhemed reduces amyloid beta plasma levels by 60 percent and brain levels of amyloid fibrils by 30 percent after eight weeks of treatment. As amyloid fibrils serve as a marker for AD, this effect may be a significant and important.

Ampalex (CX516) is a modulator of glutaminergic AMPA-type receptors (see Chapter 3). In studies in schizophrenic patients, ampalex was noted to improve both negative symptomatology and cognitive functioning. This finding implies potential usefulness in AD, although clinical trials have not been reported.

NS-2330 is a new compound that increases the activity of dopaminergic, noradrenergic, and cholinergic neurons. It is currently being evaluated for the treatment of AD (Thatte, 2001). Other information on this agent has not yet been reported.

STUDY QUESTIONS

1. What is Parkinson's disease?
2. What does it share in common with traditional neuroleptic drugs? Why?
3. List the various ways that dopaminergic action in the brain might be augmented or potentiated.
4. Explain how carbidopa potentiates the action of levodopa.
5. Explain how a COMT inhibitor potentiates the action of levodopa.
6. Differentiate the newer from the older dopamine receptor agonists.

7. How does selegiline work in the treatment of Parkinson's disease?

8. Besides drugs, how might parkinsonism be managed? List the nonpharmacologic options.

9. What is the currently accepted hypothesis for the genesis of Alzheimer's disease?

10. What are the currently available medications used to treat Alzheimer's disease?

11. Differentiate cholinesterase inhibitors from each other and from memantine.

12. How is glutamate involved in the action of memantine and how does this involvement relate to neuroprotection?

REFERENCES

Bar-Am, O., et al. (2004). "Contrasting Neuroprotective and Neurotoxic Actions of Respective Metabolites of Anti-Parkinson Drugs Rasagiline and Selegiline." *Neuroscience Letters* 355: 169–172.

Ben-Shlomo, Y., et al. (1998). "Investigation by Parkinson's Disease Research Group of United Kingdom into Excess Mortality Seen with Combined Levodopa and Selegiline Treatment in Patients with Early, Mild Parkinson's Disease: Further Results of Randomized Trial and Confidential Inquiry." *British Medical Journal* 316: 1191–1196.

Bianchetti, A., et al. (2003). "Aggressive Behavior Associated with Donepezil Treatment: A Case Report." *International Journal of Geriatric Psychiatry* 18: 657–658.

Bilsland, J. G., and S. J. Harper (2003). "CEP-1347 Promotes Survival of NGF Responsive Neurons in Primary DRG Explants." *Neuroreport* 14: 995–999.

Colcher, A., and T. Simuni (1999). "Clinical Manifestations of Parkinson's Disease." *Medical Clinics of North America* 83: 327–347.

Danysz, W., and C. G. Parsons (2003). "The NMDA Receptor Antagonist Memantine as a Symptomatological and Neuroprotective Treatment for Alzheimer's Disease: Preclinical Evidence." *International Journal of Geriatric Psychiatry* 18, Supplement 1: S23–S32.

Darreh-Shori, T., et al. (2002). "Sustained Cholinesterase Inhibition in AD Patients Receiving Rivastigmine for 12 Months." *Neurology* 59: 563–572.

Doody, R. S. (2003). "Current Treatments for Alzheimer's Disease: Cholinesterase Inhibitors." *Journal of Clinical Psychiatry* 64, Supplement 9: 11–17.

Factor, S. A. (1999). "Dopamine Agonists." *Medical Clinics of North America* 83: 415–443.

Finberg, J. P., and M. B. Youdim (2002). "Pharmacological Properties of the Anti-Parkinson Drug Rasagiline: Modification of Endogenous Brain Amines, Reserpine Reversal, Serotonergic and Dopaminergic Behaviors." *Neuropharmacology* 43: 1110–1118.

Frucht, S., et al. (1999). "Falling Asleep at the Wheel: Motor Vehicle Mishaps in Persons Taking Pramipexole and Ropinirole." *Neurology* 52: 1908–1910.

Giacobini, E. (2003). "Cholinergic Function and Alzheimer's Disease." *International Journal of Geriatric Psychiatry* 18: S1–S5.

Grossberg, G. T. (2003). "Diagnosis and Treatment of Alzheimer's Disease." *Journal of Clinical Psychiatry* 64, Supplement 9: 3–6.

Hartman, S., and H. J. Mobius (2003). "Tolerability of Memantine in Combination with Cholinesterase Inhibitors in Dementia Therapy." *International Clinical Psychopharmacology* 18: 81–85.

Hauser, R. A. (2004). "Levodopa/Carbidopa/Entacapone (Stalevo)." *Neurology* 62, Supplement 1: 564–574.

Hauser, R. A., and T. A. Zesiewicz (1999). "Management of Early Parkinson's Disease." *Medical Clinics of North America* 83: 393–414.

Holm, K. J., and C. M. Spencer (1999). "Entacapone: A Review of Its Use in Parkinson's Disease." *Drugs* 58: 159–177.

Hughes, A. J. (1997). "Drug Treatment of Parkinson's Disease in the 1990s: Achievements and Future Possibilities." *Drugs* 53: 195–205.

Jones, R. W. (2003). "Have Cholinergic Therapies Reached Their Clinical Boundary in Alzheimer's Disease?" *International Journal of Geriatric Psychiatry* 18: S7–S13.

Lyketsos, C., et al. (2003). "Treating Depression in Alzheimer's Disease. Efficacy and Safety of Sertraline Therapy, and the Benefits of Depression Reduction: The DIADS." *Archives of General Psychiatry* 60: 737–746.

Lu, C., and L. Tune (2003). "Chronic Exposure to Anticholinergic Medications Adversely Affects the Course of Alzheimer's Disease." *American Journal of Geriatric Psychiatry* 11: 458–461.

Mahmood, I., (2002). "Selegiline Transdermal System: Somerset." *Current Opinions on Investigational Drugs* 3: 1230–1233.

Medical Letter (2000). "Entacapone for Parkinson's Disease." *Medical Letter on Drugs and Therapeutics* 42 (January 24): 7–8.

Medical Letter (2003). "Memantine for Alzheimer's Disease." *Medical Letter on Drugs and Therapeutics* 45 (September 15): 73–74.

Mintzer, J. E. (2003). "The Search for Better Noncholinergic Treatment Options for Alzheimer's Disease." *Journal of Clinical Psychiatry* 64, Supplement 9: 18–22.

Mobius, H. J. (2003). "Memantine: Update on the Current Evidence." *International Journal of Geriatric Psychiatry* 18, Supplement 1: S47–S54.

Nussbaum, R. L., and C. E. Ellis (2003). "Alzheimer's Disease and Parkinson's Disease." *New England Journal of Medicine* 348: 1356–1364.

Orgogozo, J. M., et al. (2002). "Efficacy and Safety of Memantine in Patients with Mild to Moderate Vascular Dementia: A Randomized, Placebo-Controlled Trial (MMM300)." *Stroke* 33: 1834–1839.

Parkinson Study Group (2002). "A Controlled Trial of Rasagiline in Early Parkinson Disease: The TEMPO Study." *Archives of Neurology* 59: 1937–1943.

Porsteinsson, A., et al. (2003). "Valproate Therapy for Agitation in Dementia: Open-Label Extension of a Double-Blind Trial." *Journal of Geriatric Psychiatry* 11: 434–440.

Reisberg, B., et al. (2003). "Memantine in Moderate-to-Severe Alzheimer's Disease." *New England Journal of Medicine* 348: 1333–1341.

Rogawski, M. A., and G. L. Wenk (2003). "The Neuropharmacological Basis for the Use of Memantine in the Treatment of Alzheimer's Disease." *CNS Drug Reviews* 9: 275–308.

Sano, M. (2003). "Noncholinergic Treatment Options for Alzheimer's Disease." *Journal of Clinical Psychiatry* 64, Supplement 9: 23–28.

Saporito, M. S., et al. (2002). "Discovery of CEP-1347/KT-7515, an Inhibitor of the JNK/SAPK Pathway for the Treatment of Neurodegenerative Diseases." *Progress in Medicinal Chemistry* 40: 23–62.

Schapira, A. H. V., and C. W. Olanow (2004). "Neuroprotection in Parkinson Disease: Mysteries, Myths, and Misconceptions." *Journal of the American Medical Association* 291: 358–364.

Simon, D. K., and D. G. Standaert (1999). "Neuroprotective Therapies." *Medical Clinics of North America* 83: 509–523.

Snijdelaar, D. G., et al. (2004). "Effects of Perioperative Oral Amantadine on Postoperative Pain and Morphine Consumption in Patients After Radical Prostatectomy." *Anesthesiology* 100: 134–141.

Standaert, D. G., and A. B. Young (2001). "Treatment of Central Nervous System Degenerative Disorders." In J. G. Hardman, L. E. Limbird, and A. G. Gilman, eds., *Goodman and Gilman's The Pharmacological Basis of Therapeutics,* 10th ed. (pp. 549–568). New York: McGraw-Hill.

Tariot, P. N., et al. (2004). "Memantine Treatment in Patients with Moderate to Severe Alzheimer Disease Already Receiving Donepezil: A Randomized Controlled Trial." *Journal of the American Medical Association* 291: 317–324.

Thatte, U. (2001). "NS-2330." *Current Opinions on Investigational Drugs* 2: 1592–1594.

Trinh, N., et al. (2003). "Efficacy of Cholinesterase Inhibitors in the Treatment of Neuropsychiatric Symptoms and Functional Impairment in Alzheimer's Disease: A Meta-Analysis." *Journal of the American Medical Association* 289: 210–216.

Wang, L. H., et al. (2004). "Mixed-Lineage Kinases: A Target for the Prevention of Neurodegeneration." *Annual Reviews of Pharmacology and Toxicology* 44: 451–474.

Wenk, G. L. (2003). "Neuropathologic Changes in Alzheimer's Disease." *Journal of Clinical Psychiatry* 64, Supplement 9: 7-10.

Wilcock, G., et al. (2002). "A Double-Blind, Placebo-Controlled Multicentre Trial of Memantine in Mild to Moderate Vascular Dementia (MMM 500)." *International Clinical Psychopharmacology* 17: 297–305.

Wilkinson, D., et al. (2003). "Donepezil in Vascular Dementia: A Randomized, Placebo-Controlled Study." *Neurology* 61: 479–486.

Wimo, A., et al. (2003). "Resource Utilization and Cost Analysis of Memantine in Patients with Moderate to Severe Alzheimer's Disease." *Pharmacoeconomics* 21: 327–340.

Special Topics in Psychotherapeutics

Part 5 focuses on four special topics in psychopharmacology. First are two chapters dealing with the pharmacology of drugs used to treat pain. Chapter 14 covers the nonnarcotic or nonopioid analgesics, such as aspirin. Important with these agents is their ability, in combination with opioids, to reduce the dose of the opioid while providing adequate pain relief. Chapter 15 concentrates on the pharmacology of opioid analgesics and the treatment of opioid dependency. Chapter 16 critically examines the literature on the pharmacology and efficacy of herbal substances used in the treatment of psychological illnesses such as depression and anxiety. Finally, Chapter 17 examines the integration of psychological therapies and pharmacotherapies in the treatment of psychological disorders.

Chapter 14

Nonnarcotic Anti-Inflammatory Analgesics

Previous chapters have described the pharmacology of drugs used to treat psychological disorders such as anxiety, insomnia, depression, mania, and psychosis. Chapters 14 and 15 address the treatment of pain and the pharmacology of analgesic drugs. We have already addressed the issue of pain in Chapters 9 and 10: the antidepressants and the anticonvulsant neuromodulators possess prominent analgesic actions and are used both as analgesics and as "morphine-sparing" agents, reducing the amounts of morphine (or other opioids) necessary to achieve pain relief. Pain and depression are often inseparable (Bair et al., 2003), and both may need to be addressed during treatment of the patient with chronic pain syndromes (for example, fibromyalgia, chronic fatigue syndrome, chronic back pain, and so on):

> The prevalence of pain in depressed cohorts and depression in pain cohorts are [sic] higher than when these conditions are individually examined. The presence of pain negatively affects the recognition and treatment of depression. When pain is moderate to severe, impairs function, and/or is refractory to treatment, it is associated with more depressive symptoms and worse depression outcomes (e.g., lower quality of life, decreased work function, and increased health care utilization). Similarly, depression in patients with pain is associated with more pain complaints and greater impairment. Depression and pain share biological pathways and neurotransmitters, which has implications for the treatment of both concurrently. (p. 2433)

There are two classes of analgesic drugs. The first consists of the centrally acting opioid analgesics, such as morphine (Chapter 15). The second consists of nonnarcotic anti-inflammatory analgesics, such as aspirin, ibuprofen (Advil, Motrin), acetaminophen (Tylenol), celecoxib (Celebrex), rofecoxib (Vioxx), valdecoxib (Bextra), and many others. These analgesics are the subject of this chapter.

All the nonnarcotic analgesics are classified as *nonsteroidal analgesic anti-inflammatory agents* (NSAIDs). These drugs act at the local (peripheral) site of tissue injury to reduce the inflammatory response associated with tissue injury and to reduce the transmission of nociception to the central nervous system. NSAIDs have classically been thought not to act within the CNS, although recent evidence is identifying receptors on which NSAIDs may act within the spinal cord to produce analgesia and potentiate the effects of morphine (Kroin et al., 2002; Seybold et al., 2003; Zhu et al., 2003). The NSAIDs do not produce euphoria, and they are not considered as drugs of abuse.

The NSAIDs are a group of chemically unrelated drugs (Figure 14.1) that produce both analgesic and anti-inflammatory effects. They block the generation of peripheral pain impulses by inhibiting the synthesis and release of chemical mediators called *prostaglandins*. NSAIDs do not bind to opioid receptors, but they exert a prominent morphine-sparing effect in improving pain relief in a variety of clinical situations (Gilron et al., 2003; Malan et al., 2003).

Prostaglandins are body hormones that perform a variety of functions including the production of local inflammatory responses. NSAIDs act by inhibiting the enzyme *cyclooxygenase*. *Cyclooxygenase* (also called *prostaglandin synthetase*) functions to convert a precursor substance (arachidonic acid) to prostaglandins. There are two isomeric forms of cyclooxygenase, COX-1 and COX-2. COX-1 primarily functions to mediate the production of prostaglandins that protect and regulate cell function in the gastrointestinal (GI) tract and in blood platelets during normal physiologic conditions. Among other things, this action permits platelets to function normally as initiators of blood clotting. COX-2 has fewer roles under normal conditions; however, in response to stressors such as inflammation, COX-2 is markedly induced by chemical mediators associated with inflammation (Ehrich et al., 1999). Such induction by immune or inflammatory stimuli leads to the production of prostaglandins that mediate inflammation and pain. COX-2 (in contrast to COX-1) is therefore considered as an *inducible enzyme*. It is induced in peripheral tissues and in the spinal cord in response to such immune instigators as autoimmune diseases (for example, osteoarthritis and rheumatoid arthritis), for which anti-inflammatory drugs are so effective therapeutically.

Older NSAIDs, such as aspirin, nonselectively inhibit the cyclooxygenase enzyme (both COX-1 and COX-2). Therefore, they would be

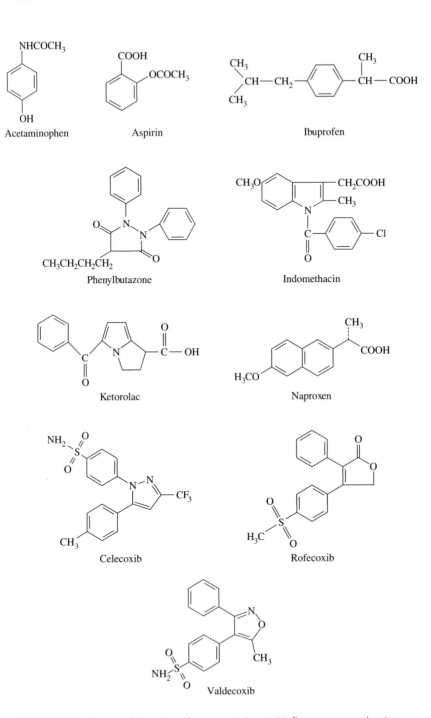

FIGURE 14.1 Structural formulas of representative anti-inflammatory analgesics.

expected to adversely affect both the GI tract and platelet function, as well as reducing pain and inflammation. Three newer (and much more expensive) prescription-only drugs, celecoxib (Celebrex), rofecoxib (Vioxx), and valdecoxib (Bextra), are selective inhibitors of the COX-2 enzyme at therapeutic concentrations. They do not inhibit the COX-1 enzyme, so they would be expected to have less effect on the GI tract and on platelet function. Adversely, the COX-2 inhibitors have recently been noted to increase the incidence of heart disease (discussed next).

The effects of anti-inflammatory analgesic drugs include:

- Reduction of inflammation (an anti-inflammatory effect)
- Reduction in body temperature when the patient has a fever (an antipyretic effect)
- Reduction of pain without sedation (an analgesic effect)
- Inhibition of platelet aggregation (an anticoagulant effect)— nonselective drugs only

The prototype nonselective NSAID is *aspirin*; hence, all nonselective NSAIDs can be referred to as aspirinlike drugs. Other nonselective NSAIDs include *acetaminophen, ibuprophen, mefenamic acid* (Ponstel), *meclofenamate sodium* (Meclomen), *tolmetin* (Tolectin), *diclofenac* (Voltaren, Cataflam), *piroxicam* (Feldene), and *nabumetone* (Relafen). These drugs are used as analgesics and for the long-term treatment of the pain and inflammation associated with arthritis.

The prototype selective COX-2 inhibitor is *celecoxib* (Celebrex). This and two other selective COX-2 inhibitors have become popular for the treatment of various forms of arthritis, largely because of their heavy promotion both to physicians and directly to patients through the mass media.

Nonselective Cyclooxygenase Inhibitors

Nonselective cyclooxygenase (COX) inhibitors are drugs that inhibit both COX-1 and COX-2 variants of the COX enzyme. COX drugs, the prototype of which is aspirin, therefore exert clinically significant effects on inflammation, blood platelets, and the GI tract. These three effects differentiate these drugs from the opioid analgesics, such as morphine (Chapter 15), and from the selective COX-2 inhibitors that are discussed later in this chapter. Opioid analgesics, while powerfully analgesic, do not exert anti-inflammatory effects and they do not affect blood platelet function. The selective COX-2 inhibitors have the same analgesic action as the nonselective agents discussed here, but they do not affect platelet function.

Aspirin

In the United States, between 10,000 and 20,000 tons of aspirin are consumed each year. *Aspirin* is the most popular and most effective analgesic, antipyretic, and anti-inflammatory drug. As an analgesic, aspirin is most effective for low-intensity pain, as increased doses rapidly reach a ceiling beyond which additional drug provides little more analgesia than do lower doses (all NSAIDs demonstrate this ceiling effect against pain). The ceiling is reached with doses of between about 650 milligrams and 1300 milligrams (a single, full-strength, regular aspirin contains 325 milligrams of drug).

Aspirin's antipyretic (fever-lowering) effect follows the inhibition of prostaglandin synthesis in the hypothalamus, a structure in the brain that modulates body temperature. However, one caution is necessary regarding the use of aspirin to reduce fever in children. An association exists between the use of aspirin for the fever that accompanies varicella (chicken pox) or influenza and the subsequent development of Reye's syndrome, including severe liver and brain damage and even death (Pinsky et al., 1988). Therefore, in children, aspirin use is precluded for the treatment of virus-induced febrile illness.

Aspirin exerts important effects on blood coagulation. For blood to coagulate, platelets[1] must first be able to aggregate, an action requiring the presence of prostaglandins. Aspirin binds to blood platelets, irreversibly inhibiting their function for the eight- to ten-day lifetime of the platelet. This results in inhibition of hemostasis, reducing the tendency for blood to clot. In daily low doses (often, 1/2 tablet/day), aspirin is used to prevent blood from clotting in diseased coronary arteries, markedly reducing the incidence of strokes and heart attacks (Gum et al., 2001).

Aspirin increases oxygen consumption by the body, which increases the production of carbon dioxide, an effect that stimulates respiration. Therefore, an overdose of aspirin is often characterized by a marked increase in respiratory rate, which causes the overdosed person to appear to pant. This overdose effect results in other severe metabolic consequences that are beyond this discussion.

Side effects of aspirin are common. First, gastric upset occurs frequently and can range from mild upset and heartburn to severe, destructive ulcerations and bleeding of the stomach or upper intestine. Second, poisoning due to aspirin overdosage is not infrequent and can be fatal. Third, mild intoxication can produce ringing in the ears,

---

[1]Platelets are small components of the blood that adhere to vascular membranes after injury to a vessel. They form an initial plug, over which a blood clot eventually forms to limit bleeding from a lacerated blood vessel.

auditory and visual difficulties, mental confusion, thirst, and hyperventilation. Fourth, in aspirin-sensitive individuals, a single dose of aspirin can precipitate an asthma attack.

Acetaminophen

Acetaminophen (Tylenol) is an effective alternative to aspirin both as an analgesic and as an antipyretic agent. However, acetaminophen has only minor actions as an anti-inflammatory agent. Therefore, it is less useful than aspirin in the treatment of acute inflammation or chronic arthritis. However, as a pain-relieving agent, acetaminophen is every bit as effective as is aspirin.

The beneficial effects of acetaminophen over aspirin are three. First, acetaminophen does not inhibit platelet function, so bruising easily is not a problem. (On the other hand, acetaminophen is not useful for preventing vascular clotting or for prophylaxis against heart attacks or stroke). Second, no reports have associated acetaminophen with Reye's syndrome; therefore, it has an improved margin of safety in children. Third, acetaminophen generally produces less gastric distress and less ringing in the ears than does aspirin.

On the negative side, an acute overdose (either accidental or intentional) might produce severe or even fatal liver damage. Alcoholics appear to be especially susceptible to the hepatotoxic effects of even moderate doses of acetaminophen. Indeed, such persons should avoid acetaminophen while they persist in heavy consumption of alcohol. Finally, there has recently been association between the use of acetaminophen (and other NSAIDs except aspirin) and the development of hypertension (high blood pressure) in a small minority of women who consume these drugs nearly daily (Armstrong and Malone, 2003; Curhan et al., 2002). It would be wise for women who are hypertensive to use these drugs with discretion and for women who use these drugs regularly to be periodically monitored for hypertension.

In summary, acetaminophen has been proven to be a reasonable substitute for aspirin when analgesic or antipyretic effectiveness is desired, especially in children and in patients who cannot tolerate aspirin.

Ibuprofen

Ibuprofen (Advil) and related drugs such as fenoprofen (Nalfon) and ketoprofen (Orudis) exert aspirinlike analgesic, antipyretic, and anti-inflammatory effects (Table 14.1) and are often better tolerated than aspirin. Their analgesic effectiveness is comparable to or greater than that of acetaminophen, aspirin, codeine, aspirin with codeine, and propoxyphene. Like other NSAIDs, ibuprofen's actions result from drug-induced inhibition of prostaglandin synthesis. The incidence and severity of side effects produced by ibuprofen are somewhat lower

TABLE I4.1 Ibuprofen and related drugs: Available formulations and recommendations for anti-inflammatory therapy

Nonproprietary name	Trade name	Formulation	Usual anti-inflammatory dose
Ibuprofen	Motrin, Advil, Nuprin, Medipren	Tablets	400 mg, three to four times a day
Naproxen	Naprosyn, Aleve, Anaprox	Tablets, suspension	250–500 mg, twice a day
Fenoprofen	Nalfon	Tablets, capsules	300–600 mg, three to four times a day
Ketoprofen	Orudis, Oravail	Capsules	150–300 mg, two to four times a day
Flurbiprofen	Ansaid, others	Tablets	50–75 mg, two to four times a day
Oxaprozin	Daypro	Tablets	600–1200 mg, once a day
Mefenamic acid	Ponstel	Tablets	250 mg, three to four times a day
Celecoxib	Celebrex	Capsules	100 mg, twice a day
Rofecoxib	Vioxx	Tablets, suspension	12.5–25 mg, once a day
Valdecoxib	Bextra	Tablets	10–20 mg, once a day

than those of aspirin, but gastric distress and the formation of peptic ulcers have occasionally been reported. Like aspirin (but unlike acetaminophen), ibuprofen and related drugs inhibit platelet aggregation and therefore interfere with the clotting process. These drugs should be used with caution in patients who suffer from peptic ulcer disease or bleeding abnormalities. Ibuprofen, unlike most other NSAIDs, is not secreted in breast milk, but in general, NSAIDs are not recommended for use in breast-feeding mothers or for use by pregnant women.

FDA-approved indications for ibuprofen include use as an analgesic and use for the symptomatic treatment of various forms of arthritis, tendonitis, bursitis, and dysmenorrhea (painful menstrual cramps). The anti-inflammatory effect is comparable to that of aspirin. The generally lower level of gastrointestinal side effects (in comparison with aspirin) must be measured against its generally greater economic expense.

Indomethacin, Sulindac, and Etodolac

Indomethacin (Indocin), available since 1963, is an effective anti-inflammatory drug that is used primarily for treating rheumatoid arthritis and similar disorders. However, its use is limited by its toxicity. Indomethacin is an analgesic, antipyretic, and anti-inflammatory agent. Its clinical effects closely resemble those of aspirin. Side effects occur in about 50 percent of the patients who take indomethacin; gastric dysfunction is the most prominent. Paradoxically, drug-induced headache limits its use in about 50 percent of patients. Other side effects are rare but potentially serious.

Sulindac (Clinoril) and *etodolac* (Lodine) are two newer NSAIDs that are structurally and pharmacologically related to indomethacin. Sulindac is itself inactive, but its metabolite (sulindac sulfide) is very active. Its efficacy is comparable to that of indomethacin but perhaps with a lower level of gastrointestinal toxicities (less than indomethacin but greater than many other NSAIDs). Etodolac is an effective analgesic and anti-inflammatory drug. Its side effects, which include skin rashes, headache, and gastrointestinal irritation and ulceration, appear to be fewer than those caused by many other NSAIDs.

Ketorolac

Ketorolac (Toradol) is an analgesic and anti-inflammatory agent available in both oral and intravenous formulations. Ketorolac is the only NSAID available for injection, although selective COX-2 inhibitors are being studied for parenteral use (for example, parecoxib) (Malan et al., 2003). Administered either intramuscularly or intravenously, ketorolac is effective in the short-term treatment of moderate to severe pain (Gillis and Brogden, 1997). Like the other NSAIDs, ketorolac inhibits prostaglandin synthesis. Its analgesic potency is comparable to that of low doses of morphine, and it offers an anti-inflammatory action not offered by morphine. Its concomitant use with morphine offers synergistic action, reducing the required analgesic dose of morphine by about 50 percent. Ketorolac is not recommended for use in obstetrics, because it and other NSAIDs can adversely affect uterine contraction and fetal circulation.

Side effects of ketorolac include excessive bleeding (due to platelet inhibition) and renal failure; the latter is minimized by limiting the use of the drug to a few days after surgery. Used orally, analgesic efficacy differs little from other orally administered NSAIDs.

Diclofenac

Diclofenac (Cataflam, Voltaren) is another nonspecific NSAID, available since 1988 and indicated for treatment of acute and chronic pain of arthritis and for the mitigation of painful menstrual periods. The half-life of diclofenac is short (about two hours), so delayed-release preparations are commonly utilized when a more prolonged analgesic action is desired. The precautions applicable to other nonspecific NSAIDs apply to diclofenac

Nabumetone

Nabumetone (Relafen) is a nonspecific NSAID available since 1991 for the treatment of arthritis and other conditions treatable with similar drugs. Nabumetone itself is inactive; it is rapidly converted in the body to a pharmacologically active metabolite that is a potent inhibitor of prostaglandin synthetase. Its gastrointestinal toxicity appears to be somewhat lower than that of aspirin or indomethacin. The drug is primarily indicated for the long-term treatment of the pain and inflammation associated with arthritis.

Miscellaneous Nonspecific NSAIDs

Several other nonspecific cyclooxygenase inhibitors are available for use in treating various forms of arthritis or painful menstrual periods. These agents include *mefenamin acid* (Ponstel), *meloxicam* (Mobic), *naproxen* (Aleve, Anaprox), *oxaprozin* (Daypro), *piroxicam* (Feldene), and *tolmetin* (Tolectin). These drugs, as well as several of those discussed earlier, were introduced in medicine in the late 1980s to early 1990s as alternatives to aspirin. Since the patent protection of most of these drugs has expired, they are available in generic form and few manufacturers promote their use today. As we will see, however, naproxin in particular may exert a cardioprotective effect not shared by most other NSAIDs. Naproxen, however, offers less protection against heart attacks than does aspirin (Hebert and Hennekens, 2000).

Selective COX-2 Inhibitors

Only since the late 1990s have the roles of cyclooxygenase enzymes in health and disease begun to be understood, in particular, the role of "inducible"[2] COX-2 in inflammation (O'Banion, 1999) and in the prevention of various cancers.

The COX-2 enzyme is expressed in certain malignant cells of epithial tissues such as colon, breast, prostate, bladder, lung, and pancreas (Singh and Lucci, 2002). Indeed, COX-2 plays a role in tumor proliferation and growth. It is best demonstrated in cancers of the colon. COX-2 inhibitors reduce the risk of these cancers and therefore have a role in cancer chemoprotection, probably as an adjunct to more traditional anticancer medications (Marnett and DuBois, 2002; Ricchi et al., 2003). Whether COX-2 inhibitors will play a beneficial role in the treatment of noncarcinogenic inflammatory diseases of the colon is as yet unclear.

Selective COX-2 inhibitors are as effective as aspirin and other nonselective NSAIDs for the relief of pain and the reduction of inflammation while halving the rate of associated gastric ulcerations. Consequently, COX-2 inhibitors became popular as modern analgesics that exhibit only 50% of the incidence of gastric ulcerations than follow the use of aspirin and other NSAIDs. Unfortunately, the COX-2 inhibitors are now associated with a 2-fold increase in the risk of heart attacks and strokes (Solomon, 2005).

By 2004, three COX-2 inhibitors were clinically available as orally administered analgesic/anti-inflammatory drugs. Because of adverse cardiovascular effects, in late 2004 one [rofecoxib (*Vioxx*)] was removed from the market and the other two may follow. It is currently unknow what will be the future of these drugs (Shaya et al., 2005).

Celecoxib

Celecoxib (Celebrex) was released in 1998 as the first selective COX-2 inhibitor. The drug is as effective as aspirin in reducing the pain and inflammation of rheumatoid arthritis and osteoarthritis without the gastrointestinal toxicity and platelet blockade produced by aspirin (Silverstein et al., 2000). The lower incidence of gastrointestinal toxicity is advantageous as celecoxib and the other two COX-2 inhibitors are associated with a 50 percent reduction in the occurrence of drug-induced gastric ulcerations and hemorrhages (Figure 14.2). On the other hand, while decreasing the incidence of skin bruising, the lack

---

[2]By "inducible" I mean that normally the level of COX-2 in the body is low, but in response to inflammation, enzyme levels increase markedly.

of effect on blood platelets causes loss of the protective effect of aspirin in reducing the incidence of heart attacks and strokes, even increasing the incidence of heart attacks over that seen in control patients (Mukherjee et al., 2001). Regarding a possible increase in the incidence of heart attacks, Howes and Krum (2002) stated:

> There are concerns that selective COX-2 inhibitors may be pro-thrombotic and increase the risk of myocardial infarction. This has largely arisen because of an unexpected finding of a higher rate of myocardial infarctions in patients receiving rofecoxib compared with patients receiving naproxen in a study of gastric toxicity. The results of this study, a similar study of celecoxib versus ibuprofen or diclofenac, and data obtained from aspirin suggest that differences in the rates of myocardial infarction between rofecoxib and naproxen may have been due to an unexpectedly low rate of myocardial infarction in patients receiving naproxen. The magnitude of this increase in risk, if real, is uncertain but it is likely to be relatively small in patients for whom cardiovascular prophylaxis with aspirin is not indicated. (p. 829)

Another series of articles (Solomon et al., 2002; Watson et al., 2002; Rahme et al., 2002) tested this possible association and found that naproxen (a nonselective NSAID) reduces the incidence of heart attacks (an aspirinlike effect not shared by other NSAIDs). An accompanying editorial (Dalen, 2002) concluded, "There is no evidence that use of COX-2 inhibitors increases (or decreases) the risk of myocardial infarction" (p. 1092). They merely exert no protective effect, unlike aspirin or naproxen. Now, in 2005, we recognize that COX-2 inhibitors can increase the incidence of adverse cardiovascular events. As with any drug, medication is a balance between therapeutic potential and adverse reactions.

Rofecoxib

Rofecoxib (Vioxx) was the second COX-2 inhibitor, introduced in the year 2000. It was approved for the treatment of osteoarthritis, acute pain, and menstrual pain. It is superior to naproxen in reducing the incidence of gastric ulcerations (Figure 14.3). Despite this, in September 2004, its manufacturer withdrew rofecoxib from sale. This was due to a doubling in the incidence of heart attacks and strokes in patients thought to be at low risk for such events (Solomon, 2005). In February 2005, a FDA advisory panel recommended continued sale of rofecoxib, with stern warning regarding this adverse effect. At present, it is unknown whether or not rofecoxib will be reintroduced for sale.

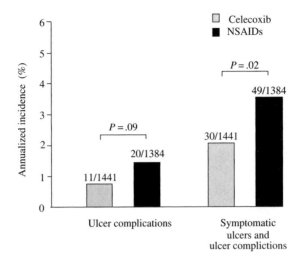

FIGURE 14.2 Annualized incidence of upper gastrointestinal tract ulcer complications alone and with symptomatic gastrointestinal ulcers. Left two bars represent ulcer complications for 1441 patient-years of celecoxib and 1384 patient-years of nonselective NSAIDs. The right two bars represent ulcer complications *plus* the presence of symptomatic ulcers in the same populations of patients. The numbers above the bars indicate events per patient-years of exposure. The annualized incidence of ulcer complications in celecoxib-treated patients was 0.76 percent (11 events per 1441 patient-years) versus an incidence of 1.45 percent (20 events per 1384 patient-years) in patients taking NSAIDs. When symptomatic ulcers were added, the percentage of complications in each group increased, but celecoxib patients still exhibited a 40 percent reduction in total complications. [From Silverstein et al., (2000), p. 1251.]

Rofecoxib is fairly rapidly absorbed orally, reaches peak plasma levels in about 3 hours, is metabolized before excretion, and has a half-life of about 17 hours. Side effects and toxicities include nausea, diarrhea, abdominal pain, and dyspepsia. As with all COX-2 inhibitors, GI toxicities are about half that seen in aspirin-treated patients. However, the adverse cardiovascular effects are serious and currently under review.

Valdecoxib

Valdecoxib (Bextra) was introduced into medicine in 2002 as the third selective COX-2 inhibitor. Like celecoxib and refecoxib, valdecoxib is indicated for the treatment of arthritis and for the treatment of menstrual pain and discomfort. It has been reported to be useful in the relief of postoperative pain (Camu et al., 2002; Daniels et al., 2002). Like celecoxib and refecoxib, valdecoxib does not impair platelet function

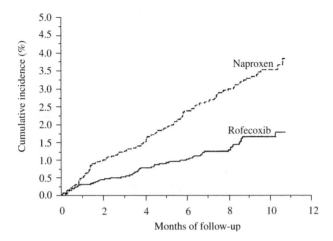

FIGURE 14.3 Cumulative incidence of a confirmed upper gastrointestinal complication among patients randomized to receive naproxen (a nonspecific NSAID) or rofecoxib (a specific COX-2 inhibitor) taken for a period of 1 year. A total of 8076 patients were studied and were randomized to one of the two groups. Naproxen-treated patients exhibited over twice the gastrointestinal complications of the rofecoxib-treated patients. [From Bombardier et al., (2000), p. 1524.]

(Leese et al., 2002). With a half-life of about 11 hours, valdecoxib is administered once daily. The *Medical Letter* (2002) concluded:

> Valdecoxib appears to be effective for the treatment of arthritis and, like celecoxib and rofecoxib, should cause less gastrointestinal toxicity than traditional NSAIDs. . . . Until there is more experience with this new drug, the older COX-2 inhibitors are preferred. For treatment of dysmenorrhea (painful menses) there is no good reason to use any of these expensive drugs rather than a traditional NSAID such as ibuprofen, unless the patient is at high risk for gastrointestinal ulceration and bleeding. (p. 40)

Parecoxib

Parecoxib (Dynastat) is a "pro-drug" (precursor agent) of valdecoxib that is administered by injection. Parecoxib is itself inactive; it undergoes rapid metabolism to valdecoxib. Parecoxib is unique in that it is the first selective COX-2 inhibitor intended for parenteral use. Currently undergoing final testing, parecoxib is expected to become commercially available in the near future. Parecoxib is intended for the treatment of postsurgical pain. Recently, Joshi and coworkers (2004) studied the analgesic effects of parecoxib administered during surgery followed by oral valdecoxib for four days following surgery. The combination of intravenous parecoxib followed by oral valdecoxib markedly reduced the amount of opioid narcotic that the patients required for their postsurgical pain and the side effects that accompany opioid ingestion (Chapter 15).

Lumiracoxib

Lumiracoxib (Prexige) is another orally administered selective COX-2 inhibitor. It is intended for the short-term treatment of postsurgical pain. It differs from the other orally administered agents in that it is more rapidly absorbed after oral administration and has a relatively short half-life. It is about half as potent as celecoxib (therefore the dose is twice as high). Clinical studies with lumiracoxib have not yet been published, but animal results (and unpublished clinical studies) report excellent analgesic effects (Fox et al., 2004).

Nonopioid Analgesics of the Future: Nitric Oxide-Releasing Aspirins

Advances beyond COX-2 inhibition are being explored and certainly are needed, especially since the COX-2 inhibitors do not block platelet action and therefore do not offer cardiac protection against thrombotic catastrophes. An interesting example of possible agents of the future is a class of drugs called *nitroaspirins* or *nitric oxide-releasing aspirins*. One example is an experimental drug code-named *NCX-4016*. This and similar drugs are new chemical entities that are obtained by adding a nitric oxide-releasing moiety to aspirin. NCX-4016 consists of a parent molecule (aspirin) linked to a "spacer" via an ester linkage, which is in turn connected to the nitric oxide-releasing moiety.

Nitric oxide is normally found in the body and contributes to protecting the lining of the walls of blood vessels and endothelial tissues such as those lining the gastrointestinal tract. Therefore, the aspirin moiety contributes the analgesic, anti-inflammatory, and antiplatelet actions while the nitric oxide protects the GI tract and coronary blood vessels (Brzozowski et al., 2003; Fiorucci et al., 2003). These drugs are also protective against carcinomas of the GI tract (Tesei et al., 2003). NCX-4016 exhibits antiatherosclerotic and antioxidant effects in the arterial walls of mice with genetic increases in cholesterol (Napoli et al., 2002) and also reduces vascular injury and repairs injured blood vessels, promoting vascular remodeling after injury (Yu et al., 2002).

Therefore, in summary, nitric oxide-releasing aspirins have wide therapeutic potential, combining aspirin's benefits without GI injury and even promoting healing of injured endothelial tissues, such as those that line the GI tract and blood vessels.

STUDY QUESTIONS

1. What is an NSAID? What does this term mean?

2. List the various actions of aspirin. How might each action be used therapeutically? Which ones might present clinical problems?

3. What is meant by the term *COX inhibitor*?

4. Differentiate between COX-1 and COX-2.

5. How is the anticoagulant action of aspirin "good"? How is it "bad"?

6. Describe the theoretical advantages of COX-2 inhibitors over NSAIDs (nonselective COX-inhibitors).

7. What is the correlation between COX enzyme and tumor genesis? How might COX inhibitors be of benefit?

8. What is a nitric oxide-releasing aspirin? What are its advantages? What might be its clinical uses?

REFERENCES

Armstrong, E. P., and D. C. Malone (2003). "The Impact of Nonsteroidal Anti-Inflammatory Drugs on Blood Pressure, with an Emphasis on Newer Agents." *Clinical Therapeutics* 25: 1–18.

Bair, M. J., et al. (2003). "Depression and Pain Comorbidity: A Literature Review." *Archives of Internal Medicine* 163: 2433–2445.

Bombardier, C., et al. (2000). "Comparison of Upper Gastrointestinal Toxicity of Rofecoxib and Naproxen in Patients with Rheumatoid Arthritis." *New England Journal of Medicine* 343: 1520–1528.

Brzozowski, T., et al. (2003). "Implications of Reactive Oxygen Species and Cytokines in Gastroprotection Against Stress-Induced Gastric Damage by Nitric Oxide-Releasing Aspirin." *International Journal of Colorectal Diseases* 18: 320–329.

Camu, F., et al. (2002). "Valdecoxib, a COX-2-Specific Inhibitor, Is an Efficacious, Opioid-Sparing Analgesic in Patients Undergoing Hip Arthroplasty." *American Journal of Therapeutics* 9: 43–51.

Curhan, G. C., et al. (2002). "Frequency of Analgesic Use and Risk of Hypertension in Younger Women." *Archives of Internal Medicine* 162: 2204–2208.

Dalen, J. E. (2002). "Selective COX-2 Inhibitors, NSAIDs, Aspirin, and Myocardial Infarction." *Archives of Internal Medicine* 162: 1091–1092.

Daniels, S. E., et al. (2002). "The Analgesic Efficacy of Valdecoxib vs. Oxycodone/Acetaminophen After Oral Surgery." *Journal of the American Dental Association* 13: 611–621.

Ehrich, E. W., et al. (1999). "Characterization of Rofecoxib as a Cyclooxygenase-2 Isoform Inhibitor and Demonstration of Analgesia in the Dental Pain Model." *Clinical Pharmacology and Therapeutics* 65: 336–347.

Fiorucci, S., et al. (2003). "Gastrointestinal Safety of NO-Aspirin (NCX-4016) in Healthy Human Volunteers: A Proof of Concept Endoscopic Study." *Gastroenterology* 124: 600–607.

Fox, A., et al. (2004). "Anti-Hyperalgesic Activity of the COX-2 Inhibitor Lumiracoxib in a Model of Bone Cancer Pain in the Rat." *Pain* 107: 33–40.

Gillis, J. C., and R. N. Brogden (1997). "Ketorolac: A Reappraisal of Its Pharmacodynamic and Pharmacokinetic Properties and Therapeutic Use in Pain Management." *Drugs* 53: 139–188.

Gilron, I., et al. (2003). "Cycooxygenase-2 Inhibitors in Postoperative Pain Management: Current Evidence and Future Directions." *Anesthesiology* 99: 1198–1208.

Gum, P. A., et al. (2001). "Aspirin Use and All-Cause Mortality Among Patients Being Evaluated for Known or Suspected Coronary Artery Disease." *Journal of the American Medical Association* 286: 1187–1194.

Hebert, P. R., and C. H. Hennekens (2000). "An Overview of the 4 Randomized Trials of Aspirin Therapy in the Primary Prevention of Vascular Disease." *Archives of Internal Medicine* 160: 3123–3127.

Howes, L. G., and H. Krum (2002). "Selective Cyclo-Oxygenase-2 Inhibitors and Myocardial Infarction: How Strong Is the Link?" *Drug Safety* 25: 829–835.

Joshi, G. P., et al. (2004). "Effective Treatment of Laparoscopic Cholecystectomy Pain with Intravenous Followed by Oral COX-2 Specific Inhibitors." *Anesthesia and Analgesia* 98: 336–342.

Kroin, J. S., et al. (2002). "Cyclooxygenase-2 Inhibition Potentiates Morphine Antinociception at the Spinal Level in a Postoperative Pain Model." *Regional Anesthesia and Pain Medicine* 27: 451–455.

Leese, P. T., et al. (2002). "Valdecoxib Does Not Impair Platelet Function." *American Journal of Emergency Medicine* 20: 275–281.

Malan, T. P., et al. (2003). "Parecoxib Sodium, a Parenteral Cyclooxygenase 2 Selective Inhibitor, Improves Morphine Analgesia and Is Opioid-Sparing Following Total Hip Arthroplasty." *Anesthesiology* 98: 950–956.

Marnett, L. J., and R. N. DuBois (2002). "COX-2: A Target for Colon Cancer Prevention." *Annual Review of Pharmacology and Toxicology* 42: 55–80.

Medical Letter (2002). "Valdecoxib (Bextra)—A New COX-2 Inhibitor." *Medical Letter on Drugs and Therapeutics* 44 (April 29): 39–40.

Mukherjee, D., et al. (2001). "Risk of Cardiovascular Events Associated with Selective COX-2 Inhibitors." *Journal of the American Medical Association* 286: 954–959.

Napoli, C., et al. (2002). "Chronic Treatment with Nitric Oxide-Releasing Aspirin Reduces Plasma Low-Density Lipoprotein Oxidation and Oxidative Stress, Arterial Oxidation-Specific Epitopes, and Artherogenesis in Hypercholesterolemic Mice." *Proceedings of the National Academy of Sciences of the United States of America* 17: 12467–12470.

O'Banion, M. K. (1999). "Cyclooxygenase-2: Molecular Biology, Pharmacology, and Neurobiology." *Critical Reviews in Neurobiology* 13: 45–82.

Pinsky, P., et al. (1998). "Reye's Syndrome and Aspirin: Evidence for a Dose-Response Effect." *Journal of the American Medical Association* 260: 657–661.

Rahme, E., et al. (2002). "Association Between Naproxen Use and Protection Against Acute Myocardial Infarction." *Archives of Internal Medicine* 162: 1111–1115.

Ricchi, P., et al. (2003). "Nonsteroidal Anti-Inflammatory Drugs in Colorectal Cancer: From Prevention to Therapy." *British Journal of Cancer* 88: 803–807.

Seybold, V. S., et al. (2003). "Cyclo-Oxygenase-2 Contributes to Central Sensitization in Rats with Peripheral Inflammation." *Pain* 105: 47–55.

Shaya, F. T., et al. (2005). "Selective Cyclooxygenase-2 Inhibition and Cardiovascular Effects: An Observational Study of a Medicaid Population" *Archives of Internal Medicine* 165: 181–186.

Silverstein, F. E., et al. (2000). "Gastrointestinal Toxicity with Celecoxib vs Nonsteroidal Anti-Inflammatory Drugs for Osteoarthritis and Rheumatoid

Arthritis. The CLASS Study: A Randomized Controlled Study." *Journal of the American Medical Association* 284: 1247–1255.

Singh, B., and A. Lucci (2002). "Role of Cyclooxygenase-2 in Breast Cancer." *Journal of Surgical Research* 108: 173–179.

Solomon, D. H. and J. Avorn (2005). "Coxibs, Science, and the Public Trust." *Archives of Internal Medicine* 165: 158–160.

Solomon, D. H., et al. (2002). "Nonsteroidal Anti-Inflammatory Drug Use and Acute Myocardial Infarction." *Archives of Internal Medicine* 162: 1099–1104.

Tesei, A., et al. (2003). "NCX-4016, a Nitric Oxide-Releasing Aspirin Derivative, Exhibits a Significant Antiproliferative Effect and Alters Cell Cycle Progression in Human Colon Adenocarcinoma Cell Lines." *International Journal of Oncology* 22: 1297–1302.

Watson, D. J., et al. (2002). "Lower Risk of Thromboembolic Cardiovascular Events with Naproxen Among Patients with Rheumatoid Arthritis." *Archives of Internal Medicine* 162: 1105–1110.

Yu, J., et al. (2002). "Nitric Oxide-Releasing Aspirin Decreases Vascular Injury by Reducing Inflammation and Promoting Apoptosis." *Laboratory Investigation* 82: 825–832.

Zhu, X., et al. (2003). "Cyclooxygenase-1 in the Spinal Cord Plays an Important Role in Postoperative Pain." *Pain* 104: 15–23.

Chapter 15

Opioid Analgesics

Pain can be defined as a highly undesirable and unpleasant sensation often associated with actual or potential tissue damage. Pain of acute onset is desirable as it functions as a warning system against real or potential damage to the body. Chronic pain differs from acute pain in that it serves no useful purpose, causes suffering, limits activities of daily living, and increases the costs of health care and disability. It also often occurs comorbid with depression, and both may need to be addressed during treatment (Bair et al., 2003). Pain is modulated, enhanced, or diminished by both cerebral and peripheral mechanisms. Cerebral factors include the placebo response, psychological phenomena, and conscious cognitive activation (Price, 2003; Solomon, 2002). These factors are powerfully affected by the opioid analgesics whereas the NSAIDs (Chapter 14) mostly affect the peripheral inflammatory responses. In addition to invoking endogenous opioids (endorphins), central mechanisms activate antinociceptive pathways beginning in the limbic forebrain and relayed through the brain stem to primary afferent nociceptive sites in the dorsal horn of the spinal cord, modulating the intensity of the pain response (Millan, 2002) as these afferent impulses enter the spinal cord.

When body tissues are damaged, tissue injury is accompanied by the activation of *nociceptive* (pain-sensing) neurons (Figure 15.1). With tissue injury or during inflammation, nociceptors become sensitized, discharge spontaneously, and produce ongoing pain. The cell bodies of the axons from these neurons are located in the dorsal root ganglia, and their bidirectional axon relays pain impulses to a synapse in the dorsal horn of the spinal cord and from there to the brain (Figure 15.2).

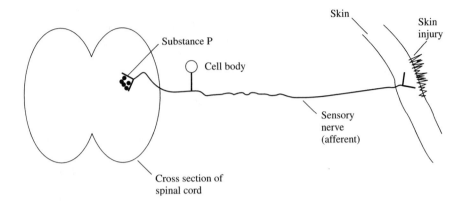

FIGURE 15.1 Activation of peripheral nociceptive (pain) fibers results in the release of substance P and other pain-signaling neurotransmitters from nerve terminals in the dorsal horn of the spinal cord. The cell body for the nerve is located in the dorsal root ganglion.

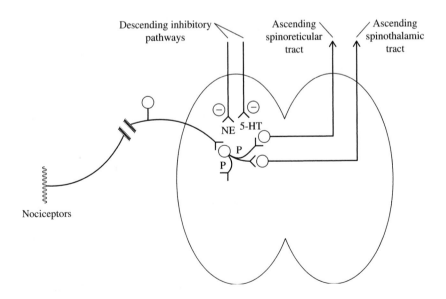

FIGURE 15.2 Release of substance P in the dorsal horn of the spinal cord with transmission of secondary relay pathways to higher centers. Descending inhibitory pathways (–) are also shown. NE = norepinephrine; 5-HT = serotonin.

There, the mechanisms associated with the modulation and transfer of pain impulses are very complex: a host of different processes involve multiple neurotransmitters and neuromodulators (DeLeo and Winkelstein, 2002). Among other events, prolonged discharge of these neurons causes release of glutamate from nerve terminals located in the dorsal horn of the spinal cord. The glutamate then activates a specific type of glutamate receptor in the spinal cord (N-methyl-D-aspartate, or NMDA receptors; Chapter 3). Activation of NMDA receptors causes the spinal cord neurons to become more responsive to all its inputs, resulting in sensitization of these neurons to painful input. When this happens, not only does the spinal cord become sensitized to pain, but these neurons also become less sensitive to the analgesic action of opioid drugs such as morphine (Bennett, 2000). One major goal of drug therapy is therefore to reduce spinal cord sensitization to pain through modulation of glutamate release. Indeed, morphine (Ostermeier et al., 2000) and cannabinoids (Rice et al., 2002) appear to act by altering the release of glutamine, albeit by slightly different mechanisms. Analgesic drugs therefore can modulate pain processes by the following actions:

1. Blocking NMDA receptors (for example, dextromethorphan and ketamine; Chapter 19)

2. Reducing glutamate release (for example, opioids, anticonvulsant "neuromodulators," Chapter 10, and cannabinoids, Chapter 18)

3. Modulating neuronal responsiveness in the spinal cord either through activation of inhibitory endorphin-secreting neurons or inhibitory GABA-secreting neurons (for example, opioid analgesics, neuromodulators)

4. Activating descending inhibitory neurons projecting from the brain stem to the dorsal horn of the spinal cord (for example, opioids or antidepressants, Chapter 9)

5. Modulating the central processing of pain stimuli, reducing the sensory and affective components of pain (for example, opioids) (Zubieta et al., 2001)

6. Reducing the peripheral inflammatory response (for example, NSAIDs, Chapter 14)

Drugs that we call *opioids* mimic the actions of our intrinsic, or endogenous, *endorphins* (the normal biological neurotransmitter at opioid or endorphin receptors). Drugs that so act are called *opioid agonists,* since they mimic the analgesic actions both of our endogenous endorphins (acting on the same set of receptors) and of morphine, the major analgesic in the opium poppy. Endorphins and opioids exert much of their analgesic action by acting presynaptically on nociceptive afferent sensory neurons to inhibit the release of pain-inducing transmitters in the spinal cord (Figure 15.3).

Chronic pain, such as that produced by nerve injury, sets up ongoing spinal processes of neuroadaptation with associated physiological changes in spinal circuitry and glutamate receptor adaptive changes. Chronic pain is thought to be poorly responsive to opioids but quite responsive to anticonvulsant neuromodulators (Chapter 10) (Schwartzman et al., 2001).

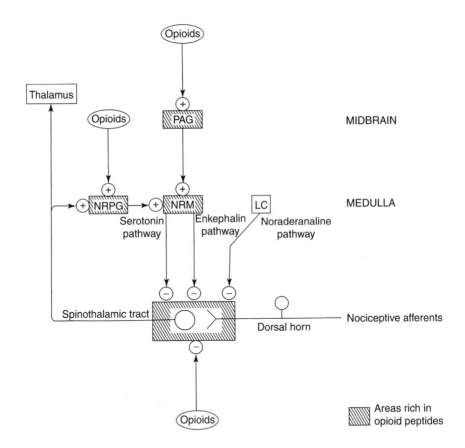

FIGURE 15.3 Sites of action of opioids on pain transmission. Opioids excite neurons in the periaqueductal gray matter (PAG) and in the midbrain and medulla. From there, serotoninergic and enkephalinergic neurons run to the dorsal horn and exert an inhibitory influence on transmission. Opioids also act directly on the dorsal horn. The locus coeruleus (LC) sends noradrenergic neurons to the dorsal horn, which also inhibits transmission. The pathways shown in this diagram represent a considerable oversimplification, but they depict the general organization of the supraspinal control mechanisms.

Besides the physical component of pain, there is an affective component that determines a person's emotional response to real or perceived distress. The affective component may be the underlying factor in the mechanism of chronic pain for which no objective cause can be identified. States of chronic pain may arise from deficits in the central processing of nociceptive afferent actions, input that might be innocuous in most people but debilitates others, and treatment with opioids is not very effective (and is sometimes harmful because dependence can develop). For people with chronic pain, treatment focuses on behavior modification, cognitive-behavioral therapy, or self-management approaches that include biopsychosocial models of therapy. Drug therapy for these patients relies on treatment algorithms (Fishbain, 1999) and judicious use of opioid analgesics as well as other adjuvant medications that reduce inflammation and/or exert a morphine-reducing effect (Savage, 1999).

History of Opioid Analgesics

Opium is extracted from poppy seeds and has been used for thousands of years to produce euphoria, analgesia, sleep, and relief from diarrhea and cough. In pre-Christian centuries, opium was used primarily for its constipating effect and later for its sleep-inducing properties (noted by writers such as Homer, Hippocrates, Discorides, Virgil, and Ovid). Even in those times, recreational abuse and addiction were common.

From the early Greek and Roman days through the sixteenth and seventeenth centuries, the medicinal and recreational uses of opium were well established. Combined with alcohol, the mixture was called *laudanum* (named by Paracelsus in 1520), meaning "something to be praised," and it was referred to as the "stone of immortality." Thereafter, opium and laudanum were used for practically every known disease. In the early 1800s, morphine was isolated from opium as its active ingredient. Since then, morphine has been used throughout the world as the premier agent for treating severe pain. Recognition of the addictive properties of opium, morphine, and other opioids has led to restrictions on their use to the treatment of conditions for which they are known to be effective.

After the Civil War (when opioid addiction was referred to as "soldier's disease") and the invention of the hypodermic needle in 1856, a new type of drug user appeared in the United States—one who self-administered opioids by injection. By about 1910, concern began to mount about the dangers of opioids and the dependence they could induce. In 1914 the Harrison Narcotic Act was passed, and the use of most opioid products was strictly controlled. Nonmedical uses of opioids were banned, although today nonmedical use continues, despite intense efforts to eradicate it. The use of opioids is deeply entrenched in society; it is widespread and impossible to stop. Opioids exert pleasurable effects, produce tolerance and physiological dependence, and have a potential for compulsive misuse, all liabilities that are likely to resist any efforts at legal control. Also, the opioids will continue to be used in medicine because they are irreplaceable as pain–relieving agents. Goldstein (1994) wrote that opioids dramatically relieve emotional as well as physical pain. This property contributes to making them extremely seductive for self-administration.

Terminology

Before proceeding, some terms, including some that we have already used, should be defined. *Opium* is a Greek word that means "juice"; more specifically, it refers to the juice or exudate from the poppy *Papaver somniferum*. An *opiate* is a drug extracted from the exudate of the poppy; the term is restricted to two drugs that are naturally found in the exudate, morphine and codeine. An *opioid* is any exogenous drug (natural or synthetic) that binds to an opiate receptor and produces agonistic, or morphinelike, effects. A couple of important opioids are classified as "weak agonists"; these drugs are analgesic like morphine, but when administered to an opioid-dependent person, withdrawal can be produced, as they are not as efficacious as morphine, the pure agonist. Conversely, an *opioid antagonist* is any drug that binds to an opiate receptor and antagonizes the effects of morphine, displacing the morphine from the receptor. In opioid-dependent persons, an opioid antagonist precipitates withdrawal signs and symptoms. Finally, several opioids are classified as *mixed agonist-antagonist opioids*, since they have a weak analgesic action at opiate receptors but (because they are "weaker" than morphine) precipitate more severe withdrawal in opioid-dependent persons.

Endorphin is an all-inclusive term that applies to an endogenous substance (a substance naturally formed in the body) that exhibits pharmacological properties of morphine. There are three families of endogenous opioid peptides—*enkephalins, dynorphins,* and *beta endorphins.* The topic of endogenous opioids is large and complex. The interested reader is referred to the review by Akil and coworkers (1998).

The term *narcotic* is derived from the Greek word *narke,* meaning "numbness," "sleep," or "stupor." Originally referring to any drug that induced sleep, the term later became associated with opioids, such as morphine and heroin. Today, it is an imprecise and pejorative term, sometimes used in a legal context to refer to a wide variety of abused substances that includes nonopioids, such as cocaine and marijuana. The term is not useful in a pharmacological context, and its use in referring to opioids is discouraged. It is not used in this chapter.

Opioids are agonists at highly specific receptor sites, and the analgesic potency of the agonist correlates with the affinity of the agonist for the opioid receptor. There is general agreement on the existence of at least three types of opioid receptors: *mu, kappa,* and *delta.* The genes encoding these three families, as well as the receptors themselves, have been cloned, sequenced, and well studied (Kieffer, 1999).

Opioids occur in nature in two places: in the juice of the opium poppy (morphine and codeine) and within our own bodies as any of the endorphins. All other opioids either are prepared from morphine (*semisynthetic opioids,* such as heroin) or are synthesized from other precursor compounds (*synthetic opioids,* such as fentanyl).

Opioid Receptors

Receptors on which endorphins and exogenous opioids act are widely distributed throughout the CNS, and each type of opioid receptor is differentially distributed. Some regions (for example, the spinal cord) have all three types of receptors; other regions have predominantly one type (the thalamus, for example, has primarily mu receptors). The clinical significance of this distribution is still unclear. However, overall, it seems that mu receptor agonists display not only the best and strongest analgesic actions but also the highest abuse liability (Kieffer, 1999).

Mu receptors are located in the brain, in the spinal cord, and in the periphery. Morphine is an example of a mu agonist. Thus, morphine exerts powerful effects on the brain (especially in the thalamus and striatum), the brain stem (where it slows respiration), and the spinal cord (where it exerts a strong analgesic action). In contrast, the delta receptor agonists exhibit little addictive potential and are also poor analgesics. Delta receptors are thought to modulate the activity of mu receptors. Kappa agonists exert modest analgesic effects, little or no respiratory depression, miosis (pinpoint pupils), and little or no dependence effects. In fact, activation of kappa receptors may serve to antagonize mu receptor-mediated actions in the brain (Pan, 1998). The use of kappa agonists is limited by strong dysphoric responses that can accompany their use (Kieffer, 1999).

In the mid-1990s the opioid receptors were first isolated, purified, cloned, and sequenced and their three-dimensional structures were modeled. All opioid receptors belong to a superfamily of G protein-coupled receptors, all of which possess seven membrane-spanning regions (Figure 15.4), similar to the receptors discussed earlier. Each receptor type (mu, kappa, delta) arises from its own gene and is expressed through a specific messenger RNA (mRNA). Each receptor is a chain of approximately 450 amino acids, and the amino acid sequences are about 60 percent identical to one another and 40 percent different

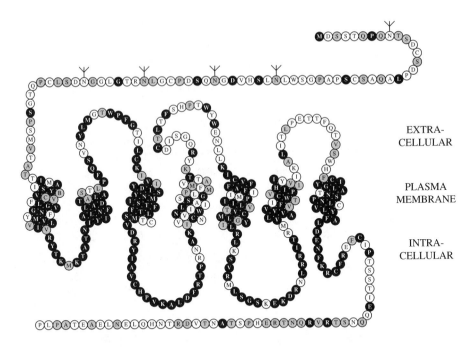

FIGURE 15.4 Two-dimensional model of the rat mu opioid receptor. The receptor is a chain of about 390 amino acids (the letter in each circle is the first letter of the individual amino acid), with seven transmembrane coils and a terminal chain both intracellular (linked to a G protein, not illustrated) and extracellular (binds the transmitter). Amino acids conserved in mu, delta, and kappa receptors are shown in black; amino acids conserved in mu and *either* delta or kappa receptors are shown in gray; amino acids preset only in the mu receptor (not in delta or kappa receptors) are shown in white. [From M. Satoh and M. Minami, "Molecular Pharmacology of the Opioid Receptors," *Pharmacology and Therapeutics* 68 (1995), pp. 343–364.]

(see Figure 15.4). The diversity is responsible for the specific fit of an endogenous endorphin or an exogenous opioid to a specific receptor. A fit for a fentanyl derivative for a mu receptor is illustrated in Figure 15.5. In this figure, note that the flat, two-dimensional drawing of the receptor shown in Figure 15.4 is now depicted more realistically as a three-dimensional receptor with seven helical coils embedded in the membrane and three amino acid loops and a terminal chain (located in the extracellular, synaptic space) forming a fit with the opioid.

What is the consequence of the binding of an opioid agonist to a mu receptor? As discussed, the primary action of opioid receptor activation (by either an endorphin or an opioid) is reduction in or inhibition of neurotransmission, which occurs largely through opioid-induced presynaptic inhibition of neurotransmitter release (Figure 15.6). Gutstein and coworkers (1997) demonstrated that opioids strongly activate important intracellular cascades, which induce changes in cellular function to the

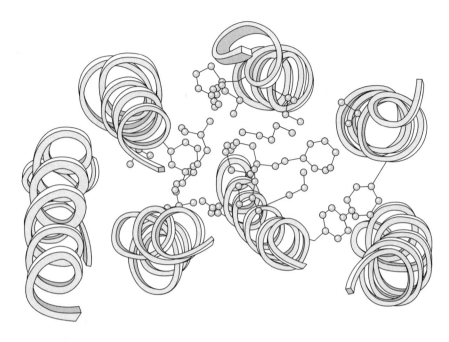

FIGURE 15.5 Speculative three-dimensional depiction of interaction of the mu opioid receptor with the potent pure mu agonist lofentanyl. Transmembrane helices are depicted by coils. The cell membrane within which the coils reside is not illustrated. Lofentanyl structure is shown by the connected small circles, which represent carbon molecules of the drug. Specific side chains of amino acids on the receptor helices bind with specific portions of the lofentanyl molecule. [Original details by H. Moereels, L. M. Kaymans, J. Leysen, and P. Janssen (Janssen Research Foundation, Beerse, Belgium).]

level of nuclear proteins. Changes were different for each receptor type and may explain the differences in receptor function (for example, mu receptor action induces euphoria and is a positive reinforcer, while kappa receptor activation causes dysphoria and is a negative reinforcer; Table 15.1).

Mu Receptors

Mu opioid receptors (and the messenger RNA that expresses the receptor protein) are present in all structures in the brain and spinal cord involved in morphine-induced analgesia. The structures include the peri-aquaductal gray, spinal trigeminal nucleus, caudate and geniculate nuclei, thalamus, and spinal cord (dorsal horn). Mu receptors are also present in brain-stem nuclei involved in control of respiration (and in morphine's depression of respiration), in brain-stem structures involved in initiation of nausea and vomiting, and in the nucleus accumbens, an

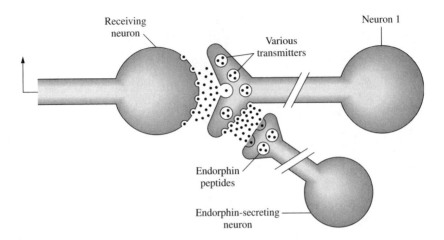

FIGURE 15.6 Simplified illustration demonstrating the presynaptic inhibition (exerted by an endorphin-secreting neuron) on neuron 1, inhibiting its release of transmitter. In the spinal cord, neuron 1 would be a primary afferent (sensory pain neuron), with enkephalin-inhibiting substance P release. In the ventral tegmentum, neuron 1 might be a GABA-secreting neuron, with an endorphin-inhibiting GABA release, disinhibiting a dopaminergic neuron, a mechanism of opioid-induced reward.

area involved in the compulsive abuse of opioids and other drugs subject to compulsive abuse. Few or no mu receptors (or its mRNA) are found in the cerebral cortex or cerebellum.

Kappa Receptors

Kappa receptors (and the mRNA that expresses the receptor protein) are found in high concentrations in the basal ganglia, nucleus accumbens, ventral tegmentum, deep layers of cerebral cortex, hypothalamus, periaquaductal gray, dorsal horn of spinal cord, and in the periphery. Binder and coworkers (2001) studied two experimental

TABLE 15.1 Responses mediated by opioid receptors

Receptor	Response on activation
μ (mu)	Analgesia, respiratory depression, miosis, euphoria, reduced gastrointestinal motility
κ (kappa)	Analgesia, dysphoria, psychotomimetic effects, miosis, and respiratory depression

kappa agonists that do not cross the blood-brain barrier but act only in the periphery. They were both very analgesic and anti-inflammatory. The researchers concluded that the agonists might well potentiate other centrally acting opioids or standard anti-inflammatory drugs (NSAIDs; Chapter 14).

As stated, kappa receptors in the CNS may actually antagonize mu receptor activity. Kappa receptors produce modest amounts of analgesia, dysphoria (as opposed to mu receptor-induced euphoria), disorientation, rare feelings of depersonalization, and only mild respiratory depression. The mixed agonist-antagonist drugs, such as pentazocine (Talwin), are agonists at the kappa receptors. Dynorphin is the endorphin with the greatest affinity for the kappa receptor.

Delta Receptors

The enkephalins are the endogenous endorphins for the delta receptors. These receptors are involved in analgesia at both the spinal and brain levels, but further pharmacologic characterization is open to investigation. Delta receptors are also found in the nucleus accumbens and limbic system, possibly playing a role in the emotional responses to opioids. As we will see in Chapter 19, the hallucinogenic agent salvidorin A (from the psychedelic mint plant *Salvia divinorum*) is a potent agonist (stimulant) of the kappa opioid receptor (Chavkin et al., 2004). How this action relates to the modulation of human perception remains to be determined.

Snyder and Pasternak (2003) present an important historical review of the development of our knowledge base about opioid receptors.

Classification of Opioid Analgesics

Classification of opioids is usually according to the receptors to which they bind and the consequences of the binding. Thus, an individual opioid is called an *agonist,* a *partial agonist,* a *mixed agonist-antagonist,* or a *pure antagonist* at the given receptor (Table 15.2). All the strong opioids, such as morphine, primarily act as agonists at mu receptors, and their pharmacological effects, including analgesia, respiratory depression, miosis, euphoria, reward, and constipation, all follow from this action.

Pure Agonists

As discussed in Chapter 1, an agonist is a drug that has an affinity for (binds to) cell receptors to induce changes in the cell characteristic of the natural ligand (here, for example, an endorphin) for the receptor. Morphine is the prototype opioid analgesic, and there are many others, including methadone, an orally active, long-acting opioid used to treat heroin dependency. All these strong opioids bind to mu receptors (Table 15.3). As stated, mu agonism invariably results in analgesia,

TABLE 15.2 Classification of opioid analgesics by analgesic properties

Pure agonists	Mixed agonist-antagonists	Pure antagonists	Partial agonists
Morphine	Nalbuphine (Nubain)	Naloxone (Narcan)	Buprenorphene (in Suboxone)
Codeine	Butorphanol (Stadol)	Naltrexone (Trexan,	Tramadol (Ultram)[a]
Heroin	Pentazocine (Talwin)	ReVia)	
Meperidine (Demerol)	Dezocine (Dalgan)	Nalmefene (Revex)	
Methadone (Dolophine)			
Oymorphone (Numorphan)			
Hydromorphone (Dilaudid)			
Fentanyl (Sublimaze)			

[a] Tramadol also blocks reuptake of norepinephrine and serotonin.

TABLE 15.3 Classification of opioid analgesics by actions at opioid receptors

Compound	Receptor types[a]		
	Mu	**Kappa**	**Delta**
Morphine	+++	+	+
Naloxone	−	−	−
Pentazocine	+/0	+	NA
Butorphanol	+/0	+	NA
Nalbuphine	−	+	NA
Buprenorphine	++	+	+
Fentanyl	+++	+	+
Dezocine	+	+	+

[a] The mu receptor is thought to mediate supraspinal analgesia, respiratory depression, euphoria, and physical dependence; the kappa receptor, spinal analgesia, miosis, and sedation. Categorizations are based on best inferences about actions in humans. See text for further explanation. Agonists are indicated by one or more plus signs, antagonists by a minus sign, and agents that have no significant action at the receptor by zero. NA = data not available.

respiratory depression, and euphoria and has a propensity to cause dependence. So far, all attempts to separate analgesia from euphoria, dependence, and respiratory depression have been unsuccessful and are likely remain so for the foreseeable future.

Pure Antagonists

Pure antagonists have *affinity* for a receptor (here, the mu receptor), but after attaching they elicit no change in cellular functioning (they lack intrinsic activity). What they do is compete with the mu agonist analgesics for the receptor, precipitating withdrawal in an opioid-dependent person and reversing any analgesia caused by the agonist. One example is the clinical use of the opioid antagonist *naltrexone* in treatment programs for heroin addicts, where heroin taken after the antagonist elicits no analgesic or euphoric effects.

Mixed Agonist-Antagonists

A mixed agonist-antagonist drug produces an agonistic effect at one receptor and an antagonistic effect at another. Clinically useful mixed drugs are kappa agonists and weak mu antagonists (they bind to both kappa and mu receptors, but only the kappa receptor is activated). In contrast to a pure agonist, a mixed agonist-antagonist usually displays a ceiling effect for analgesia; in other words, it has decreased efficacy compared to a pure agonist and usually is not so effective in treating severe pain. Also, when a mixed agonist-antagonist is administered to an opioid-dependent person, the antagonist effect at a mu receptor precipitates an acute withdrawal syndrome. *Pentazocine* (Talwin) is the prototype agonist-antagonist.

Partial Agonists

A partial agonist binds to opioid receptors but has a low intrinsic activity (low efficacy). It therefore exerts an analgesic effect, but the effect has a ceiling at less than the maximal effect produced by a pure agonist. *Buprenorphine* (in Suboxone) is the prototype partial opioid agonist. When administered to a naive individual, analgesia is observed; when administered to an opioid-dependent individual, however, blockade of the pure agonist can occur and withdrawal can be precipitated. Compared to a mixed agonist-antagonist, the partial agonist buprenorphine binds to all three types of opioid receptors with higher efficacy at mu receptors than do the mixed agonist-antagonist agents. Its potential for producing respiratory depression is reduced when compared with that produced by morphine.

Morphine: A Pure Opioid Agonist

Two analgesics (morphine and codeine) are found in the opium poppy. Morphine (Figure 15.7) is the more potent and represents about 10 percent of the crude exudate. Codeine is much less potent and constitutes only 0.5 percent of the crude exudate. Despite decades of research, no other drug has been found that exceeds morphine's effectiveness as an analgesic, and no other drug is clinically superior for treating severe pain.

Pharmacokinetics

Morphine is usually administered by injection, but it may also be given orally or rectally. Orally, morphine is available in immediate-release formulation and as a long-acting, time-release product (MS Contin). In general, absorption of morphine from the gastrointestinal tract is slow and incomplete compared to absorption following injection or inhalation. Absorption through the rectum is adequate, and several opioids (morphine, hydromorphone, and oxymorphone) are available in suppository form. (This kind of preparation might be indicated in patients suffering from muscle-wasting diseases who cannot tolerate other routes of administration.)

The action of opioids in the spinal cord has led to the administration of morphine directly into the spinal canal (through small catheters), placing the drug right at its site of action and avoiding its

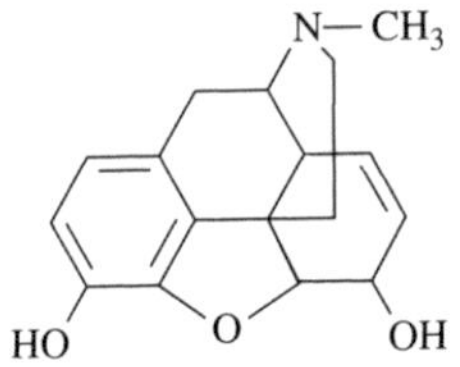

Morphine

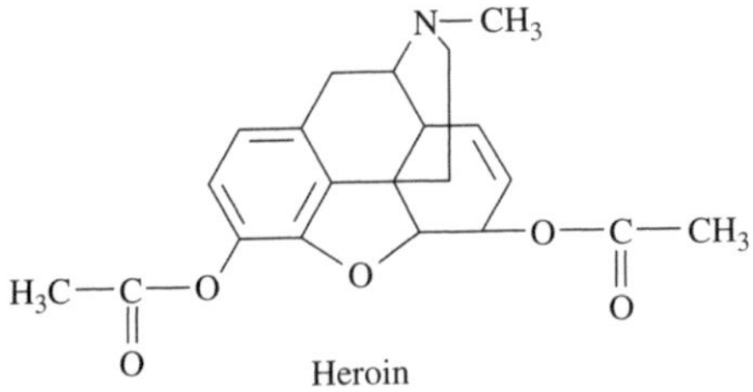

Heroin

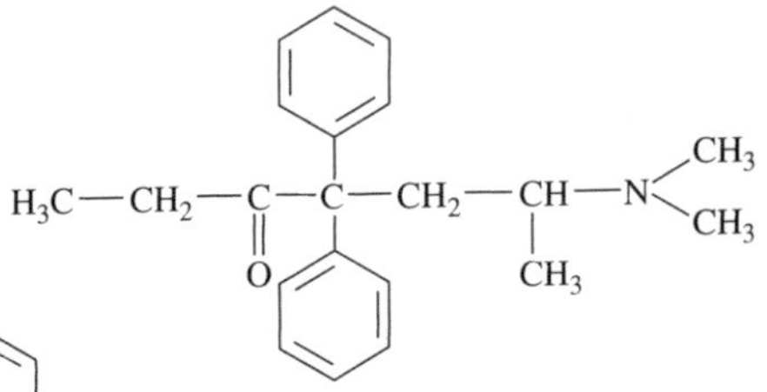

Methadone (Dolophine)

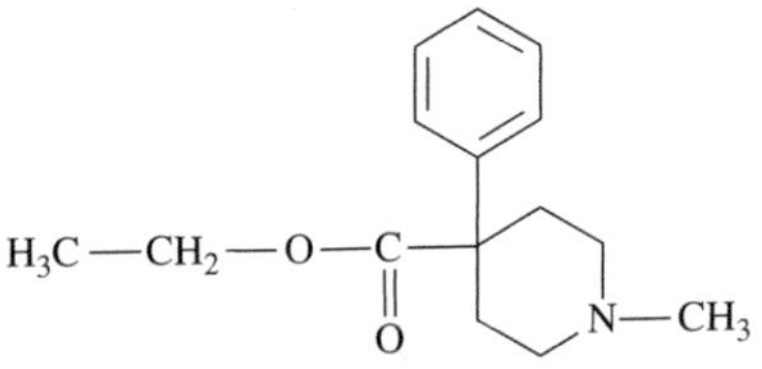

Meperidine (Demerol)

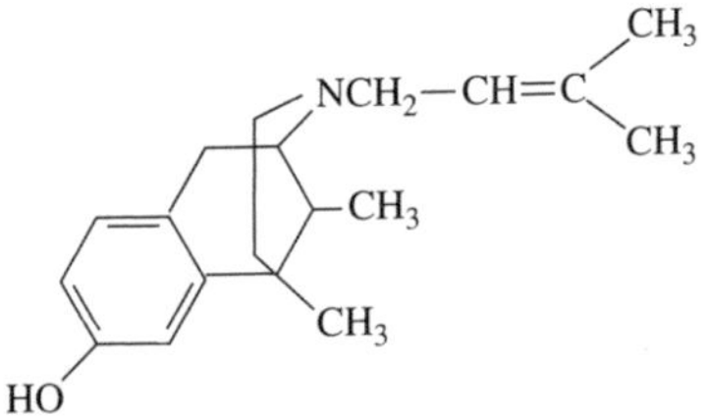

Pentazocine (Talwin)

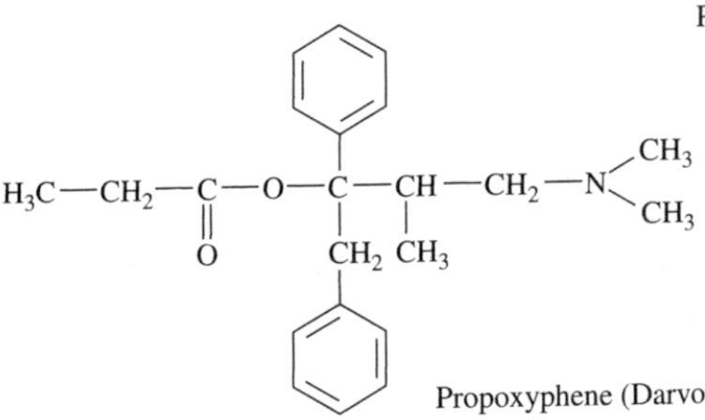

Propoxyphene (Darvon)

FIGURE 15.7 Structures of morphine, heroin, and four synthetic analgesics.

effects both on higher CNS centers (maintaining wakefulness and avoiding respiratory depression) and in the periphery (avoiding drug-induced constipation). In medicine, this technique is used to control the pain of obstetric labor and delivery, to treat postoperative pain, and (for long-term use) to relieve otherwise intractable pain associated with terminal cancer and chronic pain problems.

Morphine administered by injection must be given with great care to avoid potentially fatal respiratory depression. Regarding inhalation, for millennia crude opium has been smoked for recreational purposes; the rapidity of onset of drug action rivals that following intravenous injection. Morphine itself is rarely abused in this manner; heroin is the preparation of choice. However, for therapeutic use, a nebulized form of morphine is currently under development (Thipphawong et al., 2003).

Morphine only fairly slowly crosses the blood-brain barrier, as it is more water soluble than lipid soluble. Other opioids (such as heroin and fentanyl) cross the blood-brain barrier much more rapidly. Only about 20 percent of administered morphine reaches the CNS. This may explain why the "flash" or "rush" following intravenous injection of heroin is so much more intense than that perceived after injecting morphine.

Opioids reach all body tissues, including the fetus; infants born of addicted mothers are physically dependent on opioids and exhibit withdrawal symptoms that require intensive therapy. The habitual use of morphine or other opioids during pregnancy does not seem to increase the risk of congenital anomalies; thus these drugs are not considered to be teratogenic. However, there are increased risks of birth-related problems and fetal growth retardation. Other delays and impairments observed in the development of opioid-exposed children may relate more to environmental and social-developmental problems.

The liver metabolizes morphine, and one of its metabolites (morphine-6-glucuronide) is actually 10 to 20 times more potent as an analgesic than morphine. Much of the analgesic action of morphine is mediated by this active metabolite. The half-lives of morphine and morphine-6-glucuronide are both three to five hours. Patients with impaired kidney function tend to accumulate the metabolite and thus may be more sensitive to morphine administration.

Urine-screening tests can be used to detect codeine and morphine as well as their metabolites. Because heroin is metabolized to monoacetylmorphine and then to morphine, and because street heroin also contains acetylcodeine (which is metabolized to codeine), heroin use is suspected when monoacetylmorphine, morphine, and codeine are present in urine. Frequently, urinalysis cannot accurately determine which specific drug (heroin, codeine, or morphine) has been used. Furthermore, codeine is widely available in cough syrups and analgesic preparations, and even poppy seeds contain small amounts of morphine. Depending on the drug that was taken, morphine and codeine metabolites may be detected in a patient's urine for two to four days.

Pharmacological Effects

Morphine produces a syndrome characterized by analgesia, relaxed euphoria, sedation, a sense of tranquility, reduced apprehension and concern, respiratory depression, suppression of the cough reflex, and pupillary constriction (see Table 15.1).

Analgesia. Morphine produces intense analgesia and indifference to pain, reducing the intensity of pain and thus reducing the associated distress by altering the central processing of pain. Morphine analgesia occurs without loss of consciousness and without affecting other sensory modalities. The pain may actually persist as a sensation, but patients feel more comfortable and are able to tolerate the pain. In other words, the perception of the pain is significantly altered.

Euphoria. Morphine produces a pleasant euphoric state, which includes a strong feeling of contentment, well-being, and lack of concern. This effect is part of the affective, or reinforcing, response to the drug. Use of exogenous opioids gives a person access to the reinforcement system, especially in the nucleus accumbens. This positive reward system, normally reserved to reward the performance of species-specific survival behaviors, once reached by opioids, provides the user with a profoundly rewarding experience. Opioid use becomes an acquired drive state that permeates all aspects of human life. With acute use, all painful feelings, emotions, and physical discomforts become tolerable. Even the knowledge that withdrawal will follow, that life and livelihood are imperiled, that only more drug will avail withdrawal, that legal apprehension or even death may follow—all this becomes tolerable as long as drug is present. Separate neural pathways that cause withdrawal events to be perceived as life-threatening and the subsequent physiologic reactions often lead to renewed opioid consumption. As discussed in the section on the treatment of chronic alcoholism, the drive to resume ingestion of drug now appears to involve the endogenous cannabinoid system, as cannabinoid receptor antagonists (Chapter 18) can block the compulsion to return to drug use. The same cannabinoid system that can propel a return to alcohol drinking probably is involved in a compulsion to return to opioid use.

Regular users of morphine describe the effects of intravenous injection in ecstatic and often sexual terms, but the euphoric effect becomes progressively less intense after repeated use. At this point, users inject the drug for one or more of several possible reasons: to try to reexperience the euphoria experienced after the first few injections, to maintain a state of pleasure and well-being, to prevent mental discomfort that may be associated with reality, or to prevent withdrawal symptoms.

The mechanism of morphine's positive reinforcing and euphoria-producing action probably involves dopaminergic as well as mu receptors. Opioids activate mu receptors within the mesolimbic dopamine reward system by means of the dopaminergic ventral tegmental--nucleus accumbens pathway that is involved in the rewarding effects of cocaine and alcohol. As stated by Narita and coworkers (2001):

> Various studies provide arguments to support substantial roles for mu-opioid receptors and the possible involvement of delta-opioid receptors in the development of physical and psychological dependence on morphine. Noradrenergic transmission originating in the locus coeruleus is most likely to play the primary causal role in the expression of physical dependence on morphine. In contrast, many studies have pointed to the mesolimbic dopaminergic pathway projecting from the ventral tegmental area to the nucleus accumbens as a critical site for the initiation of psychological dependence on opioids. (p. 1)

In the ventral tegmental area, morphine inhibits GABA neurons via mu opioid receptors, thus disinhibiting dopaminergic neurons and increasing dopamine input in the nucleus accumbens and in other areas; this phenomenon may be involved in the mechanism of reward, that is, the positive reinforcer to opioid addiction.

Sedation and Anxiolysis. Morphine produces anxiolysis, sedation, and drowsiness, but the level of sedation is not so deep as that produced by the CNS depressants. Although persons who are taking morphine will doze, they can usually be awakened readily. During this state, "mental clouding" is prominent, accompanied by a lack of concentration, apathy, complacency, lethargy, reduced mentation, and a sense of tranquility. Obviously, in such a state, cognitive impairment results.

Depression of Respiration. Morphine causes a profound depression of respiration by decreasing the respiratory center's sensitivity to higher levels of carbon dioxide in the blood. Respiratory rate is reduced even at therapeutic doses; at higher doses, the rate slows even further, respiratory volume decreases, breathing patterns become shallow and irregular, and, at sufficiently high levels, breathing ceases. Respiratory depression is the single most important acute side effect of morphine and is the cause of death from acute opioid overdosage. The combination of morphine (or other opioid) with alcohol or other sedatives is especially dangerous. Bailey and coworkers (2000) review the effects of morphine on respiration.

Suppression of Cough. Opioids suppress the "cough center," which is located in the brain stem. Opioids have historically been used as cough suppressants, codeine being particularly popular for this purpose.

Today, however, less addicting drugs are used as cough suppressants; opioids are inappropriate choices for treating persistent cough. One of these substitute products is *dextromethorphan*; this drug will be discussed later in this chapter and in Chapter 19.

Pupillary Constriction. Morphine (as well as other mu and kappa agonists) causes pupillary constriction (miosis). Indeed, pupillary constriction in the presence of analgesia is characteristic of opioid ingestion.

Nausea and Vomiting. Morphine stimulates receptors in an area of the medulla that is called the chemoreceptor trigger zone. Stimulation of this area produces nausea and vomiting, which are the most characteristic and unpleasant side effects of morphine and other opioids, but they are not life threatening.

Gastrointestinal Symptoms. Morphine and the other opioids relieve diarrhea as a result of their direct actions on the intestine, the most important action of morphine outside the CNS. Opioids cause intestinal tone to increase, motility to decrease, feces to dehydrate, and intestinal spasm (and cramping) to occur. This combination of decreased propulsion, increased intestinal tone, decreased rate of movement of food, and dehydration hardens the stool and further retards the advance of fecal material. All these effects contribute to the constipating effect of opioids. Nothing more effective than the opioids has yet been developed for treating severe diarrhea. In recent years two opioids have been developed that only very minimally cross the blood-brain barrier into the CNS. The first is *diphenoxylate* (the primary active ingredient in Lomotil), and the second is *loperamide* (Imodium). These two drugs are exceedingly effective opioid antidiarrheals but are not analgesics, nor are they prone to compulsive abuse because they do not reach the CNS.

Other Effects. Morphine can release histamine from its storage sites in mast cells in the blood, which can result in localized itching or more severe allergic reactions, including bronchoconstriction (an asthmalike constriction of the bronchi of the lungs). Opioids also affect white blood cell function, perhaps producing complex alterations in the immune system. It is advisable, perhaps, to avoid the use of morphine in patients with compromised immune function.

Tolerance and Dependence

The development of tolerance and dependence with repeated use is a characteristic feature of all opioid drugs, including morphine. The use of all mu agonist opioids is severely limited because of the development of tolerance, the presence of uncomfortable side effects, and the potential for compulsive abuse.

The molecular basis of tolerance is now thought to involve gluta-minergic mechanisms (Celerier et al., 2000; Gies et al., 1997). It appears that glutaminergic NMDA receptors may regulate mu receptor mRNA, accounting for the development of tolerance to the continuous presence of opioid. Akil and coworkers (1998) review the intracellular alterations induced by morphine and their relation to the development of tolerance after prolonged exposure to opioids. Christensen and coworkers (2000) review the current understanding of the complex interaction among glutamate, NMDA receptor blockade, analgesia, and the development of tolerance and dependence.

The rate at which tolerance develops varies widely. When morphine or other opioids are used only intermittently, little, if any, tolerance develops, and the opioids retain their initial efficacy. When administration is repeated, tolerance may become so marked that massive doses have to be administered to either maintain a degree of euphoria or prevent withdrawal discomfort (avoidance of discomfort is more common). The degree of tolerance is illustrated by the fact that the dose of morphine can be increased from clinical doses (50 to 60 milligrams per day) to 500 milligrams per day over as short a period as 10 days.

Tolerance to one opioid leads to cross-tolerance to all other natural and synthetic opioids, even if they are chemically dissimilar. Cross-tolerance, however, does not develop between the opioids and the sedative hypnotics. In other words, a person who has developed a tolerance for morphine will also have a tolerance for heroin but not for alcohol or barbiturates.

Physical dependence was described in Chapter 1 as an altered state of biology induced by a drug whereby withdrawal of a drug is followed by a complex set of biological events typical for that class of drugs. Acute withdrawal from opioids has been well studied, since it can be easily precipitated in drug-dependent individuals by injecting the opioid antagonist naloxone (Narcan). Withdrawal results in a profound reduction in the release of dopamine in the nucleus accumbens and a threefold increase in the release of norepinephrine in various structures, including the hippocampus, nucleus accumbens, and locus coeruleus. The firing rate of neurons located in the locus coeruleus is actively inhibited by morphine, returns to baseline levels with tolerance, and rises dramatically during withdrawal; these phenomena may be involved in the mechanism of dependence—the negative reinforcer to opioid addiction.

Symptoms of withdrawal are, in general, the opposite of pharmacological effects (Table 15.4) and include restlessness, dysphoria, drug craving, sweating, extreme anxiety, depression, irritability, fever, chills, retching and vomiting, increased respiratory rate (panting), cramping, insomnia, explosive diarrhea, and intense aches and pains. The magnitude of these acute withdrawal symptoms depends on the dose of opioid that had been used, the frequency of previous drug administration,

TABLE 15.4 Acute effects of opioids and rebound withdrawal symptoms

Acute action	Withdrawal sign
Analgesia	Pain and irritability
Respiratory depression	Hyperventilation
Euphoria	Dysphoria and depression
Relaxation and sleep	Restlessness and insomnia
Tranquilization	Fearfulness and hostility
Decreased blood pressure	Increased blood pressure
Constipation	Diarrhea
Pupillary constriction	Pupillary dilation
Hypothermia	Hyperthermia
Drying of secretions	Lacrimation, runny nose
Reduced sex drive	Spontaneous ejaculation
Peripheral vasodilation; flushed and warm skin	Chilliness and "gooseflesh"

From R. S. Feldman, J. S. Meyer, and L. F. Quenzer, *Principles of Neuropsycholpharmacology* (Sunderland, MA: Sinauer, 1997), Table 12.8, p. 533.

and the duration of drug dependence. Acute opioid withdrawal is not considered to be life threatening, although it can seem unbearable to the person experiencing it.

To help alleviate the symptoms of acute withdrawal, several approaches have been tried. One newer method is termed *rapid opioid detoxification* or, perhaps more appropriately, *rapid anesthesia-aided detoxification* (RAAD) (Gold et al., 1999). A pure opioid antagonist, such as naloxone or naltrexone, and the sympathetic blocker clonidine are administered intravenously to the opioid-dependent person while he or she is asleep under general anesthesia. The procedure goes on for one to two days, during which time the withdrawal signs are blunted. The objective is to enable the patient to tolerate high doses of an opioid antagonist and thus undergo complete detoxification while unconscious, rather than over several days or weeks while awake and suffering from severe withdrawal symptoms. After awakening, the patient is maintained on orally administered naltrexone to reduce opioid craving and undergoes supportive psychotherapy and group therapies for relapse prevention and to address the underlying causes of addiction. The RAAD technique is controversial, in part because it is expensive, it involves the risks of anesthesia, and it focuses only on short-term dependence rather than on long-term cravings and social adjustments.

No matter the method of opioid withdrawal, following acute withdrawal, focus is directed toward a protracted *abstinence syndrome*, beginning when the acute phase of opioid withdrawal ends and persisting for up to six months. Symptoms of this syndrome include depression, abnormal responses to stressful situations, drug hunger, decreased self-esteem, anxiety, and other psychological disturbances. Complicating the diagnosis of prolonged abstinence syndrome is the high prevalence of other psychiatric disorders (for example, affective and personality disorders) in opioid-dependent patients. Brooner and coworkers (1997) documented psychiatric comorbidity in 47 percent of 716 treatment-seeking opioid abusers; antisocial personality disorder (25 percent) and major depression (15 percent) are the most common diagnoses. Nunes and coworkers (1998) reported a "robust antidepressant effect of *imipramine*" (Chapter 9) in 57 percent of 84 depressed opioid-dependent people. Oliveto and coworkers (1999) reported that another antidepressant, *desipramine*, increased opioid (and cocaine) abstinence in opioid-dependent cocaine abusers. Several behavioral theories have been posited to account for continued opioid use:

- Continued use avoids the distress and dysphoria associated with withdrawal (a negative reinforcing effect).

- The euphoria produced by the opioids leads to their continued use (a positive reinforcing effect).

- Preexisting dysphoric or painful affective states are alleviated. This presumes that the opioids were initially used as a type of self-medication to treat these symptoms, and dependence gradually developed.

- The euphoric response is an atypical response to opioids that occurs in individuals with preexisting psychopathology.

- Preexisting psychopathology may be the basis for initial experimentation and euphoria, but repeated use is prompted by the desire to avoid withdrawal.

- Some individuals have deficient endorphin systems that are corrected by the use of opioids.

- Repeated use of opioids leads to permanent dysfunction in the endorphin system to the point that normal function requires the continued use of exogenous opioids.

- Drug effects and drug withdrawal can become linked through environmental cues and internal mood states. Emotions and external cues recall the distress of withdrawal or the memory of opioid euphoria or opioid reduction of dysphoria or painful affective states.

To varying degrees, all these theories are probably involved in a given individual's use of opioids. Opioid tolerance and dependence lie not merely in a few predisposed individuals; they can develop in anyone who uses the drugs repeatedly, not necessarily people who are abusing them. A patient in the chronic pain of terminal illness should not be denied opioids, despite the inevitable development of tolerance and dependence.

Other Pure Opioid Agonists

As discussed earlier, pure opioid agonists are stimulants of the mu opioid receptor. The prototype pure opioid agonist is morphine. However, other naturally occurring opioids (for example, codeine) and several synthetic and semisynthetic opioids are also agonists of the mu opioid receptor. Those drugs are discussed here.

Codeine

Codeine occurs naturally in opium and is one of the most commonly prescribed opioid drugs. For medical use, it is usually combined with aspirin or acetaminophen for the relief of mild to moderate pain. These products are frequently sought drugs of abuse. About 40 percent of people who use them meet the criteria for codeine dependence (Sproule et al., 1999), and the use of codeine-containing products is strongly associated with endogenous depression—a dual-diagnosis problem (Romach et al., 1999). The plasma half-life and duration of action is about three to four hours.

Pharmacokinetically, codeine is metabolized by hepatic cytochrome CYP2D6 enzymes to morphine, and many of the clinical effects attributed to codeine (for example, pain relief and euphoria) may, in fact, result from the actions of morphine. Selective serotonin antidepressants can block the pain relief of codeine because they block the conversion of codeine to morphine. For patients taking an SSRI, an analgesic drug other than codeine may have to be selected.

Heroin

Heroin (diacetylmorphine) is three times more potent than morphine and is produced from morphine by a slight modification of chemical structure (see Figure 15.7). The increased lipid solubility of heroin leads to faster penetration of the blood-brain barrier, producing an intense rush when the drug is either smoked or injected intravenously. Heroin is metabolized to monoacetylmorphine and morphine; the latter is eventually metabolized and excreted. Heroin is legally available in Great Britain and Canada, where it can be used clinically. The drug is not legal in the United States, but it is widely used illicitly. When heroin is smoked together with crack cocaine, euphoria is intensified, the anxiety and paranoia associated with cocaine are tempered, and the depression that follows after the effects of cocaine wear off is reduced. Unfortunately, this combination creates a multidrug addiction that is extremely difficult to treat.

Hydromorphone and Oxymorphone

Hydromorphone (Dilaudid) and *oxymorphone* (Numorphan) are both structurally related to morphine. Both drugs are as effective as morphine, and they are six to ten times more potent than morphine. Somewhat less sedation but equal respiratory depression is observed.

Meperidine

Meperidine (Demerol) is a synthetic opioid whose structure differs from that of morphine (see Figure 15.7). Because of this structural difference, meperidine was originally thought to be free of many of the undesirable properties of the opioids. However, meperidine is addictive; it can be substituted for morphine or heroin in addicts and is widely prescribed medically. It is one-tenth as potent as morphine, produces a similar type of euphoria, and is equally likely to cause dependence. Meperidine's side effects differ from morphine's and include more excitatory effects, such as tremors, delirium, hyperreflexia, and convulsions. These effects are produced by a metabolite of meperidine (normeperidine) that appears to be responsible for the CNS excitation. Meperidine and normeperidine can accumulate in individuals who have kidney dysfunction or who use only meperidine for their opioid addiction. Withdrawal symptoms develop more rapidly than with morphine because of the shorter duration of action of meperidine.

Methadone

Methadone (Dolophine) is a synthetic mu agonist opioid, the pharmacological activity of which is very similar to that of morphine. Methadone was first shown to cover for and block the effects of heroin withdrawal in 1948. In 1965 it was introduced as substitution treatment for opioid dependency, and since then it has become the principal pharmacologic agent for prevention of abstinence symptoms and signs. The outstanding properties of methadone are its effective analgesic activity, its efficacy by the oral route, its extended duration of action in suppressing withdrawal symptoms in physically dependent individuals, and its tendency to show persistent effects with repeated administration.

The main objectives of methadone maintenance treatment programs are rehabilitation of the dependent individual and reduction of needle-associated diseases, illicit drug use, and crime. Randomized controlled trials of methadone maintenance programs have shown that they generally fulfill these aims. Although there are a number of predictors of the success of a program, the most important is the magnitude of the daily methadone dose. Programs that prescribe average daily doses exceeding 50 milligrams have higher retention rates and lower illicit drug use rates than those in which the average dose is less than 50 milligrams (Preston et al., 2000). Even where liberal doses are used, about one-third of the clients regularly experience withdrawal (they are called *nonholders*) and two-thirds (called *holders*) do not on a once-daily dosing schedule. Thus, to maintain compliance, prescribers must be free to regulate doses to meet individual requirements. (The generally accepted half-life of methadone is 24 hours.) Dyer and coworkers (1999) determined that this variability was a pharmacokinetic (not a receptor or pharmacodynamic) consequence, as some clients appear to metabolize methadone more quickly; small changes in plasma concentration can lead to relatively large changes in clinical effect (for example, withdrawal). Dyer and his colleagues concluded that (1) once-daily dosage is not suitable for at least one-third of clients; (2) dividing the daily dose may be more appropriate for nonholders; (3) use of a longer-acting opioid might be considered. Here, levo-alpha acetylmethadol (LAAM) and slow-release morphine are promising candidates.

Federal regulations until very recently restricted the care of opioid-dependent persons to federally licensed narcotic treatment programs (methadone maintenance programs) with little or no involvement by community-based health care workers. As well as some of these programs work, they reach only 170,000 of the estimated 810,000 opioid-dependent persons in the United States. Fiellin and coworkers (2001a) studied stable methadone maintenance program clients and offered data showing that they can be well cared for by community physicians; the researchers suggest steps to take in order to achieve this. These programs will be discussed later in this chapter.

LAAM

LAAM (levo-alpha acetylmethadol) is related to methadone. It is an oral opioid analgesic that was approved in mid-1993 for the clinical management of opioid dependence in heroin addicts. LAAM is well absorbed from the gastrointestinal tract. It has a slow onset and a long duration of action (about 72 hours). It is metabolized to compounds that are also active as opioid agonists. Its primary advantage over methadone is its long duration of action; in maintenance therapy it is administered by mouth three times a week. With LAAM, a major controversy relates both to dose-related efficacy and to comparative efficacy with methadone. Eissenberg and coworkers (1997) studied the problem of dose efficacy. They noted that heroin use decreased as the LAAM dose was increased (presumably fewer people were experiencing withdrawal symptoms as the dose increased) to 100/100/140 mg, Monday, Wednesday, and Friday. At this dose, opioid use, opioid craving, and withdrawal symptoms were all reduced. Johnson and coworkers (2000) compared LAAM with methadone and with a new drug, buprenorphine, for opioid maintenance. LAAM and buprenorphine were administered three times a week, methadone daily. Low doses of methadone (20 mg/day) were ineffective. Higher doses of methadone (60–100 mg), 75–115 mg doses of LAAM, and 16–32 mg doses of buprenorphine all substantially reduced the use of illicit opioids (heroin).

Oxycodone

Oxycodone (Percodan, OxyContin) is another semisynthetic opioid similar in action to morphine. The short-acting preparation (Percodan) is primarily prescribed for the treatment of acute pain. Usual doses are about 5 milligrams every 4 to 6 hours. Percodan has been associated with widespread abuse, dependence, and deaths from overdosage. OxyContin is a long-acting product intended for the treatment of chronic or long-lasting pain, such as the pain that often accompanies cancer and persistent musculoskeletal problems. Drug tolerance usually develops and doses are high (tablets contain from 10 to 160 milligrams). OxyContin goes by many street names: poor man's heroin, hillbilly heroin, oxy, OC, killer, and oxycotton, among others. Street prices are ten times the prescription price. Abusers crush the pills, destroying the time-release mechanisms, and either snort the powder or dilute it in water and inject it. Thus, while chronic pain patients are certainly physically dependent on the drug, high-dose abusers are true addicts. Currently, because of immense abuse of OxyContin, efforts are under way to add an opioid antagonist to the product so that injection would precipitate withdrawal. To date, the manufacturer has been slow to respond to the problem of widespread abuse, possibly because yearly sales of OxyContin have approached $1 billion, making the drug a larger seller than Viagra!

Propoxyphene

Propoxyphene (Darvon) is an analgesic compound that is structurally similar to methadone (see Figure 15.7). As an analgesic for treating mild to moderate pain, it is less potent than codeine but more potent than aspirin. When propoxyphene is taken in large doses, opioidlike effects are seen; when it is used intravenously, addicts recognize it as an opioid. Taken orally, propoxyphene does not have much potential for abuse. Some cases of drug dependence have been reported, but to date they have not been of major concern. Because commercial intravenous preparations of propoxyphene are not available, intravenous abuse is encountered only when someone attempts to inject solutions of the powder that is contained in capsules, which are intended for oral use.

Fentanyl and Its Derivatives

Fentanyl (Sublimaze) and three related compounds, *sufentanil* (Sufenta), *alfentanil* (Alfenta), and *remifentanyl* (Ultiva), are short-acting, intravenously administered opioid agonists that are structurally related to meperidine. These four compounds are intended to be used during and after surgery to relieve surgical pain. Fentanyl is now also available both in a transdermal skin patch (Durapatch) (Muijsers and Wagstaff, 2001; Viscusi et al., 2004) and as an oral lozenge on a stick (a "lollipop"). The transdermal route of drug delivery offers prolonged, rather steady levels of drug in blood; the lollipop is used for the short-term treatment of surgical pain in children and for breakthrough pain in chronic pain patients who are intolerant of injections.

Fentanyl and its three derivatives are 80 to 500 times as potent as morphine as analgesics and profoundly depress respiration. Death from these agents is invariably caused by respiratory failure. In illicit use, fentanyl is known as "china white." Numerous derivatives (such as *methylfentanyl)* have been manufactured illegally; they emerge periodically and have been responsible for many fatalities.

Partial Opioid Agonists

Pure agonists (such as morphine) have strong activity at mu opioid receptors. In contrast to morphine, two drugs, buprenorphine and tramadol, have a lower level of activity at these same receptors. Since they retain some of the analgesic activity of morphine, they have been referred to as *partial opioid agonists*

Buprenorphine

Buprenorphine (Buprenex) is a newer, semisynthetic, partial opioid agonist whose action is characterized by a limited stimulation of mu receptors, which is responsible for its analgesic properties. As a partial agonist, however, there is a ceiling to its analgesic effectiveness as well as to its potential for inducing euphoria and respiratory depression. Buprenorphine has a very long duration of action (about 24 hours) because it binds very strongly to mu receptors, limiting its reversibility by naloxone when reversal is considered necessary. The most common side effects are flulike symptoms, headache, sweating, sleeping difficulties, nausea, and mood swings.

As discussed, Johnson and coworkers (2000) found buprenorphine comparable to methadone and LAAM for treatment of opioid-dependent persons. Kakko and coworkers (2003) reported that buprenorphine was safe and effective as a maintenance medication in treating heroin addiction. Petry and coworkers (1999) found that, because of its ceiling effect, doses four times the daily maintenance dose could be given twice weekly without either agonist effects or withdrawal symptoms occurring. Following much delay, buprenorphine has recently been approved and marketed for the maintenance treatment of heroin or other opioid dependence. *Subutex* is buprenorphine as a sole ingredient; *Suboxone* is a combination product of buprenorphine and naloxone.

Buprenorphine (classified by the FDA as a Schedule III agent) is the first drug approved for office-based opioid dependency treatment under the Federal Drug Addiction Treatment Act of 2000. Therefore, unlike methadone and LAAM, a physician in his or her office can prescribe buprenorphine. Methadone can be prescribed only by especially licensed physicians for opioid-dependent patients through a federally licensed methadone clinic. Also, patients can take home buprenorphine instead of appearing at the clinic every day. Resnick (2003) discusses this new legislation. Fiellen and coworkers (2001b, 2002) discuss the role of buprenorphine as an office-based treatment option. Fudala and coworkers (2003) and Clark (2003) further discuss this new treatment option, encouraging physicians to undergo training to use these agents and to administer them comfortably as part of their medical practice.

Umbricht and coworkers (1999) used buprenorphine as a "tapering" medication for rapid opioid detoxification, following buprenorphine with successful opioid antagonist therapy (naltrexone). The researchers concluded that the combination was an acceptable and safe treatment for shortened opioid detoxification and induction of naltrexone maintenance. The availability of buprenorphine offers clinicians a new option for the treatment of opioid dependence.

Bai-Fang and coworkers (2004) report positive results with the use of a newly developed depot preparation of buprenorphine in opioid detoxification.

Tramadol

Tramadol (Ultram), available in Europe for many years, became available for use as an analgesic in the United States in 1995. The drug exhibits a unique dual analgesic action: (1) it is a partial agonist at mu receptors, and (2) it blocks the presynaptic reuptake of norepinephrine and serotonin, producing both an antidepressant and an analgesic action (Naguib et al,, 1998). In the United States, tramadol is available only for oral use. Well absorbed orally, the drug undergoes a two-step metabolism, and the first metabolite (monodemethyl tramadol) is as active or more active than the parent compound. As a partial agonist, the drug exhibits a ceiling effect on analgesia (it is not so analgesic as morphine), which limits respiratory depression and abuse potential. Side effects are considerable and include drowsiness and vertigo, nausea, vomiting, constipation, and headache. Additive sedation with CNS depressants is observed. Reports of its use in treating opioid dependency are not available.

There has been concern about the combination of tramadol and serotonin-type antidepressant drugs: the combination may increase the toxicity of the antidepressants (causing a serotonin syndrome; Chapter 9). This drug combination should probably be avoided, if possible.

Mixed Agonist-Antagonist Opioids

There are four commercially available drugs classified as mixed agonist-antagonist opioids: pentazocine, butorphanol, nalbuphine, and dezocine (Figure 15.8). Each of these drugs binds with varying affinity to the mu and kappa receptors. The drugs are weak mu agonists; most of their analgesic effectiveness (which is quite limited) results from their stimulation of kappa receptors (see Table 15.3). Low doses cause moderate analgesia; higher doses produce little additional analgesia. In opioid-dependent individuals, these drugs precipitate withdrawal. A high incidence of adverse psychotomimetic side effects (dysphoria, anxiety reactions, hallucinations, and so on) are associated with the use of these agents, limiting their therapeutic use but increasing their attraction for illicit use.

Pentazocine (Talwin) and *butorphanol* (Stadol) are prototypical mixed agonist-antagonists. Neither has much potential for producing respiratory depression or physical dependence. In 1993 butorphanol, previously available for use by injection, became available as a nasal spray, the first analgesic so formulated. After spraying into the nostrils, peak plasma levels (and maximal effect) are achieved in one hour, with a duration of four to five hours. Use of the nasal spray can be euphoric and abuse of this preparation appears to be increasing.

The abuse of pentazocine has also been increasing, particularly in combination with tripelennamine, an antihistamine. This combination of drugs, called "Ts and blues," has caused serious medical complications, including seizures, psychotic episodes, skin ulcerations, abscesses, and muscle wasting. (The latter three effects are caused by the repeated injections rather than by the drugs themselves.)

Nalbuphine (Nubain) is primarily a kappa agonist of limited analgesic effectiveness. Because it is also a mu antagonist, it is not likely to produce either respiratory depression or patterns of abuse.

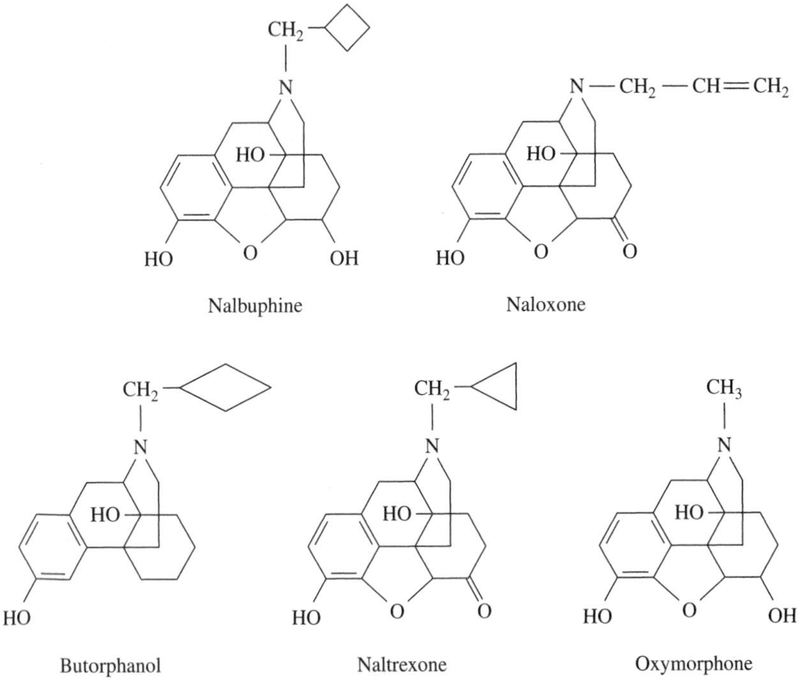

FIGURE 15.8 Structural formulas of oxymorphone and four analogues. Oxymorphone is a pure mu agonist. Nalbuphine and butorphanol have mixed agonistic and antagonistic properties, while naloxone and naltrexone are pure antagonists.

Dezocine (Dalgan) was introduced in 1990 as the newest of the agonist-antagonist drugs. As a moderate mu agonist and a weak delta and kappa agonist, dezocine can substitute for morphine. Its clinical efficacy and potential for abuse appear limited.

Pure Opioid Antagonists

Three clinically available drugs, naloxone, naltrexone, and nalmefene, are structural derivatives of oxymorphone, a pure opioid agonist (see Figure 15.8). All three have an affinity for opioid receptors (especially mu receptors), but after binding they exert no agonistic effects of their own. Therefore, they antagonize the effects of opioid agonists and are termed *pure opioid antagonists*.

Naloxone (Narcan) is the prototype pure opioid antagonist: it has no effect when injected into non-opioid-dependent people, but it rapidly precipitates withdrawal when injected into opioid-dependent people. Naloxone is neither analgesic nor subject to abuse. Because naloxone is neither absorbed from the gastrointestinal tract nor absorbed across the oral mucosa, it must be given by injection. Furthermore, its duration of action is very brief, in the range of 15 to 30 minutes. Thus, for continued opioid antagonism, it must be reinjected at short intervals to avoid "renarcotization." Naloxone is used to reverse the respiratory depression that follows acute opioid intoxication (overdoses) and to reverse opioid-induced respiratory depression in newborns born of opioid-dependent mothers. The limitations of naloxone include its short duration of action and its parenteral route of administration.

Naltrexone (Trexan, ReVia) became clinically available in 1985 as the first orally absorbed, pure opioid antagonist approved for the treatment of heroin dependence. The actions of naltrexone resemble those of naloxone, but naltrexone is well absorbed orally and has a long duration of action, necessitating only a single oral daily dose of about 40 to 100 milligrams. Naltrexone is used clinically in treatment programs when it is desirable to maintain a person on chronic therapy with an opioid antagonist rather than with an agonist such as methadone. In people who take naltrexone daily, any injection of an opioid agonist such as heroin is ineffective. Naltrexone can cause nausea (which can be quite severe in some persons) and dose-dependent liver toxicity, which can be a problem in patients with preexisting liver disease.

One problem with naltrexone is that the drug must be taken in order to be effective. Trite as that sounds, the opioid-dependent person must choose between taking naltrexone or returning to heroin use. Therefore, treatment compliance is poor and only highly motivated addicts take the drug. Recently, Comer and coworkers (2002) injected a "depot" preparation of naltrexone (the drug is suspended in an oil preparation that, when injected intramuscularly, slowly releases the drug over a period of weeks or months) into 12 recently detoxified heroin addicts. The injection completely antagonized heroin-induced subjective effects for a period of five weeks. Side effects were limited to discomfort at the injection site. A depot preparation might improve naltrexone's efficacy in less compliant individuals, requiring only monthly administration to facilitate prolonged abstinence.

As discussed in Chapter 4, naltrexone is approved by the FDA for use in the treatment of alcoholism to reduce the craving for alcohol during the maintenance period of treatment. It is thought that such action follows from the antagonism of endorphin action rather than from an as yet unidentified action outside the opioid system. As was also discussed, however, some reports (Krystal et al., 2001) indicate that in severe alcoholics, naltrexone may be no better than placebo. Also, cessation of naltrexone therapy results in loss of any positive effects (Anton et al., 2001). Carroll and coworkers (2001) reported that contingency management (mainly voucher rewards) significantly improved the response to naltrexone.

Naltrexone has also been reported to have some limited efficacy in the treatment of autism (although the antipsychotic drug *risperidone*, Chapter11, is more effective) and borderline personality disorder—two disorders where some evidence points to a role of the endogenous opioid system. Although naltrexone does not treat any core etiology of autism or bipolar disorder, it can reduce characteristic hyperactivity, irritability, and self-injurious behaviors.

Naltrexone may have a specific preventative role in reducing self-injurious behaviors (White and Schultz, 2000). It is thought that self-injurious behavior can be used to maintain a high level of endogenous opioids, either to prevent decreases in endorphins or to experience the euphoric effect of opioid stimulation following injury. Roth and coworkers (1996) reported that the self-injurious behaviors of six out of seven female patients ceased entirely during naltrexone therapy, with resumption of injurious behavior when the drug was withdrawn.

Nalmefene (Revex), introduced in 1996, is an injectable pure opioid antagonist with a half-life of about 8 to 10 hours, in contrast to the short half-life of injected naloxone. The drug is useful by injection for the treatment of acute opioid-induced respiratory depression caused by overdosage. With its long half-life, the incidence of "renarcotization" is greatly reduced. If administered to an addict, however, the precipitation of withdrawal can be prolonged and require additional medical treatment. Mason and coworkers (1999) studied the effects of orally administered nalmefene[1] as an alternative to naltrexone in alcoholic patients (see Figure 4.9). Treatment for 12 weeks was effective in preventing relapse. The oral preparation is not yet available commercially.

Opioid Combinations

Opioids are irreplaceable as strong and effective pain-relieving agents. However, their dependency potential is enormous, as is the problem of diversion of the drug to illicit users. The major problems, therefore, are twofold: (1) how to maintain efficacy while reducing dependence potential and (2) how to reduce diversion, or use of the drug by others than those for whom the drug was intended.

The first problem has been addressed for years, first by developing analgesics thought to have less dependency potential. Unfortunately, most attempts have failed. For example, heroin was initially developed

---

[1]Nalmefene is currently available only in injectable form. For this study, experimental tablets of nalmefene were supplied by the manufacturer.

as a semisynthetic alternative to morphine (naturally occurring from opium). Meperidine and numerous other drugs were similarly developed. As yet, it has been impossible to separate analgesia, dependence, and respiratory depression, and abuse continues to be a huge problem.

Another approach was to combine the opioid with an analgesic that did not induce dependency. The second analgesic is used to potentiate opioid-induced analgesia using less opioid. For example, for decades, codeine has been combined with aspirin or acetaminophen as a less addicting analgesic product. Currently, a combination of morphine and dextromethorphan is being evaluated for the treatment of moderate to severe pain. Preliminarily, this product is called *MorphiDex*. Dextro-methorphan has been available as an over-the-counter antitussive cough medication for over 40 years. It is now known that dextromethorphan is a glutamate NMDA receptor antagonist that enhances the analgesic properties of morphine. In an oral preparation, analgesia is achieved with about a 50 percent reduction in the dose of morphine. Several reports attest to the effectiveness of this combination (Caruso, 2000; Weinbroum et al., 2002). Other "morphine-sparing" analgesic regimens combine morphine (or another opioid) with an anticonvulsant neuromodulator (Chapter 10) such as lamotrigine (Arguelles et al., 2002) or gabapentin (Matthews and Dickenson, 2002).

Note that abuse of dextromethorphan is increasing. Common products that contain dextromethorphan include Nyquel (which also contains alcohol), various Coricidin products, Robitussin DM, Vicks 44, Tylenol DM, and others. It is also available illicitly through the mail as a powder called DXM. Using dextromethorphan to get high is called "roboing" or "robo-copping." At higher than recommended doses, adverse effects include sedation, agitation, dissociative symptoms, and visual hallucinations (Zawertailo et al., 1998). The effects are quite similar to those produced by phencyclidine and ketamine (Chapter 19), a not surprising fact since phencyclidine and ketamine are both glutamate NMDA receptor blockers, as is dextromethorphan.

The second problem (diversion and abuse of the drug) is persistent, as shown by the wide abuse of oxycodone, fentanyl, morphine, and other opioids. We are, however, learning. When buprenorphine was first developed as a partial opioid agonist in the late 1990s, abuse of the drug was encountered. However, combining the drug with naloxone in 2003 (as *Suboxone*) maintained analgesic efficacy while reducing diversion. The reason is as follows. Buprenorphine is effective given orally, sublingually, or by injection. Naloxone is not absorbed orally or sublingually and is effective as an antagonist only when it is injected. Therefore, when Suboxone is taken sublingually, the buprenorphine is absorbed (and is effective) while the naloxone is not absorbed and is ineffective. However, when this product is crushed, dissolved, and injected, the naloxone is placed in the bloodstream and precipitates withdrawal. Therefore, it is not attractive as a product of abuse. Obviously, intravenous abuse is markedly reduced (Amass et al., 2001; Strain et al., 2000).

Several years ago, the same idea was applied to the mixed agonist-antagonist *pentazocine* (Talwin). Pentazocine was widely abused soon after its introduction. A combination pentazocine/naloxone preparation (Talwin Nx) was marketed, essentially ending abuse of pentazocine. Addition of naloxone to Oxycontin is desperately needed in order to reduce the widespread intravenous abuse of oxycodone.

Pharmacotherapy of Opioid Dependence

Opioid dependence is a brain-related medical disorder (characterized by predictable signs and symptoms) that can be effectively treated with significant benefits for the patient and for society. However, society must make a commitment to offer effective treatment for opioid dependence to all who need it. Everyone dependent on opioids should have access to methadone, LAAM, or buprenorphine maintenance therapy in a methadone clinic or in a physician's office. Not only must governmental policies ensure availability of the programs, but insurance (or Medicare/Medicaid) coverage for these programs should be a required benefit in public and private insurance programs. In any treatment of opioid dependence, pharmacotherapy is the foundation. Medicines are used for the following functions:

1. Maintain dependence on orally administered medications (methadone, LAAM, or buprenorphine/naloxone), thus reducing the use of heroin or other injected agonists

2. Maintain detoxification in predisposed persons (oral naltrexone), combined with random urine checks and vouchers to ensure compliance

3. Maintain detoxification in less compliant persons (intramuscular injections of depot naltrexone, a developing therapy), hoping to eliminate the positive reinforcement of heroin should that drug be smoked or injected

4. Treat comorbid disorders, especially affective disorders such as depression, that complicate recovery

In addition to appropriate pharmacotherapy, nonpharmacologic supportive services are pivotal to successful therapy, whether the therapy is agonist maintenance or detoxification. How much nonpharmacologic supportive service is optimal? Can there be too little? Can there be too much? Kraft and coworkers (1997) determined that large amounts of support to methadone-maintained clients were not cost-effective, but moderate amounts of support are better than minimal amounts. They concluded that there is a floor below which supplementary support should not fall. Similarly, Avants and coworkers (1999) reported that intensive day-treatment programs for unemployed, inner-city methadone patients cost twice as much and were no more effective than a program of enhanced methadone maintenance services, which consisted of standard methadone maintenance plus a weekly skills training group and referral to on-site and off-site services.

What about the duration of methadone or buprenorphine maintenance? Should a goal be eventual withdrawal from agonist therapy? Although data are poor, it is felt that total abstinence from all opioids need not be an objective for all addicts. Goals, however, must include prevention of major relapse to the use of illicitly obtained, injectable opioids (such as heroin). Continuing medically managed supportive opioid therapy may be necessary for many addicts, an approach that follows models of medical illness.

Until recently, the objective has been medically managed withdrawal to an opioid-free state. This goal can be reached successfully in patients who are highly motivated to remain opioid-free. Examples include addicted medical personnel whose continued licensure to practice their profession is contingent on complete abstention from opioids. The continued ingestion of naltrexone implies that an opioid agonist will be ineffective. In many addicts, however, naltrexone therapy is unacceptable, and continued opioid therapy is needed. For these patients, the benefits of maintenance therapy, including significant reductions in illicit opioid use, increases in treatment retention, and improved psychosocial functioning, have been clearly demonstrated within the methadone maintenance model.

Goldstein (1994) reviewed more than 20 years of administering methadone maintenance therapy to 1000 heroin addicts in New Mexico. More than half of the patients were traced and analyzed. Of the 500, more than one-third are now dead; causes include violence, overdosage, and alcoholism. About one-quarter are still enmeshed in the criminal justice system. Another one-quarter go on and off methadone maintenance, indicating that opioid dependence, whether on heroin or on methadone, is a lifelong condition for a considerable fraction of the addict population. With half of the treated population of 1000 addicts unaccounted for, the data are obviously incomplete. It is likely that many of these unaccounted-for former addicts are either drug-free or are stabilized on an opioid and are functional in their communities. The successful graduates of therapy are the most difficult to track, usually preferring to remain anonymous in their communities.

Hser and coworkers (2001) reported a remarkable 33-year follow-up of 581 male heroin addicts who were first identified in the early 1960s.

At follow-up in 1996–1997, 284 were dead and 242 were interviewed; the mean age at interview was 57 years. Of the 242, 20 percent tested positive for heroin (an additional 9.5 percent refused to provide a urine sample, and 14 percent were incarcerated, for whom urinalysis was unavailable); 22 percent were daily alcohol drinkers; 67 percent smoked; many reported illicit drug use (heroin, cocaine, marijuana, amphetamines). The group also reported high rates of health, mental health, and criminal justice problems. Long-term heroin abstinence was associated with less criminality, morbidity, psychological distress, and higher employment.

It therefore appears that setting total abstinence as a goal is seldom accompanied by positive outcomes and leads to a productive life-style in only a minority of cases. If detoxification to a drug-free state is chosen, as soon as opioid-withdrawn individuals relapse, they must be readmitted to agonist maintenance programs immediately and receive both adequate doses and the necessary supportive therapies. The most interesting data now support prolonged opioid maintenance (e.g., methadone or buprenorphine/naloxone) as a treatment goal. Unfortunately, many people still see physical dependence on an opioid as "bad" in and of itself. These attitudes must be changed before widespread attempts at long-term opioid maintenance can be fully evaluated.

STUDY QUESTIONS

1. Describe the location of opioid receptors in the brain and in the spinal cord.

2. How are pain impulses modulated as they enter the spinal cord?

3. What is substance P and how is it influenced by opioid analgesics?

4. What might be the effects of the endorphins?

5. What is an opioid agonist? What is an opioid antagonist? What is a mixed agonist-antagonist? A partial agonist? Give an example of each.

6. What might lead a person to misuse or abuse opioids? What are the signs of opioid misuse/abuse?

7. Differentiate between naloxone and naltrexone. How might each be used?

8. Describe the various ways that opioid dependence might be handled or treated.

9. Why are tricyclic antidepressants analgesic?

10. Differentiate between the opioid modulation of afferent pain impulses and the affective component of pain.

11. Give your thoughts for and against the existence of endogenous opioid peptides (endorphins) that serve as natural opioids.

12. If a patient suffers from chronic pain, what two classes of drugs should be optimized before starting opioid therapy? If opioid therapy is started, how should the opioids be administered?

13. Differentiate the use of opioids in individuals with chronic, nonmalignant pain and in those with pain due to a terminal malignancy.

14. What is buprenorphine? What are its potential uses? Why combine it with naloxone?

15. What allows this drug to be used in medical clinics located in the community and outside licensed methadone clinics?

16. Discuss the various options in the pharmacological management of opioid withdrawal and in the prevention of relapse.

REFERENCES

Akil, H., et al. (1998). "Endogenous Opioids: Overview and Current Issues." *Drug and Alcohol Dependence* 51: 127–140.

Amass, L., et al. (2001). "Thrice-Weekly Supervised Dosing with the Combination Buprenorphine-Naloxone Tablet Is Preferred to Daily Supervised Dosing by Opioid-Dependent Humans." *Drug and Alcohol Dependence* 61: 173–181.

Anton, R. F., et al. (2001). "Posttreatment Results of Combining Naltrexone with Cognitive Behavioral Therapy for the Treatment of Alcoholism." *Journal of Clinical Psychiatry* 21: 72–77.

Arguelles, C. F., et al. (2002). "Peripheral Antinociceptive Action of Morphine and the Synergistic Interaction with Lamotrigine." *Anesthesiology* 96: 921–925.

Avants, S. K., et al. (1999). "Day Treatment Versus Enhanced Standard Methadone Services for Opioid-Dependent Patients: A Comparison of Clinical Efficacy and Cost." *American Journal of Psychiatry* 156: 27–33.

Bai-Fang, et al. (2004). "Open-Label Trial of an Injection Depot Formulation of Buprenorphine in Opioid Detoxification." *Drug and Alcohol Dependence* 73: 11–22.

Bailey, P. L., et al. (2000). "Effects of Intrathecal Morphine on the Ventilatory Response to Hypoxia." *New England Journal of Medicine* 343: 1228–1234.

Bair, M. J., et al. (2003). "Depression and Pain Comorbidity: A Literature Review." *Archives of Internal Medicine* 163: 2433–2445

Bennett, G. J. (2000). "Update on the Neurophysiology of Pain Transmission and Modulation: Focus on the NMDA-Receptor." *Journal of Pain and Symptom Management* 19, Supplement 1: S2–S6.

Binder, W., et al. (2001). "Analgesic Antiinflammatory Effects of Two Novel Kappa-Opioid Peptides." *Anesthesiology* 94: 1034–1044.

Brooner, R. K., et al. (1997). "Psychiatric and Substance Abuse Comorbidity Among Treatment-Seeking Opioid Abusers." *Archives of General Psychiatry* 54: 71–80.

Carroll, K. M., et al. (2001). "Targeting Behavioral Therapies to Enhance Naltrexone Treatment of Opioid Dependence: Effects of Contingency Management and Significant Other Involvement." *Archives of General Psychiatry* 58: 755–761.

Caruso, F. S. (2000). "MorphiDex® Pharmacokinetic Studies and Single-Dose Analgesic Efficacy Studies in Patients with Postoperative Pain." *Journal of Pain and Symptom Management* 19 (1: Proceedings Supplement): S31–S36.

Celerier, E., et al. (2000). "Long-Lasting Hyperalgesia Induced by Fentanyl in Rats: Preventive Effect of Ketamine." *Anesthesiology* 92: 465–472.

Chavkin, C., et al. (2004). "Salvinorin A, an Active Component of the Hallucinogenic Sage *Salvia divinorum*, Is a Highly Efficacious Kappa-Opioid Receptor Agonist: Structural and Functional Considerations." *Journal of Pharmacology and Experimental Therapeutics* 308: 1197–11203.

Christensen, D., et al. (2000). "Complete Prevention but Stimulus-Dependent Reversion of Morphine Tolerance by the Glycine/NMDA Receptor Antagonist (+)-HA966 in Neuropathic Rats." *Anesthesiology* 92: 786–794.

Clark, H. W. (2003). "Office-Based Practice and Opioid-Use Disorders." *New England Journal of Medicine* 349: 928–930.

Comer, S. D., et al. (2002). "Depot Naltrexone: Long-Lasting Antagonism of the Effects of Heroin in Humans." *Psychopharmacology* 159: 351–360.

DeLeo, J. A., and B. A. Winkelstein (2002). "Physiology of Chronic Spinal Pain Syndromes: From Animal Models to Biomechanics." *Spine* 27: 2526–2537.

Dyer, K. R., et al. (1999). "Steady-State Pharmacokinetics and Pharmacodynamics in Methadone Maintenance Patients: Comparison of Those Who Do and Do Not Experience Withdrawal and Concentration-Effect Relationships." *Clinical Pharmacology and Therapeutics* 65: 685–694.

Eissenberg, T., et al. (1997). "Dose-Related Efficacy of Levomethadyl Acetate for Treatment of Opioid Dependency." *Journal of the American Medical Association* 277: 1945–1951.

Fiellin, D. A., et al. (2001a). "Methadone Maintenance in Primary Care: A Randomized Controlled Trial." *Journal of the American Medical Association* 286: 1724–1731.

Fiellin, D. A., et al. (2001b). "Office-Based Treatment for Opioid Dependence: Reaching New Patient Populations." *American Journal of Psychiatry* 158: 1200–1204.

Fiellin, D. A., et al. (2002). "Office Based Treatment of Opioid-Dependent Patients." *New England Journal of Medicine* 347: 817–823.

Fishbain, D. A. (1999). "Approaches to Treatment Decisions for Psychiatric Comorbidity in the Management of the Chronic Pain Patient." *Medical Clinics of North America* 83: 737–757.

Fudala, P. J., et al. (2003). "Office-Based Treatment of Opioid Addiction with a Sublingual-Tablet Formulation of Buprenorphine and Naloxone." *New England Journal of Medicine* 349: 949–958.

Gies, E. K., et al. (1997). "Regulation of Mu Opioid Receptor mRNA Levels by Activation of Protein Kinase C in Human SH-SY5Y Neuroblastoma Cells." *Anesthesiology* 87: 1127–1138.

Gold, C. G., et al. (1999). "Rapid Opioid Detoxification During General Anesthesia: A Review of 20 Patients." *Anesthesiology* 91: 1639–1647

Goldstein, A. (1994). *Addiction: From Biology to Drug Policy*. New York: Freeman.

Gutstein, H. B., et al. (1997). "Opioid Effects on Mitogen-Activated Protein Kinase Signaling Cascades." *Anesthesiology* 87: 1118–1126.

Hser, Y.-I., et al. (2001). "A 33-Year Follow-Up of Narcotic Addicts." *Archives of General Psychiatry* 58: 503–508.

Johnson, R. E., et al. (2000). "A Comparison of Levomethadyl Acetate, Buprenorphine, and Methadone for Opioid Dependence." *New England Journal of Medicine* 343: 1290–1297.

Kakko, J., et al. (2003). "1-Year Retention and Social Function After Buprenorphine-Assisted Relapse Prevention Treatment for Heroin Dependence in Sweden: Randomized, Placebo-Controlled Trial." *Lancet* 361: 662–668.

Kieffer, B. L. (1999). "Opioids: First Lessons from Knockout Mice." *Trends in Pharmacological Sciences* 20: 19–26.

Kraft, M. K., et al. (1997). "Are Supplementary Services Provided During Methadone Maintenance Really Cost-Effective?" *American Journal of Psychiatry* 154: 1214–1219.

Krystal, J. H., et al. (2001). "Naltrexone in the Treatment of Alcohol Dependence." *New England Journal of Medicine* 345: 1734–1739.

Mason, B. J., et al. (1999). "A Double-Blind, Placebo-Controlled Study of Oral Nalmefene for Alcohol Dependence." *Archives of General Psychiatry* 56: 719–724.

Matthews, E. A., and A. H. Dickenson (2002). "A Combination of Gabapentin and Morphine Mediates Enhanced Inhibitory Effects on Dorsal Horn Neuronal Responses in a Rat Model of Neuropathy." *Anesthesiology* 96: 633–640.

Millan, M. J. (2002). "Descending Control of Pain." *Progress in Neurobiology* 66: 355–474.

Muijsers, R. B., and A. J. Wagstaff (2001). "Transdermal Fentanyl: An Updated Review of Its Pharmacological Properties and Therapeutic Efficacy in Chronic Cancer Pain Control." *Drugs* 61: 2289–2307.

Naguib, M., et al. (1998). "Perioperative Antinociceptive Effects of Tramadol. A Prospective, Randomized, Double-Blind Comparison with Morphine." *Canadian Journal of Anaesthesia* 45: 1168–1175.

Narita, M., et al. (2001). "Regulations of Opioid Dependence by Opioid Receptor Types." *Pharmacology and Therapeutics* 89: 1–15.

Nunes, E. V., et al. (1998). "Imipramine Treatment of Opiate-Dependent Patients with Depressive Disorders." *Archives of General Psychiatry* 55: 153–160.

Oliveto, A. H., et al. (1999). "Desipramine in Opioid-Dependent Cocaine Abusers Maintained on Buprenorphine vs. Methadone." *Archives of General Psychiatry* 56: 812–820.

Ostermeier, A. M., et al. (2000). "Activation of Mu- and Sigma-Opioid Receptors Causes Presynaptic Inhibition of Glutamatergic Excitation in Neocortical Neurons." *Anesthesiology* 93: 1053–1063.

Pan, Z. Z. (1998). "Mu-Opposing Actions of the Kappa-Opioid Receptor." *Trends in Pharmacological Sciences* 19: 94–98.

Petry, N. M., et al. (1999). "A Comparison of Four Buprenorphine Dosing Regimens in the Treatment of Opioid Dependence." *Clinical Pharmacology and Therapeutics* 66: 306–314.

Preston, K. L., et al. (2000). "Methadone Dose Increase and Abstinence Reinforcement for Treatment of Continued Heroin Use During Methadone Maintenance." *Archives of General Psychiatry* 57: 395–404.

Price, D. D. (2003). "Central Neural Mechanisms That Interrelate Sensory and Affective Dimensions of Pain." *Molecular Interventions* 2: 392–402.

Resnick, R. B. (2003). "Food and Drug Administration Approval of Buprenorphine-Naloxone for Office Treatment of Addiction." *Annals of Internal Medicine* 138: 360.

Rice, A. S., et al. (2002). "Endocannabinoids and Pain: Spinal and Peripheral Analgesia in Inflammation and Neuropathy." *Prostaglandins, Leukotrienes, and Essential Fatty Acids* 66: 243–256.

Romach, M. K., et al. (1999). "Long-Term Codeine Use Is Associated with Depressive Symptoms." *Journal of Clinical Psychopharmacology* 19: 373–376.

Roth, A. S., et al. (1996). "Naltrexone as a Treatment for Repetitive Self-Injurious Behavior: An Open-Label Trial." *Journal of Clinical Psychiatry* 57: 233–237.

Savage, S. R. (1999). "Opioid Use in the Management of Chronic Pain." *Medical Clinics of North America* 83: 761–785.

Schwartzman, R. J., et al. (2001). "Neuropathic Central Pain: Epidemiology, Etiology, and Treatment Options." *Archives of Neurology* 58: 1547–1550.

Snyder, S. H., and G. W. Pasternak (2003). "Historical Review: Opioid Receptors." *Trends in Pharmacological Sciences* 2: 198–204.

Solomon, S. (2002). "A Review of Mechanisms of Response to Pain Therapy: Why Voodoo Works." *Headache* 42: 656–662.

Sproule, B. A., et al. (1999). "Characteristics of Dependent and Nondependent Regular Users of Codeine." *Journal of Clinical Psychopharmacology* 19: 367–372.

Strain, E. C., et al. (2000). "Effects of Buprenorphine versus Buprenorphine/Naloxone Tablets in Non-Dependent Opioid Abusers." *Psychopharmacologica* 148: 374–383.

Thipphawong, J. B., et al. (2003). "Analgesic Efficacy of Inhaled Morphine in Patients After Bunionectomy Surgery." *Anesthesiology* 99: 693–700.

Umbricht, A., et al. (1999). "Naltrexone-Shortened Opioid Detoxification with Buprenorphine." *Drug and Alcohol Dependence* 56: 181–190.

Viscusi, E. R., et al. (2004). "Patient-Controlled Transdermal Fentanyl Hydrochloride vs Intravenous Morphine Pump for Postoperative Pain: A Randomized Controlled Trial." *Journal of the American Medical Association* 291 (2004): 1222–1341.

Weinbroum, A. A., et al. (2002). "Dextromethorphan for the Reduction of Immediate and Late Postoperative Pain and Morphine Consumption in Orthopedic Oncology Patients." *Cancer* 95: 1164–1170.

White, T., and S. K. Schultz (2000). "Naltrexone Treatment for a 3-Year-Old Boy with Self-Injurious Behavior." *American Journal of Psychiatry* 157: 1574–1580.

Zawertailo, L. A., et al. (1998). "Psychotropic Effects of Dextromethorphan Are Altered by the CYP2D6 Polymorphism: A Pilot Study." *Journal of Clinical Psychopharmacology* 18: 332–337.

Zubieta, J. K., et al. (2001). "Regional Mu Opioid Receptor Regulation of Sensory and Affective Dimensions of Pain." *Science* 293: 311–315.

Chapter 16

Herbal Medicines Used in the Treatment of Psychological Disorders

Writing a review of the pharmacology of herbal medicines used to treat psychological disorders presents unique challenges. On the one hand, some people feel that, because they are found in nature, herbals are safe, effective, and nontoxic. Is this true? Are they efficacious? Are they "safe"? Should they be freely available for purchase and use? What is their potential for causing toxic reactions or producing compulsive abuse? Should these compounds be regulated by the government? In the case of *drugs*, the FDA must ascertain that they are both safe and effective before they can be marketed. This does not mean that they are not without side effects or that problems will not emerge in the future. However, the FDA decides whether or not the potential usefulness of a drug justifies the side effects. In the case of herbal medications, the FDA has little regulatory authority and few such safeguards exist.

The approach taken in this chapter is to describe what is known about the pharmacokinetics, pharmacodynamics, side effects, toxicities, and drug interactions for each of the herbal compounds that are commonly used in the treatment of psychological disorders or that might have significant CNS actions. Much information exists about the effectiveness of the compounds discussed in this chapter. However, the quality of this information is extremely variable (Dennehy and Tsourounis, 2001).

Many drugs derived from natural plant sources are covered elsewhere in this text, including caffeine, nicotine, cocaine, morphine, codeine, tetrahydrocannabinol, scopolamine, myristicin, elemicin, and mescaline (Table 16.1). Certainly no reasonable person would advocate the free availability of cocaine, morphine, or psychedelics. Regulatory control is essential and has already been implemented for many "herbal," drugs such as cocaine and morphine. Whether controls should be exerted over other herbal medications is discussed in this chapter.

Covered here are herbal medications with presumed or claimed CNS effects that are otherwise not covered in this text. Often, their actions are not clearly delineated and their efficacy is debated. Nonetheless, they are heavily promoted and used for the treatment of various psychological disorders. In some cases, promotion may be warranted. In other cases, regulation is either currently needed (ephedrine, for example) or perhaps will be needed should widespread use become a societal problem (for example, kava).

Over the past decade, herbal medications have attracted enormous interest, almost as if they were something new. Of course, herbal medicines are ancient; they've been with us for thousands of years. Since the isolation of morphine from crude opium extract in the 1860s,

TABLE 16.1 Some of the naturally occurring psychoactive drugs already covered in this book

Drug	Chapter	Used in therapeutics	Drug of abuse
Cocaine	7	Rarely	Yes
Caffeine	8	Occasionally	Probably
Nicotine	8	No	Yes
Lithium	10	Yes	No
Morphine	15	Yes	Yes
Codeine	15	Yes	Yes
Tetrahydrocannabinol	18	Rarely	Yes
Scopolamine	19	Occasionally	Occasionally
Mescaline	19	No	Yes
Myristicin/Elemicin	19	No	Yes
Psilocybin/Psilocin	19	No	Yes
Dimethyltryptamine	19	No	Yes
Bufotenine	19	No	Yes
Ololiuqui	19	No	Yes
Harmine	19	No	Yes
Omega-3 fatty acids	10	Possibly	No

scientists called *pharmacognosists* have sought to identify pharmacologically active ingredients in natural materials. This area of study is called *pharmacognosy*.

In this chapter the focus is primarily on herbal medicines that are used to treat psychiatric symptoms or disorders; that produce changes in mood, thinking, or behavior as a side effect; or that interact with psychiatric medications (Wong et al., 1998). A specialty edition of the *Physician's Desk Reference* is devoted to herbal medicines, although it does not contain critical analysis of potential or claimed efficacy (*PDR for Herbal Medicines,* 2000). Each herb discussed in this chapter presumably contains an active ingredient that accounts for its clinical use. In some instances, the presumed active ingredient has not been conclusively identified, so discussion is oriented to the plant material and the safety, side effects, drug interactions, and efficacy in treating symptoms or diagnoses (Table 16.2).

The efficacy of many herbal medications is difficult to evaluate due to incomplete knowledge of active ingredients, absence of standardization, different purities, and so on. The final composition of a plant product varies according to what part of the plant is used, where it was grown, what time of year it was grown or harvested, the reputation of the grower, processor, packager, marketer, promoter, and so on. The widespread, largely unregulated availability and promotion of herbal products is not new. Herbals have been used from the time of Hippocrates, and patent medicines were widely promoted in the United States until the early part of the twentieth century. Federal regulations in the 1920s severely restricted the sale and nonprescription use of such products, most of which contained large amounts of alcohol as well as "natural" drugs such as cocaine and opium. But then the passage of the Dietary Supplement Health Education Act of 1994 severely restricted the Food and Drug Administration's ability to exert control over herbal products. Thus, since 1994, any product could be labeled a "supplement" as long as the product made no claim to affect a "disease." Thus, a manufacturer cannot claim that a product "alleviates depression"; the manufacturer can claim that it "promotes emotional balance." An herbal product cannot be claimed to alleviate the signs and symptoms of Alzheimer's disease; rather, it "enhances mental sharpness." Even though some herbal products can have significant adverse neuropsychiatric reactions (Pies, 2000), manufacturers must demonstrate neither safety nor efficacy. Promotion of many herbals addresses the fact that fatigue, headache, insomnia, depression, and anxiety—the symptoms and complaints most often underappreciated and untreated by medical doctors—are the most common reasons patients cite for seeking treatment from alternative practitioners.

TABLE 16.2 Herbal remedies commonly used to treat psychiatric symptoms*

Herb	Common usage	Quality of evidence category†	Adverse effects	Cautions/ contraindications	Drug interactions
Black cohosh	Menopause symptoms, PMS, Dysmenorrhea	I, II, III	GI upset (rare), headaches, CV depression	Pregnancy, lactation	Hormonal treatments (theoretical)
German chamomile	Insomnia, Anxiety	III, III	Allergy (rare)	Allergy to sunflower family of plants	None reported
Evening primrose	Schizophrenia, ADHD, Dementia	IV, IV, IV	None reported	Mania, epilepsy	Phenothiazines, NSAIDs, corticosteroids., ß blockers, anticoagulants
Ginkgo	"Cerebrovascular insufficiency" symptoms, Dementia	I, I	Headache, GI upset	Pregnancy, lactation, potential bleeding (e.g., PUD)	Anticoagulants
Hops	Insomnia	III	Allergy, menstrual irregularity	Depression, pregnancy, lactation	Sedative-hypnotics, alcohol (both theoretical)
Kava	Insomnia, Anxiety, Seizures	III, III, IV	Scaling of skin on extremities	Pregnancy, lactation	Benzodiazepines, alcohol
Lemon balm	Insomnia, Anxiety	IV, III	None reported	Thyroid disease, pregnancy, lactation	CNS depressants, thyroid medications

TABLE 16.2 Herbal remedies commonly used to treat psychiatric symptoms* *(continued)*

Herb	Common usage	Quality of evidence category[†]	Adverse effects	Cautions/ contraindications	Drug interactions
Passion flower	Insomnia Anxiety	III III	Hypersensitivity vasculitis, sedation	Pregnancy, lactation	Insufficient data
Skullcap	Insomnia Anxiety	IV IV	Sedation, confusion, seizures	Pregnancy, lactation	Insufficient data
St. John's wort	Depression	I	Photosensitivity, GI upset, sedation, anticholinergic	CV disease, pregnancy, lactation, pheochromocytoma	Drugs that interact with MAOIs
Valerian	Insomnia Anxiety	III III	Sedation	Pregnancy, lactation	CNS depressants

From Wong et al., 1998.

*PMS = premenstrual syndrome; GI = gastrointestinal; CV = cardiovascular; ADHD = attention deficit with hyperactivity disorder; NSAIDs = nonsteroidal anti-inflammatory drugs; PUD = peptic ulcer disease; CNS = central nervous system; MAOIs = monoamine oxidase inhibitors.
†Quality of evidence: I = evidence from at least two properly randomized controlled trials; II = evidence from well-designed trials without randomization; III = opinions of respected authorities based on clinical experience, descriptive studies, or reports of expert committees; IV = insufficient evidence to warrant conclusions about efficacy or safety.

St. John's Wort

St. John's wort is the common name for the flowering plant *Hypericum perforatum*. It is named after St. John the Baptist because it blooms around his feast day (June 24) and exudes a red color symbolic of his blood. It has many constituents with biological activity, including naphthodianthrones, flavinoids, and xanthones. *Hypericin* (Figure 16.1) (and possibly *pseudohypericin* and/or *hyperforin*) is generally considered to be the active ingredient, and dosage of the herb is based on its presumed hypericin content. The term *hypericin* is from the Greek *hyper* and *eikon*, which mean "to overcome an apparition"; the ancients believed in its ability to ward off evil spirits (O'Hara et al., 1998). The amount of hypericin varies widely in different parts of the plant under different growth conditions and at different times of the year.

Draves and Walker (2003) analyzed the summed total of hypericin and pseurohypericin in commercially available St. John's wort preparations. The percentage of drug relative to the claimed amount varied from 0 to 108 percent for capsules and from 31 to 80 percent for tablets. Only two products had an amount within 10 percent of the label amount. Tinctures (alcohol extracts) varied from 0 to 118 percent of the label amount. On average, most labels overstated the amount by a factor of almost two (thus contained only 50 percent of the labeled amount).

Indications

St. John's wort is licensed in Germany for the treatment of anxiety, depression, and insomnia. In the United States, no claims of effectiveness in treating these disorders may be made; it is legally sold only as a

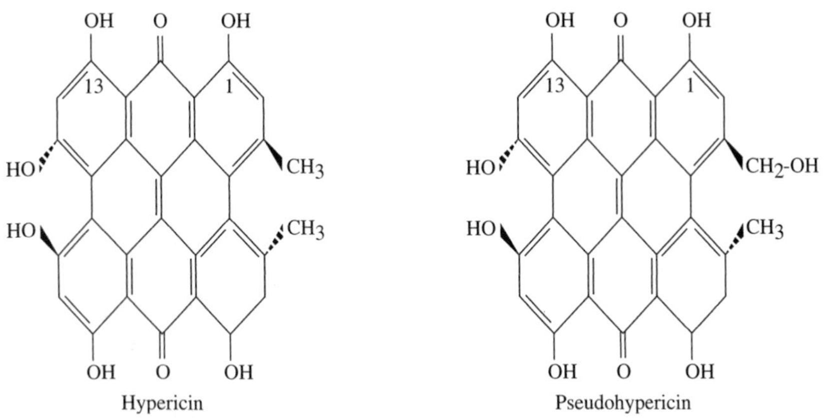

FIGURE 16.1 Structural formulas of hypericin and pseudohypericin.

dietary supplement, perhaps to promote emotional balance. Despite this, the herbal is widely used for its presumed efficacy as a mild antidepressant.

Pharmacokinetics

Hypericin has been shown to be absorbed following oral administration, with peak blood levels achieved in about 5 hours (Figure 16.2). Hypericin has an elimination half-life of about 25 hours; it thus

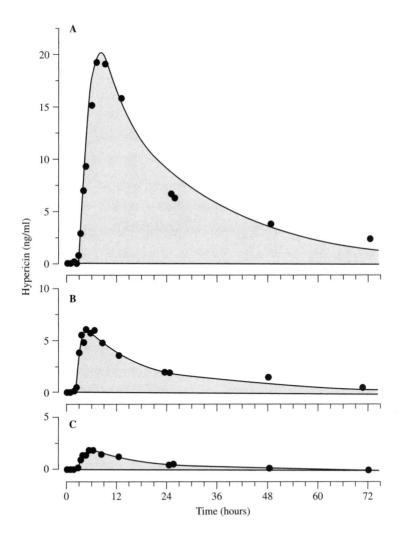

FIGURE 16.2 Time course of concentration of hypericin in plasma in three subjects after receiving a single dose of (**A**) 300 milligrams, (**B**) 900 milligrams, or (**C**) 1800 milligrams. [From Staffeldt et al. (1994), p. S49.]

achieves steady-state concentrations in the brain in about 4 to 6 days (Figure 16.3) (Staffeldt et al., 1994). Only about 15 to 20 percent of the administered hypericin reaches the central circulation and is available systemically. Whether hypericin is metabolized, how it is metabolized, what its metabolites are, and routes of excretion are unknown.

St. John's wort contains bioflavinoids, one of which is *quercitin*. Quercitin inhibits the drug-metabolizing enzyme CYP1A2. Hyperforin is a potent inhibitor of CYP2D6 and CYP2C9 (Obach, 2000). The use of St. John's wort could therefore result in numerous adverse interactions when combined with other drugs. For example, it may reduce the effectiveness of codeine (blocking conversion to morphine) and increase the blood levels of caffeine and several psychoactive medications, including tricyclic anti-depressants and antipsychotic drugs. St. John's wort has also been reported to induce certain hepatic

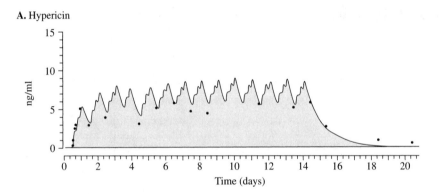

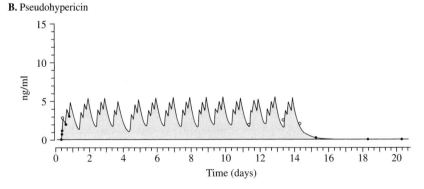

FIGURE 16.3 Time course of concentrations of (**A**) hypericin and (**B**) pseudohypericin in a subject taking one 300-mg tablet of hypericum extract three times daily for 14 days. [From Staffeldt et al. (1994), p. S50.]

drug-metabolizing enzymes, increasing activity of CYP3A4, for example, thereby reducing the blood levels of certain cardiac and anti-inflammatory medicines (Durr et al., 2000). As stated by Markowitz and coworkers (2003):

> A 14-day course of St. John's wort significantly induced the activity of CYP3A4. . . . This suggests that long-term administration of St. John's wort may result in diminished clinical effectiveness or increased dosage requirements for all CYP3A4 substrates, which represent at least 50% of all marketed medications. (p. 1500)

Pharmacodynamics

The mechanism of action of hypericin and hypericum extracts is unclear. Initially, it was thought that inhibition of monoamine oxidase (Chapter 9) would account for its antidepressant action. However, while MAO inhibition can be demonstrated in vitro at high concentrations, the effect is too weak to account for clinical efficacy. More recent reports hypothesize a hypericin-induced blockade of the presynaptic reuptake of serotonin, norepinephrine, and dopamine. Other reported effects of hypericin include binding to GABA receptors, benzodiazepine receptors, and glutaminergic NMDA-type receptors (Wong et al., 1998). Rats treated for six months with hypericum extract showed a 50 percent increase in serotonin-1A and -2A receptors without changes in receptor affinity (Teufel-Mayer and Gleitz, 1997).

Thus, the mechanism may involve blockade of neurotransmitter reuptake; it may involve increases or decreases at a transcriptional level involving receptor expression; or it may involve another as yet unrecognized and perhaps unique action. Gambarana and coworkers (1999) reported that, in rats, *Hypericum perforatum* extract

> acutely protected animals from the sequelae of unavoidable stress; . . . *H. perforatum* reverted the escape deficit maintained by repeated stressors and preserved the animal's capacity to learn to operate for earning a positive reinforcer. It was concluded that *H. perforatum* contains some active principle(s) endowed with antidepressant activity. (p. 247)

In essence, the mechanisms of the antidepressant action of St. John's wort remains unexplained (Butterweck, 2003).

Clinical Efficacy

As early as 1996, Linde and coworkers conducted a meta-analysis of the clinical efficacy of St. John's wort for depression. They concluded that, over a period of two to four weeks of treatment, hypericum extract was superior to placebo. Commenting on this review, DeSmet and Nolen (1996) stated:

> Although promising, these studies are not sufficient to accept the use of hypericum extract in major depression. . . . [S]pecific studies in severely depressed patients are still missing, as are longer-term studies to assess the risk of relapse and the possibility of late side effects. Of the four trials that have compared a hypericum monopreparation with a synthetic antidepressant, none lasted longer than six weeks. All tested the comparator drug . . . at the lower end of the usual dose range, and none of the reports described a homogenous patient group with major depression defined by the criteria of the *Diagnostic and Statistical Manual of Mental Disorders*. (p. 241)

In 1998, Wong and coworkers concluded:

> Overall, there are inadequate data regarding long-term use and efficacy in severe depression. There are concerns regarding the standardization and quality control of commercial preparations. Clearly, more research is needed to address these shortcomings in the literature. (p. 1033)

Kim and coworkers (1999) conducted a similar meta-analysis. From a total of 651 patients, they concluded that "*Hypericum perforatum* was more effective than placebo and similar in effectiveness to low-dose tricyclic antidepressants in the short-term treatment of mild to moderately severe depression" (p. 532). However, they were careful to state that "serious questions remain regarding the research design of the studies analyzed."

Philipp and coworkers (2000) reported that hypericum extract (1 g/day) was comparable in efficacy to imipramine (100 mg/day) and superior to placebo. Commenting, Linde and Berner (2000) noted that the study "confirms the existing evidence that hypericum extract is more effective than placebo in mild and moderately severe depression." Linde and Berner added, however, that the dose of hypericum was high, the dose of imipramine was low, and the superiority of both drug treatments over placebo was "not impressive," with placebo responses being quite robust.

In 2001, Sheldon and coworkers conducted the first large-scale, multicentered, randomized, double-blinded, placebo-controlled trial of St. John's wort extract and placebo in the treatment of major depression. In this study, St. John's wort (900 to 1200 mg/day) was no more effective than placebo (Figure 16.4), at least in this population of depressed patients with relatively chronic symptoms who obtain psychiatric care in academic medical centers and who did not initially self-treat their depression with herbal preparations.

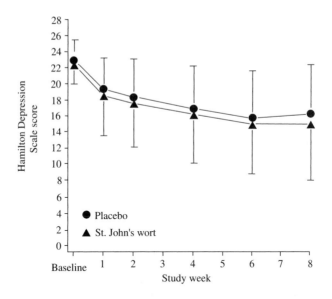

FIGURE 16.4 Effects of St. John's wort and placebo on the Hamilton Rating Scale for Depression over eight weeks of study. [From Sheldon and coworkers (2001), p. 1983.]

In 2002, the results were reported of the second and largest multi-centered, randomized, double-blinded, placebo-controlled trial of St. John's wort extract versus both placebo and sertraline (an SSRI-type antidepressant) in the treatment of major depression (Hypericum Depression Trial Study Group, 2002). Neither St. John's wort not sertraline were superior to placebo (Figure 16.5). The researchers concluded:

> This study fails to support the efficacy of *H. perforatum* in moderately severe major depression . . . the complete absence of trends suggestive of efficacy for *H. perforatum* is noteworthy. (p. 1807)

A 2002 research study in Germany (Volz et al., 2002) reported efficacy of 600 mg/day of St. John's wort extract in the treatment of somatoform disorders[1] in nondepressed patients. Should this study be replicated, it may provide an interesting, although limited, use for this product.

---

[1]Somatoform disorder involves a history of many physical complaints beginning before age 30 years that occur over a period of several years and results in treatment being sought or significant impairment in social, occupational, or other important areas of functioning. Pain, gastrointestinal, sexual, and pseudoneurological symptoms are present (American Psychological Association, 2000).

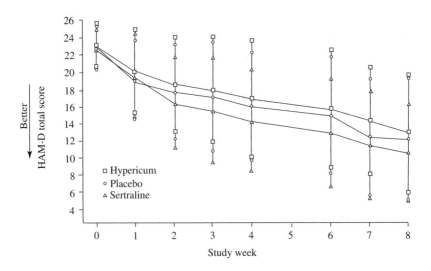

FIGURE 16.5 Effects of St. John's wort, sertraline, and placebo on the Hamilton Rating Scale for Depression over 8 weeks of study. Graphed values are means with vertical bars extending to one standard deviation. [From Hypericum Depression Trial Study Group (2002), p. 1811.]

Findling and coworkers (2003) conducted an 8-week, open-label trial of St. John's wort (dosed to 900 mg/day) in 33 youths (mean age = 10.5 years) with major depression. Twenty-five met criteria for a positive response. They stated that controlled trials in youths appear to be indicated.

Side Effects

The real and potential side effects of St. John's wort are not insignificant. The extract has been shown to cause photosensitivity, especially in fair-skinned persons taking large doses. Fortunately, the effect is reversible, usually within a few days. There are also several reports of St. John's wort precipitating hypomanic states when used either with or without other antidepressant drugs. Used with SSRI-type antidepressants, a serotonin syndrome can occur. Other, usually mild, side effects include sedation, lethargy, and gastrointestinal upset. The potential for involvement in potentially serious drug interactions was discussed earlier. St. John's wort, at least until proven safe, should not be used during pregnancy or with other psychoactive agents (Goldman et al., 2003). Lee and coworkers (2003) found little adverse effect of St. John's wort on the breast-feeding infants of mothers taking the product.

Since St John's wort induces the CYP450 enzymes that metabolize oral contraceptives, there is concern about unwanted pregnancies, despite the mother's taking contraceptive medication (Hall et al., 2003; Schwarz et al., 2003). Pfunder and coworkers (2003) noted no evidence of ovulation during low-dose oral contraceptive therapy, although women treated with St. John's wort experienced more intracycle bleeding episodes. In addition, reduced levels of the oral contraceptive products may enhance the risk of unintended pregnancies.

Ginkgo

The ginkgo tree (*Ginkgo biloba*) is one of the oldest deciduous tree species on earth. The extract of ginkgo is referred to as EGb-760 and is one of the most popular plant extracts used in Europe to alleviate symptoms associated with a range of cognitive disorders, including dementia. In the United States, the extract can be promoted not to treat cognitive dysfunctions but, for example, to provide "mental sharpness," provide antioxidant protection, maintain healthy circulatory perfusion, and so on. Purported medical indications for use include dementia, chronic cerebrovascular insufficiency (insufficient blood flow to the brain), and brain protection secondary to cerebral or head trauma.

The active ingredients in ginkgo extracts are not completely known. The standardized commercial preparation contains 24 percent ginkgo flavinoids and 6 percent terpenoids. As noted in the discussion of St. John's wort, flavinoids inhibit CYP1A2 and create drug interactions with many medications.

Flavinoids and terpenoids are antioxidants that "scavenge" free radicals that have been implicated as the mediators of the cellular damage observed in Alzheimer's disease. Ginkgolide B (a terpenoid) inhibits a platelet-activating factor, interfering with platelet aggregation and slowing blood clotting (as does aspirin). This antiplatelet action by itself provides therapeutic effectiveness by limiting abnormal clot formation in small arteries (as aspirin does). Adversely, it may increase the tendency to bleed and it may well interact with other blood thinners (again, as does aspirin). Presumed antioxidant effects have not been convincingly demonstrated to correlate well with efficacy in treating cognitive dysfunction.

Pharmacokinetics

Taken orally, *Ginkgo biloba* extracts appear to be readily absorbed, although blood levels of any of the substances found in the extract have not been reported. Plasma concentrations of ginkgo flavinoids peak in plasma at two to three hours after ingestion. The mechanisms of elimination of these substances from the body is not known. It is also not known whether any of these flavinoids or terpenoids are metabolized before excretion. Kleijnen and Knipschild (1992) reported that portions of the extract are excreted in the urine and feces and through the lungs. The half-life is thought to be about five hours.

Pharmacodynamics

The EGb-761 extract of ginkgo contains multiple compounds that are thought by some individuals to act on unidentified processes involved in the homeostasis of inflammation and oxidative stress, presumably providing membrane protection and neurotransmission modulation (LeBars et al., 1997). EEG studies (Itil et al., 1996) demonstrate an activating effect with increased alpha wave activity, indicative of increased alertness and perhaps of improved cognitive performance (perhaps similar to the effects of caffeine on the EEG).

Clinical Efficacy

Most early studies on ginkgo extract were too poorly conducted to merit conclusions. Kleijnen and Knipschild (1992) reviewed these studies, noting a general conclusion that ginkgo produced significant improvement in memory loss, concentration difficulties, fatigue, anxiety, and depression in patients severely affected with Alzheimer's disease; there was no significant improvement in individuals with mild to no memory impairment.

LeBars and coworkers (1997) conducted a 52-week study of EGb-761 in 309 patients with mild to severe Alzheimer's disease or multi-infarct dementia. Extract-treated patients exhibited modest improvements in objective testing of cognitive performance and in the caregiver's evaluation of social functioning. A "clinician's global impression of change" was unaffected. O'Hara and coworkers (1998) stated that while statistically significant, such modest effects are of uncertain clinical benefit.

Oken and coworkers (1998) reviewed 50 studies on *Ginkgo biloba* for neurological disorders and concluded that patients function slightly better than those taking placebo. Wong and coworkers (1998) concluded that there is no clear evidence of efficacy in the treatment of depression, impotence, or brain injury. Van Dongen and colleagues (2000) reported on a 24-week study of EGb 761 in 214 elderly patients in the Netherlands. Ginkgo had no positive effects as a treatment for older people with mild to moderate dementia or age-related memory impairment. The authors' meticulous attention to detail sets a new standard for the study of herbal preparations.

In 2002, Solomon and coworkers conducted a 6-week, randomized, placebo-controlled trial on the effects of ginkgo on 220 patients over the age of 60 years in order to assess drug effects on memory function. The authors found that ginkgo had no beneficial effects on standard neuropsychological tests of learning, memory, attention, or concentration. They concluded that "ginkgo, when taken following the manufacturer's instructions, provides no measurable benefit in memory or related cognitive function" (p. 835).

In contrast to the results provided by Solomon and coworkers, Mix and Crews (2002) performed a nearly identical set of memory and cognitive experiments in 262 persons aged 60 years or older. These authors reported modest improvements in memory and cognition, evaluated both objectively and subjectively. These authors concluded that their studies "provided complementary evidence of the potential efficacy of *Ginkgo biloba* Egb 761 in enhancing certain neuropsychological/memory processes of cognitively intact older adults, 60 years of age and over" (p. 267).

Side Effects and Precautions

Side effects of ginkgo include headache and GI upset, but they are mild and infrequent. Headache is most common and can be minimized by starting with a low dose and increasing it gradually. There is concern about increased bleeding and the potential for interaction with aspirin and other anticoagulants (Leak, 1999). Safety in pregnancy and during lactation has not been established

Kava

Preparations made from the roots of kava (*Piper methysticin*) have been used for ceremonial and social purposes by the peoples of the South Pacific for thousands of years. Captain James Cook first described kava in the account of his voyage in 1768. Further scientific study was not made until the early days of pharmacology and pharmacognosy in 1886.

Kava is used by the Oceanic peoples as an antianxiety drug, similar to our use of ethyl alcohol. Kava induces relaxation, improves social interaction, promotes sleep, and plays an important role in the sociocultural life of the islanders of the South Pacific. At higher doses, kava produces sleep and stupor, again like alcohol. Standardized extracts of kava are used for the therapy of anxiety, tension, and restlessness.

Chemistry

There are multiple agents with pharmacological activity in kava. Most interest centers on the alpha pyrones commonly referred to as kava lactones, found in the fat-soluble portions of the plant root. Other compounds in kava contribute to efficacy, and the sedative activity of a crude preparation exceeds that of extracted kava lactones. However, as the kava lactone content of the root varies from 3 to 20 percent, preparations standardized for kava lactone content are preferred to crude preparations.

Pharmacokinetics

When taken as the extract, kava lactones appear to be well absorbed; much less is absorbed when the isolated substances are taken (why this is so is unknown). Little is known about the distribution, metabolism, and excretion of the ingredients.

Pharmacodynamics

The mechanism of action of ingredients in kava is poorly elucidated. Kava pyrones appear to bind to various GABA receptors or to the benzodiazepine-binding site, a likely action since kava produces effects similar to those produced by the benzodiazepines and alcohol. A kava lactone has been shown to block sodium channels, an anestheticlike effect. Kava has been shown in animals to be anticonvulsant, muscle relaxant, and neuroprotective (much as are benzodiazepines and barbiturates). The EEG alterations induced by kava resemble those induced by benzodiazepines. Uebelhack and colleagues (1998) reported that kava, either in extract form or as pure kava lactones, was a reversible inhibitor of monoamine oxidase-B (MAO-B). The significance of this action is unknown, since the antidepressant effect of MAO inhibitors results from MAO-A inhibition (Chapter 15), while the food interactions result from MAO-B inhibition. The Uebelhack group stated, however, that the inhibition of MAO-B by kava pyrone-enriched extracts might be an important mechanism for their psychotropic activity. Therefore, tentatively, one can hypothesize that kava's action should closely resemble that of ethyl alcohol and the traditional sedative-hypnotic compounds.

Clinical Effects

At a dose of up to 70 milligrams of kava lactone, an anxiolytic effect is noted. At higher doses (125 to 210 milligrams), drowsiness, sedation, and a feeling of intoxication are produced. In Oceanic cultures, doses of 250 milligrams are consumed, often more than once, and inebriation is quite rapidly induced. Pittler and Ernst (2000) reviewed kava studies and concluded that "data imply that kava extract is superior to placebo as a symptomatic treatment for anxiety." However, "important caveats exist, which prevent firm conclusions" (p. 84).

- Contemporary medical research may finally allow us to separate the traditional remedies that can effectively treat disease from those that are superstition and myth. (p. 1033)

- In addition, research . . . may uncover novel treatments for psychiatric illness or yield fresh insights into basic disease mechanisms. (p. 1033)

Over the next few years we will undoubtedly see many studies relating to the safety, efficacy, and drug interactions associated with herbals. Until then, caution is warranted: patients should tell prescribing physicians of their use of herbal medications, and most herbals should probably be avoided in pregnancy until they can be proven safe.

Although significant numbers of children and adolescents are receiving one or more herbal medications, studies of these compounds in this age population are unavailable. In some cases, youths may purchase the drugs themselves, as the drugs are easily available, relatively inexpensive, and widely advertised or endorsed by their peers. In other cases, the young people may be dosed by their parents in attempts to medicate such disorders as ADHD, depression, anxiety, or insomnia. Reasonable medical practitioners recognize that few data exist to support the use of herbals in the treatment of psychiatric disorders in children. Until such evidence becomes available, these agents probably should not be administered to children, especially for long periods of time or in the presence of other medications.

STUDY QUESTIONS

1. Describe the recent legislation changing the herbal industry. How has it helped society? How has it hurt?

2. List some of the herbals discussed in other chapters in this book. Which of them should be more freely available? Defend your answer.

3. What is hypericin? Describe its pharmacokinetics. What is the evidence for its efficacy?

4. What is ginkgo? What are its claimed actions? What evidence is there for efficacy to improve memory? For other uses?

5. What is kava? Does it have therapeutic potential? Does it have abuse potential? What drug does it appear to most resemble? Should there be legal restrictions on its use? Defend your answer.

6. What is ma-huang? What is its active ingredient? Does it have a potential for abuse? Might it induce toxicity? Should its use be regulated? Defend your answer.

Side Effects and Complications

Side effects of kava are generally mild and include drowsiness, nausea, muscle weakness, blurred vision, and (with chronic use) yellow skin discoloration. Since kava is a sedative/intoxicant, it should not be combined with alcohol, benzodiazepines, barbiturates, THC, or other CNS depressants. Kava should not be taken before driving or operating machinery.

Campo and coworkers (2002) reported a case of fulminant liver failure (requiring liver transplantation) in a 14-year-old girl. This and other cases of liver failure both in the United States and in Europe have prompted an ongoing FDA investigation of this substance.

Since kava is an intoxicant, it is interesting that barbiturates and benzodiazepines are restricted to prescription use, alcohol has age restrictions, marijuana is illegal, but kava is available without restriction. Its chief deterrent to more widespread use as an alcohollike anxiolytic/intoxicant is its expense.

Ephedrine (Ma-Huang)

Ephedrine is the naturally occurring psychoactive drug found in *Ephedra sinica*, also called ma-huang. The medicinal parts are the young canes collected in autumn and the dried rhizome with roots. Ephedrine is a potent psychostimulant that acts by releasing the body's own stores of the catecholamine neurotransmitters, epinephrine (adrenaline), norepinephrine, and dopamine.

Pharmacologically, ephedrine closely resembles the amphetamines, although the duration of action of ephedrine is considerably shorter. Because of this, ephedrine-containing products (Metabolife 356 and many others) should not be considered as metabolic supplements, dietary supplements, or any other designation implying that it is not a drug. Ephedrine is a potent psychostimulant that should be under regulation of the FDA.

Deaths from ephedrine now number in the dozens. The adrenaline and other catecholamines released by ephedrine increase blood pressure, heart rate, the force of cardiac contraction, and cardiac output of blood. Cardiac arrhythmias can be serious and potentially fatal. As with any adrenaline-releasing drug, it relieves bronchoconstriction and therefore provides relief from mild asthma, although tolerance rapidly develops. Like amphetamines, ephedrine temporarily reduces appetite, is a cardiovascular stimulant, and is a psychostimulant. Its disadvantages, however, far outweigh any therapeutic utility. In athletics, ephedrine is a "doping" substance. Numerous drug interactions occur and many are serious and potentially fatal. Several herbal preparations contain both ephedrine and caffeine: this is a combination that should be avoided because caffeine increases the cardiovascular toxicity of ephedrine. In April 2004, the FDA, in response to 155 deaths and dozens of heart attacks and strokes, initiated a ban on the sale of ephedrine-containing products as too dangerous for use. It is the U.S. government's first ban of a dietary supplement. Consumer's Union (2004a, 2004b) further discusses the problems with ephedrine and other dietary supplements.

Other Herbals That Act on the CNS

A variety of other herbals have been used to treat signs and symptoms of CNS dysfunction. A few are described here. Complete descriptions may be found in the *PDR for Herbal Medicines* (2000) and in the review by Wong and coworkers (1998).

Valerian (*Valeriana officalis*) has a long history of use as a mild sedative and as an anxiolytic as well as an antidepressant. The mechanism behind this action is obscure; some data indicate that it may affect GABA receptors, thus acting as a type of mild benzodiazepine. GABA itself is a component of valerian, leading some to state that valerian is a source of naturally occurring GABA, which it is. The problem is that GABA only very poorly crosses the blood-brain barrier, and it is unlikely that this source of GABA affects the CNS. Other postulated actions invoke it as a 5-HT$_{1A}$ agonist and as a monoamine oxidase inhibitor. They are reviewed by Wong and coworkers (1998) and by Yager and coworkers (1999). Reported side effects of valerian include liver toxicity, headache, excitability, and uneasiness. There are potential drug interactions between valerian and SSRI-type antidepressants, perhaps precipitating a serotonin syndrome (Chapter 9). Nevertheless, it is generally concluded that valerian can produce anxiolysis and CNS depression similar to that produced by benzodiazepines. There is no evidence to indicate that valerian is superior to existing sedative-hypnotic agents for the treatment of insomnia. The safety of valerian during pregnancy has not been delineated, so valerian probably should not be used by pregnant women. It would be expected that valerian would potentiate the effects of other CNS depressants, such as ethyl alcohol, and caution is warranted. Valerian should not be taken before driving or in other situations when alertness is required. The usual precautions that apply to other sedatives apply as well to valerian. As does St. John's wort, valerian contains quercitin; this substance inhibits the drug-metabolizing enzyme CYP1A2 and can possibly result in clinically significant drug interactions.

German chamomile (*Matricaria recutita*) is used to treat mild insomnia and anxiety. The herb contains flavinoids that are postulated to have affinity for the benzodiazepine receptor and perhaps for a histamine receptor, either perhaps inducing a sedative effect. No controlled clinical trials have investigated these properties.

Evening primrose (*Oenothera biennis*) has been promoted for the treatment of schizophrenia and ADHD, but little scientific evidence or cultural tradition backs up these claims. Primrose contains a variety of fatty acids, and these substances are postulated to be deficient in both schizophrenia and ADHD. If omega-3 fatty acids have therapeutic usefulness in the treatment of bipolar disorder (Chapter 10), evening primrose may be a productive area for future research. Primrose may exacerbate epilepsy and has been reported to cause drug interactions with a variety of other compounds.

Hops (*Humulus lupulus*) are used in the brewing industry as a component in beer. Hops also have a long history of use as a sedative-hypnotic agent. No clinical studies support the use of hops as a single agent to treat either insomnia or anxiety. Used as a sedative, drug interactions occur, especially potentiation of the effects of other sedatives such as alcohol and benzodiazepines. Use of hops should be avoided in depression, in pregnancy, and during lactation.

Lemon balm (*Melissa officinalis*), *passion flower* (*Passiflora incarnata*), and *skullcap* (*Scutellaria laterifolia*) are all thought to possess CNS sedative properties and are promoted for use as sedatives and anxiolytics. Data on efficacy are lacking, as is information on active ingredients and mechanisms of action. As sedatives, the usual precautions apply, including those concerning drug interactions and both cognitive and motor impairments.

Conclusions

Wong and coworkers (1998) made the following statements that appear to hold true today:

- With the exception of St. John's wort for depression and ginkgo for dementia, there is insufficient evidence to recommend the use of herbal medicines in the treatment of psychiatric illness.

- None of these herbal remedies is clearly superior to current conventional treatments.

- Because these products are widely available and often used by the general public, more clinical research is needed to establish safety and efficacy.

- The advances of modern medicine . . . are greater than at any other time in history. . . . However, the experience and healing traditions of other cultures, whether in less developed countries or in history, should not be ignored.

7. What in valerian might result in drug interactions?

8. Are there any unaddressed concerns about the use of herbals in pregnancy or in women who might become pregnant? What about in breast-feeding females?

REFERENCES

American Psychological Association (2000). *Diagnostic Criteria from DSM-IV-TR.* Washington, DC: APA.

Butterweck, V. (2003). "Mechanism of Action of St John's Wort in Depression: What Is Known?" *CNS Drugs* 17: 539–562.

Campo, J. V., et al. (2002). "Kava-Induced Fulminant Hepatic Failure." *Journal of the American Academy of Child and Adolescent Psychiatry* 41: 631.

Consumer's Union (2004a). "Dangerous Supplements: Still at Large." *Consumer Reports,* May: 12–17.

Consumer's Union (2004b). "Ephedra: Heart Dangers in Disguise." *Consumer Reports,* January: 22–23.

Dennehy, C. E., and C. Tsourounis (2001). "Botanicals ('Herbal Medications') and Nutritional Supplements." In B. G. Katzung (ed.), *Basic and Clinical Pharmacology,* 8th ed. (pp. 1088–1103). New York: Lange Medical Books.

DeSmet, P., and W. A. Nolen (1996). "St. John's Wort as an Antidepressant." *British Medical Journal* 313: 241–242.

Draves, A. H., and S. E. Walker (2003). "Analysis of the Hypericin and Pseudohypericin Content of Commercially Available St. John's Wort Preparations." *Canadian Journal of Clinical Pharmacology* 10: 114–118.

Durr, D., et al. (2000). "St John's Wort Induces Intestinal P-Glycoprotein/MDR1 and Intestinal and Hepatic CYP3A4." *Clinical Pharmacology and Therapeutics* 68: 598–604.

Findling, R. L., et al. (2003). "An Open-Label Pilot Study of St. John's Wort in Juvenile Depression." *Journal of the American Academy of Child and Adolescent Psychiatry* 42: 908–914.

Gambarana, C., et al. (1999). "Efficacy of an *Hypericum perforatum* (St. John's Wort) Extract in Preventing and Reverting a Condition of Escape Deficit in Rats." *Neuropsychopharmacology* 21: 247–257.

Goldman, R. D., et al. (2003). "Taking St John's Wort During Pregnancy." *Canadian Family Physician* 49: 29–30.

Hall, S. D., et al. (2003). "The Interaction Between St. John's Wort and an Oral Contraceptive." *Clinical Pharmacology and Therapeutics* 74: 525–535.

Hypericum Depression Trial Study Group (2002). "Effect of *Hypericum perforatum* (St. John's Wort) in Major Depressive Disorder: A Randomized Controlled Trial." *Journal of the American Medical Association* 287: 1807–1814.

Itil, T. M., et al. (1996). "Central Nervous System Effects of *Ginkgo biloba,* a Plant Extract." *American Journal of Therapeutics* 3: 63–73.

Kim, H. L., et al. (1999). "St. John's Wort for Depression." *Journal of Nervous and Mental Disease* 187: 532–539.

Kleijnen, J., and P. Knipschild (1992). "*Ginkgo biloba.*" *Lancet* 340: 1136–1139.

Leak, J. A. (1999). "Herbal Medicine: Is It an Alternative or an Unknown? A Brief Review of Popular Herbals Used by Patients in a Pain and Symptom Management Practice Setting." *Current Review of Pain* 3: 226–236.

LeBars, P. L., et al. (1997). "A Placebo-Controlled, Double-Blind, Randomized Trial of an Extract of Ginkgo Biloba for Dementia." *Journal of the American Medical Association* 278: 1327–1332.

Lee, A., et al. (2003). "The Safety of St. John's Wort (*Hypericum perforatum*) During Breastfeeding." *Journal of Clinical Psychiatry* 64: 966–968.

Linde, K., and M. Berner (2000). "Commentary: Has *Hypericum* Found Its Place in Antidepressant Treatment?" *British Medical Journal* 319: 1534–1539.

Linde, K., et al. (1996). "St. John's Wort for Depression—An Overview and Meta-Analysis of Randomized Clinical Trials." *British Medical Journal* 313: 253–258.

Markowitz, J. S., et al. (2003). "Effect of St. John's Wort on Drug Metabolism by Induction of Cytochrome P450 3A4 Enzyme." *Journal of the American Medical Association* 290: 1500–1504.

Mix, J. A., and W. D. Crews (2002). "A Double-Blind, Placebo-Controlled, Randomized Trial of *Ginkgo biloba* Extract Egb 761 in a Sample of Cognitively Intact Older Adults: Neuropsychological Findings." *Human Psychopharmacology* 17: 267–277.

Obach, R. S. (2000). "Inhibition of Human Cytochrome P450 Enzymes by Constituents of St. John's Wort, an Herbal Preparation Used in the Treatment of Depression." *Journal of Pharmacology and Experimental Therapeutics* 294: 88–95.

O'Hara, M. A., et al. (1998). "A Review of Twelve Commonly Used Medicinal Herbs." *Archives of Family Medicine* 7: 523–536.

Oken, B. S., et al. (1998). "The Efficacy of *Ginkgo biloba* on Cognitive Function in Alzheimer's Disease." *Archives of Neurology* 55: 1409–1415.

PDR for Herbal Medicines, 2nd ed. (2000). Montvale, NJ: Medical Economics Company.

Pfunder, A., et al. (2003). "Interaction of St. John's Wort with Low-Dose Oral Contraceptive Therapy: A Randomized Controlled Trial." *British Journal of Clinical Pharmacology* 56: 683–690.

Philipp, M., et al. (2000). "*Hypericum* Extract Versus Imipramine or Placebo in Patients with Moderate Depression: Randomized Multicentre Study of Treatment for Eight Weeks." *British Medical Journal* 319: 1534–1539.

Pies, R. (2000). "Adverse Neuropsychiatric Reactions to Herbal and Over-the-Counter 'Antidepressants'." *Journal of Clinical Psychiatry* 61: 815–820.

Pittler, M. H., and E. Ernst (2000). "Efficacy of Kava Extract for Treating Anxiety: Systematic Review and Meta-Analysis." *Journal of Clinical Psychopharmacology* 20: 84–89.

Schwarz, U. I., et al. (2003). "Unwanted Pregnancy and Self-Medication with St John's Wort Despite Hormonal Contraception." *British Journal of Clinical Pharmacology* 55: 112–113.

Sheldon, R. C., et al. (2001). "Effectiveness of St. John's Wort in Major Depression: A Randomized Controlled Trial." *Journal of the American Medical Association* 285: 1978–1986.

Solomon, P. R., et al. (2002). "Ginkgo for Memory Enhancement: A Randomized Controlled Trial." *Journal of the American Medical Association* 288: 835–840.

Staffeldt, B., et al. (1994). "Pharmacokinetics of Hypericin and Pseudohypericin After Oral Intake of the *Hypericum perforatum* Extract LI 160 in Healthy Volunteers." *Journal of Geriatric Psychiatry and Neurology* 7, Supplement 1: S47–S53.

Teufel-Mayer, R., and J. Gleitz (1997). "Effects of Long-Term Administration of *Hypericum* Extracts on the Affinity and Density of the Central Serotoninergic 5-HT$_{1A}$ and 5-HT$_{2A}$ Receptors." *Pharmacopsychiatry* 30: 113–116.

Uebelhack, R., et al. (1998). "Inhibition of Platelet MAO-B by Kava Pyrone-Enriched Extract from *Piper methysticum forester* (Kava-Kava)." *Pharmacopsychiatry* 31: 187–192.

van Dongen, M., et al. (2000). "The Efficacy of Ginkgo for Elderly People with Dementia and Age-Associated Memory Impairment: New Results of a Randomized Clinical Trial." *Journal of the American Geriatric Society* 48: 1183–1194.

Volz, H.-P., et al. (2002). "St. John's Wort Extract (LI 160) in Somatoform Disorders: Results of a Placebo-Controlled Trial." *Psychopharmacology* 164: 294–300.

Wong, A. H. C., et al. (1998). "Herbal Remedies in Psychiatric Practice." *Archives of General Psychiatry* 55: 1033–1044.

Yager, J., et al. (1999). "Use of Alternative Remedies by Psychiatric Patients: Illustrative Vignettes and a Discussion of the Issues." *American Journal of Psychiatry* 156: 1432–1438.

Chapter 17

Integration of Drugs and Psychological Therapies in Treating Mental and Behavior Disorders

Over the past few years it has become quite apparent that the treatment of psychological illnesses requires more than medication therapy. Only rarely should psychoactive medications be prescribed as the sole treatment, although they too often are. It has now been shown that combining pharmacological therapy with psychological therapy provides more effective treatment than the use of medication alone (Barlow et al., 2000; Chilvers et al., 2001; Druss et al., 2001; Kampman et al., 2002; Keller et al., 2000; Ward et al., 2000; Zajecka et al., 2002). This chapter explores the complex interaction between pharmacotherapies and psychological therapies in the treatment of psychological disorders that are commonly encountered in clinical practice.

Undertreatment of Mental and Psychological Disorders

In December 1999 the Surgeon General of the United States released a report that criticized the state of mental health treatment (U.S. Department of Health and Human Services, 1999). The report began with definitions of mental health and mental illness:

> *Mental health* is a state of successful performance of mental function, resulting in productive activities, fulfilling relationships with other people, and the ability to adapt to change and to cope with adversity.

> *Mental illness* is the term that refers collectively to all diagnosable mental disorders. Mental disorders are health conditions that are characterized by alterations in thinking, mood, or behavior (or some combination thereof) associated with distress and/or impaired functioning.

Alzheimer's disease exemplifies a mental disorder largely marked by alterations in thinking (especially forgetting). Depression exemplifies a mental disorder largely marked by alterations in mood. Attention deficit hyperactivity disorder exemplifies a mental disorder largely marked by alterations in behavior (overactivity) and/or thinking (inability to concentrate). Alterations in thinking, mood, or behavior contribute to a host of problems—patient distress, impaired functioning, heightened risk of death, pain, disability, substance abuse/dependence, and personal loss of freedom. A few facts the Surgeon General's report put forth follow.

- The mental health field is plagued by disparities in the availability of and access to its services.
- A key disparity often hinges on a person's financial status: formidable financial barriers block off needed mental health care from too many people, from those who have health insurance with inadequate mental health benefits to the 44 million Americans who have no insurance at all.
- About one in five Americans experiences a mental disorder over the course of a year.
- Mental illness represents more than 15 percent of the overall burden of disease from all causes and slightly more than the burden associated with all forms of cancer.
- Mental illness, including suicide, ranks second in the burden of disease, second only to cardiovascular disease.
- Depression ranks second only to ischemic coronary artery (heart) disease in the magnitude of disease burden. Schizophrenia, bipolar disorder, obsessive compulsive disorder, panic disorder, and posttraumatic stress disorder also contribute significantly to the burden represented by mental illness.
- Stigmatism is the most formidable obstacle to future progress in the arena of mental illness and health.

- Nearly two-thirds of all people with diagnosable mental conditions do not seek treatment, although mental disorders can be effectively treated in about 75 percent of cases.

- About 20 percent of American adults are afflicted with a mental or psychological disorder at one point or another in their lifetime.

A U. S. Presidential Commission on Mental Health report (U.S. Department of Health and Human Services, 2003) noted that care for the mentally ill must go beyond prescribing medication and managing symptoms in crisis management fashion. Call was made for counselors to help patients lead a fuller life, including, but moving beyond, administering drugs. The report was, in fact, a call for complete integration of mental health care. The commission issued a vision statement as well as six goals for treatment, along with recommendations for achieving these goals. The vision statement and goals follow:

Vision statement

We are committed to a future where recovery is the expected outcome and when mental illness can be prevented or cured. We envision a nation where everyone with mental illness will have access to early detection and the effective treatment and supports essential to live, work, learn, and participate fully in their community.

Goals of the report

1. *Mental health is essential to health.* Every individual, family, and community will understand that mental health is an essential part of overall health.

2. *Early mental health screening and treatment in multiple settings.* Every individual will have the opportunity for early and appropriate mental health screening, assessment, and referral to treatment.

3. *Consumer/family-centered care.* Consumers and families will have the necessary information and the opportunity to exercise choice over the care decisions that affect them. Continuous healing relationships will be a key feature of care.

4. *Best care science can offer.* Adults with serious mental illness and children with serious emotional disturbance will have ready access to the best treatments, services, and supports leading to recovery and cure. Accelerate research to enhance prevention of, recovery from, and ultimate discovery of cures for mental illnesses.

5. *Information infrastructure.* The mental health system will develop and expand its information infrastructure. That infrastructure has many purposes:

   a. Inform consumers, providers, and public policy

   b. Improve access, quality, accountability

6. *Eliminate disparities in mental health care.* Promote well-being for all people regardless of race, ethnicity, language, place of residence, or age and ensure equality of access, delivery of services, and improvement of outcomes for all communities.

These are obviously idealized goals, with little consideration for manpower, facilities, or costs of implementation. However, they do provide a set of ideals to guide future decisions. Note that symptom reduction via pharmacological means is a very small part of the plan: all mental health care should be delivered in an integrated fashion. This is an area in which many prescribing physicians and other prescibers are uncomfortable. (Prescribers include physicians, mental health nurse practitioners, and specially certified psychologists who recently have been granted limited prescription privileges in New Mexico and Kentucky, a practice that will expand to other states.) It also places a burden on nonprescribing mental health personnel to understand their clients' medications well enough to allow them to interact meaningfully with prescribers.

Depression

Up to a third of patients sitting in a physician's office have a diagnosable psychiatric disorder that largely goes undiagnosed and untreated, and 75 percent are anxiety or depressive disorders (Frank et al., 1998). Cognitive, emotional, and behavioral symptoms not part of a diagnosable disorder are also common; the modal psychiatric condition most often seen in general medical practice settings is the DSM-IV-TR category of *mixed anxiety-depression* (Table 17.1). Distressed high users of medical care certainly have even higher rates of psychopathology.

Undertreatment of Depression

Attention to the undertreatment of depression was emphasized as early as 1993 with publication of two clinical practice guidelines devoted to the treatment of depression. In 1998, the American Academy of Child and Adolescent Psychiatry (1998a) published a guideline titled "Practice Parameters for the Assessment and Treatment of Children and Adolescents with Depressive Disorders." In 2000, the American Psychiatric Association updated its practice guideline for major

---

TABLE 17.1 Mixed anxiety-depression

Persistent or recurrent dysphoric mood lasting at least 1 month

Dysphoric mood is accompanied by at least 1 month of ≥4 of the following symptoms:

    Difficulty concentrating or mind going blank

    Sleep disturbance (difficulty falling or staying asleep or restless unsatisfying sleep)

    Fatigue or low energy

    Irritability

    Worry

    Being easily moved to tears

    Hypervigilance

    Anticipating the worst

    Hopelessness (pervasive pessimism about the future)

    Low self-esteem or feelings of worthlessness

Symptoms caused clinically significant distress or impairment in social,
    occupational, or other important areas of functioning

---

depressive disorder in adults (American Psychiatric Association, 2000c). That the recommendations in these guidelines have not been implemented has been reported regularly (Cabana et al., 1999). Lack of compliance exists despite demonstrated reductions in depression when the guidelines are followed (Melfi et al., 1998; Wells et al., 2000). Furthermore, as discussed in Chapter 9 and emphasized by Sheline and coworkers (2003), depression is now viewed as an organic problem, involving loss of hippocampal volume and cellular neurogenesis. This pathology can be reversed by both pharmacological and psychological interventions (Russo-Neustadt et al., 1999). Therefore, depression is a manageable, neurological disorder, the pathology of which is controllable through therapy. While it may not be *curable*—it may recur without long-term interventions—its patholological cause is certainly manageable with resultant symptomatic improvements. In this case, depression resembles other long-term illnesses such as hypertension, diabetes, and hypothyroidism.

Depression affects an estimated 11 million Americans, or about 6 percent of the population, each year. The associated costs, including everything from treatment costs to loss of workplace productivity, are estimated at $44 billion per year. Particularly undertreated are depressed individuals in ethnic minority communities (Sclar et al., 1998), in direct contradiction to the recently released presidential goals listed earlier. This also holds true for the treatment of low-income persons with anxiety disorders (Jones et al., 2001).

Treatment of Depression

There is now general consensus that depression can be best treated by a combination of pharmacotherapy and psychological interventions (Figure 17.1). To understand the reason, it is necessary to tie together the etiology, pharmacotherapy, and neurobiological basis of the psychological or behavioral therapies of both anxiety and depression. This topic was covered in Chapter 9 and is briefly summarized here.

Antidepressant drugs result in an up regulation by the messenger RNA for the protein *brain-derived neurotrophic factor,* or BDNF) in hippocampal neurons. The result is a reversal of neuronal dysfunction and relief from depression. The slow onset of action of antidepressant drugs results from the need to increase BDNF by increasing the expression of this protein by increasing its messenger RNA (mRNA) levels. Antidepressant drugs are also extremely effective in reducing anxiety disorders and stress (Chapter 9), although physicians continue to prescribe benzodiazepines for these disorders. As hypothesized by Bruce and coworkers (2003), they may do so because few head-to-head comparisons of antidepressants and benzodiazepines in the treatment of anxiety disorders have been published.

Treating anxiety and/or depression (with either antidepressant medication or psychotherapeutic interventions) acutely increases synaptic concentrations of neurotransmitters and reduces stress and anxiety. The acute change leads to increased expression of BDNF mRNA, increasing

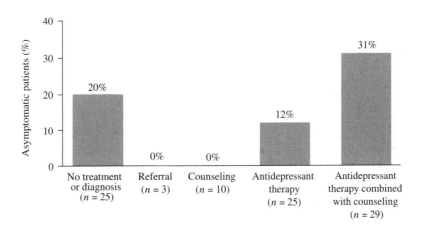

FIGURE 17.1 Percentages of patients who were treated with usual care and who were judged to be asymptomatic at month 8 in relation to the primary treatment pattern during the preceding months. [From H. C. Schulberg et al., "The Usual Care of Major Depression in Primary Care Practice," *Archives of Family Medicine* 6 (1997), pp. 334–339, with permission.]

BDNF within the neuron. Increased BDNF improves neuronal trophism, promotes repair of injured hippocampal neurons, and leads to improved neuronal function with relief of both anxiety and depression and with improvements in memory and cognitive functioning. These "repairs" set the stage for the introduction of psychological therapies and help explain the synergistic effects of combined pharmacotherapy and psychotherapy in relieving the distress of affective disorder.

Role of Drugs as Cotherapy

In addition to treating the acute symptoms associated with a mental disorder, medications serve a *prophylactic function*, altering brain chemistry to prevent the onset of a symptom complex (reducing the frequency of recurrence of symptomatology). Thus, drugs can be used to ameliorate debilitating symptoms of illness, to restore hippocampal neurons to more "normal" levels of function, and to prevent the development of additional symptoms, allowing the introduction of behavioral or psychological interventions.

The prescription of a psychotherapeutic medication is only the first step in treatment. In the treatment of affective disorders such as depression, dysthymia, or any of the anxiety disorder subtypes, medication is not necessarily superior to psychological therapies and the two are complementary. However, the medications frequently allow more rapid control of symptomatology and allow the earlier introduction of psychological interventions. Interventions can provide more than symptom relief; they may have effects that persist long after therapy ceases. In disorders such as bipolar disorder and schizophrenia, drug therapy is essential as primary therapy and psychological therapies are introduced following control of symptomatology.

Role of Psychotherapy as Cotherapy

Before the 1970s, only modest scientific evidence showed that psychotherapy was superior to placebo or that prolonged psychotherapy was superior to merely waiting for the patient to spontaneously recover. Today, it is widely recognized that psychological therapies are efficacious both as monotherapy for affective disorders and as cotherapy to pharmacological therapies. Research on psychological therapies is attempting to do several things:

- Tailor specific psychotherapeutic interventions to specific psychiatric conditions and specific patients
- Determine the appropriate duration, intensity, and complexity of effective therapies

- Assess the interaction between psychotherapeutic interventions with drug therapy

Some conclusions are becoming evident:

- In the treatment of panic disorder, agoraphobia, simple phobias, and, to a lesser extent, social phobias, behavioral and cognitive-behavioral therapies have traditionally been thought to have more consistent and longer-lasting effects than medications.

- Psychotherapy, specifically panic-focused cognitive-behavioral therapy, and medications (SSRIs, TCAs, benzodiazepines, and MAO inhibitors) are equally effective in the acute treatment for panic disorder (Work Group on Panic Disorder, 1998; Barlow et al., 2000).

- Combining cognitive-behavioral therapy and medication in the treatment of panic disorder has now been shown to be superior to either therapy alone, especially as the length of therapy continues (Barlow et al., 2000).

- Medications and behavioral techniques are equally effective in the treatment of obsessive compulsive disorder, posttraumatic stress disorder, and generalized anxiety disorder.

- In the treatment of major depressive disorder, antidepressant medications and cognitive-behavioral therapy are equally effective and display additional efficacy when used in combination (DeRubeis et al., 1999; Keller et al., 2000; Zajecka et al., 2002).

- At the very least, cognitive-behavioral therapy added to pharmacological management of depression reduces relapse rates for acute major depression and persistent severe residual symptoms (Paykel et al., 1999).

- In the treatment of eating disorders such as bulimia nervosa, cognitive-behavioral therapy is the psychological treatment of choice and medication with fluoxetine (an SSRI) adds modestly to the benefit of psychological treatment (Walsh et al., 1997).

- The positive effects of cognitive-behavioral therapy in treating depression in adults are also seen in adolescents, and treatment gains in adolescents are maintained over time (Reinecke et al., 1998).

Role of the Treatment Team

No individual should be the sole caregiver for a patient with mental or psychological illness. A team of caregivers, with members from several disciplines, should collaborate in treatment. One team member is usually a clinician with prescription privileges (a physician, a mental health nurse practitioner, or a prescribing psychologist). Other clinicians who do not prescribe medication may have responsibility for psychotherapeutic interventions. Other caregivers may include nurses, pharmacists, counselors, vocational rehabilitation counselors, physical or occupational therapists, dieticians, spiritual counselors, family members, and psychiatric, occupational, or recreational assistants. In 1996, Miller and Keitner presented a team approach, suggesting a "sequential" or "cascading" model when providing combined treatment. Various treatments (medication or psychotherapy) are administered in a sequential fashion based on the patient's response or lack of response to a previous treatment. If the patient responds to one treatment, no other may be needed; if there is no response, then a second treatment is added to the first. Continued nonresponse may lead to additional or substitute types of treatments.

Because the prescribing clinician has for so many years acted alone, it might reasonably be asked whether the treatment team concept is overly expensive or can actually deliver a higher quality of care with a better quality of life for the patient at a manageable cost to society. Several studies in the late 1990s addressed this issue, concluding that a treatment team relieves the prescriber of drugs of responsibility for handling psychological interventions, reduces hospitalizations, and provides longer, more intensive, more cost-effective case management.

In a psychiatrist/primary care model, the patient alternates visits with a psychiatrist and a primary care physician; both professionals assist in the education and pharmacologic treatment of the patient. In the psychiatrist/psychologist team model, the psychiatrist works with a psychologist to improve adherence to and effectiveness of treatment, and the psychologist also provides brief behavioral treatment in the primary care clinic. This collaborative model is associated with improved adherence to treatment, increased patient satisfaction with care, and improved outcome compared with usual care by primary care physicians alone (Katon et al., 1997).

How might a treatment team function? Nonprescribing members of the team should be familiar with the pharmacology, uses, limitations, and side effects of the drugs being used by their clients. They should also know about alternative medications that may provide equal or superior effectiveness with a more reasonable spectrum of side effects for the particular client. These clinicians must be able to professionally converse with the prescribing physician, monitor drug therapy, and institute psychological therapies appropriate to the condition under treatment. They should monitor for both positive and negative effects and be sensitive to the meaning medications have to their clients, for effective psychotherapy depends on the ability of patients to comply with treatment requirements (Sprenger and Josephson, 1998).

Regardless of their individual roles, all team members share certain basic functions. Most important is that of ongoing assessment, the purpose of which is to obtain an objective report of the patient's signs and symptoms and, as much as possible, to relate them to possible causes. Assessment may include a formal diagnosis, or it may be a description of the development of the client's behavior. Either type of assessment should address both the strengths and the weaknesses of the patient. Most beneficial is an assessment that includes the probable etiology of the problem.

The clinician may list the possible explanations for the observed behaviors in a comprehensive format called the *differential diagnosis,* from which the causes may be determined. Frequently, further assessment is necessary to rule out some of the possible causes. Less plausible causes usually can be readily eliminated. The differential diagnosis then guides further assessment and treatment. Possible causal factors in the differential diagnosis often have markedly different treatments. Consequently, an accurate assessment and diagnosis of the causes of the patient's behavior must precede any treatment planning or therapeutic intervention. Evaluation by mental health professionals is often formalized into a standard diagnostic format. Most often used is the diagnostic system of the fourth edition of the *Diagnostic and Statistical Manual of Mental Disorders,* or DSM-IV-TR (American Psychiatric Association, 2000a).

DSM-IV-TR Classification of Mental Disorders

Diagnosis is the practice of distinguishing one disease from another. In clinical psychology, diagnosis is based on the signs and symptoms of a mental disorder, regardless of the morbid changes producing them. The DSM-IV-TR classification provides a shorthand description of the patterns of behavior that can be expected with each disorder.

DSM-IV-TR is a categorical classification that divides mental disorders into types based on criteria sets with defining features. In DSM-IV-TR there is no assumption that each category of mental disorder is a complete discrete entity with absolute boundaries dividing it from other mental disorders or from no mental disorder. There is also no assumption that all individuals described as having the same mental disorder are alike in all important ways. This outlook allows more flexibility in the use of the system, encourages more specific attention to boundary cases, and emphasizes the need to capture additional clinical information that goes beyond diagnosis.

In the DSM-IV-TR classification system, each patient being diagnosed is not merely assigned a single diagnostic category (for example, bipolar disorder). Instead, the patient is characterized by clinically relevant factors that are grouped into five "axes":

- Axis I: Primary classification (diagnosis) of the major problem requiring attention (for example, alcohol dependence)
- Axis II: Mental retardation and personality disorders generally believed to begin in childhood or adolescence and persisting into adult life
- Axis III: Any physical disorder that seems relevant to a case and that may have implications for present treatment (for example, asthma that is exacerbated by psychological factors)
- Axis IV: Psychosocial and environmental problems that may affect the diagnosis, treatment, and prognosis of the mental disorders listed under Axes I and II (for example, illiteracy or unemployment)
- Axis V: Global assessment of psychological functioning, social relationships, and occupational activities (including ratings of both the current level of functioning and the highest level of functioning during the past year)

In emergencies, a preliminary classification is made even though much information is lacking. In such situations, any assessment is considered tentative and subject to revision as additional medical, psychological, and psychosocial assessments are made.

The first three axes constitute official diagnostic categories of the American Psychiatric Association. Axes IV and V are regarded as supplementary categories for use in clinical and research settings. It is common practice, however, to describe a case using all five axes. The major categories of Axis I classification are listed in Table 17.2. Here we consider four of the sixteen Axis I categories—mood (or affective) disorders, schizophrenia, anxiety disorders, and eating disorders. These four were chosen because of their prevalence and because they are the disorders most frequently treated with a combination of medication and psychotherapy.

Mood (Affective) Disorders

The term *mood* refers to a perceptual bias that alters how one views the world. Mood disorders may include major depressive, manic, or hypomanic episodes, dysthymia, or alternating recurrences of one or more such moods. DSM-IV groups mood disorders into *depressive disorders, bipolar disorders, substance-induced mood disorders,* and *mood disorders due to general medical conditions.* One of these, depression, was discussed earlier in this chapter.

TABLE 17.2 DSM-IV-TR Axis I categories

Category	Examples
Disorders usually first diagnosed in infancy, childhood, or adolescence	Attention deficit and disruptive behavior disorders, learning disorders, certain eating disorders
Delirium, dementia, and amnestic and other cognitive disorders	Transient or permanent brain dysfunction, attributable to such factors as aging, dementia due to head trauma, or Alzheimer's, and amnestic disorders (memory loss)
Substance-related disorders	Disorders related to alcohol, all chemical withdrawal syndromes, and some disorders related to or caused by substances such as substance-induced psychotic disorders
Schizophrenia and other psychotic disorders	Chronic disorganized behavior and thought of psychotic proportions (delusions, hallucinations), incoherence, and social isolation; disorders that are well-organized systems of delusions without the incoherence, bizarreness, and other social isolation seen in schizophrenia
Mood disorders	Depression and bipolar disorder
Anxiety disorders	Anxiety, tension, and worry without psychotic features (delusions, hallucinations); posttraumatic (reactive, stress-caused) disorders, whether brief or chronic
Somatoform disorders	Physical symptoms for which no medical causes can be found (symptoms apparently not under voluntary control and linked to psychological factors or conflicts)
Factitious disorders	Physical or behavioral symptoms that are voluntarily produced by the individual, apparently in order to play the role of patient and often involving chronic, blatant lying
Dissociative disorders	Sudden, temporary change in the normal functions of consciousness (for example, loss of memory, sleepwalking)
Sexual and gender identity disorders	Deviant sexual thoughts and behavior that are either personally anxiety provoking or socially maladaptive

TABLE 17.2 DSM-IV-TR Axis I categories *(continued)*

Category	Examples
Eating disorders	Disorders of eating such as anorexia nervosa
Sleep disorders	Insomnia or difficulty in going to sleep or staying asleep, excessive daytime sleeping, complaints of sleep disturbance without objective evidence, impairment of respiration during sleep, disturbance of sleeping schedule, sleepwalking, sleep terrors
Impulse-control disorders, not classified elsewhere	Maladaptations characterized by failure to resist impulses (for example, pathological gambling, chronic stealing of desired objects, habitual fire setting)
Adjustment disorders	Maladaptive reactions to identifiable life events or circumstances that are expected to lessen and cease when the stressor ceases; reaction may be dominated by depressed mood, anxiety, withdrawal, conduct disorder such as truancy, or a lessening in work or job performance
Mental disorders due to general medical condition, not classified elsewhere	Disorders that may be due to a medical condition, such as a psychotic disorder that emerges in response to renal failure
Other conditions that may be a focus of clinical attention	Includes such things as medication-induced movement disorders such as tardive dyskinesia or partner or parent/child relational problems

Abstracted from American Psychiatric Association (2000a), pp. 13–25.

All of us experience mood shifts, such as mild anxiety, depression, sadness, and grief, in response to difficult life events. These responses are natural and certainly do not constitute a mood disorder. The DSM-IV-TR classification pertains to distinct, severe processes that interfere with daily activities. These dysfunctional processes are, however, amenable to treatment. A normal course of bereavement due to environmental factors (for example, death of a loved one) is not classified as a mood disorder, even though it may temporarily incapacitate the individual and necessitate either pharmacological or psychological interventions.

In general, mood disorders are subclassified by type and duration of the mood episode. For example, two weeks of severely depressed mood (as indicated by a specific set of four additionally related symptoms) is required for a diagnosis of a major depressive episode. Two years of mildly depressed mood and the presence of two related symptoms are required for diagnosis of dysthymic disorder.

Assessment and Diagnosis. Careful assessment of psychological disorders is the initial step in effective treatment planning, whether the planned treatment is pharmacological, psychological, or a combination of both. Thorough assessment is helpful in distinguishing between functional and organic causes. In other words, not only is a DSM-IV-TR classification of symptom-based behavioral dysfunction developed, a differential diagnosis of all possible causative factors for the observed behaviors is made. This list is then narrowed to one or perhaps a few possibilities so that the likely cause can be identified and effectively treated. A thorough assessment also includes an investigation of social and psychological factors that may contribute to pathology. Other sociopsychological conditions may exacerbate existing physical or psychological problems. For example, cigarette smoking can be antidepressant (discussed in Chapter 8), and cessation of smoking may lead to the emergence or exacerbation of major depressive episodes.

Treatment. The biological, psychological, and social factors in mood disorders must be addressed in a comprehensive treatment plan. As stated earlier, pharmacotherapy and psychotherapy effectively treat depression, and combining the two further improves efficacy and reduces the probability of relapse. Even reactive (exogenous) depression, adjustment mood disorders, and dysthymia have biological components that require intervention with pharmacological agents along with psychotherapy.

A person's basic perceptual beliefs, cognitive and intellectual processing, and experiences affect the person's interaction with the environment and with other individuals. Eventually a person develops a sense of how self interacts with others. Individuals suffering from a mood disorder learn a pattern of behavior that may cause their problems to become worse and make the disorder resistant to treatment and intervention. Psychological therapies can change the pattern of behavior. There are many techniques, from simple education to supportive counseling to insight-oriented, dynamically based therapy. Cognitive therapy, behavioral therapy, brief psychodynamic psychotherapy, group therapies, and others are frequently used and are effective interventions.

Children and adolescents are being increasingly diagnosed with mood disorders, including major depressive disorder and bipolar disorder. Whether this trend reflects an increased recognition of the disorders or an actual increase in their incidence is unclear. The pharmacological treatment of mood disorders in children and adolescents is discussed in Chapter 12. Behavioral therapies and family interventions are perhaps preferred over pharmacologic interventions, at least for early intervention in less severe cases.

Schizophrenia

The formal DSM-IV-TR definition of schizophrenia is presented in Table 17.3. Positive symptoms of schizophrenia include hallucinations, delusions, disorganized speech, and bizarre behavior. Negative symptoms include impaired social interactions, impoverished and blunted affect, an absence of motivation, and significant social withdrawal. The disorder often begins in adolescence or young adulthood, frequently followed by a progressively deteriorating course; few patients make a complete recovery.

Antipsychotic Medication. The drugs used to reduce the symptomatology of schizophrenia are discussed in Chapter 11. Advances in this area occurred rapidly through the 1990s and are continuing to today. In 1993 it was stated:

> All of the symptoms associated with schizophrenia are affected to some degree by neuroleptics. Positive symptoms, including hallucinations, delusions, and disorganized thoughts, are more responsive to drug treatment than are negative symptoms, such as blunted affect, emotional withdrawal, and lack of social interest. . . . A substantial proportion of schizophrenic patients—about 10 to 20 percent—fail to demonstrate substantial improvement when they are treated with neuroleptics. This subgroup of treatment-refractory schizophrenic patients often requires long-term institutionalization in state hospitals and similar facilities. Clozapine and other atypical antipsychotic drugs may be particularly effective for these patients. (Marder et al., 1993 pp. 567–568.)

Clozapine and some new-generation antipsychotic drugs are effective in at least 30 percent of patients who are severely disabled by negative symptoms. In addition, these new drugs have become accepted as first-line agents because of their effectiveness and their lack of extrapyramidal side effects. By relieving negative symptomatology, they make patients "reachable" and more amenable to psychosocial interventions in efforts to improve their social functioning and their integration into society.

Psychotherapy and Rehabilitation. The new-generation antipsychotic drugs have made it possible for psychotherapy and other interventions to be effective, particularly in the outpatient setting. Having established the primary role of antipsychotics, there is evidence that psychosocial

TABLE 17.3 DSM-IV-TR categories of schizophrenia and related disorders

Schizophrenia is a disturbance that lasts for at least 6 months and includes at least 1 month of active-phase symptoms (i.e., two [or more] of the following: delusions, hallucinations, disorganized speech, grossly disorganized or catatonic behavior, negative symptoms). Definitions for Schizophrenia subtypes (Paranoid, Disorganized, Catatonic, Undifferentiated, and Residual) are also included in this section.

Schizophreniform Disorder is characterized by a symptomatic presentation that is equivalent to Schizophrenia except for its duration (i.e., the disturbance lasts from 1 to 6 months) and the absence of a requirement that there be a decline in functioning.

Schizoaffective Disorder is a disturbance in which a mood episode and the active-phase symptoms of Schizophrenia occur together and were preceded or are followed by at least 2 weeks of delusions or hallucinations without prominent mood symptoms.

Delusional Disorder is characterized by at least 1 month of nonbizarre delusions without other active-phase symptoms of Schizophrenia.

Brief Psychotic Disorder is a psychotic disturbance that lasts more than 1 day and remits by 1 month.

Shared Psychotic Disorder is a disturbance that develops in an individual who is influenced by someone else who has an established delusion with similar content.

In **Psychotic Disorder Due to a General Medical Condition,** the psychotic symptoms are judged to be a direct physiological consequence of a general medical condition.

In **Substance-Induced Psychotic Disorder,** the psychotic symptoms are judged to be a direct physiological consequence of a drug of abuse, a medication, or toxin exposure.

Psychotic Disorder Not Otherwise Specified is included for classifying psychotic presentations that do not meet criteria for any of the specific Psychotic Disorders defined in this section or psychotic symptomatology about which there is inadequate or contradictory information.

Abstracted from American Psychiatric Association (2000a), pp. 298–343.

therapies, when administered with these agents, improve long-term prognosis. Because chronically psychotic patients have difficulties with social adjustment, reason dictates that they and their families could benefit from such interventions. Regardless of theoretical orientation, it is clear that practitioners should provide psychosocial therapy as part of a comprehensive treatment strategy. In general, most cost-benefit studies find that the addition of psychological therapies in an outpatient setting encourages drug compliance. Therapeutic interventions improve social skills and assist in the rehabilitation of cognitive functions. Psychological therapy in conjunction with drug therapy also extends relapse time and reduces the intensity of relapse episodes. Typically, the most beneficial strategy is a sociopsychological therapy emphasizing self-esteem, social skills, and cognitive rehabilitation. This emphasis addresses the interaction between the client's symptoms and their social and psychological consequences. These strategies develop and rehabilitate cognitive functions, resulting in a more positive self-image and more effective social and cognitive functioning.

Norman and Townsend (1999) discussed the role of cognitive-behavioral interventions in reducing psychosis. Sensky and coworkers (2000) studied 90 patients with schizophrenia with medication-resistant symptoms, comparing cognitive-behavioral therapy (9 months of therapy) with a nonspecific befriending control intervention. Both therapies were effective in the short term, reducing both positive and negative symptoms. Cognitive-behavioral therapy produced longer-lasting results; continuing improvement was observed even 9 months after treatment was stopped. Cognitive-behavioral interventions were thought to be cost-effective, with an average of 24 hours of therapist time spent per clinically successful outcome. Medication addresses the biophysical component of the disorder. Social therapy, with structured or supported living, teaches and reinforces social skills. Psychological therapy addresses the intrapsychic and psychodynamic issues. Vocational rehabilitation is important in developing self-esteem and establishing financial independence.

Functions of the Treatment Team. The treatment team should teach the client the positive and negative effects of any prescribed drugs; it also answers any questions and relieves any doubts a patient has about any medication. Helping the client remain drug compliant is important in reducing the rate of relapse. In addition, monitoring of drug levels in plasma can provide important information, improve drug effectiveness, and reduce unwanted side effects. The client should also understand the limitations of his or her medication. A team member should help the client understand that motivation, medication, and psychological therapy are all important in stabilization and recovery.

Schizophrenia in children and adolescents is discussed in Chapter 12 and practice parameters have been published (American Academy of Child and Adolescent Psychiatry, 1997).

Anxiety Disorders

Symptoms of anxiety are normal and serve as an early warning system that helps a person avoid potentially dangerous situations. Excessive anxiety, however, may be a source of significant suffering and require intervention. Anxiety is subtle and pervasive; it accompanies almost every psychiatric disorder. Because anxiety touches everyone, it becomes a disorder only when it is objectively uncomfortable or is perceived to be out of control; the usual feelings of anxiety increase and interfere with normal functioning. Severe symptoms of anxiety require assessment and treatment. Understanding the underlying causes and formulating a differential diagnosis help the clinician determine which drugs and which psychological interventions will be the most effective.

The chronicity of anxiety disorders is similar to that of mood disorders, more enduring than that of substance abuse disorders, but less deep-seated than that of the schizophrenias. Only about 30 percent of individuals with anxiety disorders receive treatment, a percentage that is even lower if generalized anxiety disorder is included. Thus, a high percentage of mental health and addictive disorders are actually anxiety disorders or have a high component of comorbid anxiety. Often, these disorders go untreated or are not treated by behavioral health specialists.

Characteristic of anxiety disorders are the symptoms of anxiety and avoidance behavior. Anxiety is a complex response that includes subjective feelings of dread, apprehension, fear, tension, and related psychomotor responses. The last may include motor tension, increases in autonomic responses (heart rate, blood pressure), vigilance, and scanning. DSM-IV-TR lists several subcategories of the anxiety disorders, which are presented in Table 17.4.

Using drugs to treat anxiety disorders is controversial. The controversy arises from diagnostic difficulties, from the chronic nature of many anxieties, and from the addictive potential associated with some of the drugs used in therapy (namely, the benzodiazepines). In the 1960s and 1970s, the benzodiazepine anxiolytics appeared to treat anxiety disorders quickly, effectively, and safely and replaced the barbiturate therapies of the 1950s. Over time, the addictive potential of benzodiazepine therapy became evident, but these drugs continue to be widely prescribed, perhaps because of demand from patients who find the drugs pleasant to take and difficult to quit (Bruce et al., 2003). Also, benzodiazepines, which reduce the outward symptoms of anxiety, might be counterproductive because they may themselves produce depression and suppress cognitive function. With the advent of the antidepressants and the observation that these drugs (especially SSRIs) effectively treat many of the anxieties, sophistication in diagnosing and treating the anxieties similarly expanded. Since 1999, almost all the SSRIs have been approved by the FDA for use in the treatment of generalized anxiety disorder and other anxiety subtypes. As was discussed in Chapter 6, important new anxiolytics are on the horizon. Again, it is imperative for both prescribing and nonprescribing clinicians to become knowledgeable about the pharmacology of these drugs, their

TABLE 17.4 DSM-IV-TR categories of anxiety disorders

A **Panic Attack** is a discrete period in which there is the sudden onset of intense apprehension, fearfulness, or terror, often associated with feelings of impending doom. During these attacks symptoms such as shortness of breath, palpitations, chest pain or discomfort, choking or smothering sensations, and fear of "going crazy" or losing control are present.

Agoraphobia is anxiety about, or avoidance of, places or situations from which escape might be difficult (or embarrassing) or in which help may not be available in the event of having a Panic Attack or panic-like symptoms.

Panic Disorder without Agoraphobia is characterized by recurrent unexpected Panic Attacks about which there is persistent concern.

Panic Disorder with Agoraphobia is characterized by both recurrent unexpected Panic Attacks and Agoraphobia.

Agoraphobia without History of Panic Disorder is characterized by the presence of Agoraphobia and panic-like symptoms without a history of unexpected Panic Attacks.

Specific Phobia is characterized by clinically significant anxiety provoked by exposure to a specific feared object or situation, often leading to avoidance behavior.

Social Phobia is characterized by clinically significant anxiety provoked by exposure to certain types of social or performance situations, often leading to avoidance behavior.

Obsessive-Compulsive Disorder is characterized by obsessions (which cause marked anxiety or distress) and/or by compulsions (which serve to neutralize anxiety).

Posttraumatic Stress Disorder is characterized by the reexperiencing of an extremely traumatic event accompanied by symptoms of increased arousal and by avoidance of stimuli associated with the trauma.

Acute Stress Disorder is characterized by symptoms similar to those of Post-Traumatic Stress Disorder that occur immediately in the aftermath of an extremely traumatic event.

Generalized Anxiety Disorder is characterized by at least 6 months of persistent and excessive anxiety and worry.

Anxiety Disorder Due to a General Medical Condition is characterized by prominent symptoms of anxiety that are judged to be a direct physiological consequence of a general medical condition.

Substance-Induced Anxiety Disorder is characterized by prominent symptoms of anxiety that are judged to be a direct physiological consequence of a drug of abuse, a medication, or toxic exposure.

Anxiety Disorder Not Otherwise Specified is included for coding disorders with prominent anxiety or phobic avoidance that do not meet criteria for any of the specific Anxiety Disorders defined in this section (or anxiety symptoms about which there is inadequate or contradictory information).

Because Separation Anxiety Disorder (characterized by anxiety related to separation from parental figures) usually develops in childhood, it is included in the "Disorders Usually First Diagnosed in Infancy, Childhood, or Adolescence" section. Phobic avoidance that is limited to genital sexual contact with a sexual partner is classified as Sexual Aversion Disorder and is included in the "Sexual and Gender Identity Disorders" section.

Reproduced with permission from American Psychiatric Association (2000a), pp. 429–436.

clinical indications, limitations, and duration of usage. Most important, their limitations must receive as much attention as their assets.

Accurate assessment and diagnosis are especially vital in planning the appropriate treatment for anxiety disorders. Generally, more diffuse and severe anxiety symptoms require some initial pharmacological intervention. Less severe, more circumscribed symptoms of phobias may be more responsive to cognitive and behavioral therapy; in such cases, it is often unnecessary to resort to pharmacotherapy.

Panic Disorder. Panic disorder is one of the most common and most disabling of the anxiety disorders. Barloon and Noyes (1997) discuss Charles Darwin, describing how disabling this disorder was in his life. Panic disorder is considered a chronic condition that requires ongoing maintenance therapy, preferably combined pharmacologic and psychological therapies (Barlow et al., 2000). An editorial accompanying the Barlow report (Glass, 2000) emphasizes a lifetime, worldwide prevalence of panic disorder in the general community at about 1.5 to 3.5 percent, along with high levels of social morbidity and health care service utilization. Other data indicate that patients with panic disorder account for more than 20 percent of emergency room visits and are twelve times more likely to visit the emergency room than the general population. Patients with panic attacks average 19 medical visits per year, a rate seven times above normal; they also account for 15 percent of total medical visits. The use of medical services and the health care costs associated with panic disorder are therefore enormous. Added to them are disability costs and unemployment expenses (25 percent of panic disorder patients are fully unemployed). Appropriate treatment is presumed to reduce these disabilities and expenditures.

Comprehensive therapy reduces the severity of the course of panic disorder and enhances outcome. Pharmacologically, the SSRI-type antidepressants are the drugs of choice, except for patients also experiencing severe agitation. For those patients, a benzodiazepine anxiolytic is more effective on a short-term basis, until the anxiety and/or agitation resolves.

An estimated 50 percent of patients with panic disorder experience an episode of major depression (Gorman and Coplan, 1996), an added impetus for the use of antidepressant medications over benzodiazepines. A growing database of evidence supports the efficacy of cognitive-behavioral therapy in panic disorder (Glass, 2000). CBT usually includes patient education, monitoring of panic symptoms, breathing retraining, cognitive restructuring of the catastrophic thinking associated with panic symptoms, and exposure and desensitization to external phobic situations. Psychological therapies should also address the comorbidity of panic disorder and depression.

Pollack (1997) reviewed the psychopharmacology for panic disorder, stating that, with the use of SSRIs, it is important to start low to minimize the increased anxiety associated with the initiation of treatment. According to Pollack, buproprion and trazodone are unique among antidepressants in their relative lack of efficacy in treating panic disorder and other anxiety conditions in contrast to most other antidepressants.

Of the benzodiazepines, alprazolam (Xanax) is the most widely studied for treating panic disorder. Other benzodiazepines that have been studied include lorazepam (Ativan) and clonazepam (Klonopin). The benzodiazepines have a favorable profile of side effects; they lack the anticholinergic side effects of the TCAs and the increased anxiety of the SSRIs. Concomitant use (benzodiazepine plus SSRI) provides rapid anxiolysis and more comprehensive relief of panic and depressive symptoms. For all antidepressant medications, treatment may need to be continued indefinitely, because there is a high rate of relapse with medication discontinuation.

Generalized Anxiety Disorder. Although considerable attention focused on anxiety disorders in the 1990s, less attention was devoted to the investigation of generalized anxiety disorder (GAD):

> The emerging picture is that GAD is a common and chronic disorder, affecting primarily women, and one that leads to significant distress and impairment. Subjects with GAD frequently utilize health care services and require medication treatment. (Brawman-Mintzer and Lydiard, 1996, p. 3.)

Formerly called *anxiety neurosis*, GAD occurs at a rate that equals or exceeds the other anxiety disorders. GAD is also comorbid with other psychological disorders, especially depression and dysthymia. GAD is associated with disability, medically unexplained symptoms, and overutilization of medical resources. Two-thirds of individuals with current GAD had an additional current psychiatric diagnosis (usually major depression or dysthymia), and 98 percent of those with lifetime GAD had another lifetime psychiatric diagnosis. GAD may be a crucial factor in modifying the presentation, course, and outcome of major depression. Patients with GAD have a moderate amount of disability and impairment in quality of life. GAD is especially common in the elderly (Lenze et al., 2000).

Treatment of GAD is currently understudied. One mainstay of self-medication for GAD is ethyl alcohol, which effectively produces a short-term anxiolytic action. Until the mid- to late 1990s, benzodiazepines were the prescribed agents of choice, but their use is associated with significant emergent (rebound) anxiety and withdrawal-related symptomatology (Rickels and Rynn, 2002; Sramek et al., 2002). About 25 percent of patients treated with benzodiazepines show rebound anxiety, and 40 percent of them resume their medication because they find drug discontinuation to be intolerable.

In the mid-1990s, buspirone (BuSpar) was demonstrated to effectively reduce symptomatology with efficacy superior to placebo and equal to lorazepam (Sramek et al., 1996). At that time, buspirone was considered to be the drug of choice for GAD in situations where a slow onset of action and a "subtle" effect was acceptable. By 1997, buspirone was widely used for persistent anxiety without panic attacks, the latter often requiring therapy with an SSRI-type antidepressant. Buspirone does not impair memory or motor coordination, is not associated with abuse or dependence, is not cross-tolerant with alcohol, and does not produce a withdrawal reaction. In addition, buspirone has a progressive onset of action and produces few adverse drug reactions when combined with other agents. It was concluded in the late 1990s that if the patient does not respond to buspirone, an antidepressant such as nefazodone, a 5-HT$_2$ antagonist, or one of the SSRIs would be indicated. In 1999, venlafaxine, a mixed serotonin-norepinephrine reuptake-inhibiting antidepressant in an extended-release dosage form (Effexor-XR) was shown to be effective (Katz et al., 2002; Montgomery et al., 2002) and has been approved by the FDA for clinical use in the treatment of GAD. In essence, any SSRI-type antidepressant may be used effectively to treat GAD. Perhaps the most studied SSRI has been paroxetine (Rickels et al., 2003; Stocchi et al., 2003).

Currently, other drugs are being evaluated for use in treating GAD. For example, tiagabine (Gabitril), a GABA-reuptake blocker in the brain, is currently in clinical trial for use in treating GAD (Lydiard, 2003; Schwartz, 2002). Pregabalin (Lyrica), a gabapentin (Neurontin) derivative, was approved in 2005 for treating peripheral neuropathies. It has been reported to be useful in treating GAD (Feltner et al., 2003; Lauria-Horner and Pohl, 2003; Pande et al., 2003).

Cognitive-behavioral psychotherapies, which teach clients to examine how their unrealistic thoughts and ruminations affect their behavioral functioning, have proven effective in treating GAD (Borkovec et al., 2003; Dugas et al., 2003; Harvey and Rapee, 1995). Relaxation therapy, biofeedback, and stress management are used to teach patients how to relax even under stress. Many anxious people worry about being unable to cope. They fear losing control, "going crazy," or being publicly embarrassed. As a consequence, the fears increase the anxiety in a vicious circle. Anxious thoughts increase anxiety symptoms, which in turn generate even more anxious thoughts. Cognitive-behavioral techniques help patients break this circle by allowing them to deal appropriately with anxious thoughts and their related behavioral expressions.

Because GAD is a chronic, relapsing, and debilitating disorder, both acute efficacy and long-term prevention of relapse must be considered when choosing both drug and psychotherapeutic interventions. Ideally, cognitive-behavioral therapies should have long-term efficacy. Durham and coworkers (2003), in a 14-year follow-up report, noted that CBT was associated with significantly lower overall severity of GAD symptomatology and fewer interim treatments. CBT had less influence over diagnostic status, probability of overall recovery, or patient perceptions of overall improvement. Therefore, although data are lacking, combinations of drug therapy and CBT may offer the most hope for long-term efficacy.

Social Phobia (Social Anxiety Disorder). Social anxiety disorder is a common illness with significant associated disability. It is frequently underrecognized and underdiagnosed. Persons with this disorder are less likely to be high achievers, have lower employment rates, and lower household incomes than persons without the disorder (Patel et al., 2002). In general, the phobias are characterized by extreme anxiety about a specific object (specific phobia) or a generalized or discrete social situation (social phobia). Patients with social phobias are at high risk for developing mood or anxiety disorders and schizophrenia. According to learning theory, individuals select the behavior that moves them from a state of stress to a state in which the stress is reduced. Thus, if a conditioned stimulus is repeatedly presented in a manner that does not produce a conditioned emotional response, the original association is extinguished. Systematic desensitization (targeted exposure therapy) pairs fear-evoking incidents with relaxation training in a sequence that finally leads to the presentation of the original fear-inducing or anxiety-arousing stimulus.

When the patient with a phobia displays severe anxiety symptoms, anxiolytics may be administered to treat acute symptoms (Jefferson, 2001). For longer-term pharmacological management, antidepressant agents, especially the SSRI-type antidepressants, are the drugs of choice. Overall, the reduction in the intensity of the disorder is probably less than 50 percent, probably because the chronic nature of the disorder is not amenable to short-term drug treatment (Versiani, 2000). Nonetheless, SSRI antidepressants have become the drugs of choice. Fluoxetine is less effective (Kobak et al., 2002), while sertraline, paroxetine, fluvoxamine, and citalopram are all effective (Blomhoff et al., 2001; Furmark et al., 2002; Van Ameringen et al., 2001). Of the non-SSRI antidepressants, bupropion has been shown to be effective (Emmanuel et al., 2000).

Cognitive-behavioral therapies appear to be significantly less effective than medication, although combination therapy may be superior to that achieved by drugs alone; positive results persist into the post-drug phase (Blomhoff et al., 2001; Fedoroff and Taylor, 2001; Heimberg, 2001; Otto et al., 2000). Furmark and coworkers (2002) studied cerebral blood flow changes in patients with social phobia and assessed the alterations in blood flow induced by both citalopram (an SSRI) and cognitive-behavioral therapy. In both instances, blood flow increased in the amygdala, hippocampus, and neighboring cortical areas (brain regions subserving bodily defense reactions to threats). Increases in blood flow correlated with clinical symptom improvements.

Obsessive Compulsive Disorder. Obsessive compulsive disorder (OCD) is characterized by recurrent and disturbing thoughts (obsessions) and/or repetitive behaviors (compulsions) that the individual feels driven to perform but recognizes as irrational or excessive. Once thought to be a rare condition, it is now estimated to be present in about 2 percent of the general population, making it the fourth most common psychiatric disorder. Although traditionally viewed as resistant to a variety of therapeutic interventions, recent advances have been made in the psychopharmacologic and behavioral therapy of OCD. In particular, the efficacy of serotonin reuptake inhibitors, such as clomipramine, fluvoxamine, fluoxetine, and sertraline, has been established in double-blind studies in patients with OCD. Consistent with these drug response data are the hypotheses that changes in serotonin function are critical to the treatment of OCD and perhaps involved in the pathophysiology of at least some patients with the disorder.

SSRIs are commonly used for treating OCD; they are effective in approximately 40 to 60 percent of OCD patients. Furthermore, current research indicates that a combination of medication and behavioral therapies is more effective than the use of either drugs or psychological interventions alone. Simpson and coworkers (1999) studied cognitive-behavioral therapy (using exposure and ritual prevention) as an adjunct to SSRIs in an open trial in six patients who remained symptomatic despite the treatment. In all six patients, there was a further reduction in OCD symptoms. It therefore appears that because significant OCD symptoms often remain or recur, even when there is substantial improvement with SSRI therapy, a combined drug-CBT approach may be an appropriate strategy. Recent studies on the pharmacotherapy for OCD include those by Davidson and Bjorgvinsson (2003), Mundo and coworkers (2001), Hollander and coworkers (2003), and Wagner and coworkers (2003). The treatment of OCD in children and adolescents is discussed in Chapter 12: OCD-specific cognitive-behavioral psychotherapy and pharmacotherapy with a serotonin reuptake inhibitor define the psychotherapeutic and pharmacotherapeutic treatments of choice (American Academy of Child and Adolescent Psychiatry, 1998b).

Posttraumatic Stress Disorder. It is generally accepted that transient and long-lasting neurological alterations may underlie acute and long-term neuronal responses to traumatic stress. Comorbidity is frequent; individuals with posttraumatic stress disorder (PTSD) experience a high incidence of GAD, phobias, depression, and substance abuse. Thus, the treatment of PTSD must be comprehensive and individualized, utilizing carefully balanced pharmacotherapeutic and psychotherapeutic interventions that address both the PTSD and any comorbid disorder. Symptom relief provided by pharmacotherapy enables the patient to participate more thoroughly in individual, behavioral, or group therapy.

Most drugs that are effective for PTSD are also useful for treating major depression and panic disorder. Thus, numerous drugs have been tried, including TCAs, MAO inhibitors, trazodone, the SSRIs, clonidine, guanfacin, brofaromine, valproate, carbamazepine, benzodiazepines, and others. No one drug or class of drugs is universally effective in treating the disorder, although most clinicians feel that a serotonergic action is necessary for good clinical effect in PTSD, analogous to the situation with OCD (Asnis et al., 2004). Therefore, the drugs most utilized are the SSRIs; sertraline has been approved by the FDA for treating this complex and often chronic illness (Davis et al., 2001; Schwartz and Rothbaum, 2002; Yehuda, 2002).

Psychological therapies are essential in treating PTSD (Adshead, 2000), and combining psychotherapy with pharmacotherapy is beneficial. Marshall and Cloitre (2000) present a treatment model involving a phase-oriented treatment approach that begins with pharmacotherapy and continues with trauma-focused psychotherapy. Some clinicians advocate the use of hypnotic techniques to facilitate working through the traumatic events. This approach is based on the frequently observed interrelationship between dissociative reactions and physical trauma. Other behavioral strategies for treating PTSD include group therapy, psychoeducation, exposure and response prevention, cognitive strategies, and family involvement (Himle et al., 2003).

Eating Disorders

Only in recent years have eating disorders (bulimia nervosa, anorexia nervosa, and binge-eating disorder) been considered amenable to pharmacologic treatment. For bulimia nervosa, in particular, the role of medication has expanded; double-blind, placebo-controlled studies demonstrate significant decrease in the frequency of binge-eating behavior in response to antidepressant medications (Kotler et al., 2003; Mitchell et al., 2003). Various classes of antidepressant medications have been tried, but a revised practice guideline for the treatment of patients with eating disorders (American Psychiatric Association, 2000b) states:

> The SSRIs are currently considered to be the safest antidepressants and may be especially helpful for patients with significant symptoms of depression, anxiety, obsessions, or certain impulse disorder symptoms or for those patients who have had a suboptimal response to previous attempts at appropriate psychosocial therapy. (p. 25)

Recently, Hedges and coworkers (2003) and Hoopes and coworkers (2003) reported on the efficacy of topiramate (Topamax; Chapter 10). They note that compared with placebo, topiramate improved several behavioral dimensions of bulimia nervosa: binge and purge behaviors were reduced, and self-esteem, eating attitudes, anxiety, and body image improved.

Short-term psychotherapies have been thought to reduce binge frequency equal to or exceeding the effects of medication treatment. Fairburn and Harrison (2003) review the use of cognitive-behavioral therapy in treating bulimia nervosa. It seems reasonable to expect that combination therapy would provide additive effects. However, recently Walsh and coworkers (2004) reported that fluoxetine (Prozac) exerted beneficial effects in female patients with bulimia, but self-help therapy (based on CBT) was ineffective. Therefore, initial treatment of bulimia perhaps should utilize fluoxetine with adjunctive psychological therapy. Fluoxetine is certainly indicated for those in whom depression or an anxiety disorder is diagnosed as a comorbid disorder. Major depression is the most common comorbid disorder; others include anxiety disorders, substance abuse, and a past history of anorexia nervosa.

Medication failure can result from poor compliance, from vomiting the medication, or from other causes. Blood level analysis may be necessary before concluding that the drug attempt was a failure. Numerous other agents have been tried, but none has been effective when subjected to carefully controlled trials. The course of bulimia may require long-term antidepressant therapy with careful monitoring of side effects and compliance.

In anorexia nervosa, pharmacologic treatment has a very limited role; psychiatric therapy is more important. Psychotherapy, often with CBT components, group therapy, family therapy, nutrition counsel-ing, and so on are all necessary. Drug therapy is primarily aimed at treating comorbid depression following weight gain. However, double-blind studies of antidepressants (versus placebo) show little improvement in weight (weight gain), mood, or body perception. Certainly, however, a trial of antidepressant therapy is warranted in patients who do not respond to psychotherapeutic interventions.

REFERENCES

Adshead, G. (2000). "Psychological Therapies for Post-Traumatic Stress Disorder." *British Journal of Psychiatry* 177: 144–148.

American Academy of Child and Adolescent Psychiatry (1997). "Practice Parameters for Assessment and Treatment of Children and Adolescents with Schizophrenia." *Journal of the American Academy of Child and Adolescent Psychiatry* 36, Supplement (October): 177S–193S.

American Academy of Child and Adolescent Psychiatry (1998a). "Practice Parameters for the Assessment and Treatment of Children and Adolescents with Depressive Disorders." *Journal of the American Academy of Child and Adolescent Psychiatry* 37, Supplement (October): 63S–83S.

American Academy of Child and Adolescent Psychiatry (1998b). "Practice Parameters for the Assessment and Treatment of Children and Adolescents with Obsessive-Compulsive Disorder." *Journal of the American Academy of Child and Adolescent Psychiatry* 37, Supplement (October): 27S–45S.

American Psychiatric Association (2000a). *Diagnostic and Statistical Manual of Mental Disorders,* 4th ed., text revision (DSM-IV-TR). Washington, DC: American Psychiatric Association.

American Psychiatric Association (2000b). "Practice Guideline for the Treatment of Patients with Eating Disorders (Revision)." *American Journal of Psychiatry* 157, Supplement (January).

American Psychiatric Association (2000c). "Practice Guideline for the Treatment of Patients with Major Depressive Disorder (Revision)." *American Journal of Psychiatry* 157 (4): 1–45.

Asnis, G. M., et al. (2004). "SSRIs Versus Non-SSRIs in Post-Traumatic Stress Disorder: An Update with Receomendations. *Drugs* 64: 383–404.

Barloon, T. J., and R. Noyes (1997). "Charles Darwin and Panic Disorder." *Journal of the American Medical Association* 277: 138–141.

Barlow, D. H., et al. (2000). "Cognitive-Behavioral Therapy, Imipramine, or Their Combination for Panic Disorder: A Randomized Controlled Trial." *Journal of the American Medical Association* 283: 2529–2536.

Blomhoff, S., et al. (2001). "Randomized, Controlled, General Practice Trial of Sertraline, Exposure Therapy, and Combination Treatment in Generalized Social Phobia." *British Journal of Psychiatry* 179: 23–30.

Borkovec, T. D., et al. (2003). "Cognitive-Behavioral Therapy for Generalized Anxiety Disorder with Integrations from Interpersonal and Experimental Therapies." *CNS Spectrum* 8: 382–389.

Brawman-Mintzer, O., and R. B. Lydiard (1996). "Generalized Anxiety Disorder: Issues in Epidemiology." *Journal of Clinical Psychiatry* 57, Supplement 7: 3–8.

Bruce, S. E., et al. (2003). "Are Benzodiazepines Still the Medication of Choice for Patients with Panic Disorder with or Without Agoraphobia?" *American Journal of Psychiatry* 160: 1432–1438.

Cabana, M. D., et al. (1999). "Why Don't Physicians Follow Clinical Practice Guidelines? A Framework for Improvement." *Journal of the American Medical Association* 282: 1458–1465.

Chilvers, C., et al. (2001). "Antidepressant Drugs and Generic Counseling for Treatment of Major Depression in Primary Care: Randomized Trial with Patient Preference Arms." *British Medical Journal* 322: 1–5.

Davidson, J., and T. Bjorgvisson (2003). "Current and Potential Pharmacological Treatments for Obsessive Compulsive Disorder." *Expert Opinion Investigational Drugs* 12: 993–1001.

Davis, L. L., et al. (2001). "Pharmacotherapy for Post-Traumatic Disorder: A Comprehensive Review." *Expert Opinion in Pharmacotherapy* 2: 1583–1595.

DeRubeis, R. J., et al. (1999). "Medications Versus Cognitive Behavior Therapy for Severely Depressed Outpatients: Meta-Analysis of Four Randomized Comparisons." *American Journal of Psychiatry* 156: 1007–1013.

Druss, B. G., et al. (2001). "Integrated Medical Care for Patients with Serious Psychiatric Illness: A Randomized Trial." *Archives of General Psychiatry* 58: 861–868.

Dugas, M. J., et al. (2003). "Group Cognitive-Behavioral Therapy for Generalized Anxiety Disorder: Treatment Outcome and Long-Term Follow-Up." *Journal of Consulting Clinical Psychology* 71: 821–825.

Durham, R. C., et al. (2003). "Does Cognitive-Behavioural Therapy Influence the Long-Term Outcome of Generalized Anxiety Disorder? An 8–14 Year Follow-Up of Two Clinical Trials." *Psychological Medicine* 33: 499–509.

Emmanuel, N. P., et al. (2000). "Bupropion-SR in Treatment of Social Phobia." *Depression and Anxiety* 12: 111–113.

Fairburn, C. G., and P. J. Harrison (2003). "Eating Disorders." *Lancet* 361: 407–416.

Fedoroff, I. C., and S. Taylor (2001). "Psychological and Pharmacological Treatments of Social Phobia: A Meta-Analysis." *Journal of Clinical Psychopharmacology* 21: 311–324.

Feltner, D. E., et al. (2003). "A Randomized, Double-Blind, Placebo-Controlled, Fixed-Dose, Multicenter Study of Pregabalin in Patients with Generalized Anxiety Disorder." *Journal of Clinical Psychopharmacology* 23: 240–249.

Frank, J. B., et al. (1998). "Women's Mental Health in Primary Care." *Medical Clinics of North America* 82: 359–383.

Furmark, T., et al. (2002). "Common Changes in Cerebral Blood Flow in Patients with Social Phobia Treated with Citalopram or Cognitive-Behavioral Therapy." *Archives of General Psychiatry* 59: 425–433.

Glass, R. M. (2000). "Panic Disorder: It's Real and It's Treatable." *Journal of the American Medical Association* 283: 2573–2574.

Gorman, J. M., and J. D. Coplan (1996). "Comorbidity of Depression and Panic Disorder." *Journal of Clinical Psychiatry* 57, Supplement 10: 34–43.

Harvey, A. G., and R. M. Rapee (1995). "Cognitive-Behavioral Therapy for Generalized Anxiety Disorder." *Psychiatric Clinics of North America* 18: 859–870.

Hedges, D. W., et al. (2003). "Treatment of Bulimia Nervosa with Topiramate in a Randomized, Double-Blind, Placebo-Controlled Trial, Part 2: Improvement in Psychiatric Measures." *Journal of Clinical Psychiatry* 64: 1449–1454.

Heimberg, R. G. (2001). "Current Status of Psychotherapeutic Interventions for Social Phobia." *Journal of Clinical Psychiatry* 62, Supplement 1: 36–42.

Himle, J. A., et al. (2003). "Group Behavioral Therapy for Adolescents with Tic-Related and Non-Tic-Related Obsessive-Compulsive Disorder." *Depression and Anxiety* 17: 73–77.

Hollander, E., et al. (2003). "A Double-Blind, Placebo-Controlled Study of the Efficacy and Safety of Controlled-Release Fluvoxamine in Patients with Obsessive-Compulsive Disorder." *Journal of Clinical Psychiatry* 64: 640–647.

Hoopes, S. P., et al. (2003). "Treatment of Bulimia Nervosa with Topiramate in a Randomized, Double-Blind, Placebo-Controlled Trial, Part 1: Improvement in Binge and Purge Measures." *Journal of Clinical Psychiatry* 64: 1335–1341.

Jefferson, J. W. (2001). "Benzodiazepines and Anticonvulsants for Social Phobia (Social Anxiety Disorder)." *Journal of Clinical Psychiatry* 62, Supplement 1: 50–53.

Jones, G. N., et al. (2001). "Utilization of Medical Services and Quality of Life Among Low-Income Patients with Generalized Anxiety Disorder Attending Primary Care Clinics." *International Journal of Psychiatry in Medicine* 31: 183–198.

Kampman, M., et al. (2002). "Addition of Cognitive-Behaviour Therapy for Obsessive-Compulsive Disorder in Patients Non-Responsive to Fluoxetine." *Acta Psychiatrica Scandinavica* 106: 314–319.

Katon, W., et al. (1997). "Collaborative Management to Achieve Treatment Depression Guidelines." *Journal of Clinical Psychiatry* 58, Supplement 1: 20–23.

Katz, I. R., et al. (2002). "Venlafaxine ER as a Treatment for Generalized Anxiety Disorder in Older Adults: Pooled Analysis of Five Randomized Placebo-Controlled Clinical Trials." *Journal of the American Geriatric Society* 50: 18–25.

Keller, M. B., et al. (2000). "A Comparison of Nefazodone, the Cognitive Behavioral Analysis System of Psychotherapy, and Their Combination for the

Treatment of Chronic Depression." *New England Journal of Medicine* 342: 1462–1470.

Kobak, K. A., et al. (2002). "Fluoxetine in Social Phobia: A Double-Blind, Placebo-Controlled Pilot Study." *Journal of Clinical Psychopharmacology* 22: 257–262.

Kotler, L. A., et al. (2003). "An Open Trial of Fluoxetine for Adolescents with Bulimia Nervosa." *Journal of Child and Adolescent Psychopharmacology* 13: 329–335.

Lauria-Horner, B. A. and R. B. Pohl (2003). "Pregabalin: A New Anxiolytic." *Expert Opions on Investigational Drugs* 12: 663–672.

Lenze, E. J., et al. (2000). "Comorbid Anxiety Disorders in Depressed Elderly Patients." *American Journal of Psychiatry* 175: 722–728.

Lydiard, R. B. (2003). "The Role of GABA in Anxiety Disorders." *Journal of Clinical Psychiatry* 64, Supplement 3: 21–27.

Marder, S. R., et al. (1993). "Schizophrenia." *Psychiatric Clinics of North America* 16: 567–588.

Marshall, R. D., and M. Cloitre (2000). "Maximizing Treatment Outcome in Post-Traumatic Stress Disorder Combining Psychotherapy with Pharmacotherapy." *Current Psychiatry Reports* 2: 335–340.

Melfi, C. A., et al. (1998). "The Effects of Adherence to Antidepressant Treatment Guidelines on Relapse and Recurrence of Depression." *Archives of General Psychiatry* 55: 1128–1132.

Miller, I. W., and G. I. Keitner (1996). "Combined Medication and Psychotherapy in the Treatment of Chronic Mood Disorders." *Psychiatric Clinics of North America* 19: 151–170.

Mitchell, J. E., et al. (2003). "Drug Therapy for Patients with Eating Disorders." *Current Drug Target CNS Neurological Disorders* 2: 17–29.

Montgomery, S. A., et al. (2002). "Characterization of the Longitudinal Course of Improvement in Generalized Anxiety Disorder During Long-Term Treatment with Venlafaxine XR." *Journal of Psychiatric Research* 36: 209–217.

Mundo, E., et al. (2001). "Fluvoxamine in Obsessive-Compulsive Disorder: Similar Efficacy and Superior Tolerability in Comparison with Clomipramine." *Human Psychopharmacology* 16: 461–468.

Norman, R., and L. A. Townsend (1999). "Cognitive-Behavioral Therapy for Psychosis: A Status Report." *Canadian Journal of Psychiatry* 44: 245–252.

Otto, M. W., et al. (2000). "A Comparison of the Efficacy of Clonazepam and Cognitive-Behavioral Group Therapy for the Treatment of Social Phobia." *Journal of Anxiety Disorders* 14: 345–358.

Pande, A. C., et al. (2003). "Pregabalin in Generalized Anxiety Disorder: A Placebo-Controlled Trial." *American Journal of Psychiatry* 160: 533–540.

Patel, A., et al. (2002). "The Economic Consequences of Social Phobia." *Journal of Affective Disorders* 68: 221–233.

Paykel, E. S., et al. (1999). "Prevention of Relapse in Residual Depression by Cognitive Therapy." *Archives of General Psychiatry* 56: 829–835.

Pollack, M. H. (1997). "Psychopharmacology Update." *Journal of Clinical Psychiatry* 58: 38–40.

Reinecke, M. A., et al. (1998). "Cognitive-Behavioral Therapy of Depression and Depressive Symptoms During Adolescence: A Review and Meta-Analysis." *Journal of the American Academy of Child and Adolescent Psychiatry* 37: 26–34.

Rickels, K., and M. Rynn (2002). "Pharmacotherapy of Generalized Anxiety Disorder." *Journal of Clinical Psychiatry* 63, Supplement 14: 9–16.

Rickels, K., et al. (2003). "Paroxetine Treatment of Generalized Anxiety Disorder: A Double-Blind, Placebo-Controlled Study." *American Journal of Psychiatry* 160: 749–756.

Side Effects and Complications

Side effects of kava are generally mild and include drowsiness, nausea, muscle weakness, blurred vision, and (with chronic use) yellow skin discoloration. Since kava is a sedative/intoxicant, it should not be combined with alcohol, benzodiazepines, barbiturates, THC, or other CNS depressants. Kava should not be taken before driving or operating machinery.

Campo and coworkers (2002) reported a case of fulminant liver failure (requiring liver transplantation) in a 14-year-old girl. This and other cases of liver failure both in the United States and in Europe have prompted an ongoing FDA investigation of this substance.

Since kava is an intoxicant, it is interesting that barbiturates and benzodiazepines are restricted to prescription use, alcohol has age restrictions, marijuana is illegal, but kava is available without restriction. Its chief deterrent to more widespread use as an alcohollike anxiolytic/intoxicant is its expense.

Ephedrine (Ma-Huang)

Ephedrine is the naturally occurring psychoactive drug found in *Ephedra sinica*, also called ma-huang. The medicinal parts are the young canes collected in autumn and the dried rhizome with roots. Ephedrine is a potent psychostimulant that acts by releasing the body's own stores of the catecholamine neurotransmitters, epinephrine (adrenaline), norepinephrine, and dopamine.

Pharmacologically, ephedrine closely resembles the amphetamines, although the duration of action of ephedrine is considerably shorter. Because of this, ephedrine-containing products (Metabolife 356 and many others) should not be considered as metabolic supplements, dietary supplements, or any other designation implying that it is not a drug. Ephedrine is a potent psychostimulant that should be under regulation of the FDA.

Deaths from ephedrine now number in the dozens. The adrenaline and other catecholamines released by ephedrine increase blood pressure, heart rate, the force of cardiac contraction, and cardiac output of blood. Cardiac arrhythmias can be serious and potentially fatal. As with any adrenaline-releasing drug, it relieves bronchoconstriction and therefore provides relief from mild asthma, although tolerance rapidly develops. Like amphetamines, ephedrine temporarily reduces appetite, is a cardiovascular stimulant, and is a psychostimulant. Its disadvantages, however, far outweigh any therapeutic utility. In athletics, ephedrine is a "doping" substance. Numerous drug interactions occur and many are serious and potentially fatal. Several herbal preparations contain both ephedrine and caffeine: this is a combination that should be avoided because caffeine increases the cardiovascular toxicity of ephedrine. In April 2004, the FDA, in response to 155 deaths and dozens of heart attacks and strokes, initiated a ban on the sale of ephedrine-containing products as too dangerous for use. It is the U.S. government's first ban of a dietary supplement. Consumer's Union (2004a, 2004b) further discusses the problems with ephedrine and other dietary supplements.

Other Herbals That Act on the CNS

A variety of other herbals have been used to treat signs and symptoms of CNS dysfunction. A few are described here. Complete descriptions may be found in the *PDR for Herbal Medicines* (2000) and in the review by Wong and coworkers (1998).

Valerian (*Valeriana officalis*) has a long history of use as a mild sedative and as an anxiolytic as well as an antidepressant. The mechanism behind this action is obscure; some data indicate that it may affect GABA receptors, thus acting as a type of mild benzodiazepine. GABA itself is a component of valerian, leading some to state that valerian is a source of naturally occurring GABA, which it is. The problem is that GABA only very poorly crosses the blood-brain barrier, and it is unlikely that this source of GABA affects the CNS. Other postulated actions invoke it as a 5-HT$_{1A}$ agonist and as a monoamine oxidase inhibitor. They are reviewed by Wong and coworkers (1998) and by Yager and coworkers (1999). Reported side effects of valerian include liver toxicity, headache, excitability, and uneasiness. There are potential drug interactions between valerian and SSRI-type antidepressants, perhaps precipitating a serotonin syndrome (Chapter 9). Nevertheless, it is generally concluded that valerian can produce anxiolysis and CNS depression similar to that produced by benzodiazepines. There is no evidence to indicate that valerian is superior to existing sedative-hypnotic agents for the treatment of insomnia. The safety of valerian during pregnancy has not been delineated, so valerian probably should not be used by pregnant women. It would be expected that valerian would potentiate the effects of other CNS depressants, such as ethyl alcohol, and caution is warranted. Valerian should not be taken before driving or in other situations when alertness is required. The usual precautions that apply to other sedatives apply as well to valerian. As does St. John's wort, valerian contains quercitin; this substance inhibits the drug-metabolizing enzyme CYP1A2 and can possibly result in clinically significant drug interactions.

German chamomile (*Matricaria recutita*) is used to treat mild insomnia and anxiety. The herb contains flavinoids that are postulated to have affinity for the benzodiazepine receptor and perhaps for a histamine

receptor, either perhaps inducing a sedative effect. No controlled clinical trials have investigated these properties.

Evening primrose (Oenothera biennis) has been promoted for the treatment of schizophrenia and ADHD, but little scientific evidence or cultural tradition backs up these claims. Primrose contains a variety of fatty acids, and these substances are postulated to be deficient in both schizophrenia and ADHD. If omega-3 fatty acids have therapeutic usefulness in the treatment of bipolar disorder (Chapter 10), evening primrose may be a productive area for future research. Primrose may exacerbate epilepsy and has been reported to cause drug interactions with a variety of other compounds.

Hops (Humulus lupulus) are used in the brewing industry as a component in beer. Hops also have a long history of use as a sedative-hypnotic agent. No clinical studies support the use of hops as a single agent to treat either insomnia or anxiety. Used as a sedative, drug interactions occur, especially potentiation of the effects of other sedatives such as alcohol and benzodiazepines. Use of hops should be avoided in depression, in pregnancy, and during lactation.

Lemon balm (Melissa officinalis), passion flower (Passiflora incarnata), and *skullcap (Scutellaria laterifolia)* are all thought to possess CNS sedative properties and are promoted for use as sedatives and anxiolytics. Data on efficacy are lacking, as is information on active ingredients and mechanisms of action. As sedatives, the usual precautions apply, including those concerning drug interactions and both cognitive and motor impairments.

Conclusions

Wong and coworkers (1998) made the following statements that appear to hold true today:

- With the exception of St. John's wort for depression and ginkgo for dementia, there is insufficient evidence to recommend the use of herbal medicines in the treatment of psychiatric illness.

- None of these herbal remedies is clearly superior to current conventional treatments.

- Because these products are widely available and often used by the general public, more clinical research is needed to establish safety and efficacy.

- The advances of modern medicine . . . are greater than at any other time in history. . . . However, the experience and healing traditions of other cultures, whether in less developed countries or in history, should not be ignored.

- Contemporary medical research may finally allow us to separate the traditional remedies that can effectively treat disease from those that are superstition and myth.

- In addition, research . . . may uncover novel treatments for psychiatric illness or yield fresh insights into basic disease mechanisms. (p. 1033)

Over the next few years we will undoubtedly see many studies relating to the safety, efficacy, and drug interactions associated with herbals. Until then, caution is warranted: patients should tell prescribing physicians of their use of herbal medications, and most herbals should probably be avoided in pregnancy until they can be proven safe.

Although significant numbers of children and adolescents are receiving one or more herbal medications, studies of these compounds in this age population are unavailable. In some cases, youths may purchase the drugs themselves, as the drugs are easily available, relatively inexpensive, and widely advertised or endorsed by their peers. In other cases, the young people may be dosed by their parents in attempts to medicate such disorders as ADHD, depression, anxiety, or insomnia. Reasonable medical practitioners recognize that few data exist to support the use of herbals in the treatment of psychiatric disorders in children. Until such evidence becomes available, these agents probably should not be administered to children, especially for long periods of time or in the presence of other medications.

STUDY QUESTIONS

1. Describe the recent legislation changing the herbal industry. How has it helped society? How has it hurt?

2. List some of the herbals discussed in other chapters in this book. Which of them should be more freely available? Defend your answer.

3. What is hypericin? Describe its pharmacokinetics. What is the evidence for its efficacy?

4. What is ginkgo? What are its claimed actions? What evidence is there for efficacy to improve memory? For other uses?

5. What is kava? Does it have therapeutic potential? Does it have abuse potential? What drug does it appear to most resemble? Should there be legal restrictions on its use? Defend your answer.

6. What is ma-huang? What is its active ingredient? Does it have a potential for abuse? Might it induce toxicity? Should its use be regulated? Defend your answer.

7. What in valerian might result in drug interactions?

8. Are there any unaddressed concerns about the use of herbals in pregnancy or in women who might become pregnant? What about in breast-feeding females?

REFERENCES

American Psychological Association (2000). *Diagnostic Criteria from DSM-IV-TR.* Washington, DC: APA.

Butterweck, V. (2003). "Mechanism of Action of St John's Wort in Depression: What Is Known?" *CNS Drugs* 17: 539–562.

Campo, J. V., et al. (2002). "Kava-Induced Fulminant Hepatic Failure." *Journal of the American Academy of Child and Adolescent Psychiatry* 41: 631.

Consumer's Union (2004a). "Dangerous Supplements: Still at Large." *Consumer Reports,* May: 12–17.

Consumer's Union (2004b). "Ephedra: Heart Dangers in Disguise." *Consumer Reports,* January: 22–23.

Dennehy, C. E., and C. Tsourounis (2001). "Botanicals ('Herbal Medications') and Nutritional Supplements." In B. G. Katzung (ed.), *Basic and Clinical Pharmacology,* 8th ed. (pp. 1088–1103). New York: Lange Medical Books.

DeSmet, P., and W. A. Nolen (1996). "St. John's Wort as an Antidepressant." *British Medical Journal* 313: 241–242.

Draves, A. H., and S. E. Walker (2003). "Analysis of the Hypericin and Pseudohypericin Content of Commercially Available St. John's Wort Preparations." *Canadian Journal of Clinical Pharmacology* 10: 114–118.

Durr, D., et al. (2000). "St John's Wort Induces Intestinal P-Glycoprotein/MDR1 and Intestinal and Hepatic CYP3A4." *Clinical Pharmacology and Therapeutics* 68: 598–604.

Findling, R. L., et al. (2003). "An Open-Label Pilot Study of St. John's Wort in Juvenile Depression." *Journal of the American Academy of Child and Adolescent Psychiatry* 42: 908–914.

Gambarana, C., et al. (1999). "Efficacy of an *Hypericum perforatum* (St. John's Wort) Extract in Preventing and Reverting a Condition of Escape Deficit in Rats." *Neuropsychopharmacology* 21: 247–257.

Goldman, R. D., et al. (2003). "Taking St John's Wort During Pregnancy." *Canadian Family Physician* 49: 29–30.

Hall, S. D., et al. (2003). "The Interaction Between St. John's Wort and an Oral Contraceptive." *Clinical Pharmacology and Therapeutics* 74: 525–535.

Hypericum Depression Trial Study Group (2002). "Effect of *Hypericum perforatum* (St. John's Wort) in Major Depressive Disorder: A Randomized Controlled Trial." *Journal of the American Medical Association* 287: 1807–1814.

Itil, T. M., et al. (1996). "Central Nervous System Effects of *Ginkgo biloba,* a Plant Extract." *American Journal of Therapeutics* 3: 63–73.

Kim, H. L., et al. (1999). "St. John's Wort for Depression." *Journal of Nervous and Mental Disease* 187: 532–539.

Kleijnen, J., and P. Knipschild (1992). "*Ginkgo biloba.*" *Lancet* 340: 1136–1139.

Leak, J. A. (1999). "Herbal Medicine: Is It an Alternative or an Unknown? A Brief Review of Popular Herbals Used by Patients in a Pain and Symptom Management Practice Setting." *Current Review of Pain* 3: 226–236.

LeBars, P. L., et al. (1997). "A Placebo-Controlled, Double-Blind, Randomized Trial of an Extract of Ginkgo Biloba for Dementia." *Journal of the American Medical Association* 278: 1327–1332.

Lee, A., et al. (2003). "The Safety of St. John's Wort (*Hypericum perforatum*) During Breastfeeding." *Journal of Clinical Psychiatry* 64: 966–968.

Linde, K., and M. Berner (2000). "Commentary: Has *Hypericum* Found Its Place in Antidepressant Treatment?" *British Medical Journal* 319: 1534–1539.

Linde, K., et al. (1996). "St. John's Wort for Depression—An Overview and Meta-Analysis of Randomized Clinical Trials." *British Medical Journal* 313: 253–258.

Markowitz, J. S., et al. (2003). "Effect of St. John's Wort on Drug Metabolism by Induction of Cytochrome P450 3A4 Enzyme." *Journal of the American Medical Association* 290: 1500–1504.

Mix, J. A., and W. D. Crews (2002). "A Double-Blind, Placebo-Controlled, Randomized Trial of *Ginkgo biloba* Extract Egb 761 in a Sample of Cognitively Intact Older Adults: Neuropsychological Findings." *Human Psychopharmacology* 17: 267–277.

Obach, R. S. (2000). "Inhibition of Human Cytochrome P450 Enzymes by Constituents of St. John's Wort, an Herbal Preparation Used in the Treatment of Depression." *Journal of Pharmacology and Experimental Therapeutics* 294: 88–95.

O'Hara, M. A., et al. (1998). "A Review of Twelve Commonly Used Medicinal Herbs." *Archives of Family Medicine* 7: 523–536.

Oken, B. S., et al. (1998). "The Efficacy of *Ginkgo biloba* on Cognitive Function in Alzheimer's Disease." *Archives of Neurology* 55: 1409–1415.

PDR for Herbal Medicines, 2nd ed. (2000). Montvale, NJ: Medical Economics Company.

Pfunder, A., et al. (2003). "Interaction of St. John's Wort with Low-Dose Oral Contraceptive Therapy: A Randomized Controlled Trial." *British Journal of Clinical Pharmacology* 56: 683–690.

Philipp, M., et al. (2000). "*Hypericum* Extract Versus Imipramine or Placebo in Patients with Moderate Depression: Randomized Multicentre Study of Treatment for Eight Weeks." *British Medical Journal* 319: 1534–1539.

Pies, R. (2000). "Adverse Neuropsychiatric Reactions to Herbal and Over-the-Counter 'Antidepressants'." *Journal of Clinical Psychiatry* 61: 815–820.

Pittler, M. H., and E. Ernst (2000). "Efficacy of Kava Extract for Treating Anxiety: Systematic Review and Meta-Analysis." *Journal of Clinical Psychopharmacology* 20: 84–89.

Schwarz, U. I., et al. (2003). "Unwanted Pregnancy and Self-Medication with St John's Wort Despite Hormonal Contraception." *British Journal of Clinical Pharmacology* 55: 112–113.

Sheldon, R. C., et al. (2001). "Effectiveness of St. John's Wort in Major Depression: A Randomized Controlled Trial." *Journal of the American Medical Association* 285: 1978–1986.

Solomon, P. R., et al. (2002). "Ginkgo for Memory Enhancement: A Randomized Controlled Trial." *Journal of the American Medical Association* 288: 835–840.

Staffeldt, B., et al. (1994). "Pharmacokinetics of Hypericin and Pseudohypericin After Oral Intake of the *Hypericum perforatum* Extract LI 160 in Healthy Volunteers." *Journal of Geriatric Psychiatry and Neurology* 7, Supplement 1: S47–S53.

Teufel-Mayer, R., and J. Gleitz (1997). "Effects of Long-Term Administration of *Hypericum* Extracts on the Affinity and Density of the Central Serotoninergic 5-HT$_{1A}$ and 5-HT$_{2A}$ Receptors." *Pharmacopsychiatry* 30: 113–116.

Uebelhack, R., et al. (1998). "Inhibition of Platelet MAO-B by Kava Pyrone-Enriched Extract from *Piper methysticum forester* (Kava-Kava)." *Pharmacopsychiatry* 31: 187–192.

van Dongen, M., et al. (2000). "The Efficacy of Ginkgo for Elderly People with Dementia and Age-Associated Memory Impairment: New Results of a Randomized Clinical Trial." *Journal of the American Geriatric Society* 48: 1183–1194.

Volz, H.-P., et al. (2002). "St. John's Wort Extract (LI 160) in Somatoform Disorders: Results of a Placebo-Controlled Trial." *Psychopharmacology* 164: 294–300.

Wong, A. H. C., et al. (1998). "Herbal Remedies in Psychiatric Practice." *Archives of General Psychiatry* 55: 1033–1044.

Yager, J., et al. (1999). "Use of Alternative Remedies by Psychiatric Patients: Illustrative Vignettes and a Discussion of the Issues." *American Journal of Psychiatry* 156: 1432–1438.

Integration of Drugs and Psychological Therapies in Treating Mental and Behavior Disorders

Over the past few years it has become quite apparent that the treatment of psychological illnesses requires more than medication therapy. Only rarely should psychoactive medications be prescribed as the sole treatment, although they too often are. It has now been shown that combining pharmacological therapy with psychological therapy provides more effective treatment than the use of medication alone (Barlow et al., 2000; Chilvers et al., 2001; Druss et al., 2001; Kampman et al., 2002; Keller et al., 2000; Ward et al., 2000; Zajecka et al., 2002). This chapter explores the complex interaction between pharmacotherapies and psychological therapies in the treatment of psychological disorders that are commonly encountered in clinical practice.

Undertreatment of Mental and Psychological Disorders

In December 1999 the Surgeon General of the United States released a report that criticized the state of mental health treatment (U.S. Department of Health and Human Services, 1999). The report began with definitions of mental health and mental illness:

> *Mental health* is a state of successful performance of mental function, resulting in productive activities, fulfilling relationships with other people, and the ability to adapt to change and to cope with adversity.

> *Mental illness* is the term that refers collectively to all diagnosable mental disorders. Mental disorders are health conditions that are characterized by alterations in thinking, mood, or behavior (or some combination thereof) associated with distress and/or impaired functioning.

Alzheimer's disease exemplifies a mental disorder largely marked by alterations in thinking (especially forgetting). Depression exemplifies a mental disorder largely marked by alterations in mood. Attention deficit hyperactivity disorder exemplifies a mental disorder largely marked by alterations in behavior (overactivity) and/or thinking (inability to concentrate). Alterations in thinking, mood, or behavior contribute to a host of problems—patient distress, impaired functioning, heightened risk of death, pain, disability, substance abuse/dependence, and personal loss of freedom. A few facts the Surgeon General's report put forth follow.

- The mental health field is plagued by disparities in the availability of and access to its services.
- A key disparity often hinges on a person's financial status: formidable financial barriers block off needed mental health care from too many people, from those who have health insurance with inadequate mental health benefits to the 44 million Americans who have no insurance at all.
- About one in five Americans experiences a mental disorder over the course of a year.
- Mental illness represents more than 15 percent of the overall burden of disease from all causes and slightly more than the burden associated with all forms of cancer.
- Mental illness, including suicide, ranks second in the burden of disease, second only to cardiovascular disease.
- Depression ranks second only to ischemic coronary artery (heart) disease in the magnitude of disease burden. Schizophrenia, bipolar disorder, obsessive compulsive disorder, panic disorder, and posttraumatic stress disorder also contribute significantly to the burden represented by mental illness.
- Stigmatism is the most formidable obstacle to future progress in the arena of mental illness and health.

- Nearly two-thirds of all people with diagnosable mental conditions do not seek treatment, although mental disorders can be effectively treated in about 75 percent of cases.

- About 20 percent of American adults are afflicted with a mental or psychological disorder at one point or another in their lifetime.

A U. S. Presidential Commission on Mental Health report (U.S. Department of Health and Human Services, 2003) noted that care for the mentally ill must go beyond prescribing medication and managing symptoms in crisis management fashion. Call was made for counselors to help patients lead a fuller life, including, but moving beyond, administering drugs. The report was, in fact, a call for complete integration of mental health care. The commission issued a vision statement as well as six goals for treatment, along with recommendations for achieving these goals. The vision statement and goals follow:

Vision statement

We are committed to a future where recovery is the expected outcome and when mental illness can be prevented or cured. We envision a nation where everyone with mental illness will have access to early detection and the effective treatment and supports essential to live, work, learn, and participate fully in their community.

Goals of the report

1. *Mental health is essential to health.* Every individual, family, and community will understand that mental health is an essential part of overall health.

2. *Early mental health screening and treatment in multiple settings.* Every individual will have the opportunity for early and appropriate mental health screening, assessment, and referral to treatment.

3. *Consumer/family-centered care.* Consumers and families will have the necessary information and the opportunity to exercise choice over the care decisions that affect them. Continuous healing relationships will be a key feature of care.

4. *Best care science can offer.* Adults with serious mental illness and children with serious emotional disturbance will have ready access to the best treatments, services, and supports leading to recovery and cure. Accelerate research to enhance prevention of, recovery from, and ultimate discovery of cures for mental illnesses.

5. *Information infrastructure.* The mental health system will develop and expand its information infrastructure. That infrastructure has many purposes:

   a. Inform consumers, providers, and public policy

   b. Improve access, quality, accountability

6. *Eliminate disparities in mental health care.* Promote well-being for all people regardless of race, ethnicity, language, place of residence, or age and ensure equality of access, delivery of services, and improvement of outcomes for all communities.

These are obviously idealized goals, with little consideration for manpower, facilities, or costs of implementation. However, they do provide a set of ideals to guide future decisions. Note that symptom reduction via pharmacological means is a very small part of the plan: all mental health care should be delivered in an integrated fashion. This is an area in which many prescribing physicians and other prescibers are uncomfortable. (Prescribers include physicians, mental health nurse practitioners, and specially certified psychologists who recently have been granted limited prescription privileges in New Mexico and Kentucky, a practice that will expand to other states.) It also places a burden on nonprescribing mental health personnel to understand their clients' medications well enough to allow them to interact meaningfully with prescribers.

Depression

Up to a third of patients sitting in a physician's office have a diagnosable psychiatric disorder that largely goes undiagnosed and untreated, and 75 percent are anxiety or depressive disorders (Frank et al., 1998). Cognitive, emotional, and behavioral symptoms not part of a diagnosable disorder are also common; the modal psychiatric condition most often seen in general medical practice settings is the DSM-IV-TR category of *mixed anxiety-depression* (Table 17.1). Distressed high users of medical care certainly have even higher rates of psychopathology.

Undertreatment of Depression

Attention to the undertreatment of depression was emphasized as early as 1993 with publication of two clinical practice guidelines devoted to the treatment of depression. In 1998, the American Academy of Child and Adolescent Psychiatry (1998a) published a guideline titled "Practice Parameters for the Assessment and Treatment of Children and Adolescents with Depressive Disorders." In 2000, the American Psychiatric Association updated its practice guideline for major

TABLE 17.1 Mixed anxiety-depression

Persistent or recurrent dysphoric mood lasting at least 1 month

Dysphoric mood is accompanied by at least 1 month of ≥4 of the following symptoms:

  Difficulty concentrating or mind going blank

  Sleep disturbance (difficulty falling or staying asleep or restless unsatisfying sleep)

  Fatigue or low energy

  Irritability

  Worry

  Being easily moved to tears

  Hypervigilance

  Anticipating the worst

  Hopelessness (pervasive pessimism about the future)

  Low self-esteem or feelings of worthlessness

Symptoms caused clinically significant distress or impairment in social,

  occupational, or other important areas of functioning

---

depressive disorder in adults (American Psychiatric Association, 2000c). That the recommendations in these guidelines have not been implemented has been reported regularly (Cabana et al., 1999). Lack of compliance exists despite demonstrated reductions in depression when the guidelines are followed (Melfi et al., 1998; Wells et al., 2000). Furthermore, as discussed in Chapter 9 and emphasized by Sheline and coworkers (2003), depression is now viewed as an organic problem, involving loss of hippocampal volume and cellular neurogenesis. This pathology can be reversed by both pharmacological and psychological interventions (Russo-Neustadt et al., 1999). Therefore, depression is a manageable, neurological disorder, the pathology of which is controllable through therapy. While it may not be *curable*—it may recur without long-term interventions—its patholological cause is certainly manageable with resultant symptomatic improvements. In this case, depression resembles other long-term illnesses such as hypertension, diabetes, and hypothyroidism.

Depression affects an estimated 11 million Americans, or about 6 percent of the population, each year. The associated costs, including everything from treatment costs to loss of workplace productivity, are estimated at $44 billion per year. Particularly undertreated are depressed individuals in ethnic minority communities (Sclar et al., 1998), in direct contradiction to the recently released presidential goals listed earlier. This also holds true for the treatment of low-income persons with anxiety disorders (Jones et al., 2001).

Treatment of Depression

There is now general consensus that depression can be best treated by a combination of pharmacotherapy and psychological interventions (Figure 17.1). To understand the reason, it is necessary to tie together the etiology, pharmacotherapy, and neurobiological basis of the psychological or behavioral therapies of both anxiety and depression. This topic was covered in Chapter 9 and is briefly summarized here.

Antidepressant drugs result in an up regulation by the messenger RNA for the protein *brain-derived neurotrophic factor,* or BDNF) in hippocampal neurons. The result is a reversal of neuronal dysfunction and relief from depression. The slow onset of action of antidepressant drugs results from the need to increase BDNF by increasing the expression of this protein by increasing its messenger RNA (mRNA) levels. Antidepressant drugs are also extremely effective in reducing anxiety disorders and stress (Chapter 9), although physicians continue to prescribe benzodiazepines for these disorders. As hypothesized by Bruce and coworkers (2003), they may do so because few head-to-head comparisons of antidepressants and benzodiazepines in the treatment of anxiety disorders have been published.

Treating anxiety and/or depression (with either antidepressant medication or psychotherapeutic interventions) acutely increases synaptic concentrations of neurotransmitters and reduces stress and anxiety. The acute change leads to increased expression of BDNF mRNA, increasing

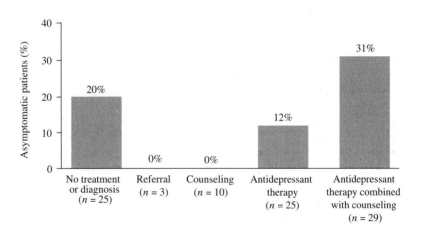

FIGURE 17.1 Percentages of patients who were treated with usual care and who were judged to be asymptomatic at month 8 in relation to the primary treatment pattern during the preceding months. [From H. C. Schulberg et al., "The Usual Care of Major Depression in Primary Care Practice," *Archives of Family Medicine* 6 (1997), pp. 334–339, with permission.]

BDNF within the neuron. Increased BDNF improves neuronal trophism, promotes repair of injured hippocampal neurons, and leads to improved neuronal function with relief of both anxiety and depression and with improvements in memory and cognitive functioning. These "repairs" set the stage for the introduction of psychological therapies and help explain the synergistic effects of combined pharmacotherapy and psychotherapy in relieving the distress of affective disorder.

Role of Drugs as Cotherapy

In addition to treating the acute symptoms associated with a mental disorder, medications serve a *prophylactic function,* altering brain chemistry to prevent the onset of a symptom complex (reducing the frequency of recurrence of symptomatology). Thus, drugs can be used to ameliorate debilitating symptoms of illness, to restore hippocampal neurons to more "normal" levels of function, and to prevent the development of additional symptoms, allowing the introduction of behavioral or psychological interventions.

The prescription of a psychotherapeutic medication is only the first step in treatment. In the treatment of affective disorders such as depression, dysthymia, or any of the anxiety disorder subtypes, medication is not necessarily superior to psychological therapies and the two are complementary. However, the medications frequently allow more rapid control of symptomatology and allow the earlier introduction of psychological interventions. Interventions can provide more than symptom relief; they may have effects that persist long after therapy ceases. In disorders such as bipolar disorder and schizophrenia, drug therapy is essential as primary therapy and psychological therapies are introduced following control of symptomatology.

Role of Psychotherapy as Cotherapy

Before the 1970s, only modest scientific evidence showed that psychotherapy was superior to placebo or that prolonged psychotherapy was superior to merely waiting for the patient to spontaneously recover. Today, it is widely recognized that psychological therapies are efficacious both as monotherapy for affective disorders and as cotherapy to pharmacological therapies. Research on psychological therapies is attempting to do several things:

- Tailor specific psychotherapeutic interventions to specific psychiatric conditions and specific patients
- Determine the appropriate duration, intensity, and complexity of effective therapies

- Assess the interaction between psychotherapeutic interventions with drug therapy

Some conclusions are becoming evident:

- In the treatment of panic disorder, agoraphobia, simple phobias, and, to a lesser extent, social phobias, behavioral and cognitive-behavioral therapies have traditionally been thought to have more consistent and longer-lasting effects than medications.
- Psychotherapy, specifically panic-focused cognitive-behavioral therapy, and medications (SSRIs, TCAs, benzodiazepines, and MAO inhibitors) are equally effective in the acute treatment for panic disorder (Work Group on Panic Disorder, 1998; Barlow et al., 2000).
- Combining cognitive-behavioral therapy and medication in the treatment of panic disorder has now been shown to be superior to either therapy alone, especially as the length of therapy continues (Barlow et al., 2000).
- Medications and behavioral techniques are equally effective in the treatment of obsessive compulsive disorder, posttraumatic stress disorder, and generalized anxiety disorder.
- In the treatment of major depressive disorder, antidepressant medications and cognitive-behavioral therapy are equally effective and display additional efficacy when used in combination (DeRubeis et al., 1999; Keller et al., 2000; Zajecka et al., 2002).
- At the very least, cognitive-behavioral therapy added to pharmacological management of depression reduces relapse rates for acute major depression and persistent severe residual symptoms (Paykel et al., 1999).
- In the treatment of eating disorders such as bulimia nervosa, cognitive-behavioral therapy is the psychological treatment of choice and medication with fluoxetine (an SSRI) adds modestly to the benefit of psychological treatment (Walsh et al., 1997).
- The positive effects of cognitive-behavioral therapy in treating depression in adults are also seen in adolescents, and treatment gains in adolescents are maintained over time (Reinecke et al., 1998).

Role of the Treatment Team

No individual should be the sole caregiver for a patient with mental or psychological illness. A team of caregivers, with members from several disciplines, should collaborate in treatment. One team member is usually a clinician with prescription privileges (a physician, a mental health nurse practitioner, or a prescribing psychologist). Other clinicians who do not prescribe medication may have responsibility for psychotherapeutic interventions. Other caregivers may include nurses, pharmacists, counselors, vocational rehabilitation counselors, physical or occupational therapists, dieticians, spiritual counselors, family members, and psychiatric, occupational, or recreational assistants. In 1996, Miller and Keitner presented a team approach, suggesting a "sequential" or "cascading" model when providing combined treatment. Various treatments (medication or psychotherapy) are administered in a sequential fashion based on the patient's response or lack of response to a previous treatment. If the patient responds to one treatment, no other may be needed; if there is no response, then a second treatment is added to the first. Continued nonresponse may lead to additional or substitute types of treatments.

Because the prescribing clinician has for so many years acted alone, it might reasonably be asked whether the treatment team concept is overly expensive or can actually deliver a higher quality of care with a better quality of life for the patient at a manageable cost to society. Several studies in the late 1990s addressed this issue, concluding that a treatment team relieves the prescriber of drugs of responsibility for handling psychological interventions, reduces hospitalizations, and provides longer, more intensive, more cost-effective case management.

In a psychiatrist/primary care model, the patient alternates visits with a psychiatrist and a primary care physician; both professionals assist in the education and pharmacologic treatment of the patient. In the psychiatrist/psychologist team model, the psychiatrist works with a psychologist to improve adherence to and effectiveness of treatment, and the psychologist also provides brief behavioral treatment in the primary care clinic. This collaborative model is associated with improved adherence to treatment, increased patient satisfaction with care, and improved outcome compared with usual care by primary care physicians alone (Katon et al., 1997).

How might a treatment team function? Nonprescribing members of the team should be familiar with the pharmacology, uses, limitations, and side effects of the drugs being used by their clients. They should also know about alternative medications that may provide equal or superior effectiveness with a more reasonable spectrum of side effects for the particular client. These clinicians must be able to professionally converse with the prescribing physician, monitor drug therapy, and institute psychological therapies appropriate to the condition under treatment. They should monitor for both positive and negative effects and be sensitive to the meaning medications have to their clients, for effective psychotherapy depends on the ability of patients to comply with treatment requirements (Sprenger and Josephson, 1998).

Regardless of their individual roles, all team members share certain basic functions. Most important is that of ongoing assessment, the purpose of which is to obtain an objective report of the patient's signs and symptoms and, as much as possible, to relate them to possible causes. Assessment may include a formal diagnosis, or it may be a description of the development of the client's behavior. Either type of assessment should address both the strengths and the weaknesses of the patient. Most beneficial is an assessment that includes the probable etiology of the problem.

The clinician may list the possible explanations for the observed behaviors in a comprehensive format called the *differential diagnosis,* from which the causes may be determined. Frequently, further assessment is necessary to rule out some of the possible causes. Less plausible causes usually can be readily eliminated. The differential diagnosis then guides further assessment and treatment. Possible causal factors in the differential diagnosis often have markedly different treatments. Consequently, an accurate assessment and diagnosis of the causes of the patient's behavior must precede any treatment planning or therapeutic intervention. Evaluation by mental health professionals is often formalized into a standard diagnostic format. Most often used is the diagnostic system of the fourth edition of the *Diagnostic and Statistical Manual of Mental Disorders,* or DSM-IV-TR (American Psychiatric Association, 2000a).

DSM-IV-TR Classification of Mental Disorders

Diagnosis is the practice of distinguishing one disease from another. In clinical psychology, diagnosis is based on the signs and symptoms of a mental disorder, regardless of the morbid changes producing them. The DSM-IV-TR classification provides a shorthand description of the patterns of behavior that can be expected with each disorder.

DSM-IV-TR is a categorical classification that divides mental disorders into types based on criteria sets with defining features. In DSM-IV-TR there is no assumption that each category of mental disorder is a complete discrete entity with absolute boundaries dividing it from other mental disorders or from no mental disorder. There is also no assumption that all individuals described as having the same mental disorder are alike in all important ways. This outlook allows more flexibility in the use of the system, encourages more specific attention to boundary cases, and emphasizes the need to capture additional clinical information that goes beyond diagnosis.

In the DSM-IV-TR classification system, each patient being diagnosed is not merely assigned a single diagnostic category (for example, bipolar disorder). Instead, the patient is characterized by clinically relevant factors that are grouped into five "axes":

- Axis I: Primary classification (diagnosis) of the major problem requiring attention (for example, alcohol dependence)
- Axis II: Mental retardation and personality disorders generally believed to begin in childhood or adolescence and persisting into adult life
- Axis III: Any physical disorder that seems relevant to a case and that may have implications for present treatment (for example, asthma that is exacerbated by psychological factors)
- Axis IV: Psychosocial and environmental problems that may affect the diagnosis, treatment, and prognosis of the mental disorders listed under Axes I and II (for example, illiteracy or unemployment)
- Axis V: Global assessment of psychological functioning, social relationships, and occupational activities (including ratings of both the current level of functioning and the highest level of functioning during the past year)

In emergencies, a preliminary classification is made even though much information is lacking. In such situations, any assessment is considered tentative and subject to revision as additional medical, psychological, and psychosocial assessments are made.

The first three axes constitute official diagnostic categories of the American Psychiatric Association. Axes IV and V are regarded as supplementary categories for use in clinical and research settings. It is common practice, however, to describe a case using all five axes. The major categories of Axis I classification are listed in Table 17.2. Here we consider four of the sixteen Axis I categories—mood (or affective) disorders, schizophrenia, anxiety disorders, and eating disorders. These four were chosen because of their prevalence and because they are the disorders most frequently treated with a combination of medication and psychotherapy.

Mood (Affective) Disorders

The term *mood* refers to a perceptual bias that alters how one views the world. Mood disorders may include major depressive, manic, or hypomanic episodes, dysthymia, or alternating recurrences of one or more such moods. DSM-IV groups mood disorders into *depressive disorders, bipolar disorders, substance-induced mood disorders,* and *mood disorders due to general medical conditions*. One of these, depression, was discussed earlier in this chapter.

TABLE 17.2 DSM-IV-TR Axis I categories

Category	Examples
Disorders usually first diagnosed in infancy, childhood, or adolescence	Attention deficit and disruptive behavior disorders, learning disorders, certain eating disorders
Delirium, dementia, and amnestic and other cognitive disorders	Transient or permanent brain dysfunction, attributable to such factors as aging, dementia due to head trauma, or Alzheimer's, and amnestic disorders (memory loss)
Substance-related disorders	Disorders related to alcohol, all chemical withdrawal syndromes, and some disorders related to or caused by substances such as substance-induced psychotic disorders
Schizophrenia and other psychotic disorders	Chronic disorganized behavior and thought of psychotic proportions (delusions, hallucinations), incoherence, and social isolation; disorders that are well-organized systems of delusions without the incoherence, bizarreness, and other social isolation seen in schizophrenia
Mood disorders	Depression and bipolar disorder
Anxiety disorders	Anxiety, tension, and worry without psychotic features (delusions, hallucinations); posttraumatic (reactive, stress-caused) disorders, whether brief or chronic
Somatoform disorders	Physical symptoms for which no medical causes can be found (symptoms apparently not under voluntary control and linked to psychological factors or conflicts)
Factitious disorders	Physical or behavioral symptoms that are voluntarily produced by the individual, apparently in order to play the role of patient and often involving chronic, blatant lying
Dissociative disorders	Sudden, temporary change in the normal functions of consciousness (for example, loss of memory, sleepwalking)
Sexual and gender identity disorders	Deviant sexual thoughts and behavior that are either personally anxiety provoking or socially maladaptive

TABLE 17.2 DSM-IV-TR Axis I categories *(continued)*

Category	Examples
Eating disorders	Disorders of eating such as anorexia nervosa
Sleep disorders	Insomnia or difficulty in going to sleep or staying asleep, excessive daytime sleeping, complaints of sleep disturbance without objective evidence, impairment of respiration during sleep, disturbance of sleeping schedule, sleepwalking, sleep terrors
Impulse-control disorders, not classified elsewhere	Maladaptations characterized by failure to resist impulses (for example, pathological gambling, chronic stealing of desired objects, habitual fire setting)
Adjustment disorders	Maladaptive reactions to identifiable life events or circumstances that are expected to lessen and cease when the stressor ceases; reaction may be dominated by depressed mood, anxiety, withdrawal, conduct disorder such as truancy, or a lessening in work or job performance
Mental disorders due to general medical condition, not classified elsewhere	Disorders that may be due to a medical condition, such as a psychotic disorder that emerges in response to renal failure
Other conditions that may be a focus of clinical attention	Includes such things as medication-induced movement disorders such as tardive dyskinesia or partner or parent/child relational problems

Abstracted from American Psychiatric Association (2000a), pp. 13–25.

All of us experience mood shifts, such as mild anxiety, depression, sadness, and grief, in response to difficult life events. These responses are natural and certainly do not constitute a mood disorder. The DSM-IV-TR classification pertains to distinct, severe processes that interfere with daily activities. These dysfunctional processes are, however, amenable to treatment. A normal course of bereavement due to environmental factors (for example, death of a loved one) is not classified as a mood disorder, even though it may temporarily incapacitate the individual and necessitate either pharmacological or psychological interventions.

In general, mood disorders are subclassified by type and duration of the mood episode. For example, two weeks of severely depressed mood (as indicated by a specific set of four additionally related symptoms) is required for a diagnosis of a major depressive episode. Two years of mildly depressed mood and the presence of two related symptoms are required for diagnosis of dysthymic disorder.

Assessment and Diagnosis. Careful assessment of psychological disorders is the initial step in effective treatment planning, whether the planned treatment is pharmacological, psychological, or a combination of both. Thorough assessment is helpful in distinguishing between functional and organic causes. In other words, not only is a DSM-IV-TR classification of symptom-based behavioral dysfunction developed, a differential diagnosis of all possible causative factors for the observed behaviors is made. This list is then narrowed to one or perhaps a few possibilities so that the likely cause can be identified and effectively treated. A thorough assessment also includes an investigation of social and psychological factors that may contribute to pathology. Other sociopsychological conditions may exacerbate existing physical or psychological problems. For example, cigarette smoking can be antidepressant (discussed in Chapter 8), and cessation of smoking may lead to the emergence or exacerbation of major depressive episodes.

Treatment. The biological, psychological, and social factors in mood disorders must be addressed in a comprehensive treatment plan. As stated earlier, pharmacotherapy and psychotherapy effectively treat depression, and combining the two further improves efficacy and reduces the probability of relapse. Even reactive (exogenous) depression, adjustment mood disorders, and dysthymia have biological components that require intervention with pharmacological agents along with psychotherapy.

A person's basic perceptual beliefs, cognitive and intellectual processing, and experiences affect the person's interaction with the environment and with other individuals. Eventually a person develops a sense of how self interacts with others. Individuals suffering from a mood disorder learn a pattern of behavior that may cause their problems to become worse and make the disorder resistant to treatment and intervention. Psychological therapies can change the pattern of behavior. There are many techniques, from simple education to supportive counseling to insight-oriented, dynamically based therapy. Cognitive therapy, behavioral therapy, brief psychodynamic psychotherapy, group therapies, and others are frequently used and are effective interventions.

Children and adolescents are being increasingly diagnosed with mood disorders, including major depressive disorder and bipolar disorder. Whether this trend reflects an increased recognition of the disorders or an actual increase in their incidence is unclear. The pharmacological treatment of mood disorders in children and adolescents is discussed in Chapter 12. Behavioral therapies and family interventions are perhaps preferred over pharmacologic interventions, at least for early intervention in less severe cases.

Schizophrenia

The formal DSM-IV-TR definition of schizophrenia is presented in Table 17.3. Positive symptoms of schizophrenia include hallucinations, delusions, disorganized speech, and bizarre behavior. Negative symptoms include impaired social interactions, impoverished and blunted affect, an absence of motivation, and significant social withdrawal. The disorder often begins in adolescence or young adulthood, frequently followed by a progressively deteriorating course; few patients make a complete recovery.

Antipsychotic Medication. The drugs used to reduce the symptomatology of schizophrenia are discussed in Chapter 11. Advances in this area occurred rapidly through the 1990s and are continuing to today. In 1993 it was stated:

> All of the symptoms associated with schizophrenia are affected to some degree by neuroleptics. Positive symptoms, including hallucinations, delusions, and disorganized thoughts, are more responsive to drug treatment than are negative symptoms, such as blunted affect, emotional withdrawal, and lack of social interest. . . . A substantial proportion of schizophrenic patients—about 10 to 20 percent—fail to demonstrate substantial improvement when they are treated with neuroleptics. This subgroup of treatment-refractory schizophrenic patients often requires long-term institutionalization in state hospitals and similar facilities. Clozapine and other atypical antipsychotic drugs may be particularly effective for these patients. (Marder et al., 1993 pp. 567–568.)

Clozapine and some new-generation antipsychotic drugs are effective in at least 30 percent of patients who are severely disabled by negative symptoms. In addition, these new drugs have become accepted as first-line agents because of their effectiveness and their lack of extrapyramidal side effects. By relieving negative symptomatology, they make patients "reachable" and more amenable to psychosocial interventions in efforts to improve their social functioning and their integration into society.

Psychotherapy and Rehabilitation. The new-generation antipsychotic drugs have made it possible for psychotherapy and other interventions to be effective, particularly in the outpatient setting. Having established the primary role of antipsychotics, there is evidence that psychosocial

TABLE 17.3 DSM-IV-TR categories of schizophrenia and related disorders

Schizophrenia is a disturbance that lasts for at least 6 months and includes at least 1 month of active-phase symptoms (i.e., two [or more] of the following: delusions, hallucinations, disorganized speech, grossly disorganized or catatonic behavior, negative symptoms). Definitions for Schizophrenia subtypes (Paranoid, Disorganized, Catatonic, Undifferentiated, and Residual) are also included in this section.

Schizophreniform Disorder is characterized by a symptomatic presentation that is equivalent to Schizophrenia except for its duration (i.e., the disturbance lasts from 1 to 6 months) and the absence of a requirement that there be a decline in functioning.

Schizoaffective Disorder is a disturbance in which a mood episode and the active-phase symptoms of Schizophrenia occur together and were preceded or are followed by at least 2 weeks of delusions or hallucinations without prominent mood symptoms.

Delusional Disorder is characterized by at least 1 month of nonbizarre delusions without other active-phase symptoms of Schizophrenia.

Brief Psychotic Disorder is a psychotic disturbance that lasts more than 1 day and remits by 1 month.

Shared Psychotic Disorder is a disturbance that develops in an individual who is influenced by someone else who has an established delusion with similar content.

In **Psychotic Disorder Due to a General Medical Condition,** the psychotic symptoms are judged to be a direct physiological consequence of a general medical condition.

In **Substance-Induced Psychotic Disorder,** the psychotic symptoms are judged to be a direct physiological consequence of a drug of abuse, a medication, or toxin exposure.

Psychotic Disorder Not Otherwise Specified is included for classifying psychotic presentations that do not meet criteria for any of the specific Psychotic Disorders defined in this section or psychotic symptomatology about which there is inadequate or contradictory information.

Abstracted from American Psychiatric Association (2000a), pp. 298–343.

therapies, when administered with these agents, improve long-term prognosis. Because chronically psychotic patients have difficulties with social adjustment, reason dictates that they and their families could benefit from such interventions. Regardless of theoretical orientation, it is clear that practitioners should provide psychosocial therapy as part of a comprehensive treatment strategy. In general, most cost-benefit studies find that the addition of psychological therapies in an outpatient setting encourages drug compliance. Therapeutic interventions improve social skills and assist in the rehabilitation of cognitive functions. Psychological therapy in conjunction with drug therapy also extends relapse time and reduces the intensity of relapse episodes. Typically, the most beneficial strategy is a sociopsychological therapy emphasizing self-esteem, social skills, and cognitive rehabilitation. This emphasis addresses the interaction between the client's symptoms and their social and psychological consequences. These strategies develop and rehabilitate cognitive functions, resulting in a more positive self-image and more effective social and cognitive functioning.

Norman and Townsend (1999) discussed the role of cognitive-behavioral interventions in reducing psychosis. Sensky and coworkers (2000) studied 90 patients with schizophrenia with medication-resistant symptoms, comparing cognitive-behavioral therapy (9 months of therapy) with a nonspecific befriending control intervention. Both therapies were effective in the short term, reducing both positive and negative symptoms. Cognitive-behavioral therapy produced longer-lasting results; continuing improvement was observed even 9 months after treatment was stopped. Cognitive-behavioral interventions were thought to be cost-effective, with an average of 24 hours of therapist time spent per clinically successful outcome. Medication addresses the biophysical component of the disorder. Social therapy, with structured or supported living, teaches and reinforces social skills. Psychological therapy addresses the intrapsychic and psychodynamic issues. Vocational rehabilitation is important in developing self-esteem and establishing financial independence.

Functions of the Treatment Team. The treatment team should teach the client the positive and negative effects of any prescribed drugs; it also answers any questions and relieves any doubts a patient has about any medication. Helping the client remain drug compliant is important in reducing the rate of relapse. In addition, monitoring of drug levels in plasma can provide important information, improve drug effectiveness, and reduce unwanted side effects. The client should also understand the limitations of his or her medication. A team member should help the client understand that motivation, medication, and psychological therapy are all important in stabilization and recovery.

Schizophrenia in children and adolescents is discussed in Chapter 12 and practice parameters have been published (American Academy of Child and Adolescent Psychiatry, 1997).

Anxiety Disorders

Symptoms of anxiety are normal and serve as an early warning system that helps a person avoid potentially dangerous situations. Excessive anxiety, however, may be a source of significant suffering and require

intervention. Anxiety is subtle and pervasive; it accompanies almost every psychiatric disorder. Because anxiety touches everyone, it becomes a disorder only when it is objectively uncomfortable or is perceived to be out of control; the usual feelings of anxiety increase and interfere with normal functioning. Severe symptoms of anxiety require assessment and treatment. Understanding the underlying causes and formulating a differential diagnosis help the clinician determine which drugs and which psychological interventions will be the most effective.

The chronicity of anxiety disorders is similar to that of mood disorders, more enduring than that of substance abuse disorders, but less deep-seated than that of the schizophrenias. Only about 30 percent of individuals with anxiety disorders receive treatment, a percentage that is even lower if generalized anxiety disorder is included. Thus, a high percentage of mental health and addictive disorders are actually anxiety disorders or have a high component of comorbid anxiety. Often, these disorders go untreated or are not treated by behavioral health specialists.

Characteristic of anxiety disorders are the symptoms of anxiety and avoidance behavior. Anxiety is a complex response that includes subjective feelings of dread, apprehension, fear, tension, and related psychomotor responses. The last may include motor tension, increases in autonomic responses (heart rate, blood pressure), vigilance, and scanning. DSM-IV-TR lists several subcategories of the anxiety disorders, which are presented in Table 17.4.

Using drugs to treat anxiety disorders is controversial. The controversy arises from diagnostic difficulties, from the chronic nature of many anxieties, and from the addictive potential associated with some of the drugs used in therapy (namely, the benzodiazepines). In the 1960s and 1970s, the benzodiazepine anxiolytics appeared to treat anxiety disorders quickly, effectively, and safely and replaced the barbiturate therapies of the 1950s. Over time, the addictive potential of benzodiazepine therapy became evident, but these drugs continue to be widely prescribed, perhaps because of demand from patients who find the drugs pleasant to take and difficult to quit (Bruce et al., 2003). Also, benzodiazepines, which reduce the outward symptoms of anxiety, might be counterproductive because they may themselves produce depression and suppress cognitive function. With the advent of the antidepressants and the observation that these drugs (especially SSRIs) effectively treat many of the anxieties, sophistication in diagnosing and treating the anxieties similarly expanded. Since 1999, almost all the SSRIs have been approved by the FDA for use in the treatment of generalized anxiety disorder and other anxiety subtypes. As was discussed in Chapter 6, important new anxiolytics are on the horizon. Again, it is imperative for both prescribing and nonprescribing clinicians to become knowledgeable about the pharmacology of these drugs, their

TABLE 17.4 DSM-IV-TR categories of anxiety disorders

A **Panic Attack** is a discrete period in which there is the sudden onset of intense apprehension, fearfulness, or terror, often associated with feelings of impending doom. During these attacks symptoms such as shortness of breath, palpitations, chest pain or discomfort, choking or smothering sensations, and fear of "going crazy" or losing control are present.

Agoraphobia is anxiety about, or avoidance of, places or situations from which escape might be difficult (or embarrassing) or in which help may not be available in the event of having a Panic Attack or panic-like symptoms.

Panic Disorder without Agoraphobia is characterized by recurrent unexpected Panic Attacks about which there is persistent concern.

Panic Disorder with Agoraphobia is characterized by both recurrent unexpected Panic Attacks and Agoraphobia.

Agoraphobia without History of Panic Disorder is characterized by the presence of Agoraphobia and panic-like symptoms without a history of unexpected Panic Attacks.

Specific Phobia is characterized by clinically significant anxiety provoked by exposure to a specific feared object or situation, often leading to avoidance behavior.

Social Phobia is characterized by clinically significant anxiety provoked by exposure to certain types of social or performance situations, often leading to avoidance behavior.

Obsessive-Compulsive Disorder is characterized by obsessions (which cause marked anxiety or distress) and/or by compulsions (which serve to neutralize anxiety).

Posttraumatic Stress Disorder is characterized by the reexperiencing of an extremely traumatic event accompanied by symptoms of increased arousal and by avoidance of stimuli associated with the trauma.

Acute Stress Disorder is characterized by symptoms similar to those of Post-Traumatic Stress Disorder that occur immediately in the aftermath of an extremely traumatic event.

Generalized Anxiety Disorder is characterized by at least 6 months of persistent and excessive anxiety and worry.

Anxiety Disorder Due to a General Medical Condition is characterized by prominent symptoms of anxiety that are judged to be a direct physiological consequence of a general medical condition.

Substance-Induced Anxiety Disorder is characterized by prominent symptoms of anxiety that are judged to be a direct physiological consequence of a drug of abuse, a medication, or toxic exposure.

Anxiety Disorder Not Otherwise Specified is included for coding disorders with prominent anxiety or phobic avoidance that do not meet criteria for any of the specific Anxiety Disorders defined in this section (or anxiety symptoms about which there is inadequate or contradictory information).

Because Separation Anxiety Disorder (characterized by anxiety related to separation from parental figures) usually develops in childhood, it is included in the "Disorders Usually First Diagnosed in Infancy, Childhood, or Adolescence" section. Phobic avoidance that is limited to genital sexual contact with a sexual partner is classified as Sexual Aversion Disorder and is included in the "Sexual and Gender Identity Disorders" section.

Reproduced with permission from American Psychiatric Association (2000a), pp. 429–436.

clinical indications, limitations, and duration of usage. Most important, their limitations must receive as much attention as their assets.

Accurate assessment and diagnosis are especially vital in planning the appropriate treatment for anxiety disorders. Generally, more diffuse and severe anxiety symptoms require some initial pharmacological intervention. Less severe, more circumscribed symptoms of phobias may be more responsive to cognitive and behavioral therapy; in such cases, it is often unnecessary to resort to pharmacotherapy.

Panic Disorder. Panic disorder is one of the most common and most disabling of the anxiety disorders. Barloon and Noyes (1997) discuss Charles Darwin, describing how disabling this disorder was in his life. Panic disorder is considered a chronic condition that requires ongoing maintenance therapy, preferably combined pharmacologic and psychological therapies (Barlow et al., 2000). An editorial accompanying the Barlow report (Glass, 2000) emphasizes a lifetime, worldwide prevalence of panic disorder in the general community at about 1.5 to 3.5 percent, along with high levels of social morbidity and health care service utilization. Other data indicate that patients with panic disorder account for more than 20 percent of emergency room visits and are twelve times more likely to visit the emergency room than the general population. Patients with panic attacks average 19 medical visits per year, a rate seven times above normal; they also account for 15 percent of total medical visits. The use of medical services and the health care costs associated with panic disorder are therefore enormous. Added to them are disability costs and unemployment expenses (25 percent of panic disorder patients are fully unemployed). Appropriate treatment is presumed to reduce these disabilities and expenditures.

Comprehensive therapy reduces the severity of the course of panic disorder and enhances outcome. Pharmacologically, the SSRI-type antidepressants are the drugs of choice, except for patients also experiencing severe agitation. For those patients, a benzodiazepine anxiolytic is more effective on a short-term basis, until the anxiety and/or agitation resolves.

An estimated 50 percent of patients with panic disorder experience an episode of major depression (Gorman and Coplan, 1996), an added impetus for the use of antidepressant medications over benzodiazepines. A growing database of evidence supports the efficacy of cognitive-behavioral therapy in panic disorder (Glass, 2000). CBT usually includes patient education, monitoring of panic symptoms, breathing retraining, cognitive restructuring of the catastrophic thinking associated with panic symptoms, and exposure and desensitization to external phobic situations. Psychological therapies should also address the comorbidity of panic disorder and depression.

Pollack (1997) reviewed the psychopharmacology for panic disorder, stating that, with the use of SSRIs, it is important to start low to minimize the increased anxiety associated with the initiation of treatment. According to Pollack, buproprion and trazodone are unique among antidepressants in their relative lack of efficacy in treating panic disorder and other anxiety conditions in contrast to most other antidepressants.

Of the benzodiazepines, alprazolam (Xanax) is the most widely studied for treating panic disorder. Other benzodiazepines that have been studied include lorazepam (Ativan) and clonazepam (Klonopin). The benzodiazepines have a favorable profile of side effects; they lack the anticholinergic side effects of the TCAs and the increased anxiety of the SSRIs. Concomitant use (benzodiazepine plus SSRI) provides rapid anxiolysis and more comprehensive relief of panic and depressive symptoms. For all antidepressant medications, treatment may need to be continued indefinitely, because there is a high rate of relapse with medication discontinuation.

Generalized Anxiety Disorder. Although considerable attention focused on anxiety disorders in the 1990s, less attention was devoted to the investigation of generalized anxiety disorder (GAD):

> The emerging picture is that GAD is a common and chronic disorder, affecting primarily women, and one that leads to significant distress and impairment. Subjects with GAD frequently utilize health care services and require medication treatment. (Brawman-Mintzer and Lydiard, 1996, p. 3.)

Formerly called *anxiety neurosis*, GAD occurs at a rate that equals or exceeds the other anxiety disorders. GAD is also comorbid with other psychological disorders, especially depression and dysthymia. GAD is associated with disability, medically unexplained symptoms, and overutilization of medical resources. Two-thirds of individuals with current GAD had an additional current psychiatric diagnosis (usually major depression or dysthymia), and 98 percent of those with lifetime GAD had another lifetime psychiatric diagnosis. GAD may be a crucial factor in modifying the presentation, course, and outcome of major depression. Patients with GAD have a moderate amount of disability and impairment in quality of life. GAD is especially common in the elderly (Lenze et al., 2000).

Treatment of GAD is currently understudied. One mainstay of self-medication for GAD is ethyl alcohol, which effectively produces a short-term anxiolytic action. Until the mid- to late 1990s, benzodiazepines were the prescribed agents of choice, but their use is associated with significant emergent (rebound) anxiety and withdrawal-related symptomatology (Rickels and Rynn, 2002; Sramek et al., 2002). About 25 percent of patients treated with benzodiazepines show rebound anxiety, and 40 percent of them resume their medication because they find drug discontinuation to be intolerable.

In the mid-1990s, buspirone (BuSpar) was demonstrated to effectively reduce symptomatology with efficacy superior to placebo and equal to lorazepam (Sramek et al., 1996). At that time, buspirone was considered to be the drug of choice for GAD in situations where a slow onset of action and a "subtle" effect was acceptable. By 1997, buspirone was widely used for persistent anxiety without panic attacks, the latter often requiring therapy with an SSRI-type antidepressant. Buspirone does not impair memory or motor coordination, is not associated with abuse or dependence, is not cross-tolerant with alcohol, and does not produce a withdrawal reaction. In addition, buspirone has a progressive onset of action and produces few adverse drug reactions when combined with other agents. It was concluded in the late 1990s that if the patient does not respond to buspirone, an antidepressant such as nefazodone, a $5-HT_2$ antagonist, or one of the SSRIs would be indicated. In 1999, venlafaxine, a mixed serotonin-norepinephrine reuptake-inhibiting antidepressant in an extended-release dosage form (Effexor-XR) was shown to be effective (Katz et al., 2002; Montgomery et al., 2002) and has been approved by the FDA for clinical use in the treatment of GAD. In essence, any SSRI-type antidepressant may be used effectively to treat GAD. Perhaps the most studied SSRI has been paroxetine (Rickels et al., 2003; Stocchi et al., 2003).

Currently, other drugs are being evaluated for use in treating GAD. For example, tiagabine (Gabitril), a GABA-reuptake blocker in the brain, is currently in clinical trial for use in treating GAD (Lydiard, 2003; Schwartz, 2002). Pregabalin (Lyrica), a gabapentin (Neurontin) derivative, was approved in 2005 for treating peripheral neuropathies. It has been reported to be useful in treating GAD (Feltner et al., 2003; Lauria-Horner and Pohl, 2003; Pande et al., 2003).

Cognitive-behavioral psychotherapies, which teach clients to examine how their unrealistic thoughts and ruminations affect their behavioral functioning, have proven effective in treating GAD (Borkovec et al., 2003; Dugas et al., 2003; Harvey and Rapee, 1995). Relaxation therapy, biofeedback, and stress management are used to teach patients how to relax even under stress. Many anxious people worry about being unable to cope. They fear losing control, "going crazy," or being publicly embarrassed. As a consequence, the fears increase the anxiety in a vicious circle. Anxious thoughts increase anxiety symptoms, which in turn generate even more anxious thoughts. Cognitive-behavioral techniques help patients break this circle by allowing them to deal appropriately with anxious thoughts and their related behavioral expressions.

Because GAD is a chronic, relapsing, and debilitating disorder, both acute efficacy and long-term prevention of relapse must be considered when choosing both drug and psychotherapeutic interventions. Ideally, cognitive-behavioral therapies should have long-term efficacy. Durham and coworkers (2003), in a 14-year follow-up report, noted that CBT was associated with significantly lower overall severity of GAD symptomatology and fewer interim treatments. CBT had less influence over diagnostic status, probability of overall recovery, or patient perceptions of overall improvement. Therefore, although data are lacking, combinations of drug therapy and CBT may offer the most hope for long-term efficacy.

Social Phobia (Social Anxiety Disorder). Social anxiety disorder is a common illness with significant associated disability. It is frequently underrecognized and underdiagnosed. Persons with this disorder are less likely to be high achievers, have lower employment rates, and lower household incomes than persons without the disorder (Patel et al., 2002). In general, the phobias are characterized by extreme anxiety about a specific object (specific phobia) or a generalized or discrete social situation (social phobia). Patients with social phobias are at high risk for developing mood or anxiety disorders and schizophrenia. According to learning theory, individuals select the behavior that moves them from a state of stress to a state in which the stress is reduced. Thus, if a conditioned stimulus is repeatedly presented in a manner that does not produce a conditioned emotional response, the original association is extinguished. Systematic desensitization (targeted exposure therapy) pairs fear-evoking incidents with relaxation training in a sequence that finally leads to the presentation of the original fear-inducing or anxiety-arousing stimulus.

When the patient with a phobia displays severe anxiety symptoms, anxiolytics may be administered to treat acute symptoms (Jefferson, 2001). For longer-term pharmacological management, antidepressant agents, especially the SSRI-type antidepressants, are the drugs of choice. Overall, the reduction in the intensity of the disorder is probably less than 50 percent, probably because the chronic nature of the disorder is not amenable to short-term drug treatment (Versiani, 2000). Nonetheless, SSRI antidepressants have become the drugs of choice. Fluoxetine is less effective (Kobak et al., 2002), while sertraline, paroxetine, fluvoxamine, and citalopram are all effective (Blomhoff et al., 2001; Furmark et al., 2002; Van Ameringen et al., 2001). Of the non-SSRI antidepressants, bupropion has been shown to be effective (Emmanuel et al., 2000).

Cognitive-behavioral therapies appear to be significantly less effective than medication, although combination therapy may be superior to that achieved by drugs alone; positive results persist into the post-drug phase (Blomhoff et al., 2001; Fedoroff and Taylor, 2001; Heimberg, 2001; Otto et al., 2000). Furmark and coworkers (2002) studied cerebral blood flow changes in patients with social phobia and assessed the alterations in blood flow induced by both citalopram (an SSRI) and cognitive-behavioral therapy. In both instances, blood flow increased in the amygdala, hippocampus, and neighboring cortical areas (brain regions subserving bodily defense reactions to threats). Increases in blood flow correlated with clinical symptom improvements.

Obsessive Compulsive Disorder. Obsessive compulsive disorder (OCD) is characterized by recurrent and disturbing thoughts (obsessions) and/or repetitive behaviors (compulsions) that the individual feels driven to perform but recognizes as irrational or excessive. Once thought to be a rare condition, it is now estimated to be present in about 2 percent of the general population, making it the fourth most common psychiatric disorder. Although traditionally viewed as resistant to a variety of therapeutic interventions, recent advances have been made in the psychopharmacologic and behavioral therapy of OCD. In particular, the efficacy of serotonin reuptake inhibitors, such as clomipramine, fluvoxamine, fluoxetine, and sertraline, has been established in double-blind studies in patients with OCD. Consistent with these drug response data are the hypotheses that changes in serotonin function are critical to the treatment of OCD and perhaps involved in the pathophysiology of at least some patients with the disorder.

SSRIs are commonly used for treating OCD; they are effective in approximately 40 to 60 percent of OCD patients. Furthermore, current research indicates that a combination of medication and behavioral therapies is more effective than the use of either drugs or psychological interventions alone. Simpson and coworkers (1999) studied cognitive-behavioral therapy (using exposure and ritual prevention) as an adjunct to SSRIs in an open trial in six patients who remained symptomatic despite the treatment. In all six patients, there was a further reduction in OCD symptoms. It therefore appears that because significant OCD symptoms often remain or recur, even when there is substantial improvement with SSRI therapy, a combined drug-CBT approach may be an appropriate strategy. Recent studies on the pharmacotherapy for OCD include those by Davidson and Bjorgvinsson (2003), Mundo and coworkers (2001), Hollander and coworkers (2003), and Wagner and coworkers (2003). The treatment of OCD in children and adolescents is discussed in Chapter 12: OCD-specific cognitive-behavioral psychotherapy and pharmacotherapy with a serotonin reuptake inhibitor define the psychotherapeutic and pharmacotherapeutic treatments of choice (American Academy of Child and Adolescent Psychiatry, 1998b).

Posttraumatic Stress Disorder. It is generally accepted that transient and long-lasting neurological alterations may underlie acute and long-term neuronal responses to traumatic stress. Comorbidity is frequent; individuals with posttraumatic stress disorder (PTSD) experience a high incidence of GAD, phobias, depression, and substance abuse. Thus, the treatment of PTSD must be comprehensive and individualized, utilizing carefully balanced pharmacotherapeutic and psychotherapeutic interventions that address both the PTSD and any comorbid disorder. Symptom relief provided by pharmacotherapy enables the patient to participate more thoroughly in individual, behavioral, or group therapy.

Most drugs that are effective for PTSD are also useful for treating major depression and panic disorder. Thus, numerous drugs have been tried, including TCAs, MAO inhibitors, trazodone, the SSRIs, clonidine, guanfacin, brofaromine, valproate, carbamazepine, benzodiazepines, and others. No one drug or class of drugs is universally effective in treating the disorder, although most clinicians feel that a serotonergic action is necessary for good clinical effect in PTSD, analogous to the situation with OCD (Asnis et al., 2004). Therefore, the drugs most utilized are the SSRIs; sertraline has been approved by the FDA for treating this complex and often chronic illness (Davis et al., 2001; Schwartz and Rothbaum, 2002; Yehuda, 2002).

Psychological therapies are essential in treating PTSD (Adshead, 2000), and combining psychotherapy with pharmacotherapy is beneficial. Marshall and Cloitre (2000) present a treatment model involving a phase-oriented treatment approach that begins with pharmacotherapy and continues with trauma-focused psychotherapy. Some clinicians advocate the use of hypnotic techniques to facilitate working through the traumatic events. This approach is based on the frequently observed interrelationship between dissociative reactions and physical trauma. Other behavioral strategies for treating PTSD include group therapy, psychoeducation, exposure and response prevention, cognitive strategies, and family involvement (Himle et al., 2003).

Eating Disorders

Only in recent years have eating disorders (bulimia nervosa, anorexia nervosa, and binge-eating disorder) been considered amenable to pharmacologic treatment. For bulimia nervosa, in particular, the role of medication has expanded; double-blind, placebo-controlled studies demonstrate significant decrease in the frequency of binge-eating behavior in response to antidepressant medications (Kotler et al., 2003; Mitchell et al., 2003). Various classes of antidepressant medications have been tried, but a revised practice guideline for the treatment of patients with eating disorders (American Psychiatric Association, 2000b) states:

> The SSRIs are currently considered to be the safest antidepressants and may be especially helpful for patients with significant symptoms of depression, anxiety, obsessions, or certain impulse disorder symptoms or for those patients who have had a suboptimal response to previous attempts at appropriate psychosocial therapy. (p. 25)

Recently, Hedges and coworkers (2003) and Hoopes and coworkers (2003) reported on the efficacy of topiramate (Topamax; Chapter 10). They note that compared with placebo, topiramate improved several behavioral dimensions of bulimia nervosa: binge and purge behaviors were reduced, and self-esteem, eating attitudes, anxiety, and body image improved.

Short-term psychotherapies have been thought to reduce binge frequency equal to or exceeding the effects of medication treatment. Fairburn and Harrison (2003) review the use of cognitive-behavioral therapy in treating bulimia nervosa. It seems reasonable to expect that combination therapy would provide additive effects. However, recently Walsh and coworkers (2004) reported that fluoxetine (Prozac) exerted beneficial effects in female patients with bulimia, but self-help therapy (based on CBT) was ineffective. Therefore, initial treatment of bulimia perhaps should utilize fluoxetine with adjunctive psychological therapy. Fluoxetine is certainly indicated for those in whom depression or an anxiety disorder is diagnosed as a comorbid disorder. Major depression is the most common comorbid disorder; others include anxiety disorders, substance abuse, and a past history of anorexia nervosa.

Medication failure can result from poor compliance, from vomiting the medication, or from other causes. Blood level analysis may be necessary before concluding that the drug attempt was a failure. Numerous other agents have been tried, but none has been effective when subjected to carefully controlled trials. The course of bulimia may require long-term antidepressant therapy with careful monitoring of side effects and compliance.

In anorexia nervosa, pharmacologic treatment has a very limited role; psychiatric therapy is more important. Psychotherapy, often with CBT components, group therapy, family therapy, nutrition counsel-ing, and so on are all necessary. Drug therapy is primarily aimed at treating comorbid depression following weight gain. However, double-blind studies of antidepressants (versus placebo) show little improvement in weight (weight gain), mood, or body perception. Certainly, however, a trial of antidepressant therapy is warranted in patients who do not respond to psychotherapeutic interventions.

REFERENCES

Adshead, G. (2000). "Psychological Therapies for Post-Traumatic Stress Disorder." *British Journal of Psychiatry* 177: 144–148.

American Academy of Child and Adolescent Psychiatry (1997). "Practice Parameters for Assessment and Treatment of Children and Adolescents with Schizophrenia." *Journal of the American Academy of Child and Adolescent Psychiatry* 36, Supplement (October): 177S–193S.

American Academy of Child and Adolescent Psychiatry (1998a). "Practice Parameters for the Assessment and Treatment of Children and Adolescents with Depressive Disorders." *Journal of the American Academy of Child and Adolescent Psychiatry* 37, Supplement (October): 63S–83S.

American Academy of Child and Adolescent Psychiatry (1998b). "Practice Parameters for the Assessment and Treatment of Children and Adolescents with Obsessive-Compulsive Disorder." *Journal of the American Academy of Child and Adolescent Psychiatry* 37, Supplement (October): 27S–45S.

American Psychiatric Association (2000a). *Diagnostic and Statistical Manual of Mental Disorders*, 4th ed., text revision (DSM-IV-TR). Washington, DC: American Psychiatric Association.

American Psychiatric Association (2000b). "Practice Guideline for the Treatment of Patients with Eating Disorders (Revision)." *American Journal of Psychiatry* 157, Supplement (January).

American Psychiatric Association (2000c). "Practice Guideline for the Treatment of Patients with Major Depressive Disorder (Revision)." *American Journal of Psychiatry* 157 (4): 1–45.

Asnis, G. M., et al. (2004). "SSRIs Versus Non-SSRIs in Post-Traumatic Stress Disorder: An Update with Receomendations. *Drugs* 64: 383–404.

Barloon, T. J., and R. Noyes (1997). "Charles Darwin and Panic Disorder." *Journal of the American Medical Association* 277: 138–141.

Barlow, D. H., et al. (2000). "Cognitive-Behavioral Therapy, Imipramine, or Their Combination for Panic Disorder: A Randomized Controlled Trial." *Journal of the American Medical Association* 283: 2529–2536.

Blomhoff, S., et al. (2001). "Randomized, Controlled, General Practice Trial of Sertraline, Exposure Therapy, and Combination Treatment in Generalized Social Phobia." *British Journal of Psychiatry* 179: 23–30.

Borkovec, T. D., et al. (2003). "Cognitive-Behavioral Therapy for Generalized Anxiety Disorder with Integrations from Interpersonal and Experimental Therapies." *CNS Spectrum* 8: 382–389.

Brawman-Mintzer, O., and R. B. Lydiard (1996). "Generalized Anxiety Disorder: Issues in Epidemiology." *Journal of Clinical Psychiatry* 57, Supplement 7: 3–8.

Bruce, S. E., et al. (2003). "Are Benzodiazepines Still the Medication of Choice for Patients with Panic Disorder with or Without Agoraphobia?" *American Journal of Psychiatry* 160: 1432–1438.

Cabana, M. D., et al. (1999). "Why Don't Physicians Follow Clinical Practice Guidelines? A Framework for Improvement." *Journal of the American Medical Association* 282: 1458–1465.

Chilvers, C., et al. (2001). "Antidepressant Drugs and Generic Counseling for Treatment of Major Depression in Primary Care: Randomized Trial with Patient Preference Arms." *British Medical Journal* 322: 1–5.

Davidson, J., and T. Bjorgvisson (2003). "Current and Potential Pharmacological Treatments for Obsessive Compulsive Disorder." *Expert Opinion Investigational Drugs* 12: 993–1001.

Davis, L. L., et al. (2001). "Pharmacotherapy for Post-Traumatic Disorder: A Comprehensive Review." *Expert Opinion in Pharmacotherapy* 2: 1583–1595.

DeRubeis, R. J., et al. (1999). "Medications Versus Cognitive Behavior Therapy for Severely Depressed Outpatients: Meta-Analysis of Four Randomized Comparisons." *American Journal of Psychiatry* 156: 1007–1013.

Druss, B. G., et al. (2001). "Integrated Medical Care for Patients with Serious Psychiatric Illness: A Randomized Trial." *Archives of General Psychiatry* 58: 861–868.

Dugas, M. J., et al. (2003). "Group Cognitive-Behavioral Therapy for Generalized Anxiety Disorder: Treatment Outcome and Long-Term Follow-Up." *Journal of Consulting Clinical Psychology* 71: 821–825.

Durham, R. C., et al. (2003). "Does Cognitive-Behavioural Therapy Influence the Long-Term Outcome of Generalized Anxiety Disorder? An 8–14 Year Follow-Up of Two Clinical Trials." *Psychological Medicine* 33: 499–509.

Emmanuel, N. P., et al. (2000). "Bupropion-SR in Treatment of Social Phobia." *Depression and Anxiety* 12: 111–113.

Fairburn, C. G., and P. J. Harrison (2003). "Eating Disorders." *Lancet* 361: 407–416.

Fedoroff, I. C., and S. Taylor (2001). "Psychological and Pharmacological Treatments of Social Phobia: A Meta-Analysis." *Journal of Clinical Psychopharmacology* 21: 311–324.

Feltner, D. E., et al. (2003). "A Randomized, Double-Blind, Placebo-Controlled, Fixed-Dose, Multicenter Study of Pregabalin in Patients with Generalized Anxiety Disorder." *Journal of Clinical Psychopharmacology* 23: 240–249.

Frank, J. B., et al. (1998). "Women's Mental Health in Primary Care." *Medical Clinics of North America* 82: 359–383.

Furmark, T., et al. (2002). "Common Changes in Cerebral Blood Flow in Patients with Social Phobia Treated with Citalopram or Cognitive-Behavioral Therapy." *Archives of General Psychiatry* 59: 425–433.

Glass, R. M. (2000). "Panic Disorder: It's Real and It's Treatable." *Journal of the American Medical Association* 283: 2573–2574.

Gorman, J. M., and J. D. Coplan (1996). "Comorbidity of Depression and Panic Disorder." *Journal of Clinical Psychiatry* 57, Supplement 10: 34–43.

Harvey, A. G., and R. M. Rapee (1995). "Cognitive-Behavioral Therapy for Generalized Anxiety Disorder." *Psychiatric Clinics of North America* 18: 859–870.

Hedges, D. W., et al. (2003). "Treatment of Bulimia Nervosa with Topiramate in a Randomized, Double-Blind, Placebo-Controlled Trial, Part 2: Improvement in Psychiatric Measures." *Journal of Clinical Psychiatry* 64: 1449–1454.

Heimberg, R. G. (2001). "Current Status of Psychotherapeutic Interventions for Social Phobia." *Journal of Clinical Psychiatry* 62, Supplement 1: 36–42.

Himle, J. A., et al. (2003). "Group Behavioral Therapy for Adolescents with Tic-Related and Non-Tic-Related Obsessive-Compulsive Disorder." *Depression and Anxiety* 17: 73–77.

Hollander, E., et al. (2003). "A Double-Blind, Placebo-Controlled Study of the Efficacy and Safety of Controlled-Release Fluvoxamine in Patients with Obsessive-Compulsive Disorder." *Journal of Clinical Psychiatry* 64: 640–647.

Hoopes, S. P., et al. (2003). "Treatment of Bulimia Nervosa with Topiramate in a Randomized, Double-Blind, Placebo-Controlled Trial, Part 1: Improvement in Binge and Purge Measures." *Journal of Clinical Psychiatry* 64: 1335–1341.

Jefferson, J. W. (2001). "Benzodiazepines and Anticonvulsants for Social Phobia (Social Anxiety Disorder)." *Journal of Clinical Psychiatry* 62, Supplement 1: 50–53.

Jones, G. N., et al. (2001). "Utilization of Medical Services and Quality of Life Among Low-Income Patients with Generalized Anxiety Disorder Attending Primary Care Clinics." *International Journal of Psychiatry in Medicine* 31: 183–198.

Kampman, M., et al. (2002). "Addition of Cognitive-Behaviour Therapy for Obsessive-Compulsive Disorder in Patients Non-Responsive to Fluoxetine." *Acta Psychiatrica Scandinavica* 106: 314–319.

Katon, W., et al. (1997). "Collaborative Management to Achieve Treatment Depression Guidelines." *Journal of Clinical Psychiatry* 58, Supplement 1: 20–23.

Katz, I. R., et al. (2002). "Venlafaxine ER as a Treatment for Generalized Anxiety Disorder in Older Adults: Pooled Analysis of Five Randomized Placebo-Controlled Clinical Trials." *Journal of the American Geriatric Society* 50: 18–25.

Keller, M. B., et al. (2000). "A Comparison of Nefazodone, the Cognitive Behavioral Analysis System of Psychotherapy, and Their Combination for the

Treatment of Chronic Depression." *New England Journal of Medicine* 342: 1462–1470.

Kobak, K. A., et al. (2002). "Fluoxetine in Social Phobia: A Double-Blind, Placebo-Controlled Pilot Study." *Journal of Clinical Psychopharmacology* 22: 257–262.

Kotler, L. A., et al. (2003). "An Open Trial of Fluoxetine for Adolescents with Bulimia Nervosa." *Journal of Child and Adolescent Psychopharmacology* 13: 329–335.

Lauria-Horner, B. A. and R. B. Pohl (2003). "Pregabalin: A New Anxiolytic." *Expert Opions on Investigational Drugs* 12: 663–672.

Lenze, E. J., et al. (2000). "Comorbid Anxiety Disorders in Depressed Elderly Patients." *American Journal of Psychiatry* 175: 722–728.

Lydiard, R. B. (2003). "The Role of GABA in Anxiety Disorders." *Journal of Clinical Psychiatry* 64, Supplement 3: 21–27.

Marder, S. R., et al. (1993). "Schizophrenia." *Psychiatric Clinics of North America* 16: 567–588.

Marshall, R. D., and M. Cloitre (2000). "Maximizing Treatment Outcome in Post-Traumatic Stress Disorder Combining Psychotherapy with Pharmacotherapy." *Current Psychiatry Reports* 2: 335–340.

Melfi, C. A., et al. (1998). "The Effects of Adherence to Antidepressant Treatment Guidelines on Relapse and Recurrence of Depression." *Archives of General Psychiatry* 55: 1128–1132.

Miller, I. W., and G. I. Keitner (1996). "Combined Medication and Psychotherapy in the Treatment of Chronic Mood Disorders." *Psychiatric Clinics of North America* 19: 151–170.

Mitchell, J. E., et al. (2003). "Drug Therapy for Patients with Eating Disorders." *Current Drug Target CNS Neurological Disorders* 2: 17–29.

Montgomery, S. A., et al. (2002). "Characterization of the Longitudinal Course of Improvement in Generalized Anxiety Disorder During Long-Term Treatment with Venlafaxine XR." *Journal of Psychiatric Research* 36: 209–217.

Mundo, E., et al. (2001). "Fluvoxamine in Obsessive-Compulsive Disorder: Similar Efficacy and Superior Tolerability in Comparison with Clomipramine." *Human Psychopharmacology* 16: 461–468.

Norman, R., and L. A. Townsend (1999). "Cognitive-Behavioral Therapy for Psychosis: A Status Report." *Canadian Journal of Psychiatry* 44: 245–252.

Otto, M. W., et al. (2000). "A Comparison of the Efficacy of Clonazepam and Cognitive-Behavioral Group Therapy for the Treatment of Social Phobia." *Journal of Anxiety Disorders* 14: 345–358.

Pande, A. C., et al. (2003). "Pregabalin in Generalized Anxiety Disorder: A Placebo-Controlled Trial." *American Journal of Psychiatry* 160: 533–540.

Patel, A., et al. (2002). "The Economic Consequences of Social Phobia." *Journal of Affective Disorders* 68: 221–233.

Paykel, E. S., et al. (1999). "Prevention of Relapse in Residual Depression by Cognitive Therapy." *Archives of General Psychiatry* 56: 829–835.

Pollack, M. H. (1997). "Psychopharmacology Update." *Journal of Clinical Psychiatry* 58: 38–40.

Reinecke, M. A., et al. (1998). "Cognitive-Behavioral Therapy of Depression and Depressive Symptoms During Adolescence: A Review and Meta-Analysis." *Journal of the American Academy of Child and Adolescent Psychiatry* 37: 26–34.

Rickels, K., and M. Rynn (2002). "Pharmacotherapy of Generalized Anxiety Disorder." *Journal of Clinical Psychiatry* 63, Supplement 14: 9–16.

Rickels, K., et al. (2003). "Paroxetine Treatment of Generalized Anxiety Disorder: A Double-Blind, Placebo-Controlled Study." *American Journal of Psychiatry* 160: 749–756.

Russo-Neustadt, A., et al. (1999). "Exercise, Antidepressant Medications, and Enhanced Brain-Derived Neurotrophic Factor Expression." *Neuropsychopharmacology* 21: 679–682.

Schwartz, A. C., and B. O. Rothbaum (2002). "Review of Sertraline in Post-Traumatic Stress Disorder." *Expert Opinion in Pharmacotherapy* 3: 1489–1499.

Schwartz, T. L. (2002). "The Use of Tiagabine Augmentation for Treatment-Resistant Anxiety Disorders: A Case Series." *Psychopharmacology Bulletin* 36: 53–57.

Sclar, D. A., et al. (1998). "What Factors Influence the Prescribing of Antidepressant Pharmacotherapy? An Assessment of National Office-Based Encounters." *International Journal of Psychiatry in Medicine* 28: 407–419.

Sensky, T., et al. (2000). "A Randomized Controlled Trial of Cognitive-Behavioral Therapy for Persistent Symptoms in Schizophrenia Resistant to Medication." *Archives of General Psychiatry* 57: 165–172.

Sheline, Y. I., et al. (2003). "Untreated Depression and Hippocampal Volume Loss." *American Journal of Psychiatry* 160: 1516–1518.

Simpson, H. B., et al. (1999). "Cognitive-Behavioral Therapy as an Adjunct to Serotonin Reuptake Inhibitors in Obsessive-Compulsive Disorder: An Open Trial." *Journal of Clinical Psychiatry* 60: 584–590.

Sprenger, D. L., and A. M. Josephson (1998). "Integration of Pharmacotherapy and Family Therapy in the Treatment of Children and Adolescents." *Journal of the American Academy of Child and Adolescent Psychiatry* 37: 887–889.

Sramek, J. J., et al. (1996). "Efficacy of Buspirone in Generalized Anxiety Disorder with Coexisting Mild Depressive Symptoms." *Journal of Clinical Psychiatry* 57: 287–291.

Sramek, J. J., et al. (2002). "Generalized Anxiety Disorder: Treatment Options." *Drugs* 62: 1635–1648.

Stocchi, F., et al. (2003). "Efficacy and Tolerability of Paroxetine for the Long-Term Treatment of Generalized Anxiety Disorder." *Journal of Clinical Psychiatry* 64: 250–258.

U.S. Department of Health and Human Services (1999). *Mental Health: A Report of the Surgeon General*. Rockville, MD: U.S. Department of Health and Human Services, Substance Abuse and Mental Health Services Administration, Center for Mental Health Services, National Institutes of Health, National Institute of Mental Health.

U.S. Department of Health and Human Services (2003). *President's New Freedom Commission on Mental Health, Final Report*. Publication SMA 03-3832, National Institute of Mental Health.

Van Ameringen, M. A., et al. (2001). "Sertraline Treatment of Generalized Social Phobia: A 20-Week, Double-Blind, Placebo-Controlled Study." *American Journal of Psychiatry* 158: 275–281.

Versiani, M. (2000). "A Review of 19 Double-Blind, Placebo-Controlled Studies in Social Anxiety Disorder (Social Phobia)." *World Journal of Biological Psychiatry* 1: 27–33.

Wagner, K. D., et al. (2003). "Remission Status after Long-Term Sertraline Treatment of Pediatric Obsessive-Compulsive Disorder." *Journal of Child and Adolescent Psychopharmacology* 13, Supplement 1: S53–S60.

Walsh, B. T., et al. (1997). "Medication and Psychotherapy in the Treatment of Bulimia Nervosa." *American Journal of Psychiatry* 154: 523–531.

Walsh, B. T., et al. (2004). "Treatment of Bulimia Nervosa in a Primary Care Setting." *American Journal of Psychiatry* 161: 556–561.

Ward, E., et al. (2000). "Randomized Controlled Trial of Non-Directive Counseling, Cognitive-Behaviour Therapy, and Usual General Practitioner Care for Patients with Depression. I: Clinical Effectiveness." *British Medical Journal* 321: 1383–1388.

Wells, K. B., et al. (2000). "Impact of Disseminating Quality Improvement Programs for Depression in Managed Primary Care: A Randomized Controlled Trial." *Journal of the American Medical Association* 283: 212–220.

Work Group on Panic Disorder (1998). "Practice Guideline for the Treatment of Patients with Panic Disorder." *American Journal of Psychiatry* 155, Supplement (May): 2–3.

Yehuda, R. (2002). "Post-Traumatic Stress Disorder." *New England Journal of Medicine* 346: 108–114.

Zajecka, J., et al. (2002). "Sexual Function and Satisfaction in the Treatment of Chronic Major Depression with Nefazodone, Psychotherapy, and Their Combination." *Journal of Clinical Psychiatry* 63: 709–716.

Agents Primarily Considered as Drugs of Abuse

Chapters 18 through 21 focus on drugs widely considered to be drugs of abuse. Previous chapters in this book have covered other drugs with high abuse potential (cocaine and amphetamines in Chapter 7 and the opioids in Chapter 15). However, those drugs have significant therapeutic uses (for example, amphetamines for treatment of ADHD and opioids for treatment of severe pain). The drugs discussed here have less therapeutic potential and have significant illicit use and abuse in our society.

The pharmacology of tetrahydrocannabinol, the active substance in marijuana, is discussed in Chapter 18 and that of the psychedelic drugs is presented in Chapter 19. Several naturally occurring psychedelics are discussed in Chapter 19 (for example, mescaline and psilocybin) as well as a variety of "designer" psychedelics including NMDA (ecstacy). Also discussed is the pharmacology of phencyclidine and ketamine, two dissociative psychedelics that also serve as model drugs for investigations into the psychobiology of schizophrenia.

Chapter 20 discusses the pharmacology and abuse of anabolic steroids, substances abused for their ability to increase muscle mass. Finally, Chapter 21 concludes this textbook with a brief discussion of other topics in drug abuse and drug abuse education.

Chapter 18

Tetrahydrocannabinol

The hemp plant *Cannabis sativa,* commonly called marijuana, grows throughout the world and flourishes in most temperate and tropical regions. The major psychoactive ingredient of the marijuana plant is *delta-9-tetrahydrocannabinol* (THC; Figure 18.1); *cannabinol* and *cannabidiol,* among other components, are present in lesser amounts. The major psychoactive effects of marijuana are due primarily to THC (Wachtel et al., 2002). THC is probably responsible also for the side effects and therapeutic effects associated with smoking marijuana. Names for *Cannabis* products include marijuana, hashish, charas, bhang, ganja, and sinsemilla. *Hashish* and *charas,* which consist of the dried resinous exudates of the female flowers, are the most potent preparations, with a THC content averaging between 10 and 20 percent. *Ganja* and *sinsemilla* refer to the dried material found in the tops of the female plants, where the THC content averages about 5 to 8 percent. *Bhang* and *marijuana* are lower-grade preparations taken from the dried remainder of the plant, and their THC content varies between 2 to 5 percent, although improved growing, harvesting, and processing techniques have boosted this content considerably, perhaps to as high as 30 percent in imported hydroponically produced product.

Until about 1990, marijuana was classified according to its behavioral effects, usually as a mild sedative-hypnotic agent, with effects similar to low doses of alcohol but without the intoxication. Unlike alcohol, however, higher doses of THC do not depress respiration and are not lethal. THC also produces a unique spectrum of pharmacologic effects, including disruption in attention mechanisms, impairment of

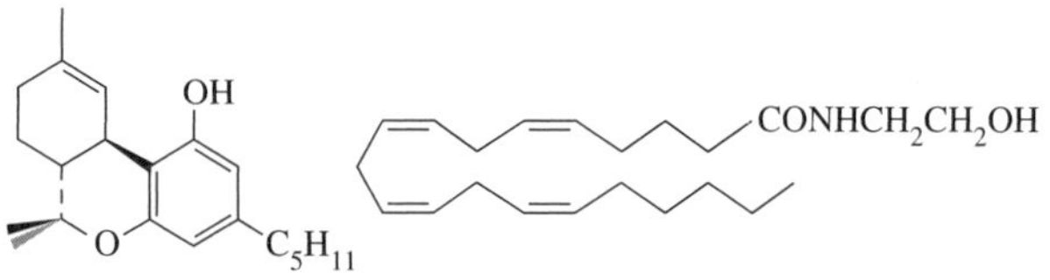

FIGURE 18.1 Structures of delta-9-tetrahydrocannabinol (THC) and anandamide, the endogenous ligand (neurotransmitter) of the cannabinoid receptor.

short-term memory, altered sensory awareness, analgesia, and altered control of motor movements and postural control.

Since the early 1990s, extensive evidence has accumulated to demonstrate that THC binds to specific *cannabinoid receptors* in the brain and in the peripheral nervous system. Indeed, THC mimics the actions of an endogenous cannabinoid (a fatty acid called *anandamide*), which exert important biological effects of their own. In addition, cannabinoid receptors exist in the brain in quantities that surpass most other G protein-coupled receptors, approaching or exceeding levels observed for the amino acid receptors glutamate and GABA (Childers and Breivogel, 1998; Felder and Glass, 1998).

History

The use of *Cannabis sativa* dates from several thousand years ago (Figure 18.2), when it was used as a mild intoxicant; it is somewhat milder than alcohol. It is much less useful for religious and psychedelic experiences than naturally occurring psychedelic drugs because it produces much less sensory distortion. Over the years, products from *Cannabis sativa* have been claimed to have a wide variety of medical uses, although few persist in native cultures.

Cannabis sativa was introduced into Western cultures probably in the 1850s. During the early 1920s, marijuana was portrayed as being an underground evil and a menace. Because it was claimed that an association existed between marijuana and crime, laws were passed to outlaw its use. By the mid-1930s, marijuana was looked on as a "narcotic" and as a drug responsible for crimes of violence. By 1940, the public was convinced that marijuana was a "killer drug" that (1) induced people to commit crimes of violence, (2) led to heroin addiction, and (3) was a great social menace. The emotional campaign against marijuana persists even today, limiting research into the possible medical uses of cannabinoid agonists and antagonists. Several facts associated with cannabis abuse are disquieting. First, marijuana is the most widely used illicit drug in the United States and the western hemisphere. In 2000, an estimated 76 percent of America's 14.8 million

A. The ancient world to the present

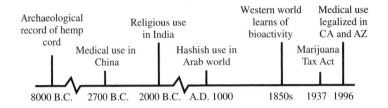

B. *Cannabis* research developments

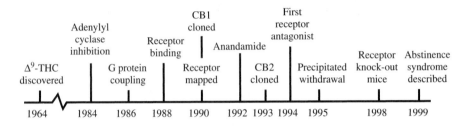

FIGURE 18.2 Two timelines of marijuana history. [Modified from Childers and Breivogel (1998), p. 174.]

illicit drug users used marijuana alone (59 percent) or in conjunction with other drugs (17 percent). Approximately 6 percent of the population 12 years and older have used marijuana in the month prior to interview. Perhaps 5 percent of high school-aged people smoke marijuana daily. Early onset of heavy use is likely to be associated with more severe psychopathology in later years (Brook et al., 2003). Alcohol and marijuana use often serves as a marker for later pathology, probably because the substances are used early to self-medicate for psychological distress. Second, a marijuana discontinuation syndrome occurs, although it is probably not as severe as that seen in alcohol withdrawal. Third, use of marijuana may serve to increase rates of relapse to the use of a more dangerous drug (DeVries et al., 2001).

Since 1996, voters in nine states have approved ballot initiatives to permit the legal use of marijuana for purported medical purposes.[1] Approval of these initiatives signaled the first time since the repeal of the Prohibition amendment some 70 years ago that the public has approved a pullback in the "war on drugs," and these initiatives place

[1]Oregon, Washington, Alaska, California, Colorado, Hawaii, Nevada, Maine, and Maryland as of 2003.

state laws in conflict with federal statutes. The medical efficacy of marijuana is controversial; however, evidence is accumulating that marijuana does have medical uses, perhaps most prominently in the relief of certain types of painful conditions (Watson et al., 2000). Canada has recently made available medical marijuana, placing the Canadian law in direct conflict with federal statutes in the United States.[2] Passage of these Canadian and state initiatives thus raises several issues:

- Should marijuana (or the active drug THC) be made available for *medical use* throughout the United States, and for what medical uses is THC (or crude marijuana) efficacious?
- Should marijuana (or the active drug THC) be made available for *recreational use by adults* in the United States?
- How should society deal with the use of marijuana (or the active drug THC) as well as ethyl alcohol by those under the age of 21 years?

Mechanism of Action: Cannabinoid Receptor

THC was isolated from marijuana as its pharmacologically active ingredient (see Figure 18.1) in 1964. Evidence gathered from then until the mid-1980s led to the hypothesis that THC and other cannabinoids act via a pharmacologically distinct set of receptors. In 1986 it was shown that THC inhibits the intracellular enzyme *adenylate cyclase* and that the inhibition requires the presence of a G protein complex, similar to the opioid receptors discussed in Chapter 15. In about 1990, it was shown that THC does *not* directly inhibit adenylate cyclase; rather, it acts on a specific receptor in such a way that the enzyme is ultimately inhibited. In 1990 the THC receptor was isolated, sequenced, and cloned. The receptor is a specific G protein-coupled receptor that both inhibits adenylate cyclase and binds THC and other cannabinoids. These receptors are primarily found on presynaptic nerve terminals and act to inhibit calcium ion flux and facilitate potassium channels. As a result, activation of cannabinoid receptors inhibits the release of other neurotransmitters, primarily the inhibitory neurotransmitter GABA (Ohno-Shosaku et al., 2001) from presynaptic nerve terminals. Ohno-Shosaku and coworkers (2002) and Iversen (2003) state that endogenous cannabinoids are "retrograde messengers" released from neurons either by increased intracellular levels of calcium

---

[2]As of this writing, Canada proposes to sell an ounce of marijuana (10 percent THC content) for about $112 to $150 for a one-month supply or a pack of 30 seeds once a year for $15.

ions or by activation of certain glutamate receptors. The release in turn inhibits GABA release.

Physically, the cannabinoid receptor is a continuous chain of 473 amino acids with seven loops through the cell membrane (Figures 18.3 and 18.4). As shown by Childers and Breivogel (1998), when THC (or an endogenous endocannabinoid) binds to the cannabinoid receptors, it activates G proteins that act on various effectors, including the second-messenger enzyme adenylate cyclase, to ultimately inhibit GABA release. In 1990, the identification of a naturally occurring ligand (an endocannabinoid) that binds to the cannabinoid receptor and thus might function as a natural THC remained to be demonstrated. In the search for this ligand, Devane and coworkers (1992) first isolated an arachidonic acid derivative named *anandamide* (see Figure 18.1), which not only bound to the cannabinoid receptor but also produced cannabinoidlike pharmacological effects. Many additional reports since then demonstrated that anandamide produces behavioral, hypothermic, and analgesic effects that parallel those caused by psychotropic cannabinoids. Anandamide is a weaker agonist than is THC and has a shorter half-life. It exhibits the essential criteria required to be classified as the endogenous ligand at cannabinoid receptors. In 1999, Ameri and colleagues verified that anandamide acting on

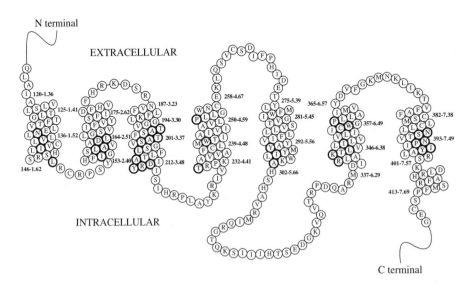

FIGURE 18.3 Two-dimensional representation of the anandamide receptor, a protein consisting of a chain of more than 450 amino acids (the first letter of each amino acid is shown). Like the opioid receptors, the anandamide receptor is a G protein-linked, seven membrane-spanning structure with three extracellular loops.

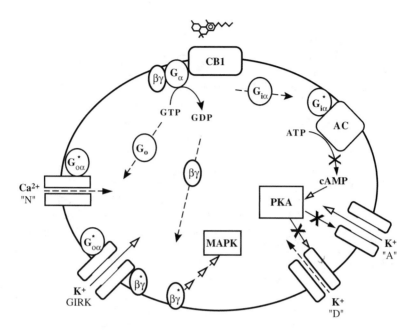

FIGURE 18.4 Several proposed signal transduction mechanisms of cannabinoid receptors. After THC (or anandamide) binds (*top*), the CB1 receptor activates G proteins, which in turn act on various effectors including adenylate cyclase (AC), calcium (Ca^2), and mitogen-activated protein kinase (MAPK). Inhibition of adenylate cyclase and subsequent decreases in cAMP decrease activation of cAMP-dependent protein kinase (PKA), which leads to decreased potassium (K^+) channel fluxes. Stimulatory effects are shown by open arrows and inhibitory effects by filled arrows. The open or closed states of the channels and X's over some arrows reflect the final effects of cannabinoid agonists. [From Childers and Breivogel (1998), p. 179.]

hippocampal cannabinoid receptors controls neuronal excitability by reducing excitatory neurotransmission at a presynaptic site. Shen and Thayer (1999) demonstrated that THC acts as a partial agonist at hippocampal glutamate-releasing neurons to "reduce, but not totally block, excitatory transmission" (p. 8). From these studies we can conclude that both THC and anandamide function as partial agonists that are unable to fully activate cannabinoid receptors at maximally effective concentrations.

There are huge numbers of cannabinoid receptors in the brain, perhaps 10 to 20 times the number of opioid receptors and perhaps more than any other type of receptor. Anandamide, as a partial agonist, activates perhaps only 50 percent of available receptors; THC activates only about 20 percent. In fact, THC is probably effective not because of any inherent efficacy but because of the tremendous number of receptors for it in the brain. Even in the spinal cord, cannabinoid receptors are expressed in sensory nociceptive cells located in the dorsal root ganglion from whence the receptors are carried by axoplasmic flow both to peripheral sensory nerve endings and to nerve terminals in the dorsal horn of the spinal cord (Hohmann and Herkenham, 1999a, 1999b).

As can be seen from Figure 18.1, anandamide is structurally dissimilar to THC. Thomas and coworkers (1996) constructed three-dimensional pharmacologic models of THC and anandamide and demonstrated that in this conformation the molecules are in actuality quite similar (Figure 18.5) and would be predicted to interact with the same receptor. As the 1990s ended, the first cannabinoid antagonist was synthesized, and mice lacking the cannabinoid receptor were bred and demonstrated no response to canninoid drugs (Ledent et al., 1999). Recently, a marijuana abstinence (or discontinuation) syndrome has been described (Smith, 2002), and cannabinoid antagonists are being used both to study this discontinuation syndrome and to develop clinical uses in treating obesity and drug craving.

Cannabinoid receptors are located throughout the brain (Figures 18.6 and 18.7). Large numbers are found in the basal ganglia and cerebellum and are involved in many forms of movement and postural control that are affected by smoking marijuana. The cerebral cortex, especially the frontal cortex, is rich in cannabinoid receptors (Ong and Mackie, 1999). Binding of THC here probably mediates at least some of the psychoactive effects of the drug, including distortions of the sense of time, sound, color, and taste; alterations in the ability to concentrate; and production of a dreamlike state. Cannabinoid receptors are also dense in the hippocampus; this fact may account for THC-induced disruption of memory, memory storage, and coding of sensory input. Because brain-stem structures do not bind cannabinoids, THC does not affect basal body functions, including respiration. The absence of cannabinoid–anandamide receptors in the brain stem explains the relative nonlethality of THC.

In 1994 Lynn and Herkenham studied the peripheral effects of cannabinoids and reported cannabinoid receptors outside the brain of a slightly different type (type 2) than those found in the brain (the brain receptors, as well as certain cannabinoid receptors in the peripheral nervous system, are termed *cannabinoid-1 receptors*). *Cannabinoid-2* receptors are thought to be all located outside the CNS. Originally thought to be located only on specific components of the lymphoid system, they are also located in the heart and in body tissues involved in inflammatory and pain responses.

In December 2003, Farquhar-Smith and Rice reported on the effects of anandamide on inflammatory responses mediated by the cannabinoid-2 receptors and immune cells. They noted that in the periphery, certain immune cells coexpress cannabinoid-2 receptors as

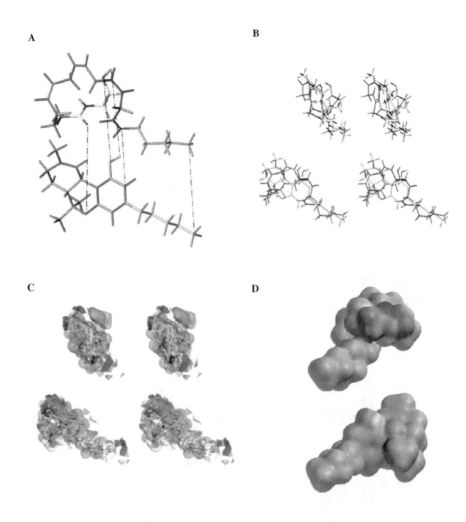

FIGURE 18.5 Several structural comparisons of anandamide and THC. **A.** Stick model showing alignment of the two molecules with dashed lines signifying the five atoms used for superpositioning. **B.** Views of the overlaid structures that predict three-dimensional similarity and thus affinity for the same receptor. **C.** Stereoviews of overlaid structures show nonoverlapping molecular volumes. **D.** Another view of the steric shape and bulk of anandamide (*top*) and THC (*bottom*). [From Thomas et al. (1996), p. 474.]

well as a receptor for a protein called *nerve growth factor*. The researchers found that anandamide (and another synthetic cannabinoid agonist) blocked nerve growth factor-induced painful and inflammatory responses and that this peripheral analgesic/anti-inflammatory response of anandamide is independent of CNS effects involving

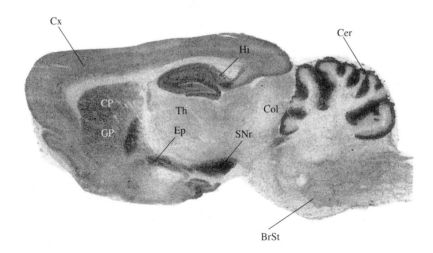

FIGURE 18.6 Autoradiographic binding of potent cannabinoid-to-cannabinoid receptors in the rat brain. BrSt = brain stem; Cer = cerebellum; Col = colliculi; CP = caudate putamen; Cx = cerebral cortex; Ep = entopeduncular nucleus; GP = globus pallidus; Hi = hippocampus; SNr = substantia nigra; Th = thalamus.

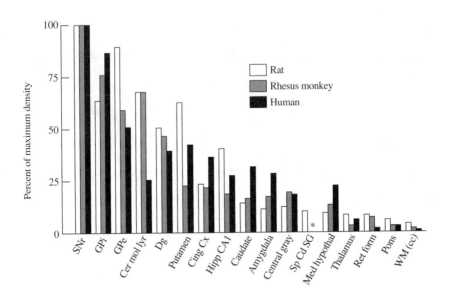

FIGURE 18.7 Relative densities of cannabinoid receptors across brain structures in rat, rhesus monkey, and human. Cer mol lyr = cerebellum, molecular layer; Cing Cx = cingulate cortex; Dg = dentate gyrus; GPe = external globus pallidus; GPi = internal globus pallidus; Hipp CA1 = hippocampal field CA1; Med hypothal = medial hypothalamus; Ret form = reticular formation; Sp Cd SG = substantia gelatinosa of spinal cord (*only rat measured); WM (cc) = white matter of corpus callosum.

cannabinoid-1 receptors (which have additional and independent analgesic involvement).

Pharmacokinetics

Most marijuana available in the United States has a THC content that does not exceed 8 percent, although some products contain much higher amounts. THC is usually administered in the form of a hand-rolled marijuana cigarette. Thus, if a marijuana cigarette contains 1.5 grams of plant material with a THC content of about 5 percent, the cigarette contains approximately 75 milligrams of THC. In general, about one-fourth to one-half of the THC present in a marijuana cigarette is actually available in the smoke. Thus, if a cigarette contains 75 milligrams of THC, about 25 milligrams are available in the smoke. In practice, the amount of THC *absorbed* into the bloodstream as a result of the social smoking of one marijuana cigarette is probably in the range of 5 to 10 milligrams. The absorption of THC from the smoking of marijuana is rapid and complete.

Besides administration by smoking, marijuana can be taken orally, and one THC preparation, dronabinol (Marinol), has been available for oral use since the mid-1980s. Taken orally, onset is delayed and "first-pass metabolism" significantly hinders the drug from reaching significant plasma concentration. Indeed, taken orally, only 10 to 20 percent of the ingested dose of THC reaches the systemic circulation. However, the first metabolite of THC (11-hydroxy-delta-9-THC) is pharmacologically active and has a prolonged half-life with a duration of action of about 4 to 6 hours.

The behavioral effects of THC in smoked marijuana occur almost immediately after smoking begins and correspond with the rapid attainment of peak concentrations in plasma (Figure 18.8). A "high" is experienced with plasma concentrations of THC of about 5 to 10 nanograms of drug per milliliter of plasma (ng/ml) of drug. Unless more is smoked, the effects seldom last longer than 2 to 3 hours. Peak blood levels of THC of 50 to 100 ng/ml occur about 10 minutes after initiation of smoking cigarettes containing 1.75 percent and 3.55 percent THC, respectively. Within 2 hours, levels fall below 5 ng/ml but remain detectable for up to 12 hours after smoking a single cigarette. THC is also absorbed when it is administered orally, but the absorption is slow and incomplete. The onset of action usually takes 30 to 60 minutes, with peak effects occurring 2 to 3 hours after ingestion.

Once THC is absorbed, it is distributed to the various organs of the body, especially those that have significant concentrations of fatty material. Thus, THC readily penetrates the brain; the blood-brain barrier does not appear to hinder its passage. Similarly, THC readily crosses

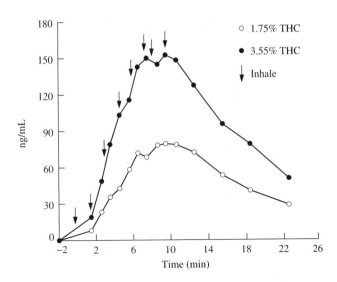

FIGURE 18.8 Mean plasma concentrations of total THC for smoked marijuana and infused THC on days 1 and 22. One marijuana cigarette was smoked from 0 to 15 minutes and was followed by intravenous infusion from 15 to 65 minutes, as indicated by arrows. Results from day 22 were obtained after daily smoking of marijuana and suggest that tolerance failed to develop. [From M. Perez-Reyes et al., "The Pharmacological Effects of Daily Marijuana Smoking in Humans," *Pharmacology, Biochemistry, and Behavior* 40 (1991), p. 693.]

the placental barrier and reaches the fetus. THC is almost completely metabolized by hepatic cytochrome P450 enzymes to an active metabolite (11-hydroxy-delta-9-THC) that is subsequently converted to an inactive metabolite (11-nor-9-carboxy-delta-9-tetrahydrocannabinol or THC-COOH or carboxy-THC) that is then excreted in the urine. The metabolism of THC itself is quite slow; an elimination half-life of about 30 hours is generally accepted, although some researchers report longer half-life. Therefore, THC can persist in the body for several days to about 2 weeks, longer in chronic smokers and obese smokers. Such a delay tends to prolong and intensify the activity of subsequently smoked marijuana, forming a type of "reverse tolerance" to the drug, where the persistent low levels are potentiated by subsequently smoked THC cigarettes.

Like most psychoactive drugs, only minute quantities of THC are found in the urine of persons who use the drug. Therefore, urine testing for THC focuses primarily on identification of its metabolite, carboxy-THC. This carboxy-THC is only slowly excreted; its half-life in urine varies from about 30 hours to 60 hours (Huestis and Cone, 1998), even longer in obese individuals. Chronic smokers, even if they smoke only two to three times weekly, have persistently positive urine tests for carboxy-THC. A heavy smoker who stops smoking may test positive for carboxy-THC in urine for about a month after cessation. Thus, a positive urinalysis can indicate either recent use or use that occurred several weeks earlier. In addition, a positive urine test does not necessarily mean that a person was under the influence of marijuana at the time the urine specimen was collected; there may be little or no correlation between the presence of carboxy-THC in urine and the presence of a pharmacologically significant amount of THC in the blood.

Pharmacological Effects of THC in Animals

THC produces a unique syndrome of behavioral effects, including analgesia, cognitive alterations, and euphoria. Mice lacking the cannabinoid receptor have increased mortality rates, lose body weight, are less active, and have lower pain thresholds (Zimmer et al., 1999). THC and anandamide are both analgesic at spinal, brain-stem, and peripheral sites, especially against the pain resulting from persistent inflammation or neuropathic pain (Farquar-Smith and Rice, 2001; Rice et al., 2002). The analgesic action of cannabinoids is similar to but distinct from the action of the opioids such as morphine (Chapter 15).

THC in rodents potentiates the analgesic action of morphine, increasing morphine's potency; this action is blocked by cannabinoid antagonists (Smith et al., 1998). As discussed, cannabinoid receptors are present in both the peripheral and central terminals of afferent nociceptive neurons. Thus THC can exert analgesic effects by modulating both sensory input from peripheral sites of tissue injury as well as reducing the release of nociceptive neurotransmitters in the dorsal horn of the spinal cord. THC therefore exerts important analgesic actions in the brain, the spinal cord, and the periphery at the site of tissue injury.

THC also exerts a variety of other effects in animals. THC decreases body temperature, calms aggressive behavior, potentiates the effects of barbiturates and other sedatives, blocks convulsions, and depresses reflexes. In primates, specifically, THC decreases aggression, decreases the ability to perform complex behavioral tasks, seems to induce hallucinations, and appears to cause temporal distortions. THC causes monkeys to increase the frequency of their social interactions. High doses can depress ovarian function, lower the concentration of female sex hormones, decrease ovulation, and possibly decrease sperm production. Finally, THC can disrupt appetite regulation, inducing overeating in rats exposed to anandamide, which provides evidence for the involvement of a central cannabinoid system in the normal control of eating (Cota et al., 2003; Williams and Kirkham, 1999).

Pharmacological Effects of THC in Humans

The investigation into the effects of THC in humans results in applicable data regarding the effects of THC on behavior, mentation, memory, and potential uses in the treatment of disease.

Central Nervous System

The CNS effects of THC in humans vary with dose, route of administration, experience of the user, vulnerability to psychoactive effects, and setting of use. In general, the senses may be enhanced and the perception of time is usually altered. Users report an increased sense of well-being, mild euphoria, relaxation, and relief from anxiety. The subjective effects include dissociation of ideas. Illusions and hallucinations occur infrequently. The effect sought after by most users is the "high" and "mellowing out." This effect is described as different from the stimulant high and the opioid high. The effects vary with dose, but the typical marijuana smoker experiences a high that lasts about two hours. During this time, there is impairment of cognitive functions, perception, reaction time, learning, and memory. Impairment of coordination and tracking behavior has been reported to persist for several hours beyond the perception of the high. These impairments have obvious implications for the operation of a motor vehicle and performance in the workplace or at school.

One of the major deleterious effects of the acute use of marijuana in humans is the short-term disruption of memory and cognition; THC disrupts both the encoding and the retrieval processes (Hampson and Deadwyler, 1999). These acute memory impairments are accompanied by reductions in blood flow to the areas of brain involved in memory formation (Block et al., 2002). Memory impairments can be attenuated by cannabinoid antagonists (Mallet and Beninger, 1998), implying that THC- and anandamide-induced memory disruption is mediated by cannabinoid receptors, not by any indirect sedative mechanism.

How severe are these memory impairments, and do they persist beyond the duration of action of the drug? During the period of intoxication, there is a modest degree of memory impairment, although amnesia, similar to the blackout seen with high-dose alcohol ingestion, is not observed and there are only minimal degredations in behavioral performance on attention tasks (O'Leary et al., 2002). Very heavy use, however, is associated with reduced performance on tests measuring memory, executive functioning, psychomotor speed, and manual dexterity (Bolla et al., 2002). Hart and coworkers (2001) studied individuals who smoked an average of 24 marijuana cigarettes per week and found that while marijuana increased the time that smokers required to complete complex tasks, it had no effect on measures of cognitive flexibility, mental calculation, and reasoning. Fried and coworkers

(2002) followed a group of youth from birth through the age of use of marijuana, thus having the advantage of evaluating them before initiation of drug use. Current marijuana use was associated in a dose-related fashion with a decline in IQ scores. Current heavy users showed decreases averaging 4.1 points compared to gains in IQ points for light current users, former users, and nonusers. Therefore, only individuals who were heavy users (five or more joints smoked per day) showed reductions in IQ, and smoking any amount did not appear to have a long-term negative impact on global intelligence. Pope and coworkers (2001) reached the same conclusions, reporting that "some cognitive deficits appear detectable at least 7 days after heavy cannabis use but appear reversible and related to recent cannabis exposure rather than irreversible and related to cumulative lifetime use" (p. 909). In contrast, Bolla and coworkers (2002) noted some persistence of neurocognitive deficits in very heavy users after 28 days of abstinence. In total, data appear to indicate that heavy marijuana smoking is associated with acute effects detrimental to cognitive functioning, effects can be detected for at least 1 month following discontinuation of heavy use, and only minimal effects are likely to persist following a 30-day period of abstinence. THC is certainly not a "dementing drug" as are ethanol or the benzodiazepines.

At very high doses, acute depressive reactions, acute panic reactions, or mild paranoia have been observed, probably brought on by drug-induced alterations in perception; some panic responses may follow the feeling of a loss of mental control. Several surveys indicate that 50 to 60 percent of marijuana users have reported at least one anxiety experience. Only at massive doses of THC do delusions, paranoia, hallucinations, confusion and disorientation, depersonalization, altered sensory perception, and loss of insight occur, and these reactions are unusual and generally short lasting. Common predisposing factors include preexisting personality disturbances or schizophrenia.

Solowij (1995) described a marijuana-induced impaired ability to focus attention and filter out irrelevant information. Users demonstrate weakness in attention and synthetic skills, difficulty making subtle distinctions in relevance and memory, decreased psychospatial skills, poor mental representations of the environment, and poor routines of daily life. These impairments are associated with feelings of alienation and that life is not under their control and lacks meaning. With cessation of drug use and with initiation of psychological treatment, users demonstrated improvement in cognitive functioning within 14 days of abstinence and functioned normally at the end of 6 weeks of therapy.

Kouri and coworkers (1995) studied cohorts of heavy versus occasional marijuana smokers in a college population. By objective measurement of psychiatric functioning (diagnosed DSM disorders), the two groups were indistinguishable. They differed, however, in the level of use of other drugs, with one-third of heavy marijuana users displaying a history of some form of substance abuse or dependence (Tables 18.1 and 18.2).

To understand the behavioral attractiveness of marijuana, Gardner and Lowinson (1991) reviewed marijuana's interactions with brain reward systems, particularly in the dopamine-mediated, medial forebrain bundle projection. They stated:

> Acute enhancement of brain reward mechanisms appears to be the single essential commonality of abuse-prone drugs, and the hypothesis that recreational and abused drugs act on these brain mechanisms to produce the subjective reward that constitutes the "high" or "rush" or "hit" sought by drug users is, at present, the most compelling hypothesis available on the neurobiology of recreational drug use and abuse. (p. 571)

Also involved are synaptic interconnections of opioid and many other neurotransmitters. Gardner and Lowinson (1991) argued that THC acts on this system as do other abused drugs, inducing the release of

TABLE 18.1 Lifetime substance use among heavy versus occasional marijuana smokers

	Heavy smokers (n = 45)	Occasional smokers (n = 44)
	n(%)	n(%)
SUBJECTS WHO HAD EVER USED		
Hallucinogens	44 (98)	23 (42)[c]
Hallucinogens >10 times	36 (80)	5 (11)[c]
Cocaine	32 (71)	8 (18)[c]
Cocaine >10 times	20 (44)	0[c]
Inhalants	11 (24)	3 (7)[a]
Stimulants	14 (31)	7 (16)
Sedative-hypnotics	27 (60)	7 (16)[c]
Opioids	12 (27)	1 (2)[b]
Any of the above	45 (100)	26 (59)[c]
SUBJECTS CURRENTLY USING		
Cigarettes ≥1 pack/day	17 (38)	5 (11)[b]
Alcohol >10 drinks/week	17 (38)	9 (20)

Significance of differences between groups: [a]$p < .05$; [b]$p < .01$; [c]$p < .001$.

TABLE 18.2 Lifetime diagnoses of substance abuse and dependence in heavy versus occasional marijuana smokers

	Heavy smokers ($n = 45$)	Occasional smokers ($n = 44$)
	$n(\%)$	$n(\%)$
SUBSTANCE		
Cannabis	45 (100)	0
Alcohol	11 (24)	5 (11)
Cocaine	6 (13)	0
Hallucinogens	3 (7)	0
Sedative-hypnotics	1 (2)	0
Polysubstance	2 (4)	0
ANY SUBSTANCE OTHER THAN CANNABIS[a]	15 (33)	5 (11)

[a]Total for heavy users is less than the sum of the individual diagnoses because some subjects reported more than one form of substance abuse or dependence.
Significance of differences: cannabis, $p < .001$; cocaine, $p = .03$; any substance other than cannabis, $p = .01$.

dopamine in reward loci including the basal ganglia, the nucleus accumbens, and the prefrontal cortex. Tanda and colleagues (1997) reported that THC increased dopaminergic activity in the nucleus accumbens, probably "through a common mu opioid receptor mechanism located in the ventral tegmentum" (p. 2048). This action may account for both the pleasurable and the analgesic actions of THC. Manzanares and colleagues (1999) expanded on this concept and concluded that there is a functional link between opioids and cannabinoid pathways, especially regarding the antinociceptive (analgesic) actions of cannabinoids. Haney and coworkers (2003a) demonstrated in humans that the opioid antagonist naltrexone actually increased the positive reinforcing effects of orally administered THC. Manzanares and colleagues (1999) suggested that cannabinoids induce the synthesis or release (or both) of opioid peptides, a potential mechanism to explain the augmentation of morphine-induced analgesia by THC as well as the ability of THC to ameliorate the symptoms of opioid withdrawal (both potential therapeutic uses of natural and synthetic cannabinoids). On the other hand, the Manzanares team stated that "the hypothesis that marijuana consumption might enhance the reinforcing potential of opioids (by increasing opioid receptor expression) needs to be more extensively studied" (p. 287).

Diana and coworkers (1998) noted that withdrawal from chronic cannabinoid administration is associated with *reduced* dopamine neurotransmission in the nucleus accumbens, similar to that seen with other addictive drugs. They postulated that "these changes in neuronal plasticity may play a role in drug craving and relapse into drug addiction" (p. 10269).

An "amotivational syndrome" has long been associated with chronic marijuana use: it compels users to "drop out" because of a loss of interest in goal-oriented endeavors. The etiology of this syndrome is unclear, although Musty and Kaback (1995) reported that between 40 and 50 percent of adolescents admitted to a treatment program were found to have depressive symptoms at admission (indicating comorbidity of substance abuse with depression). They concluded that the amotivational symptoms observed in heavy marijuana users in treatment are due to depression and that a causal relationship does not exist between marijuana smoking and these behavioral characteristics.

The major acute side effects associated with marijuana use are dose-related extensions of its recreational uses: sedation, altered motor coordination, impaired cognition, and reduced short-term memory. Marijuana impairs a person's ability to drive an automobile safely, much as alcohol does. With marijuana intoxication, however, impairment can persist well beyond the time of actually feeling impaired. This is perhaps due to the presence of the active metabolite 11-hydroxy-delta-9-THC. Unperceived impairment can persist for several hours.

Cardiovascular System

Marked increases in heart rate and mild increases in blood pressure are two commonly observed physiological effects of THC. During periods of intoxication, the combined effect can increase the workload (increasing oxygen requirements) of the heart and simultaneously reduce blood flow to the heart muscle. Ischemia of the heart can follow, perhaps similar to that seen during exercise. Although the increased heart rate could be a problem for people with cardiovascular disease, dangerous physical reactions to marijuana are almost unknown. There is no association of marijuana use with cardiovascular disease hospitalizations or mortality (Jones, 2002; Sidney, 2002). By extrapolation from animal experiments, the ratio of lethal to effective (intoxicating) dose is estimated to be on the order of thousands to one. Interestingly, peripheral cannabinoid-2 receptors in the heart function in an intrinsic defense of the heart against potentially fatal ischemic attacks (Bouchard et al., 2003). This protective effect of cannabinoids may eventually be an important therapeutic intervention in the prevention of heart attacks.

Blood vessels of the cornea can dilate, which results in bloodshot eyes that can be observed in someone who has just smoked marijuana. THC users frequently report increased appetite, dry mouth, occasional dizziness, and slight nausea. Respiratory depression is not observed.

Pulmonary System

The gaseous and particulate components of both marijuana and tobacco smoke provide some insights into the potential for marijuana to cause pulmonary damage. With the exception of the presence of THC in marijuana and nicotine in tobacco, both inhalants are remarkably similar; marijuana smoke contains more tars and many of the same carcinogenic compounds identified in tobacco smoke. A single marijuana cigarette may be more harmful than a single tobacco cigarette because more tar is inhaled and retained from marijuana. Also, THC can act as a tumor-promoting agent and molecular alterations of lung tissues can be demonstrated, showing evidence of bronchial irritation and inflammation. Tashkin and coworkers initially noted changes in heavy marijuana smokers consistent with tobacco-induced lung injury, although a 1997 study by the same researchers noted that tobacco smoking but not marijuana smoking is associated with a decline in lung function. Long-term follow-up studies have shown that marijuana use is not associated with increased rates of all cancers (including head and neck cancers) or smoking-related cancers (Hashibe et al., 2002).

Immune System

As noted earlier, cannabinoid-2 receptors are found primarily in the immune system. Long-term marijuana use is associated with a degree of immunosuppression, which might be thought to potentially render the smoker susceptible to infections or disease. Although data in this area are controversial and implications have not been proven, marijuana smoking, in some circumstances, may partially suppress immunity. The clinical significance of this occurrence is not known, but it should be noted that other depressant drugs, such as alcohol, barbiturates, benzodiazepines, and anticonvulsants, share this immunosuppressive action.

Because both the spleen and the lymphocytes (white blood cells) are important to the body's immune response, they have been investigated to determine how they are affected by cannabinoids. Zhu and coworkers (2000) reported that THC is capable of promoting tumor growth by inhibiting a specific mediator of cancer immunity, exerted via the cannabinoid-2 receptors. The implications of such actions and the physiological role of anandamide in immunomodulation are unknown. To put the immunosuppressive action of marijuana in perspective, in humans marijuana-induced immune suppression is subtle and in most cases insignificant. There is, at this time, little evidence for cannabinoid-induced immunosuppression as a causative agent in disease.

Reproductive System

Evidence of THC-induced suppression of sexual function and reproduction is controversial. The chronic use of marijuana by males can reduce levels of the hormone testosterone while reducing sperm formation. Reductions in male fertility and sexual potency, however, have not been reported. In females, the levels of follicle-stimulating hormone (FSH) and luteinizing hormone (LH) are reduced by the use of marijuana. Menstrual cycles can be affected and anovulatory cycles have been reported. All these actions reverse when drug use is discontinued. In animals, anandamide can decreases female sex hormone levels and is postulated to be a central neuromodulator of reproduction (Wenger et al., 1999).

Marijuana freely crosses the placenta, so its use probably should be avoided during pregnancy. However, estimated prevalence rates of cannabis use during pregnancy range from 3 percent to more than 20 percent of pregnant women (Little et al., 1998). To date, the only medical risk reasonably ascribed to marijuana use during pregnancy appears to be mild fetal growth retardation and maternal lung damage (both similar to that seen with tobacco smoking).

One of the greatest risks appears to be the high probability that a pregnant female who smokes marijuana during pregnancy may also use other, more fetotoxic drugs (including nicotine cigarettes). Infants born of marijuana-smoking mothers display mild withdrawal signs, including tremulousness and abnormal responses to stimuli. These signs appear to be transient in nature.

Important evaluations of the long-term effects of prenatal marijuana exposure on child development have been reported by Fried (2002a, 2002b) and by Cornelius and coworkers (2002). Prenatal marijuana use resulted in somewhat shorter stature in offspring; IQ was about the same; basic visuoperceptual skills were about the same. However, problem solving involving visual interpretations and analytical skills was adversely affected. Marijuana exposure in utero had modestly adverse effects on executive functioning in offspring at ages 9 to 12 years. Maternal nicotine cigarette smoking contributed to more problems in offspring than did exposure to marijuana smoke. Richardson and coworkers (2002) noted that at age 10 years, children whose mothers smoked marijuana during pregnancy were significantly impaired in measurements of learning, memory, and impulsivity.

Mereu and coworkers (2003), in a series of studies in rats exposed prenatally to a cannabinoid agonist, noted that offspring showed increased behavioral activity and decreased memory functioning. These same offspring also had lower levels of hippocampal glutamate than did control rats (those not exposed to the cannabinoid agonist in utero). These effects on memory and glutamate occurred in the absence of any external evidence of birth defects. These data strongly argue against the use of marijuana during pregnancy.

Tolerance and Dependence

Tolerance to *Cannabis sativa* does occur, and it appears to result from two separate mechanisms. The first involves a cannabinoid-induced down regulation and desensitization of brain cannabinoid receptors (Breivogel et al., 1999). The second is more complicated and involves a rapid receptor internalization following agonist binding and receptor activation (Hsieh et al., 1999). Potent synthetic cannabinoid agonists cause rapid internalization; THC causes little, if any. Thus, with the weak agonist THC, down regulation is the primary mechanism of tolerance and withdrawal of THC results in rapid normalization of receptor responsiveness.

Until recently, it was generally thought that physical dependence on THC probably did not develop, and if it did, any symptoms were mild and transient. Today, a more extensive literature has developed that more clearly defines a *marijuana withdrawal syndrome* that, by definition, implies that body functioning is altered by marijuana use and that uncomfortable symptoms occur when the drug is withdrawn (Budney et al., 2001; Kouri and Pope, 2000; Lichtman and Martin, 2002; Smith, 2002). The withdrawal symptoms, however, are generally thought not to be so severe as to call marijuana (or THC) capable of causing "addiction" or a state of strong physical dependence. People seldom use the drug to avoid withdrawal.

Withdrawal symptoms consist of craving for marijuana, restlessness, irritability, agitation, anxiety, depressed mood, reduced food intake, insomnia, sleep disturbances, nausea, and cramping. Aggression, anger, irritability, restlessness, and strange dreams can sometimes be observed, but these symptoms are not always present. Withdrawal symptoms occur in over 50 percent of regular users who discontinue the drug. Symptoms begin within 48 hours after cessation of drug administration and last at least 2 days, more usually about 7 to 10 days and perhaps longer, as EEG changes associated with withdrawal persist for at least 28 days (Herning et al., 2003). Budney and coworkers (2001) conclude that these withdrawal effects appear similar in type and magnitude to those observed in studies of nicotine withdrawal. In treating people who smoke marijuana, significant withdrawal symptoms should be identified and intervention provided as required, including brief admission, extended care, and/or pharmacotherapy, if necessary. Haney and coworkers (2003b) reported that nefazadone (Remeron; Chapter 9), an antidepressant drug with prominent sedative properties, did not alter the acute subjective effects associated with marijuana smoking. During withdrawal, nefazadone decreased ratings of anxiety and muscle pain but had no effect on ratings of irritability and general discomfort (feelings of being "miserable"). Thus, nefazadone relieved certain discomforts associated with marijuana withdrawal, but individuals still reported substantial discomfort.

Brook and coworkers (1999) conducted a five-year study of 1182 youths of African American and Puerto Rican ancestry in East Harlem, New York, with marijuana use (used at least monthly) as the only independent variable. An increase in marijuana use was associated with a reduced likelihood of graduating from high school, with delinquency, with a tripling of the risk of self-deviancy, and with an increase in the risk of multiple other problem behaviors. While marijuana smoking in early adolescence is correlated or associated with later educational, job, and psychosocial problems, no causal inferences can be drawn. Marijuana use may indeed predispose one to future problems, or it may merely be one of many factors incorporated into the life of adolescents who choose one pathway versus another. The cognitive effects of THC, however, would, at a minimum, interfere with academic success. In any case, no one of reasonable mind advocates the availability of marijuana to minors.

DeWit and coworkers (2000) studied 2729 lifetime marijuana users as part of the larger Ontario Mental Health Supplement program. Early and frequent use was associated with highly persistent use and rapid progression to marijuana-related harm. There was a level of use (100 to 200 times) associated with the elevated risk. Females had a lower threshold for risk (50 to 100 times). They concluded: "Required are preventive programs aimed at delaying the onset of first use as well as harm reduction strategies that encourage cessation or reduced levels of consumption among those already using" (p. 455). However society moves toward or away from marijuana availability for medical or recreational use, availability to youth must be restricted.

Until recently, few treatment programs were oriented solely toward marijuana abuse, as both multidrug dependence and comorbid disease are invariably present. Perhaps the recent recognition of a distinct marijuana withdrawal syndrome may draw more attention to the need for specific programs. Historically, treatments such as psychotherapy can be appropriate for frequent users of marijuana, but the therapy is not for marijuana abuse but for an underlying psychopathology (such as depression; Bovasso, 2001), one symptom of which is the abuse of cannabis. Grinspoon and Bakalar (1997) wrote:

> Being attached to cannabis is not so much a function of any inherent psychopharmacologic property of the drug as it is emotionally driven by the underlying psychopathology. Success in curtailing cannabis use requires dealing with that pathology. (p. 204)

Diamond and coworkers (2002), Stephens and coworkers (2002), and French and coworkers (2002) described treatment models for marijuana dependence in adolescents. Models included motivational enhancement therapy, cognitive-behavioral therapy, community reinforcement approaches, and multidimensional family therapy. Most were effective, although adolescents with higher levels of externalizing disorders and internalizing disorders continued to experience more substance abuse problems. Following treatment, relapses are common and to be expected (Moore and Budney, 2003).

Therapeutic Uses

The medical applications of marijuana have long been a focus of public and scientific interest, but until recently there was little scientific basis for establishing medical uses. This situation is now changing. Currently, there is one approved medical use and a basis established for additional medical uses for marijuana and its active ingredient THC. Additionally, cannabinoid *antagonists* (such as rimonabant) have been shown to have important medical actions (remember, THC is a cannabinoid *agonist*).

Dronabinol (Marinol), which is synthetic THC formulated in sesame oil, has been available for more than 10 years for use as an appetite stimulant in patients with AIDS and for use in the treatment of nausea and vomiting associated with chemotherapy in cancer patients. In 1997, Schwartz and coworkers reviewed the use of smoked marijuana and oral dronabinol in this population of patients and compared the THC-containing products with physician-prescribed antiemetic compounds. Traditional antiemetics fared better than did THC in treating chemotherapy-induced nausea and vomiting. Bagshaw (2002) reviewed more recent literature in this area and concluded that while cannabinoids have modest antiemetic properties, oral cannabinoids would not be recommended as first-line antiemetics. Cannabinoids may only prove effective for refractory nausea or as an adjunct to other antiemetics. Smoked marijuana was not superior to orally administered drug.

Cannabinoids have very specific analgesic properties; analgesic actions have been best described in animal studies. The same animal studies also demonstrate that our endogenous cannabinoid systems have a role in the normal day-to-day modulation of pain (Hohmann et al., 2004). For example, Farquhar-Smith and Rice (2001) demonstrated that anandamide reduces pain associated with inflammation of the bladder (suggesting a clinical use of THC in treated interstitial cystitis—painful irritation of the bladder—as well as in other types of visceral pain—pain originating from internal organs). It appears that neuronal cell bodies that produce anandamide reside in the dorsal root ganglion (which lies outside the spinal canal). The gene encoding the production of anandamide resides in the nucleus of the cell and stimulates production of the anandamide, which then travels by axoplasmic flow both to the bladder (a peripheral site of action) and to the dorsal horn of the spinal cord (exerting a central analgesic action). Cannabinoid receptors can be found both in the bladder and in the spinal cord. Gardell and coworkers (2002) and Clayton and coworkers (2002) note that the spinal analgesic action of cannabinoids is exerted through action on its own cannabinoid receptors rather than indirectly through actions on opioid receptors. Furthermore, the cannabinoid-analgesic system is tonically active as a modulator of pain. This modulating effect on pain is also discussed by Lever and Malcangio (2002), Walker and coworkers (2001), and Pertwee (2001). Cannabinoid agonists, like THC, will probably have an important role in modulating visceral and inflammatory pain, providing analgesia, and reducing the necessary quantities of opioids in the control of severe pain. Quartilho and coworkers (2003) note that an experimental cannabinoid-2 receptor agonist (AM1241) exerted a peripheral anti-inflammatory effect in the absence of CNS actions. Therefore, nonpsychedelic analgesic cannabinoid is possible. These results will certainly lead to exciting new concepts in the treatment of pain.

Another claimed use of dronabinol is reduction of the muscle spasms and pain of multiple sclerosis. Cannabis has long been noted to suppress certain symptoms of multiple sclerosis, including pain, spasticity, tremor, and nocturia (Pertwee, 2003). Animal studies verify these clinical results and impressions, but Killestein and coworkers (2004), after reviewing available data, concluded: "Convincing evidence that cannabinoids are effective in multiple sclerosis is still lacking" (p. 267).

THC has long been known to increase appetite in patients with AIDS-related wasting disease (Croxford, 2003). Cannabinoids do stimulate appetite, especially for sweet and palatable foods (Cota et al., 2003). In fact, one physiological role of the endogenous cannabinoid system is to maintain the stimulus of appetite; a role of endocannabinoids in obesity can be postulated in reward processes contributing to the normal control of appetite (Kirkham and Williams, 2001).

Preliminary evidence has been accumulated that cannabinoids and anandamide have neuroprotective effects following brain injury

(Mechoulam et al., 2002). Cannabinoid agonists (like THC) inhibit glutaminergic transmission and reduce reactive oxygen intermediates, which are factors in causing neuronal injury after head injury. One experimental cannabinoid, HU211, is undergoing trials as a protective agent after head trauma (Williamson and Evans, 2000).

Cannabinoids have long been reported to reduce intraoccular pressure and therefore might be clinically useful in the treatment of glaucoma. Results are inconclusive, however, and clinical utility is probably minimal and limited by the side effects discussed earlier in this chapter.

Historical use and anecdotal reports indicate that marijuana might have use as symptomatic and prophylactic therapy for migraine. To date, no randomized clinical trials have been conducted to scientifically study this claim (Bagshaw, 2002). Nevertheless, self-medication for this use probably will continue.

Cannabinoids can be shown in animals to have antiepileptic effects. This action should not be unexpected from a drug that increases GABA and inhibits glutamate activity. A few case reports indicate that antiepileptic action might occur in humans (Bagshaw, 2002).

Antidepressant effects have been claimed of marijuana. Also, claims of use in treating intractable hiccups have appeared. However, there is little or no scientific evidence to justify these uses (at least at present). The acute intoxicant effects of marijuana may contribute to a perception of effects. The relatively short duration of effect of THC also would lead to either rapid loss of effect or else a need to continue use. CNS side effects including altered perception, forgetfulness, impaired psychomotor skills, and reduced reaction times also limit clinical utility in cases where efficacy is difficult to demonstrate (Sharpe, 2000).

Cannabinoid Antagonists

As discussed, activation of cannabinoid receptors underlies the psychological effects of THC and other cannabinoid agonists. Huestis and coworkers (2001) demonstrated for the first time in humans that a specific *antagonist* for cannabinoid receptors would produce a dose-dependent blockade of marijuana-induced intoxication and tachycardia (Figure 18.9). This led to speculation about potential clinical uses of cannabinoid antagonists (D'Souza and Kosten, 2001). Such drugs might be used to reverse cannabinoid intoxication in people who experience unpleasant reactions to marijuana (for example, panic and psychosis), similar to the use of parenteral naloxone to reverse the effects of opioids (Chapter 15). This use, however, would probably be infrequent and often unpleasant as it would precipitate a

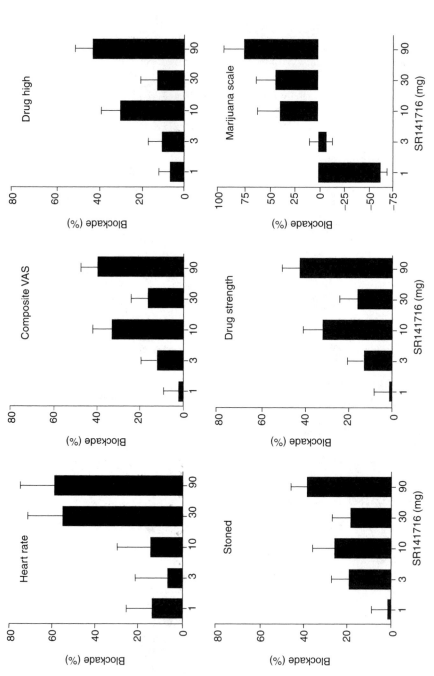

FIGURE 18.9 Percent blockade of peak marijuana effects produced by single oral doses of 1 mg, 3 mg, 10 mg, 30 mg, or 90 mg of the cannabinoid antagonist SR141716A. VAS indicates visual analog scale. Asterisk = percent blockade of marijuana effects by 90 mg SR141716A compared with placebo SR141716A (placebo response not illustrated; means and standard deviations shown). [From Huestis et al. (2001), p. 326.]

cannabinoid withdrawal syndrome. Antagonists, however, might be useful in individuals who wish to stop using marijuana, blocking any positive effects should marijuana be used, analogous to the use of oral naltrexone to prevent the effects of subsequently taken opioids (Chapter 15).

Because cannabinoid receptor activation also reduces learning, reduces memory formation, and enhances food intake, other potential uses of cannabinoid antagonists might include enhancement of learning and memory (as in the early stages of dementia) and the treatment of obesity. In addition, cannabinoid receptors and opioid receptors are intimately related and overlap in function. Also, cannabinoid receptors have been implicated in opioid-induced reward, suggesting a possible role of cannabinoid antagonists in the treatment of addiction to opioids and perhaps psychostimulants (such as cocaine).

As discussed, THC stimulates appetite, especially for sweet and palatable food (Cota et al., 2003). Therefore, cannabinoid antagonists might be used in the therapy of obesity and other eating disorders by inhibiting the reward processes that contribute to the normal control of appetite (Kirkham and Williams, 2001). In animal studies, cannabinoid antagonists lead to maintenance of weight loss as long as the drug is given; withdrawal leads to increased feeding and significant weight gain (Vickers et al., 2003). Therefore, chronically taken, these receptor antagonists are effective, although the effect disappears when the drug is withdrawn (as are the effects of most drugs for their intended uses). Currently, rimonabant, the cannabinoid antagonist SR141716, is under intense investigation as an antiobesity agent. Probably to be marketed under the trade name Acomplia, rimonabant is expected to become available clinically in 2005. Rimonabant is claimed to help people drop 20 pounds in a year and to double a smoker's success at quitting cigarettes. It will probably also be used in efforts to help drug- and alcohol-dependent people maintain abstinence by reducing the positive reinforcing effects of drug and alcohol use.

Acute intoxication with THC leads to dose-dependent alterations in learning and memory formation, and these deficits are reversible by cannabinoid antagonists (Da and Takahashi, 2002). Therefore, cannabinoid antagonists might be useful in the treatment of learning and memory disorders. Much remains to be done in this area.

Cannabinoid antagonists block the psychological effects of smoked marijuana and block the rewarding effects of food (both discussed earlier). The overlap between cannabinoid and opioid receptors, their structural similarity, and the antireward actions of both cannabinoid and opioid antagonists suggest roles for cannabinoid antagonists in the treatment of drug craving by blocking the positive rewarding effects of such drugs as alcohol (Wang et al., 2003), opioids (Navarro et al., 2001; Solinas et al., 2003), nicotine

(Cohen et al., 2002), and psychostimulants, such as cocaine (DeVries et al., 2001). Rimonabant may soon become one of the premier pharmacological treatments for the treatment of drug and alcohol dependence/relapse.

STUDY QUESTIONS

1. How are the effects of THC similar to those of the nonselective depressants? How are they dissimilar?

2. How are the effects of THC similar to those of the psychedelic drugs? How are they dissimilar?

3. How does the half-life of THC reflect a person's ability to become intoxicated more easily and with a smaller amount of drug after its repeated use?

4. Discuss some of the concerns and side effects that are associated with varying degrees of THC use by young people.

5. What does THC do to cognition?

6. Are there any long-term effects of marijuana on the brain? The body? Society?

7. Are there any potential long-term effects that might be associated with chronic use of marijuana?

8. Does dependence on marijuana develop? Discuss both views.

9. Discuss the cannabinoid receptor, its location, and its endogenous neurotransmitter.

10. How might a treatment program be organized for persons who become dependent on marijuana?

11. What do you think society's response should be to the continued illicit use of marijuana? Should marijuana be legalized for either medical or recreational use? If so, how should it be regulated or restricted?

12. Discuss evidence for or against medical uses of marijuana. If it has medical uses, how might efficacy and societal acceptance be improved?

13. How do you see the future of marijuana and cannabinoid research?

14. What are some of the potential therapeutic uses of cannaboid agonists? Antagonists?

REFERENCES

Ameri, A., et al. (1999). "Effects of the Endogenous Cannabinoid, Anandamide, on Neuronal Activity in Rat Hippocampal Slices." *British Journal of Pharmacology* 126: 1831–1839.

Bagshaw, S. M. (2002). "Medical Efficacy of Cannabinoids and Marijuana: A Comprehensive Review of the Literature." *Journal of Palliative Care* 18: 111–122.

Block, R. I., et al. (2002). "Effects of Frequent Marijuana Use on Memory-Related Cerebral Blood Flow." *Pharmacology, Biochemistry and Behavior* 72: 237–250.

Bolla, K. I., et al. (2002). "Dose-Related Neurocognitive Effects of Marijuana Use." *Neurology* 59: 1337–1343.

Bouchard, J. F., et al. (2003). "Contribution of Endocannabinoids in the Endothelial Protection Afforded by Ischemic Preconditioning in the Isolated Rat Heart." *Life Sciences* 72: 1859–1870.

Bovasso, G. B. (2001). "Cannabis Abuse as a Risk Factor for Depressive Symptoms." *American Journal of Psychiatry* 158: 2033–2037.

Breivogel, C. S., et al. (1999). "Chronic Delta-9-Tetrahydrocannabinol Treatment Produces a Time-Dependent Loss of Cannabinoid Receptors and Cannabinoid Receptor-Activated G-Proteins in Rat Brain." *Journal of Neurochemistry* 73: 2447–2459.

Brook, J., et al. (1999). "The Risks for Late Adolescence of Early Adolescence Marijuana Use." *American Journal of Public Health* 89: 1549–1554.

Brook, J. S., et al. (2003). "Earlier Marijuana Use and Later Problem Behaviors in Colombian Youths." *Journal of the American Academy of Child and Adolescent Psychiatry* 42: 485–492.

Budney, A. J., et al. (2001). "Marijuana Abstinence Effects in Marijuana Smokers Maintained in Their Home Environment." *Archives of General Psychiatry* 58: 917–924.

Childers, S. R., and C. S. Breivogel (1998). "Cannabis and Endogenous Cannabinoid Systems." *Drug and Alcohol Dependence* 51: 173–187.

Clayton, N., et al. (2002). "CB1 And CB2 Cannabinoid Receptors Are Implicated in Inflammatory Pain." *Pain* 96: 253–260.

Cohen, C., et al. (2002). "SR141716, a Central Cannabinoid (CB91) Receptor Antagonist Blocks the Motivational and Dopamine-Releasing Effects of Nicotine in Rats." *Behavioral Pharmacology* 13: 451–463.

Cornelius, M. D., et al. (2002). "Alcohol, Tobacco, and Marijuana Use Among Pregnant Teenagers: 6-year Follow-Up of Offspring Growth Effects." *Neurotoxicology and Teratology* 24: 703–710.

Cota, D., et al. (2003). "Endogenous Cannabinoid System as a Modulator of Food Intake." *International Journal of Obesity and Related Metabolic Disorders: Journal of the International Association for the Study of Obesity* 27: 289–301.

Croxford, J. L. (2003). "Therapeutic Potential of Cannabinoids in CNS Disease." *CNS Drugs* 17: 179–202.

Da, S., and R. N. Takahashi (2002). "SR 141716A Prevents Delta 9-Tetrahydrocannabinol-Induced Spatial Learning Deficit in a Morris-Type Water Maze in Mice." *Progress in Neurophychopharmacology and Biological Psychiatry* 26: 321–325.

Devane, W. A., et al. (1992). "Isolation and Structure of a Brain Constituent That Binds to the Cannabinoid Receptor." *Science* 258: 1946–1949.

DeVries, T. J., et al. (2001). "A Cannabinoid Mechanism in Relapse to Cocaine Seeking." *Nature's Medicine* 7: 1151–1154.

DeWit, D. J., et al. (2000). "The Influence of Early and Frequent Use of Marijuana on the Risk of Desistance and of Progression to Marijuana-Related Harm." *Preventive Medicine* 31: 455–464.

Diamond, G., et al. (2002). "Five Outpatient Treatment Models for Adolescent Marijuana Use: A Description of the Cannabis Youth Treatment Interventions." *Addiction* 97, Supplement 1: 70–83.

Diana, M., et al. (1998). "Mesolimbic Dopaminergic Decline After Cannabinoid Withdrawal." *Proceedings of the National Academy of Sciences of the United States of America* 95: 10269–10273.

D'Souza, D. C., and T. R. Kosten (2001). "Cannabinoid Antagonists: A Treatment in Search of an Illness." *Archives of General Psychiatry* 58: 330–331.

Farquhar-Smith, W. P., and S. Rice. (2001). "Administration of Endocannabinoids Prevents a Referred Hyperalgesia Associated with Inflammation of the Urinary Bladder." *Anesthesiology* 94: 507–513.

Farquhar-Smith, W. P., and A. S. C. Rice (2003). "A Novel Neuroimmune Mechanism in Cannabinoid-Mediated Attenuation of Nerve Growth Factor-Induced Hyperalgesia." *Anesthesiology* 99: 1391–1401.

Felder, C. C., and M. Glass (1998). "Cannabinoid Receptors and Their Endogenous Agonists." *Annual Review of Pharmacology and Toxicology* 38: 179–200.

French, M. T., et al. (2002). "The Economic Cost of Outpatient Marijuana Treatment for Adolescents: Findings from a Multi-Site Field Experiment." *Addiction* 97, Supplement 1: 84–97.

Fried, P. A. (2002a). "Adolescents Prenatally Exposed to Marijuana: Examination of Facets of Complex Behaviors and Comparisons with the Influence of *In Utero* Cigarettes." *Journal of Clinical Pharmacology* 42, Supplement 11: 97S–102S.

Fried, P. A. (2002b). "Conceptual Issues in Behavioral Teratology and Their Application in Determining Long-Term Sequelae of Prenatal Marijuana Exposure." *Journal of Child Psychology and Psychiatry and Related Disciplines* 43 (2002): 81–102.

Fried, P., et al. (2002). "Current and Former Marijuana Use: Preliminary Findings of a Longitudinal Study of Effects on IQ in Young Adults." *Canadian Medical Association Journal* 166: 887–891.

Gardell, L. R., et al. (2002). "Dynorphin-Independent Spinal Cannabinoid Antinociception." *Pain* 100: 243–248.

Gardner, E. L., and J. H. Lowinson (1991). "Marijuana's Interaction with Brain Reward Systems: Update 1991." *Pharmacology, Biochemistry, and Behavior* 40: 571–580.

Grinspoon, L., and J. B. Bakalar (1997). "Marijuana." In J. H. Lowinson, P. Ruiz, R. B. Millman, and J. G. Langrod, eds., *Substance Abuse: A Comprehensive Textbook*, 3rd ed. (pp. 199–206). Baltimore: Williams & Wilkins.

Hampson, R. E., and S. A. Deadwyler (1999). "Cannabinoids, Hippocampal Function and Memory." *Life Sciences* 65: 715–723.

Haney, M., et al. (2003a). "Interaction Between Naltrexone and Oral THC in Heavy Marijuana Smokers." *Psychopharmacology* 166: 77–85.

Haney, M., et al. (2003b). "Nefazodone Decreases Anxiety During Marijuana Withdrawal in Humans." *Psychopharmacology* 165: 157–165.

Hart, C. L., et al. (2001). "Effects of Acute Smoked Marijuana on Complex Cognitive Performance." *Neuropsychopharmacology* 25: 757–765.

Hashibe, M., et al. (2002). "Marijuana Smoking and Head and Neck Cancer." *Journal of Clinical Pharmacology* 42, Supplement 11: 103S–107S.

Herning, R. I., et al. (2003). "EEG Deficits in Chronic Marijuana Abusers During Monitored Abstinence: Preliminary Findings." *Annals of the New York Academy of Sciences* 993: 75–79.

Hohmann, A. G., and M. Herkenham (1999a). "Cannabinoid Receptors Undergo Axonal Flow in Sensory Nerves." *Neuroscience* 92: 1171–1175.

Hohmann, A. G., and M. Herkenham (1999b). "Localization of Central Cannabinoid CB1 Receptor Messenger RNA in Neuronal Subpopulations of Rat Dorsal Root Ganglia: A Double-Label In Situ Hybridization Study." *Neuroscience* 90: 923–931.

Hohmann, A. G., et al. (2004). "Selective Activation of Cannabinoid CB2 Receptors Suppresses Hyperalgesia Evoked by Intradermal Capsaicin." *Journal of Pharmacology and Experimental Therapeutics* 308: 446–453.

Hsieh, C., et al. (1999). "Internalization and Recycling of the CB1 Cannabinoid Receptor." *Journal of Neurochemistry* 73: 493–501

Huestis, M. A., and E. J. Cone (1998). "Urinary Excretion Half-Life of 11-Nor-9-Carboxy-Delta9-Tetrahydrocannabinol in Humans." *Therapeutic Drug Monitoring* 20: 570–576.

Huestis, M. A., et al. (2001). "Blockade of Effects of Smoked Marijuana by the CB1-Selective Cannabinoid Receptor Antagonist SR141716." *Archives of General Psychiatry* 58: 322–328.

Iversen, L. (2003). "Cannabis and the Brain." *Brain* 126: 1252–1270.

Jones, R. T. (2002). "Cardiovascular System Effects of Marijuana." *Journal of Clinical Pharmacology* 42, Supplement 11 (November): 58S–63S.

Killestein, J., et al. (2004). "Cannabinoids in Multiple Sclerosis: Do They Have a Therapeutic Role?" *Drugs* 64: 1–11.

Kirkham, T. C., and C. M. Williams (2001). "Synergistic Effects of Opioid and Cannabinoid Antagonists on Food Intake." *Psychopharmacology* 153: 267–270.

Kouri, E. M., and H. G. Pope, Jr. (2000). "Abstinence Symptoms During Withdrawal from Chronic Marijuana Use." *Experimental and Clinical Psychopharmacology* 8: 483–492.

Kouri, E., et al. (1995). "Attributes of Heavy Versus Occasional Marijuana Smokers in a College Population." *Biological Psychiatry* 38: 475–481.

Ledent, C., et al. (1999). "Unresponsiveness to Cannabinoids and Reduced Addictive Effects of Opiates in CB_1 Receptor Knockout Mice." *Science* 283: 401–403.

Lever, I. J., and M. Malcangio (2002). "CB (1) Receptor Antagonist SR141716A Increases Capsaicin-Evoked Release of Substance P from the Adult Mouse Spinal Cord." *British Journal of Pharmacology* 135: 21–24.

Lichtman, A. H., and B. R. Martin (2002). "Marijuana Withdrawal Syndrome in the Animal Model." *Journal of Clinical Pharmacology* 42, Supplement 11: 20S–27S.

Little, B. B., et al. (1998). "Cannabinoid Use During Pregnancy." In L. C. Gilstrap and B. B. Little, eds., *Drugs and Pregnancy,* 2nd ed. (pp. 413–417). New York: Chapman & Hall.

Lynn, A. B., and M. Herkenham (1994). "Localization of Cannabinoid Receptors and Nonsaturable High-Density Cannabinoid Binding Sites in Peripheral Tissues of the Rat: Implications for Receptor-Mediated Immune Modulation by Cannabinoids." *Journal of Pharmacology and Experimental Therapeutics* 268: 1612–1623.

Mallet, P. E., and R. J. Beninger (1998). "The Cannabinoid CB1 Receptor Antagonist SR141716A Attenuates the Memory Impairment Produced by Delta-9-Tetrahydrocannabinol or Anandamide." *Psychopharmacology* 140: 11–19.

Manzanares, J., et al. (1999). "Pharmacological and Biochemical Interactions Between Opioids and Cannabinoids." *Trends in Pharmacological Sciences* 20: 287–294.

Mechoulam, R., et al. (2002). "Cannabinoids and Brain Injury: Therapeutic Implications." *Trends in Molecular Medicine* 8: 58–61.

Mereu, G., et al. (2003). "Prenatal Exposure to a Cannabinoid Agonist Produced Memory Deficits Linked to Dysfunction in Hippocampal Long-Term Potentiation and Glutamate Release." *Proceedings of the National Academy of Sciences of the United States of America* 100: 4915–4920.

Moore, B. A., and A. J. Budney (2003). "Relapse in Outpatient Treatment for Marijuana Dependence." *Journal of Substance Abuse Treatment* 25: 85–89.

Musty, R. E., and L. Kaback (1995). "Relationships Between Motivation and Depression in Chronic Marijuana Users." *Life Sciences* 56: 2151–2158.

Navarro, M., et al. (2001). "Functional Interaction Between Opioid and Cannabinoid Receptors in Drug Self-Administration." *Journal of Neuroscience* 21: 5344–5350.

Ohno-Shosaku, T., et al. (2001). "Endogenous Cannabinoids Mediate Retrograde Signals from Depolarized Postsynaptic Neurons to Presynaptic Terminals." *Neuron* 29: 729–738.

Ohno-Shosaku, T., et al. (2002). "Cooperative Endocannabinoid Production by Neuronal Depolarization and Group I Metabotropic Glutamate Receptor Activation." *European Journal of Neuroscience* 15: 953–961.

O'Leary, D. S., et al. (2002). "Effects of Smoking Marijuana on Brain Perfusion and Cognition." *Neuropsychopharmacology* 26: 802–816.

Ong, W. Y., and K. Mackie (1999). "A Light and Electron Microscopic Study of the CB1 Cannabinoid Receptor in Primate Brain." *Neuroscience* 92: 1177–1191.

Pertwee, R. G. (2001). "Cannabinoid Receptors and Pain." *Progress in Neurobiology* 63: 569–611.

Pertwee, R. G. (2003). "Cannabinoids and Multiple Sclerosis." *Pharmacology and Therapeutics* 95: 165–174.

Pope, H. C., et al. (2001). "Neuropsychological Performance in Long-Term Cannabis Users." *Archives of General Psychiatry* 58: 909–915.

Quartilho, A., et al. (2003). "Inhibition of Inflammatory Hyperalgesia by Activation of Peripheral CB2 Cannabinoid Receptors." *Anesthesiology* 99: 955–960.

Rice, A. S. C., et al. (2002). "Endocannabinoids and Pain: Spinal and Peripheral Analgesia in Inflammation and Neuropathy." *Prostaglandins, Leukotrienes and Essential Fatty Acids* 66: 243–256.

Richardson, G. A., et al. (2002). "Prenatal Alcohol and Marijuana Exposure: Effects on Neuropsychological Outcomes at 10 Years." *Neurotoxicology and Teratology* 24: 309–320.

Schwartz, R. H., et al. (1997). "Marijuana to Prevent Nausea and Vomiting in Cancer Patients: A Survey of Clinical Oncologists." *Southern Medical Journal* 90: 167–172.

Sharpe, P. (2000). "Cannabis: Time for Scientific Evaluation of this Ancient Remedy?" *Anesthesia and Analgesia* 90: 237–240.

Shen, M., and S. A. Thayer (1999). "Delta9-Tetrahydrocannabinol Acts as a Partial Agonist to Modulate Glutamatergic Synaptic Transmission Between Rat Hippocampal Neurons in Culture." *Molecular Pharmacology* 55: 8–13.

Sidney, S. (2002). "Cardiovascular Consequences of Marijuana Use." *Journal of Clinical Pharmacology* 42, Supplement 11: 64S–70S.

Smith, F. L., et al. (1998). "The Enhancement of Morphine Antinociception in Mice by Delta9-Tetrahydrocannabinol." *Pharmacology, Biochemistry, and Behavior* 60: 559–566.

Smith, N. T. (2002). "A Review of the Published Literature into Cannabis Withdrawal Symptoms in Human Users." *Addiction* 97: 621–632.

Solinas, M., et al. (2003). "The Cannabinoid CB1 Antagonist SR-141716A Differentially Alters the Reinforcing Effects of Heroin Under Continuous-Reinforcement, Fixed-Ratio and Progressive-Ratio Schedules of Drug Self-Administration in Rats." *Journal of Pharmacology and Experimental Therapeutics* 306: 93–102.

Solowij, N. (1995). "Do Cognitive Impairments Recover Following Cessation of Cannabis Use?" *Life Sciences* 56: 2119–2126.

Stephens, R. S., et al. (2002). "The Marijuana Treatment Project: Rationale, Design and Participant Characteristics." *Addiction* 97, Supplement 1: 109–124.

Tanda, G., et al. (1997). "Cannabinoid and Heroin Activation of Mesolimbic Dopamine Transmission by a Common Mu Opioid Receptor Mechanism." *Science* 276: 2048–2054.

Tashkin, D. P., et al. (1997). "Heavy Habitual Marijuana Smoking Does Not Cause an Accelerated Decline in FEV_1 with Age." *American Journal of Respiratory and Critical Care Medicine* 155: 141–148.

Thomas, B. F., et al. (1996). "Structure-Activity Analysis of Anandamide Analogs: Relationship to a Cannabinoid Pharmacophore." *Journal of Medicinal Chemistry* 39: 471–479.

Vickers, S. P., et al. (2003). "Preferential Effects of the Cannabinoid CB (1) Receptor Antagonist SR 141716 on Food Intake and Body Weight Gain of Obese (fa/fa) Compared to Lean Zucker Rats." *Psychopharmacology* 167: 103–111.

Wachtel, S. R., et al. (2002). "Comparison of the Subjective Effects of Delta(9)-Tetrahydrocannabinol and Marijuana in Humans." *Psychopharmacology* 161: 331–339.

Walker, J. M., et al. (2001). "Cannabinoids and Pain." *Pain Research and Management* 6: 74–79.

Wang, L., et al. (2003). "Endocannabinoid Signaling via Cannabinoid Receptor 1 Is Involved in Ethanol Preference and Its Age-Dependent Decline in Mice." *Proceedings of the National Academy of Sciences of the United States of America* 100: 1393–1398.

Watson, S. J., et al. (2000). "Marijuana and Medicine: Assessing the Scientific Base: A Summary of the 1999 Institute of Medicine Report." *Archives of General Psychiatry* 57: 547–552.

Wenger, T., et al. (1999). "The Effects of Cannabinoids on the Regulation of Reproduction." *Life Sciences* 65: 695–701.

Williams, C. M., and T. C. Kirkham (1999). "Anandamide-Induced Overeating: Mediation by Central Cannabinoid (CB1) Receptors." *Psychopharmacology* 143: 315–317.

Williamson, E. M., and F. J. Evans (2000). "Cannabinoids in Clinical Practice." *Drugs* 60: 1303–1314.

Zhu, L. X., et al. (2000). "Delta-9-Tetrahydrocannabinol Inhibits Antitumor Immunity by a CB2 Receptor-Mediated, Cytokine-Dependent Pathway." *Journal of Immunology* 165: 373–380.

Zimmer, A., et al. (1999). "Increased Mortality, Hypoactivity, and Hypoalgesia in Cannabinoid CB1 Receptor Knockout Mice." *Proceedings of the National Academy of Sciences of the United States of America* 96: 5780–5785.

Chapter 19

Psychedelic Drugs: Mescaline, Ecstasy, LSD, and Other Hallucinogens

This chapter introduces a group of heterogeneous compounds that act on various neurotransmitters in the CNS to produce visual hallucinations and "out-of-body" experiences. As such, their actions are also charactereized by marked alterations in cortical functioning, including cognition, perception, and mood (Davis et al., 2002). Because of the wide range of psychological and physiological effects they produce, the single term that might best be used to classify these agents has long been debated. The term *hallucinogen* is used because these agents can, in high enough doses, induce hallucinations. However, that term is somewhat inappropriate because illusory phenomena and perceptual distortions are more common than are true hallucinations. The term *psychotomimetic* has also been used because of the alleged ability of these drugs to mimic psychoses or induce psychotic states. However, most of these drugs do not produce the same behavioral patterns that are observed in people who experience psychotic episodes. Others have used a descriptive term, such as *phantasticum* or *psychedelic*, to imply that these agents all have the ability to alter sensory perception. In this book the term *psychedelic* is used because it allows for more flexibility in grouping together a disparate array of effects into a quantifiable and recognizable syndrome.

Abraham and coworkers (1996) defined a psychedelic drug as "any agent that causes alterations in perception, cognition, and mood as its primary psychobiological actions in the presence of an otherwise clear sensorium" (p. 285). This definition separates the pure psychedelic drugs from other substances that can cause altered states of thinking and perception, such as *poisons* that affect the mind (not discussed in this book) and *deliriants* (such as ethyl alcohol) that produce clouding of consciousness and amnesia. This chapter covers both the true psychedelics and certain other abused deliriants (e.g., scopolamine, phencyclidine, and ketamine).

Many psychedelic agents occur in nature; others are synthetically produced. Naturally occurring psychedelic drugs have been inhaled, ingested, worshipped, and reviled since prehistory. Some may even be viewed as having magical or mystical properties. Prior to the 1960s, most Americans were barely aware of their existence. During the late 1960s and the 1970s, however, some people advocated their use to enhance perception, expand reality, promote personal awareness, and stimulate or induce comprehension of the spiritual or supernatural. These drugs heighten awareness of sensory input, often accompanied by both an enhanced sense of clarity and diminished control over what is experienced. Frequently, there is a feeling that one part of the self seems to be a passive observer, while another part of the self participates and receives the vivid and unusual sensory experiences. In this state, the slightest sensation may take on profound meaning. Today, many of these drugs, such as the "rave" drugs, are used not only for sensory expansion but also for an intoxicating effect.

Many psychedelic drugs structurally resemble one of four neurotransmitters: acetylcholine, two catecholamines (norepinephrine and dopamine), and serotonin. These structural similarities lead to three of the five classes for categorizing psychedelic drugs (Table 19.1): *anticholinergic, catecholaminelike,* and *serotoninlike.* The fourth and fifth classes of psychedelic drugs are the *glutaminergic NMDA receptor antagonists* (two psychedelic anesthetics as well as dextromethorphan) and the *opioid kappa receptor agonist* salvinorin A. The *deliriants*—for example, alcohol (Chapter 4), GHB (Chapter 5), kava (Chapter 16), and the inhalants of abuse (Chapter 4)—do not produce hallucinations or profound sensory distortion in doses below intoxicating doses; therefore they are not considered to be psychedelic drugs.

Anticholinergic Psychedelics: Scopolamine

Scopolamine, an acetylcholine receptor antagonist, is the classic example of an anticholinergic psychedelic drug (Figure 19.1). Having receptor affinity but devoid of intrinsic activity, scopolamine blocks the access of acetylcholine to its receptors—hence the term *anticholinergic.* This term implies a constellation of effects, including dry mouth, blurred vision, increased heart rate, and urinary retention. If the anticholinergic drug

TABLE 19.1 Classification of psychedelic drugs

• ANTICHOLINERGIC PSYCHEDELIC DRUG
Scopolamine

• CATECHOLAMINELIKE PSYCHEDELIC DRUGS
Mescaline
DOM, MDA, DMA, MDMA (ecstasy), TMA, MDE
Myristin, elemicin

• SEROTONINLIKE PSYCHEDELIC DRUGS
Lysergic acid diethylamide (LSD)
Dimethyltryptamine (DMT)
Psilocybin, psilocin, bufotenine
Ololiuqui
Harmine

• GLUTAMINERGIC NMDA RECEPTOR ANTAGONISTS
Phencyclidine (Sernyl)
Ketamine (Ketalar)
Dextromethorphan

• OPIOID KAPPA RECEPTOR AGONIST
Salvinorin A

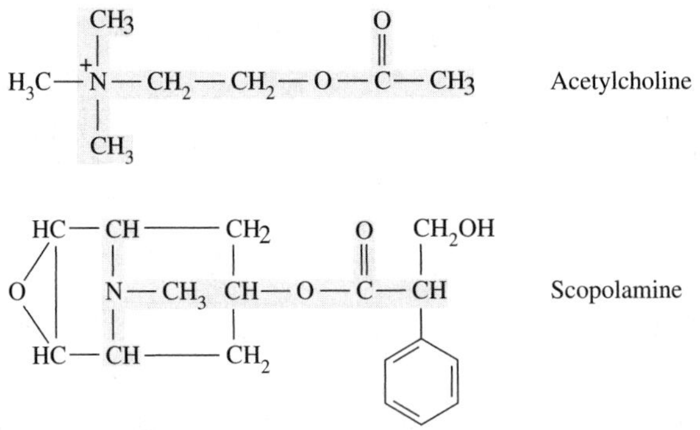

FIGURE 19.1 Structural formulas of acetylcholine (a chemical transmitter) and the anticholinergic psychedelic scopolamine, which acts by blocking acetylcholine receptors. The shaded portion of each molecule illustrates structural similarities, which presumably contribute to receptor fit.

crosses the blood-brain barrier and reaches the brain, it causes sedation, amnesia, and delirium. Medically, scopolamine is found in some travel-sickness products including motion-sickness skin patches. Besides scopolamine, another deliriant anticholinergic is *guaifenesin*, a secretion-drying agent found in many cough and cold syrups (Wogoman et al., 1999). Abuse of guaifenesin is occasionally encountered, especially as guaifenesin is found in products frequently also containing dextromethorphan (discussed at the end of this chapter).

Historical Background

The history of scopolamine is long and colorful (Holzman, 1998). The drug is distributed widely in nature, found in especially high concentrations in the plants *Atropa belladonna* (belladonna, or deadly nightshade), *Datura stramonium* (Jamestown weed, jimsonweed, stinkweed, thorn apple, or devil's apple), and *Mandragora officinarum* (mandrake). Both professional and amateur poisoners of the Middle Ages frequently used deadly nightshade as a source of poison. In fact, the plant's name, *Atropa belladonna*, is derived from Atropos, the Greek goddess who supposedly cuts the thread of life. Belladonna means "beautiful woman," which refers to the drug's ability to dilate the pupils when it is applied topically to the eyes (eyes with widely dilated pupils were presumably a mark of beauty). Accidental ingestion of berries from *Datura* has even been associated with the incapacitation of whole armies, for example, the defeat of Marc Antony's army in 36 B.C. and the defeat of British soldiers by settlers in the rebellion known as Bacon's Revolution near Jamestown, Virginia, in 1676 (hence the name Jamestown weed).

Scopolamine-containing plants have been used and misused for centuries. For example, the delirium caused by scopolamine may have persuaded certain people that they could fly—and that they were witches (associated with the Halloween customs involving flying witches). Marijuana and opium preparations from the Far East were once fortified with material from *Datura stramonium*. Today, cigarettes made from the leaves of *Datura stramonium* and *Atropa belladonna* are smoked occasionally to induce intoxication. Throughout the world, leaves of plants that contain atropine or scopolamine are still used to prepare intoxicating beverages.

Pharmacological Effects

As introduced, scopolamine acts on the peripheral nervous system to produce an anticholinergic syndrome consisting of dry mouth, reduced sweating, dry skin, increased body temperature, dilated pupils, blurred vision, tachycardia, and hypertension. Scopolamine in the CNS functions as a deliriant and intoxicant. Low doses produce drowsiness, mild euphoria, profound amnesia, fatigue, delirium, mental confusion, dreamless sleep, and loss of attention. Rather than expanding consciousness, awareness, and insight, scopolamine clouds consciousness and produces amnesia; it does not expand sensory perception. The amnesia produced is quite intense (Mintzer and Griffiths, 2003). As doses of scopolamine progress, psychiatric symptoms include restlessness, excitement, hallucinations, euphoria, and disorientation.

In higher and much more toxic doses, a behavioral state that resembles a toxic psychosis occurs. Delirium, mental confusion, stupor, coma, and respiratory depression dominate. While scopolamine intoxication can convey a sense of excitement and loss of control to the user, the clouding of consciousness and the reduction in memory of the episode render scopolamine rather unattractive as a psychedelic drug. It is probably more appropriate to refer to it as a somewhat dangerous intoxicant, amnestic, and deliriant. Scopolamine is classically stated to make one "hot as a hare, blind as a bat, dry as a bone, red as a beet, and mad as a hen." Typically, sensorium and psychosis usually clear within 36 to 48 hours.

Catecholaminelike Psychedelics

Norepinephrine and dopamine receptors are important sites of action for a large group of psychedelic drugs that are structurally similar to both catecholamine neurotransmitters and the amphetamines (Figure 19.2). They differ structurally from the normal neurotransmitters by the addition of one or more methoxy (OCH_3) groups to the phenyl ring structure. These methoxy groups, varied as they are, confer psychedelic properties on top of their amphetaminelike psychostimulant properties. Methoxylated amphetamine derivatives include mescaline, DOM (also called STP), MDA, MDE, MDMA (ecstasy), MMDA, DMA, and certain drugs that are obtained from nutmeg (myristin and elemicin).

As would be predicted from their structures, catecholamine psychedelics exert amphetaminelike psychostimulant actions, presumably on dopaminergic neurons (Chapter 7). As such, they can enhance energy, endurance, sociability, and sexual arousal (Kalant, 2001). However, their psychedelic actions are probably ultimately exerted by augmentation of serotonin neurotransmission; they are probably agonists at postsynaptic serotonin 5-HT_{2A} receptors. This action would account for their LSD-like effects. The combination of catecholamine and serotonin actions points to a complex interaction between dopamine and serotonin and explains their intermediate position between stimulants and (LSD-like) hallucinogens (Gouzoulis-Mayfrank et al., 1999).

As early as the late 1960s, most psychedelics were known to produce a remarkably similar set of effects, including enhanced emotional

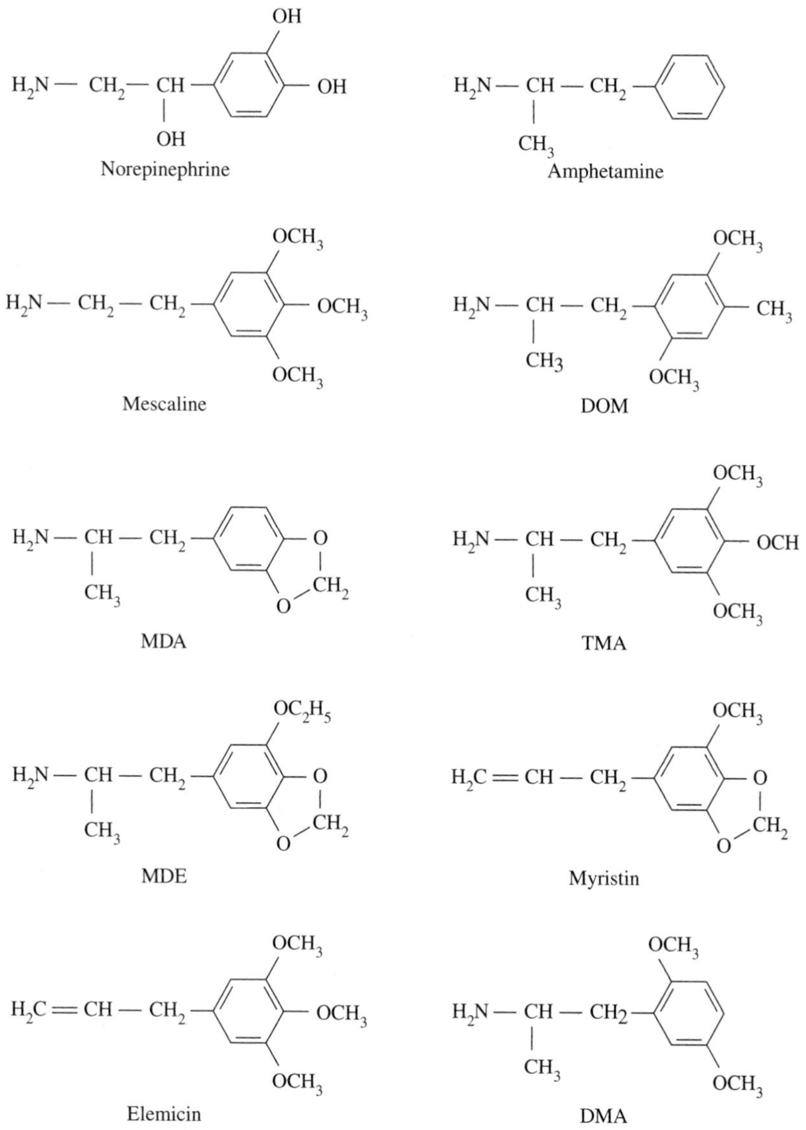

FIGURE 19.2 Structural formulas of norepinephrine (a chemical transmitter), amphetamine, and eight catecholaminelike psychedelic drugs. These eight drugs are structurally related to norepinephrine and are thought to exert their psychedelic actions by altering the transmission of nerve impulses at norepinephrine and serotonin synapses in the brain.

responses; sensory-perceptual distortion; altered perceptions of colors, sounds, and shapes; complex hallucinations; dreamlike feelings; depersonalization; and somatic effects (tingling skin, weakness, tremor, and so on). During the 1980s, it was noted that psychedelic drugs produce marked alterations in brain serotonin. As serotonin receptors were characterized in the early 1990s, it became clear that LSD was a serotonin receptor agonist and that the catecholaminelike psychedelics functioned ultimately as indirectly acting serotonin agonists. Today, the focus of attention has been on activation of a subgroup of the 5-HT$_2$ receptors, specifically the 5-HT$_{2A}$ receptor. These psychedelics can therefore be safely classified as *mixed dopamine and serotonin agonists*, with 5-HT$_2$ receptors certainly involved.

Mescaline

Peyote (*Lophophora williamsii*) is a common plant in the southwestern United States and in Mexico. It is a spineless cactus that has a small crown, or "button," and a long root. When the plant is used for psychedelic purposes, the crown is cut from the cactus and dried into a hard brown disk. This disk, which is frequently referred to as a "mescal button," is later softened in the mouth and swallowed. The psychedelic chemical in the button is mescaline.

Historical Background.   The use of peyote extends back to pre-Columbian times, when the cactus was used in the religious rites of the Aztecs and other Mexican Indians (Bruhn et al., 2002). Currently, peyote is legally available for use in the religious practice of the Native American Church of North America, whose members regard peyote as sacramental. The use of peyote for religious purposes is not considered to be abuse, and peyote is seldom abused by members of the Native American Church. Today, the federal government and 23 states permit its sacramental use.

Pharmacological Effects.   Early research on the peyote cactus led in 1896 to the identification of mescaline as its pharmacologically active ingredient. After the chemical structure of mescaline was elucidated in 1918, the compound was produced synthetically. Because of its structural resemblance to norepinephrine, a wide variety of synthetic mescaline derivatives have now been synthesized, and all have methoxy (OCH_3) groups or similar additions on their benzene rings (see Figure 19.2). Methoxylation of the benzene ring apparently adds psychedelic properties to the drug, presumably due to increased affinity and full agonist activity at the 5-HT$_{2A}$ receptor subtype.

When taken orally, mescaline is rapidly and completely absorbed, and significant concentrations are usually achieved in the brain within

1 to 2 hours. Between 3.5 and 4 hours after drug intake, mescaline produces an acute psychotomimetic state, with prominent effects on the visual system (Hermle et al., 1998). The effects of a single dose of mescaline persist for approximately 10 hours. The drug does not appear to be metabolized before it is excreted. In functional brain imaging using SPECT, mescaline produced in healthy volunteers a "hyperfrontal" pattern with an emphasis on the right hemisphere, which was correlated with mescaline-induced psychotomimetic psychopathology.

Interest in mescaline focuses on the fact that it produces unusual psychic effects and visual hallucinations. The usual oral dose (5 mg/kg) in the average normal subject causes anxiety, sympathomimetic effects, hyperreflexia of the limbs, tremors, and visual hallucinations that consist of brightly colored lights, geometric designs, animals, and occasionally people; color and space perception is often concomitantly impaired, but otherwise the sensorium is normal and insight is retained. The psychotic effects are mainly concerned with the dissolution of ego boundaries, visual hallucinations, and dimensions of boundlessness, often mixed with anxious passivity experiences.

Synthetic Amphetamine Derivatives

DOM, MDA, DMA, MDE, TMA, AMT, 5-MeO-DIPT, and MDMA are structurally related to mescaline and methamphetamine and, as might be expected, produce similar effects. They have moderate behavioral stimulant effects at low doses, but like LSD, psychedelic effects dominate as doses increase. These derivatives are considerably more potent and more toxic than mescaline.

DOM (dimethoxy-methamphetamine) has effects that are similar to those of mescaline; doses of 1 to 6 milligrams produce euphoria, which is followed by a 6- to 8-hour period of hallucinations. DOM is 100 times more potent than mescaline but much less potent than LSD. The use of DOM is associated with a high incidence of overdose (because it is potent and street doses are poorly controlled). Acute toxic reactions are common; they consist of tremors that may eventually lead to convulsive movements, prostration, and even death. Because toxic reactions are common, the use of DOM is not widespread.

MDA (methylene-dioxy-amphetamine), *DMA* (dimethoxy-methyl-amphetamine), *MDE* (methylene-dioxy-ethylamphetamine, or Eve), *TMA* (trimethoxy-amphetamine), and other structural variations of amphetamine are encountered as "designer psychedelics." MDA is also a metabolite of MDMA and much of MDMA's effect may be due to the presence of MDA. In general, the pharmacological effects of these drugs resemble those of mescaline and LSD; they reflect the mix of catecholamine and serotonin interactions. Side effects and toxicities (including fatalities) are similar to those of MDMA. MDA is sometimes represented as MDMA; when this occurs, MDA is more lethal in lower doses and its effects are longer lasting than those of MDMA.

Gouzoulis-Mayfrank and colleagues (1999), in their SPECT-scan study of MDE, noted that MDE induced hypermetabolism in the cerebellum and right anterior cingulate with hypometabolism in the cortex. They referred to MDE as an *entactogen*,[1] constituting an intermediate position between stimulants and hallucinogens. This name probably reflects a complex set of actions at both dopaminergic and serotoninergic 5-HT$_{1A}$ and 5-HT$_{2A}$ receptors.

AMT and 5-MeO-DIPT.   In April 2003, the Drug Enforcement Administration (DEA) designated alpha-methyltryptamine (AMT) and 5-methoxy-isopropyltryptamine (5-MeO-DIPT, or Foxy) as Schedule I substances under the Controlled Substances Act (Drug Enforcement Division, 2003). Such scheduling for these new "designer" psychedelics implies high abuse potential with no therapeutic usefulness. Administered orally, both cause hallucinations, mood elevation, nervousness, insomnia, and pupilary dilation. AMT is of slow onset (3 to 4 hours) after oral administration and prolonged duration (12 to 24 hours). Foxy is of more rapid onset (20 to 30 minutes) and shorter duration (3 to 6 hours). These new drugs are popular at dance "raves."

MDMA.   MDMA (methylene-dioxy-methamphetamine, also called ecstasy, XTC, X, E, and Adam) resembles MDA in structure but may be less hallucinogenic, inducing a less extreme sense of disembodiment and visual distortion. MDMA is also a potent and selective serotonin neurotoxin in animals. Kish and coworkers (2000) and Croft and coworkers (2001) reported that serotonin dysfunction occurs in human users of MDMA who used the drug for prolonged periods of time. The dysfunction is related to dose and duration of use. Dysfunction is also independent of marijuana use. Reneman and coworkers (2001) verified the neurotoxicity of MDMA on serotonin neurons, adding that women might be more susceptible than men and that while the effects on serotonin neurons might be reversible with time, detrimental effects on memory function might be long-lasting (a year or more). Kalant (2001) summarized persistent MDMA-induced psychiatric problems:

- Impairments in memory, both verbal and visual
- Impairments in decision making ("executive functioning")

---

[1]Gouzoulis-Mayfrank and colleagues use the term *entactogen* to distinguish mechanisms of drug-induced enhancement of emotional responses (entactogenic effects) from mechanisms responsible for hallucinogenic effects and stimulant effects (such as increased drive and energy).

- Greater impulsivity and lack of self-control
- Panic attacks following withdrawal
- Recurrent paranoia, depersonalization, and flashbacks
- Depression, sometimes resistant to treatment with other than SSRI-type antidepressants (Chapter 9)

Morgan (2000) reviewed the neuropsychological problems with ecstasy and concluded:

> There is growing evidence that chronic, heavy, recreational use of ecstasy is associated with sleep disorders, depressed mood, persistent elevation of anxiety, impulsiveness, and hostility, and selective impairment of episodic memory, working memory, and attention. There is tentative evidence that these cognitive deficits persist for at least 6 months after abstinence, whereas anxiety and hostility remit after a year of abstinence. . . . Residual neurotoxicity and decline of serotonergic function with age may result in recurrent psychopathology and premature cognitive decline. (p. 230)

Montoya and coworkers (2002) stated that repeated use of ecstasy is associated with sleep, mood, and anxiety disturbances, elevated impulsiveness, memory deficits, and attention problems, which may persist for up to two years after cessation.

Sprague and coworkers in 1998 developed a hypothesis stating that MDMA induces a sequence of events that ultimately results in serotonergic neurotoxicity:

1. MDMA induces an acute release of serotonin and dopamine.
2. This is followed by depletion of intraneuronal serotonin stores.
3. Released serotonin activates postsynaptic serotonin-2 receptors located on GABA intraneurons, resulting in decreased GABAergic neurotransmission and increased dopamine release and synthesis.
4. The excessive amounts of dopamine are transported into depleted serotonin nerve terminals.
5. The dopamine is broken down by the enzyme monoamine oxidase located in the serotonin terminals.
6. This results in free-radical formation and selective degeneration of serotonin axons, nerve terminals, and reuptake transporter proteins.

Although this hypothesis has not been verified, PET scan studies on human users suggest memory impairment and reduced serotonin transporter binding, and ultimately destruction of the presynaptic serotonin transporter (Yuan et al., 2002). Ricaurte and coworkers (2002) feel that, in addition to serotonergic neurotoxicity, MDMA may also cause dopaminergic neurotoxicity. More research in this area is needed.

Despite generally positive emotional effects of single uses at "rave" parties, "somatic" effects can be significant. Two examples are dramatic increases in blood pressure and body temperature, increases that are generally well tolerated by most young users but undesirable in persons with cardiovascular disease. Other somatic effects include jaw clenching, suppressed appetite, restlessness, insomnia, impaired gait, and restless legs. Adverse sequelae after 24 hours include lack of energy and appetite, fatigue, restlessness, difficulty concentrating, and brooding.

Concern about MDMA is increasing as use of this "club drug"[2] increases around the world, especially at dance clubs and "raves." Surveys indicate that between 1.5 and 3.5 percent of 15- to 30-year-olds have used ecstasy within the last year. In an Australian study, Topp and colleagues (1999) noted that early studies of ecstasy users found generally self-limiting patterns of use, low levels of intravenous use, and few adverse health effects. In their recent study, the situation was radically different. Extensive polydrug use was the norm (Table 19.2), high rates of intravenous drug use were reported, and many physical, psychological, financial, relationship, and occupational problems occurred as a result of ecstasy use (Tables 19.3 and 19.4). Twenty percent of users had received treatment for an ecstasy-related problem, and 15 percent wanted formal treatment.

MDMA is potentially too dangerous for human use: abuse of MDMA certainly leads to severe toxicities, including fatalities. When it is used during periods of intense activity, such as skiing and dancing at "rave" parties, symptoms include hyperthermia, tachycardia, disorientation, dilated pupils, convulsions, rigidity, breakdown of skeletal muscle, kidney failure, cardiac arrhythmias, and death (Kalant, 2001). The pathology for these serious effects is unclear, although it may well represent induction of a fatal syndrome called "malignant hyperthermia" (Fiege et al., 2003). Fiege's group demonstrated that MDMA would precipitate malignant hyperthermia in susceptible pigs and that this response could be blocked by a drug called dantrolene. It is hoped that, should an MDMA-intoxicated, hyperthermic patient be taken to an

---

[2]Ecstasy, gamma hydroxybutyrate (GHB, Chapter 5), ketamine (discussed later in this chapter), and methamphetamine (Chapter 7) are four examples of "club drugs" that are increasing in popularity. Ecstasy is a psychostimulant/hallucinogen, GHB is a sedative, ketamine is a dissociative anesthetic, and methamphetamine is a psychostimulant.

TABLE 19.2 Patterns of drug use of 329 ecstasy users

Drug class	Ever used (%)	Used in last 6 months (%)	No. days used in last 6 months (median)[a]
Ecstasy	100	100	10
Alcohol	99.1	93.6	24
Cannabis	98.8	92.1	48
Amphetamine	94.2	81.8	10
LSD	93.3	68.1	4
Tobacco	85.4	74.8	180
Amyl nitrate	75.4	46.5	3
Cocaine	61.4	40.7	2
Nitrous oxide	61.1	35.3	4
Benzodiazepines	56.8	43.2	5.5
MDA	50.5	31.3	3
Other opiates	32.0	20.7	3
Heroin	30.1	17.3	12
Antidepressants	23.1	13.4	6
Ketamine	18.2	10.0	4
Ethyl chloride	10.0	5.8	2
Methadone	7.3	2.7	20
Anabolic steroids	4.3	1.5	20
GHB	2.7	1.8	1.5
Other drugs[b]	—	5.2	2

[a]Among those who had used.
[b]Other drugs included hallucinogenic mushrooms, DMT, and PCP.
From Topp et al. (1999), p. 108.

emergency room in time, dantrolene would be administered and a life saved. Despite these consequences, the "intense euphoric high" promotes continued use.

Myristin and Elemicin. Nutmeg and mace are common household spices sometimes abused for their hallucinogenic properties. Myristin and elemicin, the pharmacologically active ingredients in nutmeg and mace, are responsible for this psychedelic action. Ingestion of large amounts (1 to 2 teaspoons—5 to 15 grams—usually brewed in tea) may, after a delay of 2 to 5 hours, induce feelings of unreality, confusion, disorientation, euphoria, visual hallucinations, acute psychotic reactions, and feelings of impending doom, depersonalization, and unreality. Considering the close structural resemblance of myristin and

TABLE 19.3 Physical side effects of ectasy (n = 329)

Symptom	Last 6 months (%)	While using ecstasy[a]	While coming down[a]	At other times[b]	Median length of worst case[b]	Only related to ecstasy(%)[b]
Loss of energy	64.9	7.7	61.2	19.4	2 days	46.0
Muscular aches	59.9	10.7	57.6	11.6	2 days	34.7
Hot/cold flushes	48.0	39.2	25.5	4.9	1 h	52.5
Blurred vision	47.1	45.9	12.5	4.0	1 h	69.0
Numbness/tingling	45.6	42.2	14.9	6.4	1 h	59.3
Profuse sweating	42.6	38.9	18.0	4.9	3 h	40.6
Weight loss	42.6				21 days	26.1
Dizziness	41.9	31.0	21.3	9.7	20 min	46.4
Tremors/shakes	41.9	30.1	25.2	8.8	2 h	46.4
Heart palpitations	40.7	37.1	16.1	7.6	30 min	38.8
Headaches	40.4	11.2	35.3	7.9	4 h	35.3
Stomach pains	37.7	25.5	22.8	6.4	2 h	48.0
Joint pains/stiffness	35.0	7.9	33.4	7.6	2 days	31.3
Inability to urinate	34.7	34.3	5.8	1.5	3 h	77.9
Vomiting	33.9	30.0	7.6	5.5	5 min	64.9
Teeth problems	33.1	15.2	23.2	12.2	2 days	44.0
Shortness of breath	26.4	22.8	6.7	2.1	30 min	34.5
Blackout/memory lapse	24.9	14.3	12.8	3.2	3 h	31.3
Chest pains	15.8	8.8	9.4	4.9	1 h	25.0
Fainting/passing out	6.4	4.9	1.8	1.5	3.5 min	47.6

[a]Proportion of total sample [b]Among those reporting the symptom
From Topp et al. (1999), p. 109.

TABLE 19.4 Psychological side effects of ectasy (*n* = 329)

Symptom	Last 6 months (%)	While using ecstasy[a]	While coming down[a]	At other times[b]	Median length of worst case[b]	Only related to ecstasy (%)[b]
Irritability	61.9	3.4	59.8	20.4	2 days	46.8
Trouble sleeping	55.9	23.1	52.0	16.1	12 h	43.2
Depression	55.6	4.6	49.8	24.3	3 days	49.7
Confusion	47.4	30.4	45.6	10.6	12 days	53.2
Anxiety	45.0	26.7	32.5	14.0	4 h	45.9
Paranoia	40.4	22.2	30.7	10.9	3 h	39.8
Visual hallucinations	28.0	27.1	8.2	5.5	1.5 h	52.2
Sound hallucinations	20.7	18.5	7.3	3.3	45 min	54.4
Flashbacks	14.6	0	4.9	12.2	5 min	52.1
Panic attacks	12.8	10.0	4.6	4.0	1 h	42.9
Loss of sex urge	12.2	8.2	7.6	5.2	24 h	52.5
Suicidal thoughts	10.3	2	8.2	6.7	24 h	26.5

[a]Proportion of total sample
[b]Among those reporting the symptom
From Topp et al. (1999), p.110.

elemicin to mescaline (see Figure 19.2), these psychedelic actions are not unexpected. Ingestion of nutmeg, however, produces many unpleasant side effects, including vomiting, nausea, and tremors. After nutmeg or mace has been taken to produce its psychedelic action, the side effects usually dissuade users from trying these agents a second time. While extremely unpleasant reactions may occur, deaths are infrequent (Sangalli and Chiang, 2000).

Serotoninlike Psychedelics

The serotoninlike psychedelic drugs include *lysergic acid diethylamide* (LSD), *psilocybin* and *psilocin, dimethyltryptamine* (DMT), and *bufotenine* (Figure 19.3). Because of their structural resemblance to each other and to serotonin, it has long been presumed that these agents somehow exert their effects through interactions at serotonin synapses, especially the 5-HT_2 receptor, and this effect seems to be the case. Almaula and coworkers (1996) first mapped the binding site for LSD on the 5-HT_{2A} receptor and correlated the binding with receptor activation. Ebersole and coworkers (2003) confirmed their results. Indeed, LSD activation of medial prefrontal cortex and anterior cingulated cortex is mediated by 5-HT_{2A} receptors, areas involved in the production of hallucinations (Gresch et al., 2002). In addition to LSD, other serotonin psychedelics also act as partial agonists at 5-HT_{2A} receptors. These drugs include DMT (Smith et al., 1998) and bufotenine (McBride, 2000).

With all this focus of agonist action on serotonin receptors, a major question remains unanswered: Why does serotonin not induce psychotomimetic effects? In particular, psychotomimetic effects are not seen after administration of SSRI-type antidepressants except as part of the serotonin syndrome or any other treatment that increases serotonin availability at its postsynaptic receptors. Even in the serotonin syndrome (Chapter 15), true psychotomimetic effects are rarely seen. Van Oekelen and coworkers (2003) discuss the role of serotonin 5-HT_{2A} and 5-HT_{2C} receptors in mediating such processes as depression, schizophrenia, anxiety, hallucinations, dysthymia, sleep patterns, feeding behavior, and neuroendocrine functions.

Regardless of receptor mechanisms, serotonin psychedelics do produce a characteristic psychedelic syndrome, with disturbances in thinking, illusions, elementary and complex visual hallucinations, and impaired ego functioning. One speculation about the process by which hallucinogens manifest their impressive alterations of mood, perception, and thought is that the pontine (dorsal) raphe, a major center of serotonin activity, serves as a filtering station for incoming sensory stimuli. It screens the flood of sensations and perceptions,

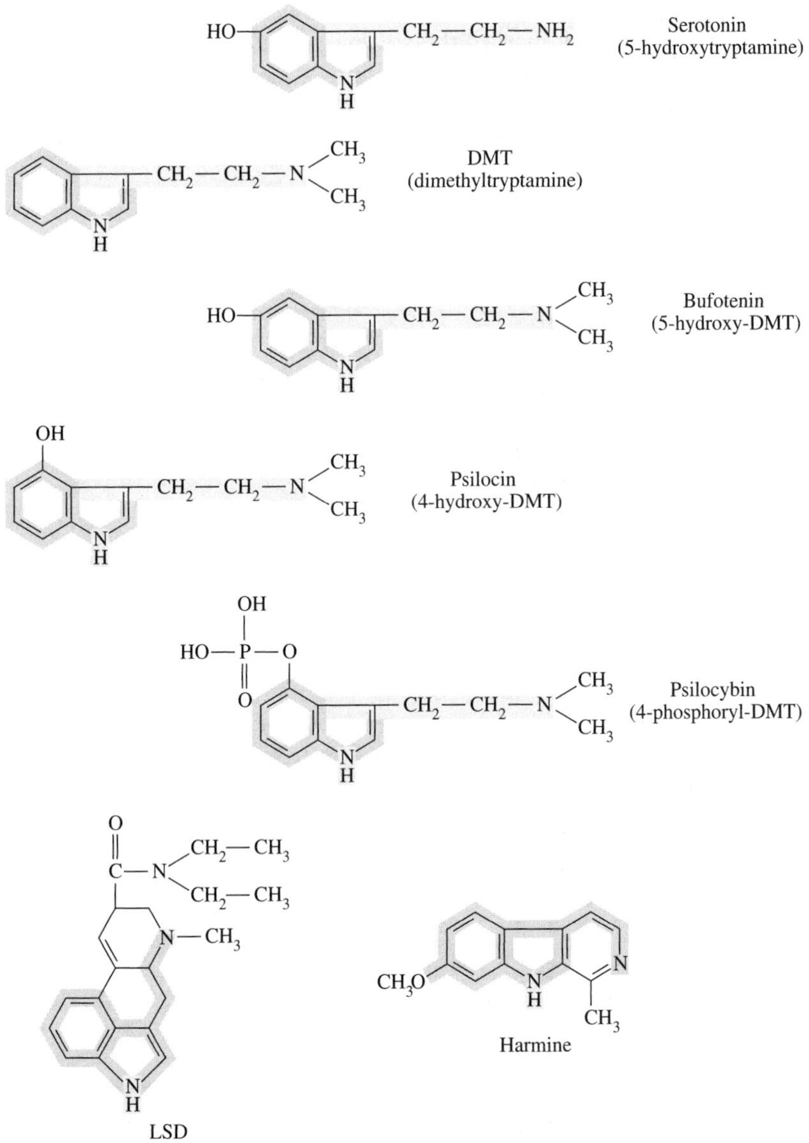

FIGURE 19.3 Structural formulas of serotonin (a chemical transmitter) and six serotoninlike psychedelic drugs. These six drugs are structurally related to serotonin (as indicated by the shading) and are thought to exert their psychedelic actions through alterations of serotonin synapses in the brain. Although LSD is structurally much more complex than serotonin, the basic similarity of the two molecules is apparent.

eliminating those that are unimportant, irrelevant, or commonplace. A drug like LSD may disrupt the sorting process, allowing a surge of sensory data and an overload of brain circuits. Dehabituation, in which the familiar becomes novel, is noted under LSD. Dehabituation may be caused by indirectly lowering the sensory gates by inhibition of the raphe activity.

Lysergic Acid Diethylamide

During the mid-1960s and early 1970s, lysergic acid diethylamide (LSD) became one of the most remarkable and controversial drugs known. In doses that are so small that they might even be considered infinitesimal, LSD induces remarkable psychological change in a person, enhancing self-awareness and altering internal reality, while causing relatively few alterations in the general physiology of the body.

Historical Background. LSD was first synthesized in 1938 by Albert Hofmann, a Swiss chemist, as part of an organized research program to investigate possible therapeutic uses of compounds obtained from ergot, a natural product derived from a fungus (*Claviceps purpurea*). Early pharmacological studies of LSD in animals failed to reveal anything unusual; the psychedelic action was neither sought nor expected. Thus, LSD remained unnoticed until 1943, when Hofmann had an unusual experience:

> In the afternoon of 16 April, 1943, . . . I was seized by a peculiar sensation of vertigo and restlessness. Objects, as well as the shape of my associates in the laboratory, appeared to undergo optical changes. I was unable to concentrate on my work. In a dreamlike state I left for home, where an irresistible urge to lie down overcame me. I drew the curtains and immediately fell into a peculiar state similar to drunkenness, characterized by an exaggerated imagination. With my eyes closed, fantastic pictures of extraordinary plasticity and intensive color seemed to surge toward me. After two hours, this state gradually wore off. (Hofmann, 1994, p. 80)

Hofmann correctly hypothesized that his experience resulted from the accidental ingestion of LSD. To further characterize the experience, Hofmann self-administered what seemed to be a minuscule oral dose (only 0.25 milligram). We now know, however, that this dose is about ten times the dose required to induce psychedelic effects in most people. As a result of this miscalculation, his response was quite spectacular:

> After 40 minutes, I noted the following symptoms in my laboratory journal: slight giddiness, restlessness, difficulty in concentration, visual disturbances, laughing. . . . Later, I lost all count of time. I noticed with dismay that my environment was undergoing progressive changes. My visual field wavered and everything appeared deformed as in a faulty mirror. Space and time became more and more disorganized and I was overcome by a fear that I was going out of my mind. The worst part of it being that I was clearly aware of my condition. My power of observation was unimpaired. . . . Occasionally, I felt as if I were out of my body. I thought I had died. My ego seemed suspended somewhere in space, from where I saw my dead body lying on the sofa. . . . It was particularly striking how acoustic perceptions, such as the noise of water gushing from a tap or the spoken word, were transformed into optical illusions. I then fell asleep and awakened the next morning somewhat tired but otherwise feeling perfectly well. (p. 80)

In 1949 the first North American study of LSD in humans was conducted, and during the 1950s large quantities of LSD were distributed to scientists for research purposes. A significant impetus for researching was the notion that the effects of LSD might constitute a model for psychosis, which would provide some insight into the biochemical and physiological processes of mental illness and its treatment. Some therapists tried LSD as an adjunct to psychotherapy to help patients verbalize their problems and gain some insight into the underlying causes, but it did not prove to be an effective treatment.

Pharmacokinetics. LSD is usually taken orally, and it is rapidly absorbed by that route. Usual doses range from about 25 micrograms to more than 300 micrograms. Because such amounts are so small, LSD is often added to other substances, such as squares of paper, the backs of stamps, or sugar cubes, which can be handled more easily. LSD is absorbed within about 60 minutes, reaching peak blood levels in about 3 hours. It is distributed rapidly and efficiently throughout the body; it diffuses easily into the brain and readily crosses the placenta. The largest amounts of LSD in the body are found in the liver, where the drug is metabolized before it is excreted to 2-oxo-3-hydroxy-LSD (Klette et al., 2000). The usual duration of action is 6 to 8 hours.

Because of its extreme potency, only minuscule amounts of LSD can be detected in urine, although the metabolite is present in concentrations 16 to 43 times greater than that of LSD. Thus, conventional urine-screening tests are inadequate to detect LSD. When the use of LSD is suspected, urine is collected (up to 30 hours after ingestion) and an ultrasensitive radioimmunoassay is performed to verify the presence of the drug.

Physiological Effects.   Although the LSD experience is characterized by its psychological effects, subtle physiological changes also occur. A person who takes LSD may experience a slight increase in body temperature, dilation of the pupils, slightly increased heart rate and blood pressure, increased levels of glucose in the blood, and dizziness, drowsiness, nausea, and other effects that, although noticeable, seldom interfere with the psychedelic experience.

LSD is known to possess a low level of toxicity; the effective dose is about 50 micrograms while the lethal dose is about 14,000 micrograms. These figures provide a therapeutic ratio of 280, making the drug a remarkably nonlethal compound. This calculation does not include any fatal accidents or suicides that occur when a person is intoxicated by LSD. Indeed, most deaths attributed to LSD result from accidents, homicides, or suicide. The use of LSD during pregnancy is certainly unwise, although a distinct fetal LSD syndrome has not been described.

Psychological Effects.   The psychological effects of LSD are quite intense. At doses of 25 to 50 micrograms, pupillary dilation and a glassy-eyed appearance may be noticed. These effects are accompanied by alterations in perception, thinking, emotion, arousal, and self-image. Time is slowed or distorted; sensory input intensifies. Cognitive alterations include enhanced power to visualize previously seen or imagined objects and decreased vigilance and logical thought. Visual alterations are the most characteristic phenomenon; they typically include colored lights, distorted images, and vivid and fascinating images and shapes. Colors can be heard and sounds may be seen. The loss of boundaries and the fear of fragmentation create a need for a structuring or supporting environment and experienced companions. During the "trip," thoughts and memories can emerge under self-guidance, sometimes to the user's distress. Mood may be labile, shifting from depression to gaiety, from elation to fear. Tension and anxiety may mount and reach panic proportions.

The LSD-induced psychedelic experience typically occurs in three phases:

1. The *somatic phase* occurs after absorption of the drug and consists of CNS stimulation and autonomic changes that are predominantly sympathomimetic in nature.

2. The *sensory* (or perceptual) *phase* is characterized by sensory distortions and pseudohallucinations, which are the effects desired by the drug user.

3. The *psychic phase* signals a maximum drug effect, with changes in mood, disruption of thought processes, altered perception of time, depersonalization, true hallucinations, and psychotic episodes. Experiencing this phase is considered a "bad trip."

Tolerance and Dependence. Tolerance of both the psychological and physiological alterations that are induced by LSD readily and rapidly develops, and cross-tolerance occurs between LSD and other psychedelics. Tolerance is lost within several days after the user stops taking the drug.

Physical dependence on LSD does not develop, even when the drug is used repeatedly for a prolonged period of time. In fact, most heavy users of the drug say that they ceased using LSD because they tired of it, had no further need for it, or had enough. Even when the drug is discontinued because of concern about bad trips or about physical or mental harm, few withdrawal signs are exhibited. Laboratory animals do not self-administer LSD.

Adverse Reactions and Toxicity. The adverse reactions attributed to LSD generally fall into five categories:

* Chronic or intermittent psychotic states
* Persistent or recurrent major affective disorder (for example, depression)
* Exacerbation of preexisting psychiatric illness
* Disruption of personality or chronic brain syndrome, known as "burnout"
* Posthallucinogenic perceptual disorder (flashbacks characterized by the periodic hallucinogenic imagery months or even years after the immediate effect of LSD has worn off)

Unpleasant experiences with LSD are relatively frequent and may involve an uncontrollable drift into confusion, dissociative reactions, acute panic reactions, a reliving of earlier traumatic experiences, or an acute psychotic hospitalization. Prolonged nonpsychotic reactions have included dissociative reactions, time and space distortion, body image changes, and a residue of fear or depression stemming from morbid or terrifying experiences under the drug. With the failure of usual defense mechanisms, the onslaught of repressed material overwhelms the integrative capacity of the ego, and a psychotic reaction results. It appears that LSD-induced disruption of long-established patterns of adapting may be a lasting or semipermanent effect of the drug. In other words, our neocortex modulates awareness of our surroundings and filters a high proportion of incoming information before it can be processed, thereby allowing only the amount of information that is necessary for survival (Goodman, 2002). LSD works to open this filter, so an increased amount of somatosensory data is processed with a corresponding increase in what is deemed important. Thus, LSD reduces a person's normal ability to control emotional reactions, and drug-induced alterations in perception can become so intense that they overwhelm one's ability to cope.

One unique characteristic of LSD and LSD-like substances is the recurrence of some of the symptoms that appeared during the intoxication after the immediate effect of the hallucinogen has worn off. These symptoms are mainly visual and the terms *flashback* and *hallucinogen persisting perception disorder* (HPPD) are used fairly interchangeably. However, a flashback is usually a short-term, nondistressing, spontaneous, recurrent, reversible, and benign condition accompanied by a pleasant affect (Lerner et al., 2002a). In contrast, HPPD is a generally long-term, distressing, spontaneous, recurrent, pervasive, either slowly reversible or irreversible, nonbenign condition accompanied by an unpleasant dysphoric affect. Halpern and Pope (1999) review evidence for and against drug-induced residual neurotoxicity that would account for HPPD, concluding that there are few, if any, long-term neuropsychological deficits attributable to hallucinogen use. In contrast, Abraham and Duffy (2001) discuss the persistent alterations in occipital cortex EEG activity in patients with HPPD, presenting evidence for a hypersynchronous state with relative isolation of the visual cortex, especially eye closure, that facilitates hallucinations and illusions.

Treatment of flashbacks and HPPD has been symptomatic. Case reports note the success of benzodiazepines (Lerner et al., 2001), reboxetine (in a patient with comorbid depression) (Lerner et al., 2002b), combinations of fluoxetine and olanzapine, clonidine, risperidone, sertraline, naltrexone, and others. Obviously, there is no consensus on appropriate therapy and no specific treatment. Infact, some of the listed agents have been reported to exacerbate HPPD! Treatment must therefore be individualized.

Other Serotoninlike Hallucinogens

DMT. DMT (dimethyl-tryptamine) is a short-acting, naturally occurring psychedelic compound that can be synthesized easily and that structurally is related to serotonin. DMT produces LSD-like effects in the user, and like LSD it is a partial agonist at serotonin 5-HT$_{2A}$ and serotonin 5-HT$_{2C}$ receptors (Smith et al., 1998). Widely used throughout much of the world, DMT is an active ingredient of various types of South American plants, such as *Virola calophylla* and *Mimosa hostilis*. Used by itself, DMT is snorted or smoked, often in a marijuana cigarette.

Ayahuasca (also called *hoasca*) is a psychoactive beverage that, as a tea, has been drunk for centuries in religious, spiritual, and medicinal contexts by Amazon Indians in the rain forest areas of South America. Two principal ingredients of ayahuasca are harmine (a beta carboline that is a potent MAO inhibitor) and DMT. Administered orally to healthy volunteers (with prior experience in the use of this tea), ayahuasca produced an experimental psychosis with onset at 30 to 60 minutes, peaked at 1 to 2 hours, and persisted for about 3 to 4 hours (Riba et al., 2001, 2002). The DMT is the active hallucinogen, and the beta carboline blocks the MAO enzyme so that it cannot break down the DMT. This action permits oral administration and prolongs the action of the DMT. In most cases, effects (changes in perceptual, affective, cognitive, and somatic spheres) are well tolerated, but one subject in the Riba study exhibited an intense dysphoric reaction with disorientation and anxiety.

In 1994, Strassman and coworkers conducted controlled investigations of DMT in "highly motivated," experienced hallucinogen users. Administered intravenously (0.04 mg/kg to 0.4 mg/kg body weight), onset of action occurred within 2 minutes and was negligible at 30 minutes. DMT elevated blood pressure, heart rate, and temperature, dilated pupils, and increased body endorphin and hormone levels. The psychedelic threshold dose was 0.2 mg/kg body weight; lower doses were primarily "affective and somaesthetic." Hallucinogenic effects included a rapidly moving, brightly colored visual display of images. Auditory effects were less common. "Loss of control," associated with a brief but overwhelming "rush," led to a dissociated state, where euphoria alternated or coexisted with anxiety. These effects completely replaced subjects' previously ongoing mental experience and were more vivid and compelling than dreams or waking awareness.

Thus, DMT produces intense visual hallucinations, intoxication, and often a loss of awareness of the user's surroundings. When DMT is injected, smoked, or taken as a snuff, after the 30-minute period of effect the user returns to normal feelings and perceptions—thus the nicknames "lunch-hour drug," "businessman's lunch," and "businessman's LSD." Administered with an MAO inhibitor (as the ayahuasca tea), it is absorbed orally and has a longer duration of action.

Bufotenine. Bufotenine (5-hydroxy DMT or dimethyl-serotonin), like LSD and DMT, is a potent serotonin agonist hallucinogen with an affinity for several types of serotonin receptors. The name bufotenine comes from the name for a toad of the genus *Bufo,* whose skin and glandular secretions supposedly produce hallucinogenic effects when ingested. Toad secretions have been used since ancient times for a variety of mythological and medicinal purposes involving magical, shamanic, or occult uses for casting spells and for divination (Lyttle et al., 1996).

After subcutaneous injection to rats, the half-life of bufotenine is about 2 hours, with MAO responsible for metabolism (as it is for DMT). Mechanistically, bufotenine is an agonist of serotonin-5-HT$_{2A}$ and 5-HT$_{2C}$ receptors, as are other serotonin psychedelics (McBride, 2000; Ebersole et al., 2003).

Bufotenine is not found in the bodies of normal people. However, it can be produced in an alternate and unusual pathway for the metabolic breakdown of serotonin. Research in the 1960s attempted to correlate the presence of bufotenine in urine with various psychiatric disorders. Takeda (Takeda, 1994; Takeda et al., 1995) reviewed the breakdown of serotonin (Figure 19.4), noting that the pathway to bufotenine is an unusual route that is associated with the production of venoms or hallucinogens and is not associated with normal homeostasis in animals. Urine specimens obtained from controls and from inpatients on a psychiatric ward revealed interesting results. Only 2 of 200 control urine specimens were positive for bufotenine; in 18 autistic patients with mental retardation and epilepsy, urine was positive in all; in autistic patients with mental retardation (no epilepsy), 32 of 47 were positive; in 18 patients with depression, urine was positive in 15; 13 of 15 schizophrenic patients tested positive for bufotenine. Takeda concluded that the presence of bufotenine in urine may serve as a marker for some psychiatric disorders.

Karkkainen and coworkers (1995) studied the urinary excretion of bufotenine in 112 Finnish male violent offenders. Suspiciousness was positively correlated and socialization was negatively correlated with urinary bufotenine excretion. This and other results indicated that violent offenders with paranoid personality traits have higher urinary levels of bufotenine than other violent offenders. These intriguing reports raise important questions about the role of altered metabolic pathways of serotonin (producing methylated derivatives) in the etiology of human psychiatric disorders such as autism, paranoia, and psychosis (Ciprian-Ollivier and Cetkovich-Bakmas, 1997).

Psilocybin.   Psilocybin (4-phosphoryl-DMT) and psilocin (4-hydroxy-DMT) are two psychedelic agents that are found in many species of mushrooms that belong to the genera *Psilocybe, Panaeolus, Copelandia,* and *Conocybe*. As Figure 19.3 shows, the only difference between psilocybin and psilocin is that psilocybin contains a molecule of phosphoric acid. After the mushroom has been ingested, phosphoric acid is enzymatically removed from psilocybin, thus producing psilocin, the active psychedelic agent. Vollenweider and coworkers (1999) noted that psilocybin is a potent hallucinogen that exerts such action through an agonist effect at serotonin 5-HT$_{2A}$ and 5-HT$_{1A}$ receptors, similar to the effects of other serotonin psychedelics. Psilocybin administration (about 0.25 mg/kg body weight, orally) produces changes

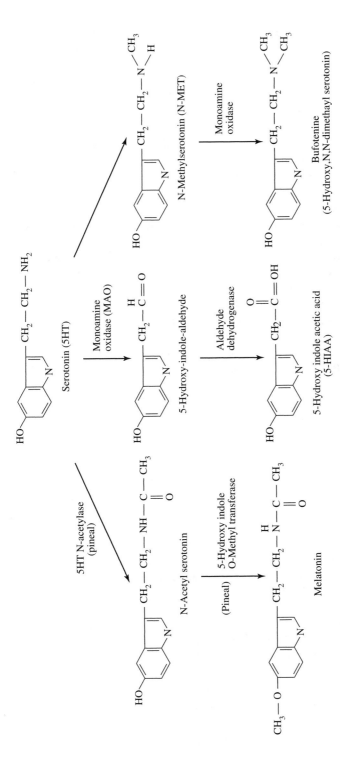

FIGURE 19.4 Metabolic pathways for serotonin (5-HT). The major pathway, shown in the center, leads to production of 5-HIAA, which is excreted by the kidneys. The pathway shown at the left occurs in the pineal gland and leads to the production of the neurohormone melatonin. The pathway at the right is an abnormal metabolic pathway leading to methylation of the terminal nitrogen group and ultimately to the formation of bufotenine, a putative psychogenic substance. See text for discussion.

in mood, disturbances in thinking, illusions, complex visual hallucinations, and impaired ego functioning, similar to the effects produced by LSD.

Psilocybin-containing mushrooms grow throughout much of the world, including the northwestern United States. Psilocin and psilocybin are approximately 1/200 as potent as LSD, peak in about 2 hours, and their effects last about 6 to 10 hours. Unlike DMT, psilocin and psilocybin are absorbed effectively when taken orally; the mushrooms are eaten raw to induce psychedelic effects.

There is great variation in the concentration of psilocybin and psilocin among the different species of mushrooms, as well as significant differences among mushrooms of the same species. For example, the usual oral dose of *Psilocybe semilanceata* (liberty caps) may consist of 10 to 40 mushrooms, while the dose for *Psilocybe cyanescens* may be only two to five mushrooms. Also, some extremely toxic species of mushrooms are not psychoactive, but they bear a superficial resemblance to the mushrooms that contain psilocybin and psilocin. Because the effects of psilocybin so closely resemble those produced by LSD, the "psilocybin" sold illicitly may be LSD, and ordinary mushrooms laced with LSD may be sold as "magic mushrooms."

Although the psychedelic effects of *Psilocybe mexicana* have long been part of Indian folklore, *Psilocybe* intoxication was not described until 1955, when Gordon Wasson, a New York banker, traveled through Mexico. He mingled with native tribes and was allowed to participate in a *Psilocybe* ceremony, in which he consumed the magic mushroom. Wasson said:

> It permits you to travel backward and forward in time, to enter other planes of existence, even to know God. . . . Your body lies in the darkness, heavy as lead, but your spirit seems to soar and leave the hut, and with the speed of thought to travel where it listeth, in time and space, accompanied by the shaman's singing. . . . At least you know what the ineffable is, and what ecstasy means. Ecstasy! The mind harks back to the origin of that word. For the Greeks, ekstasis meant the flight of the soul from the body. Can you find a better word to describe this state? (Crahan, 1969, p. 17).

Weil (1980, pp. 73–79) narrates his experiences with psilocybin mushrooms. Some view psilocybin intoxication as inducing a schizophrenialike psychosis via a serotonin 5-HT$_{2A}$ agonist action with a hyperfrontal metabolic pattern in the cerebral cortex (Umbricht et al., 2003). Gouzoulis-Mayfrank and coworkers (1999) described psilocybin-induced alterations in "prepulse inhibition" of the startle reflex in humans, further indication of a drug-induced schizophrenialike effect and of psilocybin producing a "model psychosis."

Ololiuqui. Ololiuqui is a naturally occurring hallucinogen in morning glory seeds that is used by Central and South American Indians both as an intoxicant and as a hallucinogen. The drug is used ritually for spiritual communication, as are extracts of most plants that contain psychedelic drugs. The use of ololiuqui seeds in Central and South America was first described by the Spaniard Hernandez, who is said to have reported, "When the priests wanted to commune with their Gods, they ate ololiuqui seeds and a thousand visions and satanic hallucinations appeared to them."

The seeds were analyzed in Europe by Albert Hofmann, the discoverer of LSD, who identified several ingredients, one of which was lysergic acid amide (not lysergic acid diethylamide, LSD). The lysergic acid amide that Hofmann identified is approximately one-tenth as active as LSD as a psychoactive agent. However, considering the extreme potency of LSD, lysergic acid amide is still quite potent.

Side effects of ololiuqui include nausea, vomiting, headache, increased blood pressure, dilated pupils, and sleepiness. These side effects are usually quite intense and serve to limit the recreational use of ololiuqui. Ingestion of a hundred or more seeds produces sleepiness, distorted perception, hallucinations, and confusion. Flashbacks have been reported, but they are infrequent.

Harmine. Harmine is a psychedelic agent that is obtained from the seeds of *Peganum harmala,* a plant native to the Middle East, and from *Banisteriopsis caapi* of the South American tropics. Intoxication by harmine is usually accompanied by nausea and vomiting, sedation, and finally sleep. The psychic excitement that users experience consists of visual distortions that are similar to those induced by LSD. Harmine probably acts through dopaminergic mechanisms as an MAO inhibitor (Chapter 9) (Iurlo et al., 2001). As discussed earlier, harmine is one of the ingredients in ayahuasca.

Glutaminergic NMDA Receptor Antagonists

Phencyclidine and Ketamine

Phencyclidine (PCP, angel dust) and ketamine (Figure 19.5) are referred to as psychedelic anesthetics because they were first developed as amnestic and analgesic drugs for use in anesthesia; later it was found that they also produced a psychedelic or dissociative state of being. These two drugs are structurally unrelated to the other psychedelic agents, and their psychedelic effects are unique: they do not involve actions on serotonin, acetylcholine, or dopamine neurons.

Phencyclidine was developed in 1956 and was briefly used as an anesthetic in humans before being abandoned because of a high incidence

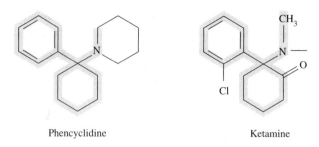

Phencyclidine   Ketamine

FIGURE 19.5 Structural formulas of the psychedelic anesthetic drugs phencyclidine and ketamine.

of psychiatric reactions, including agitation, excitement, delirium, disorientation, and hallucinatory phenomena (considered undesirable in the surgical patient!). The altered perception, disorganized thought, suspiciousness, confusion, and lack of cooperation that were exhibited resembled a schizophrenic state that consisted of both positive and negative symptoms (Jentsch and Roth, 1999). In fact both phencyclidine and ketamine can induce symptoms that are almost indistinguishable from those associated with schizophrenia (Murray, 2002). Phencyclidine is still used as a veterinary anesthetic, primarily as an immobilizing agent.

Ketamine (Ketalar) structurally resembles phencyclidine and was developed shortly after the prominent psychedelic properties of phencyclidine were identified. Introduced in 1960, ketamine induces a phencyclidinelike anesthetic state in low doses with fewer bothersome psychiatric side effects. The anesthetic state is characterized by amnesia and analgesia, combined with maintenance of blood pressure and respiration. Ketamine is occasionally used as anesthesia in patients who cannot tolerate the cardiovascular depressant effects of other anesthetics. Ketamine causes psychiatric reactions similar to but not as severe as those caused by PCP, including brief, reversible positive and negative schizophrenialike symptoms. Both PCP and ketamine can exacerbate psychosis in schizophrenia.

Abuse of phencyclidine and ketamine began in the mid-1960s. Today, abuse of phencyclidine and ketamine still persists, with periodic resurgences in popularity. Phencyclidine is the more commonly abused of the two and has appeared in the form of powders, tablets, leaf mixtures, and "rock" crystals. It is commonly sold as crystal, angel dust, hog, PCP, THC, cannabinol, or mescaline. When phencyclidine is sold as crystal or angel dust (terms also used for methamphetamine), the drug is usually in concentrations that vary between 50 and 90 percent. When it is purchased under other names or in concoctions, the amount of phencyclidine falls to between 10 and 30 percent; the typical street dose is about 5 milligrams (Zukin et al., 1997). Phencyclidine can be eaten, snorted, or injected, but it is most often smoked, sprinkled on tobacco, parsley, or marijuana. Frequently, phencyclidine is sold as a "club drug," although its pharmacology is entirely distinct from other club drugs such as ecstasy or GHB. As a club drug PCP is an analgesic/anesthetic/amnestic/ psychedelic.

Pharmacokinetics.   PCP is well absorbed whether taken orally or smoked. When it is smoked, peak effects occur in about 15 minutes, when about 40 percent of the dose appears in the user's bloodstream. Oral absorption is slower; maximum blood levels are reached about 2 hours after the drug has been taken. The elimination half-life is about 18 hours but ranges from about 11 to 51 hours. A positive urine assay for PCP is assumed to indicate that PCP was used within the previous week. Because false-positive test results are common, a positive assay requires secondary confirmation.

Mechanism of Action.   Phencyclidine and ketamine both exert their psychotomimetic, analgesic, amnestic actions and schizophrenic actions primarily as a result of binding as noncompetitive antagonists of the N-methyl-D-aspartate (NMDA)/glutamate receptors.[3] Several lines of evidence now implicate involvement of NMDA receptor dysfunction in the pathophysiology of schizophrenia (Chapter 11). Adler and coworkers (1999) conducted a neuropsychological comparison of normal volunteers to whom ketamine was administered and patients with schizophrenia. The results are illustrated in Figure 19.6. As can be seen, the ketamine-induced thought disorder is not dissimilar to that seen in patients with schizophrenia, providing support for the involvement of NMDA receptor dysfunction in the disease. Although acute doses of PCP and ketamine can induce a toxic psychosis, repeated doses induce a more persistent schizophrenic symptomatology, including psychosis, hallucinations, flattened affect, delusions, formal thought disorder, cognitive dysfunction, and social withdrawal.

Orser and coworkers (1997) concluded that ketamine inhibits NMDA receptors by two mechanisms: (1) blockade of the open channel by occupying a site within the channel in the receptor protein (as discussed earlier for phencyclidine) and (2) reduction in the frequency of

---

[3]The NMDA/PCP receptor complex has a molecular weight of 203,000 and is composed of four membrane-spanning polypeptides (molecular weights of 67,000, 57,000, 46,000, and 33,000), which cluster together to form an ion channel that resembles the benzodiazepine-GABA receptor. Here, however, the drug-binding site (the PCP receptor) is located within the lumen of the ion channel. Attachment of PCP to the receptor occludes the channel and inhibits calcium ion influx when the transmitter (glutamate) attaches to its receptor on the outer surface.

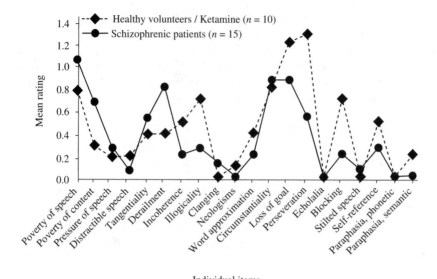

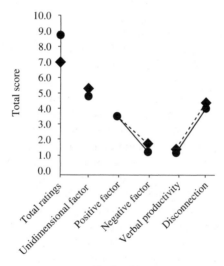

FIGURE 19.6 Comparison of total, factor, and individual item scores for the assessment of thought, language, and communication of 10 healthy volunteers with ketamine-induced thought disorder and 15 patients with schizophrenia (schizophrenic patients were ketamine-free). [From Adler et al. (1999) p. 1647.]

NMDA channel opening by drug binding to a second attachment site on the outside of the receptor protein. Phencyclidine probably shares this duality of action.

As noted, PCP and ketamine are powerful analgesic drugs. The mechanism seems to be twofold: these two drugs (1) activate NMDA-glutamate receptors in the spinal cord and (2) activate descending analgesic pathways, pathways that appear to involve norepinephrine and dopamine (Kawamata et al., 2000). Ketamine and PCP have complex interactions with dopamine in the CNS, interactions that probably are involved in both the schizophrenic and the analgesic actions of these drugs (Balla et al., 2003; Kapur and Seeman, 2002).

Psychological Effects.   Phencyclidine (and ketamine) dissociates individuals from themselves and their environment. It induces an unresponsive state with intense analgesia and amnesia, although the subject's eyes remain open (with a blank stare); the subject may even appear to be awake. When not used under controlled conditions, phencyclidine in low doses produces mild agitation, euphoria, disinhibition, or excitement in a person who appears to be grossly drunk and exhibits a blank stare. The subject may be rigid and unable to speak. In many cases, however, the subject is communicative but does not respond to pain.

PCP acutely induces a psychotic state in which subjects become withdrawn, autistic, negativistic, and unable to maintain a cognitive set; they manifest concrete, impoverished, idiosyncratic, and bizarre responses to questions. People under the influence of PCP exhibit profound alterations of higher emotional functions affecting judgment and cognition.

High doses of phencyclidine induce a state of coma or stupor. However, abusers tend to titrate their dose to maximize the intoxicant effect while attempting to avoid unconsciousness. Blood pressure usually becomes elevated, but respiration does not become depressed. The patient may recover from this state within 2 to 4 hours, although a state of confusion and cognitive poverty may last for 8 to 72 hours. The disruption of sensory input by PCP causes unpredictable exaggerated, distorted, or violent reactions to environmental stimuli. These reactions are augmented by PCP-induced analgesia and amnesia. Massive oral overdoses, involving up to 1 gram of street-purchased phencyclidine, result in prolonged periods of stupor or coma. This state may last for several days and may be marked by intense seizure activity, increased blood pressure, and a depression of respiration that is potentially lethal. Following this stupor, a prolonged recovery phase, marked by confusion and delusions, may last as long as 2 weeks. In some people, this state of confusion may be followed by a psychosis that lasts from several weeks to a few months.

Side Effects and Toxicity.   The course of recovery from a PCP-induced psychotic state is variable for reasons that are poorly understood. The intoxicated state may lead to severe anxiety, aggression, panic, paranoia, and rage. A user can also display violent reactions to sensory input, leading to such problems as falls, drowning, burns, driving accidents, and aggressive behavior. Self-inflicted injuries and injuries sustained while physical restraints are applied are frequent, and the potent analgesic action certainly contributes to the lack of response to pain.Respiratory depression, generalized seizure activity, and pulmonary edema have all been reported.

PCP is the only psychedelic drug self-administered by monkeys. In humans, this pattern of compulsive abuse is also seen. By inference, therefore, phencyclidine seems to stimulate brain reward areas and therefore places the user at risk of compulsive abuse despite negative health consequences.

Treatment of Intoxication.   Therapy for PCP intoxication is aimed at reducing the systemic level of the drug, keeping the individual calm and sedated, and preventing any of several severe adverse medical effects. It involves the following:

- Minimization of sensory inputs by placing the intoxicated individual in a quiet environment
- Oral administration of activated charcoal, which can bind any PCP present in the stomach and intestine and prevent its reabsorption
- Precautionary physical restraint to prevent self-injury
- Sedation with either a benzodiazepine (such as lorazepam) for agitation or an antipsychotic (such as haloperidol, clozapine, or olanzapine) for psychosis

Hyperthermia, hypertension, convulsions, renal failure, and other medical consequences should be treated as necessary by medical experts. PCP-induced psychotic states may be long-lasting, especially in individuals with a history of schizophrenia.

Dextromethorphan

The pharmacology of dextromethorphan (DXM) as an analgesic drug was discussed in Chapter 15. Mention is made of the drug here, however, because of a recent increase in DXM abuse, an event that appears to follow from high-dose DXM-induced NMDA receptor blockade, an action similar to that produced by PCP and ketamine. Indeed, in rats and monkeys, DXM and its metabolite dextrorphan (DXO) can substitute for PCP and exert PCP-like effects (Nicholson et al., 1999). In cough and cold preparations such as Coricidin and Robitussin, abuse of DXM is increasing (Baker and Borys, 2002: Banerji and Anderson, 2001) and is often referred to as "roboing," "dexing," "robo-tripping," or "robo-copping." Most abusers are in their teen years, and males exceed the number of females. Symptoms associated with intoxication include tachycardia, hypertension, sleepiness, agitation, disorientation, slurred speech, hallucinations, and tremor. The NMDA-glutamate blockade appears to ultimately result in augmentation of dopaminergic activity in the reward centers of the brain (Jahng et al., 2001).

Opioid Kappa Receptor Agonist: Salvinorin A

Salvia divinorum, a member if the mint family of perennial herbs, is a psychoactive plant that has been used for curing and for divination in traditional spiritual practices by the Mazatec peoples of Oaxaca, Mexico, for many centuries. More recently, young people in Mexico have smoked the dried leaves of the plant as a marijuana substitute. *Salvia* also grows in California and other parts of the United States as well as in other countries, such as Switzerland (Giroud et al., 2000). *Salvia* has been used as a short-acting, legal hallucinogen for several years because neither the "magic mint" nor its active compound are banned (yet!). *Salvia* is comparable in hallucinogenic efficacy to other hallucinogens such as psilocybin-containing mushrooms. In use, the fresh leaves of the plant are moistened and chewed as a quid and kept in the mouth. Alternatively, the dried leaves are smoked in the manner of marijuana or cocaine free base. The fresh leaves may also be eaten raw or prepared as an aqueous solution (Valdes, 1994). Parenteral injection of the solution has not been reported. The mint is essentially inactive if taken orally; the compound is effective when smoked in doses of 200 to 500 micrograms of active drug. Thus, *Salvia* contains the most potent naturally occurring hallucinogen thus far isolated (Valdes, 1994).

The main active ingredient of *Salvia divinorum* is a novel "diterpene" called *salvinorin A*. The molecular structure and mechanism of action of salvinorin A (Figure 19.7) are distinct from all other naturally occurring hallucinogens (such as DMT, psilocybin, and mescaline) as well as synthetic hallucinogens such as LSD and ketamine. Salvinorin A is reported to induce an intense hallucinatory experience in humans, with a typical duration of action of several minutes to an hour or so. Until recently, the mechanism of action of salvinorin A was unknown.

Roth and coworkers (2002) studied the molecular binding profile of salvinorin A at a large number (50) of cloned human G protein receptors, channels, and transporters known to be involved in psychopharmacology. Of all these, salvinorin A was active at only one receptor, the kappa opioid receptor, upon which it exerted an agonist action. Salvinorin A had no action at the serotonin 5-HT$_{2A}$ receptor, which is the principal molecular target responsible for the actions of classical hallucinogens such as LSD (Figure 19.8). Salvinorin A can

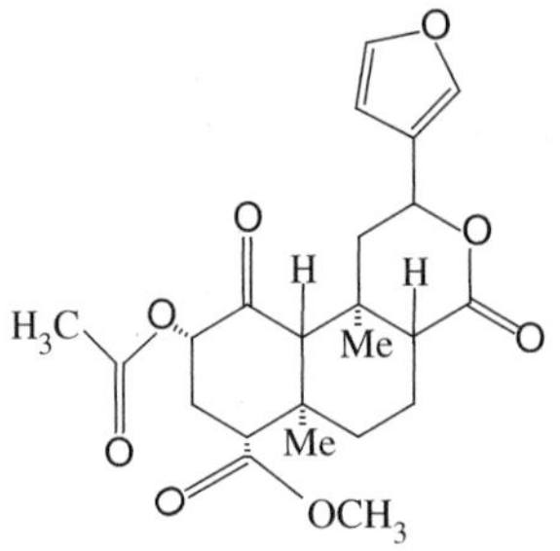

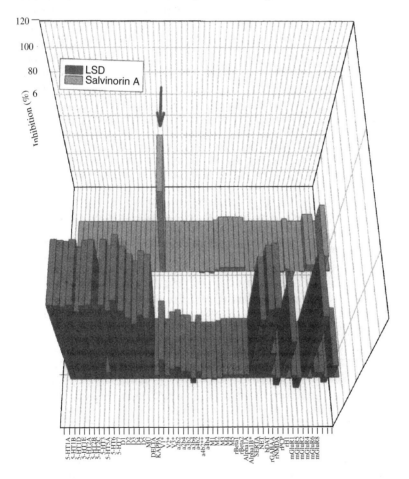

FIGURE 19.7 Structure of salvinorin A, the active drug in *Salvia divinorum*.

FIGURE 19.8 Large-scale screening of LSD and salvinorin A against many cloned G protein-type receptors. LSD binds to many receptors, especially those involving serotonin. Salvinorin A binds specifically to the kappa opioid receptor and is classified pharmacologically as a specific kappa opioid agonist. [From Roth et al. (2002), p. 11937.]

therefore now be classified as a *kappa opioid agonist*, the first naturally occurring compound to exhibit such an action. Roth and coworkers (2002) speculated that because of this action, kappa opioid receptors (see Chapter 15) may play a role in the regulation of human perception, and they suggest that kappa opioid antagonists (the opposite of salvinorin A) could represent a novel class of drugs with beneficial activity in diseases in which alterations in perception are predominant. Regardless, their results imply that the kappa opioid system may function to modulate human perception and cognition.

Finally, in a case report, Hanes (2001) reported on one patient with severe depression unrelieved by traditional antidepressant medications. This person obtained *Salvia* through a mail order house. She chewed two or three leaves at a time three times per week and claimed total remission of depressive symptoms. Continued use was accompanied by continued effectiveness, "engendering a kind of psychospiritual awakening, characterized by the discovery of her sense of self, greater self-confidence, increased feelings of intuitive wisdom, and connectedness to nature" (p. 634).

STUDY QUESTIONS

1. What is a psychedelic drug?
2. What differentiates a psychedelic drug from a behavioral stimulant? Discuss from both structural and behavioral viewpoints.
3. List the four classes of psychedelic drugs presented in this chapter.
4. Differentiate between mescaline and LSD.
5. How does LSD exert psychedelic actions?
6. What is the psychedelic syndrome?
7. What are some of the problems associated with LSD use?
8. How does phencyclidine work? Discuss the state of psychosis it produces.
9. What properties characterize the clinical usefulness of phencyclidine and ketamine?
10. Discuss the therapeutic and abuse potentials of dextromethorphan.
11. Compare salvinorum A with other psychedelic drugs.

REFERENCES

Abraham, H. D., and F. H. Duffy (2001). "EEG Coherence in Post-LSD Visual Hallucinations." *Psychiatry Research* 107: 151–163.

Abraham, H. D., et al. (1996). "The Psychopharmacology of Hallucinogens." *Neuropsychopharmacology* 14: 285–298.

Adler, C. M., et al. (1999). "Comparison of Ketamine-Induced Thought Disorder in Healthy Volunteers and Thought Disorder in Schizophrenia." *American Journal of Psychiatry* 156: 1646–1649.

Almaula, N., et al. (1996). "Mapping the Binding Site Pocket of the Serotonin 5-Hydroxytryptamine$_{2A}$ Receptor." *Journal of Biological Chemistry* 271: 14672–14675.

Baker, S. D., and D. J. Borys (2002). "A Possible Trend Suggesting Increased Abuse from Coricidin Exposures Reported to the Texas Poison Network: Comparing 1998 to 1999." *Veterinary and Human Toxicology* 44: 169–171.

Balla, A., et al. (2003). "Subchronic Continuous Phencyclidine Administration Potentiates Amphetamine-Induced Frontal Cortex Dopamine Release." *Neuropsychopharmacology* 28: 34–44.

Banerji, S., and I. B. Anderson (2001). "Abuse of Coricidin HBP Cough and Cold Tablets: Episodes Recorded by a Poison Center." *American Journal of Health-System Pharmacy* 58: 1811–1814.

Bruhn, J. G., et al. (2002). "Mescaline Use for 5,700 Years." *Lancet* 359: 1866.

Ciprian-Ollivier, J., and M. G. Cetkovich-Bakmas (1997). "Altered Consciousness States and Endogenous Psychosis: A Common Molecular Pathway?" *Schizophrenia Research* 28: 257–265.

Crahan, M. E. (1969). "God's Flesh and Other Pre-Columbian Phantastica." *Bulletin of the Los Angeles County Medical Association* 99: 17.

Croft, R. J., et al. (2001). "Electrophysiological Evidence of Serotonergic Impairment in Long-Term MDMA ('Ecstasy') Users." *American Journal of Psychiatry* 158: 1687–192.

Davis, K. L., et al., eds. (2002). *Psychopharmacology—The Fifth Generation of Progress.* Philadelphia: Lippincott, Williams & Wilkins.

Drug Enforcement Division (DEA), U. S. Department of Justice (2003). "Schedules of Controlled Substances: Temporary Placement of Alpha-Methyltryptamine, and 5-Methoxy-N,N-Diisopropyltryptamine in Schedule I. Final Rule." *Federal Register* 68 (65, April 4): 16427–16430.

Ebersole, B. J., et al. (2003). "Molecular Basis of Partial Agonism: Orientation of Indoleamine Ligands in the Binding Pocket of the Human Serotonin 5-HT$_{2A}$ Receptor Determines Relative Efficacy."*Molecular Pharmacology* 63: 36–43.

Fiege, M., et al. (2003). "Induction of Malignant Hyperthermia in Susceptible Swine by 3,4-Methylenedioxymethamphetamine ('Ecstasy')." *Anesthesiology* 99: 1132–1136.

Giroud, C., et al. (2000). "*Salvia divinorum:* A Hallucinogenic Mint Which Might Become a New Recreational Drug in Switzerland." *Forensic Science International* 112: 143–150.

Goodman, N. (2002). "The Serotonergic System and Mysticism: Could LSD and the Nondrug-Induced Experience Share Common Neural Mechanisms?" *Journal of Psychoactive Drugs* 34: 263–272.

Gouzoulis-Mayfrank, E., et al. (1999). "Neurometabolic Effects of Psilocybin, 3,4-Methylenedioxyethylamphetamine (MDE) and d-Methamphetamine in Healthy Volunteers: A Double-Blind, Placebo-Controlled PET Study with [18F]FDG." *Neuropsychopharmacology* 20: 565–581.

Gresch, P. J., et al. (2002). "Lysergic Acid Diethylamide-Induced Fos Expression in Rat Brain: Role of Serotonin-2A Receptors." *Neuroscience* 114: 707–713.

Halpern, J. H., and H. G. Pope, Jr. (1999). "Do Hallucinogens Cause Residual Neuropsychological Toxicity?" *Drug and Alcohol Dependence* 53: 247–256.

Hanes, K. R. (2001). "Antidepressant Effects of the Herb *Salvia divinorum:* A Case Report." *Journal of Clinical Psychopharmacology* 21: 634–635.

Hermle, L., et al. (1998). "Blood Flow and Cerebral Laterality in the Mescaline Model of Psychosis." *Pharmacopsychiatry* 31, Supplement 2: 85–91.

Hofmann, A. (1994). "Notes and Documents Concerning the Discovery of LSD." *Agents and Actions* 43: 79–81.

Holzman, R. S. (1998). "The Legacy of Atropos, the Fate Who Cut the Thread of Life." *Anesthesiology* 89: 241–249.

Iurlo, M., et al. (2001). "Effects of Harmine on Dopamine Output and Metabolism in Rat Striatum: Role of Monoamine Oxidase-A Inhibition." *Psychopharmacology* 159: 98–104.

Jahng, J. W., et al. (2001). "Effects of Dextromethorphan on Nocturnal Behavior and Brain c-Fos Expression in Adolescent Rats." *European Journal of Pharmacology* 43: 47–52.

Jentsch, J. D., and R. H. Roth (1999). "The Neuropharmacology of Phencyclidine: From NMDA Receptor Hypofunction to the Dopamine Hypothesis of Schizophrenia." *Neuropsychopharmacology* 20: 201–225.

Kalant, H. (2001). "The Pharmacology and Toxicology of 'Ecstasy' (MDMA) and Related Drugs." *Canadian Medical Association Journal* 165: 917–928.

Kapur, S., and P. Seeman (2002). "NMDA Receptor Antagonists Ketamine and PCP Have Direct Effects on the Dopamine D-2 and Serotonin 5-HT2 Receptors: Implications for Models of Schizophrenia." *Molecular Psychiatry* 7: 837–844.

Karkkainen, J., et al. (1995). "Urinary Excretion of Bufotenin (N,N-Dimethyl-5-hydroxytryptamine) Is Increased in Suspicious Violent Offenders: A Confirmatory Study." *Psychiatry Research* 58: 145–152.

Kawamata, T., et al. (2000). "Analgesic Mechanisms of Ketamine in the Presence and Absence of Peripheral Inflammation." *Anesthesiology* 93: 520–528.

Kish, S. J., et al. (2000). "Striatal Serotonin Is Depleted in Brain of a Human MDMA (Ecstasy) User." Neurology 55: 294–296.

Klette, K. L., et al. (2000). "Metabolism of Lysergic Acid Diethylamide (LSD) to 2-Oxo-3-Hydroxy LSD (O-H-LSD) in Human Liver Microsomes and Cryopreserved Human Hepatocytes." *Journal of Analytical Toxicology* 24: 550–556.

Lerner, A. G., et al. (2001). "LSD-Induced Hallucinogen Persisting Perception Disorder Treated with Clonazepam: Two Case Reports." *Israel Journal of Psychiatry and Related Sciences* 38: 133–136.

Lerner, A. G., et al. (2002a). "Flashback and Hallucinogen Persisting Perception Disorder: Clinical Aspects and Pharmacological Treatment Approach." *Israel Journal of Psychiatry and Related Sciences* 39: 92–99.

Lerner, A. G., et al. (2002b). "LSD-Induced Hallucinogen Persisting Perception Disorder with Depressive Features Treated with Reboxetine." *Israel Journal of Psychiatry and Related Sciences* 39: 100–103.

Lyttle, T., et al. (1996). "Bufo Toads and Bufotenine: Fact and Fiction Surrounding an Alleged Psychedelic." *Journal of Psychoactive Drugs* 28: 267–290.

McBride, M. C. (2000). "Bufotenine: Toward an Understanding of Possible Psychoactive Mechanisms." *Journal of Psychoactive Drugs* 32: 321–331.

Mintzer, M. Z., and R. R. Griffiths. (2003). "Lorazepam and Scopolamine: A Single-Dose Comparison of Effects on Human Memory and Attentional Processes." *Experimental and Clinical Psychopharmacology* 11: 56–72.

Montoya, A. G., et al. (2002). "Long-Term Neuropsychiatric Consequences of 'Ecstasy' (MDMA): A Review." *Harvard Review of Psychiatry* 10: 212–220.

Morgan, M. J. (2000). "Ecstasy (MDMA): A Review of Its Possible Persistent Psychological Effects." *Psychopharmacology* 152: 230–248.

Murray, J. B. (2002). "Phencyclidine (PCP): A Dangerous Drug, but Useful in Schizophrenia Research." *Journal of Psychology* 136: 319–327.

Nicholson, K. L., et al. (1999). "Evaluation of the Reinforcing Properties and Phencyclidine-like Discriminative Stimulus Effects of Dextromethorphan and Dextrorphan in Rats and Rhesus Monkeys." *Psychopharmacology* 146: 49–59.

Orser, B. A, et al. (1997). "Multiple Mechanisms of Ketamine Blockade of N-methyl-D-aspartate Receptors." *Anesthesiology* 86: 903–917.

Reneman, L., et al. (2001). "Cortical Serotonin Transporter Density and Verbal Memory in Individuals Who Stopped Using 3,4-Methylenedioxymethamphetamine (MDMA or 'Ecstasy')." *Archives of General Psychiatry* 58: 901–906.

Riba, J., et al. (2001). "Subjective Effects and Tolerability of the South American Psychoactive Beverage Ayahuasca in Healthy Volunteers." *Psychopharmacology* 154: 85–95.

Riba, J., et al. (2002). "Effects of Ayahuasca on Sensory and Sensory-Motor Gating in Humans as Measured by P50 Suppression and Preimpulse Inhibition of the Startle Reflex, Respectively." *Psychopharmacology* 165: 18–28.

Ricaurte, G. A., et al. (2002). "Severe Dopaminergic Neurotoxicity in Primates After a Common Recreational Dose Regimen of MDMA ('Ecstasy')." *Science* 297: 2260–2263.

Roth, B. L., et al. (2002). "Salvinorin A: A Potent Naturally Occurring Nonnitrogenous Opioid Selective Agonist." *Proceedings of the National Academy of Sciences of the United States of America* 99: 11934–11939.

Sangalli, B. C., and W. Chiang (2000). "Toxicology of Nutmeg Abuse." *Journal of Toxicology—Clinical Toxicology* 38: 671–678.

Smith, R. L., et al. (1998). "Agonist Properties of N,N-dimethyltryptamine at Serotonin 5-HT2A and 5-HT2C Receptors." *Pharmacology, Biochemistry and Behavior* 61: 323–330.

Sprague, J. E., et al. (1998). "An Integrated Hypothesis for the Serotonergic Axonal Loss Induced by 3,4-methylenedioxymethamphetamine." *Neurotoxicology* 19: 427–441.

Strassman, R. J., et al. (1994). "Dose-Response Study of N,N-dimethyltryptamine in Humans. II: Subjective Effects and Preliminary Results of a New Rating Scale." *Archives of General Psychiatry* 51: 98–108.

Takeda, N. (1994). "Serotonin-Degradative Pathways in the Toad (*Bufo japonicus*) Brain: Clues to the Pharmacological Analysis of Human Psychiatric Disorders." *Comparative Biochemistry and Physiology Part C: Pharmacology, Toxicology and Endocrinology* 107: 275–281.

Takeda, N., et al. (1995). "Bufotenine Reconsidered as a Diagnostic Indicator of Psychiatric Disorders." *NeuroReport* 6: 2378–2380.

Topp, L., et al. (1999). "Ecstasy Use in Australia: Patterns of Use and Associated Harm." *Drug and Alcohol Dependence* 55: 105–115.

Umbricht, D., et al. (2003). "Effects of the 5-HT2A Agonist Psilocybin on Mismatch Negativity Generation and AX-Continuous Performance Task: Implications for the Neuropharmacology of Cognitive Deficits in Schizophrenia." *Neuropsychopharmacology* 28: 170–181.

Valdes, L. J. (1994). "*Salvia divinorum* and the Unique Diterpene Hallucinogen, Salvinorin (Divinorin) A." *Journal of Psychoactive Drugs* 26: 277–283.

Van Oekelen, D., et al. (2003). "5-HT$_{2A}$ and 5-HT$_{2C}$ Receptors and Their Atypical Regulation Properties." *Life Sciences* 72: 2429–2449.

Vollenweider, F. X., et al. (1999). "5-HT Modulation of Dopamine Release in Basal Ganglia in Psilocybin-Induced Psychosis in Man: A PET Study with [^{11}C]raclopride." *Neuropsychopharmacology* 20: 424–433.

Weil, A. (1980). *The Marriage of the Sun and the Moon*. Boston: Houghton Mifflin.

Wogoman, H., et al. (1999). "Acute Intoxication with Guaifenesin, Diphenhydramine, and Chlorpheniramine." *American Journal of Forensic Medicine and Pathology*, 20: 199–202.

Yuan, J., et al. (2002). "Effect of Depleting Vesicular and Cytoplasmic Dopamine on Methylenedioxymethamphetamine Neurotoxicity." *Journal of Neurochemistry* 80: 960–969.

Zukin, S. R., et al. (1997). "Phencyclidine (PCP)." In J. H. Lowinson, P. Ruiz, R. B. Millman, and J. G. Langrod, eds., *Substance Abuse: A Comprehensive Textbook*, 3rd ed. (pp. 238–246). Baltimore: Williams & Wilkins.

Chapter 20

Anabolic Steroids

"Anabolic steroids" is the familiar name for synthetic substances related to the male sex hormone testosterone (National Institute on Drug Abuse, 2003). Anabolic steroids have both muscle-building (anabolic) and masculinizing effects, and illicit use is a common practice among adolescents and adults, both male and female, athletes and nonathletes. While it may not be surprising that 55 percent of 27-year-old male and 10 percent of 24-year-old female bodybuilders use anabolic steroids, the prevalence of anabolic steroid injection in college athletics may be as high as 20 percent, and anabolic steroid use in high schools has been estimated as high as 7 percent for males and 3 percent for females. Lifetime use is 4.9 percent for males and 2.4 percent for females, and the numbers are likely to increase (Yesalis et al., 1997). More than 1 million Americans have used these hormones illicitly either to improve athletic performance or to improve personal appearance, and more than 50 percent are age 26 years or older; the prevalence of use of anabolic steroids is equal in both athletes and nonathletes (Naylor et al., 2001).

In both athletes and nonathletes, anabolic steroids promote increased muscle mass and enhance physical strength, endurance, physical appearance, and athletic performance. The use of the testosterone precursor *androstenedione* by baseball home run record holder Mark McGwire focused even more attention on steroid use by athletes. In the year 2003, the previously undetectable anabolic steroid *tetrahydro-gestrinone (THG)* incited a furor in the written press when high-profile professional athletes admitted to using this muscle-building, performance-enhancing drug. Subsequently, in March 2004 the federal Food and Drug Administration classified this drug as an illegal substance. Tests are now available to detect the drug in urine.

As well as illicit use, anabolic steroids have well-recognized uses in prescription medicine (Dobs, 1999). Uses of these agents include the treatment of delayed puberty and the prevention of weight loss both in renal failure patients undergoing hemodialysis and in males with HIV (AIDS)-related weight loss. Rabkin and coworkers (2000) studied the effects of weekly injections of testosterone in 70 males with symptomatic HIV illness. The majority reported improved libido and energy, improvements in mood, and increases in muscle mass.

Much of the controversy over anabolic steroid use, medical and illicit, involves the documented health risks associated with steroid use as well as the "unfair advantage" a performance-enhancing drug offers the competitive athlete. Also, adolescent nonathletes who use steroids as cosmetic enhancers place themselves at risk for long-term health problems, and they also may suffer from serious body self-image problems that should be attended to.

Testosterone is the primary male sex hormone. Normally, the levels of testosterone in the body are tightly regulated by a negative feedback system involving the testes (where testosterone is synthesized), the hypothalamus, and the pituitary gland (Figure 20.1). When the plasma level of testosterone falls, cells in the hypothalamus (which has receptors sensitive to the circulating amount of testosterone) sense the decrease and begin producing a releasing factor called *gonadotropin-releasing factor* (GRF). GRF circulates in blood to the pituitary gland and stimulates the pituitary to produce and release *follicle-stimulating hormone* (FSH) and *luteinizing hormone* (LH). In turn, FSH and LH act on the testes to induce both spermatogenesis (the production of sperm) and synthesis and release of testosterone. (A similar process in the female regulates fertility.)

As testosterone levels in blood increase, the hypothalamus decreases its production of GRF; the pituitary decreases production of FSH and LH; the testes decrease production of testosterone and sperm; and the process repeats. Administering anabolic steroids overwhelms this system; abnormally high levels of steroids shut off production of GRF, FSH, LH, and testosterone and shut off the process of spermatogenesis. Therefore, anabolic steroids (1) block the normal process that regulates testosterone, male fertility, and spermatogenesis, (2) exert peripheral hormone actions to increase muscle

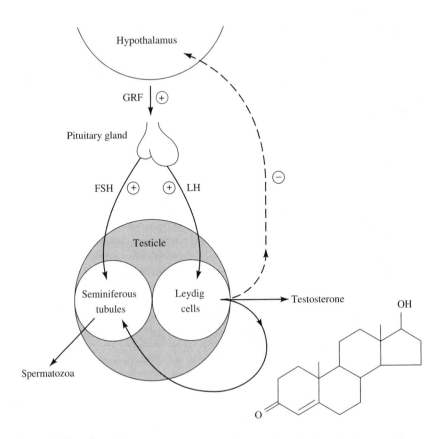

FIGURE 20.1 Hormonal regulation of male fertility. The brain (hypothalamus and pituitary gland) is involved in the control of fertility. However, fertility in the male is not subject to periodic cycling as it is in the female. The structure of naturally occurring testosterone is shown. GRF = gonadotropin-releasing factor; FSH = follicle-stimulating hormone; LH = luteinizing hormone. Solid arrows = stimulation; dashed arrows = inhibition.

mass and produce a more masculine appearance, and (3) exert central effects that increase aggression.

Mechanism of Action

The structures of testosterone and several synthetically produced anabolic steroids are illustrated in Figure 20.2. The structures of two related substances are not illustrated. They are (1) androstenedione, thought to be a precursor to testosterone, and (2) dehydroepiandrosterone (DHEA),

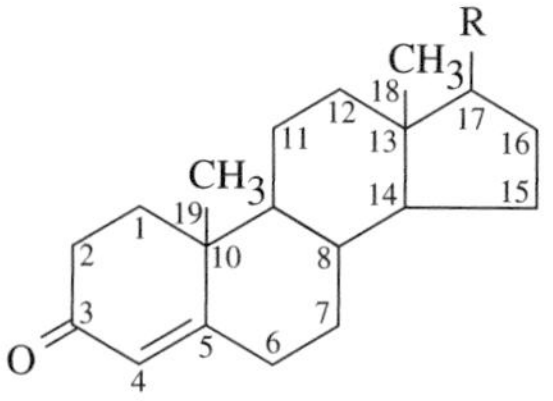

Compound	R
Testosterone	–OH
Testosterone propionate	–O–COCH$_2$CH$_3$
Testosterone enanthate	–O–CO(CH$_2$)$_5$CH$_3$
Testosterone cypionate	–O–COCH$_2$CH$_2$– (cyclopentane) 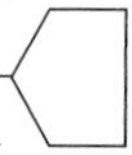
Nandrolone decanoate	–O–CO(CH$_2$)$_8$CH$_3$ (no methyl group at position 19)
Nandrolone phenpropionate	–O–CO(CH$_2$)$_2$  – (phenyl) (no methyl group at position 19)

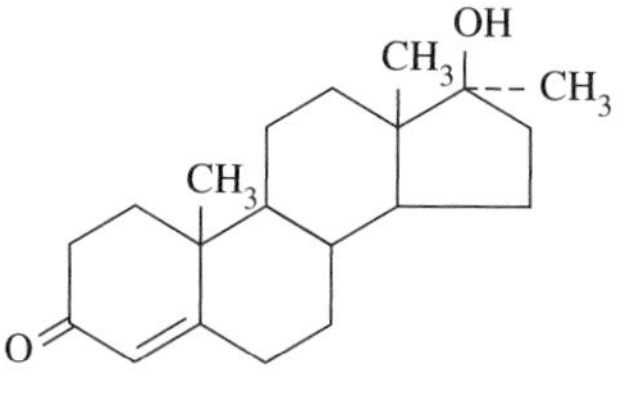

Methyltestosterone

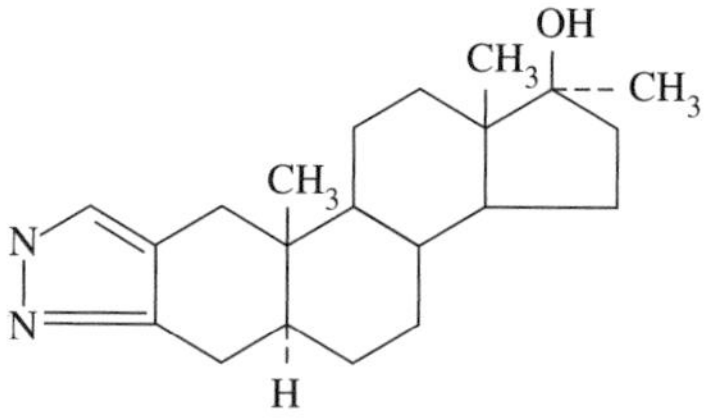

Stanozolol

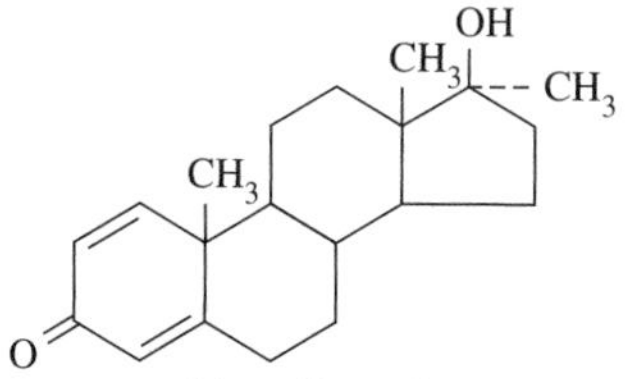

Metandienone

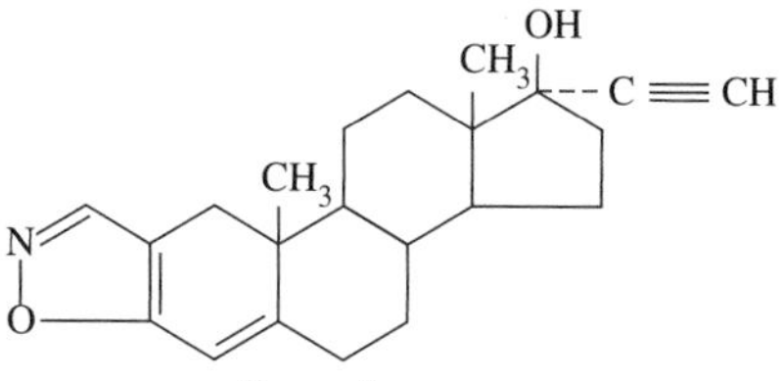

Danazol

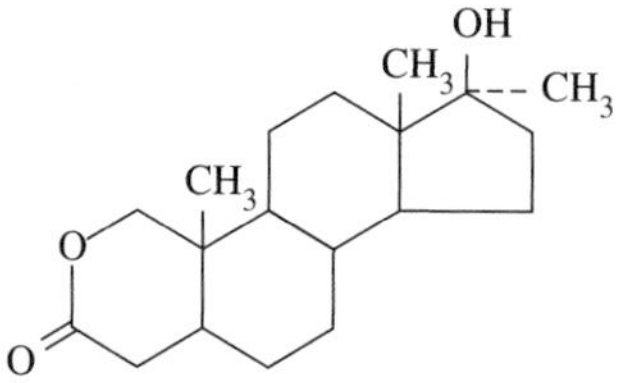

Oxandrolone

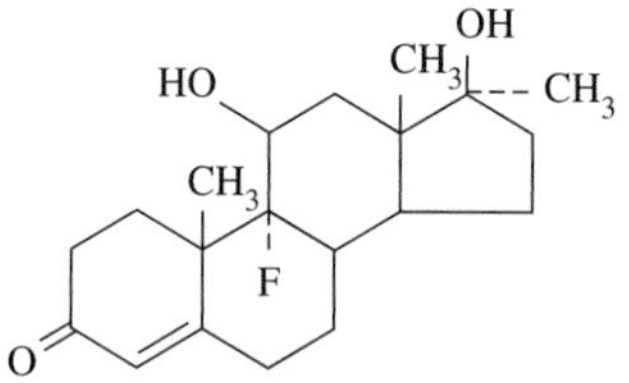

Fluoxymesterone

FIGURE 20.2 Structures of some common parenteral (*left*) and oral (*right*) anabolic-androgenic steroids. [From S. E. Lucas, "Current Perspectives on Anabolic-Androgenic Steroid Abuse," *Trends in Pharmacological Sciences* 14 (1993); p. 62.]

an androgen released by the adrenal glands. Their structures are not included in Figure 20.2 because, as stated by Yesalis and Bahrke (2002):

> Androstenedione is an anabolic-androgenic steroid used to increase blood testosterone levels for purposes of increasing strength, lean body mass, and sexual performance. However, there is no research indicating androstenedione or its related compounds significantly increase strength and/or lean body mass by increasing testosterone levels. . . . Dehydroepiandrosterone (DHEA) is a weak androgen also used to elevate testosterone levels. DHEA is also advertised as an anti-obesisty and anti-aging supplement capable of improving libido, vitality, and immunity levels. However, research demonstrates that DHEA supplementation does not increase serum testosterone concentrations or increase strength in men and it may have virilizing effects in women. (p. 246)

All anabolic steroids differ from each other not so much in structure as in their individual resistance to metabolic degradation by liver enzymes. After oral administration, testosterone is effectively absorbed from the intestine. Following absorption, it is rapidly transported in the blood to the liver, where it is immediately metabolized. As a result, little testosterone reaches the systemic circulation. Administered by injection, some of this first-pass metabolism is blunted, and it is the metabolic product, androstanolone, that is most active as an anabolic substance. Structural modification of the testosterone molecule reduces this rapid metabolic breakdown and thus improves the effectiveness of both oral and intramuscular administration.

Not all anabolic steroids are illicit substances. Eight synthetic anabolic steroids (Table 20.1) are approved in the United States for therapeutic uses, including testosterone replacement in hypogonadal males, the treatment of certain blood anemias and severe muscle loss following trauma, HIV, renal dialysis, and, in females, the treatment of endometriosis and fibrocystic disease of the breast. In malnourished males with severe pulmonary disease (chronic obstructive pulmonary disease), 27 weeks of oral androgen therapy increased lean body mass and muscle mass even though endurance capacity was not changed (Ferreira et al., 1998). Therefore, in states of malnutrition, anabolic steroid therapy increases muscle mass, an effect that hopefully will reduce mortality and improve quality of life.

The mechanism of action of testosterone and the various anabolic steroids is quite well understood. Testosterone is synthesized principally in a specialized type of cell (the Leydig cell) of the testes (see Figure 20.1) under the influence of GRF released from the hypothalamus, which stimulates the synthesis and release of LH from the pituitary gland; LH acts on the Leydig cells to stimulate testosterone production.

Table 20.1 Anabolic-androgenic steroids

Name	Route	Brand name
APPROVED IN UNITED STATES		
Testosterone cypionate	im	Depo-Testosterone, Virilon
Nandrolone phenpropionate	im	Durabolin
Nandrolone decanoate	im	Deca-Duraboli
Danazol	po	Danocrine
Fluoxymesterone	po	Halotestin
Methyltestosterone	po	Android, Metandren, Testred, Virilon
Oxymetholone	po	Anadrol-50
Slanozolol	po	Winstrol
APPROVED OUTSIDE UNITED STATES		
Testosterone enanthate	im	Delatestryl
Testosterone propionate	im	Testex, Oreton propionate
Methenolone enanthate	im	Primobolan Depot
Ethylestrenol	po	Maxibolan
Mesterolone	po	
Methandrostenolone	po	Dianabol
Methenolone	po	Primobolan
Norethandrolone	po	
Oxandrolone	po	Anavar
Oxymesterone	po	Oranabol
APPROVED FOR VETERINARY USE		
Bolasterone	im	Finiject 30
Boldenone undecylenate	im	Equipoise
Stanozolol	im	Winstrol
Mibolerone	po	

im = intramuscular; po = oral.

Once in the bloodstream, testosterone (or an anabolic steroid) passes through the cell walls of its target tissues and attaches to steroid receptors in the cytoplasm of the cell (Figure 20.3). This hormone-receptor complex is translocated into the nucleus of the cell and attaches to the nuclear material (the DNA). A process of genetic transcription follows, and new messenger RNA is produced. Translation of this RNA results in the production of specific new proteins that leave the cell and mediate the biological functions of the hormone. Thus, the

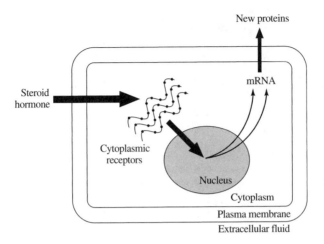

FIGURE 20.3 Mechanism of action of steroid hormones on cells. The hormone passes through the cell wall of its target tissue and binds to steroid receptors in the cytoplasm. The hormone-receptor complex moves into the nucleus and binds to sites on the chromatin, which is transcribed to give specific messenger RNA (mRNA). The mRNA is translated into specific new proteins that mediate the function of the hormone. [From S. E. Lucas, "Current Perspectives on Anabolic-Androgenic Steroid Abuse," *Trends in Pharmacological Sciences* 14 (1993); p. 63.]

effects of anabolic steroids on target cells are mediated by intracellular receptors and the synthesis of new proteins. The increased levels of circulating testosterone (or anabolic steroid) exert a negative feedback effect on the hypothalamus, inhibiting further stimulation of testosterone release.

Effects

People use anabolic steroids for many reasons. Commonly, steroids are used to improve athletic performance because they increase body muscle and reduce body fat. Both competitive bodybuilders and other athletes take advantage of this effect, using either the steroids themselves or their precursors. Nonathletes use these agents to achieve a desired shape when they have a skewed perception of their body habitus. None of these people recognize the breadth of the effects of these agents on the body, the brain, and behavior.

Effects on Athletic Performance

Because testosterone and anabolic steroids increase protein synthesis, they increase muscle mass and strength and produce a more masculine appearance. The assumption that this is what happens has been around for decades, but a 1996 report by Bhasin and coworkers was the first to demonstrate that supraphysiologic doses of testosterone, with or without strength training, increase fat-free mass, muscle size, and strength in normal men. As shown in Figure 20.4, exercise alone or testosterone alone produced increases in strength, triceps and quadriceps size, and fat-free mass. The combination of testosterone

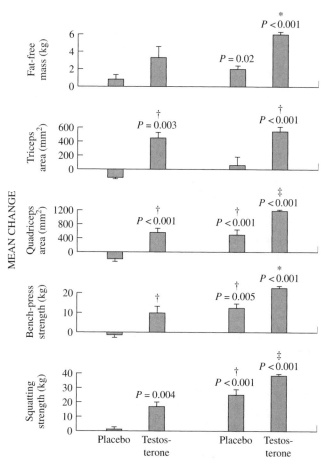

FIGURE 20.4 Changes from baseline in mean (±SE) fat-free mass, triceps, and quadriceps cross-sectional areas, and muscle strength in the bench-press and squatting exercises over 10 weeks of treatment with testosterone. The P values shown are for the comparison between the change indicated and a change of zero. The asterisks indicate $P < 0.05$ for the comparison between the change indicated and that in either no-exercise group; the daggers indicate $P < 0.05$ for the comparison between the change indicated and that in the group assigned to placebo with no exercise; the double daggers indicate $P < 0.05$ for the comparison between the change indicated and the changes in all three other groups. [From Bhasin et al. (1996), p. 6.]

and exercise produced additive increases. Despite these beneficial effects of testosterone, the authors concluded:

> Our results in no way justify the use of anabolic-androgenic steroids in sports, because, with extended use, such drugs have potentially serious adverse effects on the cardiovascular system, prostate, lipid metabolism, and insulin sensitivity. Moreover, the use of any performance-enhancing agent in sports raises serious ethical issues. (p. 6)

Hartgens and coworkers (2002) studied the increased muscle fiber size in experienced male athletes. Compared with controls, polydrug regimens of anabolic steroids at supratherapeutic dosages increased the size of deltoid muscle fibers in experienced strength-trained athletes, while a therapeutic dose of an anabolic steroid (nandrolone) did not exert any effect. In rats trained to weight lift, anabolic steroids enhance the rate of protein synthesis, enhance work capacity, and reduce fatigue (Tamaki et al., 2001).

Thus, anabolic steroids increase both the size and the strength of the athlete and thereby improve performance in athletic activities that require size, strength, and endurance. They have no positive effects on aerobic performance (Haupt, 1993). Therefore, athletes who depend on aerobic energy expenditure (for example, long-distance runners) benefit less from anabolic steroids than do athletes who depend on bulk size and short bursts of energy expenditure (football players and sprint runners, for example).

Anabolic steroids exert effects through anticatabolic, anabolic, and motivational effects on the athlete. Table 20.2 summarizes the constellation of effects and side effects. In the *anticatabolic effect,* the anabolic steroids block the action of natural cortisone, which normally functions to increase energy stores during periods of stress and training. Cortisone makes energy stores available by breaking down proteins into their constituent amino acids. Carried to excess, muscle wasting can occur. This action is blocked by the anabolic steroids. The anticatabolic action may be the major mechanism by which these drugs increase body mass.

The *anabolic effects* follow both the synthesis of new protein in muscle cells and steroid-induced release of endogenous growth hormone. However, the doses commonly used by athletes are 10 to 200 times the therapeutic dosage for testosterone deficiency. These doses often involve the "stacking" or "pyramiding" of several drugs, even combining oral and injectable substances through cycles of several weeks' duration (Galloway, 1997).

In the female athlete, anabolic steroids exert the same anabolic and anticatabolic effects found in male athletes. However, these drugs also induce in females masculinizing and related effects, including increases

Table 20.2 Effects of anabolic-androgenic steroids

POSITIVE EFFECTS
   Transient increase in muscular size and strength
   Treatment of catabolic states
      Trauma
      Surgery
ADVERSE EFFECTS
   Cardiovascular
      Increase in cardiac risk factors
         Hypertension
         Altered lipoprotein fractions
         Increase in LDL/HDL ratio
      Reported strokes/myocardial infarctions
   Hepatic effects associated with oral compounds
      Elevated liver enzymes
      Peliosis hepatis (greater than 6 months' use)
      Liver tumors
         Benign
         Malignant (greater than 24 months' use)
   Reproductive system effects
      In males
         Decreased testosterone production
            Abnormal spermatogenesis
            Transient infertility
            Testicular atrophy
      In females
         Altered menstruation
   Endocrine effects
      Decreased thyroid function
   Immunologic effects
      Decreased immunoglobulins IgM/IgA/IgC
   Musculoskeletal effects
      Premature closure of bony growth centers
      Tendon degeneration
         Increased risk of tendon tears
   Cosmetic
      In males
         Gynecomastia
         Testicular atrophy
         Acne
         Acceleration of male-pattern baldness
      In females
         Clittoral enlargement
         Acne
         Increased facial/body hair
         Coarsening of the skin
         Male-pattern baldness
         Deepened voice
   Psychologic
      Risk of habituation
      Severe mood swings
      Aggressive tendencies
      Psychotic episodes
      Depression
      Reports of suicide
   Legislation
      Classified as Schedule III controlled substance

From Haupt (1993), p. 471.

in facial and body hair, lowered voice, enlarged clitoris, coarser skin, and menstrual cycle cessation or irregularity. Cessation of steroid use results in a variable and often incomplete reversal of the altered functions. Tuiten and colleagues (2000) administered sublingual testosterone to eight healthy females and evaluated its effects on sexual arousal. Testosterone achieved maximal plasma levels in 15 minutes, returning to baseline levels by 90 minutes. At about 4.5 hours, significant increases in arousal and genital responsiveness occurred. Alterations in "central" hormonal mechanisms were postulated to account for the discrepancy between plasma levels and physiological responses.

Effects on Physical Appearance

Anabolic steroids are widely used (and abused) by young male (usually noncompetitive) athletes who take them to develop the muscular physique considered fashionable. As many as 250,000 to 500,000 young adult males may take steroids. Regardless of the exact number, a significant number of teenagers and young adults, primarily male, use suprahysiologic doses of anabolic steroids to give them more muscle strength and a more powerful, masculine appearance. Unlike competitive athletes who often choose to terminate drug use when competition ends, nonathlete youths may continue to take steroids in order to maintain the cosmetic effect. As stated by Schwerin and coworkers (1996):

> Physique and physical appearance are ever important in how people are viewed in their social environment. With these come the spoils: social acceptance, admiration, and opportunity. To a certain extent, an attractive physique is related to enhanced self-esteem and perceived social competence. . . . Sometimes the drive reaches an unhealthy extreme . . . taking the form of anorexia, bulimia, and anabolic steroid use. (p. 1)

Furthermore:

> Anabolic steroid users present an appearance of healthfulness, strength, "sex appeal," and physical attractiveness. Other illicit drugs do not present such an image of healthfulness. . . . It may be this contradiction of increased steroid use leading to increased appearance of healthfulness and physical attractivenes which may allow the seriousness of steroid use to remain underappreciated. . . . Anabolic steroids are the only addictive substance over the short to middle term that enhances a user's physical appearance and whose purpose is to allow the user to work harder and longer (though stimulants share the latter characteristic). (pp. 6–7)

Endocrine Effects

Males taking anabolic steroids experience a hypogonadal state, which is characterized by atrophy of the testicles, impaired production of sperm, and infertility, causing reduced libido and impotence (Torres-Calleja et al., 2001). In addition, gynecomastia (enlargement of the breasts in males) may occur and may require surgical treatment (Babigian and Silverman, 2001). In females, puberty is delayed and estrous cyclicity is adversely affected. These effects are usually reversible within a few months after cessation of drug use.

Cardiovascular Effects

Adverse effects of anabolic steroids on the cardiovascular system have been of concern, and reports of fatal myocardial infarctions (heart attacks) occurring in users of anabolic steroids implicate arteriosclerosis-induced coronary artery disease as a cause of death. Thus, analysis of the potential correlation between anabolic steroids and arteriosclerosis is important. The effect of these steroids on blood cholesterol as a predisposing factor to atherosclerotic coronary artery disease must be considered. Cholesterol is of two types: "bad" cholesterol (low-density lipoprotein cholesterol, or LDL) and "good" cholesterol (high-density lipoprotein cholesterol, or HDL). Decreasing HDL and increasing LDL are strongly correlated with an increased risk of coronary artery disease.

All anabolic steroids induce a reduction in serum HDL cholesterol and an elevation in LDL cholesterol. This effect suggests that individuals taking these drugs are at greater risk of developing atheromatous plaques within arteries, which places such individuals at increased risk of coronary artery disease. This condition can be expressed as myocardial infarctions, thromboembolic disease (blood clots and emboli), strokes, and hypertension. The actual risk of cardiovascular disease is unknown, largely due to the young age of users, their relatively lean or muscular physiques, and the intermittent pattern of drug use. Once these users are adults, it can be determined whether using anabolic steroids during their earlier years harmed them. Hartgens and coworkers (2002), Heriex and Kuipers (2003), and Karila and coworkers (2003) review the cardiovascular effects of the anabolic steroids and propose several models to explain their toxicity, including new information on drug-induced hypertrophy of the left ventricular muscle.

Effects on the Liver

The use of oral anabolic steroid preparations has been associated with a risk of liver disorders, especially jaundice and tumors. Increases in the blood levels of liver enzymes, indicative of possible liver dysfunction, are quite common among steroid users. Such adverse effects appear to resolve within a year after cessation of drug use (Urhausen et al., 2003). Hepatitis is also common, perhaps as a result of reusing needles (Aitken et al., 2002). In addition, several dozen cases of liver carcinomas of unusual types have been reported. The incidence of developing these potentially fatal carcinomas is estimated to be 1 to 3 percent within two to eight years of exposure to drugs.

Psychological Effects

Anabolic steroids are centrally acting drugs, involved in the regulation of sexuality, aggression, cognition, emotion, and personality. Thus, drug-induced increases in aggression, competitiveness, and combativeness can be predicted in people who use large doses of these drugs. It is now well established that areas of the brain that influence mood and judgment contain steroid receptors and that sharp fluctuations in the levels of steroid hormones have important psychological effects.

The *motivational* and *behavioral effects* are profound: athletes taking anabolic steroids often develop very aggressive personalities, a condition nicknamed "roid rage." For some sports, such as football, the enhancement of combativeness can be desirable. But for most purposes, the adverse behavioral effects associated with anabolic steroids are detrimental. These effects include anger, violent feelings, irritability, forgetfulness, and distractibility (Daly et al., 2003). Clearly, users of anabolic steroids tend to be less in control of their aggression, and increases in aggression are reported by 60 percent of steroid users (Midgley et al., 2001). However, it is unclear whether steroid use causes aggression or whether aggressive individuals are attracted to steroid use. The prevalence of extreme cases of violence and behavioral disorders seems to be low (National Institute on Drug Abuse, 2003).

Pope and colleagues (2000) conducted a six-week trial of testosterone in 56 males, increasing the weekly dose to 600 milligrams. Their goal was to assess drug effects on mood and aggression. Doses of up to 300 mg/week produced few psychiatric effects; doses of 500 to 600 mg/week produced prominent effects in some individuals. Under these "laboratory" conditions, 84 percent exhibited minimal psychiatric effects, 12 percent became mildly hypomanic, and 4 percent became markedly hypomanic or manic. Two participants withdrew when they became "alarmingly hypomanic and aggressive." From these results it appears that in small and unpredictable numbers of users, high doses of anabolic steroids may produce marked signs of mania and/or aggression. This report is perhaps the first to quantify these effects and provide statistics on the possible numbers of users who might be expected to display these symptoms. The authors of the study state that the statistics may understate the incidence in the real world: doses may be even higher and drug takers may have preexisting psychiatric conditions and/or may use other illicit drugs while using steroids. All these conditions would increase the probability of adverse reactions. Why some individuals were markedly and dangerously affected while the majority were not is unknown.

Kanayama and coworkers (2003) interviewed 223 male substance abusers admitted to a substance abuse program. Twenty-nine men (13 percent) reported prior steroid use (only 4 of these men were identified on the physicians' referral forms). Among 88 men who listed opioids as their drug of choice, 22 (25 percent) acknowledged steroid use. Only 7 of the remaining 135 men in the program admitted to steroid use. Many of the opioid-dependent men who used steroids first encountered opioids from friends at the gyms and obtained opioids from the same person who sold them the injectable steroids. Four of the 29 men with steroid abuse histories (17 percent) reported severe aggressiveness or violence during their periods of steroid use.

Thus, anabolic steroids administered in regular large doses are indeed mood-altering chemicals. They do, however, have a delayed onset of effect. This delay occurs because their mechanism of synthesizing new proteins takes days or weeks. Because their effects are not immediate, the effects may not be perceived as being a consequence of drug ingestion. Haupt (1993) summarized:

> There are significant adverse psychological effects associated with the use of anabolic steroids although the effects are not easily measured by current psychological inventories. Athletes taking anabolic steroids suffer some degree of personality change that may range from simple mood swings to a psychosis requiring hospitalization for treatment. A Jekyll-and-Hyde personality is common, where even the slightest provocation can cause an exaggerated, violent, and often uncontrolled response. The users of anabolic steroids often suffer disturbed personality relationships that may include separations from family and friends and even divorce. Arrest records are not uncommon. Fortunately these psychological effects are reversible when the steroids are discontinued, but the social scars may be permanent. (p. 470)

Galloway (1997) reviewed these psychological effects at length, adding that about half of a small population of interviewed weightlifters experienced depression and an even higher percentage experienced paranoid thoughts and some psychotic behaviors, experiences consistent with the study conducted by Pope and coworkers (2000). Withdrawal from steroid use is frequently accompanied by moderate to severe depression, and suicidal thoughts and actual suicides are not uncommon during the period of withdrawal.

Physical Dependence

Physical dependence is characterized by withdrawal symptoms when a drug is removed. Withdrawal from large doses of anabolic steroids can be accompanied by psychological depression, fatigue, restlessness, insomnia, loss of appetite, and decreased libido. Other withdrawal symptoms that have been reported include drug craving, headache, dissatisfaction with body image, and suicidal ideation (Brower, 2002). Despite these observations, no defined psychiatric withdrawal syndrome has been described; withdrawal psychosis or bipolar illness has not been reported, although depression is commonplace.

Abuse and Treatment

The use of anabolic steroids for athletic or cosmetic purposes constitutes drug abuse because the doses used far exceed those needed for medical indications. Abuse persists despite recognized, unavoidable side effects and negative consequences for the physical and psychological health of the user. The mechanisms responsible for dependence are largely unknown and may be psychological and/or physiological.

Testosterone is the most potent hormonal determinant of physical and behavioral masculinization. It has been implicated for decades in the stimulation of sexual behavior, as well as in the activation of dominance and aggressive behaviors in male primates, including humans (Schaal et al., 1996). The attraction to the use of supraphysiologic doses of testosterone derivatives is strong, with significant numbers of young persons succumbing to their attractiveness.

As with all other psychoactive drugs, treatment of steroid dependence requires drug abstinence, treatment of any signs of withdrawal, and maintenance of abstinence. Behavioral and cognitive approaches are possible treatment tools. Supportive therapy, including reassurance, education, and counseling, remains the mainstay of treatment. Antidepressants may be indicated when dependency is complicated by major depression. A physician trained in endocrinology can best prescribe other therapies for hormonal alterations.

One societal response to the use of anabolic steroids has been to ban their use in athletics. Since the beginning of organized competition, athletes have tried to gain every possible advantage over their competitors. Sometimes this competitive edge is gained fairly by training harder or developing new and improved methods. Sometimes, however, athletes seek an advantage by using substances that affect the body in ways that can improve athletic performance.

The National Collegiate Athletic Association (NCAA) and the United States Olympic Committee (USOC) have declared the use of anabolic steroids illegal, not only because of their ability to artificially increase muscle mass and competitiveness but also because of their serious and sometimes permanent side effects. Olivier (1996) argued in favor of the ban, stating that these drugs not only harm the user but create a climate of subtle coercion toward their use by others, as well as placing others (for example, partners of steroid users) at risk of violence from users while they are on the drug. Olivier concludes:

> I have argued that prohibition of harmful practices is justified by potential harm to others (rather than just to one's self). One must bear in mind the powerful effects of subtle coercion and influence and the consequent limitations placed on choice. So, on the grounds that it is wrong to harm others or to coerce them into potentially harmful situations, this paper takes issue with sports libertarians who claim that banning performance-enhancing substances is an unjustified paternalistic action that violates the principle of autonomy. (p. S45)

Education has to be the mainstay of anabolic steroid abuse prevention, especially since the drugs initially promote a more healthy, masculine appearance as well as increasing muscle mass and strength. Goldberg and coworkers (2000) designed and tested a team-based, educational interventional program to reduce the intent of adolescent athletes to use steroids. Conducted with 702 football players in 31 high schools, seven weekly classroom sessions, seven weekly weight-room sessions, and one evening parent session led to increased understanding of anabolic steroid effects, greater belief in personal vulnerability to the adverse consequences of steroids, improved drug refusal skills, less belief in steroid-promoting media messages, increased belief in the team as an information source, improved perception of athletic abilities and strength-training self-efficacy, improved nutritional and exercise behaviors, and reduced intentions to use steroids.[1]

The abuse of anabolic steroids by athletes, bodybuilders, and body-conscious individuals poses a special challenge to society in general. Perhaps the desire of adolescents and young adults to take steroids has been fostered largely by our societal fixations on winning and physical appearance. Thus, successful intervention must go beyond education, counseling, law enforcement, and drug testing: the social environment that subtly encourages steroid abuse may have to be changed.

Certainly, professional sports have fostered the notion that steroid use may be acceptable, as long as the goal is to win athletic competitions. Perhaps most notorious is major league baseball, which only in

---

[1]The title of the program is *The ATLAS Program*. It is available from its publisher, Jones and Bartlett, 40 Tall Pine Drive, Sudburg, MA 01776 (800-832-0034).

2004 began testing for anabolic steroid use (many baseball players have acknowledged steroid use); however, penalties are less than stringent and allow for some positive tests. Testing in professional basketball is more stringent (perhaps because anabolic steroids are of less use in athletes who need prolonged endurance). Professional football bans steroid use. Professional hockey does not have a mandatory drug-testing policy and tests only players already in the league's substance abuse aftercare program. Players who seek help the first time are neither exposed nor suspended. As long as professional athletics "allows" the abuse of anabolic steroids, the example will pass both to fans and to younger athletes.

Androstenedione

Androstenedione is promoted as a testosterone precursor and anabolic steroid and is available as a "dietary supplement," outside FDA regulation. It became prominent as a result of its use by Mark McGwire as a performance-enhancing substance (Yesalis, 1999). Currently, the drug is not outlawed in major league baseball, but the International Olympic Committee, the National Football League, and the National Collegiate Athletic League ban it. Adolescents, however, are drawn to the drug because of its availability (as a "natural" alternative to testosterone or synthetic anabolic steroids) and because of its popularization.

King and coworkers (1999) studied 30 young men not taking nutritional supplements, anabolic steroids, or engaging in resistance training. Twenty received intermittent schedules of androstenedione and 10 received placebo; all underwent 8 weeks of whole-body resistance training. Androstenedione supplementation did not increase serum testosterone concentrations and did not enhance skeletal muscle adaptations to resistance training. This result was consistent with the statement by Yesalis and Bahrke (2002) discussed at the beginning of this chapter. The test doses given were 100 mg of androstenedione; it is unclear whether massive doses would have produced different results. This study, however, questions the efficacy of androstenedione as an anabolic substance and leaves open the question of possible long-term toxicity. Testing of over-the-counter preparations of androstenedione contained trace contaminants of other, more potent banned substances (Catlin, 2000).

STUDY QUESTIONS

1. What are androgenic-anabolic steroids?

2. How do these substances affect body functions?

3. How do these agents increase muscle mass?

4. Describe the similarities and differences between dependence on anabolic steroids and on the more traditional drugs of abuse.

5. Describe the two groups of persons who are the most frequent users of these substances. How are they similar? How are they different?

6. Describe the anticatabolic, anabolic, and motivational effects of these drugs.

7. What are the side effects associated with use of these agents?

8. What are the psychological effects associated with use of these agents?

9. How might the misuse of these substances be prevented?

REFERENCES

Aitken, C., et al. (2002). "Pumping Iron, Risking Infection? Exposure to Hepatitis, Hepatitis B, and HIV Among Anabolic-Androgenic Steroid Injectors in Victoria, Australia." *Drug and Alcohol Dependence* 65: 303–308.

Babigian, A., and R. T. Silverman (2001). "Management of Gynecomastia Due to Use of Anabolic Steroids in Bodybuilders." *Plastic and Reconstructive Surgery* 107: 240–242.

Bhasin, S., et al. (1996). "The Effects of Supraphysiologic Doses of Testosterone on Muscle Size and Strength in Normal Men." *New England Journal of Medicine* 335: 1–7.

Brower, K. J. (2002). "Anabolic Steroid Abuse and Dependence." *Current Psychiatry Reports* 4: 377–387.

Catlin, D. H., et al. (2000). "Trace Contamination of Over-the-Counter Androstenedione and Positive Urine Test Results for a Nandrolone Metabolite." *Journal of the American Medical Association* 284: 2618–2621.

Daly, R. C., et al. (2003). "Neuroendocrine and Behavioral Effects of High-Dose Anabolic Steroid Administration in Male Normal Volunteers." *Psychoneuroendocrinology* 28: 317–331.

Dobs, A. S. (1999). "Is There a Role for Androgenic Anabolic Steroids in Medical Practice?" *Journal of the American Medical Association* 281: 1326–1327.

Ferreira, I. M., et al. (1998). "The Influence of Six Months of Oral Anabolic Steroids on Body Mass and Respiratory Muscles in Undernourished COPD Patients." *Chest* 114: 19–28

Galloway, G. P. (1997). "Anabolic Steroids." in J. H. Lowinson, P. Ruiz, R. B. Millman, and J. G. Langrod, eds., *Substance Abuse: A Comprehensive Textbook*, 3rd ed. (pp. 380–395). Baltimore: Williams & Wilkins.

Goldberg, L., et al. (2000). "The Adolescents' Training and Learning to Avoid Steroids Program: Preventing Drug Use and Promoting Health Behaviors." *Archives of Pediatrics and Adolescent Medicine* 154: 332–338.

Hartgens, F., et al. (2002). "Misuse of Androgenic-Anabolic Steroids and Human Deltoid Muscle Fibers: Differences Between Polydrug Regimens and Single Drug Administration." *European Journal of Applied Physiology* 86: 233–239.

Haupt, H. A. (1993). "Anabolic Steroids and Growth Hormone." *American Journal of Sports Medicine* 21: 468–474.

Heriex, A., and H. Kuipers (2003). "Prospective Echocardiographic Assessment of Androgenic-Anabolic Steroids: Effects on Cardiac Structure and

Function in Strength Athletes." *International Journal of Sports Medicine* 24: 344–351.

Kanayama, G., et al. (2003). "Past Anabolic-Androgenic Steroid Use Among Men Admitted for Substance Abuse Treatment: An Underrecognized Problem?" *Journal of Clinical Psychiatry* 64: 156–160.

Karila, T. A., et al. (2003). "Anabolic Androgenic Steroids Produce Dose-Dependent Increase in Left Ventricular Mass in Power Athletes, and This Effect Is Potentiated by Concomitant Use of Growth Hormone." *International Journal of Sports Medicine* 24: 337–343.

King, D. S., et al. (1999). "Effect of Oral Androstenedione on Serum Testosterone and Adaptations to Resistance Training in Young Men: A Randomized Controlled Trial." *Journal of the American Medical Association* 281: 2020–2028.

Midgley, S. J., et al. (2001). "Levels of Aggression Among a Group of Anabolic-Androgenic Steroid Users." *Medicine, Science, and the Law* 41: 309–314.

National Institute on Drug Abuse (2003). "Anabolic Steroid Abuse." Research Report Series. NIH publication 00-3721.

Naylor, A. H., et al. (2001). "Drug Use Patterns Among High School Athletes and Nonathletes." *Adolescence* 36: 627–639.

Olivier, S. (1996). "Drugs in Sport: Justifying Paternalism on the Grounds of Harm." *American Journal of Sports Medicine* 24: S43–S45.

Pope, H. C., et al. (2000). "Effects of Supraphysiologic Doses of Testosterone on Mood and Aggression in Normal Men: A Randomized Controlled Trial." *Archives of General Psychiatry* 57: 133–140.

Rabkin, J. G., et al. (2000). "A Double-Blind, Placebo-Controlled Trial of Testosterone Therapy for HIV-Positive Men with Hypogonadal Symptoms," *Archives of General Psychiatry* 57: 141–147.

Schaal, B., et al. (1996). "Male Testosterone Linked to High Social Dominance but Low Physical Aggression in Early Adolescence." *Journal of the American Academy of Child and Adolescent Psychiatry* 34: 1322–1330.

Schwerin, M. J., et al. (1996). "Social Physique Anxiety, Body Esteem, and Social Anxiety in Bodybuilders and Self-Reported Anabolic Steroid Users." *Addictive Behaviors* 21: 1–8.

Tamaki, T., et al. (2001). "Anabolic Steroids Increase Exercise Tolerance." *American Journal of Physiology—Endocrinology and Metabolism* 280: E973–E981.

Torres-Calleja, J., et al. (2001). "Effect of Androgenic Anabolic Steroids on Sperm Quality and Serum Hormone Levels in Adult Male Body Builders." *Life Sciences* 68: 1769–1774.

Tuiten, A., et al. (2000). "Time Course of Effects of Testosterone Administration on Sexual Arousal in Women." *Archives of General Psychiatry* 57: 149–153.

Urhausen, A., et al. (2003). "Reversibility of the Effects on Blood Cells, Liver Function, and Hormones in Former Anabolic-Androgenic Steroid Abusers." *Journal of Steroid Biochemistry and Molecular Biology* 84: 369–375.

Yesalis, C. E. (1999). "Medical, Legal, and Societal Implications of Androstenedione Use." *Journal of the American Medical Association* 281: 2043–2044.

Yesalis, C. E., and M. S. Bahrke (2002). "Anabolic-Androgenic Steroids and Related Substances." *Current Sports Medicine Report* 1: 246–252.

Yesalis, C., et al. (1997). "Trends in Anabolic-Androgenic Steroid Use Among Adolescents." *Archives of Pediatric and Adolescent Medicine* 151: 1197–1206.

Chapter 21

Topics in Drug Abuse

Drug abuse has been a societal problem for thousands of years, ever since grain was fermented (ethyl alcohol) and natural substances were found that produced euphoria (cocaine), relieved pain (morphine), or produced altered states of consciousness for divination (psychedelics). As history suggests, as long as these drugs persist in society (and they always will), their use will be associated with compulsive use and abuse as well as with dependency and addiction. This chapter reviews the mechanisms responsible for producing compulsive drug abuse and dependency. It also reviews the literature on the current concepts of treatment of dependency and abuse. The individual drugs discussed in their own chapters are brought together in a chapter devoted to general concepts that apply to all drugs of abuse.

Historical and Current Perspectives

In all of recorded history, every society has used drugs to produce alterations in mood, thought, feeling, or behavior or to provide temporary alterations in reality. Moreover, some people have always digressed from social custom with respect to the time, the amount, and the situation in which drugs were used. Abuse of psychoactive drugs has always produced problems for the individual taking the drug, for those in direct contact with the user, and for society at large.

Alcohol is the classic psychoactive drug used throughout history primarily for recreational purposes, but it is not the only such agent. Naturally occurring substances are used to alleviate anxiety, produce relaxation, provide relief from boredom, communicate with the gods, alleviate pain, and/or increase strength or work tolerance. In most cultures, only very few naturally occurring substances were available and their use was closely monitored, so just a relatively small minority of individuals abused them. Today, patterns of abuse differ considerably from traditional patterns:

- We currently have available at one time (now) and in one culture (ours) virtually all of the naturally occurring psychoactive and psychedelic drugs ever identified. For example, the naturally occurring divination substance *Salvia divinorum*, until recently unknown outside a geographically isolated area of Mexico, has become more widely known (see Chapter 19).

- In most cases, the pharmacologically active ingredient in each natural product has been isolated, identified, and made available to those who desire it.

- Organic chemistry has made possible synthetic derivatives of naturally occurring drugs. In many cases, the synthetic derivatives magnify the psychoactive potency of the natural substance 100 times or more.

- Users have adopted new methods of drug delivery, starting with the invention of the hypodermic syringe in the 1860s, and new drugs, the most recent of which are crack cocaine, ice methamphetamine, and "designer" derivatives of both fentanyl and mescaline. These developments have markedly increased the delivered dose, decreased the time to onset of drug action, and increased both the potency and the toxicity of these agents compared with their naturally occurring counterparts.

As in past decades, caffeine, nicotine, and ethyl alcohol are the addictive drugs used by the vast majority of people. Caffeine use is nearly universal; 90 percent of Americans over the age of 11 use the drug at least once weekly. Thankfully, little harm seems to follow. Nicotine and alcohol are the next most widely used and abused addictive drugs, and their economic toll on lives, productivity, and health are enormous. The probability that an American living today has a drug abuse or dependence disorder is 36 percent for nicotine, 14 percent for alcohol, and 4 percent for marijuana (now the most commonly used illicit drug).

Extent of the Drug Problem

The total yearly economic costs of substance abuse are estimated at $430 billion: alcohol abuse makes up $175 billion of this amount, substance abuse $114 billion, and cigarette smoking $138 billion. A 2002 national survey on drug use and health (U.S. Deptartment of Health and Human Services, 2003) noted that 22 million Americans suffered from dependence on or abuse of drugs, alcohol, or both. There were 19.5 million Americans (8.3 percent of the population age 12 or older) who currently used drugs, 54 million who participated in binge drinking in the previous 30 days, and 15.9 million who were heavy drinkers. Almost 8 million people (3.3 percent of the total population age 12 or older) needed treatment for a diagnosable drug problem, and 18.6 million (7.9 percent of the population age 12 or older) needed treatment for a serious alcohol problem. Yet only 1.4 million persons received specialized substance abuse treatment for an illicit drug problem and 1.5 million received treatment for an alcohol problem. Over 94 percent of people with substance abuse disorders who did not receive treatment did not believe they needed treatment.

The 2002 national survey reported that marijuana is the most commonly used illicit drug. Over 14 million Americans, one-third of whom used it on 20 or more days in the previous month, use it. There is a continuing decline in the yearly number of adolescents initiating use of marijuana, with 1.7 million new users in youth ages 12 to 17 years in the year 2002.

The second most popular category of drug use after marijuana is the nonmedical abuse of prescription drugs. An estimated 6.2 million people (2.6 percent of the population age 12 or older) were current users of prescription drugs taken nonmedically. About 60 percent used opioids, 20 percent used anxiolytics, 15 percent used prescription stimulants not prescribed for them, and 10 percent used sedatives. An estimated 1.9 million persons ages 12 or older had used the painkiller OxyContin at least once.

At any given time in 2002, about 2 million people used cocaine, of whom "hard-core" crack cocaine users numbered over 500,000. Hallucinogens were used by 1.2 million persons, half of them users of ecstasy. The were about 160,000 current heroin users. Among young people ages 12 to 17 years, inhalant use was higher than the use of cocaine.

Substance abuse is age related. Current illicit drug use is highest among people ages 18 to 25 years; 20 percent use drugs. Second are people ages 12 to 17; 11 percent use drugs. Third are people ages 26 and older—only 5.8 percent use drugs. Binge drinking and driving under the influence of drugs and alcohol affected millions. Initiation to drug and alcohol abuse begins almost universally before the age of 21 years; most occurs in the 14-to-16-years range. Although some people who develop a substance abuse disorder in adulthood did not expose themselves to recreational drugs until after the age of 21 years, it is unusual, Should these people develop a problem with dependence, they are much more successfully treatable than are people who initiate drug use in the early teenage years. The age of first exposure is an important predictor and estimate of the likelihood of developing both a substance abuse problem and a need for treatment for illicit drug abuse problems. Whether initial use of a drug represents self-medication for an underlying mental health disorder or whether it represents a progression in drug experimentation is not clear. Based on current estimates of early-age drug exposure, substance abuse treatment needs will increase by 57 percent by the year 2020 (Gfroerer and Epstein, 1999). To stem this tide of substance dependence, early-age initiation to alcohol, cigarettes, and marijuana must be curbed to minimize the progression to the eventual development of a substance abuse disorder.

On September 9, 2003, the Institute of Medicine of the National Academy of Sciences published and presented to the U.S. Congress a report addressing underage drinking (National Academy of Sciences, Institute of Medicine, 2003). This report details the extent of the problem and causes of underage drinking ($53 billion per year) and presents a comprehensive societal strategy to reduce underage drinking.

Substance abuse is also related to mental health (Havassy et al., 2004). Over 23 percent of people with a serious mental health problem were dependent on or abused alcohol or illicit drugs. This compares with 8 percent of persons without mental illness. Of adults with substance dependence, over 20 percent had serious mental illness, compared with 7 percent of adults who were not dependent on or abusing drugs or alcohol.

Nosology and Psychopathology of Substance Abuse

Published in 2000 in its revised fourth edition, the *Diagnostic and Statistical Manual of Mental Disorder* (DSM-IV-TR) (American Psychiatric Association, 2000) presents commonly accepted criteria for what constitutes substance dependence and substance abuse (Table 21.1). The two substance use disorders involve maladaptive patterns of substance use, leading to clinically significant impairments or distress. The distinctions between abuse and dependence are listed in the table and discussed by Bucholz (1999) and by Cami and Farre (2003).

Approximately one-third of individuals with a drug or alcohol addiction have a diagnosed *comorbid* (Axis I) psychiatric disorder, a situation covered by the term *dual diagnosis*. This term is one of convenience, used to capture the concept that many patients have a substance use disorder in addition to another psychiatric disorder (Goldsmith, 1999). (The reverse is, of course, also true; many patients have a psychiatric disorder, often undiagnosed, in addition to a diagnosed substance use disorder.) The epidemiology of this comorbidity is striking. Of people

---

TABLE 21.1 DSM-IV criteria for substance dependence or abuse

CRITERIA FOR SUBSTANCE DEPENDENCE:

A maladaptive pattern of substance use, leading to clinically significant impairment or distress, as manifested by three (or more) of the following, occurring at any time in the same 12-month period:

(1)   tolerance, as defined by either: (a) need for markedly increased amounts of the substance to achieve intoxication or desired effect; (b) markedly diminished effect with continued use of the same amount of substance

(2)   withdrawal, as manifested by either: (a) the characteristic withdrawal syndrome for the substance; (b) the same (or a closely related) substance is taken to relieve or avoid withdrawal symptoms

(3)   the substance is often taken in larger amounts or over a longer period than was intended

(4)   there is a persistent desire or unsuccessful efforts to cut down or control substance use

(5)   a great deal of time is spent in activities necessary to obtain the substance, use the substance, or recover from its effects

(6)   important social, occupational, or recreational activities are given up or reduced because of substance use

(7)   the substance use is continued despite knowledge of having a persistent or recurrent physical or psychological problem that is likely to have been caused or exacerbated by the substance

CRITERIA FOR SUBSTANCE ABUSE:

A.   A maladaptive pattern of substance use leading to clinically significant impairment or distress, as manifested by one (or more) of the following occurring within a 12-month period:

(1)   recurrent substance use resulting in a failure to fulfill major role obligations at work, school or home

(2)   recurrent substance use in situations in which it is physically hazardous

(3)   recurrent substance-related legal problems

(4)   continued substance use despite having persistent or recurrent social or interpersonal problems caused or exacerbated by the effects of the substance

B.   The symptoms have never met the criteria for Substance Dependence for this class of substance.

Adapted from American Psychiatric Association (2000), pp. 181–183.

---

with a lifetime diagnosis of schizophrenia or schizophreniform disorders, 47 percent have met criteria for substance abuse or dependence; of those with an anxiety disorder, 23.7 percent; obsessive compulsive disorder, 32.8 percent; bipolar disorder, 50 percent; and depression, 32 percent, with distribution equal for males and females (McCance-Katz and

Kosten, 1998). Jacobsen and coworkers (2001) and Kilpatrick and coworkers (2003) review the complex interactions between substance abuse and PTSD. Hasin and coworkers (2002) discuss the interactive effects of major depression on the remission and relapse of substance use and dependence. Skodol and coworkers (1999) noted that close to 60 percent of subjects with substance abuse disorders had personality disorders, including borderline personality disorder, antisocial personality disorder, and conduct disorder. Leshner (1997) stated:

> Comorbidity is reality! Estimates vary by disorder, but more than 50 percent of people with mental disorders have also been found to abuse drugs, including alcohol; there is also a widespread belief that many mentally ill people who abuse drugs may be actually attempting to medicate themselves. We do not know if this is actually true, but the sequence of onset between the mental disorder and substance use favors the hypothesis for many patients. . . . Many of our causative models ignore the almost inevitability of comorbidity or at best treat it superficially. Worse, many of our treatment approaches ignore comorbidity or insist that mental and addictive disorders be treated separately. (p. 692)

There are serious deficiencies in the diagnosis and provision of services for patients with dual or comorbid illnesses. Making the correct diagnosis is a pivotal component in the successful treatment of dual-diagnosis patients. It is important to maintain a high level of suspicion of dual disorders and gather information about the patient from as many sources as possible. A key clinical issue is that the underlying psychiatric disorder and the substance use disorder must be treated concomitantly, and the dual-diagnosis program should include pharmacotherapy, psychoeducation, behavioral intervention, skills training, and case management. It is essential that both diseases be addressed simultaneously, with appropriate communication and coordination among the treatment providers and corroboration from significant others in the patient's environment.

Psychoactive Drugs as Behavioral Reinforcers: The Neurobiology of Addiction

One of the newer areas of interest in the field of chemical dependencies is the neurobiology of addiction. With the possible exception of the benzodiazepine anxiolytics (Chapter 6), drugs that are prone to compulsive abuse activate brain mechanisms involved in reward and positive reinforcement by increasing the level of dopamine in the mesolimbic system (Cami and Farre, 2003; Lingford-Hughes and Nutt, 2003). Indeed, increased dopamine in the nucleus accumbens is the key in mediating the rewarding effects or positive reinforcement of drugs of abuse (Bonci et al., 2003; Koob and LeMoal, 2001). For example, alcohol and morphine do not have rewarding effects in mice that lack the dopamine-2 receptor. In humans, cocaine and methylphenidate (Ritalin) increase dopamine levels in the brain, an effect associated with euphoria and pleasurable experiences (Volkow et al., 1999). People with the lowest control dopamine levels have the greatest pleasure responses to cocaine. Subjects with the highest control dopamine levels experience less pleasurable responses to cocaine, and some even experience dysphoric responses.

Nucleus Accumbens

In the past dozen years it has become apparent that there are specific circuits in the brain dedicated to the neural mediation of reward and pleasure (Wise, 1998). These circuits are shown in Figure 21.1 A primary system comprises descending (caudally projecting) fibers of

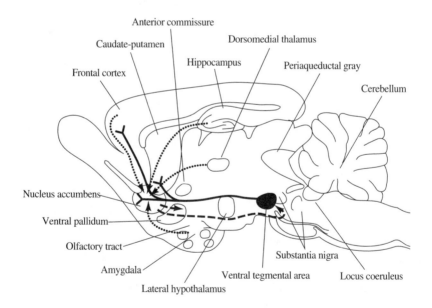

FIGURE 21.1 Sagittal rat brain section illustrating a cocaine and amphetamine neural reward circuit that includes a limbic-extrapyramidal motor interface. Dotted arrows indicate limbic afferents to the nucleus accumbens and dashed arrows represent efferents from the nucleus accumbens thought to be involved in psychomotor stimulant reward. Solid arrows indicate projections of the mesocorticolimbic dopamine system thought to be a critical substrate for psychomotor stimulant reward. This system originates in the ventral tegmental area and projects to the olfactory tubercle of the nucleus accumbens and the ventral striatal domains of the caudate putamen. [Adapted from Koob (1992), p. 181.]

dopaminergic neurons whose cell bodies are located in the nucleus accumbens and several limbic structures. These fibers run within the medial forebrain bundle and synapse onto second-stage dopaminergic neurons whose cell bodies are located in the ventral tegmental area (VTA) of the midbrain. The second-stage fibers are the axons of these VTA cells, and they ascend (travel rostrally) in the medial forebrain bundle and project into neurons of the forebrain, largely in the nucleus accumbens, frontal cortex, amygdala, and septal area. In essence, this two-neuron system is a dopaminergic loop between the forebrain and the ventral tegmentum.

Cocaine and the amphetamines act on both the first- and the second-stage neuronal terminals; the drugs mimic the effects of direct electrical stimulation of these areas. Other behavior-reinforcing drugs act only on the second-stage neurons, probably through action on the endogenous opioid, cannabinoid, or serotonin circuitry. As early as 1992, Koob stated:

> Dopamine forms a critical link for all reward, including opiates and sedative/hypnotics. While open to multiple neurotransmitter inputs and outputs, this view still holds a centrist position for dopamine in all reward. An emphasis on multiple independent neurochemical elements, . . . places the focus on the nucleus accumbens and its circuitry as an important, perhaps critical, substrate for drug reward. (p. 181)

Role of Dopamine in Anticipation and Craving

Childress and coworkers (1999) extended earlier studies of brain circuitry underlying drug experiences, identifying limbic structures activated during cocaine craving. They pointed out that during craving, the user is gripped by a visceral emotional state, experiences a highly focused incentive to act, and is unencumbered by the memory of negative consequences of drug taking. Sensory "cues," even more than food or reinforcing drugs, increase dopamine in the brain. Nucleus accumbens dopamine is involved in responsiveness to conditioned stimuli and the activational aspects of motivation (Salamone et al., 2003). After the cue increases dopamine, if a drug is not administered, dopamine drops and dysphoria follows (an unfulfilled cue). This fall in dopamine is proposed to increase the drive to obtain the drug. In both adolescents and adults who have an alcohol use disorder, brain activation to alcohol-related cues is greater than in persons who do not have an alcohol use problem. Youth who drink more per month and who have more desire to drink have the greatest degree of brain activation to cues (Tapert et al., 2003). This certainly is one major drive behind some of the recommendations of the 2003 Institute of Medicine report to make alcohol advertising less appealing to underaged youth who might be excessively vulnerable to such advertising.

Dopamine and Withdrawal

Reductions in brain dopamine, especially in the mesolimbic circuitry, are observed in the early stages (perhaps 6 months) of abstinence from drugs of abuse. These reductions are associated with reduced levels of dopamine receptors, which slowly up regulate over a period of several months of abstinence. This period of a hypodopaminergic state leads to drug craving and an increased risk of relapse. Reinitiating drug use increases dopamine levels and provides relief from withdrawal and craving (as would be predicted).

Tremblay and coworkers (2002) studied the role of the nucleus accumbens brain reward system in depression. These authors administered a single oral dose of dextroamphetamine to control nondepressed patients and patients with major depressive disorder. Both by self-reports of feelings and by measured autonomic responses, depressed patients had exaggerated responses to the amphetamine, perhaps reflecting a hypofunctional state of the nucleus accumbens in depression. Thus, depression may be associated with a hypofunctional dopamine state that exhibits greater responsiveness to stimulants. The patients with the most severe states of depression exhibited the greatest psychological responsiveness to amphetamine.

Since replacement of dopamine activity reduces the symptoms of withdrawal and the associated drug craving, might there be a way to replace dopamine without resorting to use of illicit drugs? Pilla and coworkers (1999) utilized an experimental dopamine-3 receptor partial agonist (BP-897) to successfully inhibit in rats cocaine-seeking behaviors in response to behavioral cues. Garcia-Ladona and Cox (2003) reviewed the potential usefulness of this experimental drug in the treatment of cocaine addiction. Available for clinical use is bupropion (Wellbutrin, Zyban), a dopamine-reuptake inhibitor that has proven effective in the treatment of nicotine dependency (Chapter 8).

Other Neurotransmitter Systems Involved in Reward: Modulators of Dopaminergic Activity

No brain system works in isolation. The dopaminergic reward system in the nucleus accumbens is under the control of many other neurotransmitter systems (Cami and Farre, 2003). Some of these systems are discussed here.

Opioids

Chapter 15 discussed the pharmacology of the opioids and the receptors on which they act. Activation of the mu receptors increases dopamine in the nucleus accumbens, and mice lacking mu receptors do not exhibit a reward response to morphine (Kieffer, 1999). This rewarding action of mu receptors underlies the action of naltrexone (Chapter 4) in treating alcohol dependence. This usefulness is thought to be a consequence of naltrexone's ability to block the actions of endorphins that are released by drinking alcohol and that mediate pleasure.

Conversely, activation of kappa receptors reduces activity in the nucleus accumbens. Kappa agonist opioids are not behaviorally rewarding, and their administration can result in a dysphoric response. Similarly, experimental delta receptor antagonists reduce alcohol self-administration. Therefore, increased delta activity should play a role in positive reinforcement.

Glutamate

Glutamate appears to be the brain's number one excitatory neurotransmitter. Glutamate-releasing neurons in the frontal cortex and amygdala project to the mesolimbic reward system and affect thought, affect, behavioral reward, and addiction (McFarland et al., 2003; Winder et al., 2002). The NMDA-type glutamate receptors have been implicated in dependence associated with nicotine, ethanol, benzodiazepines, and marijuana. Antagonists of these same NMDA receptors inhibit responsiveness to stimulants such as cocaine and the amphetamines and the development of opioid dependence. Memantine, a nonpsychedelic NMDA antagonist that is used in the treatment of moderate to severe dementia (Chapter 13), attenuates naloxone-precipitated withdrawal (Bisaga et al., 2001). Glutamate receptors are proposed to be involved in cocaine self-administration (McFarland et al., 2003).

During ethanol withdrawal, one observes increases in activity in NMDA-type glutamate receptors along with increases in glutamate release. These increases in glutamate activity are thought to be involved in alcohol withdrawal seizures and in the loss of neurons during long-term alcoholism with repeated detoxifications. Acamprosate (Chapter 4) is an NMDA antagonist that is awaiting FDA approval for use in treating alcoholism. Acamprosate may be neuroprotective (Dahchour and DeWitte, 2000; Olive, 2002). Perhaps acamprosate therapy should be initiated with the onset of ethanol detoxification (Lingford-Hughes and Nutt, 2003), although the same can be said for initiation of therapy with anticonvulsant neuromodulators such as topiramate (Chapter 10).

Cannabinoids

As discussed in Chapter 18, cannabinoid receptors and opioid receptors are remarkably similar, and cannabinoid-opioid interactions are becoming very important in current concepts of addiction and drug reward mechanisms. It is now widely recognized that cannabinoids act on brain reward mechanisms and processes in strikingly similar fashion to other drugs of abuse (Gardner, 2002; Mechoulam and Parker, 2003). Cannabinoids are capable of increasing endorphin synthesis or release, and opioid antagonists, such as naloxone, can block some of the effects of THC as well as inducing withdrawal in THC-dependent animals. Smoking marijuana may also reduce opioid withdrawal. In mice lacking cannabinoid receptors, the rewarding and withdrawal responses to morphine (but not cocaine) are reduced. Therefore, cannabinoid CB-1 receptors are involved in dependence not only on THC but on opioids such as morphine. The cannabinoid antagonist rimonabant (Chapter 18) blocks cravings for sweets, fattening foods, and many drugs of abuse. It or similar drugs yet to be discovered may have a prominent role in the future treatment of both drug dependence and obesity.

Drug Availability

Over the years, laws have been passed to limit the availability of drugs and to punish drug users deemed dangerous to themselves or to society. When these laws are strictly enforced, they can reduce drug use by people who fear reprisal, but aggressive legislation does not control a person's craving for mind-altering drugs. This is true whether or not the person seeks the drug as self-medication for psychological distress, as pain relief for physical or psychological pain, or as anything else. Moreover, legislation often fails to address the legal drugs that cause the greatest amount of harm to individuals and society—ethanol and nicotine. Legalization of currently illegal drugs (for example, tetrahydrocannabinol) is not likely to solve drug abuse problems, and it certainly is politically unlikely. Simple legalization of the currently illegal drugs, if properly implemented, could solve much of the drug traffic-related crime problem. However, it would do nothing to solve the substance abuse problem, especially the major part of it caused by tobacco and alcohol.

Besides legislation, other traditional techniques for reducing drug abuse include education and developing negative attitudes toward drugs in both users and potential users. Such efforts have brought limited results, although the antianabolic steroid intervention (ATLAS program) described in Chapter 20 is encouraging. Perhaps it is time to take a public health approach to the problem of drug abuse, an approach that attempts to minimize danger to the individual and society. The primary goal of this approach is to reduce the use and abuse of all the recreational mood-altering drugs to a level of safe, pleasurable use consistent with centuries-old human experience, while minimizing to the greatest degree possible their harmful effects in individuals, the family, and society as a whole.

A second major goal is the elimination of the use of alcohol, cigarettes, and marijuana by individuals under the age of 21 years. Given a historical perspective of human use of psychoactive drugs, these are reasonable social goals. The first step is to agree on the need to implement them, and the second step is implementation of measures to achieve them. Certainly, the 2003 National Academy of Sciences Institute of Medicine report on underage drinking is an important start, especially if it serves to reduce advertising intended as an ethanol cue to susceptible youth.

Addiction as a Chronic, Relapsing Illness

In past years, success of treatment programs for substance abuse has often been measured by the percentage of individuals who, after detoxification, remain drug-free, or abstinent from drug use. In essence, drug dependency has been treated as an acute illness, and treatment success is measured by successful abstinence. Relapse to drug use has been considered as treatment failure, and individuals have often been lost to treatment following relapse. With so much dependent on the success of treatment, efforts have traditionally involved lengthy and costly residential treatment programs aimed at drug detoxification. These programs were usually followed by a "graduation ceremony" that recognized those who completed the detoxification program and were preparing to make the transition from the residential program to the "real world."

As we have discussed elsewhere in this book, however, one of the goals of pharmacotherapy of drug dependency (on alcohol, cocaine, opioids, marijuana, and so on) is the long-term prevention of craving and relapse, recognizing that relapses can and probably will occur. Therefore, the current trend in addiction treatment involves treating drug dependency as a chronic disease, subject to relapses and setbacks. Medically, this is no different than treating medical illnesses such as hypertension, diabetes, asthma, thyroid deficiency, and so on. In those situations, relapses occur periodically, often involving noncompliance with prescribed medicines or necessary life-style changes. When relapses occur, the physician counsels the patient, usually in brief periods of counseling, and therapy is started over again. These lapses are considered not treatment failures but merely temporary lapses or setbacks. The long-term goals are to help the patient with chronic illness maintain as healthy and productive a life and life-style as possible. As examples, the long-term consequences of diabetes or hypertension are reduced, not eliminated. Long-term consequences of these diseases are unavoidable, but their impact early in life can be moderated and a productive life-style can be maintained for as long as possible. The same should hold true for the treatment of drug dependency.

Positive treatment outcomes should not be measured by abstinence alone but should involve such factors as family life, employment, and decreased involvement with the criminal justice system. Treatment of drug dependency should involve the same standards of success used to measure the effectiveness of treatment of chronic medical illnesses, where periodic relapses and noncompliance with therapy and medications are common and expected. In essence, this is a *disease management model* for addiction treatment that requires that success be measured in incremental improvements and that relapses be considered as temporary setbacks, not total failures.

Relapse rates for drug dependency are about the same as relapse rates during the treatment of chronic medical illnesses, ranging from 90 percent for very brief relapses to 50 percent for major setbacks. In essence, periodic relapses are a part of the lifelong management of chronic illnesses. Treatment is therefore prolonged, usually lifelong, and outcomes are measured by incremental improvements in the patient's life. The potential for relapse is part of chronic disease.

If we adopt the model of substance dependency, or addiction, as a chronic illness, the model of prolonged residential treatment is inappropriate. As with the treatment of chronic medical illnesses, brief therapeutic interventions are appropriate and effective. Here we do not mean only one intervention, or two, or several. We mean lifelong, continuing treatment, like the treatment of a patient with diabetes. Although each intervention may be brief, the patient is engaged in the system for life (Stout, 2002). What form would such interventions take in drug abuse treatment? Certainly they would include regular patient-medical personnel visits. Mental health personnel as well as support groups such as Alcoholics Anonymous would be involved. Family support therapy would also be essential.

Another reason for bringing treatment of addictive diseases into the medical mainstream is the fact that many, if not most, people with substance dependence also suffer from comorbid disorders such as major depression, dysthymia, bipolar illness, schizophrenia, or anxiety disorders. Personality disorders, such as antisocial personality disorder, also are frequently encountered. Unless comorbid illnesses are controlled and control is maintained, relapse is probable. Pharmacological and behavioral treatment for both substance dependence and other comorbid illnesses can and must occur together.

One example of an advance in this direction was the passage in the year 2000 of legislation that allows a physician to treat opioid dependency in an office setting; the practitioner can now prescribe Schedule III drugs (such as buprenorphine) for this purpose (Chapter 15). Many opioid-dependent people can now be treated in a medical clinic rather than in a methadone clinic.

Major factors that may inhibit a move to treating substance dependence as a chronic medical illness include the following:

1. Lack of availability of physicians trained in the treatment of substance dependence and its associated comorbid illnesses
2. Lack of established relationships between prescribers of psychotherapeutic medications and personnel trained to diagnose and treat mental/behavioral disorders
3. Poor financial reimbursement from insurance companies for long-term mental health treatment
4. Poor support from local, state, and federal governments to adequately fund this model of care

Each of these factors can be overcome. It only needs commitment from all involved. In July 2003, the New Freedom Commission on Mental Health presented to President George W. Bush its final report on the mental health changes that need to be made in America. The report calls for a transformation of mental health care in America, bringing mental health care into the mainstream of society. The commission's vision statement was as follows:

> We envision a future when everyone with a mental illness will recover, a future when mental illness can be prevented or cured, a future when mental illness can be detected early, and a future when everyone with a mental illness at any stage of life has access to effective treatment and supports—essentials for living, working, learning, and participating fully in the community. (p. 1)

The statement indicates that the integration of substance dependence into mental health treatment objectives is understood.

Drug Education

Drug education and dependency treatment programs must consider the extent of a person's behavioral and physiological involvement with psychoactive drugs. Although educational programs may be useful approaches, formal treatment programs are necessary for people who are compulsive abusers or addicts.

One approach to drug education is to teach the pharmacology of psychoactive drugs, as this book does. Even though this approach can be seen as providing directions for taking drugs, it can also be seen as providing accurate information for people to use in examining and modifying their own risk-taking behavior and thus making the informed decisions necessary to lead a healthy life in the community.

No program of drug education can guarantee to reduce the use of psychoactive drugs. A drug education program can, however, teach individuals the beneficial and harmful effects of a given drug (whether licit or illicit). Education may limit experimentation by some individuals. It will not dissuade those already involved in drugs, nor will it dissuade those who seek pharmacologic relief from their own psychiatric symptoms or disorders. In other words, it will not dissuade self-prescription for symptom relief.

To alter the behavior of youths requires both education and examples set by teachers, peers, parents, and the whole community, including government officials. Three steps are necessary:

1. Basic information—truthful information—has to be imparted to generate motivation for behavior change. Only honest, straightforward, and full information about the health risks of the addictive drugs will meet this requirement.

2. The means for behavior change have to be provided. Many techniques have proven effective, especially teaching children how to resist peer pressure. It is important to promote a redefinition of drug-using peers as not "cool."

3. Methods for reinforcing the new behaviors have to be employed. This means that children need recognition, praise, and other rewards for not using drugs. Emphasis on how drugs detract from a healthy body and an attractive appearance, for example, appeals to adolescents' interest in athletics as well as to their developing sexuality and their striving for intimate peer relationships.

In essence, this approach is directed toward building self-esteem in a drug-free environment. While praiseworthy, the approach works best for those least likely to abuse drugs. Recently, a Project ALERT program has been demonstrated to be an effective method for reducing drug use in middle school students (Ellickson et al., 2003). Project ALERT seeks to motivate students against using drugs and give them the skills to translate motivation into effective resistance behavior.

Prevention of drug abuse requires adults to be willing to set a consistent example by responsibly using or minimizing their own use of psychoactive drugs. In addition, legislation must be consistent and in agreement with accepted, documented scientific evidence. This action is particularly important regarding cigarettes and alcohol. The casualness with which these drugs are used and promoted, distributed, and sold demonstrates both ignorance and societal hypocrisy about the use of addicting drugs.

Treatment Issues

In past years, many people equated physical dependence with addiction. In older views, the defining problem of addiction was physical dependence, implying that fear of withdrawal following drug removal was the "engine driving addictive substance use" (Gold and Eaton, 1996, p. 1365). Detoxification was seen as the principal treatment for addiction: free the addicted individual from the clutches of the drug by assisting him or her through withdrawal and the grip of the addiction was broken. It is not surprising that treatment focused on detoxification, often in a clinical, residential, or hospital setting. Even today, detoxification is often a primary goal of addiction treatment. But physical dependence (as defined by existence of a withdrawal syndrome with drug removal) is not equated with "addiction", as study of the effects of the serotonin-type antidepressants makes clear. None would argue that these drug are prone to compulsive abuse or are "addicting," yet a well-characterized, multifaceted withdrawal syndrome can follow cessation of their use (Chapter 9).

A mid-1990s view of addiction treatment followed the observation that most individuals who go through detoxification eventually relapse to drug use. The focus was on drug-induced reward rather than on drug withdrawal as the engine driving addiction. Clearly, the positive aspects of the drug experience support drug self-administration. The reinforcing properties of drugs are powerful motivational forces that are preferred by the subjects to natural reinforcers. Thus, *drug reinforcement* becomes the unifying feature of drug abuse and dependence (DuPont and Gold, 1995). *Drug abstinence* can then be viewed as a behavioral and physical state induced by the absence of the drug of abuse to which the addict has adapted. It is behaviorally reinforcing to reverse the abstinence state by the readministration of a drug (relapse is behaviorally reinforcing). The state of abstinence is, therefore, not a return to "normal," as presumed by old models of addiction and withdrawal. Abstinence is characterized by a mental state of apathy, boredom, depression, malaise, anhedonia, and craving for relief. The individual needs the drug to feel normal. Thus, relapse is driven both by the negative reinforcement of abstinence and the positive reinforcement of the drug.

Now researchers are looking beyond the rather simplistic concepts of reward and withdrawal as the engines driving addiction. Not all individuals who experiment with drugs develop a substance abuse disorder; risk factors become an important predisposing variable to the expression of the genetically influenced, complex, chronic, and relapsing disease that we call "addiction" or "substance dependence." In adolescents, there are several broad classes of risk factors for the development of substance use disorders (SUDs), including parent and family risk factors, peer-related risk factors, individual risk factors (including biogenetic variables), and community risk factors. SUDs often are associated with other psychiatric diagnoses, such as disruptive behavior, mood and anxiety disorders, and with problematic behaviors, including risk taking, aggression, and suicidal behavior.

Just as focus cannot be solely on the drug of dependence and its rewarding and withdrawal effects as the principal factor involved in and driving abuse of the drug, neither can it be only on pharmacotherapy for treatment of the addiction. Focusing just on physical brain changes is not adequate; addicts will have to be able to handle later exposure to craving-eliciting cues in the environment and will need rehabilitation to either learn or relearn social skills or job skills. Moreover, it is likely that combined behavioral and pharmacological treatments will be truly synergistic, not just complementary in nature.

Comprehensive treatment does work (Marwick, 1998), and it can be provided in a cost-effective manner (Shepard et al., 1999). In general, regular outpatient treatment programs are the most cost-effective, while long-term residential treatment programs provide little extra benefit at a fivefold increase in expenses. Uniformly placing individuals in more intensive types of treatment is not the most cost-effective strategy, and incarceration as a treatment modality is prohibitively expensive. Any reasonable treatment strategy, even 5 to 10 minutes of physician counseling on several visits, is more effective than no treatment (Friedman et al., 1998). Friedman and coworkers (1998) summarized the techniques that can be used to manage adults recovering from substance abuse problems (Table 21.2). They present a practical approach to the support of a substance-free life-style,

TABLE 21.2 Relapse prevention strategies in the primary care setting

Identify patients in recovery
Establish a supportive patient-physician relationship
Schedule regular follow-up
Mobilize family support
Facilitate involvement in 12-step recovery groups
Help recovering patients recognize and cope with relapse precipitants and craving
Advise recovering patients to develop a plan to manage early relapse
Facilitate positive lifestyle changes
Manage depression, anxiety, and other comorbid conditions
Consider adjunctive pharmacotherapy
Collaborate with addiction specialty professionals

From Friedman et al. (1998), p. 1228.

centering on patients who are early into recovery and at the highest risk of relapse, although many of the principles also apply to longer-term recovery.

Pharmacotherapy of Substance Use Disorders

It must be acknowledged that drugs have limited usefulness in most cases of substance use disorders; they should be used to augment psychosocial therapies. Despite this limitation, pharmacological treatment options for individuals with substance use disorders are many:

- Use a substitute drug to ameliorate or reduce the intensity of any withdrawal effects or to reduce the risk of relapse to illicit drug use.
- Substitute a "legal," usually medically prescribed, longer-acting agonist for an illicit one to ameliorate some of the acute withdrawal effects, maintain an agonist effect, and reduce craving and relapse (so-called *relapse prevention pharmacology*).
- Treat the substance abuse with a receptor antagonist so that taking the illicit drug will be without effect.
- Treat comorbid psychiatric disorders with appropriate psychotherapeutic agents.

Complete details of the use of specific pharmacological agents to manage dependence on specific drugs of abuse can be found in the chapters devoted to specific drugs of abuse (benzodiazepines, alcohol, opioids, nicotine, psychostimulants, and so on).

STUDY QUESTIONS

1. What is meant when a particular drug is called a "behavioral reinforcer"?
2. Why might the evaluation of drug-reinforcing properties in animals be valuable in the assessment of human experiences?
3. Is a propensity for abusing drugs caused by a psychopathological process in the user, or is it a property of the particular drug?
4. On a physiological level, what might explain the lack of self-reinforcing action of phenothiazines or antidepressants?
5. What is the mechanism that underlies the behavioral reinforcing properties of abused drugs?
6. List several key principles that underlie a positive approach toward drug education.

7. Where has drug education failed? How might drug education be used successfully?

8. What is the relationship between age of first use of drugs and development of a substance use disorder? What are the limitations to this relationship?

9. List, from most harmful to least harmful, the classes of psychoactive drugs presented in this book. Defend your choices.

10. Should certain drugs be more readily available? How should legislation be directed?

11. Are current efforts to limit cigarette smoking likely to prove successful? How should we change our approach?

12. Where should alcohol education be aimed? Defend your position.

REFERENCES

American Psychiatric Association (2000). *Diagnostic and Statistical Manual of Mental Disorders*, 4th ed., text revision (DSM-IV-TR). Washington, DC: American Psychiatric Association.

Bisaga, A., et al. (2001). "The NMDA Antagonist Memantine Attenuates the Expression of Opioid Physical Dependence in Humans." *Psychopharmacology* 157: 1–10.

Bonci, A., et al. (2003). "The Dopamine-Containing Neuron: Maestro or Simple Musician in the Orchestra of Addiction?" *Trends in Pharmacologic Sciences* 24: 172–177.

Bucholz, K. K. (1999). "Nosology and Epidemiology of Addictive Disorders and Their Comorbidity." *Psychiatric Clinics of North America* 22: 221–240.

Cami, J., and M. Farre (2003). "Drug Addiction." *New England Journal of Medicine* 349: 975–986.

Childress, A. R., et al. (1999). "Limbic Activation During Cue-Induced Cocaine Craving." *American Journal of Psychiatry* 156: 11–18.

Dahchour, A., and P. DeWitte (2000). "Ethanol and Amino Acids in the Central Nervous System: Assessment of the Pharmacological Actions of Acamprosate." *Progress in Neurobiology* 60: 343–362.

DuPont, R. L., and M. S. Gold (1995). "Withdrawal and Reward: Implications for Detoxification and Relapse Prevention." *Psychiatric Annals* 25: 663–668.

Ellickson, P. L., et al. (2003). "New Inroads in Preventing Adolescent Drug Use: Results From a Large-Scale Trial of Project ALERT in Middle Schools." *American Journal of Public Health* 93: 1830–1836.

Friedman, P. D., et al. (1998). "Management of Adults Recovering from Alcohol and Other Drug Problems." *Journal of the American Medical Association* 279: 1227–1231.

Garcia-Ladona, F. J., and B. F. Cox (2003). "BP 897, a Selective Dopamine D3 Receptor Ligand with Therapeutic Potential for the Treatment of Cocaine Addiction." *CNS Drug Reviews* 9: 141–158.

Gardner, E. L. (2002). "Addictive Potential of Cannabinoids: The Underlying Neurobiology." *Chemistry and Physics of Lipids* 12: 267–290.

Gfroerer, J. C., and J. F. Epstein (1999). "Marijuana Initiates and Their Impact on Future Drug Abuse Treatment Need." *Drug and Alcohol Dependence* 54: 229–237.

Gold, M. S., and D. H. Eaton (1996). "Drugs in History." *Journal of the American Medical Association* 275: 1364–1365.

Goldsmith, R. J. (1999). "Overview of Psychiatric Comorbidity: Practical and Theoretical Considerations." *Psychiatric Clinics of North America* 22: 331–349.

Hasin, D., et al. (2002). "Effects of Major Depression on Remission and Relapse of Substance Dependence." *Archives of General Psychiatry* 59: 375–380.

Havassy, B. E., et al. (2004). "Comparisons of Patients with Comorbid Psychiatric and Substance Use Disorders: Implications for Treatment and Service Delivery." *American Journal of Psychiatry* 161: 139–145.

Jacobsen, L. K., et al. (2001). "Substance Use Disorders in Patients with Posttraumatic Stress Disorder: A Review of the Literature." *American Journal of Psychiatry* 158: 1184–1190.

Kieffer, B. L. (1999). "Opioids: First Lessons from Knockout Mice." *Trends in Pharmacological Sciences* 283: 19–26.

Kilpatrick, D. K., et al. (2003). "Violence and Risk of PTSD, Major Depression, Substance Abuse/Dependence, and Comorbidity: Results from the National Survey of Adolescents." *Journal of Consulting and Clinical Psychology* 71: 692–700.

Koob, G. F. (1992). "Drugs of Abuse: Anatomy, Pharmacology, and Function of Reward Pathways." *Trends in Pharmacologic Sciences* 13: 177–182.

Koob, G. F., and M. LeMoal (2001). "Drug Addiction, Dysregulation of Reward, and Allostasis." *Neuropsychopharmacology* 24: 97–129.

Leshner, A. I. (1997). "Drug Abuse and Addiction Treatment Research: The Next Generation." *Archives of General Psychiatry* 54: 691–694.

Lingford-Hughes, A., and D. Nutt. (2003). "Neurobiology of Addiction and Implications for Treatment." *British Journal of Psychiatry* 182: 97–100.

Marwick, C. (1998). "Physician Leadership on National Drug Policy Finds Addiction Treatment Works." *Journal of the American Medical Association* 279: 1149–1150.

McCance-Katz, E. F., and T. R. Kosten (1998). *New Treatments for Chemical Addictions.* Washington, DC: American Psychiatric Press.

McFarland, K., et al. (2003). "Prefrontal Glutamate Release into the Core of the Nucleus Accumbens Mediates Cocaine-Induced Reinstatement of Drug-Seeking Behavior." *Journal of Neuroscience* 23: 3531–3537.

Mechoulam, R., and L. Parker. (2003). "Cannabis and Alcohol: A Close Friendship." *Trends in Pharmacological Sciences* 24: 266–268.

National Academy of Sciences, Institute of Medicine (2003). "Reducing Underage Drinking: A Collective Responsibility." Washington DC: National Academic Press.

New Freedom Commission on Mental Health (2003, July). *Achieving the Promise: Transforming Mental Health Care in America: Final Report.* U.S. Department of Health and Human Services Publication SMA-03-3832. Rockville, MD.

Olive, M. F. (2002). "Interactions Between Taurine and Ethanol in the Central Nervous System." *Amino Acids* 23: 345–357.

Pilla, M., et al. (1999). "Selective Inhibition of Cocaine-Seeking Behavior by a Partial Dopamine D3 Recetor Agonist." *Nature* 400: 371–375.

Salamone, J. D., et al. (2003). "Nucleus Accumbens Dopamine and the Regulation of Effort in Food-Seeking Behavior: Implications for Studies of Natural Motivation, Psychiatry, and Drug Abuse." *Journal of Pharmacology and Experimental Therapeutics* 305: 1–8.

Shepard, D. S., et al. (1999). "Cost-Effectiveness of Substance Abuse Services: Implications for Public Policy." *Psychiatric Clinics of North America* 22: 385–400.

Skodol, A. E., et al. (1999). "Axis II Comorbidity of Substance Use Disorders Among Patients Referred for Treatment of Personality Disorders." *American Journal of Psychiatry* 156: 733–738.

Stout, R. (2002, October). "Treatment Failure Is the First Step to Success." *Brown University Digest of Addiction Theory and Application,* p. 8.

Tapert, S. F., et al. (2003). "Neural Response to Alcohol Stimuli in Adolescents with Alcohol Use Disorder." *Archives of General Psychiatry* 60: 727–735.

Tremblay, L. K., et al. (2002). "Probing Brain Reward System Function in Major Depressive Disorder: Altered Response to Dextroamphetamine." *Archives of General Psychiatry* 59: 409–416.

U.S. Department of Health and Human Services, Substance Abuse and Mental Health Services Administration (2003, September). "National Survey on Drug Use and Health 2002." Washington DC: USDHHS.

Volkow, N. D., et al. (1999). "Imaging Studies on the Role of Dopamine in Cocaine Reinforcement and Addiction in Humans." *Journal of Psychopharmacology* 13: 337–345.

Winder, D. G., et al. (2002). "Synaptic Plasticity in Drug Reward Circuitry." *Current Molecular Medicine* 2: 667–676.

Wise, R. A. (1998). "Drug Activation of Brain Reward Pathways." *Drug and Alcohol Dependence* 51: 13–22.

Abstinence syndrome   State of altered behavior that follows cessation of drug administration.

Acetylcholine   Neurotransmitter in the central and peripheral nervous systems.

Additive effect   Increased effect that occurs when two drugs that have similar biological actions are administered. The net effect is the sum of the independent effects exerted by the drugs.

Adenosine   Chemical neuromodulator in the CNS, primarily at inhibitory synapses.

Adenylate cyclase   Intracellular enzyme that catalyzes the conversion of cyclic AMP to adenosine monophosphate.

Affective disorder   Type of mental disorder characterized by recurrent episodes of mania, depression, or both.

Agonist   Drug that attaches to a receptor and produces actions that mimic or potentiate those of an endogenous transmitter.

Aldehyde dehydrogenase   Enzyme that carries out a specific step in alcohol metabolism: the metabolism of acetaldehyde to acetate. This enzyme may be blocked by the drug disulfiram (Antabuse).

Alzheimer's disease   Progressive neurological disease that occurs primarily in the elderly. It is characterized by a loss of short-term memory and intellectual functioning. It is associated with a loss of function of acetylcholine neurons.

Amphetamine   Behavioral stimulant.

Anabolic steroid   Testosteronelike drug that acts to increase muscle mass and produces other masculinizing effects.

Anandamide   Endogenous chemical compound that attaches to cannabinoid receptors in the CNS and to specific components of the lymphatic system.

Anandamide receptor   Receptor to which anandamide and tetrahydrocannabinol bind.

Anesthetic drugs   Sedative-hypnotic compounds used primarily in doses capable of inducing a state of general anesthesia that involves both loss of sensation and loss of consciousness.

Antagonist   Drug that attaches to a receptor and blocks the action of either an endogenous transmitter or an agonistic drug.

Anticonvulsant Drug that blocks or prevents epileptic convulsions. Some anticonvulsants (for example, carbamazepine and valproic acid) are also used to treat certain nonepileptic psychiatric disorders.

Antidepressant Drug that is useful in treating mentally depressed patients but does not produce stimulant effects in nondepressed persons. Subdivided into several categories.

Antipsychotic drugs Drugs that have the ability to calm psychotic states and make the psychotic patient more manageable. Two classes are defined: classical and new generation (or *atypical*).

Anxiolytic Drug used to relieve the symptoms associated with defined states of anxiety. Classically, refers to the benzodiazepines and related drugs.

Attention deficit hyperactivity disorder (ADHD) Learning and behavioral disability characterized by reduced attention span and hyperactivity.

Atypical antipsychotic Drug that ameliorates the symptoms of schiophrenia without necessarily causing abnormal motor movements. Also used in the treatment of mania.

Autonomic nervous system Portion of the peripheral nervous system that controls, or regulates, the visceral, or automatic, functions of the body, such as heart rate and blood pressure.

Barbiturates Class of chemically related sedative-hypnotic compounds that share a characteristic six-membered ring structure.

Basal ganglia Part of the brain that contains vast numbers of dopamine-containing synapses. Forms part of the extrapyramidal system. Parkinson's disease follows dopamine loss in this structure.

Benzodiazepines Class of chemically related sedative-hypnotic agents of which chlordiazepoxide (Librium) and diazepam (Valium) are examples.

Bipolar disorder Affective disorder characterized by alternating bouts of mania and depression. Also referred to as *manic-depressive illness.*

Blackout Period of time during which one may be awake but memory is not imprinted. It frequently occurs in persons who have consumed excessive alcohol or to whom have been administered (or who have taken) large doses of sedative drugs.

Brain syndrome, organic Pattern of behavior induced when neurons are either reversibly depressed or irreversibly destroyed. Behavior is characterized by clouded sensorium, disorientation, shallow and labile affect, and impaired memory, intellectual function, insight, and judgment.

Brand name Unique name licensed to one manufacturer of a drug. Contrasts with **generic name,** the name under which any manufacturer may sell a drug.

Caffeine Behavioral and general cellular stimulant found in coffee, tea, cola drinks, and chocolate.

Caffeinism Habitual use of large amounts of caffeine.

Cannabis sativa Hemp plant; contains marijuana.

Carbidopa Drug that inhibits the enzyme dopa decarboxylase, allowing increased availability of dopa within the brain. Contained in Sinemet.

Central nervous system (CNS)   Brain and spinal cord.

Cirrhosis   Serious, usually irreversible liver disease. Usually associated with chronic excessive alcohol consumption.

Clonidine (Catapres)   Antihypertensive useful in ameliorating the symptoms of narcotic withdrawal.

Cocaine   Behavioral stimulant.

Codeine   Sedative and pain-relieving agent found in opium. Structurally related to morphine but less potent; constitutes approximately 0.5 percent of the opium extract.

Comorbid disorder   Psychiatric disorder that coexists with another psychiatric disorder (for example, multisubstance abuse in a patient with a major depressive disorder).

Convulsant   Drug that produces convulsions by blocking inhibitory neurotransmission.

COX inhibitors   Aspirinlike analgesic drugs that produce their actions by inhibiting the enzyme cyclooxygenase. Two variants of the enzyme occur: COX-1 and COX-2. Some drugs are specific for COX-2; others are nonspecific inhibitors.

Crack   Street name for a smokable form of potent, concentrated cocaine.

Cross-dependence   Condition in which one drug can prevent the withdrawal symptoms associated with physical dependence on a different drug.

Cross-tolerance   Condition in which tolerance of one drug results in a lessened response to another drug.

Delirium tremens (DTs, "rum fits")   Syndrome of tremulousness with hallucinations, psychomotor agitation, confusion and disorientation, sleep disorders, and other associated discomforts, lasting several days after alcohol withdrawal.

Dementia   General designation for nonspecific mental deterioration.

Detoxification   Process of allowing time for the body to metabolize and/or excrete accumulations of drug. Usually a first step in drug abuse evaluation and treatment.

Differential diagnosis   Listing of all possible causes that might explain a given set of symptoms.

Dimethyltryptamine (DMT)   Psychedelic drug found in many South American snuffs.

Disinhibition   Physiological state of the central nervous system characterized by decreased activity of inhibitory synapses, which results in a net excess of excitatory activity.

Dopamine transporter   Presynaptic protein that binds synaptic dopamine and transports the neurotransmitter back into the presynaptic nerve terminal.

Dose-response relation   Relation between drug doses and the response elicited at each dose level.

Drug   Chemical substance used for its effects on bodily processes.

Drug absorption   Mechanism by which a drug reaches the bloodstream from the skin, lungs, stomach, intestinal tract, or muscle.

Drug administration Procedures through which a drug enters the body (oral administration of tablets or liquids, inhalation of powders, injection of sterile liquids, and so on).

Drug dependence State in which the use of a drug is necessary for either physical or psychological well-being.

Drug interaction Modification of the action of one drug by the concurrent or prior administration of another drug.

Drug misuse Use of any drug (legal or illegal) for a medical or recreational purpose when other alternatives are available, practical, or warranted or when drug use endangers either the user or others with whom he or she may interact.

Drug receptor Specific molecular substance in the body with which a given drug interacts to produce its effect.

Drug tolerance State of progressively decreasing responsiveness to a drug.

DSM-IV, DSM-IV-TR *Diagnostic and Statistical Manual of Mental Disorders,* Fourth Edition, was published by the American Psychiatric Association in 1994. The Text Revision of the Fourth Edition was published in 2000.

Dual-action antidepressants Antidepressant drugs that act by inhibiting the active presynaptic reuptake of norepinephrine and serotonin

Electroconvulsive therapy (ECT) Nonpharmacological treatment used for major depression.

Endorphin Naturally occurring protein that causes endogenous morphine-like activity.

Enkephalin Naturally occurring protein that causes morphinelike activity.

Enzyme Large organic molecule that mediates a specific biochemical reaction in the body.

Enzyme induction Increased production of drug-metabolizing enzymes in the liver, stimulated by certain drugs that increase the rate at which the body can metabolize them. It is one mechanism by which pharmacological tolerance is produced.

Epilepsy Neurological disorder characterized by an occasional, sudden, and uncontrolled discharge of neurons.

Fetal alcohol syndrome Symptom complex of congenital anomalies, seen in newborns of women who ingested high doses of alcohol during critical periods of pregnancy.

G protein Specific intraneuronal protein that links transmitter-induced receptor alterations with intracellular second-messenger proteins or with adjacent ion channels.

Gamma aminobutyric acid (GABA) Inhibitory amino acid neurotransmitter in the brain.

Generic name Name that identifies a specific chemical entity (without describing the chemical). Often marketed under different brand names by different manufacturers.

Glutamic acid An excitatory amino acid neurotransmitter.

Hallucinogen Psychedelic drug that produces profound distortions in perception.

Harmine Psychedelic agent obtained from the seeds of *Peganum harmala*.

Hashish Extract of the hemp plant (*Cannabis sativa*) that has a higher concentration of THC than does marijuana.

Heroin Semisynthetic opiate produced by a chemical modification of morphine.

Hypothalamus Structure located at the base of the brain, above the pituitary gland.

Hypoxia State of relative lack of oxygen in the tissues of the body and the brain.

Ice Street name for a smokable, free-base form of potent, concentrated methamphetamine.

Levodopa Precursor substance to the transmitter dopamine, useful in ameliorating the symptoms of Parkinson's disease.

Limbic system Group of brain structures involved in emotional responses and emotional expression.

Lithium Alkali metal effective in the treatment of mania and depression.

Lysergic acid diethylamide (LSD) Semisynthetic psychedelic drug.

Major tranquilizer Drug used in the treatment of psychotic states.

Mania Mental disorder characterized by an expansive emotional state, elation, hyperirritability, excessive talkativeness, flights of ideas, and increased behavioral activity.

MAO See **Monoamine oxidase.**

Marijuana Mixture of the crushed leaves, flowers, and small branches of both the male and female hemp plant (*Cannabis sativa*).

Mescaline Psychedelic drug extracted from the peyote cactus.

Minor tranquilizer Sedative-hypnotic drug promoted primarily for use in the treatment of anxiety.

Mixed agonist–antagonist Drug that attaches to a receptor, producing weak agonistic effects but displacing more potent agonists, precipitating withdrawal in drug-dependent persons.

Monoamine oxidase (MAO) Enzyme capable of metabolizing norepinephrine, dopamine, and serotonin to inactive products.

Monoamine oxidase inhibitor (MAOI) Drug that inhibits the activity of the enzyme monoamine oxidase.

Mood stabilizer Drug used in the treatment of bipolar illness. Examples are lithium and any of the neuromodulator anticonvulsants.

Morphine Major sedative and pain-relieving drug found in opium, composed of approximately 10 percent of the crude opium exudate.

Muscarine Drug extracted from the mushroom *Amanita muscaria* that directly stimulates acetylcholine receptors.

Myristin Psychedelic agent obtained from nutmeg and mace.

Neuromodulator   Antiepileptic drug used to treat bipolar illness, aggressive disorders, chronic pain, and a variety of other disorders.

Neurotransmitter   Endogenous chemical released by one neuron that alters the electrical activity of another neuron.

Nicotine   Behavioral stimulant found in tobacco.

Norepinephrine-specific reuptake inhibitor   See **Selective norepinephrine reuptake inhibitor.**

Off-label   Term applied to the clinical use of a drug for an indication other than that for which the drug was approved by the U.S. Food and Drug Administration. Use is usually justified by medical literature, even though formal approval for the use was not sought by the manufacturer of the drug. The manufacturer may not promote a drug for an off-label use.

Ololiuqui   Psychedelic drug obtained from the seeds of the morning glory plant.

Opioid   Natural or synthetic drug that exerts actions on the body similar to those induced by morphine, the major pain-relieving agent obtained from the opium poppy (*Papaver somniferum*).

Opium   Crude resinous exudate from the opium poppy. Contains morphine and codeine as active opioids.

Parkinson's disease   Disorder of the motor system characterized by involuntary movements, tremor, and weakness.

Partial agonist   Drug that binds to a receptor and exerts only part of the action exerted by the endogenous neurotransmitter or that produces a submaximal receptor response.

Peptide   Chemical composed of a chain-link sequence of amino acids.

Peyote   Cactus that contains mescaline.

Pharmacodynamics   Study of the interactions of a drug and the receptors responsible for the action of the drug in the body.

Pharmacokinetics   Study of the factors that influence the absorption, distribution, metabolism, and excretion of a drug.

Pharmacology   Branch of science that deals with the study of drugs and their actions on living systems.

Phencyclidine (Sernyl, PCP)   Psychedelic surgical anesthetic. Acts by binding to and inhibiting ion transport through the NMDA-glutamate receptors.

Phenothiazine   Class of chemically related compounds useful in the treatment of psychosis.

Physical dependence   State in which the use of a drug is required for a person to function normally. Such a state is revealed by withdrawing the drug and noting the occurrence of withdrawal symptoms (abstinence syndrome). Characteristically, withdrawal symptoms can be terminated by readministration of the drug.

Placebo   Pharmacologically inert substance that may elicit a significant reaction largely because of the mental set of the patient or the physical setting in which the drug is taken.

Potency   Measure of drug activity expressed in terms of the amount required to produce an effect of given intensity. Potency varies inversely with the amount of drug required to produce this effect—the more potent the drug, the lower the amount required to produce the effect.

Psilocybin Psychedelic drug obtained from the mushroom *Psilocybe mexicana.*

Psychedelic drug Drug that can alter sensory perception.

Psychoactive drug Chemical substance that alters mood or behavior as a result of alterations in the functioning of the brain.

Psychological dependence Compulsion to use a drug for its pleasurable effects. Dependence may lead to a compulsion to misuse a drug.

Psychopharmacology Branch of pharmacology that deals with the effects of drugs on the nervous system and behavior.

Psychopharmacotherapy Clinical treatment of psychiatric disorders with drugs.

Psychotherapy Nonpharmacological treatment of psychiatric disorders utilizing a wide range of modalities from simple education and supportive counseling to insight-oriented, dynamically based therapy.

Receptor Location in the nervous system at which a neurotransmitter or drug binds to exert its characteristic effect Most receptors are members of genetically encoded families of specialized proteins.

Reye's syndrome Rare CNS disorder that occurs in children; associated with aspirin ingestion.

Risk-to-benefit ratio Arbitrary assessment of the risks and benefits that may accrue from administration of a drug.

Schizophrenia Debilitating neuropsychiatric illness associated with disturbances in thought, perception, emotion, cognition, relationships, and psychomotor behavior.

Scopolamine Anticholinergic drug that crosses the blood-brain barrier to produce sedation and amnesia.

Second messenger Intraneuronal protein that, when activated by an excitatory G protein, initiates the neuronal response to the initial neurotransmitter attachment to an extracellular receptor.

Sedative-hypnotic drug Chemical substance that exerts a nonselective general depressant action on the nervous system.

Selective norepinephrine reuptake inhibitor Drug that blocks the active presynaptic transporter for norepinephrine. Clinically used to treat ADHD, depression, and other disorders, including seasonal affective disorder.

Selective serotonin reuptake inhibitor (SSRI) Second-generation antidepressant drug.

Serotonin (5-hydroxytryptamine, 5-HT) Synaptic transmitter in both the brain and the peripheral nervous system.

Serotonin syndrome Clinical syndrome resulting from excessive amounts of serotonin in the brain. Can follow use of excessive doses of SSRIs. Characterized by extreme anxiety, confusion, and disorientation.

Serotonin withdrawal syndrome Clinical syndrome that can follow withdrawal or cessation of SSRI therapy. Characterized by mental status alterations, severe flulike symptoms, and feelings of tingling or electrical shock in the extremities.

Side effect Drug-induced effect that accompanies the primary effect for which the drug is administered.

Substance P Protein neurotransmitter that regulates affective behavior, increasing the perception of pain. Substance P antagonists exhibit analgesic and antidepressant actions.

Tardive dyskinesia Movement disorder that appears after months or years of treatment with neuroleptic (antipsychotic) drugs. It usually worsens with drug discontinuation. Symptoms are often masked by the drugs that cause the disorder.

Teratogen Chemical substance that induces abnormalities of fetal development.

Testosterone Hormone secreted from the testes that is responsible for the distinguishing characteristics of the male.

Tetrahydrocannabinol (THC) Major psychoactive agent in marijuana, hashish, and other preparations of hemp (*Cannabis sativa*).

Therapeutic drug monitoring (TDM) Process of correlating the plasma level of a drug with therapeutic response.

Tolerance Clinical state of reduced responsiveness to a drug. Can be produced by a variety of mechanisms, all of which require increased doses of drug to produce an effect once achieved by lower doses.

Toxic effect Drug-induced effect either temporarily or permanently deleterious to any organ or system of an animal or person. Drug toxicity includes both the relatively minor side effects that invariably accompany drug administration and the more serious and unexpected manifestations that occur in only a small percentage of patients who take a drug.

INDEX